Hymnal Companion to *Sound the Bamboo*

G-7700

Hymnal Companion to
Sound the Bamboo
Asian Hymns in Their
Cultural and Liturgical Contexts

I-to Loh

GIA Publications, Inc.
Chicago

G-7700

7404 South Mason Avenue
Chicago, IL 60638
www.giamusic.com

ISBN: 978-1-57999-781-6

Layout by Martha Chlipala

Bible translations are from the New Revised Standard Version unless otherwise noted.

Table of Contents

GENERAL INTRODUCTION

Part One
ASIAN HYMNS IN THEIR HISTORICAL PERSPECTIVES

Part Two
ASIAN HYMNS IN THEIR CULTURAL AND LITURGICAL CONTEXTS

Part Three
BIOGRAPHIES

Preface 1

It is a great pleasure and honor to write a foreword for a good friend and long-respected Asian theologian and colleague in theology education. My sincere congratulations to Professor I-to Loh for the great work accomplished. This companion to *Sound the Bamboo* is a mission that has been made possible after much effort and time. This is a great contribution to the project of doing theology in Asia. One way to convey the multiple facets of Asian cultures is through music. Since time immemorial, music has been one of the best cultural and religious expressions for people's inner feelings, including joy, sadness, hatred, and praises. As the Israelites did in ancient times, today we construct an Asian theology through musical and other cultural resources. As in the Psalms, the songs of the people, the culture, and the history become the theology of the era. Likewise, the companion to *Sound the Bamboo*, which collates folk songs and music by Asian people expressing expectations and sorrows, is a useful and masterful work of theological education. I strongly recommend it to all Christian communities, especially theological schools in Asia.

My first ten years of church ministry was as a missionary to a tribal ethnic minority in Sabah, in Malaysia. At that time, traditional musical instruments and folk songs were prohibited because the church thought they were related to evil spirits, and Western music and hymns were instead introduced. The church worship services that I attended were solemn and dull. A trip to Africa for a conference and church visit inspired me, as I was touched by the African expressions of worship. The integration of local music and dances is not just beautiful and exciting but creates a holistic worship with body, mind, and spirit. Due to church tradition and my limited talent in music, I could not do much for the church where I served. Local theology through music is something that I regard as essential, but it is often missing from church life.

With this point of view, I invited church musicians to compose a theme song for our seminary. Three times I had to reject contributions from various experts, which delayed the process for a few years. I am so grateful to I-to, who finally gave birth to our theme song about three years ago, when he served as a visiting professor in our seminary. The song was chosen because both the music and the lyrics speak through the cultural and ethnic context. The combination of Kadazan music with Chinese rhythm is an example of how a mission theology in a multi-ethnic context should be developed. This is a theology of acculturation. As Aylward

Shorter says, "acculturation means the encounter between one culture and another, or the encounter between cultures, and it is the communication between cultures on a footing of mutual respect and tolerance and a necessary condition of a Church that claims to be universal" (Shorter 1988, 7f).

Local music is a prerequisite for local theology. They are two phenomena but one approach. To ignore the former will be to neglect the latter. Sabah Theological Seminary is trying to overcome the traditional, exclusive model of the church that has influenced generations of Christians in Malaysia. Since the inception of the seminary, I have dreamed to set up a music department highlighting local music. How and when to make this dream come true will depend on committed leaders who are well-versed in Asian music, such as I-to Loh.

Music is also ecumenical. I met I-to for the first time in 1983 during the WCC General Assembly held in Vancouver, where he was one of the leaders of the liturgy and music of the Assembly. I was so impressed and touched by the liturgy and worship presented. I think it was the first time that Asian hymns were so widely and ecumenically introduced and integrated into the BEM (Baptism, Eucharist, and Ministry) liturgy, to be sung together by all Christians regardless of their background. Since then, the Vancouver Assembly remains a fond memory because of the beauty of ecumenicity and unified spirituality expressed through music, specifically in the various ethnic melodies. There are no boundaries in music. Theology through music is both cross-cultural and ecumenical.

The main objectives of this companion are in tune with the mission and vision of ATESEA: to teach and to write Asian theology. Our senior leaders and gurus in Asia are making numerous contributions in their attempts at restructuring Asian theology. For example, Shoki Coe, C. S. Song, Kosuke Koyama, and others have written books highlighting local Asian songs. However, Asian Christian hymnals such as *Sound the Bamboo* remain rare.

Asian churches in quest of their identities must work through Asian expressions of Christian faith, of which Asian music is a decisive force. The great majority of our hymnals were translated and the liturgies were copied from the mother churches of the missionaries. Churches that regard local music as secondary to the Western products, as unacceptable to the sacred temple, are resisting their local identities.

Over thousands of years, hundreds of secular and folk songs from the West have been introduced and accommodated into the traditional church worship and liturgy, which we are still using. If these cultural elements were accepted by Western churches, music composers, and theologians, can we not do the same with our Asian cultural sources? Are they inferior to the Western ones? Surely, the Asian soil that has given birth to and has nurtured the major religions in the world has an ample and beautiful variety of music that is pleasing to God and has yet to be introduced for Christian worship. We envision that more Asian theologians and church musicians will treasure and promote the richness of our cultures and spirituality, so that in due time more Asian theologies, liturgies, and hymns will be created for the nurture and growth of all Asian churches.

—Dr. Thu En Yu
Chairman, ATESEA

Preface 2

Sing a new song to the LORD!
Sing to the LORD the entire world!
Sing to the LORD and give praise!
Proclaim every day the good news that God has saved us.
(Psalm 96:1–2, TEV)

One of God's missions for the Christian Conference of Asia (CCA) is to promote Asian cultures and spirituality in songs and instrumental works that proclaim the gospel.

Indigenous songs and musical instruments have been largely ignored and seldom used in Asian churches, especially in the countries where Christians are a minority. Some years ago, questions about indigenous music and songs were raised within CCA member churches: To what extent have Asian music and songs been used in worship? Have churches been successful in promoting Asian hymns and music?

In 1963, the East Asia Christian Conference (now the Christian Conference of Asia) published the *EACC Hymnal*. Later in 1990, in cooperation with the Asian Institute for Liturgy and Music (AILM), CCA published *Sound the Bamboo: CCA Hymnal 1990*. The book was jointly edited by I-to Loh, James Minchin, and Francisco Feliciano. *Sound the Bamboo* was revised and enlarged in the year 2000; it has also been reprinted in the United States by GIA Publications. Even today, churches and publishers around the world continue to ask for CCA's permission to reproduce hymns from this hymnal.

CCA is pleased to recommend this companion volume, *Hymnal Companion to* Sound the Bamboo: *Asian Hymns in Their Cultural and Liturgical Contexts*. It seeks to glorify God and proclaim the gospel with Asian music and songs. This book introduces the background of the hymns, their writers, and composers, which will help readers to understand and interpret hymns in their cultural and liturgical contexts. I am honored to write this preface, and I trust that churches will find this volume a useful resource. I profoundly thank Dr. I-to Loh for his efforts in making possible the production of the new hymnal companion. And now, it is in your hand.

May God bless you.

—Prawate Khid-arn
General Secretary
Christian Conference of Asia

Foreword

Asian Voices in the Christian Story

Hymns are part of our Christian family history. By "family," I mean those who at their baptism have accepted the label "Christian" as a sign of their bond to Christ and as a result are brothers and sisters in Christ. At the cusp of the twenty-first century, we have the opportunity to know more of our worldwide Christian family than any past generation. To be ecumenical Christians is by definition to embrace "the whole inhabited earth." This volume adds immensely to our understanding of what it means to be ecumenical Christians.

This is a book about Asian hymns—about those who have conceived the words and music sung by Asian Christians, about the cultures from which they come, and about the liturgical context in which these hymns appear. A hymn can have a greater significance if one understands its meaning in its original setting, even if this is far removed from one's own culture. Western hymnological studies have validated this assumption for many years. But what about the many voices outside the West? What do they bring to the Christian story?

Those of us who come from Western contexts or from Christian traditions that use primarily Western hymns may have a preconception about the nature of a hymn. When discussing Asian hymnody, we must broaden our understanding of the term "hymn." Philip Bohlman acknowledges that any discussion of world music raises the ontological question: what is music?[1] From the perspective of a Western hymnologist, the study of global congregational song prompts an analogous ontological question: what is a hymn? This is more than an academic question. This is a matter of identity both as a Christian and as a human being from a particular cultural context. Understanding the nature of Asian hymns is a window onto understanding how Asian Christians pray and how they understand God's work in the world. As you read these stories and sing these hymns, be prepared to broaden your understanding of the basic question ("what is a hymn?"). Be open to exploring the nature, diversity, and complexity of Asian hymns and, as a result, to pray and sing in new ways.

---

1   Philip V. Bohlman, *World Music: A Very Short Introduction* (New York: Oxford University Press, 2002), 6.

I attended a symposium sponsored by the Christian Conference of Asia (CCA) in 1996. Delegates from more than twenty Asian countries gathered in Kuala Lumpur, Malaysia, under the theme of using Asian theological resources and biblical perspectives to better understand the difficult economic issues faced by many countries throughout the region. I was privileged to be the only non-Asian observer. The central question of this gathering and others held by the CCA might be summarized by one question: how can we be truly Asian and truly Christian?

There was no doubt that those gathered were grateful for the witness of Christian missionaries from North America and Europe who had brought the gospel to Asian lands. Their dilemma was centered on the Western cultural context that embraced the kernel of the gospel and limited the possibility of viewing Christ's incarnation from an Asian perspective.

I will never forget the plea of a Christian woman from Malaysia who asserted to the group in Kuala Lumpur that Asian Christians had experiences, resources, and biblical insights that were different from those offered by Western Christians. "People," she said, "we must never forget that Jesus was born in far western Asia— Asia Minor—and sought refuge in Egypt in northern Africa; he never traveled to the United States!"

Though I had been on a journey for several years to understand the musical contributions of Christians beyond the European/North American context, it was at that precise moment that I experienced my own Copernican revolution: Christianity in the twenty-first century would revolve much less around Western ideas and assumptions. The spectrum of Christian thought that would shed light on the nature of Christ's incarnation in this century would be much deeper and broader. Rather than continuing a "West versus the rest" approach, twenty-first century Christians now have the opportunity to experience a fuller understanding of the one who came in a specific place and time for all places and times.

In the mid-twentieth century, the famous Sri Lankan ecumenist Daniel Thambyrajah Niles (1908–1970) captured the need to understand and experience God's revelation to humanity on our own cultural terms with an insightful simile:

> The Gospel is like a seed and you have to sow it. When you sow the seed of the Gospel in Palestine, a plant that can be called Palestinian Christianity grows. When you sow it in Rome, a plant of Roman Christianity grows. You sow the Gospel in Great Britain and you get British Christianity. The seed of the Gospel is later brought to America and a plant grows of American Christianity. Now when missionaries came to our lands they brought not only the seed of the Gospel, but their own plant of Christianity, flower pot included! So, what we have to do is to break the flower pot, take out the seed of the Gospel, sow it in our own cultural soil, and let our own version of Christianity grow.[2]

---

2   As quoted by Mortimer Arias in "Contextual Evangelization in Latin America: Between Accommodation and Confrontation." *Occasional Bulletin*, January 1978, pp. 19–28.

Hymnal Companion to Sound the Bamboo: *Asian Hymns in Their Cultural and Liturgical Contexts* contains the stories of pot-breakers—poets and musicians who have voiced their faith in the cultural idioms closest to their hearts. In doing so they have not only given voice to a continent of diverse peoples teeming with potential and poverty, splendor and suffering, but they have also expressed their faith in tongues and tones that bear witness to the exclamation, "O LORD, our Sovereign, how majestic is your name in all the earth!" (Psalm 8:1, NRSV)

Sound the Bamboo (published in 1990 and 2000) followed an earlier attempt to plant the gospel in Asian soils. Niles led the way with the *EACC Hymnal*, published in 1963 by the East Asia Christian Conference (EACC). The co-founder and first general secretary of the EACC, Niles edited a volume that consisted largely of his own hymns in Western musical idioms. Yet, these songs moved closer to the heart of Asian people. The *EACC Hymnal* was more popular in ecumenical than Asian circles, with four printings by 1966.

Niles attempted to unite Asian churches in ecumenical song using Western harmonization in the style of the missionaries' music, which was familiar to all countries. I-to Loh has attempted to highlight the distinctiveness of Asian churches through the incorporation of a wide range of Asian musical styles. In retrospect, Niles's hymnological efforts only cracked the cultural pot (to use his metaphor) brought to Asia by Western missionaries. The 1990 publication of *Sound the Bamboo*, under the general editorship of Dr. Loh, broke the pot and reassembled the pieces in a way that gave a new shape to congregational singing for Christians throughout Asia and, potentially, to the rest of the world.

Sound the Bamboo represents arguably the most labor-intensive hymnal publication by one person in the twentieth century. Over three-fourths of the songs were recorded by Dr. Loh "amid the traffic noise of busy streets, beside the village fire at night, in huts and homely settings all over the Asian region."[3] Dr. Loh has generously given time to many Western musicians over the years, guiding them song-by-song through the pages of the hymnal. Virtually every hymn serves as an entry point for a story about the place and persons associated with the hymn, the various versions recorded, the selection of the text to accompany the melody, and performance suggestions for a more accurate presentation of the hymn. Loh's heroic efforts in the collection, transcription, production, and revision of songs in the hymnal, along with the information in this companion, have few if any twentieth-century hymnological parallels.

The collection of the songs was followed by countless hours of transcription, translation, and paraphrasing. It is doubtful that any hymnal published in the twentieth century has included so much material that had not previously appeared in print. Feedback on the hymns was sought from "musicians, theologians, poets and writers, pastors, liturgists, and other representatives of Asian churches, including women and youth."[4] The 1990 publication of the trial edition of *Sound the Bamboo*

---

3   Loh, *Sound the Bamboo: CCA Hymnal 2000* (Chicago: GIA Publications, 2006), xi.
4   Ibid.

allowed for further input and cross-fertilization of these hymns among the peoples of Asia.

In spite of a busy administrative schedule during his years as the president of Tainan Theological College and Seminary, I-to Loh made extensive corrections and modifications to *Sound the Bamboo* for a revised edition that was published in 2000. The executive editorial committee of the new edition remained the same as that of the 1990 edition: Francisco F. Feliciano (Philippines), James Minchin (Australia), and Loh as general editor. In the beautiful, slightly larger format of the 2000 edition, twenty-two countries are represented. The 2000 edition contains forty-four languages, including English. Thirteen hymns were dropped from the original 280 hymns published in the 1990 edition. Forty-eight new hymns were added for a total of 315 in the 2000 edition.[5]

Hymnal Companion to Sound the Bamboo: *Asian Hymns in Their Cultural and Liturgical Contexts* represents the next step in breaking the pot and reshaping it in Asian ways. One of the important responsibilities of a hymnologist is to "put a face" on the hymns that appear in a hymnal. Songs are the result of someone's creativity and inspiration. Composers and poets are part of a larger cultural setting.

Dr. I-to Loh and the Cultivation of Asian Hymnody

Though countless individuals have had a role in the preparation of this seminal text, undoubtedly the central figure is I-to Loh. Loh's work has many influences, but among the two most important are the personal and political contexts that have shaped his life and work. The personal influences are largely those of his family, especially his father. The political context is the role that his church, the Presbyterian Church of Taiwan (PCT), has had in advocating for self-determination for the people of Taiwan, Loh's home country.

Loh's father, Loh Sian-chhun (1905–1984), was a missionary among the indigenous people of Taiwan and also a hymnal editor for PCT.[6] Loh Sian-chhun frequently uprooted his family to accept various appointments in the PCT. This ministry often took him away from home for extended periods. I-to Loh comments on his father's travel:

> My father would often come home late at night, and when we left for school, he would still be in his room. When we came back from school, he was gone . . . He was often up in the mountain area, gone for more than a month and un-contactable.[7]

---

5   For a more extensive background, see Part 1, Section 3 of this volume, "History and the Development of CCA Hymnal: *Sound the Bamboo*."

6   The definitive work on I-to Loh is by Lim Swee Hong, "Giving Voice to Asian Christians: An Appraisal of the Pioneering Work of I-to Loh in the Area of Congregational Song," (PhD diss., Caspersen School of Graduate Studies, Drew University, 2006).

7   Ibid., 34.

Lim Swee Hong, Dr. Loh's student and primary biographer, notes that "these treks into tribal villages accompanying his father nurtured his spirituality and strengthened his personal commitment to the Church."[8] Though descended from the cultural majority Han people from mainland China, Loh's family provided the context for his compassion and love of the indigenous peoples of Taiwan, their cultures, and their music. This influence is evident in his work as a compiler of hymnals.

Loh Sian-chhun was the editor for the 1936 PCT hymnal *Sèng-si* and a hymnal committee member for the later edition of *Sèng-si* in 1964. I-to Loh, while a student at Tainan Theological College, assisted the secretary of the committee and served as the executive music editor for the 1964 edition. Loh Sian-chhun encouraged tribal groups to contribute hymns and attempted to adapt tribal music for use in the hymnal. I-to Loh returned as an ethnomusicologist to many of these villages and adapted tribal songs for a broader Taiwanese Christian audience.[9] Several of the songs in *Sound the Bamboo* come from tribes that I-to Loh visited during his early years with his father. Loh continues his contribution to the PCT with a new edition of *Sèng-si* that was published in 2009.

While Loh's family life had a profound impact on his future ministry, so did the political reality of growing up in a country occupied first by Japan and later by the Chinese Nationalists (KMT) led by Chiang Kai-shek, who instituted martial law. The occupiers' persecution of the Taiwanese people and their attempts to obliterate Taiwanese culture instilled in I-to Loh a love for his homeland and a passion for promoting the self-determination for all peoples. The PCT and Tainan Theological College and Seminary were leaders in the resistance against political domination. I-to Loh's family, the Presbyterian Church of Taiwan, and political oppression formed the matrix that has influenced the direction of his life.[10]

A long list of people influenced I-to Loh, but one person deserves special mention: his wife Hui-chin. In any conversation with Loh, one becomes immediately aware of the importance of his family and the many sacrifices they have made for his studies. His wife Hui-chin is a full partner in all of his activities, as expressed here in his own words:

> Hui-chin is a woman of wisdom, an excellent mother and wife, advisor, and educator. She sacrificed her own career as a Christian Education specialist just to accommodate my needs—taking full responsibility for raising our three fine children while I was an old graduate student and, later on, a wandering husband, leaving home for more than half of the time of the year: traveling, collecting materials, researching, conducting workshops, attending conferences, and teaching. She is my best critic, always helping

---

8   Ibid., 14.
9   Two examples of Taiwanese tribal music adapted by Loh are "O Give Thanks to the Lord" (*STB* #120) from the Ami tribe and "Let All Nations Praise the Lord" (*STB* #121) from the Puyama tribe.
10 For more information on the political context of these years, see C. Michael Hawn, *Gather into One: Praying and Singing Globally* (Grand Rapids, MI: Wm. B. Eerdmans, 2003), 74–78.

me to see things from different angles, always demanding more and better and higher standards. She typed my dissertation twice and helped me with all the clerical work, indexing all my major publications: *New Songs of Asian Cities* (1972), *Hymns from the Four Winds* (1983), *Sound the Bamboo* (1990), etc. She proofread and commented on all my writings, even my compositions. If I have any achievement or contribution, it is because of her help; she deserves more than half of my credit. I sometimes joke that I have passed my Ph.D. examinations, but I cannot graduate from her expectations.[11]

Lim Swee Hong offers this appraisal of Hui-chin's role:

In my estimate, many of Loh's pioneering publications would be less than user-friendly if not for the indomitable efforts of Hui-chin. In fact, the whole realm of Loh's publishing undertakings relied heavily on Hui-chin's handiwork of typesetting, data processing, index creation, and proofreading. Therefore, it would be a misconception to think of Hui-chin as the "woman behind the man." In many instances, she is the collaborator to Loh's work in Asian church music. This collaboration started with Hui-chin typing Loh's doctoral dissertation twice, and continued thereafter to her editorial work on the many hymn collections that Loh has created thus far.[12]

I-to Loh: Ethnomusicologist, Composer, Editor, Teacher, and Church Leader

Dr. Loh's contributions to Asian hymnody are a small part of a long list of accomplishments. His education at Tainan Theological College culminated with graduation in 1963. His thesis, "Praise from Jerusalem to Formosa: History and Development of Christian Hymns, with Special Emphasis on the History of Church Music in Taiwan," was an indication of his future direction. Even as a student, he was marked by his teachers Isabel Taylor and Kathleen Moody as a potential future faculty member. From 1964 to 1967, Loh continued his study at Union Theological Seminary in New York. As a candidate in the Master of Sacred Music program, Loh focused on composition. His graduation project was a 1966 composition entitled *Cycle of Psalms*, a three-movement work that included contrapuntally treated Han-Taiwanese melodic motives with Western harmonies.[13] Compositional study at Union Seminary proved to be important for his future vocation.

Following graduation from Union Seminary, Loh returned to Tainan Theological College to teach. He was granted a sabbatical in 1974 and chose to pursue studies as a special student in the Department of Ethnomusicology at University of California,

---

11   Correspondence with I-to Loh on November 22, 1996.
12   Hong, "Giving Voice to Asian Christians," 43.
13   Ibid., 20.

Los Angeles (UCLA). Mantle Hood, a leading figure in ethnomusicology and chair of the department, encouraged him to apply for doctoral work, and Loh chose to pursue a Ph.D. in this field. The breadth of non-Western music fascinated him. He applied the knowledge and experience gained at UCLA to his compositions and to future fieldwork in collecting Asian song.

As a result of his compositional study at Union Seminary and his exposure to the diversity of global music at UCLA, Loh mastered a variety of stylistic approaches. These are reflected in *Sound the Bamboo* (2000), ranging from "Hunger Carol" (*STB* #144) based on a Javanese *pelog* scale with a Balinese accompaniment, and "Loving Spirit" (*STB* #220) using a Bhairav raga ("gypsy scale") from India, to "The God of us all" (*STB* #181) drawing on a Japanese musical tradition, and "Child of Christmas story" (*STB* #141) based upon a Nepalese folk tradition. Loh also experimented with a Middle Eastern style in "Song to the Spirit" (*STB* #222), written for the 1991 World Council of Churches (WCC) Canberra Assembly, at a time marked by continuing clashes between Jews and Palestinians.[14]

Following Loh's graduation from UCLA, the twenty-year period between 1982 and 2002 was filled with an outpouring of activity for hymnal publications. Before going to UCLA, he already had traveled Asia, collecting songs for *New Songs of Asian Cities*, published in 1972. A later volume, *Hymns for the Four Winds*, a 1983 collection prepared for the United Methodist Church in the United States, established Loh as the preeminent international voice in Asian hymnody. This volume influenced many denominational hymnals published in the United States in the late 1980s and 1990s, as evidenced by the increasing number of Asian hymns in North American hymnals.

With support provided by the General Board of Global Ministries (GBGM) of the United Methodist Church, Loh was commissioned in 1982 as a teaching missionary to the Asian Institute for Liturgy and Music (AILM) in Manila. Loh's years at AILM (1982–1994) were a time for shaping a generation of Asian students with a love for church music and an appreciation for Asian songs from many cultures. Students from this period are now leaders in their respective cultures and faith traditions throughout Asia. Loh's publications of Asian Christian music from these years are numerous, culminating in the trial edition of *Sound the Bamboo* in 1990. Following the pattern established by his father, Loh traveled extensively during this time: collecting, recording, notating, and compiling hymns for this collection.

During this period, Loh also became a principal figure on the international ecumenical stage as a leader of Asian congregational song. Ecumenical bodies such as the World Council of Churches (WCC), the Christian Conference of Asia (CCA), Asia Alliance of YMCAs, and the Lutheran World Federation called upon Loh to lead songs for worship during their assemblies. His compositions were often chosen as theme songs for these gatherings, and the program and worship books prepared for these events disseminated his songs and songs by other Asian

---

14   Ibid. See pages 114–71 for a thorough treatment of the many styles used in Loh's compositions.

composers to a broader world audience. Although his first contact with the WCC was in 1972, his leadership at the 1983 Vancouver Assembly with Pablo Sosa from Argentina and Patrick Matsikenyiri from Zimbabwe assured a primary role for the music of the world church (beyond the West) in future events. He also participated in the worship committees for the WCC 1991 Canberra and 1998 Harare Assemblies.

Evidence of Loh's international and ecumenical reputation may be seen in the following two examples. He is a participant in the Global Praise Project sponsored by the General Board of Global Ministries of the United Methodist Church of the United States. Beginning in 1992, as an original and continuing member of the Global Praise Working Group, Dr. Loh contributed extensively to one of the most prolonged and thorough efforts in North America to collect and publish songs of the world church. As a hymnologist, Loh was made a Fellow of the Hymn Society in the United States and Canada in 1995. This is a recognition bestowed only on those who have made significant and enduring contributions to the field of hymnology. Dr. Loh is the only Asian to have received this honor.

While active in Asian song collection, composition, publication, and worship leadership, Loh also assumed major administrative roles during these years. Loh's service to Tainan Theological College and Seminary continued in 1994 when he returned to his alma mater as a professor of ethnomusicology and director of the church music program, where he instituted a master's level degree in church music. In 1995 he was asked to become the president of the institution; he accepted and held this position until 2002.

Academic Contributions to Ethnomusicology and Global Song

Such a full and productive public life as a composer, editor, teacher,[15] worship leader, and administrator would be daunting enough for most people. Dr. Loh also leaves a wealth of scholarly publications and compositions.

The sheer output of materials edited, authored, or composed by I-to Loh to date is staggering by any measure:[16]

- 25 musical collections and hymnals
- 8 extended musical compositions or liturgical musical settings
- 32 anthems
- Over 100 hymn tunes or hymn settings
- 9 folksong arrangements
- Dozens of organ preludes, fantasias, fugues, Chinese instrumental pieces, children's songs, and school songs

---

15 For a complete list of teaching posts held by I-to Loh through 2005, see Hong, "Giving Voice to Asian Christians," 243–44.

16 For a complete listing of publications by I-to Loh through 2005 as well as several articles translated from Chinese to English, see Hong, "Giving Voice to Asian Christians," 247–337.

- Translations of over 300 hymns and anthems, from English and other languages into Taiwanese and/or Mandarin
- 15 academic monographs and major articles in dictionaries and encyclopedias
- 30 articles in academic journals in Chinese and/or English
- 19 papers delivered at academic conferences

Further evidence of Dr. Loh's scholarly work is available in this volume in the Prologue and the seven articles that compose Part I, "Asian Hymns in Their Historical Perspectives." These essays are a distillation of Dr. Loh's lifework and offer cultural, musical, contextual, historical, theological, and liturgical insights into the panoply of Asian cultures and musical expressions. Beyond this foundational work, the discussions of each hymn and the biographies of the contributors to this publication are invaluable. Taken as a whole, this volume provides a glimpse into Asian Christian spirituality that will make it a landmark for years to come.

Assessing I-to Loh's Contributions

It is difficult to summarize the contributions that I-to Loh, a visionary prophet, has made in so many fields. Does one measure his life in the number of his compositions or in his hymns? Does one evaluate his achievements from his vast scholarly output? Does one assess his importance from the invitations to lead international events or the recognitions and honors that he has received? Can one judge his life through the many students that he has inspired and who now serve creatively and faithfully throughout Asia?

The answer to each of these questions is a resounding "YES!" Perhaps the most important concern is that Asian people understand what his lifework is about and sing Asian Christian songs as they praise and pray to God. Terry MacArthur, a former United Methodist missionary and worship consultant for the World Council of Churches including the Canberra and Harare Assemblies, has worked closely with Dr. Loh for many years. He offers this assessment of Loh's work among Asian Christians:

> One needs to be aware that he [collected and promoted Asian Christian songs] at a time when most Asians were looking to the West as the source of music for the church. I-to's work showed the possibility that Christian music in Asian styles already existed and could be used in Christian worship. Even if many of the songs he unearthed never became popular, it was no longer possible to insist that the only music appropriate for worship came from Europe or North America.
>
> Even when his work was not valued, he continued. When there was a dearth of material, he convinced students of his to write new songs in Asian styles, even when they doubted that it would be used or acknowledged

in their home churches. How much good material his students produced shows the powers of his persuasion.

He has not succeeded in breaking the dominance of Western music in Asian churches. But he has at least shown there is another option. At the very least he has left behind some work that people can return to when they get tired of being "imitation Westerners."[17]

This volume is perhaps the greatest fulfillment of I-to Loh's life and work. As with the preparation of the hymnal *Sound the Bamboo*, bringing together the stories of so many poets, composers, translators, and arrangers is a daunting task. Dr. Loh has worked with many of his former students at the Asian Institute for Liturgy and Music (AILM) and friends around the world to gather the information for this volume. Recalling the metaphor of D. T. Niles earlier in this foreword, the pot that has been reshaped in this volume is distinctly Asian, even though the collaborators come from around the world. Asian Christianity has been shaped in part by interaction with Western missionaries and music, and this volume acknowledges this fact by citing Western contributors. The difference is that Asian soils have been mixed with those from the rest of the world to produce a pot that carries the sung faith and theology of Asian peoples. Through this volume, their stories are now a part of the witness of the world church. The church is also more universal in its scope because we may now sing prayers and praise of Asian Christians. Western Christians in the twenty-first century now have an unparalleled opportunity to receive the gifts of Asian Christians and to enlarge their perspective of God who is at work throughout the world.

The following stanza from a hymn by the Filipina Natty G. Barranda offers twenty-first-century Christians a way express unity and ecumenical faith, of the whole inhabited earth:

> O many people of all lands
> now come to God with praise;
> together shall we praise our God,
> LORD of all culture's ways.
> —*Sound the Bamboo* #21

May the seeds sown through the composers and poets in this volume bear much fruit in the soils of Asia—and beyond.

—C. Michael Hawn
Perkins School of Theology
Southern Methodist University
Dallas, Texas, USA

---

17   Ibid., 246.

Introduction

John Julian's monumental *Dictionary of Hymnology*, 1892 and revised in 1907, included the first attempt to trace the sources, authors, and texts of hymns from global perspectives, including non-Western traditions. W. A. Stevenson's twenty-page essay "Foreign Missions" devotes fourteen pages to Asian hymns. Subsequent research and commentary on pan-Asian hymns was generally restricted to developments in specific cultures.

Twentieth-century Asian hymnals mainly consisted of translated western hymns set to western-style tunes. The first collection with a significant number of Asian hymns was the *E. A. C. C. Hymnal*, 1963 (Daniel Thambyrajah Niles, general editor; John Milton Kelly, musical editor), which was compiled for the E. A. C. C. Bangkok Assembly of 1964. This landmark collection included 202 hymns, 98 by Asian poets and composers. Asian hymns were mainly translated and versed by Niles, and texts were set to indigenous melodies in four-part accompaniments. The use of this collection—and its three supplements, in academic, denominational and ecumenical settings—opened new insights, visions, and promises and helped a new generation of Asian Christians lyrically explore and express the dynamics between theology and culture.

Niles's passion for Asian hymnody and liturgy would have died with him in 1970 was it not for scholar-composer-hymnist I-to Loh and his distinctive, four-decade contributions to Asian hymnic pedagogy and bibliography. Dr. Loh's work culminates in *Sound the Bamboo*, 2000, and its magisterial *Hymnal Companion to* Sound the Bamboo: *Asian Hymns in Their Cultural and Liturgical Context*. The latter, seven years in the making, carefully traces and pictorially documents the history, geography, culture, languages, musics and music history, musical instruments, vocal performance practices, images, and hymnic developments of twenty-three Asian countries and their cultures. The author's commentary on each text and tune adds to the unique story of Asian musicians and poets who have implemented Niles's famous metaphor by lyrically sowing the seed of the gospel in their own cultural soil and let their own versions of Christianity grow. The biographies and photographs of Asian authors and poets greatly enrich the often vague and anecdotal coverage found in standard reference volumes, and literally put a new face on hymnic research.

The comprehensiveness of this volume places it in a class with other one-author, labor-intensive, magisterial works such as Louis F. Benson's *The English Hymn*,

1915, and Egon Wellesz's *History of Byzantine Music and Hymnography*, 1949. However, this volume is distinguished from these because the author-historian is also the prime enabler of the hymnic repertories and liturgies he chronicles and discusses. Given this dynamic the reader will appreciate the author's struggle to craft an objective account of Asian hymns, their poetic forms, imageries, symbols, and their musical settings—the newest contributions to the vast repertory of Christian hymns.

In his introduction the author states a three-fold purpose for writing this work:

1. To help Asian Christians understand their own hymns and Christian heritages
2. To provide a scholarly and timely reference book on Asian hymnody
3. To help churches around the world gain understandings about Asian church music and spirituality

Two of the three goals are met. First, since the volume is the distillation and conveyance of the author's knowledge and wisdom, it will inform and inspire his many students and colleagues in Asia and elsewhere, who in turn will impart it to their students and colleagues. Second, it will become the standard reference work in Asian hymnology.

The third goal will be realized incrementally as local church musicians and pastors, particularly those in North America, seek resources to help break their congregations' long bondage to traditional Euro-Anglo ethnocentric worship forms and congregational song, and help rehabilitate those addicted to show-biz-style worship and minimalist worship-song to join with Christians elsewhere who pray, sing, and read Scripture in several languages and whose liturgies include intercultural images, drama, and dance.

In the meantime let us all raise a glass and a hallelujah in celebration for this distinctive work and its distinguished author!

—Carlton R. Young, editor
The United Methodist Hymnal

Prologue

Make a joyful noise to the Lord,
all the earth.
(Psalm 100:1, ESV)

Sound the Bamboo: CCA Hymnal 2000 is the official hymnal of the Christian Conference of Asia (CCA) and contains 315 hymns from twenty-two Asian countries. The texts, which were originally in forty-four languages, have been translated into English. The volume's diverse expressions of faith are unique in the history of Christian missions in Asia.

The main purpose of this companion volume is to provide basic information to Asians and non-Asians about Asian musical styles, the hymns in *Sound the Bamboo*, and their development in various Christian contexts.

To further this purpose, three objectives have been set:

1. **Mission and evangelism**: To help Asian Christians understand their own hymns and Christian heritages, deepen their appreciation of God's gifts, and develop their own ways of witness, so as to more fully contribute to the mission and evangelistic work of the Christian Conference of Asia and its member churches.
2. **Contextualization and theological education**: To provide a reference for church leaders, including pastors, church musicians, theologians, theological educators, and theological students, and to promote the understanding and the development of contextual theology, liturgy, and music.
3. **Unity in diversity**: To help churches around the world gain understanding about Asian church music and spirituality, as a way of strengthening their unity in diversity.

The Significance of
Sound the Bamboo and
the Hymnal Companion to *Sound the Bamboo*

O sing to the LORD a new song, for he has done
marvelous things.
(Psalm 98:1, NRSV)

Diverse Ethnic Traditions in Asia
Most Asian countries, except Japan and Korea, are inhabited by dozens of ethnic groups whose songs are formed and expressed in distinct languages and musical styles. By studying and singing the hymns derived from these rich Asian musical traditions, one learns to appreciate the gifts of God.

From Oral Traditions to Written Forms
Most indigenous folk songs, ballads, and many folk hymns exist in oral traditions and are passed down by memory from generation to generation. One of the most important features of *Sound the Bamboo* is that many Asian hymns appear in written form for the first time. Thus, they are preserved.

Personal Witness to the Hymns
Between the years 1968 to 1994, I had the privilege of visiting many Asian countries and meeting with the many authors, composers, and singers of these hymns. Additional information about hymns and their authors and composers was collected between 2004 and 2007. Personal witnesses, vital for understanding these hymns, also shed new light on the authors', composers', and commentator's understandings and interpretations of the gospel.

Proper Interpretation of Contextualized Church Music
This companion volume attempts to place all the hymns in *Sound the Bamboo* in their proper historical, cultural, musicological, theological, and liturgical contexts, so that the rich Asian musical traditions may be introduced, understood, and interpreted not only by Asians but also by their sisters and brothers around the world.

Mission to Other Parts of the World

The new Asian hymns—expressed in indigenous poetic forms, imagery, symbols, musical idioms, sounds, instruments, moods, and feelings—have created new ways of interpreting the Christian gospel that are meaningful not only to Asians but also to their "mother" and "sister" churches, in that they bring new messages and challenges. This constitutes a new phase of mission to the West and other parts of the world.

Vivid Symbol of the Church in Unity and Diversity

Christians all around the world have been deeply influenced both by liturgies, theologies, and hymns from the West and by Christian faith as preached, studied, and practiced through Western culture. The emergence of new Asian hymns offers new insights, visions, and promises. While the unity of the church was formerly expressed through singing Western hymns and accepting Western theologies, Asians and others can now witness a new unity by singing Asian-style hymns.

The First Major Resource on Asian Church Music

With this book, theological schools in Asia will now be able to test their critical Asian principles in practice.

Acknowledgments

From when I began to collect Asian songs/hymns in 1968 to the completion of this work, a span of nearly thirty-nine years, I have been helped, advised, and hosted by innumerable friends and strangers in their churches and schools, at their homes, along the streets, and through phone calls, letters, and electronic correspondences. Without their kind support and assistance, this work could not have been completed. I especially thank all of the authors, composers, translators, paraphrasers, arrangers, and performers whose kind assistance was crucial to the production of *Sound the Bamboo: CCA Hymnal 2000* and this companion. Through the recommendation and introduction of Rev. George Todd, who has been my mentor since seminary days, Takenaka Masao requested me to collect songs for the Urban Rural Mission Committee (URM) of CCA, and Rev. Harry Daniel and Rev. Oh Jae Shik helped me to establish initial contacts in Asia. In addition, Tosh Arai played a major role in the editing of *Sound the Bamboo*.

Since it is impossible to name all the contributors to these volumes, only a few are listed, by country:

Japan: Rev. Sōji Kitamura, Yasuhiko Yokosaka, Taihei Satō,
    George Gish
Korea: Geonyong Lee, Seondae Kim, Young Jo Lee, Paul Huh,
    In Pyong Chun, Jae Woong Ahn, Rev. Jae Shik Oh, Ok Youn Kim,
    Yong Bock and Marion Kim, Seung Hyon Min
China and Hong Kong: Shen-yin Wang, Rev. Sheng-ben Lin, Daniel Law,
    Rev. Zhe-sheng Ji, Lung-kwong Lo
Cambodia: Rev. Chhun Eang
Thailand: Inchai Srisuwan, Solot Kuptarat
Myanmar: Anna May Saypa, Saw Si Hae, Saw Tun Meh
Bangladesh: Bart Shaha, Samar Das
Nepal: Loknath Manaen
India: Thomas Thangaraj, Sharada Schaffter, John Barathi, Ashly William Joseph,
    Sudhakar and Rouilla Doraiswamy, Prabhakar Samson, Kiran and Mrinalini
    Sebastian, E. C. John, Anto Armanad, Roger Gaikwad, Christianna Singh,
    Kumar Santosh, Immanuel Solomon, Rev. Cyril Hans
Pakistan: Bishop John Samuel, Sherazi Almoos Hizqial, Farhana Nazir
Sri Lanka: Bishop Kumara Illangasinghe, Chitra Fernando
Malaysia: Thu En Yu, Rev. Lu Chen Tiong

Singapore: Swee Hong Lim, Rev. Samuel Liew, Bishop Dr. Robert Solomon
Indonesia: Henriette Hutabarat, Sientje Merentek-Abram, Bishop Wayan Mastra,
    I Nyoman Darsane, Father Karl Prier, Ruth Kadarmanto, Christina Mandang,
    Rev. Christian I. Tamaela, Marcius Tinambunan, Timotheus Gunawan,
    Rev. Paul Urlich Munthe
Australia: Father James Minchin
New Zealand: Rev. John and Shirley E. Murray, Colin Gibson,
    Rev. Ron O'Grady, Rev. Bill (W. L.) Wallace
Philippines: Francisco F. Feliciano, Beth Nacion-Puyot, Dean Tom Maddela,
    Rev. Delbert Rice, Ronald Hines, Romeo del Rosario, Grace Roble-Tabada,
    Cobbie Palm

I thank Wallace M. Alston, Jr., the director of the Center of Theological Inquiry on the campus of Princeton Theological Seminary, for offering me a membership at the center from September 2003 to August 2004, which enabled me to devote the whole year to researching and writing this companion. It was the most luxurious year of my life—any scholar would dream to have such a beautiful environment in which to live and study. In conclusion, I am very grateful to Robert Batastini, vice-president of GIA Publications, for the generous grant that enabled me to return to Asia and visit many of the contributors in Japan, Korea, Hong Kong, the Philippines, Malaysia, India, Cambodia, and Indonesia (which I visited twice) and to search for pertinent information about the hymns. GIA has also reprinted *Sound the Bamboo* in the United States for wider distribution and will publish this companion. Without these two special forms of support, this project would never have seen completion. I am grateful to Leng and Lisa for the photographs of my instrumental collection. I also thank Deanna Lee, the copyeditor of this book.

A number of friends and scholars have read and commented on drafts of this book: Carlton R. Young (for Parts One and Two), Rev. Sōji Kitamura (Japan), Francisco Feliciano (Philippines), Thomas Thangaraj (India and Pakistan), Rev. Loknath Manaen (Nepal), Shanta Premawardhana (Sri Lanka), Bart Shaha (Bangladesh), Paul Huh (Korea), Lim Swee Hong (Singapore), Father James Minchin (Australia and New Zealand), and Rev. Lu Chen Tiong (Malaysia). I greatly value their suggestions, which have improved the texts; any possible failings of this book are entirely my responsibility.

I would like to express my gratitude to Datuk Thu En Yu, chairperson of the Association for Theological Education in South East Asia (ATESEA); Prawate Khid-Arn, general secretary of the Christian Conference of Asia; and Michael Hawn, professor of church music and director of the Sacred Music Program, Southern Methodist University, for contributing the Foreword and Prefaces. Most of all, I thank Carlton R. Young, a distinguished composer, musicologist, hymnologist, hymn editor and all-around church musician, for writing the Introduction.

My life and my work would not be as meaningful and rewarding if I did not have the love, sacrifice, support, advice, and encouragement of my wife Hui-chin. The understanding and support of our children Tun-bin, Tun-khian, and Tun-leng is also greatly appreciated; this work is affectionately dedicated to them, their spouses, and their children. I hope that our children and grandchildren find interest and inspiration in this book as a step toward searching for their Asian roots.

General Introduction

Geographical and Cultural Groupings

Asian countries—excluding those in former Soviet republics and the Middle East, which for this study are not considered part of Asia—cover approximately 23.5% of the world's surface area. Asia's nearly 3,550 ethno-linguistic peoples compose twenty-eight of the world's seventy-one ethno-linguistic families. The 2,240 distinct languages spoken in these countries constitute about 31% of the world's languages. It is estimated that 24.69% of Asian populations are Muslim, 22.8% are Hindu, 10.70% are Buddhists, and only 8.58% are Christians (Johnstone 2001, 41).

Sound the Bamboo: CCA Hymnal 2000 contains 315 hymns and liturgical responses in forty-four languages from twenty-two countries in Asia and the Pacific. The broad span of the geographical area and its diversity of cultures dictate the grouping of the hymns by country within five regions.

> **Northeast Asia:** China, Hong Kong (SAR), Japan, Korea, Taiwan
> **Mainland Southeast Asia:** Cambodia, Laos, Malaysia, Myanmar, Singapore, Thailand, Vietnam
> **Island Southeast Asia**: Indonesia, the Philippines
> **South Asian Subcontinent**: Bangladesh, India, Nepal, Pakistan, Sri Lanka
> **Southwest Pacific Ocean**: Australia, New Zealand, Papua New Guinea

The countries in each region are listed in alphabetical order, and hymns from each country are discussed in alphabetical order. Hymn texts and tunes created by authors and composers from different countries are listed under the country of the author, with a cross reference. For each country, an introduction describes its people and culture, includes basic facts and statistics for a general understanding of its present situation, and provides a brief history of Christian mission in that country. Commentaries on hymn texts and an analysis of musical styles and their usage in liturgy constitute the major portion of this volume. The names of authors, translators, paraphrasers, composers, and arrangers are included in or at the end of the texts, and their biographies appear in alphabetical order by last name in Part Three. Unfortunately, even after extensive travel and diligent searches and inquiries, many of the works still remain anonymous, and the biographies of many authors and composers are still unavailable. Any assistance or corrections for possible future editions would be appreciated.

Transliterations and Pronunciation

The hymns' diversity of languages, written forms, and unique spelling systems led the editorial committee to adopt two approaches.

Standard Romanization System

The committee considered using the International Phonetic Alphabet but found it too complicated for most users of the hymnal. In this collection, transliterated texts are based on the following standard or official transliteration systems: Burmese (including Kachin, Karen), Pilipino (including Tagalog, Ikalahan, Cebuano), Cambodian (Khmer), Laotian, Vietnamese, Indonesian (including Balinese), Japanese (including Okinawan), Korean, Mandarin Chinese, Malaysian (including Kadazan), Nepali, Taiwanese (including Hokkien [Amoy], Amis, Bunun, Paiwan), Maori, and Pidgin English in Papua New Guinea.

A Compromised System for the South Asian Subcontinent

Due to the lack of uniformity in transliteration systems in the languages of India, Pakistan, Sri Lanka, Bangladesh, and Nepal, we have unified the transliteration of vowels while adapting the use of consonants particular to the following languages: Hindi, Tamil, Kannada, Malayalam, Mizo, Mundari, Sanskrit, Telegu, Punjabi, and Urdu. Sinhala and Bengali still need further modification. The following chart provides a general guideline to the short and long vowel sounds:

Vowels:	a	e	i	o	u
Pronounced:	ah	l_e_t	h_i_t	f_o_r	p_u_t
Long vowels:	aa	ee	ii	oo	uu
Pronounced:	f_a_r	a_i_r	h_ee_l	oh	f_oo_l

When "h" is added to the consonant, such as "th" or "dh," one places the tip of the tongue against the back of the upper teeth when pronouncing the "t" and "d."

In Thamilz, the "lz" is like the American "r" as in "fur."

In Urdu, Karen, and Burmese, "añ" or "eñ" are pronounced with a nasal sound, similar to French, without actually pronouncing the "n."

In Taiwanese (Hokkien), "oa" or "ia" etc. with a small "n" on the top right are also pronounced like the "ñ" sound.

The above short vowels are also applicable to all East Asian countries.

In Korean, however, one should take note of the following:

ŭ is close to a shwa "ə", ŭi = "e", ŏ = "aw"

In Japanese, vowels are lengthened by adding a line on top: ō, ū.

Vowels and Final Consonants in Mainland and Island Southeast Asia

The above guidelines of short and long vowels in the South Asian Subcontinent are also applicable to Vietnam, Cambodia, Laos, Thailand, Myanmar, and Malaysia; additional sounds are "ae" as in "apple," "aw" as in "law," and "e" in a weak syllable is treated like a shwa "ə."

In Thai, "oe" is also pronounced as "ə," and "eu" as "i" or "u" (with a sideways slash). In Myanmar, "ey" or "ay" are the equivalent of a long "ee."

In Khmer, the final consonants "s," "t," "d," and "k" are silent.

For other consonants, see the explanations below.

Initial Consonants

Initial consonants are more complicated among Asian languages. This table provides a general guide:

Imploded, unaspirated:	k	p	t	in most Asian languages
but spelled:	g	b	d	in Mandarin
Exploded, aspirated:	kh	ph	th	in most Asian languages
but spelled:	hk	hp	ht	in Burmese, and "th" is like "the"
and spelled:	k	p	t	in Mandarin

An initial "c" in Indonesian and Burmese is pronounced like the final "ch" of "chur<u>ch</u>."

In Pilipino, "ng" alone is pronounced "nang."

In Indonesian, "yg" is an abbreviation of "yang."

Mandarin consonants are more complicated: "qi" is pronounced like "chee" and "xi" is pronounced like "she" but more frontally and with less air. "Z" is like the "tz" in "Heifetz," and "c" is like an exploded "z." "Sh" and "r" have no English equivalents; "sh" is similar to the English pronunciation but with the tongue curled, and "r" is like the initial sound of "rite."

Commentary and Analysis of Hymns

This companion is written for the general public, especially people in Asia and the Pacific for whom English is not their first language; these users may have difficulty understanding some of the hymns. Therefore, efforts have been made to highlight or summarize the main contents of every hymn, and some hymns have suggestions as to how the hymn or liturgical response may be sung and used in liturgies. For the musical analysis, a few basic musical terms and very straightforward language are used to explain the styles; these analyses are written for musicians, theological students, pastors, and theological educators with a basic knowledge of music. But this by no means precludes the general public or lay audience from reading these analyses. In fact, the cultural backgrounds, the liturgical contexts, and some of the interpretations of text, tunes, and text-tune relationships (or what is called "doing theology with music") will be helpful to all readers in understanding these hymns and using them in their liturgies or in "doing contextual theologies." The following explanation will facilitate the basic tools for analyzing the music.

Cipher Notation

Cipher notation is used in this book for two reasons: the majority of the people in Asia are not familiar with Western staff notation, and it is very difficult to insert staff notation examples within the text. Cipher notation was developed in France in 1742 by J. J. Rousseau (1712–1778) (Liu 1991, 129f). This system uses Arabic numerals to represent pitches and durations and is commonly employed in China, Hong Kong, Taiwan, Indonesia, Myanmar, and Thailand. Each number corresponds to the pitch in the movable *do* system. The following illustration shows the Western staff notation, cipher notation, tonic sol-fa system (solfege), and the Western pitch names of three scales: A = 6, C = 1, and G = 1:

6	7	1	2	3	4	5	6	7	i	2	3	4♯	5
la	si	do	re	mi	fa	sol	la	si	do'	re'	mi'	fi'	sol'
A	B	c	d	e	f	g	a	b	c'	d'	e'	f♯	g'
						G=1	2	3	4	5	6	7	1
						do	re	mi	fa	sol	la	si	do'

The movable *do* system means 1 (*do*) can be anywhere on the staff; it represents the tonic of the major scale or key. For instance: G = 1 means G is the tonic of the G diatonic scale (1 2 3 4 5 6 7), and E = 6 denotes E as *la*, i.e. the E-minor scale (6 7 1 2 3 4 5 or ♯5). A dot above the number indicates that the pitch is one octave higher, and a dot below equals one octave lower. Since it is difficult to add the dot above or below the number when citing examples in the text, they have been omitted in most cases. All the scales are listed in ascending order from low to high; it is understood that in a 5 6 1 2 3 scale, 5 and 6 are lower than 1, so there is no need to mark which notes are higher or lower. Where there is a possibility of confusion, a comma indicates a lower note (such as 5,) and an apostrophe indicates a higher note (1'), thus differentiating these notes from the others. In citing musical examples, each numeral represents one count, or a quarter note. Adding a hyphen (3-) lengthens the value by one more count. As in staff notation, a period on the right (5.) adds one-half the value. An underline cuts the value in half: $\underline{1}$ and $\underline{2}$ are one half-count each; combined, they become one count ($\underline{1\ 2}$). Sixteenth notes are indicated by double underlines ($\underline{\underline{1\ 2}}$).

Scales

One of the most important factors affecting the style of a tune is the scale; thus, the initial tone, the number of tones in the scale, and the final tone are identified for each tune. For those who may not be familiar with Western staff notation, the first note of each song has been identified for easy singing.

For instance, the first hymn in *Sound the Bamboo: CCA Hymnal 2000*, "Come, O come, let us praise parent God" (*STB* #1), is in A = 5 seven-tone scale (D = 1 2 3 4 5 6 7) with final on 1: A = 5 means the first pitch of the melody (the initial) is A, which is to be sung as *sol* (5) in the D = *do* diatonic scale (1 2 3 4 5 6 7), and the ending pitch (the final) is on 1 (*do*). When there are altered tones, they are indicated by accidentals. For example, "Now let us tell of your victory" (*STB* #22), is in E = 3 seven-tone scale (C = 1 2 3 4 5 6 7) plus a raised fourth (♯4, F♯) and a flattened seventh (♭7, B♭), with final on 1 (C).

Structure and Form

The terms "structure" and "form," denoting the organization of phrases in a tune or within a section, are used loosely and interchangeably. For easy understanding, the construction a a' b a" describes the organization of a tune in four phrases: a' is a variation of a; b represents new ideas, and a" is a further variation of a'. In certain pieces where phrases are extended and/or not clearly separated, the long phrase is combined as one unit, a or b. When capital letters (A, B, C) are used, they represent larger sections or parts, each of which may contain two to four or more phrases. For instance, *STB* #276, "Blest are the poor folk," has the following form:

Verse: 3x

//:A://BA//:   C A   ://BA//

//:A:// means the whole A section is repeated. //:CA:// is the verse, which is repeated three times with different stanzas of text. The final section //BA// is not repeated.

Harmony and Multipart Setting

The tunes with traditional Western harmonic settings are not analyzed in this volume, since they are already familiar to most musicians. For settings in other styles, the following general terms describe their harmonic treatments or relationships between parts.

Initial: the first note of the melody
Final: the last note of the melody, usually the most important tone in deciding the nature of the melody, the tonal center, tonality, or modality

    Counterpoint: an independent line, creating a countermelody against the
        main melody; may or may not follow Western musical theory
    Imitation: more or less imitating the shape of the main melody
    Sequence: a melodic figure repeating a few times either in higher or lower
        sequences with the same shape, such as 1 2 3 1, 2 3 4 2, or 6 7 1 6
    Reiterated drone: same note repeated a few times: 1 1 1 1
    Ostinato: same melodic and rhythmic figure repeating n times exactly
        without change: 6 1 6 1 6 1

Unless a hymn utilizes Western traditional harmony, it is not identified as being in a major or minor key. When appropriate, the hymn's tonal center or even the name of a church mode will indicate the hierarchical importance of the pitch.

    With this introduction, the reader is prepared to journey into the world of Asian hymns, to join Asian Christians in making a joyful noise, and to sing new songs to proclaim God's marvelous works in Asia today.

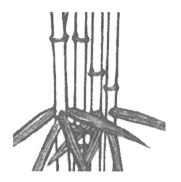

Part One

Asian Hymns in Their Historical Perspectives

But you will receive power when the Holy Spirit has come upon you;
and you will be my witnesses in Jerusalem,
in all Judea and Samaria,
and to the ends of the earth.
(Acts 1:8)

Part One

Asian Hymns in
Their Historical Perspectives

Asian Identities and Their Expression
of Christian Faith

Asia covers such a broad geographic area and is so culturally diverse that no simple statement or general description could do justice. This discussion is therefore limited to the cultural aspects that have a direct bearing on the formation of Asian Christian expression, on the words and music of hymns, and to a lesser degree on their liturgical contexts. Bishop Emerito P. Nacpil, former director of the Association of Theological Education in Southeast Asia (ATESEA) and dean of the Southeast Asia Graduate School of Theology (SEAGST) lists seven characteristics, which, though somewhat outdated, still provide insight for understanding certain Asian cultures:

1) Plurality and diversity of races, peoples, cultures, social institutions, religions, and ideologies
2) Experience as a former colony
3) In the process of nation building, development, and modernization
4) Desire to achieve authentic self-identity and cultural integrity in the modern world
5) Home of the world's living religions (Buddhism, Hinduism, Confucianism, Taoism, etc.)
6) Searching for a form of social order beyond the current options
7) Christian community is the minority (except in the Philippines)

(ATESEA Handbook 2000–2001, 68–69)

This list suggests the complex state of many Asians caught between contrasting worlds: native and global, traditional and contemporary. While most Asian countries have completed the nation-building process, many are still far from achieving an ideal situation. Development and modernization have positive and negative aspects. For example, most Asian countries that have emerged from colonization are now trapped by globalization. Asian as well as Third World countries constantly struggle to affirm their identities in an ever-changing world.

Searching for New Asian Identities

Many Asians have had vivid experiences of the region's dramatic changes since the end of World War II: the sweetness and agony of new freedom and democracy, the rapid social transformation, the pressure toward industrialization and commercialism, the development of mass media, the amazing ability and power of computers, the tremendous speed of travel and communications, and the inevitable formation of the "global village." While all of these factors compel Asians to cooperate with one another, they have also made it more difficult for Asians to maintain ethnic identities, traditions, and values. It appears the closer we are to contemporary global culture, the less we are able to retain our national heritages. It is with little wonder that many Asians today have difficulty finding their roots and convincing others of their own cultural identities.

One of the most significant changes in South and Southeast Asia is the freedom from colonial rule by imperialistic Asian neighbors and/or Western European countries, the latter often abetted by the Christian church and its missionary activities. A notable exception is Thailand, which for several centuries has maintained its sovereignty and cultural identity. In most cases, colonization, dictatorship, and political oppression were accompanied by cultural genocide. People were forced to accept and learn the cultural values of their colonizers or dictators, including their language, arts, and music. However, many Asian nations seized opportunities to fight for freedom, and they eventually gained their independence from colonizing countries, as shown in the following list:

> Bangladesh: from Pakistan, 1971
> Cambodia: from France, 1949; full independence, 1953
> Hong Kong: from the United Kingdom, 1997
> India: from the United Kingdom, 1947
> Indonesia: from the Netherlands, 1945
> Korea: from Japan, 1945
> Laos: from France, 1954
> Philippines: from the United States, 1946; from Marcos dictatorship, 1986
> Malaysia: from the United Kingdom, 1957
> Myanmar: from the United Kingdom, 1948
> Pakistan: from the United Kingdom, 1947
> Singapore: from the United Kingdom, 1957; separated from Malaysia, 1965
> Taiwan: from Japan, 1945; from Chinese Nationalist dictatorship, 1996
> Vietnam: from France, 1954

After these countries acquired freedom, democracy, and prosperity, their institutions re-educated the citizens to respect their own cultures, arts, and traditions. Consequently, many Asians have gained new understanding of their history, cultures, and ideologies, and they no longer accept or rely exclusively on the views of their former colonizers or Western scholars. At the same time that these countries have gradually gained confidence and self-esteem in developing their own democracies and cultivating their artistic heritages, they have been confronted by global political and economic structures, as well as the powerful mass media. These global forces have exploited each country's shortcomings and have created consumers' desires for the perceived lifestyle of the West. Slowly, Asian countries have entered the trap of globalization.

General Expression of Asian Christian Faith

Struggling to define their old and new identities, Asian churches are also discerning the impact of globalization while reviving their cultural heritages to recreate Christian arts and expressions. In 1988, I was invited to give a lecture in Hong Kong for the Conference of the World Association of Chinese Church Music. This lecture articulated widely held impressions of Chinese-speaking churches:

1. The concept of "banana churches": All Chinese-speaking Christians around the world appear "yellow" from their skin, but deep in their hearts and minds they long to be as "white" as Caucasians in the West. Their Christian faith is expressed by the wholesale acceptance, imitation, and replication of Western models.
2. Translated and borrowed theologies: The churches learn and express Western theologies translated into Chinese and accept them with little or no critical evaluation regarding contextual applicability. They do not develop their own theologies.
3. Copied music: The great majority of Chinese composers imitate Western styles of composition and harmony. They also copy and translate Western anthems without acquiring permission from the composer, author, or publisher.
4. Second-hand liturgies: Church leaders who resist contextualization have absolutized liturgies introduced over a century ago by missionaries.

(Loh 1992, 120–22)

In conclusion, I challenged musicians and pastors attending the conference, essentially asking, "Where is the rice? Where are the staple foods, the substance of a Chinese Christian expression?"

Unfortunately, the above observations and comments reflect the general situation and attitude in today's Asian churches, seminaries, and other institutions. Exceptions are found in India (United Theological College in Bagalore, Thamilnadu Theological Seminary in Madurai, and the [Roman Catholic] National Biblical, Catechetical and Liturgical Center in Bangalore); the Philippines (Asian Institute for Liturgy and Music); Taiwan (Tainan Theological College and Seminary, Yushan Theological College and Seminary); Thailand (Isaan Community Church); and Indonesia (Yamuger, Duta Wacana, and Protestant Church in Bali). Of course, there are likely many others. Also, during the past two to three decades, a few Asian theologians in the West and in Asia have written on Asian theologies or their interpretations. For example, C. S. Song wrote *The Tears of Lady Meng* (WCC

Risk Books, 1981), *Third-Eye Theology* (Orbis Books, 1979), *The Compassionate God* (Orbis Books, 1982), *Theology From the Womb of Asia* (Orbis Books, 1986), and three volumes on Christology: *Jesus, the Crucified People* (Orbis Books, 2001, paperback), *Jesus and the Reign of God* (Orbis Books, 1993, paperback), and *Jesus in the Power of the Spirit* (Orbis Books, 1994, paperback). Other contributions have been made by Kosuke Koyama's *Water Buffalo Theology* (Orbis Books, 1974, revised and expanded 1999), Yong-Bock Kim's *Messiah and Minjung* (CCA, 1992), and Thomas Thangaraj's in-depth dialogues about Hinduism, *The Crucified Guru* (Abingdon, 1994). More Asian Christians, including church musicians, pastors, and theologians, will continue to learn from these and other writers, so that more contextual theologies, liturgies, and hymns (including music) will be created for the nurture and growth of all Asian churches.

Recent Impact of Globalization

The central theme of my life's work has been the struggle between Asian contextualization and Westernization, and more recently the phenomenon of globalization. Having emerged during the past two decades, globalization has affected people around the world in many ways. This discussion will be restricted to the impact of globalization on music and worship. Seen as a positive force, globalization brings new ideas, stimuli, and challenges that lead to progress. It has created and sped the sharing of resources through all kinds of media, all of which impact Christian music and worship. But globalization can also be seen as a new invasion of Western powers. Because the effects of globalization are often too strong for local people to resist, it has been difficult to contextualize their music and worship within their own cultures. The following are a few examples of globalization's effect on local churches in Taiwan and other parts of Asia.

1. The wholesale importation of Western praise choruses and pop-style hymns has caused a host of problems. First, church leaders use these styles of music to warm-up the congregation for a half-hour or longer without considering its relevancy to the liturgy. Second, the music weakens the congregation's musical ability and discourages interest in other types of music; consequently, native traditions and newly composed songs in ethnic styles have little chance to be taught and thus to survive. Third, by using this music, the church loses its historical and ecumenical links, resulting in narrow-minded Christians and neglected and distorted doctrines of God and the church.

2. Entertainment-oriented worship services of "success theology" formulated after globalization have become the primary mode for preaching and evangelism.

3. Some Western editors/compilers have recorded songs from Asia and other parts of the Third World and published them under their own names as arrangers. But in fact, they have only transcribed existing tunes, changed a few notes at best, and then claimed ownership of the music.

4. Some Western composers have arranged simple Asian or Third World songs into larger Western-style choral works, altering the original styles such that their uniqueness is lost. Even worse, the arrangers then copyright the songs, and the original composers have to pay fees to access their own diluted music.

To summarize: The West has the knowledge and the financial resources to appropriate the musical works of Asia and the Third World. Composers randomly apply Western harmony to render Asian and the Third World songs more palatable for Western consumption. This is akin to forcing the poor or people in hot climates to wear formal suits and ties before allowing them to worship God. Asian or Third World people have been led to feel pride in music that is no longer anything to be proud of, and some of them do not understand how their music has been manipulated (Loh 2005c, 125f).

I frequently tell my Asian colleagues and students that modernization is not the equivalent of Westernization. If you copy others all the time, then you lose your sense of self. In the Christian context, this has occurred primarily in two ways. First, the early missionaries initially transplanted the gospel to Asia with little or no regard for local cultural context. Even if the missionaries had good intentions, they did not have better expressions to contextualize their theology. This was the fundamental cause of the problem. Second, rapid globalization is compounding the situation. Local people have come to see their own culture as having little or no value; local culture is being thrown out in favor of Western ideas. This is by no means a new concern.

The Causes of the Problem: Transplantation of the Gospel

Daniel Thambyrajah Niles (1908–1970), the cofounder of the Christian Conference of Asia and its first general secretary, recognized this problem decades ago. Although he did not live to experience the phenomenon of globalization, his observations and suggestions for solutions are still valid. Niles used an elegant metaphor to explain the problem of transplanting the gospel:

> The Gospel is like a seed and you have to sow it. When you sow the seed of the Gospel in Palestine, a plant that can be called Palestinian Christianity grows. When you sow it in Rome, a plant of Roman Christianity grows. You sow the Gospel in Great Britain and you get British Christianity. The seed of the Gospel is later brought to America and a plant grows of American Christianity. Now when missionaries came to our lands they brought not only the seed of the Gospel, but their own plant of Christianity, flower pot included! So, what we have to do is to break the flower pot, take out the seed of the Gospel, sow it in our own cultural soil, and let our own version of Christianity grow (Hawn 2003, 32).

Here, Niles points to the heart of the problem, not only of the gospel but also of Asian expression of faith through music and worship. The majority of efforts in Asia today, unfortunately, are still focused on translating, imitating, and copying Western ways of singing and worship, with the belief that they are the only authentic Christian expressions. Instead, efforts should be focused not only on breaking the Western flowerpot but also on taking out the seed of the gospel and figuring out how to plant this seed. Asians need to cultivate a version of Christianity that is appropriate to their cultural soil.

From Acculturation and Inculturation
to Contextualization

The cultivation of Asian Christian faith and forms of worship has not been an easy task, primarily because it was thought the only authentic Christian expressions were those taught by missionaries. In addition, church leaders have assumed that a ritual will lose its meaning and power if one does not rigidly follow it. Consequently, early Asian Christians had to learn Western culture, music, and hymns; to accept Western doctrines; to imitate the Western ways of life; and even to wear Western clothes. A paradox of Christian expression and native culture emerged: "The closer the Christian expression to the Western culture, the easier for the traditional Christians to accept; the closer to the native culture, the more resistance it causes" (Loh 1993a, 55). Thus, many Christians who were reconciled with God and were assimilated to Western culture became alienated from their own people and rejected their own culture. This was often regarded as a "true conversion." It is no wonder the Christians in Bali were called the "Black Dutch," for they showed much pride in dressing, thinking, and acting like the white Dutch missionaries (Loh 1988, 7).

The African specialist Albert Nolan has commented, "One of the biggest problems with Western theology is that it thought it was a universal theology" (Hawn 2003, 140). It may still be so, but it is not only a problem for the West. Many Christians in Asia and the Third World today still believe that Western theologies, music, and liturgies are universal and still want to follow, protect, and propagate them.

During the early stage of missionary endeavor, the new converts' superficial assimilation into Western Christian culture was not very difficult. But it was not easy for some Asians to sing Western hymns, because the scale system, rhythms, and harmony were foreign to them. They had to change or modify them; this is the problem of acculturation.

Acculturation

Aylward Shorter defines acculturation as "the encounter between one culture and another, or the encounter between cultures, and it is the communication between cultures on a footing of mutual respect and tolerance and a necessary condition of a Church that claims to be universal" (Shorter 1988, 7f).

Here is one example of acculturation: When missionaries introduced early Korean Christians to Western hymns, the Koreans had to change the melodies to suit their folk singing style. Korean traditional music is usually in a compound meter, 9/8 or 6/8, and usually the tunes do not repeat the same note in the melody but prepare or anticipate the next tone. According to Seongdae Kim, the hymn tune NETTLETON ("Come thou fount of every blessing") was sung like this (Kim 1999, 194):

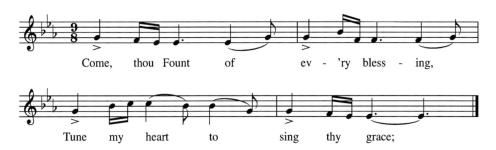

Here, the Koreans not only changed the rhythms and time signature and anticipated the next tone on the weak beat (the last eighth note) but also removed the seventh degree of the scale because it is not in the traditional five-tone scale.

Another example is H. W. Baker's text "Lord, thy word abideth," set to the tune RAVENSHAW, which was originally a Bohemian Christmas carol (Loh 1993a, 51) and uses a diatonic scale, 1 2 3 4 5 6 7. But the Indonesian *pelog* scale is 1 3 4 5 7. So Indonesian Christians removed tones 2 and 6 and altered the tune as follows, in cipher notation:

Original version: 1 1 3 4 5- 5- 6 7 i 5 3 #4 5- 4 2 3 4 3 2 1- 7 1 2 3 2- 1-
Indonesian version: 3 1 3 4 5- 5- 7 i 5 4 3 4 5- 4 3 1 4 3 1 3- 7 1 3 5 4- 3-

The Indonesians not only substituted 7 for 6 and 3 or 1 for 2 (because 6 and 2 are not in the *pelog* scale) but also changed the melodic shapes: 3 1 3 for 1 1 3, 7 i 5 4 for 6 7 i 5, and 4 3 1 4 3 1 3- for 4 2 3 4 3 2 1; they also removed the sharp from 4. The most dramatic change, however, is the cadence 7 1 3 5 4- 3-. Although the melodic shape remains similar, the cadential formula has been changed to satisfy Indonesian music theory, i.e. with final on 3. With all of these Indonesian style changes, this RAVENSHAW has become almost totally Indonesian. The original Western tune is almost unrecognizable. This example of musical acculturation is different from what I have referred to as Western exploitation.[1] There may have only been a small change in the musical language, but it was sufficient to change the style of the hymn and make it accessible to the traditional Indonesian. In this case, the pot that D. T. Niles mentioned was not broken, but native soil was added to the pot, so the plant grew slightly differently than the original; the native soil nourished and changed the features and the life of the plant to be more Indonesian. But this is not enough; the further goals are inculturation and/or contextualization.

Inculturation

Shorter defines inculturation as "the ongoing dialogue between faith and culture or cultures" or "the creative and dynamic relationship between the Christian message and a culture or cultures" (Shorter 1988, 11). Brian Wren further suggests that inculturation is "a two-way process, whereby Christians reach out to a culture different from their own, respect it, enter it, and interact with it, neither losing their identity nor remaining unchanged" (Wren 2001, 153). It seems that acculturation and inculturation are two necessary processes that will lead toward the ideal of contextualization, a term initially coined by my mentor Shoki Coe in the late 1960s.

Contextualization

In my initial attempt (1984) to define the meaning of contextualization, I summarized that

> Contextualization is, above all, the manifestation of the Imago Dei in human kind. It is the revelation of the mystery of God's creative power as shown in God's creation, including human minds that formulate various art forms. And it is our participation in God's continuous creation, letting God transform our culture and arts into dynamic media that will effectively communicate and express the meanings of the gospel to our people. (Loh 1991a, 93)

Today, the ultimate goal of contextualization is the realization of incarnation in any given context. Incarnation means that God in Christ takes on a native form. When the Word and gospel are expressed and interpreted in native forms, they should no longer be contained in Niles's flowerpot. If they are, the pot has to be broken and the seed planted so it can grow in the native soil.

---

1   These examples of musical acculturation occurred about a century ago, when Asians had no knowledge of Western notation or theory. Hymns were taught by rote by missionaries and were passed on orally. People gradually and unconsciously changed the melodies according to the familiar Asian styles, hence the acculturation. "Western exploitation" refers to today's Western composers or arrangers who take Asian music and intentionally change and impose Western harmony on Asian music to suit Western tastes.

Therefore, the task of contextualization involves breaking the pot, planting the seed of the gospel in Asian soils, interpreting the meaning of the Word, worshiping God in native forms and symbols, composing and singing hymns/songs in native tongues and musical dialects, and creating theologies and interpreting Christian faith in Asian contexts. But the problem is that many Asian Christians do not know or have lost hold of their identities. Culturally, some have become like the "Black Dutch" in Bali or yellow- and brown-skinned virtual-Caucasians in other parts of Asia. Therefore, before actual contextualization takes place, one must recover one's identity and how one expresses one's Christian faith in context.

History and Development of Sound the Bamboo

Altogether, the search for Asian Christian identities, the effort of worshiping God and communicating the meanings of the gospel through Asian cultural expressions, and the contextualization of theology, liturgy, and church music has been a long journey, one that with the publication of a collection of Asian hymns by the East Asia Christian Council in 1963.

The Formation of CCA Hymnals

The East Asia Christian Council (EACC) was formed in 1957 in Parapat, Indonesia.[2] The founders and leaders of this ecumenical organization realized that there were no Asian hymns that they could sing together in English. Fulfilling the council's goal of "life together in a common obedience," they requested member churches to submit hymns for the proposed *EACC Hymnal,* which was published in 1963. The text's editor was the Reverend D. T. Niles, who was a widely recognized theologian and a prolific writer and poet. The music editor was John Kelley, an American missionary in Japan. The *EACC Hymnal* contained 200 hymns: ninety-seven were written by Asians and 103 were translations of Western hymns. Niles contributed forty-five Asian hymns, ten original hymns, and thirty-five paraphrases or adaptations from other Asian authors. According to Masao Takenaka (1925–2006), one of the pioneers of Asian ecumenism, the publication of such an international and ecumenical collection of hymns was "an epoch-making event" (Loh 1972, i) in the history of the Asian church. Perhaps the only shortcoming was that the music of many of these hymns was not Asian in style but imitated Western four-part harmony.

The first institutional effort to develop Asian liturgy and music began in Hong Kong in 1965, when John Fleming of the Foundation for Theological Education held the South East Asian Theological Study Institute with the theme "Worship and Music in the Asian Church Today." One of the workshop participants, Francisco F.

---

2   I was privileged to attend the celebration of the EACC's fiftieth anniversary in Parapat, March 3–8, 2007.

Feliciano, was a young organist at St. Andrew's Theological Seminary in Manila; he embraced the vision and nearly fifteen years later founded with Father Ellsworth Chandlee the Asian Institute for Liturgy and Music (AILM) on the Manila campus. Under the sponsorship of the Christian Conference of Asia (CCA), which is the new name of the EACC, and some ecumenical organizations in the West, the institute became the headquarters for training Asian church musicians. In 1986, CCA requested AILM to compile a hymnal, and I volunteered to undertake the task. The result was *Sound the Bamboo: CCA Hymnal 1990*. This collection brought together words and music from many sources, including *New Songs of Asian Cities*, published in 1972 by the Urban Rural Mission Committee (URM) of the CCA. The collection was the result of my URM-sponsored travels in Asian countries from 1968 to 1972, during which I visited churches, schools, factories, streets, and slums and recorded raw material: songs being sung by contemporary Asian city people. Most of these songs were notated and printed for the first time in *New Songs of Asian Cities*.

The twenty-five contributors to Sound the Bamboo and five of the original animateurs
(Fr. Robert, France; Pablo Sosa, Argentina; Patrick Matsikenyiri, Zimbabue;
Lyn Lethgoe, Canada; I-to Loh, Taiwan) for the WCC assemblies are shown
in this 1987 photo.

Other sources for the hymns in *Sound the Bamboo* (*STB*) were supplements produced by ecumenical workshops on liturgy and music in Manila in 1980 and 1987 and an Asian American collection of hymns entitled *Hymns from the Four Winds* (published in 1983 by Abingdon and edited by I-to Loh). However, the great majority of the hymns in *Sound the Bamboo* resulted from extensive trips to most of the Asian countries between 1982 and 1990. The chart below shows the number of hymns gathered from each source:

EACC Hymnal (ed. D. T. Niles)	22
New Songs of Asian Cities (ed. I-to Loh)	8
Hymns from the Four Winds (ed. I-to Loh)	2
CCA Hymnal Supplement I (ed. Francisco Feliciano)	14
CCA Hymnal Supplement II (ed. I-to Loh)	16
CCA Hymnal Supplement III (ed. I-to Loh)	36
Collected from the field (1982–90)	83
Existing hymns translated or arranged for *STB*	42
Reprinted from published hymnals	32

In short, of the 280 hymns in the 1990 edition of *Sound the Bamboo*, approximately 240 (85.7%) were collected, transcribed, translated, or composed for it.[3]

The Most Recent Edition of *Sound the Bamboo*

Sound the Bamboo: CCA Hymnal 2000 is the revised and enlarged version of the 1990 edition. In addition to standardizing the diverse spelling systems and improving many of the translations, eleven hymns from the 1990 edition were removed, forty-six were added, a few were rewritten, and one tune (*STB* #116) was changed. The collection includes 315 hymns in forty-four languages from twenty-two countries of the CCA member churches in Asia and the Pacific. The original team of editors served on the editorial committee: Francisco F. Feliciano, founder and president of Samba Likhaan, of which AILM is a part; Father James Minchin, an Anglican priest from Australia, who was responsible for paraphrasing most of the hymns; and myself as the general editor.

The following lists the number of *STB* hymns from each country:

Australia	8
Bangladesh	6
Cambodia	4
China	18
Hong Kong SAR, China	1
India	39
Indonesia	35
Japan	20
Korea	23
Laos	1
Malaysia	9

---

3   Cf. Loh 1993b, "A Survey of Texts and Musical Styles in *Sound the Bamboo: CCA Hymnal 1990*."

Myanmar	11
Nepal	5
New Zealand	22
Pakistan	11
Papua New Guinea	2
Philippines	41
Singapore	7
Sri Lanka	15
Taiwan	39
Thailand	13
Vietnam	1
Total	331 (315)[4]

Rationale and Theology for the Structure of *Sound the Bamboo*

MEANINGS OF THE TITLE OF THE HYMNAL

Bamboo grooves are an important part of the Asian landscape. They appear as recurring motifs in poetry and painting, and they suggest the essence of peace and harmony with nature. Bamboo is also an excellent material for making musical instruments. From the simple flute of a boy riding on a water buffalo to the complicated bamboo pipe organ (as seen in Las Pinas in the Philippines and in Indonesia), bamboo can be a vehicle for the most naive outpouring of emotions as well as the most sophisticated artistic expression. The title of the hymnal, therefore, uses the imperative verb "sound" as a call for all Asian peoples to utilize their rich native resources—like bamboo as well as their poetic and musical heritages—to make joyful noises to the LORD.

THEOLOGY OF THE STRUCTURE OF *SOUND THE BAMBOO*

Two section headings of this hymnal also utilize imperative verbs, summoning the people of God to "Enter God's house with praise," and to "Proclaim God's works to all peoples." The former comes from Psalm 100:4: "Enter his gates with thanksgiving, and his courts with praise. Give thanks to him, bless his name." The latter echoes Psalm 96:3: "Declare his glory among the nations, his marvelous works among all the peoples."

To "enter God's house with praise" is to worship God; thus, all the hymns within this section are arranged according to their general subjects as well as liturgical sequences—i.e., from the historical/classical order of worship, such as psalms and canticles, Alleluia, Creed, Kyrie, Gloria, Sanctus, and Agnus Dei—and the Christian year, times, and occasions. Unfortunately, there are gaps in the order because of the lack of resources.

---

4   Sixteen hymns were written by composers and lyricists from different countries; hence, they are counted twice. The total number of hymns is 315.

The act of worship is not confined within the church building; it is the responsibility of the worshipers to "proclaim God's works to all peoples." Therefore, the second half of the hymnal exhorts worshipers to declare God's love and mercy through God's constant presence in all creation and the gift of God's son Jesus Christ and to witness the gospel through committing themselves in their service and struggle for justice, peace, and integrity of creation. This affirms the conviction of the CCA that the salvation of Jesus Christ concerns both physical and spiritual aspects (Luke 4:18–19) and that the mission of the church and the kingdom of God on earth may be realized by the power of the Holy Spirit through the balanced faith and deeds of Christians, as a witness that "worship and work must be one" (*STB* #229).[5]

Texts and Prominent Themes in Asian Hymns[6]

In analyzing hymns, both the music and the original text should be taken into consideration. Before dealing with the musical aspects, one has to study the content, imagery, poetic structure, literary style, theology, and treatment of the text as well as the intricate relationship between text and tune. This can be achieved only if one is fluent in the original language of the text. (Although I am fluent in a few languages, it is beyond my ability and the scope of this volume to engage in a detailed analysis of the original texts.)

Many have heard the Latin phrase "traductor traditor" (meaning roughly that a translator is a traitor)[7]; hymn translations are probably the best proof of this conundrum. Even translators who are competent in both English and the original language of the hymn and pursue the goals of fidelity, clarity, and beauty find it difficult to maintain the poetry of the original form and to perfectly match the original musical setting. This is a challenge to all who have accepted this task as a life-long career. For the hymns in *Sound the Bamboo*, excepting some Japanese, Chinese, and Taiwanese hymns and a few others that were analyzed from their original languages, the editors relied on English translations or paraphrases to better understand their poetic structure, imagery, or text-tune relationships.

Many of the hymns in *Sound the Bamboo* were written by amateurs with limited Christian experiences; hence, their theological interpretations may be simplistic. The imagination and skills of the paraphrasers (especially of Father James Minchin) enrich the content of these hymns and bring them to a deeper level of spirituality.

The texts in *Sound the Bamboo* (and a few from other collections) reflect four prevalent themes among Asian Christians: Devotion and Personal Salvation,

---

5   Abridged from Loh's article in *Dictionary of Hymnology,* edited by J. R. Watson, forthcoming.

6   This section is partially abridged from Loh 1993b.

7   I am indebted to Dr. Peter Casarella for this phrase.

Christmas, Social Concerns: Justice and Human Rights, and Images of God and Christ.

Devotion and Personal Salvation

Devotion and personal salvation are dominant themes; the authors of the hymns contemplate God's mercy for sinful human beings, the redemption of Christ, and the need for personal salvation by renouncing worldly things and seeking heavenly blessings. These themes are found in hymns from most countries and seem to prevail in those from South Asia (India, Pakistan, Bangladesh, and Sri Lanka). This emphasis on devotion and personal salvation recalls the role of the gospel song as a powerful medium for conversion and spiritual nourishment in the nineteenth-century missionary movement. The prevalence of these hymns may be a phenomenon of younger churches in which the ministry is largely confined to the inner circle of the church; a few of these hymns are included in the 2000 hymnal (see *STB* #63).

Christmas through Asian Eyes

Because Jesus' advent, nativity, and epiphany are favorite topics for poets and composers around the world, twenty-two hymns in *Sound the Bamboo* are related to these events. In addition to the romantic description or the retelling of the nativity, there is the traditional longing for the star, the light, the salvation, and the urge to bring gifts. Less familiar images that are uniquely Asian are also used. In "Child of Christmas Story" (*STB* #141), a New Zealand poet, Shirley Erena Murray, expresses her maternal experience and perceptions, giving Christmas a new dimension:

> Child whose baby finger, round our own is curled,
> come to melt our hearts, and come to change the world.

Murray describes the "Upside-down Christmas" (*STB* #143) in Asia, especially in New Zealand where "snow is not falling and trees are not bare," the opposite of the holiday setting usually depicted in the West. Yet one can still celebrate Christmas, for:

> Right side up Christmas belongs to the universe,
> made in the moment a woman gives birth;
> hope is the Jesus gift, love is the offering,
> everywhere anywhere, here on the earth.

Another striking text, with a theme not found in other Christmas carols, challenges us to reconsider the real meaning of Christmas. If we are not mindful of the hungry children, the poet warns us, we are crucifying the newborn Christ on the Christmas tree! One cannot help trembling and feeling chilled when singing these lines:

Son of poverty shame us till we see
self-concerned, how we deny you,
by our greed we crucify you
on a Christmas tree, Son of poverty.

—*STB* #144

Responding to the Asian reality of poverty and suffering children, Walter Marasinghe, a Sri Lankan poet-composer, pleads to the newborn baby:

Little master, hear the children everywhere cry out;
you can feel for what they suffer, what they weep about:
Huddled in their huts and clinging to their mothers' breast,
rags they wear against the cold and cannot hope for rest.

—*STB* #273

Social Concerns: Justice and Human Rights

Hymns expressing the Christian concern for human rights, poverty, and suffering have received much attention among Asian poets since the late sixties, evidenced by the large number of hymns on these themes in collections such as *New Songs of Asian Cities* (*NSAC*). *Sound the Bamboo* includes fourteen hymns in the section "Justice, Peace and the Integrity of Creation." In one example from *New Songs of Asian Cities* (Loh 1972), the conflict and struggle between closing and opening one's eyes to reality led the Reverend Samuel Liew from Singapore to question:

My God, why can't you leave me be?
Why shake me up this sight to see?

—*NSAC* #15

In their daily lives, Christians are constantly faced with the choice between remaining faithful to Christian principles or performing acts that discredit the Lord. The Taiwanese poet John Jyigiokk Tin prays:

make me brave; I would be salt and light,
a witness true

—*NSAC* #17

Reflecting on human tragedies in India, Elisha Soundararajan is perplexed and asks God:

Why should you create such bliss,
yet tolerate man's evil?

The poet continues and laments:
status, caste, family pride keep the rich aloof,
while poor women have no choice
but sell themselves for food

—*NSAC* #27

17

This hymn vividly reflects one of the most serious problems in Asia today: prostitution.

Dealing with the huge gap between the rich and the poor, the Filipina poet-composer Elena Maquiso calls out:

> And to the wealthy, we implore you
> vast portions of your land to share.
> The poor have more need for it, truly;
> the right to land is for us all.
>
> *—STB #266*

Confronted with the devastating human suffering in Asia, another New Zealand poet, the Reverend Ron O'Grady, refers to Christ in a way unheard of in traditional hymns:

> Jesus, the beggar lives in the slum,
> [. . .] suffering insults, looking for work,
> all the world's agony, etched on his face.

O'Grady urges us to:

> fight against bondage and greed,
> [. . . by] living with people in every deed.
>
> *—STB #202*

Images of God and Christ

In addition to the traditional Western images of God and Christ as alpha and omega, guide and leader, bridegroom, judge, king, etc., some of the new Asian hymns also use the following metaphors: lover (*STB* #71), friend and kindred (*STB* #26, #55, #220), healer and health (*STB* #55, #262), "Noble One" (*STB* #162), the spring wind (*STB* #174), "Morning Bird" (*STB* #305), rice (*STB* #190), water (*STB* #209), road and map (*STB* #230), the Big Dipper (*STB* #52). The feminine character of God is especially expressed in images of a hen (*STB* #161), a mothering bird (*STB* #222), and a mother (*STB* #26, #84, #181, #220). All of these indicate that some Asian poets are liberating themselves from traditional Western views and relate to God through their daily experiences. The British poet Brian Wren has also employed some of these metaphors, as in his 1987 hymn "Bring many names, beautiful and good."

Other Themes
FILIAL PIETY AND RESPECT FOR THE ELDERLY

Filial piety and respect for the elderly are important cultural attitudes in Asian societies, which is expressed by a Chinese poet who writes, "One commandment teaching me to filial be." He describes Jesus as, "dying, he entrusts to John his mother there" (*Hymns from the Four Winds*, #92).

THE FEMININE CHARACTER OF GOD

Although sexism is less apparent in Asian languages, some poets are still quite sensitive to this concern and have spent much effort to use sex-inclusive language. The feminine images of God listed above may be a breakthrough. For even on the Indian subcontinent, which has traditionally described God as Mother (as in *STB* #26), it is still almost inconceivable to use a feminine pronoun for God. But it is gradually being accepted. One can even understand God's love more vividly through the following lines by Ron O'Grady:

> The God of us all is our Mother,
> she teaches us her truth and beauty,
> she shows us a love beyond duty.
>
> —*STB* #181

Shirley Murray addresses the "Loving Spirit" even more intimately:

> Like a mother, you enfold me, hold my life within your own,
> feed me with your very body, form me of your flesh and bone.
> —*STB* #220

These poems/hymns are likely the first to equate the relationship of a mother and her baby with that of the Holy Spirit and the faithful. No relationship in the world is more intimate than a mother bearing a baby in her womb: forming and nourishing it until its birth, then nursing it afterward. Murray's hymn indeed provides a compact course on the doctrine of God and Holy Spirit!

ECOLOGY AND STEWARDSHIP

Deploring our ecological violations, which he equates with dividing Christ's body (or mantle), the New Zealand poet Bill Wallace writes:

> In nature as in Jesus, all life is truly one,
> but we divide Christ's mantle and drown creation's song.
> —*STB* #233

Sensing the urgency for environmental protection, I call for good stewardship:

> Join, all people of good will,
> while there's time, live modestly,
> guard each trace of paradise,
> keep alive things heavenly.
>
> —*STB* #257

Characteristic Features
and Performance Styles of Asian Hymns

Most traditional Asian music is monophonic, i.e., it has melody without harmony. The beauty of the music is contained in a single melodic line composed of individual pitches, ornamentation, timbre, and rhythm. Harmony is absent, with the exception of some folk expressions, such as the multipart songs of the tribal people of Taiwan, Japanese court music (*gagaku*), and the Indonesian gamelan. However, because of the influence of missionaries and Western educational systems, most Asian musical cultures have been affected to varying degrees by Western harmony. Therefore, to understand the characteristic features of Asian music and singing styles, one must analyze their rhythms, scales, melodic characters, and any harmonic aspects employed. But before dealing with these features of Asian music, one should take into account the basic aesthetic views and fundamental differences from the West regarding pitch and performance practices.

The Beauty in Asian Monophony

JAPANESE AESTHETICS OF MUSIC

According to Shigeo Kishibe, the most influential music scholar in Asia, Japan formulated its aesthetic ideal during the Kamakura period (1185–1333). It comprised four aspects: *wa* (harmony), *kei* (respect), *sei* (purity,) and *jaku* (tranquility); the concepts of *wa* and *kei* were adopted from Chinese culture, *sei* was an indigenous development, and *jaku* was influenced by the Buddhist discipline of the Jōdo sect (Kishibe 1984, 15f). Kishibe insightfully observes Eastern and Western differences concerning the philosophy of aesthetics: "In the conflicts of logic versus emotion and science versus nature, emotion and nature usually triumph." He compares the basic elements of Western musical structure, three movements in the sonata form, to the three Japanese elements described as *jo-ha-kyū* Musically speaking, they represent "slow introduction—exposition in a brighter tempo—fast conclusion," which "may have been influenced by the Chinese philosophical idea of the three elements, Heaven, Earth and Man" (Kishibe 1984, 16f). These concepts are used in *gagaku* and the more expressive music of *noh, kabuki*, and *bunraku* theatrical forms. Kishibe concludes by saying:

> [While] Western music aims to "conquer nature," Japanese music aspires to the harmony of nature and man, as is the case in the music of India. The fondness of the refinement of "free rhythm" may have stemmed from a love of nature. The well-controlled harmonic structure of modern Western music may be understood as a triumph of science and logic, while the delicate melodic structure of Japanese music, decorated by delicate colors of sound and microtones, can be regarded as a triumph of nature and human sensitivity (Kishibe 1984, 17).

I believe that Kishibe's interpretation of the Japanese aesthetic principle is also applicable to most traditional Asian music. Pointing out the contrasting aesthetic views of the East and the West, I have counseled many Asian composers searching for insights and techniques for harmonic treatment to return to the basic concepts: to reconsider the implications of *wa-kei-sei-jaku* and *jo-ha-kyū* for the inner beauty of Asian music. With regard to harmony, many uniquely Asian multipart musical treatments are available.[8]

CONCEPT OF PITCH AND INTERVALS

Pitch is one of the basic elements of music. The standard reference pitch in the West is A, at a frequency of 440 cycles per second (or 435 in Europe). However, there is no standard pitch in most Asian cultures, i.e., any pitch can be used as 1 (*do*) or the fundamental pitch in an instrument or a given performance. In India, ensembles are tuned to the flute or to the singer's preferred pitch, whatever that may be. The concept of "correct pitch" or "being in tune" is also quite different in Asian music. In the *nanguan* ensembles of Taiwan and Southeast Asia, stringed instruments are tuned to the pitch given by a vertical, notched flute (*dongxiao* or *xiao*). When tuning a pipe organ, the pitch is considered correct and tuned when the pipes stop vibrating. But in Balinese gamelan, the metallophones (*gangsa*) are purposefully tuned slightly higher or lower than each other; when all are played together, the rapid sonic vibrations create a shimmering sound. To Western ears, this often seems out of tune and perhaps even ugly. But according to Balinese aesthetics, the vibrating, shimmering sound is the ideal, a lively and beautiful tone. Therefore, since musical aesthetics are culturally based, one point of view should not be used to judge other cultures.

Western tones and intervals are standardized with well-tempered tuning, making the intervals between pitches equal, i.e. 100 cents for a half-step, 200 cents for a major second, 300 cents for a minor third, 400 cents for a major third, etc. But in Thailand, for example, the octave is divided into seven equidistant intervals. A Thai second is 171.4 cents; a third is 342.8, which is larger than a Western minor third but smaller than a Western major third, so it is called a neutral third. This is why Thai music may seem out of tune to Western ears. But in fact, the Western ears are out of tune with Thai music. Similarly, Western ears often have difficulty finding tonal references in Indian music with its twenty-two *srutis* (the small microtonal units) in the octave, its microtones, its glides, and its embellishments. Meanwhile, trained Indian musicians appreciate and enjoy the beauty of microtonal ornamentation and rhythmic complexity. (For further discussion, see the sections for Thailand and India.)

---

8   If interested, please refer to Loh 1987, 258–73.

MONOPHONIC NATURE OF ASIAN MUSIC

Some of the most typical Asian hymns are monophonic. Their beauty flows from indigenous qualities of timbre and vocal production, attack and decay, microtones and embellishments, particular idioms, motifs, melodic shapes, and progressions. In addition, they feature intricate rhythms, the intrinsic unity of text and tune, and special instrumental effects. Most of these characteristics cannot be adequately described with the English vocabulary or traditional Western notation. These songs are beautiful in their own right, and perhaps only the people who are familiar with the particular cultural styles are able to fully comprehend and enjoy their beauty. The music communicates a deep spiritual quality, and some of the hymns represent the best of the ethnic styles. Attempts to alter or adapt this music to Western styles only impair their beauty and integrity.[9] Therefore, musicians and scholars outside of the culture should refrain from harmonizing or arranging the music, unless they are very familiar with the culture in question.

The analysis of a song from Pakistan, "Have mercy on us, Lord" (*Khudaayaa, raeham kar*) (*STB* #120), illustrates this point. The melody is in a natural minor scale (6 7 1 2 3 4 5 6), and it is well organized. Musically, like most Kyries, it has three sections, A B A, each with three phrases. The musical and text organization are as follows:

Structural form:	A	B	A
Musical phrases*:	a b a	b c a	a b a
Text:	Lord	Christ	Lord
	have mercy	have mercy	have mercy

*Phrase cadences: a: closed; b: open; c: to climax and open

The climaxes of both the music and the text coincide at phrase c, which jumps to the highest point, begging the Messiah (*masii*) for mercy, and glides down slowly to the word *kar*, as if one's heart is torn by the earnest plea. This is an excellent example of a piece of music that perfectly matches the original text and also makes a powerful theological statement of one's deepest quest for and total reliance on God's mercy.

RHYTHMIC FEATURES

Generally speaking, rhythm is less complex in East Asia than in South Asia:

> The polyphonic stratification of the Balinese gamelan and the Indian tabla (a pair of two drums) accompaniment probably represent the highest rhythmic density in Asian music, even though the main melody may be very simple. No single description of a particular rhythm or rhythmic character can represent the general quality of rhythm in a given country, let alone that of Asia. We have, however, identified a few rhythmic features prevalent within certain cultures, which may provide us with a picture of these unique characters. (Loh 2001, 571f)

---

9   Cf. Loh 2001, 571.

For instance, triplets formed by an eighth note and a quarter note (♪♩ ♪♩) are popular among the Kurukh of India, Burmese, and Koreans. But they all vary in their own ways. The Kurukh use two pairs of such triplets to lead to quarter notes or other values, as seen in PUNA BINKO (*STB* #133). This is further reinforced by the drum patterns preceding them. The effect is an almost constant alternation between two rhythmic patterns. When singing a series of eighth notes, the Burmese are fond of shortening the first of the two (♪♩ ♪♩). This is quite prominent in their folk tradition, as exhibited in HP'YA SHIN (*STB* #57). Compound, complex time marks one of the most typical rhythms of Korean folk traditions: it uses the same pattern as above but reverses it immediately, revealing a very strong syncopation and rhythmic vitality (♪♩ ♩♪). These two sets of patterns are frequently reversed again with variations (♪.♪♪ ♪♩); see HON-SHIN (*STB* #75) and CHOO-SOO (*STB* #245). NAUI DOUM (*STB* #53) is a good example of native rhythmic patterns with heterophonic accompaniment.

One feature of Indian rhythm is complex accompaniment, usually of the tabla.[10] THIS EARTH (*STB* #276) illustrates how the Indian composer uses an additive rhythm of 3 + 2 + 2 in the entire piece (♪♪♪♩ ♩). After singing and listening to so many songs in regular duple, triple, or quadruple times, such a rhythm is refreshing.

Scales and Melodic Characters

The scale (or the consecutive enumeration of pitches), the shape or figure of melodic construction, the phrase structures, and the cadences are integral parts of a song; the combination of these elements determines the musical style. One of the most important characteristics of Asian hymns is their use of scales, which range from three to seven tones. The following examples illustrate how song styles are determined by the use of five-tone scales, their respective initial and final tone of cadence (both of which may be the tonal center or determine the mode), and time signature, all of which relate to the rhythms or rhythmic patterns of the song.

The anhemitonic penta scale, or five-tone scale without a half step, is more common in Northeast Asia or the countries using the Chinese system (China, Korea, Japan, and Taiwan), but it is also found in Thailand, Vietnam, and the Philippines.

Although some songs may employ the pitches in the same G A C D E (5 6 1 2 3) or C D E G A (1 2 3 5 6) grouping, the emphasis of a certain pitch hierarchy (initial or final) differentiates them from one mode to another. Likewise, the use of different idioms makes music in the same mode sound differently. All the above songs use the same five tones, but the Chinese tune (*STB* #80) is apparently in a *chih* (*sol*, 5) mode, similar to the Mixolydian mode of the West, and the Japanese

---

10   Although the tabla is important for almost all of Indian music, the enormous complexity and the highly
     specialized skills for performance prevented the inclusion of proper notations of tabla accompaniments in
     Sound the Bamboo. The omission of the tabla accompaniments for hymns from the Indian subcontinent is
     regrettable.

tune (*STB* #242) is similar to the Dorian mode (*re*, 2), but both of them are without the *fa* (4) and *si* (7) of the Western scale. The scale used in the songs above is one of the most popular Asian anhemitonic penta scales.

Mode	Scale	Initial	Final	Time	Country	STB #
G (*sol*)	G A C D E	G	G	2/4	China	80
5	5 6 1 2 3	5	5	(cipher notation as used in this book)		
A (*la*)	A C D E G	E	A	6/8	Korea	245
6	6 1 2 3 5	3	6			
C (*do*)	C D E G A	E	G	4&6	Philippines	102
1	1 2 3 5 6	3	5			
D (*re*)	D E G A C	A	D	4/4	Japan	242
2	2 3 5 6 1	6	2			

(Loh 2001, 572)

The hemitonic penta scale is popular in Japan and Indonesia; the following examples show their differences in scale, initial, final, and time signature:

Scale	Initial	Final	Time	Country	STB #
E F GB C	B	E	4/4	Indonesia	201
3 4 5 7 1	7	3			
E F AB D	E	A	3/4	Japan	189
3 4 6 7 2	3	6			

The first example is set in the Indonesian *pelog* scale, which features one large gap (G B or 5 7) and two small intervals (E F or 3 4; B C or 7 1). The Japanese *in* scale shows more variety: a minor second (E F or 3 4), a major third (F A or 4 6), and a minor third (B D or 7 2); although 1 does not appear on the ascent, it occurs on the descent: 3 1 7. While the differences between Japanese *in* and Javanese *pelog* may seem subtle, a trained ear can instantly perceive the contrasts and the countries of origin (Loh 2001, 572).

Hymns written in a diatonic scale but with a flattened seventh degree, C D E F G A B♭ C (1 2 3 4 5 6 ♭7 1), such as THEVARAM (*STB* #74) from Sri Lanka, are quite popular on the Indian subcontinent. A changing second degree is also common in this region. For example, "Sarennam, O the divine light" (*STB* #47) from India uses ♯2 (A♯) and ♯1 (G♯) in between descending and ascending (3 ♯2 3, 2 ♯1 2) almost like a lower auxiliary, but switches back to the natural 2(A) and 1(G) when descending to 1 (G) or 6 (E): 3 2 1, 2 1 6. This example shows one aspect of raga, an organizing principle of Indian melodies.

The Indian octave is divided equally into twenty-two *srutis*, or microtonal intervals. The actual sizes of intervals in a given raga depend on the sizes and the number of *srutis* employed. Furthermore, the melodic intervals may change in ascending or descending order. Unfortunately, no Western musical vocabulary can adequately describe the minute yet subtle tonal arrangements found in a raga; hence the terms "scale," "mode," "melodic shape," "ornamentation," and "mood," are needed to explain the phenomena and meanings of raga. Hymns employing the raga concept suggest a rich resource that awaits serious study and analysis.[11] Meanwhile, a simple hymn with slight embellishments such as "O come to us, pastor of the flock" (*STB* #162) demonstrates the beauty of Indian melodies.

The Use of Non-Lexical Syllables

TOO DEEP FOR WORDS

Words have specific meanings. But words are sometimes insufficient to communicate certain ideas, feelings, and concepts. Hence, some cultures use non-lexical syllables, i.e., words or vocables that are without specific meanings but are not meaningless.

Many times, I have heard the Ami tribe in Taiwan proudly sing one of their songs with non-lexical syllables and with melodic variations and multipart treatments. However, at various occasions and localities, they provided different titles for this song:

1. "Old Song" (an archaic song, the meaning of which has been forgotten)
2. "Song without a Title" (the meaning and function of the song are unknown)
3. "Drinking Song" (for entertainment or celebration)
4. "Amis no Kimigayo" (the Ami national anthem, only sung after victory against enemies; "Kimigayo" is the title of the Japanese national anthem.)

Therefore, the non-lexical syllables in this song may carry any of the above meanings, depending on the occasion or purpose. The Paiwan of Taiwan frequently begin a song with a phrase of non-lexical syllables, in order to mark the identity or purpose of the song, followed by a singer who improvises other texts to suit the occasion or purpose. The hymn "Hear now, God's own people" (*STB* #215) retains the non-lexical-syllable phrase but also offers new texts to call the attention of the listeners. Here, the non-lexical syllables "a-la-i-yo-a-i" not only identify the type of song but also invite people to do something together; thus they are appropriate for summoning people to listen to God's important words. The Bunun tribe of Taiwan also sings with non-lexical syllables (*STB* #224). The congregation responds to the soloist by singing "u-i-hi," which could mean "I agree." Thus, non-lexical syllables gain meanings from the words sung before or after them.

The Kalinga people of the Philippines sing "dong-dong-ay" or "sa-li-dum-may" songs at all occasions; sometimes these non-lexical syllables express joy, praise, and thanksgiving; at other times, they convey feelings of loneliness or sadness. In "Sing a song to the Lord"(*STB* #92), the syllables represent joyful praise. In MARY'S SALIDUMMAY (*STB* #102), which is the Virgin Mary's response to the angel's annunciation, each stanza also ends with the same non-lexical syllables;

---

11   Cf. Loh 2001, 572f. For further detail, see the section on India in this volume.

thus, the syllables reflect the moods of the respective texts. A recording of another song sounded melancholy, so I wrote the new text "Green the wild fields, blue the sky" (*STB* #257) to express feelings of guilt for destroying the ecology and to urge people to conserve energy. In a new hymn, "Sound a mystic bamboo song," I incorporated non-lexical syllables and their respective musical phrases from the Philippine Kalingas ("dong-dong-ay-si-dong-i-lay") and the Taiwan Ami tribe ("na-lu-an-na-hoi-an") to encourage reconciliation and cooperation between them.[12]

A similar use of non-lexical syllables is found in a song from Myanmar: OHLELEGOI (*STB* #285), a joyful praise to God's creation and thanksgiving. In the Thai hymn "I sing a song of victory" (*STB* #151), the last phrase ends with "uh"; this non-lexical syllable has no particular meaning, but it is important for the identity of the song.

To summarize, one may understand and interpret non-lexical syllables (NLS) according to four characteristics:

1. NLS have no specific meanings, but they are not meaningless.
2. NLS express what words cannot, but the meanings may be hidden or ambiguous.
3. NLS may gain meanings through the title, function, or purpose of the song.
4. NLS may gain meanings through context (the words sung before or after the NLS), thus they may have multiple meanings.

The phenomenon of non-lexical syllables might be compared to St. Paul's reference to the work of the Holy Spirit in Romans 8:27, "The Spirit intercedes with sighs too deep for words." One's limited vocabulary or inability to express oneself necessitates the use of something that is beyond comprehension—to un-speak through music in order to communicate deeper meanings or emotions. These unspeakable elements exceed the limitations of language, intellect, and reasoning; they are "too deep for words" and can become vehicles for the wondrous work of the Holy Spirit.

This discussion is not meant to encourage everyone to sing "la-la-la" or just any non-lexical syllables at worship but simply to point the reader's attention to some cultures that use non-lexical syllables to express their faith and to nourish their spirituality. The proper use of non-lexical syllables may stimulate new thoughts and expressions of faith.

TRANSFORMING NON-LEXICAL SYLLABLES

Non-lexical syllables can be transformed. For example, the Korean song OHORADIYA (*STB* #101) was originally associated with farmers' shouts of joy and excitement as they danced during festivals. Geonyong Lee has adapted this singing

---

12   Text by Bill Wallace; see #103 in *Global Praise 2: Songs for Worship and Witness* (GBGMusik, 2000).

style by transforming the non-lexical syllables "o-ho-ra-di-ya-sang-sa-di-ya" into "Hallelujah." In this version of Psalm 150, Korean instruments have replaced all the biblical instruments. In this way, the composer has contextualized the psalm, by transforming the non-lexical folk song into a hymn of highest praise.

LET SILENCE SPEAK

Bengali music, a part of the Indian musical system, features microtones, rhythmic cycles, and drones accompanied by the harmonium (a small, pumped, reed organ) and a pair of tabla drums. A rhythmic cycle is a set pattern of rhythm within a certain number of beats. For example, in the prayer of confession "Lord, we did not live up to your teachings" (*STB* #43), each phrase has a cycle of twelve counts. The composer, Bart Shaha, twice inserted half-cycles of rests, creating six counts of silence after the phrases "Lord, forgive us" and "Christ, forgive us" are repeated three times. Silent meditation is important in Asian culture; total silence in this music does not signify the end of praying but has at least two meanings:

1. Silence allows one to meditate on the meaning of the words just sung or the purpose for singing them. Silence provides time to examine and reflect on whether one is genuinely sincere and honest in asking for God's forgiveness. It also may provide time to confess one's sins, to ask more earnestly for forgiveness, to express what is inexpressible, and to hear God speaking the words of forgiveness or consolation. Silence in music can become the agent of "the still small voice" (I Kings 19:13), awakening one's conscience to see one's true self. Madeleine L'Engle defined this experience as "the deepest communion with God [which] is beyond words, [and] on the other side of silence" (L'Engle 1980, 128).

2. In the above example, since one cycle is twelve counts, the six-count silence is an incomplete rhythmic cycle; this imbalance may be uncomfortable for those in the musical culture of the South Asian subcontinent. One wonders whether the composer cut short the cycle to underscore the singer's urgent and repeated pleads for mercy—that the singer so needs assurance of God's forgiveness that she/he cannot wait for another six counts.

As many of today's churches in Asia (and other parts of the world) lack silence in song and during worship, they could learn from this Bengali song.

Harmonic Treatment in Asian Hymns

Western music has greatly influenced Asian students of musical composition, who find it easy to imitate Western idioms; many Asian musicians mistakenly equate modernization with Westernization. However, some Asian composers express their identities by adapting existing folk tunes or imitating traditional styles in their compositions. Some composers are more innovative, bypassing ethnic boundaries and integrating indigenous elements into international styles. But Asian composers seldom can resist the fascination of traditional Western harmonies. In addition to the aspects of rhythm and scale described earlier, Asian musical styles can be identified through their various harmonic languages, as the following examples will show.

Indigenous/Traditional Harmony

Of the twenty-two countries represented in *Sound the Bamboo*, only two have contributed hymns with indigenous/traditional harmony. The first one is Indonesia (specifically the province formerly named Irian Jaya), whose songs are frequently sung in choruses based on one major chord, *do-mi-sol* (1-3-5) (see *STB* #305). The other is Taiwan, whose tribal harmonic practices I addressed in a paper (Loh 1987). A few of the tribal musical techniques are: the free contrapuntal harmony of the Ami (as seen in *STB* #99), the sectional canon of the Pinuyumayan (*STB* #96), the reiterated drone of the Paiwan (*STB* #182), the double-third singing of the Bunun (*STB* #224), and the parallel fourths of the Saisiat (*STB* #121).

As one example, the Bunun tribe builds their choral singing in the harmonic series *do mi sol* (1 3 5), as seen in "From this time onward" (*STB* #224). Technically, the three tones are the seventh, eighth, and ninth partials of the fundamental pitch *do*. Sometime in prehistory, the Bunun developed four- to six-part singing in more or less homophonic harmony, which is unique in choral practices. In *STB* #224, a soloist sings one phrase at a time. Following each phrase, the chorus sings "u-i-hi" in harmony and sustains this chord while the soloist sings the next phrase.

Adopted Western Harmony

Some Asians have so adopted Western musical styles and harmony into their repertoire that these qualities have become part of their national style. The result is that native people instinctively harmonize any song with three chords: tonic (I), subdominant (IV), and dominant (V). This practice is common for people in all parts of Asia. One exception is the Maori of New Zealand, who have developed their own characteristics, such as in the performance of the hymn "Son of God, whose heart is peace" (*STB* #60), which combines Western harmony with Maori open-throat singing. The Batak people of northern Sumatra, Indonesia, adopted the European (particularly the German) chorus, but some of them create three-part choruses without the bass part, which Europeans regard as the most important. The Ambonese hymn "O come quickly, Holy Spirit" (*STB* #7) is one exception, as it was influenced by the Portuguese and has a bass part. Burmese choral singing (as in "God of region and of world," *STB* #61) uses only tonic and supertonic chords. An interesting feature is that the chords are almost all second inversions and in parallel motion. Although the Burmese claim that such harmonic techniques are of indigenous origin, without more evidence one might suspect that they are adopted Western styles. Further, the style of contemporary Filipino urban songs and hymns, which include such elements as triple rhythm and minor tonality and harmony (see "O many people of all lands," *STB* #21, and "In the lands of Asia," *STB* #263), displays remnants of a style adopted from the former Spanish colonizers. Filipinos have internalized this Spanish style, accepting it as one of their national musical styles.

Contextual Harmony

The following examples demonstrate contextual harmony: the harmonic techniques may have grown out of native melodic material, they may have been borrowed from other Asian traditions, or they may be the composer's innovations. Originating from various countries, they reveal new Asian musical identities (cf. Loh 2001, 573).

CHINESE

The beauty of Chinese melody depends largely on its lyrical flow. An effective accompaniment for Chinese tunes is an imitative counterpoint that echoes the line of the melody and is not dependent on Western harmonic progression. Occasional doubling of the melody and heterophonic variations also reinforce this style; an example can be seen in "Holy Night, Blessed Night" (*STB* #140). The melody of MEI-HUA SAN-NONG (*STB* #93) is taken from the *qin* or *zheng* zither. Here, the arranger imitates the zither to provide counterpoint and create a linear beauty. In these examples, harmony is derived from the melodic context.

INDONESIAN

Indonesian gamelan music is organized in a colotomic structure, in which the music is marked off into "temporal units according to the entrance of specific instruments in a specific order at specific times" (as defined by David Morton; Malm 1977, 43). TONDO (*STB* # 202) is a piano reduction of a simplified pseudo-gamelan version. The main melody is outlined in octaves by the *saron* (metallophones) while the *bonang* (kettle gongs) anticipate and decorate the melody in a Javanese style. With haunting repetitive figures, LAGU KASIH (*STB* #203) is an enchanting new hymn with an accompaniment in the style of a Javanese *celempung,* Javanese zither.

JAPANESE

The tune TOKYO (*STB* #242) is adapted from a *gagaku* melody. Instead of following the ancient *gagaku* harmony, it is set in a series of fourths and fifths, with free figurations in the alto part. Another example, KAMITAKATA (*STB* #27), uses parallel fourths and fifths in such a way that the inner voices and outer voices are paired respectively in octaves or double duet, concluding with a big surprise: a major chord!

KOREAN

Melodies in typical Korean idioms are frequently harmonized in parallel fourths and fifths, with the occasional use of contrary motion and other intervals. The *changgo* (hourglass drum) accompaniment adds further excitement to the tune CHOO-SOO (*STB* #245).

FILIPINO

Filipino folk music, as mentioned earlier, was influenced by nearly four hundred years of Spanish colonization. Its characteristics include triple meter, minor mode, and a sudden modulation to the tonic major at the refrain or in the second half of a song (as in ILAW, *STB* #278). The Filipinos' love for guitar and *banduria* (a mandolin-like instrument) can be seen in all varieties of music. For instance, simple hymns have a two-guitar accompaniment, some with thin textures (CATUROG NA NONOY, *STB* #82) and others with thick textures (DAPIT HAPON, *STB* #161) (cf. Loh 2001, 573).

TAIWANESE

Taiwanese, Chinese, and Thai are tonal languages. While setting their texts to music, one must be sensitive to natural inflections, so that the meaning of the words is clearly communicated. The music of the Taiwanese hymns HUI-HIONG (*STB* #308) and SU-KONG-PAN (*STB* #254) follow the natural intonation of the language. The harmony is either in free counterpoint (*STB* #308) or formed by two imitative melodies interwoven together (*STB* #254), resulting in a style similar to that of J. S. Bach's *Two-Part Inventions* (according to Routley 1981,183).

Contemporary Asian Styles

Sound the Bamboo includes a number of new hymns whose styles are not bound by any particular culture or country. The music may show certain native or Asian traits, but the harmonic treatments are innovative; thus, they may be regarded as having a contemporary Asian style.

For example, in a lullaby from the Philippines (*STB* #277), Francisco F. Feliciano uses a simple two-tone folk motive but develops it into a five- to six-part chorus in contemporary harmony. The music is complex and haunting and evokes the feeling of a mother rocking her baby.

Another example of innovation, "Still, I search for my God" (*STB* #176), is a mysterious, meditative hymn that marvels at God's creation, its diversity, harmony, and perfection. Here, Feliciano uses an image of ripples on a lake to inspire sonic symbolism. When one throws a small rock into a calm lake, it creates small and then bigger ripples that eventually fade. *STB* #176 is evolved from this image. The melodic construction suggests ripples expanding and then fading: 3- 34323- 36644323- 366- 6767- 67664322- 22423-. Feliciano also makes innovative use of two guitars, one playing only four tones (3 4 6 7) and the other playing the accompaniment in arpeggios.

More examples of inventive works are "Hunger Carol" (*STB* #144), "Loving Spirit" (*STB* #220), and "God of the Bible, God in the Gospel" (*STB* #255).

Some Symbols and Symbolic Acts in Asian Worship

Two Asian centers of worship, in Bali and Thailand, are known for their use of symbols and symbolic acts.

Dance and Symbolism in the Balinese Church

The Protestant church in Bali is distinguished for witnessing Christ through various art forms, as seen from their church architecture and dance forms (cf. Loh 1988, 7f).

1. The Balinese associate mountains with the presence of God as well as the source of life, which has prompted them to build churches that resemble mountains.
2. In the Balinese tradition, a temple gate symbolizes one's coming into the presence of God. Thus, a traditional temple gate is constructed behind the communion table, and a cross is set in the middle, affirming that Christ is the way to God.
3. Balinese dance is a powerful medium that communicates ideas and emotions. The highly stylized gestures and eye, finger, arm, and foot movements are the keys to understanding the dance, as they represent deeper meanings. The chart below outlines various body parts employed in the dance, their traditional Balinese interpretations, and newer Christian interpretations.

These Christian interpretations have added new dimensions to communicating the gospel to the Balinese through dance (cf. Loh 1988, 15).

The famous painter, dancer, musician, and composer I Nyoman Darsane wrote *Anak Dara* (The Parable of the Ten Virgins) in 1987 to urge diligent preparations to welcome the imminent coming of the groom, Jesus. Darsane's use of the gamelan to accompany the singing was rare at the time. The composition begins with an overture of dance; unfortunately, no video documentation of the performance exists (for more details, see the Indonesia section in this volume).

Body Part	Traditional Interpretation	Christian Interpretation
thumb	wisdom	God's wisdom, providence
index finger	power, position	God's omnipotence
middle finger	wealth	richness of God
ring finger	beauty, blessings	God's grace, blessings
pinkie	trust	faithfulness, eternal life
eyes	heaven, the watching eyes of the gods	Heaven, God's loving care, God's watching eyes
hands	human beings	God's children
feet	the world, the earth	God's world
symmetrical movements	the balance between good and evil, and right and wrong	God's justice and mercy, Judgment and grace

Liturgy of the Isaan Community Church in Thailand

The community churches in Isaan, in northeastern Thailand, have developed native forms of worship that utilize local hymns, music, and musical instruments. An ordinary Sunday worship, which is conducted in a family church, comprises the following:

> Prelude (performed by a native ensemble of mouth organ, lutes, flutes, xylophones, and drums)
> Call to worship (in song and dance)
> Reading of the scriptures
> Bible study or sermon
> Prayer of confession
> Holy Communion
> > Apostle's Creed (sung)
> > Words of institution (I Corinthians 11:23–26)
> > Prayer

Distribution of the elements (sticky rice loaves and rosella tea)
Communion
Singing of communion hymn and dancing
Prayer of thanksgiving
Offering (with song and dance)
Prayer of intercession
Postlude (performed by the native ensemble)

(Loh 1988, 19)

This is one of the most indigenous liturgies in Asia, in that none of the liturgical ideas, communion elements, or hymns were borrowed from the West. The expressions of faith in the Isaan church have emerged from their experiences and context. (For more information, see the next section and the section on Thai hymns.)

Other Symbols and Symbolic Acts in Asian Worship

While many Asian churches show little creativity in their liturgies, some utilize various cultural expressions, symbols, and symbolic acts in their worship. During the past two decades, I have experienced some of these acts in their liturgical contexts or learned of them from Asian colleagues. Below, they are briefly described according to the liturgical order.[13]

CALL TO WORSHIP: CONCH SHELLS

For many Pacific cultures, conch shells symbolize longevity; they are blown in rituals to call for ancestor spirits or rain. The shells, which can be heard from a great distance, are also blown to announce the arrival of a chief, of an important person, and other important events. Therefore, it is natural for Christians in the Moluccas of Indonesia and other Pacific islands to use conch shells on Sunday mornings as a call to worship God.

A conch from the Moluccas.

GREETINGS AND SIGNS OF PEACE

Namaskar

The Indian act of greeting, *namaskar*, is performed by pressing together one's palms in front of one's chest, with the fingers pointing up, bowing slightly, and saying "*namaste*," which literally means "I greet the divinity that is in you." This posture represents humility, respect, and reverence and has become a general Christian greeting as well as a sign of peace during worship services. Since handshaking

---

13   A portion of this section has appeared in a similar article. See Loh 1994a, 217–21.

and embracing may be considered too intimate in some Asian cultures, *namaskar* is a good alternative greeting. One can find the same use of *namaskar* in northern Sumatra in Indonesia. Many people around the world have adopted this salutation as a sign of respect, gratitude, and/or greeting.

Christians in Thailand have also embraced this Indian sign of reverence in their prayers. Instead of responding "amen," they further bow their head to touch the tip of their fingers, which signifies "So be it."

Hongi

The traditional greeting of the Maori of New Zealand to hold each other's arms and rub noses together a few times, while warmly looking into the other's eyes. This tradition has also been adopted in the church as a sign of peace. When practicing the *hongi*, Christians move around and greet everyone present at the church; care is taken to ensure that no one in the room has been left out of this friendly ritual. This greeting can also be used after the prayer of confession, as a sign of mutual forgiveness and acceptance and thus of reconciliation.

Bulath Chewing

Many people in Asia chew *bulath* leaves wrapped around areca nuts, spices, and lime. The Sinhalese in Sri Lanka believe that the *bulath* was given to humans by the gods and that it has a healing power. When a Sri Lankan host welcomes a guest, he first peels a small piece of *bulath* for the gods, then a piece for the guest, and then one for himself. As host and guest sit and quietly chew the *bulath*, they contemplate their friendship, the bond between them, and their acceptance of each other. Christians have adopted this custom in worship. At the beginning of the service, after peeling a small piece for God, the participants pass the *bulath* to their neighbors. As they chew the leaf, they feel a sense of healing and acceptance, and they reflect on the meaning of *koinonia* and wholeness in Christ.

Bulath Offering

As a part of the Sinhalese new-year ritual on November 14, children offer a stack of neatly piled *bulath* to their parents. As the children kneel and ask forgiveness for possible wrongs they may have done, the parents quickly raise them from their knees and embrace them, as a sign of acceptance, forgiveness, and reconciliation. This custom has been adopted into Christian worship. The congregation performs the same actions, offering a sheaf of *bulath* to one another during the service as a symbol of greeting, peace, and reconciliation.

PAYING OBEISANCE TO GOD: *Parikrama*

Some of the churches in southern India have created a particular ritual during their worship service to pay obeisance to God. First, they set up a mandala, a place in the sanctuary usually decorated with a cross, pebbles, a vase, and lotus flowers (a sign of purity). The mandala represents the Holy of Holies, which acknowledges God's presence. Worshipers bring gifts of flowers or any objects of God's creation and walk slowly in a meditative posture three times around the mandala, each time placing one gift on the mandala, and performing *namaskar* (see above). This action also symbolizes thanksgiving, praise, and offering oneself to God. After these actions, the worshipers return to their seats (on the floor) and continue their meditation or sing *bhajan*s, which are spiritual songs praising the attributes of God.[14]

PENITENCE

Coconut Smashing

The Tamils in Malaysia are mostly Hindus. In their festive processions, some throw down coconuts (which symbolize their hearts) along the road to express their penitence about sins they have committed. Since the hard shell of the coconuts has already been removed, the impact breaks the coconut into small pieces, and the juice and the fragments of white meat splash all around. This represents the resolution of the penitent, as if saying, "May I perish like this coconut, if I commit the same sin again!" Then they pick up one or two pieces of the kernel that symbolizes the pure heart or conscience, and they go home in peace. Some Christians have adopted this practice in the liturgy: after their confession of sin, they smash the coconut and, following the assurance of pardon, they pick up a kernel as a sign of peace of heart.[15] Here, a pagan ritual has been inculturated to a new Christian context with powerful effect.

Sugarcane Breaking

In Papua New Guinea, a host breaks sugarcane into pieces to share with guests as a gesture of welcome and a token of assurance that any possible barriers between them have been removed. Christians have utilized this custom in their worship. After the confession of sins, they break sugarcane and distribute the pieces to all participants as a symbol of eliminating walls of division, of mutual forgiveness, and of total acceptance and unity in the Lord. The sweetness of the sugarcane reinforces the feeling of communal love and thanksgiving for being united in God and with one another.

---

14 Cf. *ATESEA Occasional Papers*, no. 8 (1989), p. 21.
15 Cf. *ATESEA Occasional Papers*, no. 8 (1989), p. 19.

Mat Covering

When Pacific Islanders want to show regret for having offended someone, they ask a respected person, preferably the head of the community or the pastor, to beg for forgiveness on their behalf. Then, the acting penitent sits in front of the offended party's house, covered with a large straw mat as a sign of sorrow and repentance, and asks for forgiveness. If the offended party accepts the apology, he/she comes out, removes the mat, and invites the "penitent" into the house, thus restoring the relationship and accepting the offender as a friend again. If the apology is not accepted, the "penitent" is literally killed. This act is similar to the Christian belief that the sinless Christ sacrificed his own life to redeem sinners and reconcile them with God. This native sign of penitence has been accepted into the liturgy: during the prayers of confession, a representative sits on the floor at the front of the congregation, covered with a mat. After the assurance of forgiveness, the pastor removes the mat as a sign of God's forgiveness and reconciliation with God and other human beings.

Unfurling Spiral

The Maori of New Zealand have another ritual that Christians have adopted for their worship services. During the prayer of confession, the congregation walks itself into a slowly tightening spiral, like the shape of a furled punga frond, and people silently confess their sins. After all are joined in a tight, crowded spiral, the assurance of pardon is pronounced. Then they reverse the movement, unfurling the spiral, as a sign of relief from the burden of sin. They express the joy of new life by walking quickly and singing a song of praise as they return to their seats.

PROCLAIMING GOD'S WORD

Batu Pamali

Batu pamali are sacred stones originally placed in front of the *baeleu*, the meetinghouse or community center in the Moluccan culture of Indonesia. These stones are regarded as living signs of the presence of the ancestor spirits; they also represent promises as well as taboos and punishment. The stones are the witnesses of the promises that people make in return for wishes. If they break the promises, the stones will punish them, bringing various disasters. Moluccan Christians have adapted this idea, relating it to the biblical concept of Christ as the rock of salvation and as an expression of Peter's faith (Matthew 16:18); they build their pulpits with stones, upon which the Bible is placed. They pray to God and preach God's word in front of these stones with authority and confidence; with God as their witness, they are responsible for preaching the truth. The communion tables are also built with these sacred stones. Therefore, conducting Holy Communion on these stones is a powerful symbol: that God-in-Christ is in their midst, making a new covenant.

Conch Pulpits

In Moluccan Indonesia, pulpits are also constructed in the shape of a large conch, from which God's word is proclaimed loudly and strongly and from which the gospel is spread to all.

Adaptations from Hindu Practice

Some Roman Catholic priests in southern India have adapted the Hindu expressions of wearing an orange robe, sitting in a yogic posture, and making with the right hand the sign that symbolizes the speaking of truth in preaching. They also place a coconut-oil lamp and flowers on a plate as an offering, which is then raised by both hands and circled three times while chanting "shanthii, shanthii, shanthii" ("peace"; see *STB* #281, "From the unreal, lead to the real"). The significance of these cultural adaptations can easily be identified and understood by many Indians, although there are some who may feel offended by these inculturated acts.

RECEIVING THE SACRED FLAME (AARTI)

South Indian families usually keep a copper lamp with five wicks lit at night. When a Hindu prays in the temple, the devotee may hold a small *aarti*-lamp while chanting prayers. For Christians, the original pagan symbol on the top of the lamp (see fig.1, left) has been replaced with a cross. Originally, the lamp's five wicks symbolized the five paths to the deity through the body of the worshiper. The flame, which had symbolized enlightenment, wisdom, and knowledge, is interpreted by Christians according to their faith: Jesus Christ is the light of the world, in him there is no darkness. The flame also represents God's word, truth, and eternal life.

aarti

In a worship service, after listening to the gospel, the congregation is invited to come forward to receive the light and to pray for wisdom and understanding. This is done by passing both hands over the flame and then touching the forehead, to symbolize the intellectual embrace of God's word and of Christ. The participants again pass their hands over the flame and then touch their eyes to symbolize prayers for the illumination of the mystery: seeing the light and understanding the truth. Finally, after a third pass over the flame, they touch their chests to indicate the receiving of Christ and his word into their hearts with emotion. This is a meaningful inculturation of an existing rite into a Christian liturgy, and it has been practiced in several ecumenical gatherings with much success.

figure 1

HOLY COMMUNION

Coconut Meat and Juice

The traditional elements of the Holy Communion, bread and wine, were originally integral parts of the Jewish as well as the Western meal, but neither of these are part of a traditional Asian meal. Coconuts have become meaningful substitutes for bread and wine because millions of Asians rely on coconuts and their products to earn a living. Therefore, to practice Holy Communion, some Filipinos consecrate the coconut and its juice. The symbolism is clear: breaking one coconut yields enough meat and juice to nourish the people. Celebrating the Holy Communion using coconut meat and juice has had a profound effect on many occasions at CCA and ecumenical gatherings.

Rice Cakes

Rice is the most important staple food in Asia; for Asians, life without rice is unthinkable.

For the famous Korean poet Kim Chi Ha, gathering together at a table to eat rice is a spiritual experience. The title of the book *God Is Rice: Asian Culture and Christian Faith* (published by WCC, 1986) by the Japanese theologian Takenaka Masao means that rice is the symbol of life for Asians just as bread is the symbol of life for Westerners.[16] The hymn "The rice of life" (*STB* #190) is a good example of this metaphor. On various occasions, including during the CCA General Assemblies (the seventh in Seoul, 1985; the eighth in Manila, 1990; and the tenth in Tomohon, 2000) and many other occasions, Asian Christians have used rice crackers or rice cakes for Holy Communion to memorable effect.

Coconut and rice wine for Holy Communion,
Mount Makiling, 1987

Rice Loaves and Rosella Tea

Sticky rice is the most important staple food for the agrarian people in northeastern Thailand. A breakfast with sticky rice will provide sufficient energy for a day of hard labor. The Christians of the Isaan community, therefore, bake the sticky rice into the shape of a loaf to be broken and shared during their Holy Communion. They also drink a red-colored tea made of rosella leaves to represent the blood of Christ. This herbal tea is believed to have a healing effect on the body; thus, it has a spiritual meaning as well. After the partaking of the elements, the communicants stand up and dance freely to show their joy and thanksgiving for the

---

16   *ATESEA Occasional Papers*, no. 6 (1988), p. 65.

spiritual food and Christ's salvation. This cultural adaptation into the Eucharistic liturgy is so meaningful to the Isaan people that the regional church has experienced astonishing growth.

Sweet Potatoes and Rice Wine or Oolong Tea

Sweet potatoes used to be the main staple food for the poor in Taiwan. The physical shape of the island also resembles that of a sweet potato. Further, the political oppression and religious persecution by the former Nationalist Chinese regime have sparked a sense of pride and self-identification of the indigenous people as Taiwanese. Hence, sweet potatoes are a synonym of the Taiwanese. A popular poem demonstrates the uplifting metaphor:

> Sweet potatoes, fearless of being rotten beneath the earth,
> only yearn for sprouting of branches and leaves for
>   generation after generation

The efforts to contextualize theology and liturgy have inspired Taiwanese Christians to substitute sweet potatoes for bread in the Holy Communion: a whole, baked potato is broken into pieces for people to share. The sacrifice implied in the poem above is also analogous to the words of Christ: "A grain of wheat falls into the earth and dies . . . it bears much fruit" (John 12:24). Taiwanese Christians believe that sweet potatoes can play the role of bread in the Eucharist without lessening the original theological implications. Furthermore, since grape wine is foreign to the culture (although imported wines are available), rice wine, which is popular for feasts as well as general cooking, or oolong tea, which Taiwanese drink daily, are served in the cup for Holy Communion. Because both the body and blood of Christ are represented by native elements that are closely related to daily life, the Eucharist is a more intimate and meaningful celebration.

Chicken Meat

It seems almost unthinkable to substitute chicken for the bread in Holy Communion, but Indonesian Christians have supported its use with the following points:

1. Chicken is the most popular meat for general consumption.
2. No matter how beautiful chickens are, they only live for people, as if sacrificing themselves to nourish human beings.
3. A rooster reminds one of the weakness in human nature, especially one's possible denial of Christ, like Peter's (Matthew 26:75).
4. A hen reminds one of God's love, as shown in Jesus' lamentation for Jerusalem:
   > "How often would I have gathered your children together
   >   as a hen gathers her brood under her wings" (Matthew 23:37).

Furthermore, chewing chicken meat during Holy Communion makes people more aware of the effort, as if they were actually digesting the body of Christ, which is less profound when simply letting bread dissolve in the mouth.

Some may see the above practices as very far from Western liturgical traditions. It is not known whether they would be accepted into the official liturgies of any mainstream Protestant or Roman Catholic church. Nonetheless, they represent the conscious effort of some Asian Christians to search for new ways to interpret their faith and for new forms of worshiping God. Some of these cultural perspectives may give one insight and encouragement to seek meaningful Christian expressions within one's own context.

Asian Christians have received the power of the Holy Spirit. New hymns have been composed and new signs and symbols have been developed not only for the worship of God but also as a witness to the people in Asia, as well as God's people around the globe (cf. Acts 1:8).

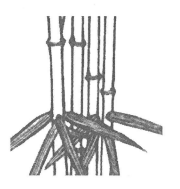

Part Two

Asian Hymns in Their Cultural and Liturgical Contexts

Northeast Asia

Northeast Asia consists of Japan, Korea, China (including the Hong Kong Special Autonomous Region [SAR]), and Taiwan and is associated with Asian high culture. The core of the culture is that of the Han Chinese, which is dominated by Buddhism and Confucian philosophies. Due to the long history of religious and cultural contacts between different peoples within the region, the music of the Tang dynasty (618–907 CE) has been preserved in and has had a lasting influence on the Japanese court music (*gagaku*), Confucian ritual and music of the Song dynasty (960–1279) is still performed in Korea today, music of the Ming dynasty (1368–1644) has been absorbed into traditional Vietnamese music, and *nanguan* music, which was specially honored by the court of the Qing dynasty (1644–1912), is popular in Taiwan as well as some Chinese communities in Singapore and the Philippines. Another cultural link is the use of Chinese written characters and calligraphy in Japan, Korea, and Taiwan (but with different rules of grammar and pronunciation). The typical Chinese five- to six-tone scales are also widely used in these countries.

 **Chinese Hymns**

A preliminary note on Romanization:

> The phonetic spelling of Chinese terms in this section follows the Pinyin system. However, the older Wade-Giles system is also used for names or terms that have been in common usage since the early twentieth century and perhaps more familiar in this form. Where necessary, both systems are provided for reference. Except for the names of widely known public figures, the order of all Chinese names have been Anglicized, i.e., the first name followed by the last name.

The Nation, People, and Music

China is a large country with a total area of 9.6 million square kilometers (about 3,706,581 square miles), and its population of over 1.3 billion is nearly one-fifth of the world population. China has fifty-six different ethnic groups; the majority (93.3%) is the Han. The second largest group is the Zhuang, numbering 13 million. The Yunnan province is the home of twenty-two ethnic groups while thirteen ethnic groups are scattered in Xinjiang Uyghur Autonomous Region (Athyal 1996, 94). All ethnic groups have their own languages, even members of the Han located in different provinces. The official language in China today is the Beijing dialect, which is commonly known as Mandarin but is called *putonghua* ("common language") among the Chinese. Overseas ethnic Chinese speak Cantonese, Hakka, Hokkien, Teochiu, and other dialects that originated from the Guangdong and Fujian provinces. Despite such differences in languages, everyone can communicate through the written Chinese characters, which can have different pronunciations, grammars, and meanings.

Some Sources of Chinese Music Theories

Archaeological finds from the Hemudu site reveal certain flutes made of bones (*gudi*) or ocarinas (*xun*) dating from about 5,000 BCE (Garland 7:106f). It is impossible to date the origin of the Chinese five-tone scale *gong shang jue zhi yu* (the equivalent of *do re mi sol la*, or 1 2 3 5 6, or relative pitches C D E G A). The *Guoyu* ("Tales of the States") records that in 522 BCE Zhou Jiu, the master of the king's music, mentioned *gong, jue*, and *yu* (1, 3, 6) and the names of twelve pitches (Garland 7:115, 117). The seven-tone scale was formed by adding *bian* ("change" or "altered") tones to *zhi* (creating *bianzhi*, or Gb, hence F#) and to *gong* (creating *biangong*, or Cb, hence B).

A set of sixty-four bells (*bianzhong*) dated 433 BCE was found in the tomb of Marquis Yi of Zheng (full name: Zheng Hou Yi) in Hubei province. Each bell can generate two pitches that are a major or minor third apart, depending on where the bell is struck, and there are inscriptions of the names of five tones on the bells. The range is from A1 to c4 in a seven-tone scale, and the middle range of the three octaves is a series of twelve semitones (Garland 7:107). If the dating of this archaeological find is accurate, it is apparent that the twelve-tone scale was in use before the middle of the fifth century BCE. Theoretically, the twelve tones were created by the *sanfen sunyi* method (adding or subtracting one-third of the length of string or pipe). The resulting twelve tones (*lü*) and their equivalent pitches, solfege, and cents are listed below.

Name	Pitch	Length	Solfege	Cents
Huangzhong	C	1	*gong*	0
Linzhong	G	*huangzhong* x 2/3	*zhi*	702
Taicu	D	*linzhong* x 4/3	*shang*	204
Nanleu	A	*taicu* x 2/3	*yu*	906
Guxian	E	*nanleu* x 4/3	*jue*	408
Yingzhong	B	*guxian* x 2/3	*biangong*	1110
Ruibin	F♯	*yingzhong* x 4/3	*bianzhi*	612
Daleu	C♯	*ruibin* x 4/3	*yingsheng*	114
Yize	G♯	*daleu* x 2/3	--	816
Jiazhong	D♯	*yize* x 4/3	--	318
Wuyi	A♯	*jiazhong* x 2/3	*qing*	1020
Zhongleu	E♯	*wuyi* x 4/3	*qingjue*	522
Qing huangzhong	c	*zhong leu* x 2/3	*shaogong*	1224

(Garland 7:118)

Historically, Chinese music has strongly influenced its neighboring countries. As mentioned earlier, the court music (*yayue*) of the Tang dynasty (618–906 CE) became the Japanese *gagaku*, the music of the Song dynasty (960–1279) is now preserved in Korean Confucian ceremonies, and the music of the Ming dynasty (1368–1644) has greatly influenced Vietnamese music. The *nanguan* music of the Qing dynasty (1644–1911) was brought to Taiwan and Southeast Asia (especially Singapore and the Philippines) by the early Hokkien migrants. Although some of these countries have contextualized their music and developed their own theories and practices, they still incorporate the basic theory and scales of Chinese music.

The following chart is a comparison of Chinese, Korean, and Japanese names of the twelve pitches in chromatic order.

Pitch	♯	Name	Sharp	Solfege/Bian	Korean	Japanese (begins with D)
C		huangzhong		gong	hwangjong	ichikotsu
	C♯		daleu		taeryo	tangin
D		taicu		shang	t'aeju	hyojo
	D♯		jiazhong		hyopchong	shosetsu
E		guxian		jue	koson	shimomu
(F)	E♯	zhongleu		qingjue	chungnyo	sojo
	F♯		ruibin	bianzhi	yubin	fusho
G		linzhong		zhi	imjong	oshiki
	G♯		yize		ich'ik	rankei
A		nanleu		yu	namnyo	banshiki
	A♯		wuyi	qingyu	muyok	shinsen
B		yingzhong		biangong	ungjong	kamimu

Each Chinese dynasty used all twelve pitches but had its own tuning system and pitch of reference. As early as the sixteenth century, the theorist Zhu Zaiyu (1536–1611) had perfected the equal-tempered, twelve-pitch scale by multiplying or dividing eleven times in succession; he revised the 2/3 ratio used when adding and subtracting thirds to 500,000,000/749,153,538, and the 4/3 ratio to 1,000,000,000/749,153,538; he generated the pitches by adding and subtracting thirds (Garland 7:119). Unfortunately, the Ming emperor did not accept the theory, so it was never put into practice. This equal-tempered tuning system was perfected more than one hundred years before J. S. Bach (1685–1750) published his first volume of *The Well-Tempered Clavier* in 1722.[1]

A Chinese notation system was developed at an early date from the *qin* repertoire. The *qin* is a long-board zither with seven silk strings and thirteen studs that mark the finger positions for the tones. This instrument, its repertory, and its performance practices have preserved the spirit, philosophy, and ideal of Chinese music for several thousand years. The *qin* notation began with the *wenzipu*, which described in prose how the pitches were to be played. It was not until the eighth century that the *wenzi* notation was changed to *jianzipu* ("abbreviated character tablature"), as seen from the earliest extant piece of *qin* music, "Youlan" ("Solitary Orchid"). This notation is unique in that it is written like a tablature that specifies the strings, pitch positions, fingerings, and the playing technique. For instance, the *wenzipu* prose statement "Use the left ring finger to stop the fourth string at the tenth marker (*hui* or "stud") and pluck the fourth string outwards with the index finger of the right hand" is transformed in *jianzipu* to four symbols that mean: "ring, 10, plucking outward, index finger, 4" (Huang 1998, 24)

---

1   *Oxford Companion to Music*, 1017. Bach composed forty-eight Preludes and Fugues ([i] BWV 846–69; [ii] BWV 870–93), two in each of the twelve major and twelve minor keys, to demonstrate a tuning system suitable for all twenty-four keys. This monument of Baroque music has been performed and studied by succeeding generations of composers and keyboardists.

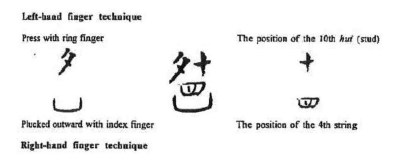

Left-hand finger technique

Press with ring finger

The position of the 10th *hui* (stud)

Plucked outward with index finger

The position of the 4th string

Right-hand finger technique

These symbols constitute one of the best and most succinct systems of notation. Unfortunately, there are no indications of time or rhythm, so interpreting the music depends on its transmission from teacher to pupil. Hence, different schools or traditions often interpret the same composition quite differently.

There are other ancient notation systems for instruments and voice, some of which are still in use today. In the early twentieth century, the Chinese adapted the Western staff notation system as well as the cipher notation system. The latter was adapted from the French tradition developed by J. J. Rousseau (1712–1778) in 1742 (Liu 1991, 129f), using 1 2 3 4 5 6 7 1 to represent the movable *do* system, and the solmization of *do re mi fa sol la si do'*. This is the easiest and most popular system, and it is widely practiced among mainland Chinese, overseas Chinese, Thais, and Indonesians, although with variations and interpretations.

Classification of Chinese Musical Instruments

Since the Zhou dynasty (1045–256 BCE), Chinese musical instruments have been classified in eight categories, according to the main material of their construction:

1. *Jin* ("metal"): *luo* (gongs with various sizes), *bianzhong* (hanging bells), *bo* (cymbals), *xiaoling* (concussion bells)
2. *Shi* ("stone"): *bianqing* (hanging stone chimes)
3. *Si* ("silk"): refers to stringed instruments such as *erhu* (two-stringed, bowed spiked lute), *sanxian* (three-stringed plucked lute), *pipa* (four-stringed, pear-shaped plucked lute), *yueqin* (two- to four-stringed, plucked moon lute); *qin* (seven-stringed, plucked board zither), *zheng* (thirteen- to twenty-five-stringed, plucked board zither)
4. *Zhu* ("bamboo"): *sona* (double-reed shawm with seven holes plus one), *dizi* (transverse flute with six holes plus one), *xiao* (vertical notched flute with six holes plus one)
5. *Bao* ("gourd"): *sheng* (free-reed mouth organ with thirteen to seventeen reed pipes)
6. *Tu* ("earth"): *xun* (ocarina with three to five holes)
7. *Ge* ("hide"): *bangu or danpigu* (single-head frame drum for accompanying Peking opera), *tanggu* (barrel drum), *biangu* (thin, large-frame drum)—all struck with mallets
8. *Mu* ("wood"): *muyu* (wooden block), *paiban* (clappers)

xiao-lu, gong

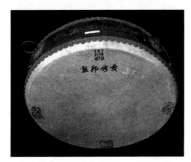

bian-gu, frame drum

bo, cymbal

sona, double-reed shawm

In a religious or Confucian ritual, instruments from all eight categories are played simultaneously to symbolize wholeness and perfection as well as the unity of *tian* (heaven) and *ren* (human beings). The performance would be considered invalid if one of the instrument classifications is missing.

The *qin* exemplifies the spirit and ideal of Chinese music, and it is considered a scholar's instrument. Since the time of Confucius (551–479 BCE), music (*yue*) has been one of the six qualifications that a scholar should acquire, along with ritual or etiquette (*li*), archery (*yi*), chariot riding (*yu*), calligraphy (*shu*), and mathematics (*shu*). Ancient paintings often show a scholar-musician playing the *qin* on a porch, surrounded by beautiful mountains, clouds, and streams; these images express the philosophy and ideal of achieving inner tranquility and the unity of human beings, nature, and heaven through music. Classical music of the *qin* and other instruments are frequently programmatic; both the players and the listeners must exercise their imaginations to perceive the meanings of the music. On the one hand, *qin* music can be introspective and contemplative; the instrument makes a soft sound, and the musician plays for oneself as an expression of tranquility and serenity or for the cultivation of character. On the other hand, the music may roar with melodic, rhythmic, and even harmonic excitement (the effect of an arpeggio or plucking multiple strings simultaneously) to depict the outburst of emotions or the rushing of waterfalls or the galloping of horses on the battleground. The listener can imagine the contents and moods of the pieces through their descriptive titles (see the discussion of *STB* #93, MEI-HUA SAN-NONG, later in this section).

Pictured are some Chinese musical instruments from I–to Loh's collection.

sheng,
free-reed
mouth organ

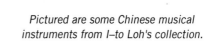

dizi, transverse bamboo flute

A History of Christian Missions in China

Early Christian Missions

When the Jesuit priest Matteo Ricci traveled to China in the sixteenth century, he found a small colony of Jews in Kaifeng (Henan Province) but no Christians.[2] However, the 1623 discovery of a tablet in Xian, the capital of the Tang dynasty, revealed that Nestorian priests had brought the gospel to China as early as 635. In *A History of Christianity in Asia*, S. H. Moffett quotes from the tablet engraved in 781, "A Monument Commemorating the Propagation of the *Ta Ch'in* Luminous Religion in China"[3]:

> When the accomplished Emperor T'ai-tsung [627–649] began his magnificent career in glory and splendour . . . behold there was a highly virtuous man named Alopen in the Kingdom of Ta-ch'in. Auguring from the azure sky he decided to carry the true Sutras with him, and observing the course of the winds, he made his way through difficulties and perils. Thus in the ninth year of the period named Chen-kuang [635] he arrived at Ch'ang-an. The Emperor dispatched his Minister, Duke Fang Hsuan-ling, with a guard of honour, to the western suburb to meet the visitor and conduct him to the Palace. The Sutras were translated in the Imperial Library. [His Majesty] investigated "the Way" in his own forbidden apartments, and being deeply convinced of its correctness and truth, he gave special orders for its propagation . . .
>
> (Moffett 1998, 291)

There is little information about the Nestorian mission. After enduring a difficult time of persecution (656–712), the priests resumed their work and erected the tablet with the above inscription in 781. By 980, they had disappeared. But according to one account, there were 30,000 Nestorians living in China by the mid-fourteenth century, the later period of the Mongol-ruled Yuan dynasty (Thomas 1978, 9).

One hymn related to the Nestorians, a "Gloria in Excelsis Deo" still sung today by Syriac Christians, was translated into Chinese. It was further translated into English by J. Foster, who said, "We of the West had to wait till the Reformation to sing this noble praise in our own tongue. Chinese Christians beat us by more than seven centuries" (quoted in Moffett 1998, 301). The hymn reads:

> The angels of the highest heavens in deepest reverence praise.
> Great earth its universal peace doth call again to mind.
> And man's own spirit-nature knows his refuge and repose.
> The Powers Three in Alaha their gracious Father find . . .

2　They were said to be Spanish Jews; some of them were forced to convert to Christianity or exiled. See Ho Wan-Li, "Jews in China: A Dialogue in Slow-Motion," *Journal of Ecumenical Studies* 40 (2003).

3　There are different interpretations of *Ta Ch'in* (or *Da Qin*), which refers to the Great Roman Empire. For further discussion, see the section on the hymnal *Zanmeishi (xinbian)*, pages 53–56.

> Great Holy-One Who art adored by all, Messiah Thou,
> We praise Thy gracious Father for His ocean-store of love.
> Great Holy-One Who dost proceed from Him, the Holy Ghost,
> We know Thy will shall here be done, all human thought above.
>
> (Moffett 1998, 301)

Another hymn, "All heaven worships in great awe," was also written by the Nestorian missionaries and will be discussed later.

According to Kuo-huang Han, the earliest Chinese hymnal appeared in 1818, and at least thirty-four hymnals were published between 1838 and 1922, some with texts only and others with tunes or four-part harmony (Garland 7:374).

Modern Christian Mission in China

According to Lee Ming Ng, the history of Christian mission in China may be divided into four periods (Thomas 1978, 9–33).

THE FIRST PERIOD: THROUGH 1840

The Nestorian mission was an early Christian presence in China. The first Chinese bishop of the Catholic Church was consecrated in 1674. By 1840, it was estimated there were over 300,000 Roman Catholics in China. Scholars believe that the Qing government was interested in the foreign missionaries not so much for their religion but for their scientific technologies: astronomy (which revised the traditional Chinese calendar), weapons production, cartography, construction of clocks, teaching of mathematics (Thomas 1978, 11). Later, antagonism between the Qing and the Christians developed when the government accused the missionaries of teachings that harmed the spirit of Confucianism.

The Protestant mission began in 1807 when Robert Morrison arrived in Canton. His work was primarily in translating the Bible and printing pamphlets that propagated the gospel. It was reported that there were fewer than one hundred Protestant converts by 1840 (Thomas 1978, 13).

THE SECOND PERIOD: 1840–1900

After the First Opium War (1839–42), China's doors were opened to foreign powers; as a result, more missionaries from the West entered China with a legal status. By 1900, there were 1,296 Protestant missionaries in 498 mission stations. After nearly one hundred years of missionary endeavor, there were 55,093 Christians by 1893 (Thomas 1978, 14).

The Taiping Rebellion (1851–64), led by Hong Xiuquan, who claimed to be the brother of Jesus Christ, took at least twenty million lives (Hoke 1975, 145). Scholars disagree over whether this movement was primarily a religious revival or a revolt against the Manchurian Qing government (cf. Hoke 1975, 145; Thomas 1978, 16); in any case, the church suffered more persecution afterward. The founding of China Inland Missions in 1865 strengthened the work of the church; by 1895, it had 641 missionaries, 462 Chinese helpers, 260 stations, and 5,211 communicants (Hoke 1975, 149).

THE THIRD PERIOD: 1900–1950

The 1900 Boxer Uprising was a violent attempt to renew Chinese sovereignty that targeted foreigners, especially missionaries, and Chinese Christians. Fifty missionaries and 30,000 Roman Catholics were killed. Of the Protestants, 200 foreigners and 2,000 Chinese Christians were slaughtered (Thomas 1978, 18). The uprising led to the invasion of Beijing by troops from eight nations (Hoke 1975, 151). It was reported that by the 1920s there were over 6,000 Protestant missionaries in China (Thomas 1978, 19).

The revolution (1894–1911) led by Sun Yat-sen eventually gave birth to the Republic of China in 1911, but ideological conflicts between Chiang Kai-shek's Kuomintang and Mao Zedong's Communists led to a bitter civil war. Mao finally won the victory in 1949 and founded the People's Republic of China while Chiang and his troops fled to Taiwan. Chiang subsequently declared Taiwan a province of China; he neither had claiming rights nor sovereignty over either country, but he held on to the former until his death in 1975. His son Chiang Ching-kuo succeeded him but died in 1988 still dreaming of overtaking China. Since Communism is basically atheist and anti-religion, the new Chinese government expelled all Christian missionaries, who subsequently competed in their work in Hong Kong, Taiwan, Singapore, and other Southeast Asian countries.

During the first quarter of the twentieth century, three indigenous sects evolved in China: the True Jesus Church, founded in 1917 by Isaac Wei; the Jesus Family, founded in 1927 by Tien-ying Ching; and the Little Flock, founded by To-sheng Ni in 1928 (Athyal 1996, 103; Hoke 1975, 173). These sects rejected foreign influences not only in terms of the structure of the church but also in the interpretation of the Bible. They were fundamentalists and were hostile to other groups with different theologies. Together with another powerful preacher and founder of the Christian Tabernacle, Ming-dao Wang (1900–1991), the leaders of these sects were imprisoned by the Communist government for opposing the Three-Self Patriotic Movement, the only state-sanctioned Christian organization in mainland China, which will be discussed below.

THE FOURTH PERIOD: 1950–1976

Being atheists, the Communists regarded Christianity as a part of Western imperialism and capitalism. According to Zhaoming Deng, Y. T. Wu (or Yaozong Wu, 1890–1979) published "The Christian Manifesto" in 1950, urging Christians to have "a new consciousness, a new awakening and a new viewpoint" in tune with the "revolutionary tide" (Athyal 1996, 105f). "Love your country/Love your church" became the slogan of the church, and patriotism meant cooperation between Christians and Communists. A recent bishop of Shanghai once wrote, "In fact, without hatred there is no true love. If we love our country, we must strongly hate the enemies of our country and people" (referring to European and American people and churches; Athyal 1996, 105f). Another prominent bishop said in 1980, "For us, patriotism is not just the love of an abstract, ancient country with a long history. It is first and foremost a love for New China" (Athyal 1996, 107). Thus the church cut itself off from the "imperialistic, bureaucratic-capitalistic, feudalistic poison and identified itself totally with the united front of the Party" (Athyal 1996, 108). When it formulated the Three-Self Patriotic Movement (TSPM), it was no surprise.

The three principles of the movement, which originated from the missionaries Henry Venn and Rufus Anderson, were: 1) self-support, 2) self-propagation, and 3) self-governance (*Asian Evangelization*, quoted in Athyal 1996, 54f). Their introduction a few decades earlier was not successful, but with a stronger political tone, the three principles became a compulsory movement. Those people who did not follow TSPM either went underground or disappeared. The underground groups met at private homes, praying and singing spiritual and gospel songs that were self-composed and transmitted orally. They never sang Western hymns (Athyal 1996, 115). During the Cultural Revolution (1966–76), most pastors were persecuted and banished to perform hard labor in China's frontier regions. Some suffered as martyrs, but the numbers of Christians continued to increase. Zhaoming Deng reports that the Roman Catholic Church in China today has about 3,500,000 members with 3,000 churches and twenty-one seminaries. The Protestant church has about 10,000,000 believers and thirteen seminaries (Athyal 1996, 122f), but other sources report a greater number of Christians and churches.[4]

China's doors were opened to the West in 1978 after the visit of the US president, Richard Nixon. The Amity Foundation was established in 1985 for printing the Bible and other Christian textbooks, and the China Christian Council joined the World Council of Churches in February 1991. The speed of church growth in China is astounding; according to some estimates, the number of Christians, including those underground, could be 70 million or more.[5]

---

4   For a more detailed analysis of the church under Communism, see Zhaoming Deng's "The Church in China," in Athyal 1996, 94–133.

5   See "Christian Statistics: The Largest Christian Populations," http://www.adherents.com/largecom/com_christian.html (accessed February 11, 2009).

Chinese Hymns: From *Putian Songzan* to *Zanmeishi (xinbian)*

In 1936, the best collection of hymns in Chinese was *Putian Songzan* ("Hymns of Universal Praise"), a joint publication of six denominations: Church of Christ in China, Chung Hwa Sheng Kung Hui (Anglican), Methodist Episcopal Church North, North China Kung Li Hui (Congregationalist), East China Baptist Convention, and Methodist Episcopal Church South. Although most of the committee members were Chinese, one of the musical editors was Bliss Wiant (1895–1975), an American Methodist missionary.

A new Chinese edition of this collection, edited by Heyward W. H. Wong and assisted by Bliss Wiant from 1963 to 1966, was published in Hong Kong in 1977 with the same title but with expanded content. An English edition was published in 1981, and a bilingual edition was released in 1986.

The New Chinese Hymnal: *Zanmeishi (xinbian)*

Zanmeishi (xinbian) ("Hymns of Praise, new edition") was published by the China Christian Council in 1983. An English-Chinese bilingual edition was printed in 1999 by the Amity Foundation. Most of the information in this volume about Chinese hymns and the biographies of the authors and composers come from the Reverend Shenyin Wang's very informative 1993 companion to the *Zanmeishi* hymnal.[6] Quotations have not been used since much of the information was not directly translated; sources are indicated at the end of each entry. The Reverend Wang is an authority on hymnology and wrote the monumental work *Shengshi Diankao* (1955); for more than a half century, this was the only scholarly work in Chinese on the sources of Western hymns and their translations.

For Chinese Christians, *Zanmeishi* represents one of the most significant achievements in terms of the development of their indigenous hymns. Ever since the Protestant mission began in China, a number of hymnals had been compiled, but most of them were translations of Western hymns and were mainly supervised by Western missionaries. *Zanmeishi*, however, was solely the work of Chinese pastors, poets, and musicians. According to the hymnal's preface, the Chinese Christian Three-Self Patriotic Movement and the China Christian Council formed an editorial committee for a new hymnal in February 1981; the committee included Shengjie Cao, Qigui Shi, Shengben Lin, and Leuming Hong. They publicized a nationwide call for new hymn texts and tunes, and the response was overwhelming. Between March 1981 and September 1982, the committee received 2,256 hymns from 423 groupings. After careful screening, 102 hymns and tunes were selected for inclusion in the new hymnal. Among the total of 400 hymns, 292 were Western, already in common usage, and taken from different hymnals such as *Putian Songzan*, *Minzhong Shenggeji*, *Shengtu Xinsheng*, *Song Zhu Shiji*, *Shige*, etc. There were six

---

6   Shenyin Wang, *Zanmeishi (xinbian) Shihua* ("Companion to Hymns of Praise, new edition") (Shanghai: China Christian Council, 1993).

new translations of hymns, which were not present in earlier publications. Among the 102 Chinese hymns, fifty-six were written after 1980. There are also forty-two short songs in the appendix, but they were not included in the bilingual edition.

One hymn in *Zanmeishi* (*ZMS*) that deserves special attention is "All heav'n worships in great awe" (Mandarin: *Wushang zhu tian shen jing tan, ZMS* #385), which was written by Nestorian missionaries, who went to China during the Tang dynasty. It was included in the original and all subsequent editions of *Putian Songzan* but with a different tune in the 1977 edition.[7] The original tune CHENG JING ZAN was composed by Jifang Liang in 1934 (see also *STB* #167):

ALL HEAVEN WORSHIPS IN GREAT AWE

(after *Zanmeishi* #385)

According to Shenyin Wang, the manuscript of this hymn text was discovered at the Dunhuang grottoes in the province of Gansu by the French sinologist Paul Pelliot (1878–1945) with the British scholar Aurel Stein (1862–1943) in 1908. Also amassed were over 5,000 items of invaluable manuscripts, documents, and artifacts that are now housed in the Guimet Museum in Paris.

The title of this hymn in classical Chinese is *Da Qin jingjiao sanwei mengdu zan*. *Da Qin*, which originally referred to the Great Roman Empire, probably denotes in this context only the eastern part of the empire, including Syria and Judea. *Jingjiao* is the name of the Nestorian church, which was formed by Nestorius, a Syrian born in Antioch and who had been the archbishop of Constantinople from 428 to 431 CE. *Sanwei* means "the majestic triune God," *mengdu* refers to "salvation through

---

7   In the 1977 edition of *Putian Songzan*, this text and the next hymn ("Lord, before our world was formed") were both sung to the tune KANG HSI, composed by the editor H. W. Wong.

grace," and *zan* is the word for praise or a song of praise. A proper translation of the title reads: "The hymn of praise for the merciful salvation of the majestic triune God of the Nestorian Church of the Great Roman Empire (Syria and Judea)." This hymn has eleven stanzas, each of which has four lines of seven characters each (7 7 7 7), a typical form of Chinese classical poetry but one not strictly rhymed according to modern Mandarin. The first two lines are probably a paraphrase of the ancient "Gloria in excelsis" (taken from Luke 2:14, "Glory to God in the highest, peace on earth to whom God is well pleased"). The translation of this hymn was attributed to Jing Jing, a priest of Persian (Syrian) origin, who was probably the author of the aforementioned historic tablet *Da Qin Jingjiao liuxing Zhongguo bei* ("The tablet of the wide-spread Nestorian Church of the Great Roman Empire in China") in 781 CE (cf. Wang 1993, 578–83). Because it adapts Buddhist terminology and imagery, this first Chinese hymn is an invaluable source for studying the history of Christian mission and the contextualization of the gospel.

English translation by A. T. Roy, 1987; altered by Ivy Balchin, 1991, 1994:

1. All heav'n worships in great awe, All men long for earth's accord,
   Man's true nature is assured, Gracious, three-powered, Yahweh, Lord.
2. Righteous men show true respect, All with wisdom sing Your praise,
   All the truthful yield in trust, Saved by You from evil ways.
3. You are peerless, constant, true, Father, Son and Spirit, one,
   Master of all other Lords, Through all time true sovereign Son.
4. Veil'd in boundless mystery, Search we fully without end,
   Never from beginning, seen, Never by us mortals sensed.
5. Only You are purest good, Only You true pow'r possess,
   Only You remain unchanged, Root of lasting righteousness.
6. Now we ponder mercy, love, Fill the nations with Your joy,
   "Messiah" is Your holy Son And salvation without alloy.
7. Ageless King and willing lamb Sharing bitter toil and pain,
   Pray, remove man's heavy guilt "Til our nature's freed again.
8. Holy Son, at Your right hand, From Your throne above the world,
   Master, hear the call from those In the fire-stream tossed and whirled.
9. Master, and most gracious Sire, Ruler and good Lord of all,
   Teacher, law creator, King Leader, who saves those who fall.
10. Lord, provide the meek with strength, Eyes on You be fixed thereto.
    Drop sweet dew upon the parched, Till our roots be fed in You.
11. Righteous and adored Messiah, Mercies wider than the seas,
    Great and humble Holy Ghost, Laws are our sure verities. (Amen.)

(Hymns of Universal Praise 1986, #679)

Another important hymn in *Zanmeishi* is "Lord, before our world was formed" (*ZMS* #386), written by Yushan Wu, who lived from 1631 to 1718, during the Ming and Qing dynasties. This hymn was also included in all of the editions of *Putian*

Songzan since 1936. It was translated by Ivy Balchin and W. H. Wong in 1994 and was originally set to a traditional melody (YUN DAN 7777D). It is in a chant style of poetry, arranged by Changnian Qiu in 1920.

English translation:

1. Lord, before our world was formed, Hov'ring high Thou judge of all;
   For the world Thou gave Thyself, Nations at Thy cross must fall.
2. Satan's power has been foiled, Heaven's ladder now is set,
   Burdens now on Christ are laid, On He leads us step by step.

(Hymns of Universal Praise 1986, #680)

Other Notable Chinese Hymns

Some other significant hymns from *Zanmeishi* are not included in *Sound the Bamboo*. These were mostly written after 1980 and exhibit Chinese contextual elements in both text and music:

"This day's work is now completed" (*ZMS* #158),
     translated by Ida Bennett Lusk, 1994; alt.
Yi ri gong wan xin huanxi by Jifa Wang, 1982.
YONG SONG XI by Weixin Zhang; harmonization by Mingzhen Li, 1982.
5 5 1 1 /2 .32 1 /5 6 5 3 /21235 - /

"Wonderful is our Creator's world" (*ZMS* #309),
     translated by Ivy Balchin & W. H. Wong, 1995.
Tienfu shijie duomo meihao! by Yanli Sun, 1982.
ZHAO XIA by Shengben Lin, 1982.
9/4 561/3- -3- - 216/5- -5- - 123/5- - 5- -653/2- -2- -

"Waxing, waning, dim, bright" (*ZMS* #193),
     translated by Wenh-in Ng, 1994.
Yue you yuanque mingan by Zhikan Zhou, 1977.
ZHUI SI (IN MEMORIAM) by Qigui Shi, 1982.
3 .33-3-/3 .55--/

"Jesus bids us to obey" (*ZMS* #354),
     translated by Bruce Chan, 1994;
     alt. Ivy Balchin, 1995.
Zhu di mingling dang zunxing by Yuzhen Duan, 1982.
AI ZHONG REN by Yuzhen Duan, 1982.
/1 5 6 1 /6 535 –

"Holy Spirit is like the wind" (*ZMS* #62),

    translated by Grace Shangkuan Koo, 1994; alt. Ivy Balchin
    and W. H. Wong, 1995.

Shengling ru feng feng he ru by Weifan Wang, 1982.

FENG XIU ZHU by Weifan Wang; harmonization by Guoren Zhong, 1982.

3.5/66 .565/3---

"Open my eyes, O my Lord" (*ZMS* #332),

    translated by Xianying Shen, 1987; alt. Ivy Balchin, 1995.

Qiu Zhu kaiqi wo yanjing by Shengjie Cao, 1982.

KAIQI by Shengben Lin, 1982.

1 1 1 /1 - 5/6 - 1 / 5--/3 3 3 /1 – 6 /2 --

"Arduous tho' our work can be" (*ZMS* #369),

    translated by Wenh-in Ng, 1994.

Women zuogong sui xinku by Banchi Liu, stanzas 1 and 3; Zichen Zhao,
    stanza 2, alt. 1981.

XIN SHENG by Wenzhen Li, 1971; harmonization by Xuexin Wang, 1982.

5 1 2 31/21655-/55112.1/1---

"Have you ever known? From the first, Christ was with God" (*ZMS* #45),

    translated by Donald Snow, 1996; alt.[8]

Ni ke ceng zhi fou? Jidu taicu yu Shen xie by Yifan Shen, 1982.

YONG CHANGJIU by Leuming Hong, 1982.

3 5 6 i2/5---/i i 6 i/5 653-/

"God so loved his world his son to give" (*ZMS* #84),

    translated by J. J. Dai, 1992; alt. Ivy Balchin & W. H. Wong, 1996.

Yesu lai renjian, Shen ai shiren by Daling Ren, 1981.

SHENGDAN GANEN by Shengben Lin, 1981.

3 – 1 5 /6 1 5 --/1 – 1 6 /2---

"God's lasting love, measureless and great" (*ZMS* #257),

    translated by Ida Bennett Luck, 1994; alt.

Shen ai chang, wan ai mo neng liang by Mingsui Shen, 1981.

HONG by Shengben Lin, 1982.

5 –5 2 3 /5---/3 5 2 6 /1---

---

8   This is an excellent hymn.

Commentary on Individual Hymns

"Amen" (*STB* #108)

Puqi Jiang adapted a Chinese folk melody for the tune of this amen and introduced it to the participants of the 1987 Asian Workshop on Liturgy and Music in Makiling, Manila; the original title is unknown. It is in an A = 3 five-tone scale (D = 6 1 2 3 5). The setting is interesting in that the second voice is a retrogression of the main melody, i.e., the melody is sung backward, but the rhythm has been adjusted for a harmonic purpose. This compositional form was invented as early as the fourteenth century by the French composer Guillaume de Machaut (about 1300–1377) in his polyphonic *rondeaux* entitled "Ma fin est mon commencement et mon commencement ma fin" ("My end is my beginning and my beginning my end") (Grout 1973, 122f). The form is a playful musical game that also shows off the composer's skills in counterpoint. In practice, it would be good for the congregation to sing the melody first at the end of a prayer of thanksgiving or praise, or at the conclusion of worship, and the second time with the choir singing the harmony.

"Brilliant spring paints beauteous landscapes"
> (Mandarin: *Chun-guang mingmei, meijing liang chen*)
> See "IN ALL THE SEASONS SEEKING GOD" (*STB* #237)

"For the beauty of the earth" (*STB* #171)
> (Mandarin: *Huan guan dadi hao feng-guang*)

Folliot S. Pierpoint's 1864 hymn has been very popular in many churches because it relates to people's daily experiences and feelings. It is like a litany: after expressing one's gratitude to God for the beauty of creation, time, and seasons; for the joy of senses and perceptions; for the mystery of harmony; for loving relations between friends and family members; and for the universal church, each stanza concludes with the refrain "Lord of all, to you we raise this our hymn of grateful praise." Each stanza of this hymn can be sung as a corresponding response to thanksgiving prayers. Originally this was a Eucharistic hymn, with the refrain ending "this our sacrifice of praise." It was altered by Ting-fang Liu to "this our hymn of praise," and it was further expanded by the arranger to "this our hymn of grateful praise" to fit the new tune.

The melody MO-LI-HUA ("jasmine flower") is one of the most famous folk songs in China. The Italian composer Giacomo Puccini (1858–1924) adapted it in his opera *Turandot*. The original text of the folk song reads:

What a beautiful jasmine flower,
What a beautiful jasmine flower,
Full of beauty and fragrance in all branches and buds,
Everyone is proud of your fragrance and brightness (being white).
Let me pick [a flower from] you, and give to someone.
Oh, jasmine flower, jasmine flower!

Like Martin Luther, who was said to have asked why the devil should have all the nice melodies, the adaptor and arranger Pen-li Chen felt that this beautiful melody that praised the beauty of flowers could be transformed into a hymn to praise the beauty of God's creation. Chen's first idea while searching for a proper text was "For the beauty of the earth." The old and new texts are similar not only in meter but also in mood. Only a slight alteration was needed at the end of the refrain, the addition of "this our hymn of grateful praise."

The melody is in a G = 3 pentatonic scale (B♭ = 5 6 1 2 3), a typical Chinese *zhidiao* (*chih* mode with final on 5), in which one exceptional cadence ends on 1. The phrase organization is a a b c d e e'; only the initial and the final phrases are repeated. The polyphonic treatment with echoes and imitative passages and the addition of the sixth tone 7 provide more color to this lovely melody. The part progressions are also intended to demonstrate harmonious interactions between nature and the human family and their unity in Christ. The concluding phrase in octaves, unison, and heterophony are typical features of the Chinese instrumental ensemble. This text and tune were matched specifically for the Asian American hymnbook project for the Chinese Caucus of the Federation of the Asian American United Methodist Church in 1980. It was included in *Hymns from the Four Winds* (translated by Tingfang Liu).

"Fount of love, our Savior God" (*STB* #65)

(Mandarin: *Ai zhi quanyuan jiushi Shen*)

This is a superb hymn in the classical poetic form *ci* (or *ts'u*, "verse"), which is commonly written with specific metric structures and certain melodic formulae to be recited or sung. The metric structure of the original poem "Man Jiang Hong" is 7 4 7 4 7 7 8 3, without rhyme. Such poems are so condensed that it is impossible to translate them into English with the same number of syllables and faithfully retain the original meanings. This is generally true for most of the Chinese and Taiwanese poems written in the classical style. Unless one is knowledgeable and fluent in these languages, it is difficult to fully appreciate the nuances and beauty of the original poem. This hymn expresses the complexity and reality of Christian life and prays for the Savior's guidance. It first appeared in an early edition of *Cantate Domino*, the World Student Christian Federation hymnal (either the first edition in 1924 or the revised edition in 1930), and also in the third edition (1951), which was translated by Margaret Barclay and harmonized by Roger Vuataz. *Sound the Bamboo* features a 1953 translation by Frank W. Price. He skillfully paraphrased the hymn and reorganized the thoughts expressed instead of translating it line by line; thus, one can still understand the main idea of the hymn.

The hymn has two sections. The first section of four lines states the work of God or various conditions and struggles of human beings; the second section of two lines is a prayer of thanksgiving or a petition to God and/or Jesus. Therefore, this hymn is appropriate for prayers after a sermon or altar calls or as a dedication. This traditional tune first appeared in 1920 in the December issue of the musical journal of Beijing University (vol. 1, nos. 9–10), and was originally set to a classical Yuan dynasty poem by Dula Sa. In 1925, this was adapted by Ernest Yinliu Yang to the tune MAN-JIANG-HONG ("All Red the River") by General Yue Fei (1103–1142) expressing the patriotic sentiment of the time (cf. *Zhongguo Yinyue Cidian* 1986, 103). Yang must have written the new Christian text to this tune around the same time, for this setting had already appeared in the 1924 or 1930 edition of *Cantate Domino*. The original adaptation by Yang ends with the third system, but the popularly known version of the MAN-JIANG-HONG melody, though considerably different, is incomplete without the refrain of the fourth system. Therefore, the hymn arrangement restores the original form of the tune. This setting was done in 1981 for the Asian American hymnbook project and published in *Hymns from the Four Winds*.

The melody is in a G♯ = 3 pentatonic scale (B = 5 6 1 2 3) and in *zhi* mode (final on 5). The arrangement sets the three- to four-part accompaniment in unison, octave doublings, imitations, echoes, and sequences with contrapuntal lines to avoid forming Western chords and to contextualize the music to a Chinese style. The song is through-composed, as is the case in many traditional Chinese tunes. It is best sung in unison, with alternating genders singing different stanzas. Although keyboards are handy for playing the accompaniment, flutes, bowed lutes of any kind, or other instruments would also be effective for doubling the melody or accompanying the hymn.

"Gentle Jesus, meek and mild" (*STB* #231)

(Mandarin: *Wenrou Yesu zhen ren-ai*)

Charles Wesley (1707–1788) originally wrote this hymn for children in 1742 with fourteen stanzas. It is a prayer to Jesus to allow children to come to him, to learn from his examples of humility, obedience, and a loving heart, and to be like him.

The tune SINIM (whose meaning is unknown) is from a Chinese folk melody in a G = 2 five-tone scale (F =1 2 3 5 6). Its simplicity and melancholy reflects well the mood of a children's prayer. The final cadence on 1 changes the character of this seemingly Hypo-Dorian mode in pentatonic scale. Lujia Xu's accompaniment with short motifs that imitate or echo portions of the melody adds interest and slightly changes the character of the song.

"God, be praised at early morn" (*STB* #156)

(Mandarin: *Qingchen zaoqi zanmei Shen*)

There is a moving story behind this hymn. When the author and composer Dawei Wang learned of the *Zanmeishi* editorial committee's call for new hymns in 1981, he considered writing but had difficulty finding good texts. But his late father had taught him to write poetry when he was young, and his mother had coached him in music theory. So, after diligent study of the Bible and renewing his intimate relations with God, he was finally able to write three hymns within one night—one for morning, one for evening, and one for God's glory. After reviewing his works, the committee decided to use the morning hymn, which originally had only two stanzas: the first stanza giving thanks for God's mercy for a good night's sleep and the third stanza asking for spiritual growth. And with Wang's agreement, they took his hymn for God's glory and condensed it to form the second stanza (cf. Wang 1993, 251–52). Because of its simplicity, this hymn has been attractive to many and has been widely used in the church.

The melody QING-CHEN meaning "early morning" (the original name being ZAO QI, "rising early," harmonized by Ming-zhen Li) is in a G = 3 five-tone scale without a half step (E♭ =1 2 3 5 6); it has been reset by Pen-li Chen in a richer Western harmony. Since the melody is in a typical Chinese style, Chen provided an alternative setting in a more contrapuntal manner to enhance the flow of the melody. One suggestion is to use the alternate setting to accompany the second stanza. If so, make sure that the pianist/organist plays a short interlude consisting of the last phrase without harmony so that the congregation can adjust to the different harmony. By the same token, after the second stanza, another interlude should be played to bring the congregation back to the Western setting for the third stanza. Of course, the leader of worship or choir director should feel free to suggest other ways of singing.

"God, we praise you for this LORD's day" (*STB* #13)

(Mandarin: *Jin zhao women gongjing qianbei*)

This is a hymn for morning worship by Tsu-chen Chao (Zichen Zhao, 1888–1979), one of the most outstanding theologian-educators in China. It asks God to forgive one's sins, acknowledges God's endless mercy, and begs the Father not to depart from one's sorrows; it also assures that the heavenly father's love is the source of joy and peace. The English version is a free paraphrase; the "LORD's day" on the first line was originally "this morning"; hence it turns into a hymn for Sunday worship.

The music PU-TO is in an E = 3 six-tone scale (C =1 2 3 5 6 7) and in a a b a' form; it was adapted from a Buddhist chant from Mount Puto. This origin provided the tune name to Bliss Wiant, who wrote the Western harmonization in the original setting. This tune first appeared in the West in an early (1924 or 1930) edition of *Cantate Domino,* the World Student Christian Federation hymnal, and was set to "Let us with a gladsome mind," a paraphrase or adaptation of Psalm 136 by John Milton (1608–1674). It was included in the 1951 edition of *Cantate Domino* without an indication of the harmonizer. Ever since Wiant's new setting in the 1936 *Putian Songzan*, it has appeared in many hymnals of Western mainline churches. In 1999, in order to maintain its original Chinese character, Pen-li Chen provided monotonous drones like punctuating gongs, and added an ostinato (0 3 6 56) with variations that resemble the chanting and colotomic accompaniments in a temple. (Colotomy refers to the use of different instruments to mark off time intervals that are nested within other time intervals or cycles, as in the Indonesian gamelan. See the Indonesian section for further explanation.)

"Golden breaks the dawn" (*STB* #155)

(Mandarin: *Qingzao qilai kan*)

This is one of the most popular hymns by Tzu-chen Chao (Zichen Zhao). Chao utilizes beautiful imagery to depict the rising sun as strong as a warrior or as handsome as a bridegroom (which is not shown in the English translation). This hymn is also a prayer for guidance and trust that God will provide in a blessed, simple life. The original translation by Mildred A. Wiant, "Rise to greet the sun," was chosen for the 1964 United Methodist hymnbook (#678 in the 1989 United Methodist Hymnal). This was considered the first Chinese hymn to have been included in an American hymnal (Wang 1993, 248). The present English version was translated by Frank W. Price in 1953.

The tune name LE PING literally means "joy peace." It was composed by Te-ngai Hu, then a student in the department of music at Yanjing University, and it was published in Chao's 1931 *Minzhong Shenggeji* ("Hymns of the People") (Wang 1993, 247). The mood of the basically five-tone melody (G = 1 2 3 5 6)—centered and ending five times on 5, which characterizes the *zhi* mode—is changed by the sudden introduction of another tone 4 (C) before reaching the climax in the third system. This tune was skillfully harmonized in a Western idiom by Bliss Wiant and was included in the 1936 *Putian Songzan*. According to Carlton Young, Wiant indicated that the composer of this tune first heard this melody played on a flute by a street musician in a market (Young 1993, 570). If that was the case, then Hu might not be the composer but the transcriber and adaptor.

"Great are your mercies, Heavenly Father" (*STB* #174)

(Mandarin: *Tianshang di fuqin zhen shi cibei*)

Tzu-chen Chao (Zichen Zhao) wrote this hymn according to the teachings of Jesus on the mountains: "Be not anxious for tomorrow" (Matthew 6:25–31). The first stanza encourages one to be humble and obedient to God and concludes with a beautiful Chinese image: "You, the spring wind, I, the grass; on me blow!" The rest of the stanzas are paraphrases of the biblical passage, ending with the statement "This world God made is your home, yours and ours." The first stanza in the original text refers to God in the third person, but the translation addresses God more intimately in the second person. To avoid confusion, make sure that the congregation is aware that the last two stanzas are sung to fellow worshipers, not to God.

The melody CHU-TOU-GE ("song of the hoe") is an adaptation of a folk melody, which is through-composed in a D = 3 five-tone scale (B♭ =1 2 3 5 6), with final on 5. According to Shenyin Wang, a pioneer in hymnological studies, this folk song was very popular during the 1930s, and the original text, "with the hoe that cuts the weeds, remove the weeds that seedlings may grow," not only described the need for farmers to weed the fields but also implied the need to root out corruption in society (Wang 1993, 64). Chao captured the spirit of the song and skillfully imitated the folk idiom to formulate this new hymn. The tune was originally harmonized by Bliss Wiant but was reset by Lujia Xu for *Sound the Bamboo* in 1989. The lively and rhythmic running figures seem to depict the busy and industrious lives of hardworking people. If this is deemed too complicated for the congregation, it will suffice to use a flute to double the main melody.

"Holy night, blessed night" (*STB* #140)
(Mandarin: *Shengye qing, shengye jing*)

This Chinese Christmas carol is full of beautiful images; its mood is so similar to Franz Gruber's STILLE NACHT that it was fondly nicknamed "the Chinese Silent Night" and has been sung all over China. The original description of the angel's song in the third and fourth lines of the second stanza is fascinating. The Mandarin consists of seventeen syllables:

> *jinqin yuzheng mantian geyun,*
> *haliluya shanhai yu qiming*

The literal English translation has thirty-one syllables:

> Golden harps and jade zithers making music over the heavens,
> Hallelujah, mountains and oceans roaring with sound [of joy].

The richly picturesque description in seventeen Chinese syllables cannot be conveyed in the final seventeen English syllables:

> Earth and heavens ring with praises,
> Alleluia, all creation sings.

This reveals the impossibility of complete translation from one language to another. But the hymn's author maintains the most important message of the hymn: the coming of Christ like a morning sun, shining his love, sacrifice, justice, and peace upon the world.

The melody of SHENG-YE JING ("holy night quiet") is constructed with a B♭ = 5 five-tone scale (E♭ =1 2 3 5 6), through-composed with simplicity and melancholy. There is an interesting series of large skips down a minor seventh, from a higher 5 to lower 6. Although it might sound unusual to Western ears, this is one of the characteristics of Chinese melodic progression. Also, the composer seems to be making tone paintings. The two large downward skips of a seventh occur

HOLY NIGHT, BLESSED NIGHT
SHENG YE JING
6.7.8.9.8

Wei-yu Zhu and Jing-ren Wu, 1921
para. Kathleen Moody

Qu-gui Shi, 1982

1. Ho - ly night, Bless - ed night, Stars shine bright - ly, earth is still: Hills and val - leys, field and wood-lands, All sur-round the small town Beth - le - hem. In a man - ger Christ the Lord sleeps.

2. Ho - ly night, Bless - ed night, An - gels sing praise, shep - herds fear. Earth and heav - en ring with prais - es, Al - le - lu - ia all cre - a - tion sings. Tell the good news: Christ is born now.

3. Ho - ly night, Bless - ed night, Christ has come down, dwells with us. Sac - ri - fice, love, peace and jus - tice Shine up - on us like the morn - ing sun. Grace and glo - ry bless the whole world. (A - men)

(after *Zanmeishi* #79)

between the words *tian* ("heaven"), *di* ("earth"), and *dansheng* ("being-born"), which describe the acts of descending and hence imply the incarnation of Christ. Whether intentional or simply coincidental, such text treatments do provide some space for imagination and interpretation, or even for doing theology with music.

The original setting was in Western four-part homophonic harmony, as shown in the illustration. Pen-li Chen rearranged it in 1988 with free contrapuntal technique—imitating, echoing, and decorating the main melody, which enhances the beauty of this Chinese tune.

According to Shenyin Wang, when Qigui Shi was young, he was under the guidance of the Reverend Weiyu Zhu at St. John's Church in Suzhou. Shi naturally had very high respect for his mentor. While on the *Zanmeishi* editorial committee in 1981, he requested Zhu to submit some of his hymn texts for consideration in the new hymnal. And to his surprise and joy, Zhu's earlier hymns survived the Cultural Revolution. Shi was impressed by this Christmas hymn, and he was inspired to compose this beautiful carol. Zhu acknowledged that he had written this text in 1921 with Jingren Wu, so he had to share the credit (Wang 1993, 142–44).

"IN ALL THE SEASONS SEEKING GOD"
("Brilliant spring paints beauteous landscapes," *STB* #237)

(Mandarin: *Chun-guang mingmei, meijing liang chen*)

In this hymn, the author Chen-chang (Zhenchang) Yang uses the four seasons—spring, summer, autumn, and winter—as analogies of the stages of life and encourages young people to pursue meaningful, responsible, and dedicated Christian lives to ensure acceptance in heaven. The tune SI-SHI ("four seasons") was composed by Chia-jen (Jiaren) Yang in an A = 5 pentatonic scale (D =1 2 3 5 6), with a simple a a' form ending on 1. Although set in Western harmony, the frequent doubling between the tenor and soprano lines and certain imitative figures have effectively reinforced the Chinese-style melody.

"Jesus loved each little child" (*STB* #200)

(Mandarin: *Yesu Jiuzhu ai xiaohai*)

Tzu-chen Chao (Zichen Zhao) was concerned for the gospel to reach out to serve all people, including farmers, students, and young children. This is evident from this children's hymn, written in 1931. It invites children to come to Jesus, as it describes Jesus' welcoming of children. It concludes with an encouragement for one to be humble and pure in heart so that one may enter the kingdom of God.

CECILIA, which is derived from the Latin word for "blind," is usually a female name. Why this simple Chinese folk melody has this name is unknown. It is in an A = 3 pentatonic scale (F =1 2 3 5 6) and commonly sung as a school song:

Now the classes are over; let's pack our bag of books to go home.

I bow my head when I see my parents; my parents see me, smiling with joy.

Chao's decision to adapt this tune to the text, relating the parents' love to Jesus' care for children, exhibits his sensitivity and ingenuity for contextualizing the gospel. Pen-li Chen's accompaniment uses reiterated tones, the intervals of fourths, fifths, and even seconds and thirds, and active contrapuntal lines in the bass to make this children's song more lively.

PSALM 100
PLUM BLOSSOM
Irregular

Arr. W. H. Wong, 1995

Chinese ancient chin tune
Arr. Ze-min Chen, 1982

1. Make a joy-ful noise un - to the Lord, all ye lands, and serve the
2. En - ter in - to His gates with thanks - giv - ing, and in - to

Lord with glad - ness; come be - fore His pres - ence with sing -
His courts with praise; be thank - ful un - to Him, and bless His

ing. Know ye that the Lord He is God: it is He that hath made us,
name. For the Lord is good; His mer - cy is ev - er - last - ing;

we are His peo - ple, and the sheep of His pas - ture.
and His truth en - dur - eth to all gen - er - a - tions. (A - men)

(after *Zanmeishi* #380)

"Make a joyful noise, all the lands" (*STB* #93)

(Mandarin: *Putianxia dang xiang Zhu huanhu*)

This is a good example of Zemin Chen's adaptation of *qin* music to create hymns. He sets the text of Psalm 100 ("Make a joyful noise, all the lands") to the melody of MEI-HUA SAN-NONG ("plum flowers in three variations"). This song is through-composed, in an F = 1 five-tone scale (1 2 3 5 6); it is only the first section of the whole *qin* piece, which is long and has many variations. Chen had originally arranged it in Western four-part harmony, as seen in the illustration. In 1988, Pen-li Chen subsequently utilized certain *qin* or *guzheng* (bridged zither) playing styles to enhance the flow of the melody. There is no actual harmony in Chinese music, but the arrangement of a counter-melody with imitations, echoes, and glissandos creates the effect of two zithers playing a duet. The *qin* piece has been transformed into a contemporary psalm praising God. Since the sounds of both the *qin* and the *guzheng* are soft, both instruments (one playing the main melody and another on the bass clef, with certain necessary transposition and/or simplification) would need to be amplified to be heard by the singers. A harpsichord or harp accompaniment can also add new life to this piece. If a *guzheng* is not available, a keyboard instrument would be acceptable. A flute of any kind to double the melody would be effective as well.

"May the Holy Spirit's sword" (*STB* #223)

(Mandarin: *Dan yuan Shengling daofu*)

This is a hymn of prayer to the Holy Spirit: to pierce one like a sword for obedience, to teach one to love God more than jewels, and to shine God's love on one's heart. It was written by one of the most outstanding theologian-educators in China, Tzu-chen Chao (Zichen Zhao).

The tune JU MENG LING (or RU MENG LING) was the original name of this ancient *ci* (or *ts'u*) melody for chant or poetry recitation. It is in basically an A = 3 five-tone scale (D = 6 1 2 3 5), but the sixth tone 7 appears near the end, which is one of the typical features of traditional Chinese melodies, breaking the monotony of a pentatonic scale. This tune is almost through-composed, with only a few spots of motivic imitation, which is another feature of traditional compositions. The harmonization was set for the Asian American hymnbook project in 1981, which was published in *Hymns from the Four Winds*. A few chords provide a sustaining effect against the flow of the melody and the occasional contrapuntal figures. The unison near the end that introduces the sixth tone 7 is almost unnoticeable because of its diatonic unison progression, but it gives a new dimension to the song. This new tone 7 (E) carries the Mandarin words *guo yu*, meaning "more than" in both the second and third stanzas: the message is to love God more than jewels and that God's love is wider than the sea of clouds. When one can identify such interesting points to do theology, hymn singing becomes more meaningful and challenging.

"May the Lᴏʀᴅ, gracious God" (*STB* #80)

(Mandarin: *Yuan quanneng Zhu Shangdi*)

This anonymous English text has been sung in the United States with the Austrian folk melody "Edelweiss," which was featured in the musical *The Sound of Music*. During the collecting and editing process of the Asian American hymnbook project, it was difficult to find new hymns composed by Chinese Americans. I (I-to Loh) was then the project director and helped the Chinese group look for new hymns. Since the 1960s, I was very fond of this beautiful ᴡᴇɴ ᴛɪ melody and wanted to find a suitable text for it. I discovered that the "May the Lᴏʀᴅ, gracious God" text and ᴡᴇɴ ᴛɪ tune almost perfectly matched in both meter and mood, with only slight adjustments needed. Thus a new prayer of benediction was born.

The title ᴡᴇɴ ᴛɪ means "listening to a flute"; originally, the first line of the song was "Who is playing the flute inside the chamber tower?" Pao-chen (Baozhen) Li composed the melody in a traditional five-tone scale without a half step (D = 5 6 1 2 3). The simple melody evokes feelings of peace and tranquility. The original choral arrangement was a Western four-part chordal harmony with piano accompaniment. But the second stanza had a beautiful descant. In order to preserve the beauty of the Chinese melody, the adaptor retained only the descant to show the contrast and eliminated the rest of the parts. After the hymn's introduction in *Hymns from the Four Winds*, it has been well received by many churches and has become one of the most popular Chinese hymns in the world. Some editors have changed the title from "May the Lᴏʀᴅ, mighty God" to "May the Lᴏʀᴅ, gracious God," which is more in line with the spirit of the song. This is a good hymn for benediction. The descant should be sung by only a few female voices so that it is not too strong. Care should be taken at the descant's big jump 3- 6 2 2-; it should have sufficient support to go up, but lightly, not loudly.

"Midnight stars make bright the sky" (*STB* #135)

(Mandarin: *Mingxing canlan ye wei yang*)

This is one of the most famous and popular Christmas carols in China, by one of the most prolific hymn writers, the Reverend Jingqiu Yang (1897–1984). Shenyin Wang, who quoted Qigui Shi's analysis of this hymn, made the following observations (cf. Wang 1993, 121–23):[9]

1. Yang uses his profound imagination to describe the biblical story objectively, then gradually relates the nativity event to more personal reflections, as shown in the last stanza: "I am prone to devilish ways, wander hopeless in a maze ... how can I a lost sheep be?" The concluding statement is more decisive and powerful: "My clean heart shall be his throne, not an inn with no more room."

---

9   For this discussion, the quotations have been translated directly from Wang's original Chinese and are not from the English translation.

2. Yang has skillfully utilized classical poetic expressions to depict the Biblical scenes. For instance, the seventh line in Chinese, *huwen lun-yin ban jiuxiao*, means "suddenly hearing the emperor's [*sic*, refers to the LORD of the universe] holy decree announcing from the highest heaven." This elegant description in classical poetic form is unfortunately not translated in the English version.

3. Yang relates the Biblical event to his context and at the same time extends it to all human beings: from "the shepherds in the field seeing a wondrous sight" to the personal statement "God has ordained a good shepherd for me" to "peace and blessings to all people on earth."

HUAN-SHA-XI (also the name of an ancient *ci* melody) was composed by Jifang Liang, who was a student at Yanjing University during the 1930s (Wang 1993, 123). The melody is in a C = 5 five-tone scale (5 6 1 2 3), with most of the cadences on 5 (the Chinese *zhi* mode); it is through-composed and is very effectively developed, especially in the second half of the song. The rhythmic running notes (6535231/ 2123165) vividly depict the angels' announcement of the joyful news, the surprise and fear of the shepherds, and the camels running thousands of miles across the dessert. The last system is a beautiful tone painting, in which the melody fluctuates around high 5 for "Glory be to God on high" and then glides down to the lower 5 in the contrasting phrase "blest are all beneath the sky." The original harmonization by Bliss Wiant has been simplified by Pen-li Chen to feature the natural flow of the melody.

"Praise our God above" (*STB* #165)

(Mandarin: *Zanmei sheng Tianfu*)

In this song of praise, Tzu-chen Chao (Zichen Zhao) has captured the spirit of the ancient Confucian ceremony, which is still conducted once a year on the sage's birthday, on September 28. (Incidentally, in Korea, celebrations are held twice each year, in February and in September.)

The ceremony is meant not only to pay homage and offer sacrifices to Confucius but also to give sacrifices in thanks for blessings from heaven (*tian*). The music for the ceremony comprises eight sections or pieces. XUAN PING (literally "proclaiming peace") is one of the *dacheng* chants. The chants are all stately in manner: slow and solemn, accompanied by the eight types of musical instruments that signify the totality of sound and music (as outlined earlier in this section). Zhao's hymn gives thanks for the harvest, praising the heavenly father, a concept similar to the Confucian *tian*. The words, images, and descriptions are very picturesque and Chinese in character. The poetic structure is eight lines of five syllables each, and the melody is in a C = 6 pentatonic scale (6 1 2 3 5), with each phrase having the same rhythmic pattern. It is through-composed and is set in a modal harmony by Heyward W. H. Wong but has been slightly altered to keep the rhythm moving toward the end. It should be sung in a solemn, stately manner.

"We assemble with joy and praise" (*STB* #167)

(Mandarin: *Jinri wo zhong huan ji songen*)

This is a hymn for the dedication of the house of worship, praying for God's glory to shine upon it and through the worshipers and concluding with a self-rededication. The author, Mingdao Wang (1900–1991), was one of the most gifted, powerful, and respected preachers in China.

The tune CHENG CHING TSAN (or CHENG JING ZAN, meaning "praising with utmost sincerity and respect") was composed by Jifang Liang in 1934. This is a famous tune, originally written for the Nestorian hymn "All heaven worship in great awe," which was discussed earlier. The composer shows his superb compositional technique in this majestic melody, which is in a B = 3 pentatonic scale (G = 1 2 3 5 6) and formed in two arches, the second of which builds upward to the climax and skips downward to the conclusion. Lujia Xu's resetting provides a more polyphonic texture.

"Winter has passed, the rain is o'er" (*STB* #71)

(Mandarin: *Dongtian yi wang yushui yi zhi*)

The Song of Solomon is rarely sung in church. Here, the passion and tender love between a man and a woman is a metaphor for the longing and intimate relationship between Christ and his beloved church. Care must be taken to differentiate the intimate terms used by the bridegroom (Christ) and his bride (the church). The words "my love" (*jiaou*, stanza 1) and "precious dove" (*gezi*, stanza 2) are terms used by the bridegroom for his bride while "my beloved" (*liangren,* stanza 3) denotes the bride addressing the bridegroom. However, the "my love" in the refrain should be understood as the Christians' address to Christ. At the beginning of the second stanza, the Chinese does not indicate clearly who is addressing whom, so it could be interpreted either way. However, according to Song of Solomon 2:14, ". . . let me see your face, let me hear your voice . . ." are the words of the bridegroom addressing the bride, not the other way around. Therefore, in order to be Biblically accurate and theologically sound, "O Lord" at the beginning of stanza 2 was changed to "My dove" to avoid possible misinterpretation.

The original hymn, written by Weifan Wang in the spring of 1957, had only three stanzas of four lines without the refrain. In the first two stanzas, the bridegroom calls for his bride, and in the third stanza, the bride (or the author) responds to the call. According to Shenyin Wang, the composer Shengben Lin and Weifan Wang were classmates at the Jinling Seminary. They wrote this hymn and published it in the third issue of the *Shengguang* ("Holy Light") journal in 1957, after a sermon with the same theme. Although this hymn was not sung in the church at that time, the Miao minority church included it in their hymnal. In 1981, after China was opened to the West and when *Zanmeishi* was being developed, Shengben Lin remembered this hymn, but he felt that something was missing: he persuaded Wang to write text for a refrain, and Lin subsequently added the climactic musical refrain (Wang

1993, 392). Only then, in 1982, were they courageous enough to publicly proclaim in the hymn, "Jesus, my Lord, my love, my all"—Chinese Christians no longer needed keep their faith a secret. Shenyin Wang relates a moving story behind this hymn, in which the author Weifan Wang professed:

WINTER HAS PASSED, THE RAIN IS O'ER
COME AWAY
Wei-fan Wang, 1957, ref., 1982
Tr. Weing W. Carroll, Jr.
LM with Refrain
Sheng-ben Lin, 1957, ref., 1982

1. Win-ter has passed, the rain is o'r, Earth is a bloom, songs
2. O Lord, your face I long to see, Your still, small voice, re-
3. O my be-loved, I'll fol-low you, Far from the rocks, the

fill the air. Ling-er no more, why must you wait?
veal to me. Your ten-der care, your joy so dear,
hills and sea. Midst all the song and blos-soms a-new,

"Rise up my love, come fol-low me."
"O Pre-cious dove, with me be near." Je-sus, my Lord,
In your firm steps, I'll fol-low you.

my love, my all, Bod-y and soul for-ev-er yours. In dale so dark,

I long for you. A-bide with me in Spring a-new. (A - men)

(after *Zanmeishi* #248)

Ever since joining the Three-Self Patriotic Movement of the Chinese Church in 1951, I have been searching for a new way to spiritual renewal. The first three stanzas written in 1957 were the conclusion of a six-year search: "departing far from the rocks and hidden places, and amid the springtime when hundreds of flowers blossom and birds burst into song, [I/we] followed Christ the Lamb, walking along and going with him." The refrain was written in the spring of 1982 after going through a long valley [of death]; it was then possible to make this yearning call in another springtime. The original poem was about spring, and the refrain was also about spring. But in between the two springs, there was a long pause of twenty-five years (Wang 1993, 392f).

Other Christians no doubt had similar experiences, and it is no wonder that church numbers are booming. The growth rate of Christian churches is probably beyond comparing to any time in the history of world mission. It is estimated that there are more than twenty million Christians in China today!

The tune name JIA-OU is a poetic expression that means "good lover/companion" or "my love;" it was composed in 6/8 time, which is not typical of Chinese rhythm, yet because of its pentatonic (F = 5, B♭ = 1 2 3 5 6) nature, it exhibits a Chinese melodic character and fits well the mood of the text. The original setting, named TONG QU ("going together"), was in Western chordal harmony (see illustration). Pen-li Chen was inspired by the image of one following Christ, and his arrangement is similar to a two-part invention that symbolizes Christians following in Christ's footsteps, sometimes well and at other times fumbling. Note that the accompaniment at the beginning of the refrain repeats the initial call of Christ. This is purposefully done to symbolize one's acceptance and response to the call while one sings, "Jesus, my Lord, my love, my all"; it is one way of doing theology with music.

Conclusion

1. Chinese poets have utilized the classical poetic forms to create new Christian hymns with vivid images and beautiful rhetoric, a contextualization that began during the Nestorian mission. The hymns written by Tzu-chen Chao (Zichen Zhao) during the 1930s are considered the best in terms of classical style or in colloquial expression. They are still popular even after more than seventy years of use and changes of context.

2. Five-tone scales without half steps are not only characteristic of Chinese music. They can be found all over Asia—Korea, Japan, Taiwan, the Philippines, Indonesia, Thailand, Vietnam, Myanmar, and India—as well as the United Kingdom and North America. But there is a certain

simplicity, melancholy, and charm in the five-tone scales that the Chinese prefer, as shown in most of the hymns analyzed. Six- or seven-tone scales are also used, especially in new compositions and those with traditional or contemporary harmony.

3. Although the melodies may demonstrate a Chinese style, the hymns show a strong tendency toward Westernization, not only in the tuning of instruments but also in melodic and harmonic treatments. A great majority of the newly composed hymns belong to this category: a Chinese melody with Western traditional four-part harmony.

4. Recently, a young composer nicknamed Xiao-min was discovered; though she had no musical training, she has composed more than one thousand hymns with Biblical or personal texts, and these are loved by Christians both young and old. The 2005 publication of *Shipian Songzan Quanji* ("The Whole Book of Psalms of Praise" by Anhui Theological Seminary) contains folk and original melodies set to the entire Book of Psalms. The hymns by Xiao-min and the *Shipian Songzan Quanji* have become the resources for the Three-Self Patriotic Movement churches, especially for the rapidly growing house churches that also call for pastoral, liturgical, and musical/hymnological training and leadership.

5. Because China is a vast country with over 1.3 billion people and such diverse cultures and musical traditions, there are tremendous resources of classical, folk, and instrumental music that await serious study by ethnomusicologists. If Christian musicians engage in serious research and dialogues with traditional musicians, other ethnomusicologists, and composers, they could exploit their great potential for developing contextual Chinese church music.

 **Hong Kong Hymns**

The Nation and Its People

Hong Kong Island was ceded to the United Kingdom in 1841 by the Chinese Qing dynasty (1644–1912), followed by the cession of the southern Kowloon peninsula and Stonecutter Island in 1861. The New Territories, New Kowloon (north of Boundary Street), and 235 adjacent islands were also leased to the United Kingdom for ninety-nine years in 1898; all of these areas composed the British crown colony. During the Second World War, from 1941 to 1945, Hong Kong was occupied by Japan. The post-war population numbered only 600,000. The Communist victory over China prompted thousands to take refuge in Hong Kong. Within seven years the population of Hong Kong increased to two million.

The population today is 7,018,636, most living within roughly 129 square kilometers (fifty square miles) of the total area of 1,085 square kilometers (about 419 square miles).[10] The residents of Hong Kong are 97% ethnic Chinese; there are 55,000 Vietnamese boat people and 50,000 Filipino domestic helpers. Hardworking professionals and laborers turned Hong Kong into a center of light industry, which is now being replaced by the electronics industry. Hong Kong now ranks fifth in the world for its exports and re-exports (Athyal 1996, 148f).

The Sino-British Accord in 1984 returned Hong Kong to China in 1997, which resulted in a mass exodus from Hong Kong. The government estimated that as many as 426,000 may have emigrated, most to North America and some to Australia. Hong Kong is now officially a Special Administrative Region (SAR) of China. Despite China's assurance of freedom and autonomy for fifty years following the handover, the Governor of Hong Kong, though chosen by local elections, in practice listens to China. This has naturally caused some to doubt the Communist

Hong Kong Chinese Christian Orchestra

---

10   Internet World Stats, "Asia Internet Usage Stats and Population Statistics," http://www.internetworldstats. com/asia.htm#hk (accessed January 6, 2009).

promises. But Hong Kong's worst situation seems to have passed. There are signs of hope and prosperity.

A Brief History of Christian Mission in Hong Kong

According to Kwok Nai Wang, the Roman Catholic Church (RCC) established its mission in Hong Kong in 1841. The British Baptists, the Reformed and Congregational London Missionary Society (LMS), and the Anglican Church Missionary Society (CMS) followed the British army chaplain to Hong Kong. The RCC, LMS, and CMS missions concentrated on educational and medical work.

Even a decade ago, churches and church organizations provided 20% of the hospital beds, 40% of the secondary, primary, and kindergarten school seats, and more than 60% of the social services (Athyal 1996, 153). All of these church institutions have earned the trust and respect of the locals. Their schools have produced many scholars and influential leaders in the Hong Kong government as well as successful business people. Although the evangelical

Kowloon Methodist Church, Hong Kong

churches have also established schools, they still emphasize evangelism and church development. Statistics in the 1990s indicated that Christians composed about 9% of the entire population, approximately 520,000 Roman Catholics and Protestants. Today, there are about 1,000 Protestant congregations and sixty Catholic parishes, sixteen seminaries and Bible schools (including one Catholic seminary), and sixteen Christian publishing houses. Also, there are nearly one hundred registered Christian organizations, such as the YMCA and the Bible Society (Athyal 1996, 155). The Hong Kong Christian Council was formed in 1954 by mainline Protestant denominations. It has been active in promoting social services and ecumenical cooperation, not only between Protestant and evangelical groups but also with Catholics. From 1993 to 2006, the presence in Hong Kong of the headquarters of the Christian Conference of Asia also strengthened such cooperation.[11] In 1988, the founding of the Hong Kong Christian Institute by 120 Christian leaders, seminary professors, pastors, professionals, and lay followers gave churches a new vision

---

11   The headquarters of CCA moved to Chiang Mai, Thailand, in 2006.

for meeting the challenges of the Special Administrative Region of China (Athyal 1996, 165).

Because of Hong Kong's century-long relationship with Great Britain, the theology, worship, and music of its churches strongly reflect those of the West; hence there are many highly qualified scholars and specialists in these fields. In 1997, a group of musicians playing traditional Chinese instruments founded the Hong Kong Chinese Christian Orchestra under the direction of Francis Fong. This group has contributed a new dimension of contextualization. They are dedicated to promoting Chinese compositions and present numerous performances every year in churches as well as public concert halls. While many churches are trying hard to imitate the West, this group of musicians diligently offers its talents to proclaim the gospel through Chinese music. This is certainly an excellent model for Hong Kong as well as for China and Asia in general.

Commentary on the Hymn

"God is here as we your people meet" (*STB* #49)

(Mandarin: *Shen zai dian zhong xintu chongjing*)

F. Pratt Green's text is an affirmation of God's presence in one's worship and daily life. Green emphasizes the importance of the word "here," which he uses six times: it is here that we share our skills and arts, take bread and wine, explore what we believe and adore, and give and receive. This excellent hymn explores the meaning and content of worship.

The text has been set to a melody in a Chinese style. The composer, Daniel Law, begins the melody in a C = 6 pentatonic scale (C = 6 1 2 3 5), harmonized in a C-minor modality, and concludes the first half of the song in its relative major (E♭). By introducing D (7) and A (♯4) in the third system, he moves to the B♭ scale (B♭ = 1 2 3 5 6 7) to create a contrast without actually modulating to G minor. The recapitulation of the initial melodic line brings the hymn to a conclusion in C minor. Although the sudden shift of the tonal center might pose problems for the congregation, a short rehearsal should overcome this difficulty. One can appreciate the beauty of a master's touch in interpreting the text through his compositional technique: the lineal counterpoint, contrary motions, individual part and chord progressions, dissonances, suspensions and resolutions, and surprises (see the Db in the alto part near the end). This work exhibits a master composer's impeccable craftsmanship. Also, this typical Chinese piece has an arrangement that in style is almost like Bach. This represents the ideal of some of today's Asian composers, the syncretization of two cultures in one hymn.

Conclusion

The fact that there is only one tune from Hong Kong included in *Sound the Bamboo* indicates the SAR's lack of contextual hymns. Most hymns from Hong Kong are in a traditional Western style. This is probably the result of more than 150 years of colonial rule; economic prosperity is deemed more important than cultural and artistic development or the cultivation of self-identity. But compared to other Asian countries, Hong Kong has a higher percentage of scholars, theologians, liturgists, church musicians, and composers who have great potential for expressing their perspectives in the church.

The 2006 edition of *Putian Songzan* ("Hymns of Universal Praise," edited by Angela Tam) marks a new era. Although Chinese contributions to this hymnal are still limited, the input from contemporary Western as well as international hymns will undoubtedly broaden the vision of church music in Hong Kong. The development of the Hong Kong Chinese Christian Orchestra also gives one hope. In addition, the conscious effort by a small group of people to develop contextual hymns composed and sung in Cantonese further strengthens the prospects of church music. Given more exchanges with and new challenges from mainland China, one may see new musical flowers from Hong Kong blooming in the near future.

 # Japanese Hymns

The Nation and Its People

Japan consists of four main islands—Hokkaidō, Honshū, Kyushū, and Shikoku—and 3,300 small islands and islets, including Okinawa, with a total area of 372,300 square kilometers (about 143,746 square miles), of which four-fifths are mountainous. The population is 127,288,416.[12] Most Japanese people are ethnically homogenous; there is an ethnic minority in Hokkaido, the Ainu, who are related to ethnic groups in the far eastern regions of Russia. For fifteen hundred years, Japan absorbed ideas from other cultures, such as: Mahayana Buddhism in the seventh and eighth centuries; the culture of the Chinese Tang dynasty (618–907 CE); Confucian concepts of social and personal ethics during the Edo period (1603–1867); Western parliamentary government in the Meiji period (1868–1912); and assimilation with Western culture and technology after 1945 (Hoke 1975, 341). The traditional religion of Japan is Shinto, which combines shamanistic animism and ancestor worship. Gordon H. Chapman describes the various religious roots of Japanese culture:

> Shinto installed a reverence for nature, all of whose parts and phenomena were identified as spirit beings, or *kami* (the generic term for divinity) . . . There was little or no ethical content to this primitive cult, except for the emphasis on ritual purity as symbolized by bodily cleanliness. Confucianism provided standards for Japanese societal structure, while Buddhism fostered notions of holiness through ascetic practices . . . The three religions were viewed as Shinto being the root, Confucianism the leaves, and Buddhism the flower and fruit of Japanese civilization (Hoke 1975, 304f).

In the 1970s, Japan became "the salesman to the world," ranking first in world shipbuilding, second in the production of radios and TV sets and automobiles, and third in the production of steel, electric energy, and petroleum refining (Hoke 1975, 341f). More recently, Japan was the leader in high-tech products: computers, robots, and video and digital cameras.

---

12   CIA, "The World Factbook, Japan," July 2008 estimate, https://www.cia.gov/library/publications/the-world-factbook/print/ja.html (accessed January 9, 2008).

A Brief History of Church Mission in Japan

Since the sixteenth century, Christians have had a presence in Japan, summarized in the following chronology.[13]

1549 Roman Catholic missionaries, including Francis Xavier, arrived in Japan.

1552 First Mass celebrated in Japanese by the Jesuits.

1553 First Japanese Mass compiled.

1555 First Japanese-conducted Mass.

1561 First Christian school opened.

1597 The Tokugawa Shōgunate began persecution of Christians.

Twenty-six martyrs crucified in Nagasaki.

Christianity moved underground. (Christian hymns/chants were taught by rote then, and some oral tradition still exists today.)

1637 The Shimabara Revolt in Kyushu; 40,000 Christians were massacred.

1638 Japan isolated itself from the rest of the world.

1853 On July 11, Commodore Perry's US flagship "Mississippi" arrived near Edō (modern Tokyo); the crew sang Psalm 100.

1858 Treaty with the West, leading to new opportunities for missionaries.

1859 First missionaries arrived: Episcopalian (J. Liggins, C. Williams), Presbyterian (J. Hepburn), Dutch Reformed (D. Simmons, G. Verbeck).

Western schools and medical clinics opened.

1864 First Japanese (Ryu Yano) baptized by a Protestant missionary.

1868 Meiji Restoration: constitutional monarchy after seven centuries of feudalism.

Beginning of Westernization and modernization.

3,304 "hidden Christians" imprisoned for six years.

1872 Ten Christians baptized.

Greek Orthodox Church began work in Sendai. Nicolai Dō Cathedral built in Tokyo; membership later grew to 30,000.

Many young converts included samurais.

After 1880 Emergence of new Japanese religious leaders: Jyo Niijima (established Dōshisha University, 1875), Kanzō Uchimura (founded the Nonchurch Movement, and was against bowing to [i.e. worshiping] the emperor), Masahisa Uemura, and Yoichi Honda.

Establishment of Christian colleges, including Dōshisha and Sapporo Agriculture College (by W. S. Clark). Christian numbers increased to 34,000.

---

13 The original source of this chronology is unknown, but it provides a succinct picture of the history of the Japanese church. For more analysis, see Akio Doi, "Christianity in Japan," in Thomas 1978, 35–81.

1905–45 Japan is ruled by militant nationalism.

Christian reformer and activist Toyohiko Kagawa, who worked in slums and was nominated for the Nobel Peace Prize (1954 and 1955).

Thirty-two church groups were forced to form the United Church of Christ in Japan (UCCJ) in support of the government war policy. The Holiness Church did not join, and its members were persecuted.

After World War II, the Anglican, Presbyterian, Reformed, Lutheran, Baptist, Free Methodist, and Holiness groups withdrew from UCCJ and formed their own denominations.

1959 The National Christian Council of Japan (NCCJ) sponsored the centennial of Protestant mission in Japan. The UCCJ (consisting of Presbyterian, Methodist, and Congregational churches) is the main member of this organization; others are the Anglican Church of Japan, the Japan Evangelical Lutheran Church, the Japan Baptist Convention, and the Japan Baptist Union. In 1968, the Japan Evangelical Association (JEA) was formed to encourage mutual cooperation among the churches.

Today there are approximately one million Christians in Japan—Protestant (600,000), Catholic (370,000), and Greek Orthodox (25,000)—i.e. about 0.8% of the total population. Two-thirds of the members are women (Athyal 1996, 27 and 32). There are fifty-one church or mission medical facilities, including hospices. Educational ministry in Japan is also very strong since the early days of mission. There are 103 denominational and interdenominational Bible schools and seminaries (eighty-one Protestant, twenty-two Catholic), fifty-one universities (such as Aoyama Gakuin, Meiji Gakuin, St. Paul's, Kantō Gakuin, Kwansei Gakuin, Dōshisha, and International Christian University), eighty-five junior colleges, 215 senior high schools, 176 junior high schools, and eighty-five primary schools.

Theologically, Barthian neo-orthodoxy has been strong in Japan since the 1930s. The dialectical theology became influential in the post-war period. One of the most famous Japanese theologians is Kazō Kitamori of Union Theological Seminary Tokyo, whose *Theology of the Pain of God* relates the Christian faith to Japanese culture in a fresh way. Masao Takenaka (1925–2006) of Dōshisha Divinity School was a leader in the research and practice of social responsibility of the Christian faith (Athyal 1996, 39–40).

Japanese artists have made significant contributions to the interpretation of Christian faith, as can be seen from many art works by Sadao Watanabe and others. One Roman Catholic church in Japan has incorporated a traditional Japanese meditative device, a box of "water-dropping sound" called *suikinkutsu*, which literally means "water harp cave." It is felt that listening to the periodic sound of water drops calms the congregation, encouraging quiet meditation. The kind Reverend Sōji Kitamura provided this explanation by Father Yoshiaki Sonoda, the principal of Nigawa Gakuin High School:

A *suikinkutsu* is an instrument, made of a water jar placed in a corner of a traditional Japanese garden, which amplifies the sound of water drops. It is said that this instrument was devised in the Edo period (1603–1867 CE). The sound of water drops leads people into quiet devotion. Recently, it is said that the sound is very good for mental healing. The box in the small chapel of Nigawa Gakuin school is

A *suikinkutsu* is to the left of the altar, covered with a white cloth.

named "Coo75 - Francesco" because the school has been managed by the St. Francis Cathedral and Monastery in Assisi, Italy, though the instrument itself was made in Kyoto, Japan.[14]

A Brief Introduction to the Music of Japan

Japan has a written history of over 2600 years. While it has its own traditional culture, Japan has also been keen on learning and adapting from the cultures of its Asian neighbors as well as the European world. Japan incorporated the Chinese writing system as early as the fourth century CE. In 453 CE, eighty Korean court musicians performed at a Japanese ruler's funeral. According to the scholar and ethnomusicologist Shigeo Kishibe, who wrote a succinct yet authoritative work on Japanese traditional music, Japan introduced Chinese Buddhism and its chanting (*shōmyō*) as early as the Asuka period (593–628 CE). It was then that the Hōryuji temple complex, with the oldest extant wooden buildings in the world, was constructed. It was also during this period that music from Korea and China began to enter Japan. The music of the Chinese Tang dynasty, which was influenced by music from India, Iran, and Central Asia, played a significant role in shaping the court music of Japan. This is one reason why Japan is included in the circle of Far Eastern intercultural music (Kishibe 1984, 3).

After the Meiji Restoration (1868), Japan opened its doors to the outside world, and strong waves of Westernization and modernization brought new sciences and industrial technologies. Following World War II, more intensive internationalism led the country into the period of "world culture" (Kishibe 1984, 1–3).

---

14   From a personal communication to the author, March 21, 2007.

Japanese Aesthetics of Music

According to Kishibe, art music of the Heian period (794–1185 CE) was mainly for the entertainment and enjoyment of the aristocrats. During the Kamakura period (1185–1333), Japanese culture was greatly influenced by its warrior class, which formulated an aesthetic composed of four principles: harmony (*wa*), respect (*kei*), pureness (*sei*) and quietness (*jaku*). The first two principles were modified from Chinese musical aesthetics, but the concept of purity in art was an early aesthetic ideal. The idea of quietness also implies elegant simplicity and refinement; the Jōdo sect of Buddhism influenced the establishment of this principle (Kishibe 1984, 15f). Other aesthetic terms came from *noh* theater: *yōgen* and *hana*. *Yōgen* denotes elegance, beauty, profundity, and the fantastic while *hana*, meaning "flower," emphasizes the contrast of simple beauty. According to Kishibe, the third genre of aesthetics in music is found in the *shamisen* music of the Edo period (1603–1867), music that was mainly created by and for the merchant class, which developed a new aesthetic ideal, *sui* or *iki*: a combination of elegance, fashion, and smartness; for women, it also meant being sexually attractive (Kishibe 1984, 15f).

Concerning the philosophy of aesthetics, Kishibe insightfully observes, "In the conflicts of logic versus emotion and science versus nature, emotion and nature usually triumph." He compares the Western concept of three basic elements of musical structure, A-B-A symmetry, to the Japanese tradition—which may have come from the Chinese philosophical ideal of heaven, earth, and man—that emphasizes the three elements *jo*, *ha*, and *kyū*. Musically speaking, these elements represent "slow introduction—exposition in a brighter tempo—fast conclusion" (Kishibe 1984, 16f). These concepts are used in *gagaku* court music, and the more expressive music of *noh*, *kabuki*, and *bunraku* theater. Kishibe concludes by saying:

> The well-controlled harmonic structure of modern Western music may be understood as a triumph of science and logic, while the delicate melodic structure of Japanese music, decorated by delicate colours of sound and microtones, can be regarded as a triumph of nature and human sensitivity. (Kishibe 1984, 17).

I feel that Kishibe's views on the Japanese aesthetic also apply to most traditional Asian music, and the above quote summarizes the contrasting aesthetic positions of the East and the West. While many Asian composers search for insights and techniques for the harmonic treatment of their music, they should reconsider the implications of *wa-kei-sei-jaku* and *jo-ha-kyū* for creating inner beauty in Asian music.

Japanese Music Theory

In the middle of the eighth century, Japanese scholars were sent to China; they returned to Japan not only with Buddhist teachings but also Chinese theories of music. These theories greatly influenced Japanese music from the eighth to the twelfth century. It is not surprising, therefore, that many of the musical terms were direct translations from early Chinese vocabularies, some of which were phonetic transcriptions from Indian, Persian, or Central Asian terminologies.

Japanese Tone System

The ideas of key and of absolute pitch are absent from the Japanese musical practice. The Japanese tone system is the same as the Chinese twelve-tone, non-tempered scale, but it has different terms:

Ichikotsu	*Tangin*	*Hyōjō*	*Shozetsu*	*Shimomu*	*Sōjō*
d	d♯	e	f	f♯	g

Fushō	*Ōshiki*	*Rankei*	*Banshiki*	*Shinsen*	*Kamimu*
g♯	a	a♯	b	c'	c'♯

(Malm 1959, 101)

Five-Tone Scales

In: The Japanese *in* scale consists of five tones with semitones and uses different tones for ascending and descending.

E f a b d' e' c' b a f e (when descending, *d* is replaced by *c*)
(3 4 6 7 2 3 1 7 6 4 3)

Yō: This scale has five tones without semitones, with differences in ascending and descending.

E f♯ a b d' e' c♯ b a f♯ e
(3 ♯4 6 7 2 3 ♯1 7 6 ♯4 3) (or 5 6 1 2 4 5 3 2 1 6 5)

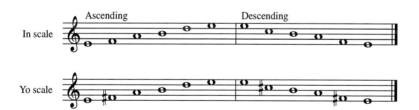

These five-tone scales have in fact six tones, but the added tone only appears in the descending order (e/c to replace d, or e/c♯ to replace d). The *in* scales are mostly used in *shamisen* (plucked lute) and *koto* (zither) music, while the *yō* scale appears more often in folk songs. Although theoretically the scales have these rules, actual practice may not observe all of them. And music for *noh* drama follows rules that are quite different from these.

Gagaku performance (kangen) ensemble
(after Kishibe 1984, p. 92, plate 1)

Seven-tone scales are mostly used in *gagaku*, which was imported from the Chinese Tang dynasty. These are classified as the *ryo* scale (5 6 7 1 2 3 4 5) and the *ritsu* scale (6 7 1 2 3 #4 5 6) in the movable *do* system.

According to Chinese music theory, all twelve tones may be used as the tonic or fundamental tone of their respective *diao* (tonality, mode, or key). During the Sui (580–618 CE) and the Tang dynasties, there were eighty-four *diao* in theory, but only fourteen were in common use during the Tang period. These fourteen *diao* were imported to Japan to become the *gagaku* repertoire; only six of them are still in use today (Kishibe 1984, 20f).

Koizumi's Theory of the Japanese Scale: Tetrachord

There have been different theories about Japanese scale systems, but in 1958, Fumio Koizumi (1927–1983) conceived a new theory: using the fourth as a unit called a "tetrachord" for analysis. Koizumi proposed that the four basic tetrachords of Japanese music are:

1. *Minyō* (found in folk songs and children's songs):   C e♭ F
2. *Ritsu* (used in *gagaku* and Buddhist chant or *shōmyō*): C d   F
3. *Miyakobushi* (common in urban centers during the Edo period):
                                                    C d♭ F
4. Okinawa (found in folk songs of Okinawa, one of the Ryukyu Islands):
                                                    C e F

There are two *minyō* tetrachord combinations:

Conjunct: D f G b♭ C
Disjunct: C e♭ F G b♭ C

Koizumi's interpretation of Uehara's ascending *in* scale:

Miyakobushi   Minyō
D e♭ G   A c D

(Garland 7:567–69)

Rhythm

According to Kishibe (1984, 21), rhythmic elements may be viewed as a beat or a non-beat, and as equal or un-equal beats with or without meter, as follows:

1. Non-beat and non-meter: used in folk songs, *shakuhachi* music, and *noh* music
2. Beat and non-meter: used in *shōmyō*
3. Beat and meter: used in most of Japanese music
4. Non-beat and meter: used in folk songs

The idea of additive and divisive meter is also present, especially in *gagaku* pieces.

There are also the concepts of absolute or relative tempo. One *koto* (zither) piece, "Uya no tsuki," which lasts about twenty-nine minutes, has twenty-eight sections including six interludes, but the tempo changes for every section (ranging from quarter note = 60 to 140), according to the mood of the text (Kishibe 1984, 23). This is an extreme case, one probably not found in any other culture.

There are complex rhythmic patterns as well in *gagaku* and *noh* music. According to Kishibe's analysis (1984, 23), *noh* uses three drums with eight beat patterns, but each drum has its own number of patterns: *ko-tsuzumi* (small hourglass drum), 170 patterns; *ō-tsuzumi* (medium hourglass drum), 200 patterns; and *taiko* (large side drum), 200 patterns.

Melody

The melody in Japanese music (except in *gagaku* and *noh*) is usually gentle and legato; staccato melodies are rare. All vocal music is monophonic, and the instrumental accompaniments are also in unison with the voice. Vocal parts are syllabic in narrative music and melismatic in other song styles.

Harmony and Multiphony

Kishibe and other scholars describe the simultaneous sounding of two or more tones as multiphony, which can be seen in heterophony, polyphony, and harmony.

In Japanese music, unison singing and playing is the general practice although heterophony occurs frequently in instruments according to their idiomatic style and playing techniques. Polyphony is also found among *koto* and *shamisen* duets. One musical occurrence rarely seen in the West is the vocal part performed slightly ahead of the instrumental accompaniment (by about one half beat, one quarter beat, or less). Kishibe says the reason for this is "the need for elasticity in the rhythm, the love of heterophony or polyphony found in this discrepancy, and the desire to let each word and syllable be heard clearly for the purpose of conveying the meaning for the text" (1984, 27). The concept of harmony as such can only be found in *gagaku*, in that "the lowest tone of each chord of the *shō* and the highest tone of each chord [in arpeggio or stylized patterns] of the *biwa* and *koto* follow the principal tones of the melody"; such harmonic structure is unparalleled in any other kind of music (Kishibe 1984, 26). (See discussion of *STB* #54, "Dawn and the light of sunrise.")

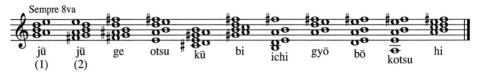

Shō chords

An interesting case of multiphony is seen in a *gagaku* piece for the entrance and exit of the dancers. When this piece, *chōshi*, is performed, the *shō* (free-reed mouth organ) ensemble plays the melody; this is followed by the Japanese oboes and flutes that each play the same melody, not in a strict canon but in "an elastic discrepancy" that creates a chaotic effect, hence coined by Kishibe as "chaophony" (1984, 27). I encountered a similar chaophony in a performance in Korea, in which about a dozen instruments all played simultaneously with different melodies and rhythms; it was unclear whether the parts were improvised or followed melodic motives.

Timbre

Chest voice is common in Japanese music; head voice and falsetto are also used. Yodeling also occurs in some folk singing. A strong and wide range of vibrato is employed in different genres, some of which use a glottal trill similar to that of the Iranian tradition (Kishibe 1984, 28). In instrumental performances, the breathy quality of the *shakuhachi* (vertical flute) and the noises made by the large plectrum on the strings of the *biwa* or *shamisen* are considered part of the beauty of the extra-musical sound and thus are integral parts of the music.

Form

Form in Japanese music also follows the aesthetic principles outlined earlier. As mentioned, Japan adopted musical concepts from the Chinese: *jo* from the Chinese *qi* (introduction, slow), *ha* from *po* (exposition, moderate), *kyū* from *ji* (conclusion, fast), *ki* from *qi* ("to rise," beginning), *sho* from *cheng* ("to succeed," continuation), *ten* from *zhuan* ("to change," modulation), and *ketsu* from *he* ("to close," conclusion). Several of these concepts can be seen in the famous Japanese piece *Etenraku*, which is in A-B-A form (Kishibe 1984, 29–30). The A section consists of a and b with eight measures each, and B has eight measures. The A section is organized in *ki-sho-ten-ketsu* form, and each section has four measures. A simplified version of the *Etenraku* melody was adapted by Hikaru Hayashi as an affirmation of faith in *STB* #54, "Dawn and the light of sunrise" by Tomotsune

Yanagida. The four phrases of four measures each clearly demonstrate the *ki-sho-ten-ketsu* form.

These musical characteristics and related views on beauty and harmony illustrate the rich diversity of Japanese traditional music. They also reveal the abundant gifts that contemporary Japanese Christian authors and composers have received from God and how they may be able to utilize those artistic gifts for proclaiming the gospel not only to their own people but also to the whole world. It is good to know that some younger composers are already conscious of this issue. Just as Japan is known for first-rate technology, perhaps the country will someday produce excellent works in church music.

Genres of Japanese Music

Kishibe divides Japanese music into eight genres:

1. *Gagaku* (court music)
2. *Shōmyō* (Buddhist chant)
3. *Biwa* music
4. *Noh* theatrical music
5. *Sōkyoku (koto* music)
6. *Kabuki* and *bunraku* theatrical music, and *shamisen* music
7. *Shakuhachi* music
8. Folk songs and folk music

Major Japanese Musical Instruments

IDIOPHONES

Atarigane (small handheld gong), *dora* (plate-shaped gong), *chappa* (cymbals), *dōbatsu* (cymbals), *shōko* (small bronze gong)

MEMBRANOPHONES

Gakudaiko or *taiko* (large frame drum), *kakko* (drum with two lashed heads), *tsuzumi* (hourglass drum in different sizes)

CHORDOPHONES

Koto (long-board zither with thirteen silk strings), *biwa* (pear-shaped plucked lute with four strings, played with a plectrum), *shamisen* (plucked lute made of cat-skin with three strings, played with a plectrum), *kokyū* (bowed lute with four strings)

AEROPHONES

Ryuteki (transverse bamboo flute with seven finger holes), *hichiriki* (bamboo oboe with seven plus two holes), *shō* (mouth organ with seventeen bamboo pipes), *shakuhachi* (end blown flute with four plus one holes), *nohkan* or *fue* (flute with seven holes)

A Brief History of *Sambika* ("Songs of Praise")

In 1860, the American Baptist missionary Jonathan Goble (1827–1896) arrived in Japan. At the time, Christians sang hymns with the accompaniment of the *shamisen* (plucked lute) and *koto* (long-board zither); it is not known how long this tradition continued. In 1872, the Reverend Nicholas Kasatkin (1836–1912) established a Greek Orthodox mission in Tokyo; the music for worship was from the Russian Orthodox tradition. Singing hymns with Western scales must have been difficult because the Japanese were used to traditional songs that were mostly pentatonic melodies (SRK1955, 32f).

The Reverend Sōji Kitamura, the chair of the Sambika committee for more than twenty years, and his wife, Kazuyo.

In the year Meiji 36 (1903), *Sambika* ("Songs of Praise") was published. This hymnbook was shared by different denominations. While some Japanese had participated in selecting texts for the compilation, American missionaries selected the tunes. The collection went through a number of revisions before the Japanese texts could be sung to the Western tunes. On many occasions, the rhythm of the music had to be altered or the harmony simplified to fit the Japanese texts. This first *Sambika* contained 483 hymns, the Apostle's Creed, the Ten Commandments, and the Japanese national anthem (SRK1955, 34). The words and music of the hymns were mostly borrowed from American gospel songs. Also, the tonic *sol-fa* system was placed on top of the staff notation for ease of learning. In 1909, *Sambika Dainihen* ("second volume") was published for children in Sunday schools.

On Christmas 1931, a new *Sambika* was published. Three musicians participated in the editing: Eizaburō Kioka, Shuichi Tsugawa (1896–1971), and Chugorō Torii (1898–1986). The collection contained 604 hymns with 654 tunes, of which twenty-four were by thirteen Japanese composers, a historically significant fact (SRK1955, 34).

In 1951, the new *Sambika* committee began compiling another edition of *Sambika*, which was published in 1954, with 567 hymns and 588 tunes, of which forty-one were by twenty-one Japanese composers. While the hymns were mostly of American and British origin, there were also a variety of hymns from other countries (SRK1955, 35).

The composers in *Sambika Dainihen* (1967) included: Masayoshi Abe, Yoshio Hayashi, Setsu Imagawa, Fukuko Kobayashi, Isao Koizumi, Shōzō Koyama, Ugo Nakada, Toshiaki Okamoto, Kōichi Matsuda, Toraji Ōnaka, Chūgorō Torii, Shuichi

Tsugawa, and William Merrell Vories (SRK1955, 35).
Other publications of *Sambika* include:
Tomo ni Utaō (1976)
Kodomo Sambika (1987)
Sambika 21 (1997), the newest edition, with 580 hymns

Commentary on Individual Hymns

"Come, smell the scent of sweet wild flowers" (*STB* #52)
(Okinawan: *Uga di uga mi busha*)

Okinawa Prefecture consists of innumerable small islands in the Ryukyu Islands chain. Although geographically and politically part of Japan, the Okinawans have maintained their own cultural and linguistic identities. In addition to working at businesses related to US airbases, many inhabitants of Okinawa are farmers and fishermen. This hymn reflects these two aspects of their daily lives. The hymn's author, Seiei Yokota, a Baptist minister, invites people to smell the scent of sweet wild flowers and enjoy the beauty of God's creation, and he relates these to the saving power of Jesus Christ. Along with many beautiful images related to Christ's love, he writes:

> With open arms on the cross out stretched,
> all earth touched by Christ's body . . . we trust such love.

Stressing the importance of navigation for sea-faring people, Yokota identifies the Big Dipper (actually the Polar Star) to represent Christ's guidance in one's wandering life:

> In dead of night our boat's sailing, the Big Dipper guides homeward.
> Seek when it's dark, the Cross shining, our Savior guides us home.

This hymn is a beautiful contextualized expression of Okinawan faith.

The tune TINSAGU NO HANA, meaning "balsam flowers," is a very popular and lovely children's song, using a typical Okinawan F♯ = 3 six-tone scale (D = 1 2 3 4 5 7). Although it may sound similar to the Indonesian *pelog* scale (1 3 4 5 7, without 2), the rhythm and idiom are quite different. Also, the Okinawans use *jabisen* for the accompaniment; a *jabisen* is a spike-plucked lute with three strings, and the sounding box is covered with snakeskin (the *shamisen* is covered with cat skin). The hymn's melody is in a b a c form. The accompaniment, providing an ostinato-like variation to the first phrase of the melody, reflects the simple folk idiom. This hymn was recorded during a worship service in August 1987; it seemed to inspire joy and intimacy in the congregation. For performance, one may use any plucked instrument (such as guitar or banjo) or a cello played with pizzicato to accompany the hymn. A flute of any kind doubling the melody will also add to its beauty. (para. Ronald Hines)

"Dawn and the light of sunrise" (*STB* #54)

(Japanese: *Hana no akebono*)

This is a hymn of thanksgiving for day and night, for the beautiful creation and seasonal changes, and for sharing love, friendship, and support in joy and sorrow. It may be sung at the end of a school semester or the close of an academic year in giving thanks for life together. The text was written in a semi-classical idiom by Tomotsune Yanagida (who was the president of Kinjo Gakuin University in 1958). The tune is an adaptation of a *gagaku* ("elegant music") piece entitled *Etenraku* (see illustrations). In a *gagaku* piece, the *ryuteki* (flute) and *hichiriki* (oboe) play the main melody, while the *shō* (mouth organ) plays six-tone chords, with the lowest tone corresponding to the melody on the downbeat, and the *biwa* (plucked lute) and *koto* (long zither) play arpeggios or stylized figures, with the highest tone corresponding to the main melody on the downbeat. Such a harmonic practice is only found in *gagaku* (Kishibe 1984, 26).

Etenraku: Banshiki chō (after Garfias 1975, 241)

BANSHIKI-CHŌ   241

Hichiriki version of Etenraku (after Malm 1959, 97)

Order: A twice, B twice, C twice, A twice, B twice.

The tempo of the original *gagaku* piece is very slow, but this hymn should be sung faster (quarter note = 88 per minute, approximately). This melody is in a G = 5 five-tone scale (A = 6 7 2 3 5) with final on 6. The form of this piece is exactly a four-phrase structure of *ki* (beginning), *shō* (continuation), *ten* (development), and *ketsu* (conclusion) in the respective systems, and with the same cadence (6 6 6 5 6---), except the third *ten* phrase, which is meant to change. But the harmonic setting by Hikaru Hayashi is similar to Western modal harmony, with certain variations.

"Distracted by the world's concerns" (*STB* #69)

(Japanese: *Kono yo no tsutome*)

Amid the busy world full of noises and distractions, Kō Yuki (1896–1985) points to Christ's retreat to the mountains to seek God's will and urges us to seek a quiet place so that "within the temple of the heart we hear [Christ's] voice of peace." In 1930, while waiting for an hour and a half for an acquaintance in a bank, the author prayed in silence; the thick wall of the waiting room blocked the street noise. There, he wrote this hymn of prayer in under ten minutes. This piece is appropriate as an opening hymn or may be sung to set the mood at the beginning of a retreat.

Shuichi Tsugawa composed this lovely tune in a B♭ = 5, E♭ major scale (E♭ = 1 2 3 4 5 6 7), with a a' b a" form. The tune name comes from the meaning of the original first line UCHI NARU MIYA ("temple of the heart"). It was first included in the 1931 *Sambika* and has been a popular hymn among the Japanese (SRK21, 310).

"Gathering round the table of the Lord" (*STB* #83)

(Japanese: *Shu no shokutaku o kakomi*)

"Come, Lord Jesus" (Revelations 22:20) is the theme and refrain of this hymn. Tsugutoshi Aragaki, an ecumenically minded Roman Catholic, wrote both text and tune of this contemporary Japanese hymn. According to Aragaki, this text is also related to the theme of the Lord's Prayer, which he contemplated for ten years. The first stanza refers to sharing the bread and cup of the Eucharist as a sign of unity; the second stanza affirms new life in Christ through his death and resurrection, and the third stanza is one's response to the call of Christ through the power of the Holy Spirit (SRK21, 66).

The tune MARANATHA (Aramaic for "come, Lord") is in a G = 3 E♭ major scale (E♭ = 1 2 3 4 5 6 7), and in a b a'c form, plus the refrain in d e d e' form. It is set with fast syllabic and reiterated tones, which feel natural when sung in Japanese but may not be as easy to sing in the English version. The longer note values and the repetition of "Maranatha" at the refrain slow the pace and lessen the tension created by the quick syllabic English verses. This can be a joyful song for celebrating the Holy Communion or a prayer of hope for the coming of God's kingdom.

"Here I am, the one who turned away from my God" (*STB* #44)

(Japanese: *Katakunani mo Shū o koba minu*)

This is a hymn of confessing one's sin and praying for God's forgiveness, through which one can find new light, hope, and joy by the salvation of Jesus and can sing praises for the goodness of God. Written by Yukiko Ishiyama, this hymn was translated by Yasuhiko Yokosaka, a young musicologist. The tune MIKOKORO (which refers to the heart of God) by Akira Tanaka uses two simple melodic lines in a D = 6 seven-tone scale (6 7 1 2 3 4 5), in a b b' a form: the a in unison and very Japanese in style, then b b' with harmony in D minor, but the a recapitulates and concludes with a Tierce de Picardie (raised third), turning it into a D-major chord for a more positive feeling.

"Here, O Lord, your servants meet" (*STB* #242)

(Japanese: *Sekai no tomo to te o tsunagi*)

This was the theme song for the fourteenth World Conference on Christian Education held in Tokyo in the summer of 1958; TokuoYamaguchi wrote this hymn, based on the theme "Jesus Christ is the Way, the Truth, and the Life," for the conference. In 1957, the launch of Sputnik, the first space satellite, triggered tensions and competition between the superpower nations. Although people expected scientific achievement to result in peace among the countries, it brought more fear and anxiety. Yamaguchi caught this sentiment and concern. In this hymn, he urges the different peoples of the world to join hands and face the cross of Jesus, who is the Way to the realm of God. He prays that through the love, truth, faith, and power from Christ, all may gain hope and new life.

The hymn was published on January 25, 1958, in *Christian News*. Two tunes were composed for this text. TOKYO CONVENTION by Eisai Ikemiya was in a Western style, which the Japanese liked very much and included in the 1967 *Sambika Dainihen* (volume 2). The other tune, TOKYO by Isao Koizumi, was in a Japanese style and was welcomed by the international participants of the conference but was not accepted in the Japanese hymnal. It was translated into English by Everett M. Stowe and was later included in *The Hymns of the Church* in 1963 (SRK21, 261f); it also appeared in the WCC hymnal *Cantate Domino* (1980). After it became popular in the ecumenical world, TOKYO finally gained its rightful place in the 1997 *Sambika 21*.

TOKYO uses the traditional *gagaku* mode (see *STB* #54, "Dawn and the light of sunrise," for further explanation) in an A = 6 five-tone scale (D = 2 3 5 6 1), in a b a' c form. Koizumi has retained part of the *shō* (mouth organ) style of harmony with parallel fifths in the accompaniment but with more florid and syncopated inner parts that depart from the original style. *Gagaku* music is usually performed at a very slow tempo, but this hymn should be sung a little bit faster (quarter note = 88–96) to match the spirit of the text. This is especially appropriate as an opening hymn for ecumenical and international gatherings and as a prayer for Christ's guidance.

"In old Galilee when sweet breezes blew" (*STB* #195)
(Japanese: *Gariraya no kaze kaoru oka de*)

With simple narratives, Nobuo Befu points to four incidents in which Jesus spoke to crowds in Galilee or to his disciples. Each stanza concludes with a prayer, asking Jesus to let us hear "those words of grace that gave them promise," "those words of power that gave them courage," those words of salvation that gave sinners hope, and "those words of life" so that we can recognize him. Shō kō Maita composed this tune, GARIRAYA NO KAZE ("the breezes of Galilee"), following the narrative style of the text, in D major (D = 1 2 3 4 5 6 7). It is through-composed without any musical repetition but with simple traditional Western harmony. Since all the last phrases are direct prayers to Jesus, a prayerful spirit is needed to sing this hymn well (SRK21, 51).

"In the dawn of the morn" (*STB* #158)
(Japanese: *No ni idete*)

Masuko Endō depicts the intimate connections between life, work, and prayer in this hymn. With vivid descriptions of the lifestyle of rural Japan, the hymn gives thanks to God for the gift of a new day, for the earth and tilling of the field, and for sharing simple meals as a family on the *tatami* (straw mat). The three stanzas

93

state, respectively, that these are "the places for prayer" (which is the meaning of the tune name INORI NO ZA) for tomorrow, at noon, and at dusk. The original text's references to three specific times or spaces were not translated to English. The third stanza may be sung as an evening hymn or at the dinner table as a grace. Endō wrote this hymn when her husband was very ill and she had to assume all the responsibilities of the family chores and farming (SRKII, 114f).

Tomoaki Bunya set this tune in a typical Japanese folk style, especially in the second system: 3335656- / 77756-. It is in an F# = 3 six-tone scale (D = 1 2 3 5 6 7) with final on 2 and is through-composed. It utilizes Western harmonic language to support the Japanese melody. Bunya wrote this tune while still a composition student in college. This beautiful hymn both musically and textually reflects a typical Japanese context and was accepted in the 1967 *Sambika Dainihen* but was not included in *Sambika 21*.

"In this world abound" (*STB* #216)
(Japanese: *Yo no naka ni*)

This is one of the earlier hymns written by a Japanese composer. Saichirō Yuya reminds one that the Word of God containing wisdom and truth was outlined by ancient sages and that the depth of truth is always a mystery; though beyond one's comprehension, it may break forth with new meanings and may be understood through prayers or after we have walked along the path of hardest truth, as did the ancient sages. Because the text affirms the importance of the Bible, it is appropriate to sing this hymn after the reading of the Scriptures. The first two stanzas were translated by Esther Hibbard and the last two were by Toshi Arai, but they were paraphrased by Terry MacArthur for this hymnal; Arai and MacArthur were Worship Desk staff members of the WCC during the 1990s.

MOSO is an old Japanese melody, probably of ancient Chinese origin; this arrangement was by Kazu Nakaseko (1908–1973). The A = 6 six-tone scale (6 7 1 2 3 5), without a half-tone progression, is through-composed with the final on 2; these are all features of an old Japanese style. The setting with unison, simple counterpoint, and fourths has preserved the beauty of the original style.

"Jesus built the church" (*STB* #68)
(Japanese: *Iesu sama ga kyō kai o*)

As suggested by the tune name CHRISTIAN HOME, this is a prayer for blessing a domicile that, like the church, is redeemed by Christ's sacrificial love. It is also a prayer that this home may become a place full of love and grace (Ephesians 5:30–32). The second stanza is a prayer for nourishing the Word of God so that the family might be blessed with joy and happiness. The third stanza prays for the children, that even when they leave home, they may continue to witness God's love. This hymn was written by Naoi Ishida, who wanted his children to share it and sing together in family worship. The text was accepted for the *Sambika Dainihen* in 1967 (SRK21, 337). This is an excellent hymn for family worship on Sunday, especially families with children.

The composer Koyama Shōzō had known of this text and liked it very much. One Christmas Eve, on the way home after caroling with his choir members, he thought of this tune in a moment of inspiration and hurried home to write it down (SRK21, 337). It is in an E♭-major scale (E♭ = 1), with a very simple a b a b' form, hence very easy for children to sing.

"Lo, now ascends the morning sun" (*STB* #194)

(Japanese: *Asahi wa noborite*)

This was probably the first Japanese Christmas hymn. It was written in 1868 and first appeared in the 1881 *Sambika*. It is not a description of the Christmas scene but a theological commentary on the meanings of the incarnation of God's son, who is the Light (hence the words "morning sun"), wisdom, power, peace, consolation, and the realization of God's redeeming love. The first printed version included four stanzas with the suggestion of the tune ANTIOCH. In 1953, Chūgorō Torii set the words to CHRISTMAS DAY. It is in a C = 5, F-major scale (F = 1), in a b c b' form; the lively rhythm and melody provide a mood of joy and give new life to this text of heavy theological statements. This has been one of the most popular Japanese Christmas carols (SRK21, 176).

Although the author's name is not shown in the hymn, Japanese scholars believe that this is the work of the Reverend Masatsuna Okuno (1823–1910). Okuno was born in Edo (the former name of Tokyo). Since the age of ten, Okuno studied Buddhism, Chinese and Japanese classics, and martial arts and music, and he served in a temple in the Ueno area. After the fall of the Tokugawa regime, Okuno lost his position and all his possessions. A few years later, he began a second career, teaching Japanese to a few American missionaries, and he assisted Nathan Brown and other missionaries in the early stages of translating the New Testament and hymns. Okuno was baptized in 1872 and became the first Japanese to be ordained as a pastor. His ministry was centered in Tokyo; after his retirement, he still served as an itinerant preacher (SRK21, 336).

"Now, let us sing a new song to the Lord" (*STB* #27)

(Japanese: *Atarashii uta o utaō*)

This lively hymn by Naoi Ishida, based on Psalm 96:1, "O sing to the LORD a new song," celebrates the beginning of a new age of love and trust. It emphasizes the joyful new day of victory of the powerful word of God and calls for all who are new creations in Christ (2 Corinthians 5:17) to praise God, whose Word will cover the whole earth.

The melody of KAMITAKATA ("Upper Takata," the name of the town where the composer lived) is almost through-composed in a typical Japanese *yō* scale: (E = 6 1 2 3 5), five tones without a half step. It utilizes lively syncopations with time changes—4, 3, 4, 3, 2, 3, 4 counts per measure—to create excitement. The composer Isao Koizumi has very skillfully utilized unison, discords, parallel fourths, and octave doublings for the first half of the piece; for the second half, he combines the voices in double duet with fourths, fifths, and octaves and concludes with a surprise: F♯ (with an open fifth) to a B-major chord with the optional fifth on top, turning it into a six-tone major piece. (Strictly speaking, the transition is not from an F♯ chord to a B-major chord, but an F♯ open fifth to a B-major chord is like the "horn fifth" progression (V–I) of the trumpets, hence the effect of a two major-chord progression cannot be denied.) With the rhythmic changes, the variety of intervallic combinations, and the final chord progression, the music vividly conveys the idea of something new.

"Plodding on with weary footsteps" (*STB* #207)
(Japanese: *Yuke domo, yuke domo*)

In this hymn, "Come to me, my weary friend," is the gentle call from Jesus to all who are wandering in the wilderness—thirsty, lonely, and near death. He offers water, peace, and a home. This was the last hymn that Nagasaka Kanjirō wrote before his death. Koyama Shōzō set this tune COME TO ME in D minor (D = 6) and in a b c b' form. The first section, a b, describes the negative condition of human experiences, but the second part, c b', modulates to F major (F = 1) as a positive assurance from the word of Christ. This reflects the typical approach of Romantic composers: a major key expresses joy, and a minor key expresses sadness. Shōzō composed this tune while a student at the Kunitachi Music University. It was accepted in the 1955 edition of *Sambika* and was one of the most popular hymns of the time (SRK21, 275).

"Praise the LORD" (*STB* #23)

Praising God for the beauty of creation is the most natural way to acknowledge God's love for human beings. The words of this hymn invite us to thank God for the gifts of friends, the church, and God's endless grace, and to give glory to the "parent God," a term that was as controversial as feminist theology at the time this hymn was written.

SAKURA ("cherry blossom," the national flower of Japan) is the country's most famous traditional melody. When Nobuaki Hanaoka told me he wanted to use the tune of SAKURA for this hymn, I immediately wrote it down because I have known it since childhood; when I was a student at UCLA, I also learned to play the tune on a *shakuhachi* (Japanese vertical flue). The melody is in a B = 6 seven-tone scale (6 7 1 2 3 4), with final on 3. SAKURA is known in many parts of the world. During World War II, this melody was played in all Japanese-occupied territories, and for many the song stirs negative memories of the occupation. Thus, strong resistance arose when the Asian American hymnbook editorial committee discussed the inclusion of this tune. For people from the Philippines and Korea, it was almost impossible to accept this melody as the setting of a song of praise. After long arguments, however, the committee understood the author's sincerity in giving thanks for God's gifts of creation, love, and salvation through Christ and finally accepted this hymn, including it in the 1983 *Hymns from the Four Winds*.

The hymn was subsequently sung in a number of Asian American hymn festivals in California, which transformed the feelings of animosity and resentment into a spirit of reconciliation between Japanese, Koreans, and Filipinos. During one of the worship services, at the 1987 General Assembly of the Asian Alliance of the YMCA in Tōzanso, Japan, it was surprising to see that some Japanese were touched by this hymn. With tears, they admitted that they never imagined that this song of national pride could become a hymn of praise and reconciliation!

"Send your word, O Lord" (*STB* #218)
(Japanese*: Mikotoba o kudasai*)

This hymn was originally written by Yasushige Imakoma to be sung on Pentecost Sunday, when he served at the Kawasaki Church. The poet believes that the crisis and wars of the world are caused by the lack of verbal communication, as shown by God's interference in the building of the Tower of Babel (Genesis 11:1–9). The only way to solve the problem is to receive the gift of the Holy Spirit, as did the people in Acts, Chapter 1, who were able to communicate with those who spoke in languages presumed unintelligible. It is also like the faith of the centurion who requested Jesus to "only speak the word, and my servant will be healed" (Matthew 8:8). This hymn is a prayer to Jesus: "Send your word, O Lord" like the rain, like the wind, and like the dew, so that your endless grace, your wondrous power, and your endless love can renew the world. The hymn is appropriate as a prayer for illumination before or after the reading of the Scriptures, and it can also be an effective hymn during revival meetings or prayers for healing.

Koyama Shōzō was so moved by this direct prayer to the Lord that he set this tune MIKOTOBA (meaning "holy word") in a minor mode (C = 6 7 1 2 3 4 5) and in a b c d d a' c form. Both the text and tune were accepted together for inclusion in the *Sambika Dainihen* in 1967 (SRK21, 51f). This was translated into English by the Reverend Tomoaki Hanaoka in San Francisco for the 1983 Asian American hymnal, *Hymns from the Four Winds*.

"To every one a call comes from yonder" (*STB* #228)
(Japanese: *Yobare te imasu itsu mo*)

This hymn is a reminder of a small voice that requires good ears to hear, a challenge to proclaim the good news that requires good lips to speak the love of Christ, and an invitation to the heavenly banquet that requires strength to walk the pilgrim path. The poem is beautifully written, using similar wording and structured like a litany. The music, STILL SMALL VOICE (a reference to 1 Kings 19:12), is skillfully set to the text by Takata Saburō, one of the most important Japanese composers, who writes for both Roman Catholic and Protestant churches.

The music is composed in an A = 6 pentatonic scale (G = 5 6 1 2 3) in a charming syllabic, narrative style with simple homophonic harmony. The first two phrases a and b are like a question and an answer. After a long third phrase c, another paired sequence with the same text leads to the end. Because of Takata's sensitivity in textual treatment, the Japanese is easily understood while sung. But for the sake of clarity, some parts of the melody in different stanzas have to be altered according to natural inflections (indicated by asterisks). When singing the hymn in English, however, there is no need to change the melody, but one should slow the tempo slightly.

"We who bear the human name" (*STB* #258)

The Urban Rural Mission Committee of the Christian Conference of Asia has always promoted justice, human rights, equal opportunity, and an involvement with society. In order to understand the problems of Asian workers and how the churches could meet their needs, the committee, under the leadership of Masao Takenaka, proposed in 1968 to collect street songs from Asian cities and invited me to undertake the task. From 1968 to 1972, I traveled around fifteen Asian countries and recorded songs sung by workers, street people, youths, choirs, individual singers, and congregations.

In the spring of 1972, the committee invited Fred Kaan (born 1929), a prominent and prolific Dutch poet in England, to Jakarta to help with paraphrasing and writing new texts to songs that had been recorded and transcribed. During one lunch conversation, Takenaka, Kaan, and I were discussing the power of folk songs; our attention was caught by one Indonesian popular song, "Becak," named after the tricycles that were the most convenient and reasonable vehicles for transportation and that thousands of people relied on for their livelihoods in the crowded city of Jakarta. This inspired Takenaka, who jotted a few lines (which had no relation to the original text of the song) in English. The structure (meter and accent) of the song was explained to Kaan, and the new song was completed within a short time. It was published later that year in *New Songs of Asian Cities.*

The text uses images of Jesus' teaching on the providence of God (Luke 12:27–31): though human beings are like flowers of the fields, trampled down and made to yield, they are precious in the eyes of the LORD, that even the richness and glory of King Solomon cannot be compared with the beauty of lilies (Matthew 6:25–34). The authors call for Asian city dwellers to join together to build communities of peace, so that the world will blossom like a field.

The tune BECAK is a contemporary urban song composed by Nj Sutisno in an F = 5 seven-tone scale (Bb = 1 2 3 4 5 6 7) with a lively, syllabic melody. Although the melody is not particularly Indonesian, it is one of the most popular songs in the country. It is almost through-composed, but the sequential development in the melody, especially in the third system (<u>55</u> <u>11</u> <u>71</u> 6, <u>66</u> <u>22</u> <u>12</u> 7) clearly marks the influence of Western idiom; hence it is best sung with guitar accompaniment, as is the common practice.

"Why am I living?" (*STB* #250)
(Japanese: *Nan no tame ikiru no ka?*)

The author Genzō Mizuno is one of the most important Christian poets in Japan. Although he suffered severe illness at the age of nine and was eventually paralyzed, he has a brilliant mind and spirit. In order for him to compose poetry, his mother posted Japanese phonetic characters on the wall and pointed to one character after another; Genzō would blink his eyes when she reached the character he wanted. Through innumerable hours of labor with love, patience, and hope, his mother helped him to write many deeply moving poems that have enlightened many hearts and given new hope and courage to live. This hymn vividly reflects his struggles to live under such a difficult condition. He asks "Why am I living . . . striving . . . going . . . seeking?" He does not know the reason, but he trusts that God has meant for him to live and is leading him ahead. He even encourages himself to love those who twist the truth because even he, in his condition, is loved by the good LORD.

The music NAN NO TAME (literally meaning "for what reasons") was composed by Taihei Satō, who uses a recitative style to set the questions to music. It is in an F = 6 natural minor scale (6 7 1 2 3 4 5) and in a b c c' form. The composer uses very romantic and chromatic harmony that provides different colors and moods to express doubts, struggles, and feelings. The slight changes in rhythm and melodic line between c and c' are subtle and effective. The last chord with a Tierce de Picardie (a raised third, turning it into a major chord) is striking. This melody resembles a Romantic tone painting in which the author has found positive answers from God; hence it ends in a major chord. Notice Satō's sensitivity in changing the melody according to Japanese intonation for stanzas 2 and 3 (marked with asterisks). These changes may be ignored when singing the hymn in English.

"Why have you forsaken me?" (*STB* #189)

Quoting the bitter cry of Jesus on the cross, "My God, my God, why have you forsaken me?" (Matthew 27:46), the author, Bill Wallace, suggests that all fears will be conquered if we trust in God's love. This hymn shows the mystery of God's love through Christ, in his weeping at the death of Lazarus and his deepest pain and agony of being forsaken. Although the first stanza depicts Christ's cry of agony, the focal point is not his suffering but his love, care, and sympathy to all who trust him.

SHIMPI is the Japanese word for "mystery." Taihei Satō composed this tune after meeting Bill Wallace at the Ecumenical Workshop on Liturgy and Music in Manila in 1980, when all participants encouraged each other in utilizing their musical talents to serve God. Satō uses a Japanese *in* scale (E = 3 4 6 7 2) ending on 6, to portray the agony of Jesus; simple textures add color to the music, which is very Japanese in style. The tritone (an augmented fourth between F and B), which is one of the most typical Japanese melodic features, is difficult to sing and should be taught carefully.

Regarding the setting, the composer makes the following theologization:

> The note *mi* is the fifth in A minor: the dominant note. My idea is that it means we're subordinate to the earth, to this world. That's why the note is so important as to appear ten times in this tune. To go half up and down between *mi* and *fa* (also *ti* and *la, mi* and *re*) expresses our wish and wavers. But it more reveals the waver of Jesus; he directly called for God and cried, wept, and prayed, and Jesus committed himself on the cross at last. I realized that *ti–re–re–ti* in the last phrase is the last breath, the last word, the thanksgiving, the prayer for forgiveness, of all the living. And then I think the last *la* leads to the salvation we are supposed to reach with Jesus. Thus I wish to sing this *la* (the main tone in A minor) as the final goal of the ten-times-repeated dominant *mi*.[15]

It is no accident that a hymn so full of theological implications has been well received among ecumenical circles. It has been included in no fewer than fourteen major hymnals in the English-speaking world.

Conclusion

The Japanese are known for their ability to adapt ideas from other cultures, most recently from the West. Their innovative skills in science and technology have few rivals in the world, as reflected in their automobiles, computers, cameras, televisions, and audio-visual products. The areas of arts and music are no exception. Although there have been various attempts in contextualization, the theology, liturgy, and church music in Japan are largely Western-oriented. Japanese Christians find honor and satisfaction in expressing their faith through European high art music. In Japan's urban churches, one can find pipe organs and high-quality choir performances. Many fine hymn tunes have been composed in Western styles. But some prominent composers, such as Hikaru Hayashi (see *STB* #54), Tomoaki Bunya (*STB* #158), and Taihei Satō (*STB* #189, *STB* #250), have contributed excellent hymn tunes that exhibit the Japanese spirit. It is hoped that the younger generation of composers will be inspired to search their roots and become more innovative in expressing their Christian faith in the years to come.

---

15   From the author's communication with Satō, January 15, 2007.

Korean Hymns

The Nation and Its People

Korea has a history of more than four thousand years; it is said the country originated from a mythical founder. The recorded history began in the first century BCE with the rise of three kingdoms. One kingdom, the gold-rich Silla dynasty (668–935) united the country; according to Samuel Hugh Moffett, its capital, Kyongju, was thought to be the fourth largest city in the world after Constantinople, Baghdad, and Chang-an of the Chinese Tang dynasty (Hoke 1975, 373). In 1446, during the Yi or Choson dynasty (1392–1910), King Sejong established the Korean alphabet, *hangul*, one of the most scientific phonetic alphabets in the world (Athyal 1996, 70). Racially, Korea has been a homogenous country for over 1300 years. Korea has historically been caught "like a shrimp among whales" in the wars of its three neighbors: China, Russia, and Japan. During the twentieth century, Korea was under Japanese control for forty years (1905–45) (Hoke 1975, 372f). Although independence was restored in 1948, the country was divided in two: North Korea, under the Russian-controlled communist regime, and South Korea, which enjoyed a freedom supported by the United States. On June 25, 1950, the North invaded the South, initiating the bitter Korean War, which ended in October 1953. There has been some political dialogue in recent years between the leaders of the South and the North, but no peace treaty has been signed. South Korea has a total area of 98,480 square kilometers (about 38,023 square miles) with a population of 49,044,790; North Korea occupies a total area of 120,540 square kilometers (about 46,541 square miles) with a population of 23,479,088.[16] (Because the North Korean state is highly inaccessible, this chapter primarily concerns the Christian activities and attitudes of South Koreans.)

Most Koreans practice Buddhism and Confucianism. Buddhism came from China in the fourth century and has dominated Korean art and folk literature. Confucianism, introduced in the seventh century from China, has molded the country's ethics and academic disciplines (Hoke 1975, 374). But the roots of Korean culture belong to animistic shamanism, as shown in fortune-telling, geomancy, and folk healing. During the 1970s, there were over twenty-seven thousand practicing shamanist sorceresses registered in the country (Hoke 1975, 375).

---

16   CIA, "The World Factbook, Korea, North," July 2008 estimate, https://www.cia.gov/library/publications/the-world-factbook/print/kn.html (accessed January 10, 2009).

A Brief Introduction to Korean Music

Classifications of Korean Music

Historically, Koreans have referred to their music as *kugak*, meaning "national music," while *umak* refers to Western-style music. Like their counterparts in China, Japan, and Taiwan, most Korean musicians received a Western education in public schools, which did not include Korean music. In present usage, *umak* refers to all music, but *kugak* refers to music of Korean origin.

The court music developed in the Choson period (1392–1910) was classified in three genres: *aak*, *tangak*, and *hyangak*.

AAK

Aak ("elegant music," *yayue* in Chinese, *gagaku* in Japanese) refers to the Confucian ritual music introduced in 1114 and 1116 during the Koryo dynasty (935–1392) by the Chinese Song emperor Huizong, who donated more than 400 musical instruments to the Korean royal court. However, because of the fall of the Song capital to the northern Jurchen invaders, the playing techniques as well as the instruments were eventually lost. Only some of the skeletal melodies survived (Garland 7:807).

Aak uses heptatonic modes. Only two tunes exist today, each of which contains thirty-two notes; each note has a duration of about four seconds, and each piece lasts about four minutes in performance (Garland 7:861f). Robert C. Provine outlines the basic sections of the "Sacrifice to Confucius":

Section	Ensemble	Key	Dance
Welcoming the Spirit	Courtyard	C, F, A, A♭	Civil
Offering of the Tribute	Terrace	A	Civil
Offering of Food	Courtyard	E	(no dance)
First Wine Offering	Terrace	A	Civil
Second Wine Offering	Courtyard	E	Military
Final Wine Offering	Courtyard	E	Military
Removing the Vessels	Terrace	A	(no dance)
Ushering out the Spirit	Courtyard	C	(no dance)

(Garland 7:862)

The following is the original notation of the Munmyo Confucian Ceremony, with Western notation provided by Chun In-pyong, in the *hwang-zhong gong* mode. It is read from top to bottom beginning at the upper right, and each square has one full note. The first column from the right contains the text, and the second column features the names of the notes: *hwang* (C), *nan* (A), *lin* (G), *gu* (E), etc. (*Gugak Chonchip* 1981, 14). For further discussion, see the section on theory and notation on page 109f.

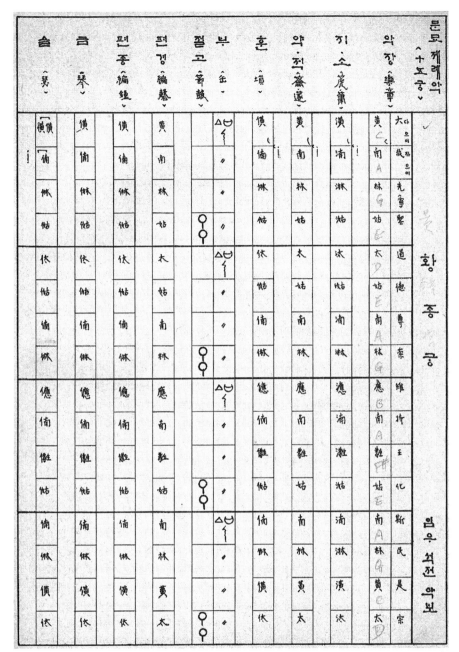

현행 문묘제례악 중 황종궁

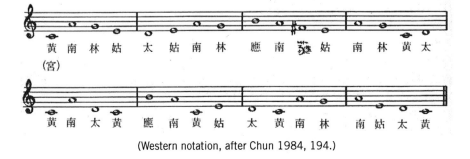

(Western notation, after Chun 1984, 194.)

103

TANGAK

Of Chinese origin, this ensemble music became very Korean in style and was performed for various court functions. Two extant pieces of *tangak* are *Pohoja* ("Pacing the Void") and *Nagyangch'un* ("Springtime in Nagyang," which uses the Korean name for the Chinese city of Luoyang). Both pieces originally had texts of sung poetry (*ci* in Chinese, *sa* in Korean), but only the instrumental parts survive today (Garland 7:866f). Although Koreans originally borrowed their music from China, they adapted and radically transformed it to meet their purposes and tastes and eventually established distinctly Korean musical styles (Garland 7:801).

HYANGAK

Hyangak refers to the native music of Korea performed in many contexts, such as ritual music for the "Sacrifice to Royal Ancestors" as well as long pieces of court music for the enjoyment of the elite. The most famous piece is *Sujech'on* ("Long life everlasting as the sky") which is characterized by aftertones (*yoŭm*) at the ends of phrases, "where the bowed strings *haegŭm* and *ajaeng* continue and decorate the final phrase pitch while the lead instrument, the *hyang p'iri*, rests" (Garland 7:868). A particular concept of beauty in sound, the *yoŭm* "spread out when a string had been plucked, just as waves ripple outward in a pond when a stone is thrown in. [Musicians] took pleasure in the idea that *yoŭm* was something mystical, and that it was analogous to nature. Because *yoŭm* is considered the most important characteristic of traditional Korean stringed instruments" (Garland 7:813f). It is interesting that the bowed string instruments, such as *haegŭm* and *ajaeng,* which do not produce *yoŭm,* are classified as wind instruments (Garland 7:813f).

Another concept is *nonghyon*; it denotes the strong vibrato that continues to sound after a tone has been plucked or bowed on stringed instruments or blown through wind instruments. *Nonghyon* is an ornament with a variety of characteristics: deep vibration, slight vibration, sliding down, sliding up, and circumflex.[17]

The *hyangak* category includes the most important genres of art songs with classical poetry (*sijŏ* , *kasa*, and *kagok*), which were patronized primarily by the affluent classes outside the court.

KAGOK

Kagok is a lyric song cycle. It is performed by a professional soloist with the accompaniment of an ensemble, which includes *komungo, sep'iri, taegŭm, haegŭm,* and *changgo*, and sometimes *kayagŭm* and *tanso*. The contemporary repertoire has twenty-six songs for male voice and sixteen for female voice. The songs are divided into five sections, each containing two to four groups of words with three to five syllables, with an interlude between the third and fourth sections. The tempo is very slow; one syllable may be as long as thirty-five seconds. There are two rhythmic cycles: a sixteen-beat regular rhythm and a ten-beat condensed rhythm played on the *changgo* (Garland 7:919–23).

---

17   From the author's email communication with In-pyong Chun, January 10, 2009.

SIJO

Sijŏ is a short classical lyric song, with three lines and forty-five syllables of text. The text is divided into three sections, each with four groups of three to five syllables. The last three syllables are usually not sung. Songs vary in length, melodic type, and register; there are also regional differences. Accompaniment is provided by a *changgo*, or the singer drums the rhythmic patterns with his hands on his knees. In formal performance, a *taegŭm*, *p'iri*, and *haegŭm* may be added (Garland 7:924–26).

KASA

Kasa is a type of long narrative song. There are twelve in all, called *sibi kasa* ("twelve *kasa*"), accompanied by *changgo*; *taegŭm*, *sep'iri*, and *haegŭm* may be added for formal presentation. The texts are strophic, with sets of three and four or four and four, some with a refrain. In the course of singing, a series of unrelated vocables such as "nouona noninaru" are sometimes added as a refrain or a whole stanza. The songs are characterized by fluid melodies, falsetto, dynamics, and a wide range of vibrato. All songs in *kasa* are in the *kyemyonjo* mode, but sometimes *ujo* is also added (Garland 7:927f).

SANJO

Sanjo is a kind of folk music performed by solo instruments, such as *kayagŭm*, *komungo*, *haegŭm*, *ajaeng*, and *taegŭm*. Pieces consist of three to six movements with different rhythmic patterns, ranging from slower to faster. The length of a piece also varies; the shortest is approximately twenty minutes long while the longest can last up to an hour in duration (Garland 7:913).

Religious Music

BUDDHIST

There are three types of Buddhist chant. The sutra-chanting *yombul* is syllabic Chinese or Sanskrit, the *hwaach'on* is in Korean, in a compound asymmetrical pattern of eight units (3 + 2 + 3), and the *pomp'ae* is an archaic, solemn chant performed only by trained musicians at special rites. The melismatic chant is performed by a solo or chorus. Today, the chant is performed at an extremely slow tempo, accompanied by a small handbell, a wooden gong (*mokt'ak*), and a large flat gong (*ching*). Because of the influence of Mahayana Buddhism, only Tibet and Korea practice Buddhist ritual dance (Garland 7:871f).

SHAMANIC

Shamans (*mudang*) and their rituals (*kut*) are very popular in Korea. A shaman is usually a woman and inherits her status from her mother or mother-in-law, who trains her. Shamanic ritual includes: invocation to the spirit by singing and dancing, speaking and listening to the wishes of the person after being possessed by the spirit, praying as a mediator to the spirit for blessings, entertaining the spirit with a dance, and finally sending off the spirit with songs (Garland 7:875f).

P'ANSORI

Developed at the beginning of the eighteenth century, *p'ansori* is a kind of folk musical drama performed by professional musicians (*kwangdae*). The performer tells the story through songs (*sori*), with dialogue or narration (*aniri*) and gesture (*pallim*), holding a fan and/or handkerchief. He or she is accompanied by a frame drum (*puk*); the drummer frequently makes calls of encouragement, or *ch'uimsae*. The audience plays an important role in the drama by also calling words of encouragement. A traditional saying about *p'ansori* is: "First the audience, second the drummer, and third the singer" (Garland 7:897). A song in *p'ansori* has a particular *jo* (mode or melodic type) and *changdan* (long and short beats that form specific rhythmic cycles), with a particular mood, character, or set of actions. *P'ansori* vocal production is full of various techniques, including straight voice (*t'ongsong*), central or principal voice (*chungangsong* or "chest voice"), a hard vocal attack with huskiness and hoarseness, head voice, falsetto, wide and narrow vibrato, "jaw voice," "teeth voice," etc. (Garland 7:819f). In 1985, the Asian Institute for Liturgy and Music (AILM) and Korea Christian Academy produced the collection *New Korean Hymns*, with a new set of *p'ansori* edited by Chay Shiwohn. A new movement in the church uses *p'ansori* for preaching and evangelism. The Reverend In-wan Chang's work in this area, as observed in June 2006, is notable.

NONGAK

The term *nongak* is probably of recent origin; it denotes the music and dance of farmers. The term *pungmul* (literally "wind-object" or "wind-matter") is also used for this genre. Both terms refer to ensemble performances, which originally had regional distinctions. The main percussion instruments include *kkwaenggwari*, *ching*, *changgo*, *puk*, and *sogo*, and the melodic instruments include *nabal* (trumpet) and *hojok* (shawm). The rhythms are very complicated, as may be seen from transcriptions (in Garland 7:936–37).

FOLK SONG

"Arirang" is one of the most popular national Korean folksongs. It is said there are over seventy versions, which are sung differently by region. The following illustration shows the 9/8 rhythmic pattern *semanch'i*.

A - ri - rang, a - ri - rang, a - ra - ri - yo;

A - ri - rang ko - gae - ro nŏ - mŏ kan - da.

Aesthetics in Korean music

The explanations of a few more terms and concepts will help one understand and appreciate the beauty of Korean music.

Han is the expression of "a profound sadness in response to a tragic life . . . Hearing such music, one feels a tragic beauty touching the heart" (Garland 7:814). The word *mot* is derived from *mat* ("taste"); it denotes something attractive that deviates slightly from the norm. "When an object of our emotion is particularly appealing, we tend to sense a rhythm in it, nothing less than magnetism; in such a situation, the word *mot* is used" (Garland 7:814f). It can refer to the spontaneous, rhythmic, and excited interjections from the audience to a folk singer (Garland 7:815).

Him means "universal vitality." Koreans feel that a musical sound must carry a "powerful, vibrant tone color, rather than a tone color that is clear, sweet or voluminous" and the sound must be "dynamic, varying delicately in tone color, volume and pitch" (Garland 7:815). *Changdan* is a basic element of traditional Korean music, similar to rhythm or a rhythmic pattern. *Chang* literally means "long," and *dan* means "short." The most essential rhythm in Korean folk music is long–short, usually 2–1 in ratio. All Korean folk songs and rhythmic patterns are derived from the variation of this combination, as shown in these *changgo* (hourglass drum) patterns:

Beats			2	3	4	5	6
Changgo	Ⓘ				O	i	
Rhythm							

- O = *kung*: left drumhead struck with open hand, making a low, *yin* sound

- | = *ttok*: right drumhead struck with a stick, making a high, *yang* sound

- i = *torururu*: (a variation of *ttok*) a rolling sound, made with a vibrating stick (all dotted)

- Ⓘ = *ttong*: *taeguk* ("great absolute sound"), produced by striking both heads simultaneously This *taeguk* marks the beginning of a cycle combining both *yin* and *yang* sounds in all the rhythmic cycles (Garland 7:815f).

One of the most prominent rhythmic patterns is *kutkori;* it combines two 6/8 patterns and is frequently associated with dance. The duration of the rhythmic cycle is approximately five seconds. The *kutkori* may be rendered in the following mnemonic:

Ttong   kidong kung   to ru ru ru ttong   kidong kung ttok

Ttong kidong kung torururu Ttong kidong kung ttok

As is the case of many folk traditions, the beats in Korean rhythmic patterns may not be very strict in the Western sense, especially at a slow tempo; rubato, lengthening or hurrying certain beats, is normal. Due to the *changdan* concept, many beats are subdivided into units of three or 2 + 1 or 1 + 2. Thus the instrumental ensemble piece *Pohoja* has the rhythmic patterns of

6 + 4 + 4 + 6   and it can be subdivided in compound time as
18/8 12/8 12/8 18/8   or simply
6/4   4/4   4/4   6/4   each beat with a triplet

(Garland 7:841–44)

The following illustration depicts gong patterns (after Garland 7:936).

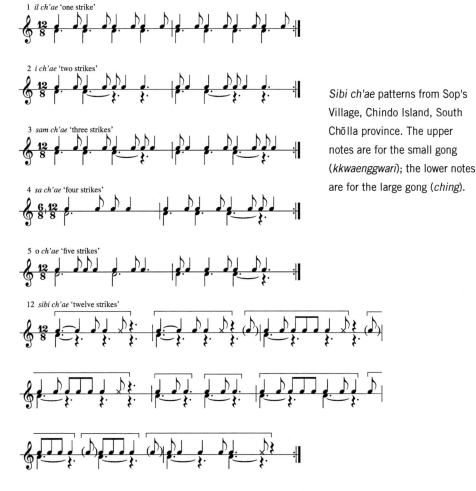

Sibi ch'ae patterns from Sop's Village, Chindo Island, South Chŏlla province. The upper notes are for the small gong (*kkwaenggwari*); the lower notes are for the large gong (*ching*).

Theory and Notation

While early Korean musical theories were influenced by Chinese traditions, practices were incorporated in *Akhak kwebom* ("Guide to the Study of Music") in 1493, beginning with the musical treatises of the Choson period (1392–1910). However, musical terms, tuning systems, and concepts such as *yin* and *yang* and the circle of fifths were still related to Chinese theories. The earliest notated Korean music dates from 1430 and is based on a Chinese *aak* piece from 1349.

The most important innovation to northeast Asian music is the Korean rhythmic notation *chongganbo*, which was developed in the middle of the fifteenth century. It consists of horizontal and vertical lines that create columns of boxes to be read from top to bottom and from right to left. Each box represents one unit of time, and the respective pitches or rhythms are inserted in the box. Initially there were thirty-two boxes; the number was later reduced to sixteen or twenty (Garland 7:833–37).

The illustrations below show the original Korean notation of *Song Gu Yeo* and the Western transcription for full orchestra. The Korean notation, read from the top right downward, shows a six-beat cycle with the *changgo* drum pattern on the far right. The right column indicates the melody and is played by the *komungo* (zither); this part is the second from the bottom in the staff notation. Notice how varied the heterophonic treatment of the melody could become, especially among the aerophones at the top of the score.

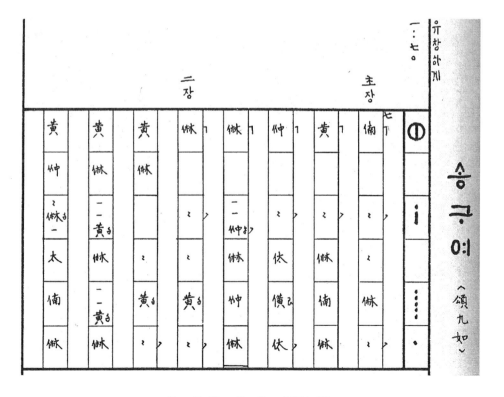

Song Gu Yeo, after Chun 1984, 92.

도 드 리 "수연장. 송구여"
Do deu ri "Su yeon jang, Song gu yeo"

After Chun 1984, 73.

110

On Modes (*akcho*)

According to Korean music theory, there are two modes (*akcho*), *p'yongjo* and *kyemyonjo*; both of these modes are related to Chinese *chidiao* (5 6 1 2 3) and *yudiao* (6 1 2 3 5), respectively. Each mode has seven scales with the same tonal structure. *Kyemyonjo* has two meanings. It denotes the expression of sadness, calm, and loneliness, contrasting against the bright and joyful mood of *p'yongjo*. Another meaning of *kyemyonjo* refers to the tonal structure of the *la* mode (6 1 2 3 5), which is considered the original mode, but at some point it was changed to the *re* mode (2 3 5 6 1), as found in *p'ansori*. Scholars have different views and interpretations of these confusing modal concepts. In-pyong Chun, a professor at the College of Korean Music, Chung Ang University and the president of the Council for Asian Musicology, does not encourage people to subscribe to the old theories as stated above. Chun prefers a new approach: understanding the Korean tonal system according to the *do* mode, *re* mode, *mi* mode, *sol* mode, *la* mode, etc.[18]

Musical Instruments

The major classifications of Korean musical instruments are:

- **Chordophones:** *kayagŭm* (half-tube zither, with twelve strings), *komungo* (half-tube zither, with six strings and sixteen frets), *ajaeng* (bowed zither, with seven to nine strings), *haegŭm* (bowed spiked lute, with two strings)

- **Aerophones:** *taegŭm* (transverse flute with membrane, with six holes), *tanso* (vertical notched flute, with six holes plus thumb-hole), *p'iri* (double-reed bamboo oboe, with eight holes)

- **Membranophones:** *changgŏ* (double-headed hourglass drum, played with the palm of the hand or a ball-headed mallet and stick), *puk* (double-headed barrel drum, played with a hardwood stick)

- **Idiophones:** *kkwaenggwari* (small knobbed gong, played with a wooden mallet), *ching* (large gong with padded beater)

Pictured below are some Korean instruments from I-to Loh's collection.

tanso

---

18   From the author's e-mail communication with In-pyong Chun, January 10, 2009.

puk

changgo and sticks

A Brief History of Christian Missions in Korea

In 1784, Roman Catholicism was introduced to Korea by the diplomat Yi Sung-hun, who had been baptized in Beijing. Subsequent evangelism was met with persecutions and martyrdom; during the Pyung Jin massacre in 1866, nine French priests and more than 2,000 Koreans were killed. Yet the numbers of converts swelled to 20,000 by the year 1885 (Athyal 1996, 53).

Protestant missions began in Korea in 1884, led by American Presbyterian missionaries, who emphasized evangelism, and American Methodist missionaries, who stressed education. The medical services of both churches had a strong impact on the Korean royal families and the greater society (Athyal 1996, 54). Since then, innumerable missionary groups and denominations from the United States, Australia, England, and Canada have entered Korea. Their success may have followed the "Nevius Method of Missions," as introduced by the British missionary John Nevius in 1890:

1. emphasis on personal evangelism through wide interaction
2. self-support
3. self-propagation
4. self-government
5. systematic Bible study for every Christian
6. strict discipline in the church
7. close cooperation with other Christian bodies
8. non-interference in lawsuits
9. general help for those who are really in economic need

(*Asian Evangelization,* quoted in Athyal 1996, 54f)

Among these methods, the "three-self" principles have had a lasting influence on the mission in Korea and China, as well as in other countries. The explosion of church growth in Korea has been astounding. Samuel Hugh Moffett reported that the number of Protestant Christians in Korea increased 900 percent between 1900 and 1910, from 18,081 to 167,352; by 1940, the number grew to 372,000 (Hoke 1975, 378f).

Bong Rin Ro offers non-spiritual reasons for the rapid church growth during the past half century:

1. Christianity introduced new ideas of political democracy.
2. Christianity filled a spiritual vacuum, which Buddhism and Confucianism could not.
3. Christianity offered comfort from the suffering experienced during the Japanese occupation (1910–45) and the Korean War (1950–53) and from the constant threat of Communism from North Korea.

These factors "encouraged the people to find their security in God rather than man" (Athyal 1996, 56f). The work of countless pastors and *minjung* theologians during the past fifty years has also contributed to the political and social reform of the country as well as to the growth of the church. Korean theologians have developed a *minjung* theology, which refers to *minjung* as "the people who are politically oppressed, economically exploited, and socially alienated" (Park 2003, 197f). Yong Bock Kim regards Jesus "as the life of the *minjung*," and they are the subjects of history (Kim 1992, 40–46). Christians from other parts of the world can learn a lot from *minjung* theology. Sixty-five church leaders from Hong Kong and the Philippines observed the following spiritual aspects of the Korean church, which may explain the church's incredible growth in that country.

1. pastoral leadership
2. prayer
3. preaching the Word
4. laity training
5. Christian education
6. upper room (small groups)
7. worship
8. missions
9. administration
10. social concerns

(Athyal 1996, 64)

During a spiritual renewal week at a Presbyterian church in Seoul in 1995, the three predawn prayer meetings (at 4:30, 5:30, and 6:30) were attended by more than 16,000 members each morning. A Full Gospel church has organized more than 40,000 cell groups for 706,000 members throughout Seoul for Bible study. There are 270 theological colleges and seminaries, six of which have more than 1,500 students each; they produce over 7,000 graduates every year for church ministries. Today, there are more than 4,000 Korean missionaries from seventy-one mission agencies working in one hundred countries (Athyal 1996, 67f). Korea's Christians account for 26.3 percent of the total population.[19] But Korean churches do have problems. There are at least 160 Protestant denominations, with fifty-six Presbyterian groups. Ecumenically oriented groups and those emphasizing evangelism have difficulty sharing their missions and services. Some believe that the churches, with their substantial resources, should adopt a more socially responsible role by serving the needy (Athyal 1996, 70–72).

Commentary on Individual Hymns

"Broken communion tore you apart" (*STB* #297)
(Korean: *Gallajin apŭmŭl*)

Junchol Hong prays, "Broken communion tore you apart. Grant us, Lord, union, close to your heart." Geonyong Lee captures this mood of grief with a wailing motif in an F = 1 four-tone scale (1 2 4 5) with final on the lower 5. The humming of the melody in the second half of the hymn provides room for meditation and prayers with one's thoughts. This prayer seems to call for unifying the divided churches, but it originally referred to the division of Korea; millions of family members have been separated because of the war and have been earnestly praying for reunion. This hymn may be sung as a response to prayers for unity and reconciliation. (para. J.M.)

"Come now, O Prince of Peace" (*STB* #241)
(Korean: *Ososŏ*)

This is one of the few hymns for which the composer Geonyong Lee has written his own text. He originally wrote this as a prayer for peace, reconciliation, and the reunification of North and South Korea. After its publication in the 1990 edition of *Sound the Bamboo*, it has been used around the world as a prayer for peace (*pyonghwa*), love (*sarang*), freedom (*chayu*), and unification (*tongil*) or a Christian unity between all peoples and all nations. Since it has a simple, repetitive poetic form, it is easy to sing in Korean with the four key words transliterated above. This can be an excellent response to prayers for peace, love, freedom, and unity, with the congregation singing the stanza of the respective theme after each prayer.

The music of ososo is in a B♭ = 1 five-tone scale (G = 6 7 1 2 3) with final on 6, in triple time, which is typical of Korean music. Although the composer has used Western harmonic language, he has freely employed dissonances and crossing inner parts and ends the hymn with an open fifth. Perhaps the harmonic treatment

---

19   CIA, "The World Factbook, Korea, South," https://www.cia.gov/library/publications/the-world-factbook/geos/ks.html (accessed March 3, 2009).

implies the breaking of barriers and rules in order to achieve peace and unity. The beginning is clearly in G minor, but the final chord is an open fifth; without the third, it is impossible to discern whether it is in a major or minor key. Perhaps the composer wished to evoke the still-missing peace and unity with the undecided final chord. Near the end of the hymn, the tenor part crossing beyond the alto part might imply that one has to go further and break rules in order to find paths to reconciliation.

This hymn stimulates conversation and encourages dialogue between groups, especially those with political, doctrinal, or ideological differences. It has been sung in many international and ecumenical gatherings with much success. This hymn brings people together, especially as a commitment to peace or a sign of peace, before or after the Eucharist. (para. Marion Pope, late 1980s)

"Cross of Christ, you stand above us" (*STB* #150)

(Korean: *Gwinadoda shipchagayŏ*)

The music committee of the Anglican Church of Korea translated this text from the Latin hymn "Pange lingua gloriosi proelium certaminis," and this hymn has been sung in Korea for a long time. Geonyong Lee set the text to a new Korean tune, and Marion Pope translated it back into English. A comparison of the texts reveals the differences. The orders of stanzas are different; the present stanza 1 was the original 4, 2 was 3, and 4 was 5; the present stanza 3 was not in the original, and the original first two stanzas were not translated. This is the original form of the hymn, with the first stanza added to the beginning:

(original stanza 1)
Sing, my tongue, how glorious battle
Glorious victory became;
And above the Cross, his trophy,
Tell the triumph and the fame:
Tell you He, the earth's Redeemer,
By His death for man o'ercome.

(original stanza 4, present stanza 1)
Faithful Cross, above all other,
One and only noble Tree,
None in foliage, none in blossom,
None in fruit compares with thee:
Sweet the wood and sweet the iron,
And thy Lord how sweet is He.

(original stanza 3, present stanza 2)
His the nails, the spear, the spitting,
Reed and vinegar and gall;
From His patient body pierced
Blood and water streaming fall:

> Earth and sea and stars and mankind
> By that stream are cleansed all.
> (original stanza 5, present stanza 4)
> Unto God be laud and honour:
> To the Father, to the Son,
> To the mighty Spirit, glory –
> Ever Three and ever One:
> Power and glory in the highest
> While eternal ages run.[20]

The tune SHIPCHAGA, meaning "cross," is in a D = 3 six-tone scale (G = 6 7 1 2 3 4) with final on 6. The phrases are very closely organized: a a' b(a) a" a a'. The b uses the same a motif but transposed to a higher range, with only a slight difference, and a" is the same as a' except for the first and the last notes. The harmony is also stylized, with repeated half notes skipping in the bass. The upward and downward quarter-note figures in the tenor seem to depict the suffering of Christ, weighed down by the heavy cross. This hymn is appropriate for Good Friday services—for contemplating the meaning of the cross and the transformation from pain and death to victory and glory.

"Dark is the night" (*STB* #253)

(Korean: *Kamkamhan bam sanaun*)

Drawing from Matthew 8:23–27, Helen Kim uses the image of Jesus stilling the storm around a small boat as a metaphor of salvation. This hymn reflects that one is frequently faced with unexpected storms and dangers, like a tiny boat tossed by the waves, threatening one's life at any moment. Carlton Young succinctly states that this hymn "effectively transfers the story's metaphors into a personal testimony of the abiding support, love, and peace afforded by God in Christ for the Christian on 'life's cruel sea'" (Young 1993, 469).

The tune BAI, meaning "ship," was composed by Dong Hoon Lee in a Bb = 5 six-tone scale (Eb = 1 2 3 5 6 7) with typical Korean 6/8 time and rhythmic patterns. The melody begins with smooth, repeated notes, like a boat just beginning to sail (555 6-/161 6-). In the third system, the sudden change of rhythmic pattern, the large melodic intervals (6 3 6 7/ 6-), and the appearance of a new tone 7 seem to depict the dramatic moment of turmoil, "straight into the swell." The music for the cry "My God, death and danger" also features different rhythms to convey this idea. The music clearly captures the Korean imagination and emotion. Meanwhile, the harmony is the familiar traditional Western style that most people enjoy.

---

20   The original text was written by Venantius Honorius Clementianus Fortunatus (ca. 530–609) and translated by William Mair (1830–1920) and Arthur Wellesley Wotherspoon (1853–?); verse 4 was translated by John Mason Neale (1818–1866). From *The Scottish Psalter 1929, Metrical Version and Scripture Paraphrases with Tunes* (London: Oxford University Press / Humphrey Milford, 1929).

Helen Kim's most famous hymn has a long history. According to Kim Seongdae, it was written in 1921 and first appeared in 1931 in the *Shinjung Chansongka*, number 126, to Joseph Barnby's tune SAVED IN THE STORM.[21] This hymnal was published by a joint committee of three denominations, headed by Henry D. Appenzeller. Dong Hoon Lee's tune BAI (with the original name "The Little Ship") was set to this text first in 1967 in *Gaepyun Chansongka*.[22] The English translation was initially by Hae Jong Kim and paraphrased by Linda and Doug Sugano in 1981, and it was published in the Asian American *Hymns From the Four Winds* (1983). The text was further revised by Hope Omachi-Kawashima and was included in the *United Methodist Hymnal* in 1989. Because this last version was too wordy and had altered the original text-tune relationships, Ok-youn Kim was requested to translate the hymn from the original Korean. Terry MacArthur paraphrased Kim's translation for the 2000 edition of *Sound the Bamboo*.

"ENDLESS GRACE"
("Time is precious, time is gold," *STB* #183)

(Korean: *Saramdŭrŭn shigani*)

Acknowledging God's grace as more precious than anything else in the world, Jong-joon Kim admonishes people to pray, to restore the power of true love for one another, and to live in faith. The refrain praises the LORD for infinite grace.

Un-yung La's tune UN-CH'ONG, meaning "grace," is in typical Korean triple time, with an F = 1 six-tone scale (1 2 3 5 6 ♭7), in which the ♭7 only appears once at the first "Hallelujah." The melody is well organized in a a' b c d d' form, of which both b and c have their respective similar figures repeated. The last two phrases function as a refrain. The harmony comprises free combinations of Western traditional as well as altered chords with some surprises, especially the appearances of E♭ and A♭ in the second half of the hymn. The composer indicates that, except at the refrain, the choir should hum, not sing, the harmony. (para. Marion Kim)

"Far and near the fields are teeming"

(Korean: *Nŏlbun dŭre igŭn gokshik*)
See "THE CALL FOR REAPERS" *(STB #245)*

"Food for pilgrim people" (*STB* #290)

(Korean: *Nagŭnee yangshik*)

---

21   From personal correspondence with the author, October 14, 2006.
22   See Kim Seongdae, "Inculturation in Korean Protestant Hymnody" (PhD diss., Drew University, 1999), 172f.

This is another Latin hymn, "O Esca Viatorum," from 1661. It had been translated into English by John Athelstan Riley (1858–1945) and was further translated into Korean. Geonyong Lee composed this setting YANG SHIK, meaning "foods," and Marion Pope retranslated the text from Korean into English. Shirley Murray assisted with the paraphrasing. This is Riley's translation, which reveals the many differences in the present version.

1. O Food of pilgrim given, O Bread of life from heaven,
     O Manna from on high!
   We hunger; Lord supply us, nor thy delights deny us,
     Whose hearts to thee draw nigh.

2. O stream of love past telling, O purest fountain, welling
     from out the Savior's side!
   We faint with thirsts; revive us, of thine abundance give us,
     And all we need provide.

3. O Jesus, by thee bidden, we here adore thee, hidden
     in forms of bread and wine.
   Grant when the veil is riven, we may behold, in heaven,
     Thy countenance divine.

(The Hymnal 1982, no. 308)

The tune is a straightforward composition in a traditional Western D = 6 five-tone scale (6 1 2 3 5) or Aeolian mode (cadence: 6 6 5 6-). The phrases have similar melodic and rhythmic patterns. The fourth line of the text is repeated but is set with different music. The composer has used both B natural (G-major chord) and B♭ (B♭-major chord) to evoke different feelings.

"Gather here, believers in Christ" (STB #243)
(Korean: *Uri modu Yesumikko*)

This is a call to people around the world, regardless of color or status, to be united and renewed in Christ and to follow him. Byong-sop Ban's text is set to the tune HAN GA JOK ("one family") by Un-yung La in a B♭ = 5 six-tone scale (E♭ = 1 2 3 5 6 7). In this basically five-tone melody, the 7 only appears in one sequential development (262 3-, 373 5-). The melody is in a typically Korean 6/8, syncopated rhythm, with an interesting accompaniment that combines parallel thirds, fourths, fifths, and other intervals. The composer has specified that the first system should be sung in unison, the second system is a solo, and the last is a chorus. The time signature of the chorus is 9/8, which alters the rhythmic patterns; all voices at first sing in unison (symbolizing all people united in one accord) and conclude with four-part harmony. The musical setting makes a powerful statement of unity in diversity. The hymn may be used to open an international gathering, especially one that celebrates new life in Christ. (trsl. Genell Poitras & J. M.)

"HARVEST THANKSGIVING"
("Picture the rugged landscape," *STB* #166)
(Korean: *Sanmada buritanda*)

In this beautiful hymn, Ok In Lim describes a scene of abundant reaping, recalls past labor with trust in God's providence, and gives heartfelt thanks for God's blessings. Then he praises God for planting a new seed and words of life in one's heart, a metaphor of expecting a spiritual harvest. The refrain is longer than the verse and contains a series of climaxes for giving thanks and praises to God. As the title indicates, it is appropriate for thanksgiving, especially after harvest.

The tune KAM-SAH, meaning "giving thanks," exhibits uniquely Korean musical features: triple time, strong rhythm with syncopation and alternating accents, and a wide range (B to high e). It is in a G = 1 five-tone scale (E = 6 1 2 3 5). The verse section with four phrases is through-composed while the six phrases of the refrain are organized in a a' b c c' form. Jae Hoon Park utilizes traditional Western four-part harmony, except for two short motifs in unison. The verse is in E minor (E = 6), but the refrain suddenly moves to its relative major, G. Park uses similar phrases to build the mood of joyful praise to the climaxes of the last two phrases and concludes in E minor. Although the time signature indicates that the hymn is in 6/4 time, it should be regarded as 6/8 time when singing (i.e., 3 + 3, not 2 + 2 + 2) so that the typical Korean 6/8 rhythm can be maintained and highlighted.

"Jesus Christ, workers' Lord" (*STB* #234)
(Korean: *Urinŭn bujirŏnhan*)

Acknowledging that all people are servants of Jesus Christ, Byung Soo Oh writes this hymn of stewardship for the trades. He believes that with the gifts of love, grace, and talent, all serve as one family, expecting harvest from this fertile land of hope.

The tune KEUN-LOH (meaning "industrious" or "hardworking") by Kook Jin Kim is in a C = 5 five-tone scale (F = 1 2 3 5 6). Although it is in 4/4, the syncopated rhythmic patterns reflect vigorous Korean folk characters. The phrases are organized in a b c b form, so the hymn is easy to sing. The setting is in Western four-part harmony in F major. This English version was paraphrased for the 1983 Asian American hymnal *Hymns from the Four Winds* by Elise Shoemaker, who was then a staff member at the Board of Discipleship of the United Methodist Church. (trsl. T. Tom Lee: para. Elise Shoemaker)

"Jesus, our true Lord of love" (*STB* #192)
(Korean: *Sarangŭi Chunim Yesu*)

This hymn, by Ke Joon Lee, is a prayer to Jesus to "come to be always with us . . . to give us new life . . . new sight . . . to free us anew." It further prays for the Emmanuel God to be born today as a baby, a brother, a king, and a savior to fill one's heart with joy and light, and to fill the world with justice, peace, grace, and love.

The tune IMMANUEL ("God with us"), by Doo Wan Kim, is in an A♭ = 1 five-tone scale (1 2 3 5 6), with the sixth tone 4 (D♭) appearing once near the climax. The typical 6/8 time signature exhibits a Korean character but is set in traditional Western chordal harmony. (trsl. Marion Pope)

"Joy found in truth surely sets the world free" (*STB* #66)

(Korean: *Jinliga urirŭl jayuhage*)

Kyung-soo Kim composed this text with a repetitive structure; the second and fourth lines of each verse end with the word *hanaida*, which is a respectful form of saying, "let something happen." The author exhorts one to seek the truth, to love one's neighbors, to be one through faith, to live the new life, to let one's light shine, to be the true salt, and to speak the truth in love. The refrain is a prayer to the God of infinite love to set one free and bring forth life.

The tune JIN-LI ("truth") was composed by Un-yung La in an A = 6 seven-tone scale (6 7 1 2 3 ♯4 5). The phrases are organized according to the poetic structure:

a x a x / y y' c c

The a and c are two measures long while x and y are each one measure. The x is set to the word *hanaida*; c is in a typical Korean rhythmic pattern. The y' is similar to y but transposed to a fifth higher. The harmony of the verse is very economical, but it becomes thicker and more rhythmic in the refrain, with a series of reiterated open fifths, followed by chords in B major with first and second inversions and a D-minor seventh chord. The final full cadence to A major (E7 to A) is a surprise. It seems that La purposefully concludes in a major tonality to symbolically "bring forth life!" (para. Marion Pope)

"Lord, as the earth welcomes showers of rain" (*STB* #90)

(Korean: *Pulbate naerinŭn danpi chŏrŏm*)

This is a paraphrase of Psalm 72:6–19 by Hye-ryon Ham, who changes the third person "he" in the Psalm to the second person "you," directly addressing the Lord: "as the earth welcomes showers of rain, so will your advent relieve human thirsting," and justice and peace will flourish, and "those who are weak and oppressed you will save, May all the earth sing your glory and praise." This Advent hymn is appropriate for occasions related to justice, peace, and the integrity of creation.

The tune JONGUIGA KKOTPINUN, which means "justice blooming," is written in a D = 6 six-tone scale (6 1 2 3 4 5), in triple time and with large intervals, features that are characteristically Korean. The song is quite long, with five phrases in a b c d c' form plus a refrain, e f. The chordal and arpeggio accompaniment, though somewhat different from the styles of Geonyong Lee's other compositions, is interesting and quite effective. (para. Rolando S. Tinio)

"Lovely star in the sky" (*STB* #132)

(Korean: *Hanŭre binnanŭn*)

This Western hymn, "Brightest and best of the stars of the morning" by Reginald Heber (1783–1826) of the United Kingdom, had been translated into Korean long ago and was in common use. Un-yung La composed this new tune, and Marion Pope retranslated the Korean text to English. For comparison, the original English text is:

1. Brightest and best of the sons of the morning,
    Dawn on our darkness, and lend us thine aid;
  Star of the east, the horizon adorning,
    Guide where our infant Redeemer is laid.

2. Cold on his cradle the dew-drops are shining;
    Low lies his head with the beasts of the stall;
  Angels adore him in slumber reclining,
    Maker and Monarch and Savior of all.

3. Say, shall we yield him, in costly devotion,
    Odours of Edom, and offerings divine,
  Gems of the mountains and pearls of the ocean,
    Myrrh from the forest or gold from the mine?

4. Vainly we offer each ample oblation,
    Vainly with gifts would his favor secure;
  Richer by far is the heart's adoration;
    Dearer to God are the prayers of the poor.

(The Church Hymnary, 1973, no. 201)

The tune HANURE BINNANUN ("in the sky . . . shining") is in an E = 6 six-tone scale (6 7 1 2 3 5) with a lyrical and mysterious melody, 6 3 3 <u>32</u> 3-/ <u>26</u> 2 3 3 -, which is developed into a through-composed piece with similar rhythm and shape. The accompaniment is very simple, with dotted half notes mostly in parallel fifths, only moving and changing near the end. Especially striking are the sudden appearances of the A♯ seventh chord (2 ♯4 6 1) in the third system and the chromatic descent of the tenor approaching the final cadence (5 ♯4--4--3--).

"O God of great love" (*STB* #64)

(Korean: *Sarangŭi Chunim*)

Hyun-chu Lee composed this prayer to Jesus, the Lord of great love, peace, and hope—the power that makes one strong and takes away fears. In the refrain, the text earnestly pleads to the Lord, like the repentant thief on the cross, to remember the faithful when his kingdom comes (Luke 23:42).

The music KIDO, meaning "prayer," was composed by Yong-cho Lee in E minor with a sharpened-4, seven-tone scale (6 7 1 2 3 #4 5), with both 6/8 and 9/8 time signatures and rich harmony. The song is in two sections; the refrain is a repetition of the verse and of equal length, with only slight variations at the beginning. But the harmonic treatment is totally different. The melody is very lyrical but earnest. It seems to be more soloistic, but with some practice, it can be sung by a congregation. The harmony is both romantic and contemporary, with mixtures of parallel thirds, fourths, and fifths, dissonances, altered seventh chords, imitations, and arpeggios. Two surprising E-major chords suddenly appear at the end of both sections. The composer has also skillfully created tension and restlessness in the middle of both sections with an altered B chord (with a diminished-fifth F, instead of F#). The melodic progression of the concluding phrase of both sections is striking: an ascending fifth from A to E instead of the usual fourth (B to E). Singers should practice this particular interval so that it does not alter the style of the song. If a church has a good choir, the refrain should be sung in four-part harmony to add vitality to this earnest prayer.

While it is no longer common to sing "Amens" at the conclusion of hymns, this music seems to require an "Amen" to provide sufficient time and an appropriate mood to conclude the prayer. (para. Jim Minchin)

"O Lord, as a deer longs for cool water" (*STB* #62)

(Korean: *Chuyŏ, sasŭmi Shinaenmul Ch'attŭt*)

The composer Geonyong Lee set his music to a paraphrase of Psalm 42:1–2: "As a deer longs for flowing streams, so my soul longs for you, O God. My soul thirsts for God, for the living God. When shall I come and behold the face of God?" Lee changed the last phrase of the text to an expression of greater piety: "When can I worship, kneel before you at last?" The melody of SASUMI ("deer") is in an E = 6 five-tone scale (6 1 2 3 5), harmonized with a second voice in free imitation, like an echo of a more diligent prayer, and ends on 6 with the harmony on 5. At the end, the clashing interval of the second implies instability. Perhaps the composer intended to depict a feeling of restlessness, for not being able to kneel before God. This reminds one of St. Augustine: " . . . restless is our heart until it comes to rest in thee."[23] (para. I. L.)

"O Lord, please have mercy on us" (*STB* #299)

(Korean: *Chuyŏ, ulirŭl*)

This is a Korean Kyrie ("Lord, have mercy"), composed by Geonyong Lee. The musical expression of the leader's call is a descending motif, <u>16</u> 6-, while

---

23   Book One, Chapter 1.1, from Saint Augustine, *The Confessions*, trans. Albert C. Outler
      (Fine Communications, 2007).

the congregation's response goes up, <u>12</u> 2-, and adds another pitch (3) to build up the prayer but returns to a similar cadence (<u>1216</u> 6-). On the second Kyrie, the melody goes up higher, <u>53</u> 3-, and reaches the climax, <u>66 56 53</u> 3-, but the congregation still responds with the same music. The third time, the word *Chuyŏ* is sung with melisma to express a more earnest plead for mercy. Except for the first statement, the two leader's phrases end with 3-; these are open phrases for the congregation's responses, and the congregation always answers and closes the phrases on the tonal center 6. Although it seems simple, the music exhibits the composer's skillful treatment of text and his sensitivity to the theology and the psychological effect of the music. In this simple yet sincere Kyrie, the setting provides musical excitement, expressing wholehearted and earnest pleading, as well as psychological satisfaction.

"Ŏgiyŏngcha, Morning sunlight beams in splendor" (*STB* #225)
(Korean:*Ŏgiyŏngcha, achim haetsal nunbushigo*)

This is the second song by Geonyong Lee that adapts a folk singing style with non-lexical syllables (for further discussion, see *STB* #101, "*Ŏhŏradiya*, In God's temple, praise the LORD God"). "Ŏ -gi-yŏng-cha" is what the boatmen call, shout, or sing while pulling ropes or rowing the boat. The rhythm of these non-lexical syllables helps them to act in unison, with more strength, and without feeling tired. Lee took this idea and integrated it into this hymn—Jesus is on a boat, sailing as a fisherman to seek people. Christ calls: "Throw your nets out, let the good news be a life line." With Jesus as a companion, one is assured that the harbor is near: "Put the anchor down." Liturgically, this hymn, which is a lyrical enactment of Jesus' call to cast the nets for abundant fishing (John 21:4–6) and of Jesus' calming of the storm (Mark 4:35–41), can be sung as an expression of faith and obedience in mission, as a witness of Christ as Lord, or as an assurance of the presence of Christ at a time of crisis.

The music OGIYONGCHA is in 6/8 throughout. It is in a B = 3 four-tone scale (E = 6 1 2 3). Musically, there are three sections of A B A form, each of which consists of four phrases of a a b a in a call-and-response manner, and the b a sub-section is repeated three times. The rhythmic contrast is not as complicated as that in *STB* #101, but the method of singing is somewhat similar. At the end of the non-lexical syllables, Lee has added slightly different texts. In each section after the initial phrase, the cantor always sings three lines of text; the congregation responds to each line before proceeding to a new "Ŏ-gi-yŏng-cha." (para. Marion Pope)

"Ŏhoradiya, In God's temple, praise the Lord God" (STB #101)
(Korean: *Ŏhŏradiya, Sŏngsŏesŏ ch'anyanghara*)

Many Asian folk cultures practice the singing of non-lexical syllables, which express various moods. The meanings of non-lexical syllables are not specific, but they may gain meanings from the title of the song, the purpose of singing, the occasion and function of the singing, the mood of the occasion, or, most likely, from the texts sung by the leader. In this respect, the syllables could mean "I agree with what you have just sung," "let us rejoice," or the equivalent of the shouted "Amen!" by African American congregations when they are moved by the preacher's sermon. (For further discussion, see "From this time onwards," *STB* #224, in the Taiwan section of this volume.)

The phrase "Ŏ-hŏ-ra-di-ya sang-sa-di-ya" is associated with Korean festivals, especially the farmers' dance. Often combined with excited dancing, the singing of "Ŏ-hŏ-ra-di-ya" can be an expression of joy and/or thanksgiving for a good harvest and a time of celebration.

The composer Geonyong Lee captures the joyful mood of Korean folk dance and matches the music with the praise in Psalm 150. He clearly matches "Hallelujah" to "Ŏ-hŏ-ra-di-ya sang-sa-di-ya," giving a new meaning to these non-lexical syllables. In effect, he has translated the syllables into "Praise the Lord!" He has further contextualized the psalm by replacing all the Biblical instruments with Korean traditional instruments: *nap'al* (cymbals), *komungo* (zither), *bip'a* (plucked lute), *puk* (frame drum), *hyonkum* (bowed lute), *p'iri* (bamboo oboe), *kkwaengkwari* (small gong), and *ching* (large gong).

The melody is in a B = 3 five-tone scale (E = 6 1 2 3 5) with a very wide range (such as a thirteenth). The composer uses two time signatures (9/8 and 6/8) and plenty of rhythmic variations. The congregation should repeat the same "ŏ-hŏ -ra-di-ya" that the leader first introduces. Then, no matter what the leader sings, the congregation still repeats the same first pattern until the leader changes to a new "Ŏ-hŏ-ra-di-ya" pattern, which is then repeated by the congregation. The climactic section of high Gs should be repeated a number of times to create the highest feeling of praise. The original text for stanza 11, "kkaeng mae kkaeng . . .," is an onomatopoeic expression that imitates the clashing sound of small gongs. For authenticity and excitement, the hymn should be sung in Korean, with Koreans playing the *changgo* (hourglass drum) and *ching* (large gong) for accompaniment. Instead of reading Psalm 150, congregations can sing this hymn to express the powerful climax of the book of Psalms. (para. Ronald Hinesz)

"Picture the rugged landscape"

(Korean: *Sanmada buritanda*)
See "HARVEST THANKSGIVING" *(STB #166)*

"THE CALL FOR REAPERS"
("Far and near the fields are teeming," *STB* #245)

(Korean: *Nŏlbun dŭre igŭn gokshik*)

This Western text by J. O. Thompson reflects a nineteenth-century missionary zeal, calling for God to send more reapers to gather the sheaves of gold before the harvest time passes. It was set to CHOO-SOO, meaning "autumn harvest," by Un-yung La in a typical Korean style. It is in a G = 3 five-tone scale (C = 6 1 2 3 5) in a a' b c form with final on 6. The rhythm is quite complicated, as seen from the first phrase. The musical setting reflects the Korean aesthetic concept of *changdan*, which is the contrasting combination of long (i.e. a quarter note) and short (an eighth note), in the first measure. While there are no identical sets of rhythm in the first system of this hymn, the patterns are repeated in the second system with a different ending. The refrain changes to a feeling of a major tonality but goes back to the feeling of a minor mode toward the end without the third, only suggesting an actual minor chord. La has skillfully integrated different harmonic techniques: chords, unison, contrary motion, parallel thirds, fourths, and fifths, and combinations of many other intervals. With the thick and homophonic harmony and with the accompaniment of the *changgo* (hourglass drum), this song may sound too busy and heavy as a call for gathering souls. So one may ignore the harmony: one may play a flute to double the melody and play a drum according to the notated six-beat patterns. Stems on the bottom indicate a lower, stronger, and heavier sound, and those on top denote a higher pitch, one short and sharp (see the earlier section about the aesthetics of Korean music). When no drums are available, the choir can be divided into two groups: one singing the melody, the other tapping the rhythmic patterns on a table or on their bodies. One should also take note of the accents that frequently fall on the weaker and shorter beats, making the rhythm tricky but exciting.

"This is my one, my lifelong wish" (*STB* #48)

(Korean: *Nae pyŏngsaeng sowŏn*)

This is an anonymous hymn expressing one's lifelong wish to serve the LORD and to see God face to face. It affirms that, with faith and trust in Jesus, one will fear no evil or trial, and it concludes by urging all to labor for the LORD with all strength of heart and mind.

The music SO-WON ("long wish") is by Un-yung La in a typical Korean style. It is in a C = 2 five-tone scale (F = 5 6 1 2 3) and in 6/8 time. The whole song grows out of a simple idea (2 2 5 6 5) and develops to a climax 12 3 21 6-. For harmony, La utilizes unison and consecutive fourths and fifths in contrary motions throughout the piece. This hymn demonstrates one of La's favorite styles of composition, in which the F in the second measure shakes like a fast trill and then drops down to C, following the folk style. (para. Marion Kim)

"This new morn, full of grace" (*STB* #153)
(Korean: *Ŭnheŭi achimi*)

Thanking God for the grace of a new day and new life, Jung-joon Kim writes, "If we walk with you, Lord, there is nought we can't do, nowhere we cannot go." Liturgically, this hymn may be sung as a morning prayer for God's guidance.

Un-yung La composed this NEW MORN tune in a B = 3 seven-tone, natural minor scale (E = 6 7 1 2 3 4 5) in 9/8 time with a typically syncopated Korean rhythm. The structure of the composition is in a a' b c form, but the b and c are natural developments of figures appearing in sequences. It is interesting that the pitches 4 and 7 only appear in the last phrase (141 7-), which, though a logical sequence from the former 252 1-, changes the character of the melody from basically pentatonic to heptatonic (seven tones). La skillfully employs unison, parallel fourths and fifths, and a repeated E in the bass like a drone or "chords" to support the melody. This hymn reminds one of the constant presence and assurance of the steadfast love and endless grace of God. (para. Marion Kim)

"Time is precious, time is gold"
(Korean: *Saramdŭrŭn shigani*)
See "ENDLESS GRACE" *(STB #183)*

"To the high and kindly hills" (*STB* #53)
(Korean: *Naega sanŭl hyanghayŏ*)

This is a setting of Psalm 121:1–2, "I lift up my eyes to the hills—from where will my help come? My help comes from the Lord, who made heaven and earth." The Korean text is by Song-suk Im. The melody NAUI DOUM, meaning "my help," is by Song-chon Lee. It is in a G = 3 five-tone scale (E♭ = 1 2 3 5 6) in 6/8 time, and it has a lively rhythm. It is interesting to see the frequently changing rhythms, with stresses moving from the first note (3 3 2.) to the second note (33 2.) and vice versa, and the dotted note on the fourth note (1 1 1 6.5 6). These are important characteristics of *changdan* rhythmic contrast. For the accompaniment, a *taegŭm* (long transverse bamboo flute) and a *kayagŭm* (board zither) play the main melody, two octaves apart and with their respective idiomatic variations, while a *changgo* (hourglass drum) plays exciting rhythmic patterns. If a *changgo* is not available, one can substitute other drums or even tap the rhythm on one's body to get the feeling of the song. In practice, one group may sing while another group may clap or tap the rhythms; the parts can then be reversed. This is the only Korean hymn in this collection that uses a traditional melodic instrument to accompany a song written in a traditional style. (para. J. M.)

"To the One Creator of all" (*STB* #75)

(Korean: *Juŭi hyŏngsang ddarasŏ*)

This is a hymn of thanks and praise to God. Won Yong Ra's text gives thanks for being created in God's image and for God's love and salvation from death to life and freedom. It also asks God to accept one's singing and one's life as offerings of thanks. This is best sung as an offering hymn.

HON-SHIN, meaning "dedication," was composed by Un-yung La in a D = 6 six-tone scale (6 7 1 2 3 5) with typical Korean 6/8 time. The frequent switch of accent between the first and second syllables (6 3 3 1/ or 5 3 6 6 /) is an important *changdan* feature of this song. The phrase structure is simple: ab ab'/ cc' db'//. For harmonic treatment, La utilizes traditional Western chords as well as open fifths and fourths, mostly in contrary motion. The d phrase introduces B♮ in the alto, which quickly returns to B♭, forming five consecutive sixths with the soprano. It seems that La attempts to move away from Western harmony, yet cannot resist it. However, the final "chord" without the third frees the hymn from having a completely Western style. This appears to be the composer's favorite technique in harmonizing Korean music. (trsl. T. Tom Lee; para. Elise Shoemaker)

Conclusion

Most of the Korean hymns in this collection exhibit characteristics that are typical of Korean folk styles: compound complex times (6/8, 9/8, etc.), the frequent shifting of *changdan* accents, and five- to six-tone scales without 7 and/or 4, with final on 6. The composers Un-yung La and Geonyong Lee have different approaches regarding harmonic treatment and the borrowing of traditional Western chords. Both choose to conclude phrases and tunes with an open fifth without the third. This signifies a departure from the rules of Western harmony. Son-chon Lee's approach to instrumental accompaniment (see *STB* #53) also points to a new way for Korean composers to develop their own styles. With so many dedicated Christian composers in Korea today, more contributions are sure to come.

Taiwanese Hymns

The Nation and the People

Taiwan is a small island situated southeast of China across the Taiwan Strait. The island is approximately 396 kilometers long (246 miles), and the widest part is only about 145 kilometers (90 miles). The shape of the island resembles a sweet potato; hence Taiwanese people call themselves "sweet potatoes." When Portuguese sailors first saw this green and mountainous island in 1590, they called it "ilha formosa," meaning "beautiful isle"; the name Formosa is still known today.

Taiwan's current population is about 23 million. The ethnic composition is approximately 70% Ho-lo (Han people who migrated about the sixteenth century from Fujian Province in southern China, speaking Ho-lo or Hokkien); 14% Hakka (Han people who migrated from Guangdong [Canton] Province after the Ho-lo people, speaking Hakka, one branch of the Cantonese dialect); 14% other Chinese (migrants and refugees who followed Chiang Kai-shek after being defeated by the Communists in China in 1949, speaking Mandarin and other Chinese dialects); and less than 2% original inhabitants of this island, who belong to the Malayo-Polynesian people.

Ethnic Groups, Their Music, and Political Realities

Taiwan has been home to aboriginal people since before recorded history. Theories and speculations locate their origins either in Southeast Asia and the Pacific islands or prehistoric Taiwan. They are generally regarded as the Malayo-Polynesians; in Taiwan, they have been divided into two categories according to their degrees of assimilation to the Han Chinese culture. The Ping-pu had acculturated to the Han before the arrival of the Dutch in 1624, and the *yuanzhumin* ("original inhabitants") are divided into a dozen recognized tribes, with a total population of approximately 450,000. The tribes are: Ami, Pinuyumayan (formerly named Puyuma), Paiwan, Rukai, Bunun, Tsou, Saisiat, Tayal (including Truku and Sejek), Tao (Yami), Thao (Sao), and Kavalan; the last two were formerly classified under the Ping-pu category. Mission work among the Ping-pu tribes began as soon as the missionaries arrived. But the work among the remote tribes was hindered by the Japanese government, which prohibited non-tribal persons from entering their villages. After 1945, the villages were partitally opened, and mission work was so successful that it has been regarded by missiologists as one of the miracles of the twentieth century. The tribes' gifts in choral singing are so richly diverse that I have called the tribes "a musical microcosmos in Taiwan" (Loh 1982, 448). It is believed that these singing styles developed without any foreign influences. The tribes' multipart singing techniques may be summarized as follows:

1. Occasional multipart: Tsou, Thao, Rukai, Paiwan, Ami
2. Melody with drone(s): Paiwan, Rukai, Pinuyumayan
3. Parallel 4ths and/or 5ths: Saisiat, Tsou, Bunun
4. Parallel 3ds: Paiwan, Tao (Yami)
5. Double thirds (*do-mi-sol,* homorhythmic): Bunun
6. Ostinato: Ami, Bunun, Tayal (Truku, Sejek)
7. Canonic imitation: Tayal (Truku, Sejek), Ami, Pinuyumayan
8. Tone clusters: Tao (Yami)
9. Hetero-rhythmic multipart: Ami, Pinuyumayan

(Loh 1982, 370f)

The details of some of these practices will be analyzed in the commentaries of specific hymns.

Little is known concerning the early contact between southern China and Taiwan. After Koxinga's defeat of the Dutch in Taiwan in the seventeenth century, large numbers of Han Chinese from the Fujian and Guangdong provinces migrated to Taiwan. The Qing dynasty, which had ruled Taiwan for over two centuries (1683–1895), ceded Taiwan to Japan in 1895 according to the Shimonosuke Treaty that ended the Sino-Japanese War, and Taiwan was officially a Japanese territory for fifty years (1895–45). At the end of World War II, Japan relinquished sovereignty over Taiwan; in 1945, Chiang Kai-shek was commissioned by the US General Douglas MacArthur to administer Taiwan on behalf of the Allies. An anti-Chinese uprising on February 28, 1947, known as the 228 Incident, resulted in Chiang Kai-shek and his troops killing tens of thousands of innocent people, potential leaders, and members of the elite. After the Communist forces overthrew the Kuomintang (KMT) in China in 1949, there was a large exodus from China to Taiwan. That same year, Chiang Kai-shek declared Taiwan a province of China. The Taiwanese, therefore, have never had an opportunity to exercise self-determination until the present day. For over three decades, the Presbyterian Church in Taiwan (PCT), the largest Taiwanese Christian denomination, spoke against the KMT dictatorship, corruption, and human rights violations. The church's witness against the KMT brought much suffering and persecution to its members.

Taiwan's political changes, the cultural influx from Japan and China, the strong industrial, economic, and cultural influences from the West, and the hard work of the island's people have combined to build it into an industrialized nation. Socially, Taiwan has experienced rapid and dramatic changes and been transformed into a unique community (Athyal 1996, 136).

A Brief History of Christian Mission in Taiwan

The Dutch colonized Taiwan in 1624 and were expelled in 1662 by the Chinese Ming dynasty general Zheng Cheng-gong, or Koxinga (1624–1662). The first Dutch Reformed missionary Georgius Candidius arrived in Taiwan in 1627 and worked among the Siraya tribe in the Tainan area. Another missionary, Robert Junius, arrived in 1629 and was said to have baptized 5,900 aborigines and officiated at the marriages of 1,000 couples. In addition, Dutch Reformed missionaries established many educational centers and programs for the natives, teaching them to sing hymns and psalms and to recite the Lord's Prayer (Loh 1982, 62–65). One of the melodies was the tune for Psalm 100, "Juich aarde, juicht alom den Herr," which was set by Louis Bourgeois in 1551 (Jiang 2001, 219f). A Roman Catholic mission was established as part of the Spanish colony in the northern part of Taiwan from 1626 to 1642. The Catholics taught the natives to read Latin and compiled a dictionary of the native languages and Spanish. The Roman Catholic mission renewed its work in Taiwan as early as 1859 in the Pintong area, seven years before that of the Protestant church.

The modern Protestant mission in Taiwan was initiated by the British Presbyterian missionary James Laidlaw Maxwell (1836–1921) in 1865 in the southern part of the island. The early missionaries also introduced Western medicines and founded the first health clinic (the present Sin-lau Christian Hospital). In Tainan, they established the first official school of Western education called Toa-oh (meaning "university"; it is now the Tainan Theological College and Seminary) in 1876. Missionaries introduced the first printing machine and published the first newspaper in Taiwan (the current Publishing House and the *Taiwan Church News*). They also introduced Western music to the island. Consequently, most of the first generation of medical doctors, musicians, and leaders in the Taiwanese society were Christians.

The Canadian Presbyterian church sent its first missionary, George Leslie Mackay (1844–1901) to Tamsui in the northern part of the island in 1872. There, Mackay established Oxford Academy, which was a forerunner of the Taiwan Theological College and Seminary now located in Taipei. The two missionary societies set the Dajia River in Taichung County as the division between the northern and southern synods, which were eventually united to form the General Assembly of the Presbyterian Church in Taiwan in 1953. Before the end of World War II, there were only two denominations, the Presbyterian and the Holiness churches; there were also a few Roman Catholic churches. The Presbyterian Church currently has 1,218 churches and nearly 230,000 members, including children. It also operates three seminaries, one Bible college, two universities, one medical college, three high schools, and three hospitals with seven additional branches.

Other denominations, mostly from evangelical traditions, entered Taiwan after World War II, especially after the missionaries were driven out of China in 1949. At one point, there were over sixty different denominations or mission groups in Taiwan. Other than the Presbyterians, statistics from 2003 showed the following numbers of congregations: the True Jesus Church (290), Saturday Christian Adventist Church (88), China Baptist Convention (197), the Little Flock (702), the Holiness Church (87), the Chinese Free Methodist Church (62), Bread of Life Christian Church (51), Taiwan Lutheran Church (49), Taiwan Episcopal Church (15), and local independent churches (598). The Christian population today is about 4.81%, including Roman

Catholics. According to Zhu Sancai's 2003 statistics, in Taiwan there are fifty-one denominations including the Catholic church, with a total of 1,082,767 members, 4,831 churches (including 774 Roman Catholic churches), thirty-eight seminaries and Bible schools, seventeen Christian universities and colleges, and twenty-eight Christian hospitals and counseling centers.[24]

Strengths of the Presbyterian Church in Taiwan

The mission of the Presbyterian Church in Taiwan (PCT) and its interpretation of the gospel began with an evangelical or conservative position. But in 1959, the American Presbyterian missionary George Todd advocated PCT churches to open their doors—to be involved in social reconstruction and to actively participate in the process of democratization.

CHRISTIAN FAITH AND SOCIAL JUSTICE

From 1971, the PCT issued a series of statements against Chiang Kai-shek's Nationalist Kuomintang (KMT) government, urging it to reform, to hold national elections, to abolish martial law, to respect human rights, and to declare Taiwan an independent country. Under the KMT martial law, such statements were courageous but offensive. Consequently, the newly translated Taiwanese Bibles were confiscated, church members were frequently harassed, and pastors were wiretapped. After pro-democracy demonstrations resulted in the 1979 Formosa Incident, the Reverend C. M. Kao, the general secretary of the PCT, was imprisoned for over four years. Six other alumni of Tainan Theological College and Seminary were also jailed; one of them, the Reverend Hsu Tian-hsian, was dragged from his pulpit during Christmas worship and was imprisoned. But during those long years of tribulation, the members of the PCT were united and stood firmly together. The Reverend Kao wrote his hymn of confession and witness, "Watch the bush of thorns" (*STB* #252), while in prison. The PCT also issued "The Confession of Faith of the Presbyterian Church in Taiwan" in 1985, stating its position of Christian faith, witness, and commitment to the people of Taiwan. The government finally abolished martial law in 1987, and Taiwan began to glimpse democracy under President Teng-hui Li, who was elected in 1996 despite the threat of Chinese missiles. With the election of Shui-bian Chen as president in 2000 and again in 2004, the Democratic Progressive Party was finally able to lead Taiwan into a new era of genuine democracy. Unfortunately, because of opposition from the People's Republic of China, Taiwan is still denied the right to join the United Nations. Even worse, as of 2009, China has positioned 1,500 missiles aimed at Taiwan.

---

24   Cf. *Taiwan Church Report*, ed. Zu Sancai (Taichung: Christian Resource Center, 2003).

CONTEXTUAL THEOLOGY, MUSIC, AND LITURGY

The term "contextualization" was coined in the late 1960s by Shoki Coe, who in 1948 was appointed the first Taiwanese president of Tainan Theological College and Seminary (TTCS). Because of Coe's ecumenical vision, TTCS has since developed a "homeland theology," a theology of self-determination, experimental liturgies, and new contextual hymn compositions. These practices have subsequently been adopted by other seminaries in Taiwan and Asia.

The PCT faces new challenges from praise choruses and charismatic movements. After publishing a 2002 hymnal supplement with 130 hymns and liturgical responses from thirty-six countries, the PCT in 2009 produced a new hymnal with 650 hymns, which includes historical, ecumenical, liturgical, contemporary, global, and indigenous contextual hymns. Fifty percent of the final product are Western hymns, and the rest are from Taiwan and the Third World; in contrast, the former hymnal contains almost ninty-five percent Western texts, more than ninety-eight percent Western tunes, and no contributions from the Third World.

Some Taiwanese musical instruments in I-to Loh's personal collection:

tong-ling (jingles; used by Han and various tribes)

tong-ling (jingles; used by Han and various tribes)

tatok (four-tone xylophone; used by Truku)

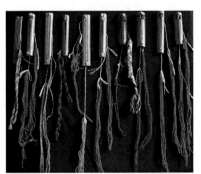

latok, haun-haun (jaw harp; used by Tayal, Truku, Bunun)

132

shuang-ling (concussion bells; used by Han)

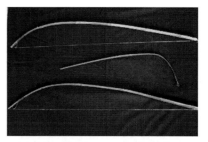

latok (musical bows; used by Paiwan, Bunun)

lalingedan (double nose flute; used by Paiwan)

so-na (shawm; used by Han)

tong-siau

xiao-luo (used by Han)

Commentary on Individual Hymns

"Although barren trees stand hopelessly"
See "MY HEAVENLY FATHER LOVES ME" (*STB* #182)

"BUILDING A JUST SOCIETY"
("Christ Jesus, you have come to us," *STB* #259)

The theme for the ninth CCA General Assembly in Manila in 1990 was "Christ our Peace: Building a Just Society." The five stanzas in this hymn represent the five respective themes and the contents of the respective morning worship services. In order to witness unity in diversity, the Worship Committee composed a tune in the Bunun choral style of Taiwan, which is slightly altered and arranged for this hymn. The hymn is appropriate for occasions when any community is pondering the meaning and strategies of mission, peace, and justice.

The leader intones the first phrase (A = 5 3 2 1) to call on Christ to "make us one," and the chorus completes the sentence. This style of singing is from the Bunun tradition: it is used to report the result of a hunt from afar. The hymn contrasts male and female participation; men sing the bass and tenor in parallel fifths in ostinato patterns while women sing the main melody. The tune BUNUNAR distinguishes the arrangement of the Bunun song.[25] The harmonic singing is based on the Bunun choral style with only a slight variation. For a similar melody with different arrangements, see the commentaries on *STB* #163 and *STB* #190.

"Christ fulfils the law of old" (*STB* #12)
(Taiwanese: *Siong-te lut-hoat te si kai*)

This traditional hymn, number 210 in the 1936 Taiwanese *Seng-si* hymnal, was taken from the Amoy hymnal (from the province of Fujian, China) and introduced to Taiwan by early missionaries. The tune name KIANG-SI should probably be pronounced "Jiangxi," the name of one of the provinces in China (it was customary for early missionaries to pronounce the "ji" sound as "ki"). The text states that God (in the fourth commandment) instructs people to observe the Sabbath as a day for rest, which is now interpreted as a day for worshiping God and receiving God's blessings. The second stanza describes the Lord's day as a celebration of Christ's resurrection and salvation. The two remaining stanzas are prayers to the Holy Spirit for transforming one's character to enable one to worship God in spirit and truth.

KIANG-SI is basically in a typical Chinese five-tone scale: $E_\flat$ = 5 6 1 2 3 with final on 6, but the sixth tone 7 appears twice at the two full cadences. The melody may look rhythmical, but it should be sung with legato without being rushed. The accompaniment, which was composed in 1963, has steady chord progressions that help the flow of the melody. This kind of traditional harmony is more acceptable to congregations in general. (trsl. I-to Loh: para. Jim Minchin)

"Christ is our peace" (*STB* #262)
See the commentary in the section for New Zealand.

"Christ Jesus, you have come to us"
See "BUILDING A JUST SOCIETY" (*STB* #259)

---

25 Regretfully, in the Asian edition, the texts became misaligned during the process of printing. But the whole song is syllabic (one note per syllable), so it should not be too difficult to adjust to this error.

"Come, Holy Spirit, renew the face of the earth" (*STB* #114)

(Taiwanese: *Kiu Seng Sin kang-lim, ho choan se-kai tit oa-sin*)

This is a prayer response, based on the theme of the seventh General Assembly of the World Council of Churches in Canberra, Australia, held in 1991. I composed the music in an Indonesian *pelog* scale, D = 3 4 5 7 1, in 1990. The chorus and congregation sing the ostinato, "Come, Holy Spirit," as an earnest prayer while the other voices cite the main purpose of the petition: to renew the face of the earth. In order to build up the spirit of prayer, the response should be sung several times with all voices ending together at the fermata. This hymn can be used as a response to short prayers, especially on peace, justice, and the integrity of creation. It may be sung once through without repeats, or it may be repeated a few times if desired.

"Find from nature proof of God's grace" (*STB* #308)

(Taiwanese: *Jin-seng chhin-chhiu chhan-ia chhau-hoe*)

This hymn was inspired by a verse from Isaiah 40:6b, 8.

> All people are grass . . .
> The grass withers, the flower fades,
> but the word of our God will stand forever.

The hymn results from the author's painful yet positive reflection on the meaning of life. On the one hand, it affirms the value of all human beings, no matter how talented or how ordinary; all are priceless jewels of God and are loved by God. On the other hand, it laments the helplessness of mortals and the mystery of human life.

This is the story behind the hymn: A woman volunteered to donate one of her kidneys to her older sister, believing that it would prolong her sister's life. But the new organ did the opposite and hastened the end of her sister's earthly days. While mourning and feeling guilt, pain, and loss, the donor restrained her own sorrows and chaired a previously scheduled workshop for curriculum writing. The donor was my wife, Hui-chin Loh. I sat beside her, praying for her and writing this hymn in February 1992; it was sung by the Taiwan Seminary Choir at the funeral a few days later. Hui-chin assisted with the editorial work of *Sound the Bamboo* and prepared all the indexes.

HUI-HIONG is the name of the sister who received the kidney transplant. The music was composed immediately after the completion of the poem. The melody, in a pentatonic scale (B = 6 1 2 3 5), follows the natural intonations of the Taiwanese poem, but the sixth tone 7 appears on the penultimate note as a climax, implying the positive aspects of life in the respective stanzas of the original Taiwanese: "fragrance," " talents," "[paradise] revived," and "never fade." Unison singing is intended to express the delicacy, fragility, and loneliness of life. The flute accompaniment for the fourth stanza suggests hope for and assurance of new life in Christ. Notice the sudden appearance of a foreign tone G♯, which appears with the passage "Christ has risen; he has given a new life, transcending all time and space, and will never decay" (as directly translated from the Taiwanese). This hymn may also be used on other occasions when contemplating the meanings of life and vocation. (trsl. I-to Loh: para. Jim Minchin)

"Flowers of the field" (*STB* #177)

(Mandarin: *Yedi di hua*)

This was one of the most popular hymns in Mandarin-speaking churches in Taiwan, Southeast Asia, and North America during the 1970s and 80s. The text, by Weixin Ye, is a paraphrase of Matthew 6:26–32; it admonishes people to learn from wild flowers and birds and not worry about their needs, for God the Father will provide and will show the way. Both the poet and the composer were then serving at Overseas Radio and Television (ORTV) in Taipei.

ORTV was founded by the American missionary Doris Brougham. Since the early 1950s, Brougham has dedicated her life to Taiwan, not only propagating the gospel through radio and television but also teaching English daily to thousands of listeners. Because of her contributions, she has been awarded governmental prizes and was recently granted an honorary Taiwanese citizenship. She plays the trumpet and directs the Heavenly Melody Choir, which used to appear every week on TV. Their televised performances popularized Christian songs like this hymn.

YEDI DI HUA, meaning "flowers of the wild field," was composed by Wendong Wu, one of the members of the Heavenly Melody Choir. It was included on the group's first album in 1979. Wu has consciously utilized Taiwanese folk idioms in many of his compositions. This tune is in an A = 3 five-tone scale (F = 1 2 3 5 6). The composer's skillful use of triplets, though foreign to Taiwanese folk idioms, provides a contemporary touch to the song. This feature is undoubtedly behind the success and popularity of this hymn, which is enjoyed by the young as well as the elderly.

"For the bread which you have broken" (*STB* #85)

(Taiwanese: *Mi-pau Chu Li ui goan lai peh*)

The original text of this tune was "On the night of betrayal, Lord Jesus took bread." It was part of an African American passion play by Marilou Taggort, which was originally performed in Harlem in New York City in the 1950s. It was introduced to Taiwan by the Reverend George Todd (born 1925). I was then a fourth-year student in theology, and I felt that both the text and the music had to be modified to the language of its audience. So after translating the play and the African American spirituals in it, I composed new "yellow spirituals" in a Taiwanese style to contextualize the work. This was done during the latter part of 1960, and the new play was performed for Passion Week in 1961 (prior to the introduction of the concept "contextualization").

The play received both positive and negative responses. One layperson was moved to tears because the passion of Jesus presented with Taiwanese-style music touched her intimately for the first time. But a theologian questioned the wisdom and relevance of using the local musical idioms, which were not accepted by the church as media to express Christian faith. But I knew then that I had found a suitable musical language to communicate the gospel to my people. This was the turning point of my views on church music, and this passion play marked the beginning of my long journey to the contextualization of music and liturgy in Taiwan as well as other parts of Asia. I still compose in this style.

"Beng-Li" was the Taiwanese name of the Canadian missionary Isabel Taylor (1909–1992), who was my mentor; on her instruction and direction, this play was translated, composed, and performed. Taylor went to Taiwan in 1931. A graduate of the Royal College of Music in Toronto, she was a pioneer in teaching classical piano technique and choral conducting to students in Taiwan. She was also the first to establish a music program in Tamsui Girls High School, which trained the first generation of church musicians. She also served as the executive secretary of the Hymnal Committee of the General Assembly of the PCT that produced the Taiwanese hymnal *Seng-si* in 1964. Together with the British missionary Kathleen Moody (born 1920), they established Taiwan's first Department of Church Music at Tainan Theological College and Seminary in 1959.

The tune BENG-LI and the other "yellow spirituals" in the play were arranged and harmonized in 1970 for more performances in the Seminary and a few churches. The tune was matched to Louis F. Benson's 1924 hymn "For the bread which thou hast broken" in 1981 for the Asian American hymnal project; it appeared first in *Hymns from the Four Winds* (1983), and it was subsequently included in a few hymnals of US mainline churches.

The simple pentatonic melody, with an A = 2 five-tone scale (E = 6 1 2 3 5), similar to a Hypodorian mode in a chorale-like movement, is harmonized in parallel fourths to portray an Eastern sound, and the counterpoint with contrary motions further adds to the beauty of Asian polyphony. The solemn melodic progression seems to fit the mysterious mood of the Lord's Supper. One suggestion is to double the melody of the first two stanzas with a flute or cello; a keyboard may play the treble parts of stanza 3. The fourth stanza concludes with the whole setting (basses con octava) with stronger conviction, as a prayer for the realization of the Lord's kingdom. (Taiwanese trsl. I-to Loh)

"From this time onwards" (*STB* #224)
(Bunun: *Pais ka lau pa ku*)

This is a hymn of discipleship and stewardship, encouraging Christians to love one another and to have deeper trust in and commitment to the victorious Jesus.

The Bunun tribe builds their choral singing in a harmonic series, 1-3-5. Technically, the three tones are the fourth, fifth, and sixth (or seventh, eighth, and ninth) partials of a fundamental pitch 1 (*do*). At some point in prehistory, the Bunun developed a way to sing up to six parts in more or less homophonic harmony, which is unique in the world of choral singing. This particular hymn is sung first by a soloist (C = 1), but after every four beats, the chorus responds in harmony with "u-i-hi" (E = 3-1-5-, with the main melody in the lower alto part) and sustains this "chord" while the soloist introduces another phrase.

"U-i-hi" are non-lexical-syllables, or vocables that have no specific meanings. But in the Bunun tribal culture, these syllables gain meanings from the texts preceding or following the solo. This is also true among the Kalinga in the Philippines.[26]

To broaden the use of this particular hymn, leaders may improvise new texts according to their context, with the congregation responding "u-i-hi." In the response, one should feel free to improvise on those three pitches in any octave and maintain them, i.e., continuing the chord softly while the soloist sings the verse. Make sure, however, that the final "chord" is an open fifth (1-5- without the 3), according to the cultural tradition.

"God created heaven and earth" (*STB* #173)
(Taiwanese: *Chin Chu Siong-te cho thi-toe*)

Most of the early Taiwanese Christian hymns were imported from Amoy in the Fujian province of China, where British or Scottish missionaries served. Since the Ho-lo (or Hokkien) language of Taiwan and Amoy are basically the same, with slightly different accents and vocabularies, it was natural that the early Taiwanese Christians would use the same 1840s hymnal *Iong Sim Sin Si* from Amoy. This anonymous hymn was clearly meant to introduce the Christian God, who is the creator of the universe and the provider of all human needs, unlike the idols that are created by people. It admonishes all people on earth to worship this true God of salvation. The text so succinctly describes the basic Christian teachings that early converts or seminarians in Taiwan would sing and explain the hymn as the main message of their evangelism.

TOA-SIA is the name of a village near Taichung, where the Ping-pu tribe used to reside. One account is that George Leslie Mackay, the first Canadian missionary to serve the people in northern Taiwan, adapted the Ping-pu melody to fit the text, but there is no evidence to substantiate this claim. "Ping-pu" refers to the aborigines in Taiwan who were more assimilated to the Han culture and lived in the plains area. This hymn has become the most popular hymn in Taiwan. It first appeared with both the tune and Romanized text in the 1926 *Seng-si* ("holy hymns"), the first hymnal produced in Taiwan with staff notation and including Taiwanese tunes. The translators, Clare and Boris Anderson, were British missionaries in Taiwan (1948–63). The melody is in a B = 6 five-tone scale (6 1 2 3 5); I harmonized the basically Western setting in 1962; it was further revised for *Hymns from the Four Winds* (1983), for other Western hymnals, and for *Sound the Bamboo*.

---

26 For further explanation, see page XXX in the section "Asian hymns in their historical perspectives."

"God of the Bible, God in the Gospel" (*STB* #255)

See the commentary in the section for New Zealand.

"God, the Lord in love and might" (STB #175)

(Taiwanese: *Siong-te chhong-cho thi kap toe*)

This is a hymn praising God for his creation, and each stanza describes different aspects of God's love and mighty acts: sun, moon, and stars; crops and sea animals; birds and insects; all of humankind—all are within the domain and loving care of God. It concludes with giving thanks and praise to the salvation of Jesus Christ. The Reverend and Mrs. Boris Anderson originally translated this hymn in 1963 for the EACC Hymnal but revised it in 1981.

This anonymous hymn was also imported from Amoy and was probably adapted by George Mackay or some other early missionaries (see the commentary on *STB* #173, "God created heaven and earth," for more information). Tamsui was the base of Mackay's mission work. He married a Ping-pu woman and founded the Oxford Academy in Tamsui. Initially established to train preachers, the college later was one of the first to educate women, at a time when Taiwanese women were not given any schooling. The tune belonged to the Ping-pu of that area, hence the tune name TAMSUI. It is in an Eb = 5 five-tone scale (5 6 1 2 3). The first harmonization was done in 1962, and it has been revised for various hymnals, as experiments to find the proper style for the tune.

I have a special relationship to the Mackays and this tune: both my parents and I were born in Tamsui; my father, Sian-chhun Loh, had been a colleague of Mackay's son at the Tamkang (formerly Tamsui) High School, a Christian institution; my mother Ang Bin was a graduate of the Oxford Women's Academy; and I had been a pupil of both Mackay's daughter-in-law (for Taiwanese Romanization) and one of his granddaughters (for singing) when I attended Sunday school in Tamsui from 1946 to 1948.

"Green the wild fields, blue the sky" (*STB* #257)

(Taiwanese: *Soa-ia chhi-chhui hoe hun-hiong*)

This folk melody is from the Cordillera region of the northern Philippines. Although the non-lexical syllables ("dong-dong-ay-si-dong-i-lay") may not have specific meanings, they are sung in such a way that sounds sad. (For further discussion of the use of non-lexical syllables, see "Let us come to worship God," *STB* #3, and "From this time onwards," *STB* #224). From the melancholy tones, one can almost feel tears being shed; for the hymn's author, the sound suggested the sighing and crying of the devastated earth. The economic growth of industrialized countries in the northern hemisphere has frequently been achieved at the expense of the underdeveloped Third World countries in the southern hemisphere. The greed and selfishness of the developed nations has led to the exploitation of the resources and the destruction of the ecologies of the Third World. The author lived in the Philippines for long enough to witness such exploitation, and he wrote this text to match the solemn melody. The original Taiwanese poem's four stanzas were so dense that five English stanzas were needed to properly express the ideas. To achieve this, Father James Minchin did a superb job with the paraphrasing.

LOK-HNG means "paradise" in Taiwanese. To achieve the feeling of the original song, which is in a C = 6 six-tone scale (6 7 1 2 3 5), one could first sing with the original non-lexical syllables to establish the mood and then sing with the text. It should be sung without any accompaniment, to imply an inner anguish, but the last stanza should be sung a little more quickly and with conviction to "guard each trace of paradise" and "keep alive things heavenly." As literally translated, the passage reads: "Be industrious and thrifty to conserve the heavenly resources, that the paradise of yours and mine may be preserved." (trsl. I-to Loh; para. Jim Minchin)

"Hear now, God's own people" (*STB* #215)

(Mandarin: *Zhu baixing dang qingting*)

ALAIYOAI is an adaptation of an old Paiwan tune in an A = 1 five-tone scale (1 2 3 5 6), which has been simplified melodically by a younger generation that has difficulty singing in the older, more traditional style. According to custom, the opening "alaiyoai" calls attention to certain issues or an important announcement; it is also an invitation, calling people to participate in certain activities. The call is followed by the singer's improvisation on the text. This recalls the "Shemah Israel" ("Hear, O Israel") in Deuteronomy 6:4–9. The original adaptor, Bai-mei Tang, must have had that in mind when she set the Psalm 19 text to ALAIYOAI as a reminder of the importance of keeping God's commandments. The melody has a short range within a fifth or sixth, with reiterated tones (1 1 2 2 2 2), each of which of the same weight, i.e., there is no distinction between strong or weak beats. In performance, therefore, it is important that every beat should have equal strength, and the final tone should have a breathy terminal glide. If desired, one could intone with "alaiyoai" to mark the identity of the song and then sing the texts.

The Chinese text is exactly the same as Psalm 19:7–8 in *Today's Chinese Version* of the Bible, which is succinct and poetic. It uses different expressions to affirm how God's law, testimony, precepts, and commandments are perfect, righteous, and pure in affecting one's soul. Bai-mei Tang was a student at the Yushan Seminary when she adapted this tune. It was first published in *Let the Hills Sing*, a collection of tribal songs (Loh 1986). (trsl. I-to Loh; para. Jim Minchin)

"Holy Spirit, Pentecost gift" (*STB* #152)
(Taiwanese: *Seng Sin kang-lim Go-sun-cheh ki*)

This is the only Pentecost hymn in *Sound the Bamboo*. It recalls the coming of the Holy Spirit that gave the disciples the courage to proclaim the risen Christ. The author, the Reverend John Jyigiokk Tin (Ji-giok Ti) has composed a prayer for courage and strength to speak against the political and religious persecutions of the corrupt Kuomintang regime that jailed many pastors and dissidents in 1979 (see *STB* #252, "Watch the bush of thorn," for further discussion of this period). This is expressed in the literal translation of the refrain:

Help us now, O Holy Spirit,
that we would be as brave as the early disciples,
to face the powers of killing and destruction,
that we may proclaim the purpose of the Lord for saving the world.

GO-SUN-CHEH is Taiwanese for "fifty-day festival," i.e., Pentecost. The tune was composed by the Reverend Raymond Adams, a British missionary who taught church music at Tainan Theological College and Seminary. He was very sensitive to the Taiwanese style of music and composed this hymn in a basically five-tone scale (D = 6 1 2 3 5) without half steps, but he introduced the sixth tone 7 to break the monotony at the end of the second system and the refrain. The melodies of the first and third phrase fit the natural inflection of the poems. Adams was an organist, and his setting in contrapuntal lines is also effective in maintaining the flow of the music.(para. Kathleen Moody)

"Hope for the children" (*STB* #260)

During the ninth CCA General Assembly in Manila in 1990, there was a morning worship service especially designed for children. While preparing for this service, I found this text, which was written by the American poet Douglas Clark. It is a prayer for a world of love, justice, and peace, so that children will have time to grow. During the service, the children cast toy guns and weapons into a fire as a symbol of the end of learning to fight in wars. When wars, crimes, and physical violence are broadcast on TV and adults give toy guns to children, one wishes that more churches and parents would pray with this hymn and teach their young to build a world of peace.

The tune name BKL represents the initials of my three children, Ben, Ken, and Leng. They were all away from home, studying in the United States, when I wrote this music. I chose the scale D = 3 4 6 7 1 3, which is similar to the Japanese *in* scale (3 4 6 7 2 3 1 7…) but is more gentle and peaceful and thus appropriate for conveying the spirit of this hymn. A simple guitar chord accompaniment is provided. The two eighth rests break the rhythmic pattern and add interest to the song.

"HUNGER CAROL"
("Child of joy and peace," *STB* #144)

See the commentary in the section for New Zealand.

"In nature as in Jesus" (*STB* #233)

See the commentary in the section for New Zealand.

"Jesus Christ sets free to serve" (*STB* #247)

The theme for the eighth General Assembly of the Christian Conference of Asia (CCA) in 1985 was "Jesus Christ Setting Free to Serve." The meeting was held in Seoul, the capital of Korea; hence, the tune is named SEOUL. I was the assembly's leader for worship and music. I wrote this text and set it to music in a Korean folk style, with the 6/8 time and lively rhythms that are the most important features of Korean folk songs. I imitated the style and the six-tone scale (D = 3 5 6 7 1 2), emphasizing two important tones (3 and 6) at the beginning with the rhythmic pattern. The accompaniment of the Korean *changgo* hourglass-shaped drum adds excitement to the song and encourages singers to serve the people and to strive for the fullness of new life in Christ. A short song like this should be sung a few times for the singers to establish the mood and the spirit. This song can be interpolated between passages of the sermon to support the message of Jesus' call for mission and service.

"Lamb of God" (*STB* #129)
(Taiwanese: *Siong-te e Iu"-ko*)

Here, the traditional Agnus Dei is set to Taiwanese music in a G = 3 six-tone scale (C = 6 7 1 2 3 4) and in free rhythm. The melody exemplifies mystery and certain Asian musical characteristics; it should be sung slowly and legato. This liturgical piece is usually sung for Holy Communion or Eucharist, especially during the passing and receiving of the elements, as a prayer to Jesus Christ, the Lamb of God, for mercy and granting of peace. Rense Wu composed this for an assignment during the 1989 Summer Church Music Workshop at Tainan Theological College and Seminary, which was sponsored by that school and the Asian Institute for Liturgy and Music. It was first published in the 1990 edition of *Sound the Bamboo*.

"Let all nations come, praise the Lord" (*STB* #96)
(Taiwanese: *Ban-kok ban-bin tioh chheng-chan Ia-ho-hoa*)

This is a setting of Psalm 117 in a three-part sectional canon composed by Shih Chen (whose original name was Panter), one of the most important composers of the Pinuyumayan tribe. Chen might have learned canonic singing technique from the Teacher's College in Taipei or from the Tayal tribe in the north, which is also fond of singing in canons. No matter the origin, the canon is innovative. Chen divides the canon into three sections: X for the initial phrase, which each part performs one measure apart; Y for the two-tone repeated pattern (5 5, and 6 1), which all the parts repeat until the third one reaches the same point; and Z, the concluding phrase in unison. Then another section begins with the same technique and sequences. That is why this form has been called a "sectional canon" (Loh 1982, 317f, 440–42; 1986, 59f). The canon can be sung in as many parts as one desires. This transcription is only for three parts.

KATIPOL is the name of the village where Chen lived. The original title of this canon is "Hai-an-o-yan," which are non-lexical syllables. The Katipol village is along the southeastern coast of Taiwan, where one can hear the sound of the ocean waves, day and night. According to the composer, the repetitive "hai-an, hai-an" represents the constant sound of the waves; hence this song is also known as "The Roaring Waves." I first learned this song in 1948 in Taitung, as taught by my father Sian-chhun Loh in Sunday school. While compiling the Asian American hymnbook *Hymns from the Four Winds*, I recalled this exciting song and decided to "baptize" it into the church as a contrafactum, as Martin Luther had done more than four hundred years earlier. The repeating Y motif reminded me of "Praise God, praise God" in Psalms, so I set this tune to Psalm 117 in English in 1981 and published it in *Hymns for the Four Winds* (1983) without the canonic setting. It was then set to a Chinese text in 1986 for the Yushan Seminary students to record for *Let the Hills Sing*; later, the Taiwanese version replaced the Mandarin one for the 1990 edition of *Sound the Bamboo*. This hymn may be sung at any occasion for praising God. When the congregation is small, it may be sung in unison or in two parts.

"Let all nations praise the Lord" (*STB* #5)
(Taiwanese: *Ban-bin ah, lin tioh o-lo*)

This setting of Psalm 117, the shortest psalm in the Bible, is also the shortest hymn in *Sound the Bamboo*, excepting the liturgical responses. The hymn was written by Xiangqi Zhang during the 1989 church music workshops sponsored by the Asian Institute for Liturgy and Music and Tainan Theological Seminary in Tainan. In one class, students composed melodies with four tones. Zhang was only fifteen years old at the time of the workshop. This simple psalm can be sung at faster or slower tempi, with vigorous shouts or with graceful summons; either approach can communicate various emotions without destroying the beauty of the song.

O-LO is Taiwanese for "praise." The English translation was altered in order to fit the music, which was originally set for a Taiwanese text. The optional simple, drone-like harmony was added later by the editor of *Sound the Bamboo*. This hymn can be sung as an antiphon after any psalm calling for people to praise God, or on other occasions of praise. It can be sung by different genders or age groups, with or without harmony.

"Let us come to worship God" (*STB* #3)

(Taiwanese: *Lan tioh keng-pai Ia-ho-hoa*)

The Ami and Pinuyumayan tribes in the Taitong area are close neighbors; hence they share some repertoires. In addition, both groups are fond of singing songs with non-lexical syllables or vocables, which may have implications that only intimate friends or people within the culture can comprehend or decipher. In daily practice, these syllables can express either sadness or joy, depending on the context or the mood of the singer. In this respect, the non-lexical syllables have as many meanings as one can imagine. This HI-A-O-HO-I-AN tune is popularly sung among members of the Pinuyumayan and the Ami tribes; it may also be found among the Paiwan tribe. It is in an A = 3 five-tone scale (D = 6 1 2 3 5) and is usually sung during joyous occasions with dancing. Gadu Masegseg, a pastor and seminary professor from the Paiwan tribe, taught this song and dance in Makiling in the Philippines, during the Asian Workshop on Liturgy and Music in 1987. I felt that this lively song could be adapted into an excellent song for worship and praise. So I matched this melody to Psalms 100:4–5 and 95:1, 3. The congregation may dance or stamp their feet on every other beat to add excitement to this hymn of praise. It is appropriate to sing this hymn as a processional and dance into the sanctuary to begin worship. Drums and jingles are also good for accompanying this hymn in a /1 1 1 1 11/ pattern.

"'Light and salt' you called your friends"

See "LIGHT OF THE WORLD, SALT OF THE EARTH" (*STB* #254)

"LIGHT OF THE WORLD, SALT OF THE EARTH"
("'Light and salt' you called your friends," *STB* #254)

(Taiwanese: *Chu Li kau-tai goa kang-tia*)

The phrase "rapid social change" was unknown to Taiwan until the 1960s, when Taiwan entered its era of industrialization, which brought a chain of effects and reactions to the traditional agrarian society. Because of urbanization, competition for jobs, desire for economic profit, and rapid Westernization, people were drawn into a massive labor force and compelled to follow the trend. Many people admitted that traditional values and Christian teachings were inadequate in the face of the new challenges. This prompted John Jyigiokk Tin (Ji-giok Ti) to write this hymn, which poses honest and sincere questions to God about how to live up to Christ's expectations of being the light of the world and salt of the earth. This hymn became the official song of the Christian Academy in the 1970s, which Tin had founded to educate laypersons on the relationship of Christian faith and ethics and the contemporary world.

SU-KONG-PAN is the Taiwanese name for the Christian Academy although it actually means "classes for ministries." I composed this hymn in 1968 according to the natural inflections of the poem. Taiwanese is a language with seven tones, and the meaning of a syllable (or word) changes with the tone. In order to make the important messages in the text understood by all who sing or listen to this song, I developed the pentatonic melody (F♯ = 3 in a D = 1 2 3 5 6 five-tone scale) according to the natural intonations of the text. To avoid Western chordal harmony, I utilized counterpoint and parallel fourths to enhance the flow of the melody, the effect of which led the eminent hymnologist Erik Routley (1981, 183) to comment:

> Observe how all three parts in this remarkable three-part invention are in the pentatonic scale. It shows that counterpoint, not block harmony, is the true context of Chinese [sic] music.

Routley was so impressed with this setting that he did a free paraphrase of this hymn into English and included this in *Cantate Domino*, published in 1980 by the World Council of Churches.

"Living in Christ with People" (*STB* #202)

See the commentary in the section for New Zealand.

"Lord, have mercy on us" (*STB* #121)

(Taiwanese: *Chu ah, kiu Li lin-bin goan*)

The Saisiat, one of the smallest tribes in the Xinzhu area in northern Taiwan, has maintained a singing style composed of parallel fourths and fifths since before recorded history. This technique of harmonization is similar to but more complicated than the organum practice in Europe about the ninth and tenth centuries, the early period of harmonic development. It is amazing that the Saisiat, a small group of people (currently numbering about 7,000) on the isolated island of Taiwan, developed such a unique way of singing. I was introduced to this piece through the Japanese ethnomusicologist Takatomo Kurozawa and confirmed this singing technique in the work of the Taiwanese scholar Tsang Houei Hsu. Further, I felt it would be a shame if such a beautiful gift from God, and certainly a treasure of Taiwan, were lost, so I transcribed the music and was eventually able to match it to the liturgical Kyrie. The Taiwanese text fits the music and the mood perfectly. This is another example of a successful contrafactum (the setting of Christian texts to existing folk tunes, or vice versa). This hymn was first introduced at the seventh General Assembly of the World Council of Churches in Canberra, Australia, in 1991, and since then it has been widely used in ecumenical communities. The main melody is in a B = 3 five-tone scale (3 5 6 1 2) ending on 6; the second voice is the same from the second phrase but a fifth lower: a C = 4 five-tone scale (G = 1 2

4 5 6) with final on 2, i.e., parallel motion in consecutive fifths. This Kyrie is best sung as response to short prayers of confession and/or intercession. According to medieval Western music theory, the intervals of the fifth and/or its inversion, the fourth, and the octave were considered in perfect consonance. Thus, a male voice should sing the second part so that the earnest pleas of men and women can be presented to God in "perfect" harmony.

"Lord, we give you heartfelt praise" (STB #112)

(Taiwanese: *Chu, goan kam-sia o-lo Li*)

This short canon was composed by Nai-chen Dai in 1989, at one of the Summer Workshops for Music and Liturgy, sponsored by the Asian Institute for Liturgy and Music and Tainan Theological College and Seminary. It was originally set to a Kyrie, but the music seemed too lively and joyful to be asking for God's mercy. With the consent of the composer, Timothy Tan wrote this new text of giving thanks and praise for God's love and mercy. The music is in a five-tone scale without half steps (G = 6 1 2 3 5); it can be sung as a two- to four-part canon, allowing the congregation's voices of thanksgiving and praise to roar and echo from all corners of the sanctuary. The hymn premiered at the concluding concert of the 1989 workshop and was included in the 1990 *Sound the Bamboo*.
(trsl. Timothy Tan)

"Lord, we thank you for this food" (STB #163)

The Bunun people have three different types of singing. The most complex is the *pashibutbut*, a prayer for the growing of millet and an abundant harvest. It is organized in a set harmonic progression with microtonal intervals: the leader's low and long tone is harmonized by a lower minor third (approximately), which moves down to a fourth. The leader then intones another pitch about one microtone higher, and the second voice harmonizes from a perfect fifth below, ending the first cycle. Then a new harmonic pattern cycle begins on a lower third, fourth, and then a fifth, until this series of progressions reaches an ideal high pitch, when the chorus stops. The genius of the Bunun song is that it portrays the growth of millet through the music, such that one can almost see the grain growing higher as the music ascends (Loh 1982, 340–45).

The second type of Bunun singing employs the overtone series 1-3-5 (see the commentary on *STB* #224, "From this time onwards," for an explanation).

The third type adds a 2 to the existing 5 3 1 melodic line, but this is rhythmically accompanied by 1-5, as in this hymn (#163). The tenor part may be divided into two groups singing "tom, tom" interlockingly (one on the beat, the other off the beat), which imitates the sounds made while pounding rice. This MOTOMASE tune prompted me to adapt it as a table grace or thanksgiving, which may be joyfully sung by a large group sharing a meal. In addition, it reminds people to serve and to love others.

146

"Loving Spirit" (*STB* #220)

See the commentary in the section for New Zealand.

"May the Lord bless you and keep you" (*STB* #79)
(Taiwanese: *Goan Chu su-hok po-ho' li*)

A benediction based on Numbers 6:24, this is written by one of the most prolific composers in Taiwan, Wang-shun Yang. The repetitive motif of the tune su-hok, which means "giving blessings," has a soothing effect. The melody, in an E = 6 six-tone scale (6 7 1 2 3 5), is set with traditional Western harmony, which is for many the most popular and favorable style. This may be sung as a benediction or as a response to sending forth with the assurance of God's blessing.

"MY HEAVENLY FATHER LOVES ME"
("Although barren trees stand hopelessly," *STB* #182)
(Paiwan: *Ku ma lia i ni ka ve nu*)

The statement by the minor prophet Habakkuk, 3:17–18, is really a test of one's faith: "Unless I have total trust, it would be impossible to declare with strong conviction that my Father loves me and cares for me even in the midst of tribulations." Drought, typhoons, floods, mudslides, earthquakes, and other natural disasters are almost yearly experiences in Taiwan. The loss of crops and human lives and poor harvests are realities of life. In this hymn, the young Paiwan pastor Vuluk Lai affirms the love of the heavenly father within the tragedies of natural disasters. It is a statement of unquestionable faith and a witness to the unchanging love of God.

The music INIKAMA VALHIT is a traditional melody of the Paiwan tribe. Vuluk has skillfully adapted it to the new text and has maintained the traditional two-part singing style. The main melody is constructed within a pentachord (five-tone scale within the interval of a perfect fifth 5–2'), E = 5 6 7 1 2, with final on 7. The Paiwan chorus utilizes a reiterated drone (the same pitch repeated) against the main melody, which moves more freely. The drone also moves up and down a major second (5 5 5 and 6 6 6), creating at times harmonious thirds or fourths

In this Paiwan church, the pulpit and communion table are built with local slate.

and, at other times, clashing seconds. The drone and the constantly moving rhythm, without any division of stronger or weaker beats, demonstrate the theology of this hymn—the conviction and trust that, in prosperity or adversity, God's steadfast love endures forever. The final tone of the song includes a Paiwan-style breathy terminal glide downward. This hymn first appeared in *Let the Hills Sing* (1986). One may compare this with the Indonesian hymn with a similar text, *STB* #313, "Oh, the cabbage price is falling." (para. Roland Tinio)

"O give thanks to the Lord" (*STB* #99)
(Mandarin: *Yao ganxie Shang Zhu*)

A call-and-response style of singing is popular among the Ami of Taiwan. Unlike "Praise be to God" (*STB* #32), in which the response is short and in unison, this tune's style belongs to the Southern Ami, whose responses are longer and in three-part contrapuntal harmony. The soloist's call has three different melodies, and the chorus responds to each in three vocal parts: the main melody remains more or less the same throughout the whole song, while the other two parts (tenor and bass) add their own "free harmony" or counterpoint. But all three voices join in unison near the end of the phrase for the cadences.

In 1972, I traveled to the east coast of Taiwan to research and record tribal music. On one Sunday, after the service at Chang-guang Presbyterian Church, about twenty members sang this song, in which I was surprised to hear my name ("Raku sensei" or "Mr. Loh" in Japanese). Later, I realized that the Ami were welcoming me and expressing their appreciation for my recording their songs. Traditionally, tribal leaders take turns improvising a text for the particular occasion, and the chorus responds in support and approval, using non-lexical syllables with the same main melody but harmonized differently in three parts at different times. Their multipart singing technique is called "free or natural harmony," in that all parts develop freely according to their styles but always join in unison or octave doublings for cadences (for further discussion, see Loh 1982, 382).

This experience reminded me of the Jewish tradition of psalm singing, in which the congregation responds with the same phrase or sentence. This also reminded me of contrafactum. My first thought was of Psalm 136, in which the leader intones, "O give thanks to the Lord, for he is good," and the congregation repeatedly responds with the phrase, "for his steadfast love endures forever." In 1981, I set the English text of Psalm 136 to the music and it was almost a perfect match. A new Ami contemporary psalm was born!

Psalm 136 recalls God's love through God's creation, God's delivery of the Israelites from slavery, and God's blessings to them. This song of praise has been used liturgically by Christians through the present. It is interesting in "the way the past impinges on the present and shapes the future" (Mays 1994, 418). While Psalm 136 has twenty-six couplets, this version only uses fifteen, omitting some verses, especially 10 and 11, which are less applicable to the present context.

This can be very effective as a hymn of praise or sung responsively as the psalm of the day. The three-part chorus refrain (one may choose one or more) may also be used as a response to any short prayers of thanksgiving. This hymn first appeared in the Asian American hymnal, *Hymns from the Four Winds*. I reset the text in Mandarin and taught it to the Yushan Theological College Choir, which in 1986 recorded my collection of tribal hymns, *Let the Hills Sing*. The bilingual version of the hymn appeared in the 1990 edition of *Sound the Bamboo*, and Michael Hawn made minor adjustments to the wording for the 2000 edition. The tune name MIHAMEK is Ami for "let us praise." (para. I-to Loh; alt. Michael Hawn)

"Praise Lord Jesus" (*STB* #20)
(Mandarin: *Zanmei Yesu*)

This call-and-response Ami song is in a B♭ = 1 five-tone scale (1 2 3 5 6). The Mandarin text was written by the Reverend Chunfa Tong, whose original Paiwan name is Gadu Masegseg. During the 1987 Asian Workshop on Liturgy and Music in Makiling, Philippines, he taught this song with dance steps to the participants, who had come from all around the world. It was an instant hit because of its simplicity and lively rhythm. The original melody was sung with non-lexical syllables, so people were free to improvise different texts. It is easy, therefore, for people to adapt such melodies to new texts in new contexts and give songs new identities. Masegseg provided a new Christian text to praise Jesus, and I then added two more stanzas for *Sound the Bamboo* in 1989.

With the congregation joined in a circle, with arms crossed, and dancing to and fro in excitement, this hymn may become a powerful praise and witness to Jesus, as the Savior who gives one freedom, the Light who gives one hope, and the true Guide whom one will follow. The main melody may be sung by the leader or by the women, and the men may respond with a strong chest voice. The bass part of the last system may be sung as a solo by the leader or by the men. For further excitement, a drum and jingles may be added using the rhythm provided.

ZANMEI is Mandarin for "praise." This tune is also popular among the Pinuyumayan and Paiwan tribes, and it is likely there are other versions of the song. (para. I-to Loh)

"Praise be to God" (*STB* #32)
(Ami: *Pahemeken no mita*)

The Ami is the largest tribe in Taiwan, with a population of approximately 150,000. They live on the east coast, in three regions, hence divided into the Northern Ami, Central Ami, and the Southern Ami. The singing styles of the three regions also vary. In the Northern Ami, there is a longer call by the leader, followed by short responses from the group; this style is shown in this hymn. The Central group has very complex multipart singing. The Southern group uses a mixture of unison and complex multipart singing.

The Ami have a well-organized social structure; all young men have to go through training stages before being admitted to the adult society, which is divided into grades according to age. Singing, dancing, and hunting are integral parts of their training.

In the Ami society, the village elders have the authority on public affairs, but families are matriarchal—the mother or grandmother has the authority. Respect for and obedience to the elderly or those who are in higher grades are absolutely required.

The call-and-response singing style reflects such social interactions between the leader and the people. This hymn should be sung with a strong chest voice (especially for the men), so that it becomes a powerful call for people to praise God, and to shout for joy because of the everlasting, merciful love of God.

PAHEMEKEN means "to give praise" in Amis. This Northern Ami traditional melody was adapted and set to the text of Psalm 136:1–3 by the Reverend Mayaw Kumud. Many of the Ami songs are in a pentatonic scale, 6 1 2 3 5, with 6 as final. This one is in a B = 6 five-tone scale. The chorus part is considered a continuation of the solo melody and therefore should be sung as one phrase. It is quite rhythmical. If soloists are not available, one part of the choir could sing this role and the rest of the choir could join at the chorus. The last two lines should be sung together. (trsl. I-to Loh; para. Rolando Tinio and J. M.)

"SONG TO THE SPIRIT"
("Spirit who broods," *STB* #222)

See the commentary in the section for New Zealand.

"The God of us all" (*STB* #181)

See the commentary in the section for New Zealand.

"The rice of life" (*STB* #190)

See the commentary in the section for Malaysia.

"Watch the bush of thorns" (*STB* #252)

(Taiwanese: *Chhi-phe ho' he sio*)

An image of the burning bush, the symbol of "burned yet unconsumed" (Exodus 3:2), is the logo of the Presbyterian Church in Taiwan (PCT). This hymn, written by the Reverend Chun-ming Kao while in prison, is a powerful confession of faith. The image of the burning bush reflects the suffering of the PCT, which endured a long period of religious and political persecution by the corrupt and authoritarian Nationalist Chinese Kuomintang (KMT) government in Taiwan. Upholding the Christian faith of the Reformed tradition and speaking the truth in love, the PCT issued statements during the 1970s and 1980s against the oppressive government, urging it to reform, to respect human rights and religious freedom, to hold national elections, to abolish martial law, and to declare Taiwan as an independent country. These statements triggered more ruthless suppressions by the government. The Reverend Kao, being the general secretary of the PCT and the signatory of all the statements, became the main target for reprisal.

On December 19, 1979, the government's aggressive presence during a peaceful celebration on Human Rights Day in Kaohsiung instigated a riot. This was known as the Formosa Incident, which became the KMT's excuse for persecuting opposition elements and arresting dissidents. The Reverend Kao was imprisoned for more than four years for harboring a dissident. Eight others, including five ministers and one elder of the PCT, were also jailed for their support of the movement (cf. Christian Conference of Asia 1990, 49–55). During their trials, all of them made public statements of their Christian convictions, of being obedient to Christ and loving others. The Reverend Kao even volunteered to sacrifice his life and pleaded to the judges to release the others. Their testimonies were full of genuine love and compassion without any hatred (even though they were tortured by the secret police) and so touching that some of the officers were moved to tears. Nonetheless, they were given sentences from three to seven years of imprisonment. But the contributions and witness of the PCT and these ministers played a significant role in the struggle for the freedom and democracy that the Taiwanese now enjoy.

While isolated in his cell, the Reverend Kao wrote this hymn as witness that Christians become stronger and more courageous during persecution.

> When fire and heat subside, seed growth soon resumes;
> the spring wakes what had died, and brings forth new blooms.

CHHI-PHE is Taiwanese for "thorns." Due to my period of study abroad, I felt guilty for not bearing the burdens with others during their persecution. When I was able to return to teach at my alma mater Tainan Theological College and Seminary for the first time in 1985, I immediately set Kao's poem to music. I adapted the wailing song motif, in an A = 3 five-tone scale (D = 6 1 2 3 5), to capture the spirit of agony combined with perseverance and courage to fight tyranny, and I developed it into a new hymn of confidence and hope. The contrapuntal lines echo, imitate, and support the main melody, creating an interconnected feeling. The 7 tone (e) appearing in the last system is a tone painting with theological significance. The sudden use of 7 in a five-tone scale (6 1 2 3 5) is considered improper, and hence it is called the "enemy tone" in Indonesian music theory, but here its appearance has a special purpose. The 7 tone is the climax of the song; not only is it the highest and most striking "enemy tone" but also it is a reversal (an ascending fifth) of the opening figure (a descending fifth), which symbolizes the transformation of adversity to prosperity—"the spring wakes what had died" and brings new life to the burning bush! This hymn is a strong witness of the gospel of hope and is my way of doing theology with music. Flutes or cellos may be used for accompaniment. Stanza 4 is the affirmation of hope and should be sung faster and with conviction. In 2006, Kao's poem, with my choral setting, won the Best Text of the Year, a national prize of the Information Bureau of the Taiwan government. (trsl. I-to Loh; para. Jim Minchin)

"Within your heart and mind, O Christ" (*STB* #188)

See the commentary in the section for New Zealand.

"You have come, Lord Christ" (*STB* #193)

(Amis: *Tayni ci Yes*)

This is one of the first Ami melodies to be adapted as a hymn. The song was originally associated with the digging of shelters for protection from US bombs during the Second World War (Loh 1986, 57f). Although the author of the text is anonymous, some Ami pastors have recently attributed this to the Reverend Sian-chhun Loh and the Reverend Liang-sheng Huang from Likiliki village, Taitong.

Due to long periods of segregation enforced by the Qing government (from about the seventeenth century to 1895) and the Japanese rulers (1895–1945), along with a distrust of the Han, the tribal people were suspicious of a Han pastor visiting their villages and giving medicine to the sick. So it was very difficult for the Reverend Sian-chhun Loh (my father) to share the gospel with tribal people when he began his ministry in 1947. Liang-sheng Huang was one of the early converts and dedicated his life to the ministry, which he served faithfully until his death. I remember that Huang would come to my home and study the Bible with my father; they would spend long hours discussing the meanings of a passage of text and finally would translate it to Amis. Huang also helped to check the hymns that my father had translated. They would sing them again and again until both were satisfied with their work. It is quite possible they wrote this hymn text and fit it to this rather new melody together.

This text recounts the tales of Jesus' ministry among the poor, the blind, and the sick and his casting out of demons and his raising of Lazarus from the dead. It concludes with an affirmation and trust in Jesus as the Way, Truth, and Life. With the exception of raising people from the dead, this hymn reflects how the Reverend Loh and his colleagues followed the ministry of Jesus to serve the poor and the outcasts from hundreds of villages. During those years, there were also a few other foreign and Han missionaries working among the tribes. It is no wonder that after nearly twenty years of evangelism, the missionary success among the tribes in Taiwan after World War II is regarded by missiologists as "a miracle of the twentieth century" (Loh 1986, 6).

TAYNI CI YES means "Jesus coming here." The melody is in the usual five-tone scale: B = 6 1 2 3 5 with initial on 3 (F♯). But the large intervals, wide range, rhythmic contrast, and uneven phrases of this tune distinguish it from other traditional Ami folk melodies; as stated earlier, this tune could well be a more recent composition.

Conclusion

The Taiwanese hymns in *Sound the Bamboo* exhibit musical diversity due to the contributions of the tribal traditions and the borrowing of musical resources from Asian neighbors. Taiwan does not lack musicians or composers, but there are two reasons for the limited number of Taiwanese names and works in this collection. First, Taiwan does lack good poets and/or hymn writers; therefore, many compositions were set to texts by New Zealand poets, especially Shirley E. Murray. Second, most composers in Taiwan have found the Western style of composition more attractive and satisfactory. It would be against the purpose of the CCA hymnal if it included too many hymns that simply imitate those from the West. Taiwan still has a long way to go in developing contextual hymns. It is hoped that some young theologians, poets, and composers will be challenged and inspired by these and other Asian hymns to create new contextual songs for God's people in Taiwan and other parts of the globe.

Mainland Southeast Asia

Mainland Southeast Asia includes the following countries: Cambodia, Laos, Malaysia, Myanmar, Singapore, Thailand, and Vietnam.

 # Cambodian Hymns

The Country, Its People, and Its Music

Cambodia, formerly known as Kampuchea, is bordered by Thailand, Laos, and Vietnam. It has an area of 181,040 square kilometers (about 69,900 square miles), with a population of 14,241,640.[27] Ninety percent of the population is Khmer and related to the Mon of Thailand and Myanmar; the remaining five percent are Vietnamese (some of them Catholics), Chinese (34,000, mostly Buddhists), Chams (about 300,000, mostly Muslim), and about twenty minority groups. Ninety-five percent of Cambodians are Theravadan Buddhists; Christians compose only 0.38% (Athyal 1996, 226f).

The back view of Angkor Wat

Bas-relief of a battle scene. Note the musicians playing the gong and oboe.

Cambodia had a glorious past. Ruling between the years 1113 and 1150, Suryavarman II united the kingdom. He gathered 600,000 workers, 40,000 elephants, and 700 bamboo rafts to construct the temple of Angkor Wat, which is one of the largest religious monuments in the world, to honor the Hindu god Vishnu.[28] It features innumerable bas-reliefs depicting the history, religion, and cosmology of the twelfth-century Khmer empire. Thousands of tourists from around the world visit Angkor Wat to admire this masterpiece of art and architecture.

The conventional history of Cambodia says that two powerful states had already been established when the early Khmer arrived in Cambodia: the Champa of Malayo-Polynesian origin and the Funan people. These two ethnic groups still control portions of Vietnam and present-day Cambodia. Since the sixteenth century, Cambodia has been invaded many times by the

---

27 CIA, "The World Factbook, Cambodia," July 2008 estimate, https://www.cia.gov/library/publications/the-world-factbook/geos/cb.html (accessed January 14, 2009).

28 This information was provided by a Cambodian tour guide.

Siamese (Thai) and Vietnamese. In 1863, Cambodia sought the protection of France, and the next year it became a French protectorate. Cambodia received nominal independence from France in 1949 and full independence in 1953. Its official name since 1993 is the Kingdom of Cambodia (Garland 4:152–54).

Cambodia has experienced civil war for nearly half a century. King Sihanouk ruled the country from 1953 to 1970 and was overthrown by the communist Khmer Rouge led by Pol Pot, but wars between factions continued. General Lon Nol, who was supported by the United States, established the Khmer Republic (1970–75), but the Khmer Rouge again overthrew this government on April 17, 1975. The Khmer Rouge regime under Pol Pot (1975–79) turned the once peaceful land into the "Killing Fields," where over two million people were executed or died of starvation, diseases, or hard labor. In 1979, Vietnamese soldiers liberated Cambodia from the Khmer Rouge and set up another communist regime (1979–91); over one million refugees escaped to Thailand. During the last decade, more churches have been established by various mission groups, and the country is now in a slow process of reconstruction.

The Music of Cambodia

The music of Cambodia is generally divided into three genres: court, folk, and religious. The court genre includes ensemble music performed for ceremonies, dramas, and dances. The folk genre is associated with regional songs, and folk ensembles usually play for various Buddhist festivals and rites of passage. The religious genre comprises music for Hindu and Buddhist rituals. Other genres include modern and Western classical and pop music (Garland 4:154–57).

Khmer musical instruments are divided into three categories: percussion, strings, and winds. Khmer music theory is based on performance and is passed from masters to pupils; written theories are yet to be found. The Khmer musical system is different from that of the Thai. While the Thai scale is based on seven equidistant pitches of 171.4 cents each (the interval of a second), the Khmer scale is without specific theory and is closer to the Western tone (200 cents) and semitone (100 cents) tuning. The ideal and the actual tuning of instruments are not necessarily the same or exact, but the tonalities of the instruments blend when played in ensembles (Garland 4:175).

The following chart compares the intervals on the *sralai* (oboe) and *roneat ek* (xylophone) (after Garland 4:175).

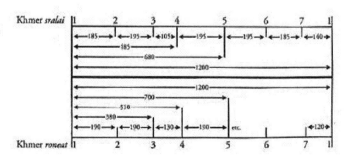

There are two types of scales: anhemitonic penta scale (G = 1 2 3 5 6 1 [G A B d e g] or C = 5 6 7 2 3 5) and heptatonic scale (G = 1 2 3 4 5 6 7 1) (Garland 4:177).

Sam-Ang Sam's analysis of fifty Khmer pieces revealed that the seventh tone F♯ never appeared: twenty-six pieces are in G-A-B-D-E-G (G = 1 2 3 5 6 1), fourteen are in D-E-G-A-B-D (D = 5 6 1 2 3 5), ten are in D-E-F-G-A-B-C-D (D = 2 3 4 5 6 7 1 2) and ten are in A-B-D-E-G-A (A = 2 3 5 6 1 2) (Garland 4:177). When the scales use G = 1, it is easier to understand the scales and their intervallic relationships.

According to Sam-Ang Sam, Khmer musicians do not have theories to guide their tunings, scales, or modes, but they have consensus and understanding of their accepted pitch levels, scales, and modes. The central pitch for the *pinn peat* (ceremonial Khmer court music) ensemble is G; for the *mohori* (secular court music) ensemble, it is C (to fit the range of vocalists) (Garland 4:177). The Khmer identify the musical mode by the final tone of the piece. They also "modulate" to another mode by shifting the tonal emphasis from one tone to the other within the same tuning or scale, usually a fourth above or fifth below. Such a change is usually referred to as a "metabole" in the music of Indochina and Vietnam in particular. In this collection, one hymn shows this occurrence well (see *STB* #206, "O Jesus Christ is True God").

The musical instruments of Cambodia are similar to those of Thailand. This may be seen from comparing a few examples:

Cambodian /	Thai /	description
Chhing	*ching*	concussion bells (o = weak beat)
Chhep	*chap*	concussion bells (+ = strong beat)
Raneat ek	*ranat ek*	xylophone
Thomm	*thong*	drum
Krapeu/chaarakhe	*ja-khe*	"crocodile" zither
Tror ou	*saw*-u	low-pitched bowed lute (with two strings)
Khloy	*khlui*	vertical flute
Ken	*khaen*	mouth organ (with multiple pipes)
Sralai	*pi*	quadruple-reed oboe

A Brief History of Christian Mission in Cambodia

The history of Christian mission in Cambodia is rather complicated. Roman Catholicism was first introduced by the Portuguese Dominicans in 1555; French Catholics entered the country in the seventeenth century, but none of them were successful in establishing churches. The first Christian and Missionary Alliance Protestant missionary arrived in 1923. Over the next decade, the Bible was translated into Cambodian, but it was not published until 1954. In 1965, Prince Sihanouk accused all Americans of working for the CIA and ordered most of the missionaries to leave the country. During the Pol Pot regime, thousands of Christians were killed. In 1989, the Vietnamese withdrew under international pressure, and in the following year, Christianity was formally legalized in Cambodia. In 1993, Cambodia held national elections, and Prince Sihanouk was restored to the throne. The new translation of the Khmer New Testament was also released (Athyal 1996, 226–36, abridged).

A note about Khmer pronunciation

The Khmer language is somewhat difficult to pronounce. Often, many letters appear in one syllable, and the consonants "s," "t," "d," and "k" at the end of a word are silent.

Commentary on Individual Hymns

"Now I know" (*STB* #289)
(Khmer: *Ey lou nis*)

The countries in the region of Indochina share certain musical features, such as the five-tone scale without half steps. Although there are differences in execution or ornamentation, melodies in this part of Asia are frequently constructed in a five-tone scale (D = 6 1 2 3 5) and end on 6. This melody, EY LOU NIS ("now I know"), is taken from a Cambodian folk song. It is in a call-and-response style with four short phrases, which the congregation repeats after the leader. The Reverend Eang Chhun, who participated in the tenth General Assembly of the Christian Conference of Asia (CCA) in Colombo in 1996, introduced this song to me; following my request, he wrote the second stanza. This hymn is a commission, with words of sending forth: "Go in peace and bring good news to all people." It is best sung by a pastor after the benediction, and the congregation should respond accordingly. If the leader of worship is unable to sing, the choir or another member may take the leader's role. (para J. M. & I. L.)

"Now my heart is sure that Jesus lives" (*STB* #312)
(Khmer: *Nouv knong duong chiet knhom*)

This hymn is about Jesus, who takes on all suffering and establishes a peace that is personal, familial, and communal. With Jesus, there are no more troubles. This anonymous hymn shows how Christians have found joy and peace through Christ during and after long wars; it is popular among Cambodians. It was sung by a small group of Cambodian delegates to the tenth General Assembly of the CCA in Colombo, Sri Lanka. Eang Chhun provided the rough translation, and Shirley Murray paraphrased it. One may sing this hymn as an expression of faith and trust in Jesus Christ, especially in times of trial.

The melody MEN PREAS YESU ("Lord Jesus lives") is basically in a B = 3 six-tone scale (E = 6 1 2 3 5 7), but the sixth tone 7 only appears near the end. Like *STB* #279, this melody also has a motif (6 1 32 1) that is repeated three times. Short recurring motifs may be a special characteristic of Cambodian music, but this conclusion has not been substantiated.

"Tell me why are you so afraid?" (*STB* #279)
(Khmer: *Neak ksoy kam Laing roeu ey*)

Taken from a Cambodian folk melody, this hymn asks four questions: "Why are you so afraid? Why are you suffering? Why are they blaming you? Why have you enemies?" But the answer to all is the same: "My beloved, come and serve the Lord. His grace is all you need." Since the author is anonymous, one wonders whether this hymn concerns the long wars of Indochina, in which millions of people have suffered constant fear and the loss of loved ones. The refrain suggests how pastors during those difficult times might have used the Biblical words to console their parishioners. Is the refrain "His grace is all you need" an expression of strong faith or of helplessness when one cannot find answers to the difficult questions in the verses? It might be both.

This tune KUN PREAS LMAUM ("the Lord's grace") was introduced to me (I-to Loh) during the tenth General Assembly of the CCA in Colombo, in 1996. It is in a B = 3 six-tone scale (E = 6 7 1 2 3 5), but the tone 7 only appears once near the beginning. The repetitive descending motif (32 21 6, with an ornament between the 2) is an important characteristic of this song; a similar style is also found in *STB* #312. It is probably one of the common features of the Cambodian folk song. (para. J. M. & I. L.)

"Oh! Jesus Christ is true God" (STB #206)
(Khmer: *Preah Yesu Krist laaw awhjaa*)

This is an excellent hymn for two reasons. First, the text is theologically sound, in that it is a succinct proclamation of God's salvation through Christ. The author states that only the kind Lord Jesus Christ can save one because he has sacrificed his own life as a ransom. But God has raised him and has given one the hope of new life. The second reason is the melodic construction. It is in a diatonic scale, but the melody is a juxtaposition of the same theme in two different keys. Basically it begins with a C-major scale (E = 34 5 4 32 1 2 34 5); at the second system, the same melody has been transposed a fourth higher in an F-major scale (A = 34 5 4 32 1 2 3), but then it returns to C major again at the second half of the phrase. At the end of the third system, it shifts naturally to F to lead into the refrain. In ethnomusicology, this practice is called a "metabole," i.e., the shifting of melody to a tonal center a fourth higher or a fifth lower without actual modulation through harmony (for further explanation, see the section for Vietnam). Both musical phrases carry the same message, "Jesus Christ is true God," but the second time is emphasized and sung in a higher register. The same is true in the remaining stanzas: "Jesus' love is so deep," "Jesus willingly died," and "how we love our dear Christ."

PREAH YESU is Khmer for "Lord Jesus." This hymn may be sung as an expression of one's trust in Jesus and obedience to his call for discipleship. One could use a bowed lute to accompany the hymn, especially to provide the bridge between the stanzas, as indicated with the smaller notes. (trsl. Alice compain; para. Jim Minchin)

Conclusion

Cambodia has rich musical traditions. The three hymns presented here suggest an affinity with those from Thailand and Vietnam. Two recent developments for churches in Indochina are the publication of a new Cambodian Methodist hymnal in 2001 and the release of another Khmer hymnal by the Overseas Missionary Fellowship, with many folk melodies newly adapted for Christian texts. Further developments are expected in the near future.

In September 1997, I visited Siemreab, Cambodia, and was privileged to meet Sokreaksa S. Himm, who is a living witness of the tragedies and the hope of the country that has suffered for more than fifty years. When Sokreaksa was thirteen years old, thirteen members of his family, including his parents and siblings, were hacked to death by hoes; Sokreaksa was with his family, but he miraculously survived. After ten more years of struggle, he immigrated to Canada and completed his education, earning a master's degree. He had originally vowed to avenge his family's deaths, but he returned to Cambodia twenty years later with the love of God. He wished not for revenge according to the Cambodian tradition but to bring the gospel of love and forgiveness to the killers of his own family and to bring about reconciliation. Sokreaksa believes only the love of God and the forgiveness of Jesus as shown on his cross can heal the wounds of millions of people in this nation. Sokreaksa has met with the only living killer of his family and forgiven him, and he has established a few churches in his hometown and other places. He has written two books describing this painful ordeal and how he has struggled to forgive his killers. They are the best books for Christians to learn how to live up to their faith.[29]

---

29 See Sokreaksa S. Himm, *The Tears of My Soul* (Oxford: Monarch Books, 2003); and Sokreaksa S. Himm, *After the Heavy Rain* (Oxford: Monarch Books, 2007).

 **Laotian Hymns**

The Nation, Its People, and Christian Mission

Laos is a long, mountainous country with an area of 236,800 square kilometers (about 91,429 square miles) and a population of 6,677,534.[30] Most Laotians reside along the Mekong River that forms much of the country's border with Thailand. As early as 1353, King Fa Ngum founded the Lao Buddhist kingdom of Lan Xang ("million elephants"), and it was a major power in southeast Asia for 350 years. In 1893, Laos joined Vietnam and Cambodia as a French protectorate. Following the French defeat in Vietnam in 1954, Laos gained full independence, but it became a pawn of the warring forces in Vietnam. In 1975, the Lao People's Representatives Congress accepted the abdication of King Sisavang Vatthana and proclaimed the formation of the Lao People's Democratic Republic (Athyal 1996, 216f). The majority of the people are farmers; most live in severe poverty, with a per capita income of US$144 (Athyal 1996, 218).

Laos has a diverse ethnic composition. According to David I. Andrianoff, it has ninety ethnic groups. Lao Loum (68%, lowlanders living along the Mekong River Valley, Buddhist) is the majority group and language; the other groups are Lao Theung (22%, Mon-Khmer speakers living on mountain slopes) and Lao Soung (9%, animist hill tribes living on mountaintops, along with the Hmong and Yao people). There are 60,000 Vietnamese, 40,000 Chinese, and 5,000 Europeans in the country (Athyal 1996, 216f).

The first Lao constitution was ratified in 1991, in which "the right and freedom to believe or not believe in religions" were specified; however, public evangelism is still prohibited (Athyal 1996, 218, 222). Roman Catholic missions began in the seventeenth century, and the Protestant church began its work in 1872. Today, the Lao government and some Lao people are still suspicious of the Catholic Church because of its former connection with the French government; Protestants are also regarded as agents of the CIA. Missions and evangelism have not been easy. In 1975, there were about 10,000 Christians in Laos. But nearly fifty percent fled the country because of war and unrest. Today, there are only 15,000 members in 150 churches (Athyal 1996, 220).

A Brief Introduction to Laotian Scales

The music of Laos is diverse. Many Laotian classical and folk instruments have counterparts in Thailand. The most popular instrument in the rural area is *khene* (*khaen* in Thai, a free-reed mouth organ with twelve to sixteen pipes), which has seven tones like the Western scale, A-B-c-d-e-f-g (6 7 1 2 3 4 5). There are

---

30   CIA, "The World Factbook, Laos," July 2008 estimate, https://www.cia.gov/library/publications/the-world-factbook/geos/la.html (accessed January 14, 2009).

two anhemitonic penta scales: the *san* scale, G-A-C-D-E (5 6 1 2 3), and the *yao* (or *nyao*) scale, A-C-D-E-G (6 1 2 3 5). There are a variety of modes on *khene*, following the northeastern Thai practice:

San modes: *lai sutsanaen*, beginning with G-A-C-D-E [G = 5 6 1 2 3]

     Lai po sai, with C-D-F-G-A [C = 5 6 1 2 3]

     Lai soi, with D-E-G-A-B [D = 5 6 1 2 3]

Yao modes: *lai yai*, A-C-D-E-G [A = 6 1 2 3 5]

     Lai noi: D-F-G-A-C [D = 6 1 2 3 5]

(Garland 4:338f, 323f)

(after Garland 4:324)

According to Terry E. Miller, "The traditional singer (*molam*) holds a special position in Lao society, not as a professional but as a person knowledgeable about culture, history, behavior, Buddhism, stories, and courtship" (Garland 4:343). *Molam* perform with the accompaniment of *khene* in rituals of healing and possession and for various entertainment occasions.

Commentary on the Hymn

"Dear friends, we're one" (*STB* #311)
(Laotian: *O phi nong oei*)

This hymn is about the sacrificial love of Jesus, "the Lord who calls us friends." Through him, one has hope and new life. The hymn summons all, Jesus' friends, to trust in him.

YESU HAK, meaning "Jesus' love," is a Laotian melody. The song is built on a C = 1 seven-tone scale (1 2 3 4 5 6 7), but 7 only occurs once in the initial phrase, and 4 suddenly appears three times in the third system and then disappears, creating an interesting style. Although all seven tones are used in the song, 4 and 7 only occur at specific phrases, making them exceptions to the scale that is basically pentatonic in nature.

This hymn was taught to me during the tenth General Assembly of the CCA in Colombo, in 1996. Until that time, there were very few hymns from the region of Indochina; the Colombo assembly was the first time that representatives from Laos and Cambodia were able to attend. I took this rare opportunity to request their help and was overwhelmed by their enthusiasm in teaching their songs of faith. Now Christians from around the world can sing and share these hymns with gratitude. If one remembers one's friends in prayers, singing "We're one in Jesus' love" will be more meaningful. This hymn can be sung on any occasion when emphasizing love and unity in Christ. It may also be effective when used on World Communion Sunday.

Conclusion

With the increased missionary work in Laos of recent years, the Laotian church should be able to make further contributions to the field of church music in the near future.

 # Malaysian Hymns

The Nation, Its People, and Its Music

The country of Malaysia comprises Peninsular Malaysia or West Malaysia, which is located on the Malay Peninsula at the southernmost tip of the Asian continent, and Malaysian Borneo or East Malaysia, which is at the top of the island of Borneo. The colonies that composed the former Federation of Malaya gained independence from the United Kingdom in 1957. In 1963, the Federation, Sabah and Sarawak (the two states on Borneo), and Singapore joined to form the new country of Malaysia. But Singapore seceded from the federation and became an independent republic in 1965. The total land area of Malaysia is 329,749 square kilometers (about 127,317 square miles), with total coastline of 5,300 kilometers (about 3293 miles). Malaysia is rich with natural resources and is one of the world's largest producers and exporters of palm oil and rubber. Tin, pepper, copper, and petroleum are also its main exports.

Malaysia is a secular democracy with a constitutional monarchy and adopts the British form of parliamentary democracy (Athyal 1996, 266f). Malaysia has thirteen states and three federal territories, with four states headed by governors: Sabah, Sarawak, Penang, and Malacca. The country has a population of 25,274,132, with at least eighty ethnic groups.[31] Malays and other indigenous groups constitute 58% of the total population; Chinese, 24%; Indians, 8%; and others, 10%. Ethnic groups in Borneo include: Dayak, Kenyah, Kayan, Iban, Bidayuh, Kajang, Punan, Penan, Melanau, Kadazan (Dusun), Bajau, Orang Sungei, Murut. Maloh, Ngaju, Barito, Malay, Javanese, Chinese, Indians, and Eurasians (Garland 4:823–25).

According to the Sabah Tourism Promotion Corporation, the Kadazan tribe (also known as Dusun) includes the following sub-tribes: Rungus, Lotud, Tambanuos, Kimarangan, Sanayo, Minokok, and Tenggera. Like the other groups in Borneo, they are ethnically not Malays but the original inhabitants or indigenous people of that large island.[32]

The religious distribution in Malaysia is: 55% Muslim; 28% Buddhist, Taoist, Confucian, and Chinese folk religion; 7% Hindus; 8% Christians; and 2% other. The Malaysian Constitution states that Islam is the religion of the Federation but other religions may be practiced in peace and harmony in any part of the Federation (Athyal 1996, 267). However, it is understood that one cannot publicly propagate the Christian gospel to a Muslim.

---

31 CIA, "The World Factbook, Malaysia," July 2008 estimate, https://www.cia.gov/library/publications/the-world-factbook/print/my.html (accessed January 14, 2009).

32 From the author's communication with Lu Chen Tiong, in 2004.

A Brief Introduction to Malaysian Music

Students of Sibu Methodist Theological School playing the engkerumong (a gong ensemble of the Iban people).

The musical traditions of Malaysia include various genres of theatrical music, story telling, ceremonial and martial arts music, music related to the life cycles, healing or religious occasions, the cultivation of rice, and entertainment (Garland 4:402). Shadow puppet (*wayang kulit*) theaters are among the most popular; the performers are Javanese descendants in the Johor area. The instruments used are the Javanese gamelan in *slendro* tuning (five tones without semitone: 1 2 3 5 6), including *saron* (metalophones in three sizes: *demung, barung, peking*), *bonang* (kettle gongs), *gambang* (wooden xylophones), *ketuk* (gong), *kenong* (large kettle gong), *kempul* (suspended gong), and *gong agung* (the largest suspended gong). The most elaborate dance drama is *mak yong*, which originated in the northeast state of Kelantan and the southeastern Thai province of Patani and Narathiwat. It includes dialogue, singing, and dancing, with the accompaniment of *gendang* (drum), *tetawak* (bossed gong), and the three-stringed *rebab* (bowed lute) as the main instruments; others, such as *serunai* (oboe), *geduk* (drum), and *canang* (gongs) may be added (Garland 4:402–07).

Since the Malay people are Muslim, their religious music is important in their daily lives. The chanting of the Qur'an (or Koran) is regarded as the highest form of art. It can be a solo or performed in unison, unaccompanied, with a syllabic or melismatic style, and with embellishments that involve glottal stops, single and double grace notes, slides, turns, and wide tremolos. Another form of cantillation is the call to prayer (*azan*) five times each day, chanted by a man amplified by loudspeakers, which everyone in the city or village can hear (Garland 4:430f).

Asli and Dondang Sayang

Asli refers to traditional Malaysian music. It may have developed from the *dondang sayang* ("melody of love") of the Malaysian Chinese community in Malacca. In *asli*, the texts are composed, but in *dondang sayang*, they are improvised. The melodies mostly move in major and minor seconds and are therefore very chromatic, and they have a binary form (AB). The typical rhythm is in an eight-beat cycle notated in two measures of 4/4 time, with a tempo of about one beat per second (Garland 4:433f).

Western and Indonesian influences on Malaysian music are strong and may be seen in contemporary and urban music. *Keroncong*, probably the oldest form of popular Malaysian music, is related to Indonesian music that originated in the former Portuguese colonies of the Moluccas and Batavia (present Jakarta). Another type of music is called *dangdut*, which is of Hindustani origin and is accompanied by the tabla (drum) and the electric

sapeh, sambe, sapi (3 strings, pecked, plucked lute)

guitar. The most popular pan-Malaysian folk songs are called *lagu-lagu rakyat*, which have diatonic scales and Western harmony but do not necessarily follow Western progressions (Garland 4:438f). See RASA SAYANG, the melody of *STB #22*, "Now let us tell of your victory," for one example.

This illustration shows the rhythms of pestles, mortar, and bamboo poles of a Central Borneo ethnic group, the Kayan (after Garland 4:832).

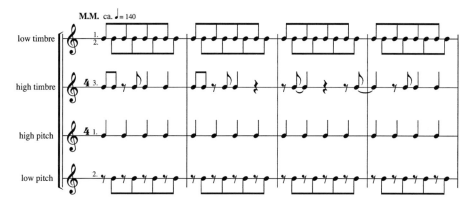

Many songs are in call-and-response forms, and the singing style is very complicated. Instrumental ensembles include many kinds of Indonesian bronze gongs, drums, and *kulintang* (xylophones, like those from the southern Philippines). They also have *togunggak* (bamboo tubes), *alu* (wooden pestles), and *gambang* (xylophones), *sapeh* (lute), *satong or lutong* (tube zithers), *suling* (flute), and mouth organs (*engkerurai, sumpotan, keledi,* etc.) (Garland 4:835f).

The *lekupa* ("dance of war") song of the Kenyah people is in two parts. The solo is syllabic and almost without ornaments, and the group joins in unison or sometimes in harmony (see illustration, after Garland 4:826).

Another style of ritual song (*kui* or *kue*) is performed before seed planting. The soloist sings a melismatic melody over the chorus's movable drones (see illustration, after Garland 4:827).

A Brief History of Christian Mission

Malaysia's earliest contact with Christianity may have taken place as early as the seventh century, through the Nestorians. Catholicism, which arrived with the Portuguese colonizers in 1511, tainted the image of Christianity for the Malaysians. The British, who arrived in the eighteenth century, were largely concerned about trade and economic exploitation; thus, Christianity was still regarded as a "conqueror" religion. In 1641, the Dutch gained control of Malaysia, and in 1753, they built the first Protestant church in Malacca, which served the needs of the Dutch settlers. In 1786, the British established colonial rule over the country (Garland 4:401), and in 1843, Benjamin Keasberry became the first to minister among the Malays and Malay-speaking Chinese. During the past 150 years, numerous mission societies from all denominations of the West have worked in this country, either in evangelism or social services. Daniel K. C. Ho reports that the Christian population is now approximately 1.1 million, of which less than fifty percent is Roman Catholic; the rest are Anglican (156,000 members), Methodist (85,000), and members of the Sidang Injil Borneo (Evangelical Church of Borneo), which is the largest Protestant denomination in Malaysia, with approximately 160,000 members and 1,300 churches. In Sabah and Sarawak, the Christian population is about thirty-five percent of the population. Ecumenical cooperation among many denominations led to the formation of the Christian Federation of Malaysia (CFM) in 1986. It comprises the National Evangelical Christian Fellowship (NECF), the Council of Churches of Malaysia (CCM), and the Catholic Church in Malaysia (Athyal 1996, 270–77). The Sabah Theological Seminary was the first institution to begin mission work and theological education among the Kadazan/Dusun people of northern Borneo.

Commentary on Individual Hymns

"Come one and all, let's follow Christ, our Lord" (*STB* #78)

(Kadazan: *Kanou kanou tumanud do Tuhan*)

This song summons all youth to follow Christ and to realize that one's body is the temple of the Lord; one may be holy and offer oneself as a living sacrifice to the Lord. This hymn is appropriate as a response to the call for discipleship or as a sending forth.

The tune KANOU (meaning "come") is a contemporary Kadazan melody. It is in a C = 1 seven-tone scale (1 2 3 4 5 6 7) with a lively rhythm. The refrain is in a b a form, and the rest of the song is through-composed. All of the phrases, except the last one, begin with 5̲ 5̲ (*sol*); the reiterated tones (2̲2̲2̲, 3̲3̲3̲, 1̲1̲1̲) and the three-note descending motive (3̲2̲1, 6.5̲4̲, 7̲6̲5̲) are prominent features in this song. The embellishments are also important elements of the folk style. (trsl. Alison Ng; para. Maria Ling)

"God has formed the church to be" (*STB* #240)

(Mandarin: *Jidu jiaohui Shen suo li*)

Both this text and the tune SIBU were written by Tiing-chang Ling, a Malaysian Chinese who was a principal of a primary school and a lay preacher in Sibu, East Malaysia. Although Ling had written a few hymns already, this was the first for which he spent a long time contemplating the meaning of the church and the ways it should relate to all Christians. The text states that all the churches of many peoples and cultures are reconciled in one body of Christ; Christians should have proof of their faith through their deeds and should shine their light of hope. The refrain is a summary of the unity in one faith and baptism in Christ, the "only Rock" of one's salvation. This hymn may be sung after the sermon as an affirmation of faith, a prayer for church unity on Ecumenical Sunday, or for Holy Communion.

Ling was invited to attend the 1987 Asian Workshop on Liturgy and Music, after which he stayed in Manila to study hymn writing. An industrious student at the age of sixty, he created many hymns and poems for his assignments, including this hymn.

The melody is in a D = 5 traditional Chinese, five-tone scale (G = 1 2 3 5 6) without half steps, and it is through-composed. The refrain incorporates syncopation to add vitality to the text. At the request of the poet/composer, Pen-li Chen treated the melody with traditional Western harmony. A few spots of unison or octave doublings are intended to portray typical Chinese melodic progressions. (trsl. I-to Loh; para. Jim Minchin)

"Hear our prayer, O Lord" (*STB* #110)

This is a prayer response, written in a Malaysian style. Due to Western influence, today's Malaysian folk music is frequently in major tonalities. The most characteristic cadence comprises four sixteenth notes within the intervals of a third or fourth before the final, which is lengthened: 3 5 4342 3-. Striking a large gong at the final note 3 would add more weight to this petition as well as reinforce the Malaysian style.

This is appropriate as a response to prayers of petition or intercession, in which the individual prayers should not be long, just a few sentences; then, all can join in singing this response to own the prayer and to add a community spirit to the prayer. This was composed by a Malaysian Tamil, Calvin Chelliah, the first graduate of the Asian Institute for Liturgy and Music (AILM), in Manila, in 1984.

"O LORD our God, have mercy on us" (*STB* #125)
   (Malay: *Ya, Tuhanku*)

This is a Malaysian Kyrie that addresses the LORD six times without addressing Christ, which is unconventional but acceptable in non-liturgical churches. The music was composed by Calvin Chelliah in a G = 1 seven-tone scale (1 2 3 4 5 6 7) with a raised fourth degree (♯4), which is only used twice as a lower neighboring tone of 5 (D). All three phrases begin on the second beat, the last part of the third phrase is syncopated, and the two cadences (four sixteenth notes 5434, 2372) are typical of a Malaysian folk style. One should not be misled by these cadences; they may sound joyful but do not necessarily convey joy. This response is best sung after prayers of intercession, and a large gong may be struck on the first beat of the last measure.

"The Lord is pure unbounded love"
   See "VOCATION" (*STB* #211)

"The rice of life" (*STB* #190)

Rice is the most popular staple food for most Asians. The Western or European Christian metaphor of Jesus as the bread of life may be foreign to many Asians, who have little or no experience of eating bread. Even Asians who live in the West are not satisfied unless they eat rice at their meals. The Reverend Andrew Fowler, an American United Methodist missionary in Malaysia, wrote this hymn to reinterpret the unfamiliar Western concept of bread in the primarily rice-oriented societies in Asia. He wrote:

For the Iban of Malaysia, rice is the basic ingredient of a meal. Other food that may be available to put on the rice is lumped together under the term *lauk*. For the traditional Iban, eating rice is considered to have a spiritual dimension, connecting them with their ancestors. From their perspective, a meal without rice, even if the person is full, leaves the person unsatisfied.

True life in Christ is a gift that satisfies. Jesus taught his disciples to pray each day for the staple food which sustains life. By example, Jesus taught his followers to feed all who are hungry, providing for physical needs, spreading the gift of his mercy, and showing his vulnerable compassion. The "rice of God," on physical/spiritual totality, is intended for all people. No one who comes is turned away.[33]

BI-NIU is Taiwanese for "rice-food," denoting all foods and nourishment for life. The melody is an adaptation of the Bunun rice-pounding song MOTOMASE from Taiwan (see *STB* #163, "LORD, we thank you for this food"), but the composer has combined two Bunun singing styles, one in B♭ = 5 3 2 1 and the other in E♭ = 1 3 5 (see *STB* #224, "From this time onwards"), making a new kind of "Bunun" music. The gliding tones up to 1, or from 2 down to 1, are important features of Bunun-style singing. Therefore, congregations are encouraged to glide naturally through these tones.

"This is the God beyond all gods" (*STB* #139)

(Thamilz: *Karthaadhi karthar iveree*)

Witnessing the birth of Jesus, the God beyond all gods, the King above all kings, D. A. Chelliah goes beyond describing the nativity scene to invite all to become cradles to hold Him, to find healing and peace. I added a stanza that states the spiritual as well as physical dimensions of the good news (Luke 4:18). This hymn may be sung as a meditation on the meaning and purpose of incarnation, especially during the Christmas season.

The Reverend D. A. Chelliah, the father of Calvin Chelliah, composed his own melody for KARTHAAR, which means "Lord." The melody is in a B = 5 seven-tone scale (E = 1 2 3 4 5 6 7) with a sharpened fourth (♯4) and in a simple a a' b b' form. The lively rhythm and the ornaments make this a joyful Christmas carol in a contemporary Indian style. This song would sound European without the ornamentation, but an Indian character emerges with the melodic embellishments. (para. I. L. & J. M.)

---

33   From the author's correspondence with Fowler, September 9, 2004.

"VOCATION"
("The Lord is pure unbounded love," *STB* #211)

This hymn is based on John 15, reflecting the idea that one is pruned by God's love so that one can bear fruit. The emphasis is to share other people's pain and joy and to offer oneself as a sacrifice, so that others can come to know God's love in Christ. The first line was borrowed from Charles Wesley's hymn, "Love divine, all loves excelling." This hymn was written by an American United Methodist missionary, the Reverend J. Andrew Fowler, and was first sung on January 4, 1982, at the Ecumenical Christian Center near Bangalore, India, during the fifth International Association for Mission Studies Conference. Concerning the singing of this hymn, Fowler wrote:

> The conference participants from five continents removed their shoes and sat on mats covering the floor of the simple chapel. The focus of attention was on a polished Indian oil lamp. The lamp burned brightly while flowers filled the tray in which the lamp stood. As we sang the hymn that night, we experienced afresh God's mission to all.[34]

Julia Chong, one of the most famous Malaysian composers, wrote the tune KUCHING (which means "cat" and is also the name of the capital of Sarawak, East Malaysia, where Chong lived). It is in a C = 3 seven-tone scale (F = 6 7 1 2 3 4 ♯5) and is through-composed in a Western style, but it has the feeling of contemporary Malaysian folk songs, especially in the triplets near the end of the two phrases. The Western harmony has been altered and simplified by Francisco F. Feliciano to suit the simplicity of this tune. Singers and/or conductors should make sure that the music is not performed too slowly. Counting once per measure, i.e., swinging one's arm once each measure, will enhance the flow of the melody. This hymn may be sung as a response to a sermon or as a dismissal after the benediction.

"We all believe in one God of love" (*STB* #51)
(Kadazan: *Kasip oko sid kinoringan*)

This is a confession of faith to the triune God of love: the Father who answers one's call for help, the Holy Spirit who guides one in the new light, and the Son the Savior who gives one new life. The refrain affirms that no other god's love can exceed God's great love for all.

The tune KASIP OKO (meaning "I believe") is a Rungus melody from Sabah, in northeast Malaysia. The melody is in an F = 1 major scale (1 2 3 4 5 6 7) and is characterized by almost isorhythmic (repeated rhythm) phrases with reiterated tones (1 11 1, 2 22 2 , 5 55 5) and descending motifs (2176, 3216, 6543). The phrase structure is a b a c , in which the b is the imitation of a but is one tone higher. The refrain is almost the replica of the first two phrases, transposed a fourth

---

34   From the author's correspondence with Fowler, September 9, 2004.

higher (almost like the metabole in *STB* #206), with only a minor difference. This hymn could be a simple way to teach young people or Sunday school children the basic concept and the roles of the three in the Trinity or the doctrine of God.

"Your word will be a lamp to guide our feet" (*STB* #46)

This anonymous Malaysian hymn, popularly sung among the Tamil Christians, was translated by Calvin Chelliah. It is an affirmation of God's word as a lamp to guide one's feet and songs of joy; God's word also proclaims the love of Jesus, the "Light of the world, and the true bread of Life." This hymn is best sung liturgically after the reading of the scriptures or after a sermon.

The melody KUTHU VILLEKU ("lamp stand") is in an F = 1 seven-tone scale (1 2 3 4 5 6 7) with a raised fourth (#4) as a lower neighboring tone of 5. The phrase structure is a b c c b' with repetitions. The glides and embellishments are important in conveying an Indian style. A pair of concussion bells may be used for accompaniment (in the pattern /o + o +/, where o = open and + = closed; for more information, see the Thai section of this volume). (trsc. and trsl. Calvin Chelliah; para. I. L. & J. M.)

Conclusion

Malaysian hymns exhibit a diversity of styles that reflect the ethnic composition of the country. Malaysian Christians (albeit Chinese, Kadazan, Iban, and Indian) can learn much from the existing folk musical traditions. I spent two months teaching at theological seminaries in Sabah and Sibu (a town in Sarawak) in 2005, and I felt very uneasy about the loss of musical traditions among most of the ethnic groups. The Westernization as well as Christianization of native people should not occur at the expense of losing indigenous musical and artistic gifts from God. It is, therefore, an urgent task for all concerned, and even more so for Christians, to investigate, preserve, develop, and promote the music of all Malaysian ethnic tribes while some indigenous art forms are still alive.

 **Myanmar Hymns**

The Country, Its People, and Their Religions

Myanmar, formerly called Burma, is surrounded by Thailand, Laos, China, Bangladesh, and India. It has a total land area of 657,740 square kilometers (253,955 square miles), which is slightly smaller than that of Texas. Its total population is approximately 48 million: 68% Burman, 9% Shan, 7% Karen, 4% Rakhine, 3% Chinese, 2% Mon, 2% Indian, and 5% others.[35] In addition, other groups such as the Chin and Kachin contribute to Myanmar's ethnic diversity; there are 107 languages spoken (Johnstone 2001, 462; Garland 4:363). The country is rich with minerals and precious stones; because of corruption and imperial theft, however, the majority of the people live in poverty.

Myanmar, after losing three wars to the United Kingdom from 1824 to 1885, was ruled by the British as part of India until 1937 and finally achieved independence in 1948. A military junta has ruled the country since 1962. There have been popular demands for democracy, including an election in 1990; despite the opposition party's winning eighty-five percent of the seats in the parliament, the government refused to relinquish power. Aung Sang Suu Kyi, the heroine of the people's nonviolent struggle for freedom, won the Nobel Peace Prize in 1991, but she was denied her right to accept the honor in person and has been repeatedly under house arrest from 1989 and was just released in 2011. Myanmar is one of the few countries that are still suffering under a military dictatorship; the people do not have the freedom to travel abroad or to participate in international conferences. The country subscribes to Theravada Buddhism, which has affected the whole culture. Yet it is no longer the official state religion.

Christianity entered Burma during the sixteenth century with Portuguese Roman Catholic priests, but the arrival of the American missionary Adoniram Judson in 1813 was the first to have an impact. According to historical accounts, Judson was only able to win the first convert after six years of hard work. His dedication and missionary success was recognized by Brown University in the United States, which awarded him an honorary doctorate, but he rejected the offer and returned the degree. In 2004, the country celebrated the 190th anniversary of Christian mission on July 11, the day before Judson's arrival 191 years earlier. I had the privilege of witnessing this day and attended a special service in a small rural church. It was unfortunately disturbed by the loud music emanating from the Buddhist temple next door. According to the leader of the church, this was a common occurrence, which illustrates the difficulties faced by Christians in Myanmar.

---

35   CIA, "The World Factbook, Burma," July 2008 estimate, https://www.cia.gov/library/publications/the-world-factbook/geos/bm.html (accessed January 15, 2009).

In Myanmar, the religions practiced are Buddhism (82.9%), Christianity (8.7%), and Islam (3.8%). Of the total Christian population of about 1.8 million, the Baptist Convention is the largest denomination, with 3,750 congregations and 617,781 members; Roman Catholics have 1,096 congregations with 372,671 members. The Assemblies of God and Churches of Christ have over 100,000 members each (Johnstone 2001, 462).

In 1966, the military regime expelled all foreign missionaries and nationalized more than 800 private schools, most of which were originally founded and administered by churches. The government does not allow the importing or printing of Christian books. All publications are censored, and paper for printing is tightly controlled. Today, there are about twenty-nine Bible schools and seminaries, which are members of the Association of Theological Education in Myanmar (ATEM). Nationwide, there are over ninety theological institutions, many of which are small and independent (Johnstone 2001, 464). It is encouraging that the churches and their educational institutions are under native leadership and that churches among the Karen and other minority groups are growing rapidly (cf. Athyal 1996, 350–55).

Burmese Music and Theory

The earliest reference to Burmese music is found in documents that tell of musicians and dancers sent by the Pyu in Burma to the Chinese Tang-dynasty court in the 800s. Only about fourteen of the musical instruments described in this chronicle correspond to modern Burmese instruments; two examples are harps and lizard-head zithers (Garland 4:365).

Burmese music is generally divided into two styles: outdoor, loud, and vigorous music and indoor, quiet chamber music. The typical outdoor ensemble is a *hsaiñwaiñ* but is usually called a *hsaiñ* and may include a *pa'waiñ* (a circle of twenty-one tuned drums hung on a wooden frame), a *ciwaiñ* (a circle of twenty-one bronze, knobbed gongs), a *pa'ma* (large drum), *yakwiñ* or *lakwiñ* (large cymbals), *si* (small cymbals), and a *hne* (multi-reed oboe).

The ensemble requires six to ten persons to play all of the instruments. It is the most important outdoor ensemble for the accompaniment of theatrical performances, rituals, religious functions, ceremonies, and funerals (Garland 4:367).

An indoor chamber ensemble may consist of a vocalist and one instrument, either a *sauñ* (arched harp)—the most important Burmese instrument—or a *pa'tala* (bamboo xylophone), and sometimes a *palwei* (bamboo flute) (Garland 4:366–78).

The *sauñ*, a fourteen-string arched harp with an elegant form resembling a swan arching its neck, is considered the most prestigious instrument and is associated with the refined and sophisticated royal courts. It is believed that the harp arrived in Burma from India (Garland 4:377f). The harp has become an important national symbol of Burmese music and is now being taught in the schools; many young female students are learning to play this elegant instrument, which is a positive sign for a brighter future.

Burmese Tuning and Theory

The Burmese system of tuning is often compared to the Western C-major scale but in descending order. The seven pitches are named according to the fingering system, or the number of holes covered when playing the oboe (*hne*): two for the pitch 7, three for 6, etc. The names of the pitches in the scale are different for the instruments of a chamber ensemble and a *hsaiñ*, as follows:

Chamber ensemble	Degree	Hsaiñ
Hnyiñlouñ	tonic	*thañ hmañ*
Pale	seventh	*hnapau'*
Duraka	sixth	*thouñpau'*
Pyidopyañ	fifth	*leipau'*
Au'pyañ	fourth	*ngapau'*
Myiñsaiñ	third	*hcau'pau'*
Hcau'thwenyuñ	second	*hkuni'pau'*

(Garland 4:386f)

In the classical Burmese tradition, the seventh and third degrees of the scale (7, 3) are slightly lower and the fourth degree (4) is slightly higher than the corresponding tones in a Western scale. But different instruments also deviate slightly from others, much like the Javanese or Balinese gamelan tuning in which there is general agreement on the shape of the scale but not the exact pitch (Garland 4:385–87). Robert Garfias lists the first four of the nine modes of the *hsaiñ* ensemble with their approximate Western equivalents:

Thañ you hcau'pau'	C E F G B [1 3 4 5 7]
Hkunithañci	G B C D F [5 7 1 2 4]
Pa'sabou	C D E G A [1 2 3 5 6]
Tahcañ pou	C E F G A [1 3 4 5 6]

(Garland 4:391)

Students of Burmese music usually study singing before learning to play instruments. As part of their training, they have to learn the "First Thirteen *Cou*" songs. A system of solfege has been developed that represents rhythm, melody, and correct strokes and pitches on two-part instruments (Robert Garfias, quoted in Garland 4:397f). The first three most important pitches of a mode are *tya* (the fundamental pitch 1), *tei* (the 7), and *tyo* (the 5). The names of the melodic patterns are *dyañ* (a falling third), *htañ* (a ninth built on the fundamental of the mode, and *htouñ* (a fifth) (Robert Garfias and Muriel Williamson, quoted in Garland 4:397f).

The following is a transcription of a *hsaiñ* piece by Robert Garfias (after Garland 4:386).

FIGURE 18 *Na'* song in version for *hsaiñ* or chamber ensemble (excerpt). Transcribed and provided by Robert Garfias.

About 3.4 million Karen live in the northern part of Myanmar, Laos, and Thailand, and they are usually divided into four subgroups. ("Karen" should be pronounced "kayiñ" just as "Rangoon" should be pronounced "yangon.") Their language has as many as six tones and belongs to the Tibeto-Burmese language family. The Karen are very musical people, and singing is related to all aspects of life. Their scales are:

D-E [2 3]; D-E-G [2 3 5], D-F-G [2 4 5], E-A-C [3 6 1];
D-F-G-C [2 4 5 1], D-E-G-A [2 3 5 6], E-G-A-C [3 5 6 1];
D-F-G-A-C [2 4 5 6 1], C-E-F-G-B [1 3 4 5 7]

(Garland 4:545)

Burmese instruments in the collection of I-to Loh:

khuang te (double-headed frame drum of
the Chin people)

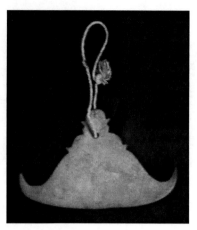

kyai si (bronze drum/bell)

sauñ (arched harp with fourteen strings)

Pronunciation guide

Although there are only two distinct tones in the Burmese language, the syllables are further differentiated by voice quality, duration, and the presence or absence of the final glottal stop. According to Ward Keeler, this results in five syllables:

1. high, short, "creaked" (with a slight, final glottal occlusion)
2. high and heavy (in final position, falling)
3. high with a full glottal stop
4. low, though sometimes pronounced as a rising tone
5. toneless

(Garland 4:383)

Because of the complexity of tone-tune relations, it is very difficult (and beyond the scope of this book) to examine the details of the art of singing in Burmese. One can find information on the Burmese treatment of melody in vocal music in the works of Muriel Williamson (1981) and Robert Garfias (1981) (Garland 4:383–85).

Commentary on Individual Hymns

"Come, O come, let us praise parent God" (*STB* #1)

(Burmese: *Lajahle, htaora Hp'ya*)

This is a short hymn inviting people to come and praise the Trinity: the Parent God for his love, Christ the King for his grace, and the Holy Spirit for his fellowship. The last phrase of each stanza repeats a part of the previous phrase. The literal translation for the first stanza is:

> Come all. Eternal God, eternal God, for whose divine love
> let us praise, whose divine love, let us praise.[36]

This hymn was chosen to be the first in *Sound the Bam*boo to put the churches in Myanmar at the forefront; perhaps more people around the globe will remember Myanmar in their prayers. This hymn is appropriate as a call to worship, inviting people to praise the triune God.

The tune LAJAHLE ("come all") was composed by Saw Gideon Tun Shwe in the Karen style. ("Saw" is the Karen honorary title for a gentleman, like "Mister" in the West, and the Karen do not specify their family names. Sometimes the composer of this hymn is called Tun Shwe or Gideon Tun Shwe.) Saw Gideon set this tune to the text he composed for the University Christian Fellowship in 1975. This tune is in an A = 5 six-tone scale (D = 1 2 3 4 5 7) without the 6. The repeated ascending motif (5 7 i-) is the important feature of this call to praise, which may be accompanied by long drums, gongs, and cymbals. (para. I. L. & J. M.)

"Glory be to the Father" (*STB* #106)

(Burmese: *Khame daw ta daw htan chi moñ*)

A mini-doxology giving glory to the Trinity, this is set to a Karen melody, which is in an F♯ = 3 four-tone scale (E = 2 3 5 6) with the final on 3. Among four short phrases in a b a c form, all three begin with 3 6; only the last phrase begins with 2. The Karen are very musical people; they are also known for singing choruses in Western harmony. One can sing this doxology following the reading of the Psalms, the Gospels, the New Testament, the forgiveness of sins, an offering, or at the close of a worship service.

According to Saw Tun Meh (see *STB* #307), this tune and text were originally a Karen blessing, *Blu he law leh, muhko ni, Ba ya didi a*, which literally means "May God's grace come down from heaven for me, more and more." The subsequent stanzas change the object to *Ba na* ("to you") and *Ba bwa* ("to all"). The music is in *hta* style, which is usually slow and lyrical with gliding notes, and it is

---

36   This demonstrates the difficult task of hymn translation. Many hymns in *Sound the Bamboo* have been paraphrased and enriched and could not have been included as literal translations.

like a lullaby without any strong beats. It is also accompanied with hand motions or gestures.

The original blessing is[37]:

3	6	65	35	2	3-	3	6	65	5 --/
Blu		*he*	*law*		*leh*	*mu*		*hko*	*ni*
May	the	grace		of	God	come	down	from	heaven,
								(triplet)	

3	6	65	35	2	3	2	12	3	3	6,-//
*Ba		*ya* - - - - - - - - - - - - - - - - - - - di*							*di*	*a.*
*to		me - - - - - - - - - - - - - - - -more							and	more.

**2nd stanza: *Ba na* = "to you"
**3rd stanza: *Ba bwa* = "to all"

"God of region and of world" (*STB* #61)
(Chin: *Leicung kan Boile khamhtu*)

This is a prayer to God to bless the country by freeing it from the greed of foes and tyrants; for leaders to be just; for the people to be compassionate and guided by God's way, truth, and wisdom; and for God to reign and prosper the land.

The traditional melody FALAM CHIN (the name of a minority group in northwestern Myanmar) was adapted and transcribed by the author Sang Maung. It is constructed in an F = 1 four-tone scale (D = 6 1 2 3), but 6 only occurs at the end, almost like an ornament. The melody is constructed in the familiar Burmese narrative style of reiterated tones. The parallel harmony is quite unusual: 3 is always harmonized in the usual 1-3-5 chord; with the exception of the second note 2 in the third system, which is also harmonized with 1-3-5, all the 2s and 1s are harmonized with the supertonic chord (2-4-6) and the tonic chord (1-3-5) in second inversions respectively, meaning 6 as the bass for the 2-4-6 chord and 5 as the bass for the 1-3-5 chord. These second inversions are considered strange or even wrong according to Western theory. But the Burmese claim this combination of tones as their style, so it should not be considered wrong in this context. Congregations can sing this beautiful hymn with parallel harmony as a prayer for peace for the people of Myanmar as well as their own countries. (para. Jim Minchin)

In 2004, I visited Kalaymyo to attend a meeting for the accreditation of theological schools in that area. On that occasion, the students of the Bethel Theological Seminary performed the original version of this parting song and dance (*Varal ah kai ee*, "crossing the other side"). The principal of the seminary, Bernard Tuan Hre, provided the tonic *sol-fa* version (transcribed in cipher notation) and text on the next page.

---

37   As taught by Saw Tun Meh to the author, July 12, 2004, Insein, Myanmar.

3 3   3 3 3 - /3   2   2 2 1 2 / 2 - 1   1 /

Varal ah kai ee   caang ee, lei cer ni thang ee raan   ee,

3   3   3 3   3 - /3 2 2 2 1 2 / 2 - 1 1 /

Thng sang lam zuan   ee   chat 'silaw kan tian lai ni ee   tawi ee,

3   2   2 2 1 2 /2 - 1   1 / 1 - - - //

Tawi ee kan tian lai ni ee   ta   wi ee.

Literal translation (phrase by phrase):

The other side crossing as soon as, the sun shining over the earth white is,
The long journey go together let us we part today short is,
Short is we part today short is.

This folk version uses only three tones (3 2 1) in AAA' form and is harmonized in a traditional Western four-part texture without any change. In Sang Maung's version, the first system is an introduction similar in melodic style to the verse in AA' form, and there are more ornaments, many with second inversions. From the above comparison, Maung's version is an apparent improvement that violates Western harmonic rules and exhibits a Burmese identity.

"Gracious Father, love divine" (*STB* #196)

    (Burmese: *Motaoñ yañ kane bouñ ci ashiñ*)

George Kya Bing's hymn talks about the gracious Father who sent Christ to fight against all poverty and injustice and finally suffer on the cross. The second stanza prays to the Trinity to make all God's children one; it concludes, "If forgiveness fills our hearts, you will vindicate our cause." This last sentence provides room for reflection on the present social and political context of Myanmar. The original language of this hymn used many beautiful inner rhymes and other pairings, such as *the ce chiñ hsa-lo chiñ* and *ko daw tha htaw pana*, and repeated words: *tha tawa tha tawa, myet ta myet ta, ko daw ko daw, htiñ sha htiñ sha.* Unfortunately, none of this beautiful poetry could be expressed in the translation.

    The melody of CHITCHIN MYETA (meaning "love") uses an F = 1 eight-tone scale (1 2 3 4 5 6 7 plus ♯4). It shows characteristic features of the Burmese style, such as the reiterated tone (1 1 1 5, 2 2 2 6), the sharpened 4 (5 ♯4 3), and the final cadence on 1 (3 2 1), and it is well constructed with repetition, imitation, sequence, and natural development. The tune is composed of two-measure phrases and may be analyzed as follows:

```
a b a' b
c d a" b
e f g
```

The first two sections are similar, in that they use a (with variations) and b while the third section is rather unusual, in that it uses all new material (e f g) and is shorter (only six measures instead of eight measures), almost like a coda. One may use this hymn as an affirmation that God through Christ is the sovereign who cares and as a prayer for mutual forgiveness and unity. (trsl. Sang Maung; para. Roland S. Tinio)

"Happy are those following Jesus Christ" (*STB* #226)
(Burmese: *Kridaw nauh laih thu mya tha*)

This hymn is an exegesis of Jesus' statement in John 14:6, "I am the way, and the truth, and the life. No one comes to the Father except through me." U Lin Sein follows the pattern of Matthew 5:3–11, matching the spirit of Jesus' teachings and explaining the three key words in the three respective stanzas. Jesus is the Way to God the Father, so "let us all follow Christ, love him, trust him, praise him through our lives." Jesus is the Truth; "Truth is his Word . . . his Truth will set us free . . ." Jesus is the Life; "life abundant his promise is . . . losing our life for him, we will surely find eternal life." This affirmation of Christ is appropriate as an affirmation of faith and trust. This hymn could also be sung as a response to a sermon or as a sending forth.

The tune NAUH LAIH THU MYA, meaning "followers," was also composed by U Lin Sein. ("U" is a Burmese honorific title for a man, like "Mister" in English.) The melody is in an A = 5 seven-tone scale (D = 1 2 3 ♯4 5 6 7). This song has many interesting Burmese features: repeated tones in a narrative style (1 1111 1, 555555 5), two-note repetitive patterns (656565, 323232), a sharpened fourth (♯4) in a descending progression (5 ♯4 3), and many gliding tones. The first three systems are repeated; each is to be sung first by the leader and then by the congregation. The last two systems should be sung in unison. Although it is not indicated in the time signature, the music flows in the pattern of four beats; two exceptions are the first phrase in the last system, with only three beats and one half, and the last phrase with six beats. The way to sing the melody in the last system is to treat the first three notes as a group (312 counting "one two three") and then 32 5 as another group (counting "one two three and"), i.e., 3 + 4. This sudden shift of rhythm and meter is dictated by the varying number of syllables.

"Hear and heed the angel's words" (*STB* #307)
(Karen: *Kanate muhko hpo sih*)

This is a different kind of hymn; it poses questions for people to choose between God and Satan. The angel invites people to stay up in heaven, where there will be no more crying and the heart will be at peace praising God. After asking Death, "Where is your sting?" the author asks one, "Hell or heaven . . . which will be your final home?" It is an important question to be asked while people are still living. Since this hymn concerns the choice of hell or heaven, it can be sung at funeral as well as other occasions when pondering the meaning of death.

The tune KANATE (meaning "hear") is a Karen melody with triple meter (3/4 time). It is basically in a G = 3 five-tone scale (C = 6 1 2 3 5) plus #5 at the final cadence. According to the translator Tun Meh, the Karen people like to end songs in a minor mode; hence the #5 suddenly appears in the final cadence. Musically, the end of the first phrase has a short echo (5 32 1 3 2-), and the second phrase is repeated to form an a b b' structure with a variation. Saw Tun Meh suggests that the initial phrase should be:

/ 3 5 3 5/ 6. 5 6 /32 1 3 / 2-...
Ka - - na-te - mu-hko hpo sih

This melody also belongs to the *hta* style; it should be sung at a slow tempo, legato and graceful with gliding tones. (trsl. Saw Tun Meh; para. Jim Minchin)

"In the beginning, God" (*STB* #285)
(Kachin: *Ohlelegoi, shing gyim masha*)

"Oh-le-le-goi" are non-lexical syllables, which do not have a particular meaning but are not without meaning. Many cultures use non-lexical syllables to identify a song type or a particular mood associated with the title, text, or occasion of singing (for further explanation, see "From this time onwards," *STB* #224, in the Taiwan section). Most likely, these syllables gain meaning from the texts following them. This hymn is a song of joy, giving thanks and praise for God's creation and providing the needs for livelihood. It concludes with the commitment to serve others with love. Therefore, when singing "oh-le-le-goi," one should express feelings of thanks and praise of God. This hymn could be sung as a response to thanksgiving prayers.

OHLELEGOI is a Kachin folk melody; it is in an A = 6 five-tone scale (6 1 2 3 5) with a very wide range (equaling a twelfth) and plenty of large intervallic skips (6–2, high 2–low 3); the final cadence is 1 6 2- (cf. *STB* #292). It is through-composed, except for the last two phrases. This hymn may be accompanied by drums, gongs, and cymbals. Playing these instruments together on the odd beats can establish a mood of joy. (trsl. Hkyen Naw; para. I. L. & J. M.)

"May the LORD bless you with joy" (*STB* #288)

(Burmese: *Mar ba zey chañ mar ba zey*)

This hymn is unlike a traditional Christian benediction. According to the Reverend Peter Joseph, the secretary of the Association of Theological Education in Myanmar (ATEM), this song was originally a Buddhist benediction. Since it had no particular references to Buddhist doctrine, some theologians adapted and contextualized the song as a Christian blessing. The literal translation of the original first stanza is:

> May you be healthy, be healthy, like fragrant flowers,
> May your life be peaceful, eternally happy may you be,
> Like cool water, sufferings be away from you.

Although these expressions may have Buddhist implications, the imagery may also be interpreted as God's blessing of good health, peace, and eternal joy. The text contains common cultural expressions that every Burmese person knows. I added the optional second stanza; it has a stronger Christian content. The hymn may be sung as a benediction by the pastor, a choir, or congregation blessing one another.

MAR BA ZEY (literally "may you be healthy") is a beautiful Burmese melody in an E♭ = 5 six-tone scale (A♭ = 1 2 3 5 6 7), which is through-composed with the final on 1. The melodic shapes, rapid syllables, and gliding tones are typical characteristics of the Burmese narrative singing style. (trsl. Anna May; para. I.L. & J.M.)

"Mighty God, power over heaven and earth" (*STB* #57)

(Burmese: *Hp'ya shiñ ye bouñ takou myatne*)

The author U Lin Sein acknowledges God's power over the heaven, earth, and the universe, yet he seems puzzled and wonders when nations will recognize this and bow before God? So he prays for the Holy Spirit to come and revive their hearts and to bring them home. So this is a prayer for acknowledging God as Lord and asking for God's guidance.

The tune HP'YA SHIÑ, meaning "Lord God," was also composed by U Lin Sein. It is in a D = 6 seven-tone scale (F = 1 2 3 ♯4 5 6 7). Note the use of ♯4, the final cadence on 1, and the narrative style, especially when two eighth notes are together—the first one only takes one-third of the value, i.e., almost like a triplet (see the first and second phrases). All of these are typical elements of the Burmese singing style. Although the first two lines are repeated with distinct cadences and there is a slight imitation in the fourth system, the song almost sounds through-composed. The melody is rather difficult; one suggestion is that a soloist sings the first section, and the congregation sings the last two systems, which should be repeated. (trsl. Sang Maung; para. Roland S. Tinio)

"There was once a time" (STB #232)

(Burmese: *Di lo achiñ yauh yiñ*)

The author Saw Si Hae recalls in this hymn how the Spirit has changed his understanding of the Lord and the Church. Now he prays that the "Church will grow into a mighty tree to shade the faithful who walk hand in hand and meet together as friends." One can imagine the implication of this hymn in the context of the Burmese people's long suffering under an oppressive rule. Even under such hardship, they are still committed to follow the faith of their forebears until they are one with God. So this hymn is appropriate as a response to the call for discipleship. (The word "Saw" is an honorific title of a man in Karen, like "Mister.")

The tune ACHIÑ (meaning "time") was also composed by Saw Si Hae in an E = 3 seven-tone scale (C =1 2 3 4 5 6 7). It is very syllabic, like the narration of a story, with a few repeated tones (<u>3335</u> 3-, <u>01117123</u> 5,-). Most important are the three reiterated tones (<u>3 3 3</u>, <u>1 1 1</u>, <u>6 6 6</u>); the second group occurs three times. It sounds like a solo and may be difficult for an ordinary congregation. So the editors suggest that this be sung as a solo, with the congregation joining in at the coda after the third stanza. Care must be taken with the Burmese: two syllables are frequently sung together as one eighth note, i.e., the first syllable "a" in *achiñ*, *ateih*, and *aliñ* should have about one-third of the note value or even shorter. (trsl. Sang Maung; para. Roland S. Tinio)

"To you, O Lord, I lift my soul" (*STB* #292)

This short song is Saw Si Hae's prayer, with words taken from Psalm 25, verses 2, 4, and 5. He prays "don't let me be put to shame . . . let no enemies triumph over me again, teach me your ways, guide me in your truth . . ."

The tune YANGON, which is the name of the capital of Myanmar (formerly spelled Rangoon), is in an A = 6 five-tone scale (D = 2 3 5 6 1), is through-composed with the final on 2, and has a very wide range equaling a twelfth. The syllabic melody, with plenty of intervallic skips and a 1 6 2- final cadence, is typically Kachin in style (see *STB* #285). This song can be sung as an antiphon when reading Psalm 25 or as a prayer for guidance. When sung alone, such a short song may be repeated a few times in order to internalize the message and feeling of the text and to strengthen one's faith and trust.

Conclusion

Although more Burmese hymns could not be collected and included in this hymnal, most of the present hymns show typical characteristics of Burmese singing styles: a narrative feeling, reiterated tones, gliding tones, and a final on 1 (*do*). I have commented on the ironic phenomenon whereby "the more authentic the hymns [or tunes] are in the ethnic styles, the more resistant the Christians become, and the more difficult they are for people within or outside of the community to sing" (cf. Loh 1993a, 55). Whether the Burmese people resist their hymns is yet to be seen, but it is apparent that some of the songs are difficult for outsiders to sing. These Burmese hymns encourage one to accept traditional styles, even though they may sound difficult at first. To paraphrase the words of Fred Pratt Green, "God is glorified through this beautiful music."

Singaporean Hymns

The Nation, Its People, and Christian Mission

Singapore is a small island country with total area of 692.7 square kilometers (about 267.5 square miles) located at the southern tip of the Malay Peninsula. It was part of Malaysia when that country was formed in 1963, but Singapore chose to become a separate republic in 1965. The population is 4,608,167: 76.8% Chinese, 14% Malay, 7.9% Indian, and 1.4% others, such as Eurasians, Armenians, and Peranakans (those with Chinese-Malay parentage).[38] In 1819, when Sir Thomas Stamford Raffles landed on "Singapura" (the Malay name for the island), there were only 150 inhabitants (thirty Chinese and 120 Malay fishermen). But migrations from India, Indonesia, southern China, England, and Scotland rapidly followed (Athyal 1996, 299). Within 150 years, this tiny city-state of industrious people became one of the "Four Asian Tigers," the others being Hong Kong, South Korea, and Taiwan.

Christian missions followed the immigrants from the West; during the nineteenth century, most of the major denominations focused on serving their own people—Anglican for the English and Presbyterian for the Scottish. But Roman Catholics and Methodists focused their work among the local Singaporeans. After the Second World War, most missionary agencies worked in India and China; after the Communists took power in China in 1949 and drove out all the missionaries, most of them fled to Taiwan and Southeast Asia. The China Inland Mission was renamed the Overseas Missionary Fellowship (OMF) in 1950 and was stationed in Singapore. According to Keith Hinton,

> The number of para-church organizations increased remarkably, from five in 1950 to nearly one hundred by 1980. With their emphasis on evangelism, follow-up, discipleship training, Bible study, and leadership development, they have played a positive role in helping revive and reactivate the Church.
>
> (Athyal 1996, 306)

During the past three decades, the charismatic movement and the Pentecostal church have greatly accelerated the growth of churches, as seen in the Church of Singapore. In 2007, the percentage of Christians in Singapore was about 16% (5% Roman Catholics and 11% Protestants); there are more than 400 churches, the largest being the Methodist, followed by the Presbyterian and then the Anglican (cf. Athyal 1996, 299–318). The most recent development is the rise of megachurches.

---

38 CIA, "The World Factbook, Singapore," July 2008 estimate, https://www.cia.gov/library/publications/the-world-factbook/print/sn.html (accessed January 27, 2009).

Most of the megachurches are independent in nature—such as City Harvest, Cornerstone, Calvary Charismatic, and Trinity Christian Center—with the exception of Faith Community Baptist Church, which still maintains its Baptist ties, albeit loosely. The Reverend Lawrence Kong leads the Faith Community Baptist Church and is most known for successfully implementing the cell-group structure within the megachurch system in Singapore. In fact, he is invited by churches in Asia and the United States to share his expertise in this area. The Reverend Kong Hee and Song He are a husband-and-wife team that pastors the City Harvest Church. Song He functions as a worship leader, and she has become a popular singer among Chinese-speaking congregations in Asia.

Commentary on Individual Hymns

"A HYMN FOR CHURCH UNITY"
("Jesus, Savior, Spirit, Sun!" *STB* #314)

See the commentary on this hymn in the New Zealand section.

"CALL ME BY MY NAME"
("Alone I am yet not alone," *STB* #265)

As one of the Four Asian Tigers during the 1970s, Singapore became a highly industrialized nation. To bring this about, corporations commonly hired large numbers of low-wage workers. The companies' most important concerns were mass production and profit. Thus, the value of a human being was determined by the amount of money one could earn or the number of products one could manufacture for the corporation. Workers were like machines wearing tags with numbers, not names. They were like treasure boxes without treasure. People longed to be recognized as individuals and to be called by their names. The author/ composer of this hymn, Samuel Liew, is a compassionate Methodist pastor. His text proclaims that the risen Christ has come to give people a life, a price, a soul, and a name; the nobody becomes a somebody. "Just call me by my name, O my Lord," can be a prayer of many laborers today.

Pastor Liew frequently condensed his sermons into short hymns. He composed the tune MY NAME is in a Western-style F♯ = 3 seven-tone scale (D major = 1 2 3 4 5 6 7), with an altered ♯4 and ♭7 and with guitar accompaniment. Liew sometimes taught his congregation to sing his songs after his sermons; in this way, they quickly learned the sermon's message. Liew recorded this song for me in 1970.

There is an anecdote associated with this hymn. At an International Youth Conference in Kuala Lumpur during the 1970s, disputes arose and the participants were divided. The debates were very emotional; hearts were torn. Amid the conflict, someone began to sing this song. The refrain "Just call me by my name" reminded the participants that they were equally valuable in the eyes of the Lord. They were drawn to join the singing, and many were moved to tears. The meeting ended in mutual acceptance, forgiveness, and reconciliation, with warm embraces and unity. This is one of the best examples of how powerful music can work beyond one's imagination.

"Grant, Lord, that we may not faint" (*STB* #185)

(Thamilz: *Thaagaththei thiirum aiyaa*)

Christians in Singapore tend to be of Chinese or south Indian (Tamil) descent. The native Malays are mostly Muslim. There are few if any publicly professed Malay Christians in Malaysia or Singapore today. This anonymous hymn in the Carnatic style and Thamilz language originated in southern India. It is a prayer for God's love and support and for God to put down tyrants. The second half asks for God's guidance for living as a Christian. It is appropriate to sing this hymn as a prayer of trust, guidance, and dedication.

The melody THAAGAM (meaning "thirst") is in a C = 3 seven-tone scale (F = 6 7 1 2 3 4 #5) with a lively rhythm. Like many Indian lyrics, it is in AB form with both phrases repeated. In the verse (the B section), the Thamilz version has different texts for each repetition, but the English version repeats the same text, apparently condensed. So, if the hymn is sung in English, one has the option of not repeating the B section. (trsl. C. R. W. David; para. Rolando Tinio)

"Jesus, Savior, Spirit, Sun!"

See the commentary on "A HYMN FOR CHURCH UNITY" *(STB #314)* in the New Zealand section.

"Lord, have mercy" (*STB* #118)

This liturgical prayer expands from an inward, self-focused orientation to an outward, other-focused perspective. This Kyrie Eleison (Greek for "Lord have mercy") reflects the various stages of the Christian life: the forgiveness of sin, the emergence of a life lived within God's grace, and the growing desire to proclaim God's grace to others. This song, in an A = 3 six-tone scale (D = 6 7 1 2 3 5), was composed in 1988, one of several works featured in Swee-Hong Lim's graduation recital at the Asian Institute for Liturgy and Music, Philippines. The tune name SINGAPURA is the Malay word for Singapore. (Comments written by Swee Hong Lim)

"May the love of the Lᴏʀᴅ" (*STB* #315)

(Mandarin: *Wei yuan Shen di ai*)

This benediction has a moving story behind its composition. Swee Hong Lim and Maria Ling were thankful to God for the birth of their first baby after many years of waiting. One day after his birth, the baby stopped breathing, but the prompt action of the nurses revived the baby. In gratitude, Ling wrote this lullaby, and Lim composed the song, whose accompaniment seems to convey a rocking crib. This hymn can be sung as a benediction at the close of a service or as a prayer for sending people off. The composer recounts the background of this work:

> The tune was created initially as a lullaby. However, as a result of God's providence in the life of our son, Soon-Ti, Maria created the English text based loosely around the Hebrew scripture (Old Testament) of Numbers 6:24–26. Dong Li, the Chinese translator of the text, was a theological student who attended Trinity Theological College, Singapore. His translation was made possible through Mary Gan, who was then his hymnology lecturer. She is currently the principal of the Methodist School of Music, Singapore. Musically speaking, with the melody having a lullaby nature, the keyboard accompaniment was deliberately kept simple and tender to strengthen the imagery of resting in God. The tune sᴏᴏɴ ᴛɪ was named after our child; it literally means "pure knowledge [of God]" in Teochew (a southern Chinese dialect). The melody is pentatonic (G, A, B, D, E [D = 5 6 1 2 3]) in design, unlike the accompaniment.[39] (Written by Swee Hong Lim)

"Now let us tell of your victory" (*STB* #22)

A paraphrase of Psalm 98, verses 1–2 and 4–6, this hymn begins with a doxological refrain. The hymn praises God's marvelous deeds, "for you have come to set us free, and in your love we all are one," and acknowledges that God will come to judge with justice, righteousness, and peace. Swee Hong Lim explains the origin of the tune:

> The tune ʀᴀsᴀ sᴀʏᴀɴɢ ("to feel love") is an Indonesian folk song. It is supposed to have come from the Moluccas region. It was subsequently adapted by the Malays and Straits Chinese (in Malaya) and sung as a *pantun* (a form of Malay repartee poetry). In the musical practice of the Straits Chinese, a *pantun* is usually sung accompanied by an instrumental ensemble. This ensemble typically features the violin, harmonium, gong, and hand drum. This particular recreational activity is known as *dondang sayang*. Here, Samuel Liew set the folk song with a Christian text. Liew's

---

39   From personal communication with the author.

text features a doxology set within the refrain of the folk song while the verses elaborate on the rationale for thanksgiving and praise.[40]

Note that the hymn is in 2/2 and should not be sung too slowly.

"Worship and praise we give" (*STB* #25)
(Thamilz: *Un paadhem pannin dheen enaallum thudhiye*)

This Thamilz lyric was recorded in Singapore in 1988. I recently learned that the text was written by Sarah Nowroji from Chennai, India, in 1969, and the tune was composed by Sathy Victor, who was from the same town. It was translated by the late professor C. R. W. David of Tamilnadu Theological Seminary in Madurai, and it was paraphrased by Rolando Tinio of the Philippines.

The lyric is in the traditional Carnatic three-part *kirtana* style (for further explanation, see the India section of this volume). It praises Jesus for his love and mercy. The first stanza is like a *bhajan* (spiritual song), listing Jesus' attributes as the reason for praise. The second stanza asks, "Jesus, be our guide." The third stanza is a prayer that Jesus will help one overcome hardships. The last stanza adopts the imagery of Psalm 23: the LORD leads one on the path of righteousness, and his rod and staff will free one from fear and give one peace, comfort, and joy. Although this text seems to have multiple themes, it is still focused on prayer for guidance and trust and thus would be appropriate for prayer meetings or as intercessory prayers.

The tune PANNIN DHEEN (meaning "I bowed down") is in a D = 1 eight-tone scale (B = 6 7 1 2 3 4 5 ♯5). The lively rhythm, skips, sequences, ornaments, and the wide range equaling an eleventh (from low B to high e) all contribute to making this a very interesting song in an Indian style.

Conclusion

The Singaporean hymns in this collection vividly demonstrate their roots in various cultures and an educational system formed by the colonial British. In these schools, English was the main language and only Western or European music was taught. So it is natural that most of the Singaporean compositions are in a Western style. But in these hymns, one finds the combined musical styles of south India, Malaysia, China, and the West.

---

40   From personal communication with the author.

 # Thai Hymns

The Nation, Its People, and Their Religions

Before 1939 and from 1945 to 1949, Thailand was named Siam. It is the only country in Southeast Asia that has never been colonized or invaded by any Western powers; thus, it is known as the "land of the free." This continuous sovereignty has enabled the Thai people to cultivate and develop their cultural heritage and artistic expressions since the thirteenth century (Loh 1989, 9). Thailand is about the size of France, with an area of 514,000 square kilometers (about 198,457 square miles), and has a population of 65,493,296.[41] The majority of the population (75%) is Thai (also called Siamese or Central Thai). Ethnic Chinese compose the largest minority group (14%), and they are integrated at every level of life, especially among the economic elite and artisans. Other ethnic groups in Thailand are Shan, Thai-Lao, Khmer, Malay, and many minority tribes.

As early as the seventh century, the ancestors of the Thai people migrated south to the fertile Chao Phraya River basin. The first Thai kingdoms were founded in the 1200s at Chiang Mai and Sukhothai, and from the mid-eighteenth century they were centered in the Bangkok area. In 1932, nearly seven hundred years of absolute monarchy ended with a bloodless coup, resulting in a constitutional monarchy. The present king Rama IX ascended to the throne in 1946. Thailand is divided into four cultural regions: center, south, north, and northeast; each is distinguished from the others in dialect, diet, housing, decorative motifs, literature, and music (Garland 4:221).

The Thai people, in general, are considered non-aggressive, polite, and restrained. The people and the country's seventy-five provinces are unified under the slogan "Nation, Religion, and King." Theravada Buddhism is the state religion. It is said, "To be a Thai is to be a Buddhist"; hence, all males must dedicate some time during their lives to serve as monks as part of their devotion to Buddha. Currently about 95% of the population is Buddhist; Muslims constitute 3.8%, and Christians compose only 0.5%.

---

41   CIA, "The World Factbook, Thailand," July 2008 estimate, https://www.cia.gov/library/publications/the-world-factbook/print/th.html (accessed January 27, 2009).

Thai Traditional Music

The influences of Thailand's powerful neighbors have resulted in similarities between Thailand's musical instruments, tunings, scales, textures, and rhythmic cycles and those of China and India. These two countries have also influenced Thai folk traditions. Nevertheless, Thai music has many unique features, such as many different kinds of ensembles. The most important ones in contemporary usage are the *piphat* ensemble and the *mahori* ensemble. These are used to accompany theatrical performances, to provide interstitial music for solo vocal performances, or to perform on their own (Garland 4:221). The ensembles are composed of the following instruments:

- **Piphat khruang ha**: *pi nai* (quadruple-reed oboe), *ranat ek* (xylophone), *khawng wong yai* (gong circle), *taphon* (double-headed barrel drum), *ching* (concussion bells), *klawng that* (double-headed drum).

- **Mahori** (originally meaning "instrumental music"): *ranat ek, khawng wong yai, saw sam sai* (three-stringed bowed lute), *saw duang* (high-pitched bowed lute), *saw u* (low-pitched bowed lute), *ja-khe* (crocodile zither with eleven frets and three strings), *khlui phiang aw* (vertical block flute in C), *thon* (goblet-shaped drum), *rammana* (shallow conical drum), *ching*.

(Garland 4:240–44)

Characteristics of Thai Traditional or Classical Music

Some of the most distinct features of Thai traditional or classical music are the intervals and formation of scales. According to Thai music theory, the octave is divided into seven equidistant intervals, each of which is 171.4 cents; in actual practice, the intervals usually fluctuate between 168 and 180 cents. This is quite different from the Western standard, which is 100 cents for a minor second and 200 cents for a major second. In effect a Thai third is 342.8 cents, which is smaller than a Western major third (400 cents) and larger than a Western minor third (300 cents); hence, it is called a "neutral third." A similar process of comparison applies to a neutral sixth. (See the following chart.) This is why a Thai traditional ensemble may sound off pitch or out of tune to Western ears. But, in fact, Western ears are out of tune with Thai music.

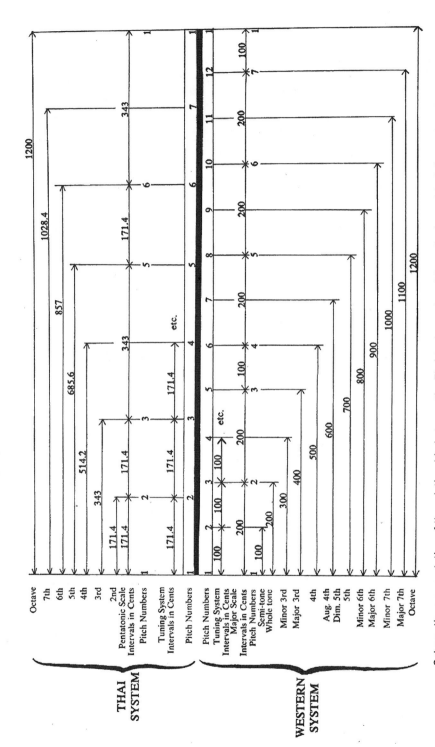

Schematic representation of the relationship between the Thai tuning system (above the heavy black line and the Wester tempered tuning system (below the line). Intervals are expressed in terms of the Ellis system which divides the octave into 1200 "cents." Each Western half step has therefore a measurement of 100 cents.

(After Morton 1976, 26)

The classical *piphat* ensemble represents the typical court tradition. Although it is regarded as playing in unison or octave doublings, the *piphat* is actually played in a manner similar to but much simpler than the polyphonic stratification of the Javanese gamelan. Certain instruments play the main melody while others decorate the tune according to their idiomatic styles, doubling or lengthening the note values, and all join periodically on the strong beats, the structural points, in unison or in octaves. This may be seen from the following example of "Sathukan" provided by the Department of Fine Arts, Bangkok (Morton 1968, 34; Loh 1989, 15–17).

* Sounding one octave higher.

There is debate over the technique of the Thai classical ensemble: whether it follows the colotomic structure of the Indonesian gong-chime or the Chinese concept of heterophonic variations. According to Terry Miller, both views are correct: the answer is somewhere between the two. But there are also antiphonal textures (imitating or almost repeating the same melody by another instrument like an echo) as well as polyphonic treatment (imitative or individual melodies crossing or overlapping each other) in Thai ensembles (Garland 4:272–75).

Music of Northeast Thailand: Isaan

One of the most popular instruments in the rural area is the *khaen* (free-reed mouth organ with twelve to sixteen pipes), which has seven tones close to the Western A-B-c-d-e-f-g. There are two groups of anhemitonic penta scales: *san*, starting from G (G-A-C-D-E [5 6 1 2 3]), and *yao* (or *nyao*) starting from A (A-C-D-E-G [6 1 2 3 5]). There are a variety of modes on the *khaen*, according to northeastern Thai practice:

San modes: *lai sutsanaen* ("melody of love"), with G-A-C-D-E [G = 5 6 1 2 3]
              lai po sai ("left-thumb mode"), with C-D-F-G-A [C = 5 6 1 2 3]
              lai soi ("fragmented mode"), with D-E-G-A-B [D = 5 6 1 2 3]

Yao modes: *lai yai* ("big mode"), with A-C-E-D-G [A = 6 1 2 3 5]
              lai noi ("little mode"), with D-F-G-A-C [D = 6 1 2 3 5]

(Garland 4:323f)

These modes are the same as those in the chart of Laotian modes, in the Laos section in this volume.

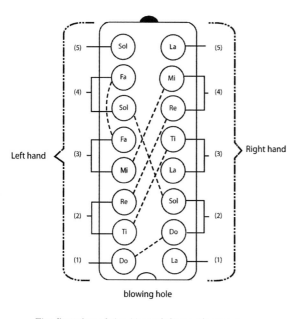

The fingering of the *khaen* (after a diagram by Inchai Srisuwan in Loh 1989, 21).

A *khaen* ensemble includes the following instruments: *khaen, phin* (three-stringed plucked lute), *pong lang* (suspended xylophones), *wod* (circular panpipes with twelve pipes), *hai song* (a pair of jars with a thick rubber band stretched across the mouth, tuned high and low and plucked), *klong* (barrel-shaped drum), *klap* (concussion sticks), *ching*, and *chap* (concussion bells). The *khaen* ensemble often accompanies singing and dancing, and the instruments usually create simple or complex multipart textures among themselves and with the singer's voice. The following illustration shows some of the ensemble's parts.

(after Loh 1989, 38)

197

Thai musical instruments in the collection of I-to Loh:

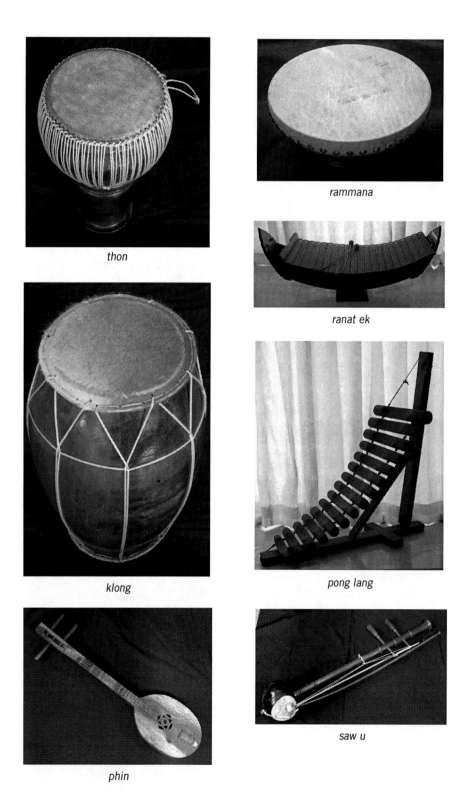

thon

rammana

ranat ek

klong

pong lang

phin

saw u

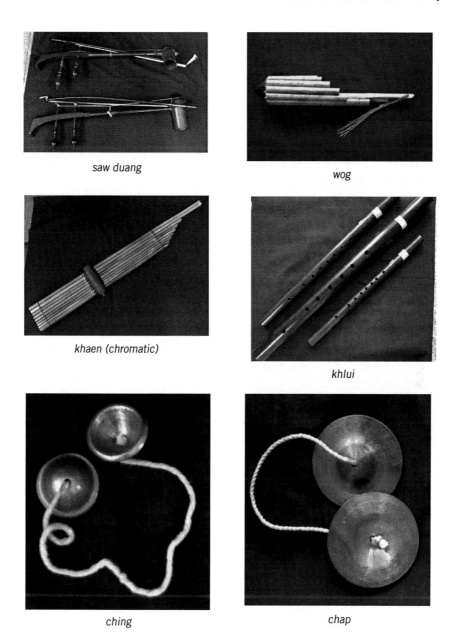

saw duang

wog

khaen (chromatic)

khlui

ching

chap

Christian Mission in Thailand

A Brief History of Christian Mission in Thailand

Roman Catholics were in Thailand as early as 1511, and the first missionary arrived in 1567. The London Missionary Society began working in Thailand in 1828. In 1859, the first Thai national was baptized; earlier baptisms were mostly of Chinese or other ethnic groups. Many missionary societies entered the country and worked in different regions. In 1934, they joined to become the Church of Christ in Thailand (CCT); twenty-five mission groups are affiliated with this body today (abridged from Athyal 1996, 238–43).

The CCT has been keen on education and social ministries; to date, it has seven hospitals, two seminaries, one university, two colleges, and thirty schools. In 1989, the membership of various Christian groups was:

Church of Christ in Thailand (CCT): 45,308
Evangelical Fellowship of Thailand (EFT),
    The [Southern] Baptist Church Association (TBCA): 101,492
Roman Catholic Church: 222,181
Others (Jehovah's Witnesses, Mormons, Children of God, etc.): . 174,105

Total: 543,086

(Cf. Athyal 1996, 249)

A New Model for Modern Mission in Isaan

In 1977, a new mission was begun at Udon Thani in northeast Thailand by the Reverend and Mrs. James Gustafson, missionaries of the Evangelical Covenant Church of America. They did not build new churches, but they established the Center for Church Planting and Church Growth (CCPCG). This institution organized ministries around the improvement of the villagers' lives by educating and supervising them in farming skills, such as raising pigs and chickens and maintaining fisheries. The staff members met every morning for Bible study; the day's scripture was interpreted within the local context, versified by Ruth Srisuwan, composed by Inchai Srisuwan into music of the traditional Isaan style, and accompanied by the group's *khaen* ensemble. These hymns were tested among the staff members regarding their theology, relevance, singability, and identification with local musical style. After further critical evaluation and improvement, the songs [were] introduced to the house churches (Loh 1989, 18).

Today, when the people and especially children of Udon Thani gather in their house churches, they are taught to play traditional musical instruments, many of which are made by Inchai Srisuwan and are used to accompany their singing in worship. Aside from the Bible, which is already translated into Thai, the only translated texts are the Apostles' Creed and the Lord's Prayer, both of which have been set to music by Srisuwan in the folk style with the accompaniment of the *khaen* ensemble. All the liturgies and hymns are indigenous.

The elements of Holy Communion are also contextualized, in that sticky rice is baked into a loaf (*khaoji*) for communion, and rosella juice (*krajiap*) is in the common cup. The *khaoji*, which symbolizes Christ's body, is the main staple food of the Isaan people, and the red *krajiap*, which symbolizes the blood of Christ, has the healing effect of an herbal medicine (for further discussion, see section V of "Asian Hymns in Their Historical Perspectives" in this volume). Both elements are the fruits of local labor and thus are meaningful. If the communicants are so moved, they may dance as an expression of their thanksgiving and praise after consuming the elements (Loh 1989, 18–20).

To date, this is the most holistic approach to mission. The gospel of Jesus Christ meets both the physical as well as the spiritual needs of the people, and all the Christian expressions—elements of the Lord's Supper, liturgies, and hymns—are grown out of the local context; nothing has been borrowed from the West. However, for the people of Isaan to experience and share the universal church, I have also encouraged them to broaden their perspectives, to learn and sing hymns from other parts of the world, so that they may feel and witness unity and diversity in Christ.

Thai Language and Poetic Forms

Thai is a tonal language, in that a change of tone alters the meaning of a spoken sound. There are five tones in Thai, as seen in the following chart (Loh 1989, 24).

Order of tone	Sign	Diagram	Description	Melodic equivalent	
1	—	⊣	(mid) level	3 -	-
2	＼	↘	low falling	1	6
3	＾	⅄	high falling	65	3
4	／	↑	high rising	5	6
5	⌄	⋏	low rising	6	1

The traditional Thai poems also have an intricate structure. A poem consists of a number of lines with eight syllables each, with the following rhyme schemes:

1. The third syllable of the even line rhymes with the end of the preceding line: aa; bb; dd
2. The end syllable of the second, sixth, and tenth lines decides the rhyme of the respective following lines and the third syllable next to them: bbb; ccc
3. The end of the sixth line rhymes with the fourth, and the tenth rhymes with the eighth: cc; ee
4. Lines 1, 5, and 9 are only matched with their respective pairs in the inner rhyme: aa; dd; ff

The illustration on the following page outlines this poetic structure; each dash represents one syllable.

Odd lines	rhyme	Even lines	Inner rhyme
1. - - - - - - - -	a	2. - -	a - - - - b
3. - - - - - - -	b	4. - -	b - - - - c
5. - - - - - - -	d	6. - -	d - - - - c
7. - - - - - - -	c	8. - -	c - - - - e
9. - - - - - - -	f	10. - -	f - - - - e

Psalm 139:1-8 as paraphrased in a typical Thai metrical poem exhibits this intricate classical form.

Kha tae phra Jao fao sam ruad	Phra ong truad tra yu ruu Jak kha
song ruu sing tii kha ram bam phen maa	Klai sud taa song khao jai nai khwaam kit
song hen kha tuk wa laa klaa tam ngaan	Mae tae kaan phak phawn phraw awn Jit
song ruu jaeg tuk yang tang cha nit	Ruu nai kit kawb kam kha tham maa
Mae wa kawn kha ja phoie oei jam nan	Song ruu than kha sai pu dai naa
Song waed lawn thuk dan tan pat jaa	Doei lit taa khawg phra ong song kriag krai
Phra ong song ruu jak kha maa thang mod	Koen kam nod leuk seug kua ruu dai
Kha ja nii phra ong pon pai hon dai	Lob tii nai ja liik ton pon phra phak
Kah phra ong mae kheun pai nai sa wan	Na tii nan song raw ta kha pra jak
Tha nawn daen maw ra naa kha pam nak	Phra ong dak yuu tii man nai suang

(after Loh 1989, 25)

Unfortunately, there is not yet a Thai hymn written in the classical form.

Commentary on Individual Hymns

"All Christians must love one another" (*STB* #213)

(Thai: *Khristian khwan rian khwaam rak pheua kaan ruujak*)

Admonishing all Christians to love one another, the author Malai Koet Keet stresses that God's love embraces all and that Christ "bought us with his blood." He states that Jesus stopped the disciples' disputes (Matthew 18:1–4) by showing them to be humble and to put their trust in God like little children.

KWAAM RAK, meaning "love," is an adaptation of a lively folk melody with frequently repeated phrases or musical ideas. It is in an E = 6 five-tone scale (D = 5 6 1 2 3) with final on 1. The most prominent motif, 5/ 3 2 3 2 1, which is set to the text about God's love, repeats several times with rhythmic and tonal variations according to the intonation of the text. Since the melody is rather fast and rhythmic, it may be too difficult for ordinary congregations to handle. Therefore, it can be sung as a solo, with the congregation joining in the refrain. The text's adaptor, who is sensitive to the natural intonation of the text, has provided another variation of the melody to suit the second stanza. When sung in English, this version may be ignored. (para. Ronald Hines)

"As the incense goes up" (*STB* #296)

(Thai: *Khaw hai kham phawana*)

This is a short prayer based on Psalm 141:2, "Let my prayer be counted as incense before you, and the lifting up of my hands as an evening sacrifice." When singing this hymn, one can chose the appropriate phrase for time of the day, either "morning's thank offering" or "evening's thank offering." The hymn may be used as a short response after each prayer of thanksgiving or praise. Notice also that the psalm has been Christianized, i.e., it adds New Testament theology, in which one offers prayers through Christ to God.

PHAWANA, meaning "prayer," was composed by Solot Kuptarat in an E = 6 six-tone scale (D = 5 6 7 1 2 3). Like rising incense smoke, the melody flows slowly and smoothly without any particular accent; hence, the lines between measures may be ignored. Flutes, bowed lutes, and concussion bells (struck on the first beat) may be used to accompany the singing. (para. JM)

"Come and worship God with songs of praise" (*STB* #2)

(Thai: *Maa thoed rao rong phleng*)

This call to worship was originally composed for a class project at the Asian Institute for Liturgy and Music. The theme was "Mary Magdalene wiping Jesus' feet," as a sign of repentance and love for Jesus. Written by Ruth Srisuwan, this short call to worship invites people to give thanks for God's love in words and deeds.

NA-MAT-SA-KAAN, meaning "worship," was composed by the author's husband, Inchai Srisuwan, in a typical Thai five-tone scale, in which D = 1 2 3 5 6. Since Thai is a tonal language, the melody develops according to the natural inflection of the poem; hence, it is through-composed without any repetition. Since the Thai traditional scale is equidistant (see the discussion earlier in this chapter), the intervals are smaller in size (171.4 cents for a second instead of 200 cents in Western tuning). When this song is sung according to the Thai tuning, it may sound out of tune to Western ears, but it shows the unique beauty of Thai music. However, if the song is sung as printed, it may also sound out of tune to traditional Thai singers. Thankfully, the untrained Thai Christians as well as the composer accept the Western tuning. This hymn will sound better if sung with a soft and lyrical voice, not an operatic or dramatic one. Let the feeling of praise be more introspective and internalized, which is a more Asian approach.

As indicated in the performance note, playing a pair of concussion bells (*ching* represented by "o" = open, light; *chap* represented by "+" = closed, accented) as accompaniment will enhance the beauty of this hymn. (para. I-to Loh)

Come children, men and women all (*STB* #209)

(Thai: *Choen thaan thanglai, thangying thangchai*)

This hymn, written by Sook Pongnoi, is a paraphrase of Jesus' calling for those who are burdened (Matthew 11:28) and thirsty (Isaiah 55:1–2) to come to him for peace, rest, and water. The asterisk in the third stanza indicates a choice of term—"rice," "wheat" or "bread" or any other staple food—appropriate to the singers' culture. Except for the fourth stanza, the poem is structured such that in the first half of each stanza, Christ uses the first person to call upon the people while in the second half of each stanza, the call is from a third person, who reaffirms the importance of receiving such drink and food of eternal life from Christ, "the Lord, the King and Savior of the world."

SOIE SON TAD, meaning "melody from Son Tad," like most of the Thai songs, is in an Eb = 5 five-tone scale (Ab = 1 2 3 5 6) with the final on 1. It has a very wide range (equaling a thirteenth) and is through-composed without any phrase repetition. This hymn is appropriate as a response to an altar call, taking refuge in Christ, or an invitation for partaking the elements during Holy Communion. It should be sung lyrically, with the accompaniment of a pair of concussion bells (+ = closed, stressed; o = open, light). (trsl. Cher Lue Vang; para. Rolando S. Tinio)

"Day of joy, let us be glad" (*STB* #11)

(Thai: *Saen suksan wan prachum nii*)

This is one of the best and most popular hymns composed by Songsan Prasopsin. In this hymn, Prasopsin exhorts people to be joyful for God's blessing and the gift of hope. The second stanza prays to God to give us love and grace to fight against sins and evil, and the last stanza gives thanks to Christ for his sacrifice and redemption and asks him to be the center of our lives forever. This hymn, therefore, is appropriate for Sunday worship as an opening hymn. It can also be sung on other occasions that focus on the meaning of the salvation of Christ.

PHLENG KRET PHA MA, which literally means "Burma melody selection," is adapted from one of the most famous Thai folk melodies of Burmese origin. It is in a D = 6 six-tone scale (F = 1 2 3 5 6 7) with a final on 1; 7 only appears once at the climax and without a half-tone progression (7–1 or 1–7). Like many other Thai songs, it is through-composed without any repetition. The repeated tone (05 5 5 5) is an important idiom in Thai folk melodies (see *STB* #72, 87, and 303). Concussion bells (o = open, + = closed) plus a drum accompaniment (see the drum pattern below) will bring out the amiable and joyful spirit of this hymn. (trsl. Boonmee Julkiree; para. Rolando S. Tinio)

"From the Bible we learn God's will" (*STB* #217)

(Thai: *Phra-kham-phii sawn hai rao ruu jak*)

Ruth Srisuwan composed this simple hymn to teach children to learn God's will from the Bible. It admonishes children to give each other love, to share the gifts of God, to offer help to all, to forgive day by day, and to come to God, who waits.

PHRA-KHAM-PHII, meaning "the Bible," was composed by the author's husband, Inchai Srisuwan, as a simple song with a C = 5 five-tone scale (F = 1 2 3 5 6). The message of each stanza is repeated three times and thus is very easy for children to learn. Teachers may also consider using signs or hand motions to interpret the meanings of the texts. An accompaniment of concussion bells (o = open, light; + = closed, accented) will add beauty and interest to the song. (para. JM)

"Happy is he who walks in God's wise way" (*STB* #87)

(Thai: *Khwaam suk yeun yong khong maa suu phuu tham chop*)

This is a free paraphrase of Psalm 1 by Erik Routley, not a translation from the Thai version. One can see Routley's favorite phrase "duty and delight" in the second stanza; the word "delight" comes from Psalm 1, verse 2: "but their delight is in the law of the LORD." In the fourth stanza, Routley changes the psalm into a direct prayer to God and uses the word "delight" again:

> LORD, in your mercy spare me, keep me still,
> let me not choose the sinner's way;
> promise and law you equally have given:
> let them be my delight today.

In this way, Routley relates the psalm directly to the singer's present context. Hence, it would be good to sing this after the responsive reading of Psalm 1 to connect the teaching of the psalm to one's daily life.

SOIE LAM PHANG (meaning "Lam Phang melody"; Lam Phang is a city in northern Thailand) is a traditional Thai folk melody, using an E♭ = 5 five-tone scale (5 6 1 2 3) with a final on 5. The melody is well constructed in a b c b' form. Both a and c use reiterated tones (5-555, 3-333) to begin the phrase; although they use different pitches, they echo each other. This hymn appeared first in the 1960s in a Thai hymnal and was included in the fourth edition of the WCC hymnal *Cantate Domino* in 1980, with Routley's setting in four-part Western harmony.

"He rules over all" (*STB* #212)

(Thai: *Ongphra Yeesuu jao*)

This hymn affirms Christ as Lord in heaven and on earth and urges people to invite Christ into their hearts. The second stanza calls one to love God with heart, mind, and soul. The third stanza reminds people to repent, for Christ has already shed his blood for their redemption. The last stanza encourages all to fight with the shield of the gospel of truth, so that they may be accepted at the foot of Christ's throne. This hymn may be sung after a sermon as a meditation and reflection of one's relationship with Christ.

THAMNAWNG SUAD, meaning "chanting melody," is in a B♭ = 5 five-tone scale (E♭ = 1 2 3 5 6). It is constructed in an a b a' b' form, with the first half of the a' phrase transposed to an octave higher. Except for the pick-up beats of b and b', all four phrases have identical rhythmic patterns and are thus very easy for congregations to sing. (para. Rolando S. Tinio)

"Holy are the Bible's many books" (*STB* #219)

(Thai: *Kam pra sird sak sit phra khrit kam pii*)

This hymn, written by the traditional folk-artist and evangelist Songsan Prasopsin, stresses the importance of the Bible, which contains the eternal truth and reveals the way of fellowship with God. The Scripture is a torch of light that drives away darkness, sins, and death and draws people to the love of God through Jesus. Finally, the hymn affirms the Bible's telling of the second coming of Christ and assures that those who have followed His commandments of love will receive the crown of life. This hymn may be sung before or after the reading of the Bible as an affirmation of the importance of God's word.

HOLY WORD is Prasopsin's composition; it is in a D = 3 six-tone scale (B♭ = 1 2 3 4 5 6) without 7, and 4 only appears twice: one occurrence is in a descending progression (6- 4 5- 4 3). This melody is through-composed without any repetition, and the melodic progression is in accord with some Thai practices. By using 3/4 meter, the composer departs from the traditional duple time of Thai music. Otherwise, the melody maintains a Thai character. (para. Roland S. Tino)

"I sing a song of victory" (*STB* #151)

(Thai: *Khaa jao banleng phleng mahachai*)

This hymn, one of the earliest Thai hymns sung outside Thailand, first appeared in *New Songs of Asian Cities* (1972). It is about the victory of Jesus Christ, who has crushed Satan's reign by his own death and resurrection. It invites all to join the praise and concludes with a commitment to trust in Christ. This Easter hymn can also be sung in funeral and memorial services to celebrate the hope and victory of life in Christ.

The tune MAHACHAI, meaning "victory," was composed by Naga Boriputt in a D = 5 six-tone scale (E = 6 7 1 2 3 5) with 6 as the final; it is through-composed. Like other six-tone scales, the 7 does not occur in an ascending progression (7–1), which is an important Thai musical feature. Although the hymn is a song of victory, its melodic flow is still rather lyrical. The inner strength of the text gives power to this song. The last phrase was originally sung with the neutral schwa "ə," but new words have been added, meaning "Praise the almighty Lord." In order to show the beauty of the original style, the congregation is encouraged to sing this phrase in Thai. A pair of concussion bells would also add appeal to this hymn. (para. JM)

"Released by love to share new life" (*STB* #72)

(Thai: *Hao mii chiiwit phraw phra jao hai*)

This hymn is a product of a husband-and-wife team, Inchai and Ruth Srisuwan. The Isaan community church in which they both served had Bible studies everyday; the day's study theme was frequently versified by Ruth, the poet; Inchai, the composer, would set music to it for all to sing. This text is a doctrinal interpretation that the love of God has given new life and that people are moved to sing beautiful songs to worship God in harmony through Jesus. Therefore, it admonishes people to worship God as a goal of life, for "Jesus intercedes to draw us close to God in peace." With this content, it is good to sing this hymn at the beginning of or during a worship service to ponder on the meaning, reasons, and purpose of worship.

CHIIWIT, meaning "life," was composed after a folk melody and is in an F♯ = 3 six-tone scale (B = 6 7 1 2 3 5) with 6 as the final. One can see the frequent use of 7 from a descending half-tone progression (1–7) but not an ascending one (7–1). It also appears in other shapes (6 7 5 6 or 676 6) a few times. This 1–7 descending half-tone progression is one major characteristic of the folk tradition; the progression rarely ascends a half step. With the refrain, the piece is quite long; the composer's arrangement can be seen in the repetition or imitation of phrases. Since Thai is a tonal language, the melody was composed according to the natural intonation of the words; hence the notes indicated in parenthesis (in the fourth system) are for the second stanza, where the texts demand the change of pitch and intonation for the sake of clarity. When singing the hymn in English, they can be ignored.

"This is the day of joy and peace" (*STB* #303)

This is an anonymous Christmas carol from Thailand, adapted by Solot Kuptarat and paraphrased by Shirley Murray. It tells not of the nativity but of the joy of meeting God's newborn child, who has everlasting power to redeem all sinners through the sacrifice of his life on the cross, so that all would be purified like angels freed from sin and pain. This is an appropriate Advent hymn and is also suitable for contemplating the meanings of salvation through Jesus.

The tune NAAMPHAI (the name of a Thai village) is in a C = 2 six-tone scale (B♭ = 1 2 3 4 5 6) with the ascending 1-5- as the final cadence, which may sound unusual to Western ears. It also has a wide range equaling a twelfth, and it consists of two identical sections of four phrases (a b c d). Although there are no exact repetitions within each section, the patterns of the repeated tones (2 2 2 2, 6 6 6 6, and 6 6 6) and the similar melodic shapes (35 32 1, 6165 4, or, reversing the second half, 61 64 5) provide a feeling of inner unity in the melodic development. The accompaniment of concussion bells (o = open and weak, + = closed and strong) is important to mark the hymn's Thai style. (para. Shirley Murray)

"Upon this day of peace" (*STB* #14)

(Thai: *Wan ni wan santisuk*)

This hymn by Songsan Prasopsin admonishes Christians to cast out sins, fears, and sorrows so that they can praise Jesus and to join the heavenly songs with the saints in harmony, praising the Lord and King. The last stanza praises Christ for his redemption through love and sacrifice—"for his love revealed to us on the tree."

LAAO-SOOM-DET, meaning "the great melody," is a traditional Thai melody in a C = 5 six-tone scale (D = 6 7 1 2 3 5). It is a typical through-composed piece without any repetition, and half-tone progressions only occur in descending motion (1-7-6). In this piece, the concussion bells accompaniment begins with a strong beat (+ = closed; o = open, weak). (trsl. Boonmee Julkiree; para. Jim Minchin)

Conclusion

Derived mainly from folk traditions, the tunes of these Thai hymns are through-composed yet they retain Thai musical characteristics. For example, an accompaniment with a pair of concussion bells is almost indispensable. Further, the tunes are basically in five-tone scales (1 2 3 5 6); when the sixth tone 7 appears, it is always in a descending motion. In this respect, the tunes are similar in style to traditional Chinese melodic idioms. Some of the Thai churches have successfully developed their church music to fit their local musical context, and they can serve as good models for churches in neighboring countries.

 # Vietnamese Hymns

The Nation, People, and Culture

The official name of Vietnam is the Socialist Republic of Vietnam. It is located south of China; the South China Sea is to the east and south, and Cambodia and Laos are to the west. It has a total area of 329,560 square kilometers (about 127,244 square miles), approximately the size of Malaysia or Norway (Garland 4:444). For about ten centuries (110 BCE–938 CE), Vietnam was ruled by China. After a succession of indigenous dynasties, Vietnam was colonized by France in the mid-nineteenth century. Efforts by communist resistance forces to expel the French in the 1940s led to the political division of the country; the communists gained control of North Vietnam in 1954. Fighting between the North and South, which was supported by the United States, continued until 1975, when North Vietnamese forces took over South Vietnam, unifying the country under communist rule. Vietnam has a population of 86,116,560, with Viet or Kinh as the largest group, composing eighty-six percent of the population.[42] The balance consists of descendents from the Chinese (thirteen percent) and fifty-three tribal groups who mostly live in the highlands (Athyal 1996, 203f).

Cross-cultural Influences

Archeologists have discovered bronze drums, bells, and lithophones (percussion instruments made of stone slabs) in Vietnam that date from the third to the first millennia BCE. The lithophones may have been the precursors of Southeast Asian xylophones, such as the *chalung* in Indonesia. The Dong Son period (700–100 BCE) bronze drums have been found throughout Southeast Asia and southern China; these drums may have led to the development of the gamelan in Indonesia. Also, it is probable that Indian and Central Asian musical instruments were introduced to Vietnam before those from China (cf. Garland 4:446f).

Musical Practice and *Metabole* in Vietnamese Music

There is no comprehensive theory of Vietnamese music, for the northern, central, and southern regions have their own systems. Since the 1700s, the Vietnamese have used a modified version of Chinese notation (*gongche pu*). Music theory and notation are mostly transmitted orally from teachers to pupils. With regard to scales, there is no absolute pitch; the fundamental pitch is decided by the performing singer or instrument. Five-tone scales are common. Pressing on strings produces

---

42   CIA, "The World Factbook, Vietnam," July 2008 estimate, https://www.cia.gov/library/publications/the-world-factbook/print/vm.html (accessed January 29, 2009).

a variety of intervallic combinations and adds additional tones. In general, the Southeast Asian whole-tones range from 165 to 175 cents. Smaller intervals or microtones are used in modulations or transmigrations of scalar units (Garland 4:456f). The term "metabole" was coined by the ethnomusicologist Constantin Brailoiu (1955, 63–75) to describe this phenomenon.

One can observe similar features in the Khmer (Cambodian) hymn "Preah Yesu" (*STB* #206). This melody is in an ordinary diatonic scale, but it is juxtaposed with the same theme in two different keys. It begins with a C scale (E = 34 5 4 32 12 34 5). At the second system, the same melody has been transposed a fourth higher in an F scale (A = 34 5 4 32 12 35), and it returns to C at the second half of the phrase. At the end of the third system, it shifts to the F scale again, leading to the refrain. This metabole shifts the melody to a higher or lower center without actual modulation through harmony.

The Vietnamese concept of mode is rather complicated. Phong T. Nguyen speculates that:

> [The modal conceptualization,] probably nurtured from time immemorial, is based on combined notions of both exact and flexible pitches, melodic patterns, specific ornamentations, timing, quality and type of vocal sound, and particular modal sentiments. (Garland 4:455)

Vietnamese music and its heritage are still propagated by the father-son musician team Tran Van Khe and Tran Van Hai, who have served in the French National Cultural Center in Paris.

Religious Music

The majority of the Vietnamese subscribe to Mahayana Buddhism; it is believed that as early as the second century CE, a Buddhist community was founded with as many as five hundred monks. But Confucianism and Taoism are also popular among the Chinese descendants. Music plays an important role in all official functions, religious rituals, the Lunar New Year festivals (usually in February), and in celebrations of life cycles. The most interesting Vietnamese religious music is related to Buddhism, Confucianism, and Taoism. Buddhist music uses three different vocal styles: cantillating sutras and mantras, singing poetic hymns, and mixing speech and song (Garland 4:502f). Chinese Confucianism and Taoism have influenced not only Vietnam's philosophical life but also certain musical ideas. But Vietnam maintains its identity within diverse musical styles.

Traditional Instruments

Some traditional Vietnamese musical instruments are: *trong dong* (bronze drum from the Dong Son period); *chieng, thanh la, tum* (large, medium, and small gongs); *dan bau* (monochord); *dan tranh* (board zithers with sixteen strings); *dan day* (three-stringed plucked lute); *dan nguyet* (moon lute); *dan nhi* (bowed lute); *sao* (horizontal bamboo flute); and *ken* (wooden oboe) (Garland 4:467–75).

The Christian Church and Its Contributions

Although it is said that Christian mission appeared in Vietnam as early as the second century, there are no historical records of this. During the seventeenth century, the French missionary Alexander de Rhodes was sent to Vietnam, mastered Vietnamese, and perfected the Romanized script of the language, which is still in use today. In 1680, Roman Catholics claimed to have 800,000 members in Vietnam. The Protestant mission began in 1911, but it has met mild persecution and opposition. Some work of the church, especially that of the evangelical missionaries since 1975, has been closely monitored by the communist government. Evangelism has been most successful in the tribal areas; in 1994, there were about 350,000 Christians among the evangelical churches and about 100,000 Viet members (Athyal 1996, 203–10).

Commentary on the Hymn

"O Lord, your mercy show" (*STB* #302)
(Vietnamese: *Xin Chua thuong xot chung con*)

The physical effects of the wars in Vietnam can still be seen throughout the country and in neighboring Cambodia and Laos. But animosity toward the West, especially the United States, has eased in recent decades with Vietnam's economic reforms and rapid growth. In the early 1970s and the 1980s, however, lingering tensions prevented I-to Loh from visiting this region and collecting material for hymns. This is why *Sound the Bamboo* features only one short Kyrie from Vietnam.

This hymn was taught by a Vietnamese pastor during the tenth General Assembly of the CCA in Colombo in 1996. It was probably taken from a Roman Catholic liturgy, as Vietnam has more Roman Catholic churches than Protestant ones. Father Jim Minchin carefully paraphrased the text to fit the music. As in most liturgical Kyries, the first two phrases are intoned initially by the priest and then repeated by the congregation. Then the priest sings the third phrase, and the congregation responds.

In ordinary worship, one can sing this Kyrie as a call to a confession of sins or as a preparation for the individual prayers of intercession. The music is in a G

= 3 six-tone scale (C = 6 7 1 2 3 5). Because of Vietnam's long relationship with China, many aspects of Vietnamese culture are similar to those of southern China. For instance, the phonetic system and pronunciation of Vietnamese are similar to those of Chinese and particularly Cantonese: "chu" is more like "zu," and "xin" is close to "xin" or "hsin," but "con" is pronounced like "gone." The melody of this hymn is also similar to a Chinese style. Uniquely Vietnamese musical features unfortunately cannot be seen from this short piece. No accompaniment is necessary for this hymn; simply intone and repeat.

Conclusion

During the past two decades, Asian and Western churches and industries have established a presence in Vietnam. Many Vietnamese Christians who have immigrated to the United States are beginning to sense the importance of maintaining and propagating their musical heritage. If more Christians pursue the study of Vietnamese traditional music and are able to interpret their faith with it, one can anticipate more Vietnamese musical and hymnal contributions in the future.

Island Southeast Asia

Island Southeast Asia includes two countries: Indonesia and the Philippines.

 Indonesian Hymns

The Nation, People, and Cultures

The Republic of Indonesia consists of five major islands and about thirty smaller island groups. There are a total of 17,508 islands, of which 6,000 are inhabited, and the total land and sea area is 1,919,440 square kilometers (about 741,100 square miles). The island chains stretch about 5472 kilometers (3,400 miles) from east to west. The estimated population in 2008 was 237,512,352, making Indonesia the fourth most populous country after China, India, and the United States.[43] The country's ethnic distribution is 94% Malay, 4% Chinese, 1.2% Irianese/Papuan people, and 0.8% others. There are 584 languages in the whole country, among which only one is extinct (Grimes 1984, 430). Among the Malay people, seventeen languages are spoken, including Javanese (42%), Sundanese (13.6%), Madurese (7%), Minangkabau (3.3%), Batak (2.9%), Sumatran Malay (2.9%), Bugis (2.8%), and Balinese (2.1%). The national language is Bahasa Indonesia or Indonesian, which is now spoken by approximately 73% of the population (Athyal 1996, 325f).

The Portuguese took over Malacca (now part of Malaysia) in 1511, and the Dutch captured it in 1641; control of this former sultanate gave the European traders access to the Maluku Islands, known as the Spice Islands, which are now part of Indonesia. The Dutch colonized Indonesia from the early seventeenth century. Japan also occupied Indonesia during the Second World War, from 1942 to 1945. Indonesia proclaimed its independence on August 17, 1945, but it was not formally recognized by the Dutch until 1949. Indonesia is the world's most populous Muslim-majority nation, with Muslims composing almost 86% of the populace. The government officially recognizes six religions: Islam, Protestantism, Catholicism, Hinduism, Buddhism, and Confucianism. According to the 2000 census, 8.7% of the population is Christian (of which roughly two-thirds are Protestant), 3% is Hindu, and 1.8% is Buddhist.[44] The motto of the nation is loosely translated as "Unity in Diversity," and the national philosophy is expressed in the Pancasila, or "five principles":

1. Belief in the one and only God
2. A just and civilized humanity
3. The unity of Indonesia
4. Democracy guided by the inner wisdom arising from deliberations among representatives
5. Social justice for all the people of Indonesia

(Athyal 1996, 326)

Effectively, this allows freedom of religious practice.

---

43   CIA, "The World Factbook, Indonesia," July 2008 estimate, https://www.cia.gov/library/publications/the-world-factbook/print/id.html (accessed January 29, 2009).

44   Wikipedia, "Indonesia," http://en.wikipedia.org/wiki/Indonesia#Demographics (accessed January 29, 2009).

A Brief History of Christian Mission

According to Iman Santoso, Nestorian Eastern Christianity reached the Indonesian archipelago by the seventh century, but the current Indonesian church was founded by Portuguese Catholic missionaries in the sixteenth century (Athyal 1996, 334). The Dutch Reformed Church arrived in the seventeenth century along with the Dutch governors and traders. In 1935, the Protestant state church was officially separated from the Dutch government, and Indonesians could take more leadership roles in its development. During the Japanese occupation (1942–45), Indonesians revolted against the policy of bowing to Japan's emperor in Sunday worship services. Thus the indigenous church matured in its faith as well as its sense of social responsibility. Many church leaders actively participated in the country's fight for independence and in nation building. During the past few decades, according to Santoso, three factors have prepared Indonesians to become Christian:

1. Huge economic problems, such as inflation and foreign debt, caused great poverty and suffering for the majority of the people.
2. The communist coup in 1965 created fear, terror, uncertainty, and restlessness in the people.
3. The first principle of the nation's ideology—to believe in one God—encourages adherence to one of the recognized religions. Because Christians contributed to the nation's development and thus improved the image of the church, many Indonesians have turned to Christ for their religious practice. (Athyal 1996, 334f)

According to the 1987 report of the Indonesian Department of Religious Affairs, there were 26,769 Protestant places of worship, 13,080 pastors, 38,857 gospel teachers, 483 missionaries, 548 orphanages, seventy-three hospitals and clinics, 5,485 Christian schools (including eight universities), sixty Protestant religious teachers' institutes, and ninety-seven Bible schools and seminaries (Athyal 1996, 340).

A Brief Introduction of Music from Sumatra and Java

Sumatra

Sumatra is the largest of the islands entirely in Indonesia, almost 2,000 kilometers (about 1242 miles) long, and is parallel to the Malay Peninsula. It is rich in natural resources such as oil and rubber, and wild tigers, elephants, and orangutans still live on the island (Garland 4:598). Sumatra's ethnic cultures are quite diverse, and the influence of Buddhist and Hindu religions and musical styles are still evident. The boat-shaped *kucapi* or *hasapi* of the Batak ethnic groups was derived from the Indian lute called *kasyapi* in Sanskrit. The Dutch and German missionaries introduced harmonic singing to the people in South Sumatra, the northern and

A *gondang* ensemble (one gong is not visible), at a reception on March 7, 2007, in Medan, coinciding with the fiftieth anniversary celebration of the founding of the Christian Conference of Asia, in Parapat.

central Batak lands, the island of Nias, and other places; accordions and violins have become popular instruments. The song "Sing-sing-so" with solo and choral responses is the best example of such influences (Garland 4:601). In 2007, I visited a Batak church service, in which four different choirs sang various choral pieces in typical Batak style and three- to four-part traditional Western harmonic settings.

"Batak" is a term for a number of ethnic groups, including the Toba (who are Christian), Simalungun, Karo, and Pakpak or Dairi subgroups in the north and the Angkola (who are Muslim) and Mandailing in the south. All Batak subgroups accompany their dances with instrumental ensembles. The Toba *gondang* ensemble consists of five graded drums (*taganing*), a bass drum (*gondang*), four gongs (*ogung*), and an oboe (*sarunei*) (Garland 4:607). Some churches are just beginning to experiment using these ensembles in worship services.

Java

Java is a long narrow island, with an area of approximately 130,000 square kilometers (about 50,193 square miles), and it is the home of two major ethnic groups: the Javanese, who compose about two-thirds of the population, and the Sundanese, who live in the western part of the island. Java's population is about 100 million (Garland 4:631). The city of Jakarta in West Java is the capital of Indonesia, and Yogyakarta in Central Java is an important center of traditional culture. The Javanese language has multiple levels of speech and corresponding honorifics. "Low Javanese" (*ngoko*) is used by persons of higher status speaking to those of lower status or by intimate friends. "High Javanese" (*krama*) is used by those of lower status when speaking to those of higher status, by younger people when speaking to their elders, and by official speech (Garland 4:631). In Javanese shadow puppetry (*wayang kulit*), the puppeteer (*dalang*) is expected to portray all the different levels of speech.

Java has 2,000 years of recorded history and has been influenced by India, China, Central Asia, Europe, and America. The Dong Son culture of Indochina (see the discussion in the section for Vietnam) left large bronze kettledrums in Java during the first and second century CE, which eventually led to the development of the Indonesian gamelan. India's influence on Javanese culture began in the fifth century through Buddhism. Carved reliefs on the monumental Buddhist *stupa* built in the eighth or ninth century in Borobudur show a large number of musical instruments, which are also seen in the ninth- or tenth-century Laro Jonggrang complex at Prambanan, a Hindu temple. Jaap Kunst, the Dutch pioneer of ethnomusicology, lists the instruments at Borobudur as: "shell and straight trumpets, side-blown flutes, end-blown flutes (or double-reed aerophones), mouth organs, lutes, bar zithers, arched harps, double-headed drums, a xylophone, bells, and a knobbed kettle-gong" (quoted by Kartomi in Garland 4:632).

View of Borobudur, March 7, 2005

Gamelan music as it is known today was derived from the court tradition of Surakarta, or Solo, in Central Java; the Solonese style emphasizes the intricate and florid vocal and instrumental lines. It is quintessentially *alus*, a term implying refinement, subtlety, and smoothness (Garland 4:633f).

Bas-relief of musicians at Borobudur, March 7, 2005

Bas-relief of musicians at Borobudur, March 7, 2005

JAVANESE GAMELAN AND ITS MUSIC

The term "gamelan" refers to the Indonesian orchestra, which consists of twelve to fifteen gong-chime instruments or as many as seventy-five or eighty instruments for the court. Jaap Kunst reported that there were as many as 17,000 gamelans around the country in the 1930s. According to Mantle Hood, the oldest type of Javanese gamelan was probably created in the second or first century BCE. Ensembles using five-note *slendro* tuning (with relatively equidistant intervals) were developed by the sixth or seventh century while ensembles using seven-note *pelog* tuning (with uneven intervals) existed as early as the twelfth century (NGDI, 9:169–70). The instrumentation or texture of gamelan music is complicated and may involve as many as thirty to forty different strata, with polyphonic relationships among the strata. Hood has described such colotomic structure as "polyphonic stratification" (Hood and Susilo 1967, 15–16). David Morton has defined this as a principle in which a "specific instrument [enters] in a specific order at a specific time" (Morton 1976, 43).

The colotomic structure of Javanese gamelan may be explained with the first section of the popular composition "Udan Mas" ("Golden Rain"), in the mode *slendro nem*. The first *gongan* (a section marked by sounding a large gong) is:

6	5	3	2	6	5	3	2	2	3	5	3	6	5	3	2	*saron*
t		t		t		t			t		t		t		t	*kethuk*
	W				P					P				P		*kempul*
			N					N					N		N	*kenong*
															G	*gong ageng*

This form can be doubled or quadrupled by adding an equal number of tones (or counts) in between the tones, but the structure is maintained.

Here, the *saron* (metallophone) plays the fixed or main melody, which is grouped in four notes (6 5 3 2) in a *gatra* (a unit of melody, like a measure of four notes or counts in Western music); the *kethuk* (small kettle gong) beats the time on every other note; the *kempul* (suspended gong) plays on every second note of the *gatra*, but the first *kempul* beat, called *wela*, is silent; the *kenong* (kettle gong) marks the end of each *gatra* and is played in between every fourth note, while the large *gong ageng* only plays once at the end to mark the complete *gongan* section. Above the main melody, the *peking* (metallophones one octave above the *saron*) and various *bonang* (kettle gongs) will double, anticipate, or decorate the main melody. For example, the first *gatra* of 6 5 3 2 is played as follows:

6 5 6 . 6 5 6 5 3 2 3 . 3 2 3 2   (*bonang panerus*, anticipating and
                                    decorating, 4x)
   6 5 6 5 3 2 3 2   (*bonang*, anticipating and doubling in a pair)
   6 6 5 5 3 3 2 2   (*peking*, echoing and anticipating, 2x faster)
      6   5   3   2   (*saron,* first *gatra*, main melody)
      (5)   (*kempul,* 5 is silent on the first *gatra*)
                 2 (*kenong*)

These notations clearly show the colotomic structure and how each instrument plays its role. If playing at a low volume (traditionally called "soft playing"), a full Javanese gamelan further features *rebab* (bowed lute), *suling* (flute), *gambang* (wooden xylophones), and voices. These parts may be seen in the following transcription (after Hood and Susilo 1967, 19).

"Sriredjeki" Kendangan Ladrang Kendangan 2, Pelog Patet Nem. Transcribed by Hardja Susilo.

PATET

Hood (1954) demonstrates the prominence of certain cadential formulas in the *saron* melody of each *patet* (or *pathet*, mode). Judy Becker argues that listeners recognize *patet* on the basis of three factors: the identity of a "melodic pattern, formula, or contour," its level of pitch, and its position within a compositional structure (Garland 4:657). The following chart compares the tonal hierarchy and *patet* and Hood's cadential formulas:

Tuning	Patet	Tones emphasized	avoided*	Hood's Cadential formula
Slendro	*nem* ("six")	2,6,5	1	6532
	sanga ("nine")	5, 1, (2)	3	2165
	manyura ("peacock")	6, 2, (3)	5	3216
Pelog	*lima* (five)	1, 5	7	
	nem (six)	5, 6	7	
	barang (things)	6, 2, (3, 5)	1	

*the "enemy tone" (Hood 1954, 245–247)
(Garland 4:657; Hood 1954, 122–124; Hood and Susilo 1967, 29–42)

Children's bamboo trumpet ensemble, Toraja,
March 6, 2005

Bamboo instruments are important in Sunda, West Java. The *angklung* is made of two to three tuned bamboo tubes set in a bamboo frame; one plays it by shaking the frame rapidly. *Angklungs* are tuned from one to three octaves and are played by a group in a melodic, interlocking, or harmonic manner (from Western influence). This instrument is very popular not only in Indonesian schools but also in schools in some other Asian countries, such as the Philippines, and most recently in Taiwan.

The Protestant Church in Bali, Its Arts, and Contextual Witnesses

Bali is a small island east of Java, with an area of 5620 square kilometers (about 2170 square miles); it has 3,750 villages and a population of approximately three million, of which ninety-eight percent is Hindu (NGDII, 12:289). According to Bishop Wayan Mastra, a Chinese evangelist began to spread the gospel in 1929 and gained more than one hundred Balinese converts within three years (Loh 1988, 7). The Dutch missionary Hendric Kraemer also worked in Bali from 1935 to 1942. It was very difficult to evangelize in this society of Hindus and animists, who believe there are spirits or gods in all natural forms— stones, trees, mountains, rivers, etc.

Front view of the Christian Church, Blimbingsari (after Takenaka 1995, 102).

The Balinese were against the establishment of Christian churches and would not allow Christians to be buried in their cemetery. On one occasion, the Reverend Mastra, who began his first term as Bishop of the Protestant Church of Bali in 1971, risked his life in a funeral procession that was blocked by the villagers. After kneeling down to pray for God's mercy and guidance, he stood up and led the march to the cemetery. Seeing the faith and courage of Mastra and his followers, the hostile and heavily armed villagers left silently without causing any harm. Christ had finally conquered Bali. It is no wonder that Mastra's motto is: "Christ is my life, but Bali is my body." There are now at least fifty-two congregations on this island (Loh 1988, 7f).

Bali is known all over the world for its rich cultural heritage of music, art, dance, and sculpture and is often called "the island of artists." Along with I Nyoman Darsane (a prolific artist, poet, dancer, puppeteer, composer, and musician), Bishop Mastra utilizes Balinese philosophy and artistic and cultural expressions to contextualize and proclaim the gospel. For example, Mastra writes:

The Balinese associate mountains with the presence of God as well as the source of life; this has prompted the conscientious Christians to build their churches resembling mountains . . . A temple gate symbolizes coming into the presence of God. Thus, a traditional temple gate is constructed behind the communion table, but a Cross is set in the middle, affirming that Christ is the Way to God (Mastra 1985; Loh 1988, 8)

The interior of the Christian Church Denpasar, looking toward the altar. Behind the communion table is a traditional temple gate with a cross in the opening, representing Jesus as "the way, the truth and the life" (after Takenaka 1995, 105).

Dance in Bali is a powerful medium for communicating ideas and emotions. The highly stylized gestures and eye, finger, arm, and foot movements are the keys to understanding Balinese dance, as they represent deeper meanings (Loh 1988, 14–15). The traditional dance movements have been reinterpreted for a Christian context as follows:

__Body Part__	__Traditional Interpretation__	__Christian Interpretation__
thumb	wisdom	God's wisdom, providence
index finger	power, position	God's omnipotence
middle finger	wealth	the richness of God
ring finger	beauty, blessings	God's grace, blessings
pinky finger	trust	faithfulness, eternal life
eyes	heaven, the watching eyes of the gods	Heaven, God's loving care, God's watching eyes
hands	human beings	God's children
feet	the world, the earth	God's world
symmetrical movements	the balance between good and evil, and right and wrong	God's justice and mercy, judgment and grace

These Christian interpretations have added new dimensions to communicating the gospel to the Balinese through dance (Loh 1988, 15; 2005c, 137).

(after Loh 1988, 33)

Kecak dance, Bali, March 11, 2005.
Photo: I-to Loh.

(after Loh 1988, 35)

I Nyoman Darsane composed *Anak Dara* ("The Parable of the Ten Virgins") to urge diligent preparations to welcome the sudden coming of the groom, Jesus Christ. Darsane's use of the gamelan to accompany the singing was rare at the time. The composition, which begins with an overture of dance, marked the beginning of a new era of Balinese Christian dance and music.

The painting "Parable of the Ten Virgins," by Darsane (after Loh 1988)

Balinese Gamelan

Balinese gamelans are more brilliant, have more dynamic contrasts, and have a greater variety of orchestration than Javanese gamelans (NGDI, 9:172). The most interesting technique is *kotekan*. In this style, the *gangsa* (metallophone) and *reyong* (kettle

225

gong) players play interlocking figures consisting of two complementary parts; the first, basic, and main part, usually played on the beat, is called *polos* (see the *gangsa* II and *reyong* II parts in the following illustration), and the part played off the beat or between the *polos* is called *sangsih* (see the *gangsa* I and *reyong* I parts). The composite melody formed by *kotekan* becomes twice as fast as the individual parts.

Darsane's composition *Anak Dara* features Balinese polyphonic stratification, *kotekan*, and other techniques. In the following example, two *gangsa* and the *reyong* play the interlocking parts (*kotekan*) against the nuclear melody of the *jublag* and *pengugal* (larger keyed metallophones with resonant tubes). The functions of other colotomic instruments (*jegogan* and gong) in the orchestra can also be seen (Loh 1988, 9–12).

A mastery of rhythmic precision is required to execute intricate passages typical of Balinese gamelan, such as this example, formed by three motives—a, b, and c—and their variants:

(after Loh 1988, 10)

Motive *a* is a descending third (3 1), *a'* is a descending second (5 4); *b* is an ascending third (1 3), *b'* is an ascending second (4 5), and *c* is a single note G (5), which marks the transition to a new pattern, i.e., the reversal of *a* (3 1) to *b* (1 3). Although this G (5) is the beginning of *a'* (5 4), it becomes the second half of the *b* motive (4 5) after the transition (the single 5). The interlocking occurs twice between *a* and *a'*, and the third time is the transition, in which the lower note of the *a* motive (1) becomes the beginning of the *b* motive (1), forming a conjunct position of the two motives; it is also where the single G note enters. This G note always forms the interval of a fifth with the lower note. The interlocking also occurs between *a'* and *b*, and *c* and *a*, and *c* and *b*, etc. Depending on how one listens to the interlocking events, one could hear groups of three-note patterns: 314 314 and 134 134 134 in the lower voice, or simply 54 54 5 45 45 4 on the top, or a combination of four tones, 5431 5431 or 1345 1345. With the addition of the other colotomic instruments to the sound, one may perceive the intricate mosaic-like activities in the gamelan (Loh 1988, 10–12).

Another passage of the same piece shows a more complicated melody with a similar technique:

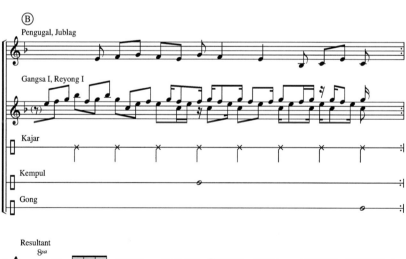

The following chart shows the various forms of Balinese notation used today: the original, traditional, and contemporary cipher notations used in Indonesia; the common cipher notation used in other parts of Asia and the world; and the Western equivalent (after Loh 1988, 14).

(after Loh 1988, 11)

West Papua

Formerly called West Irian Jaya, West Papua is an Indonesian province on the western end of the island of New Guinea. The province has a population of about two million, with more than 250 distinct ethnic groups. Some of them, especially the highlanders, sing in drones, in thirds, or in other tonal combinations, such as double thirds; see "Bird call announces morning" (*STB* #305).

Some Indonesian musical instruments in the collection of I-to Loh:

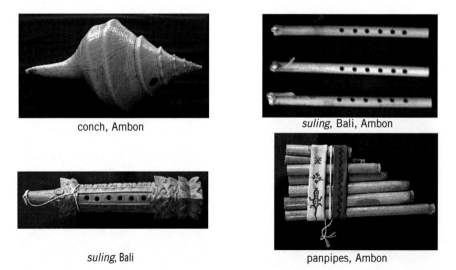

conch, Ambon

suling, Bali, Ambon

suling, Bali

panpipes, Ambon

monochord, Ambon

kacapi (2-string plucked lute), Sumatra

kacapi (2-string plucked lute), Sumatra

sasandu (tube zither with resonator), Timor

gamelan *angklung*, Bali:
kempul (suspended gong)
jegogan x2
remade x2 (metalophone)

trompong
reyong (kettle gongs)
kantilan x6

kendang (drum)
cheng cheng (turtle cymbals)
kajar (kettle gong)

kajar (kettle gong) (seen from above)

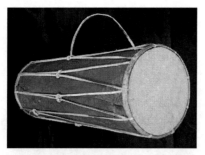

kendang, Gamelan Anklun, Bali

kendang, Gamelan Anklun, Bali

gong, Java

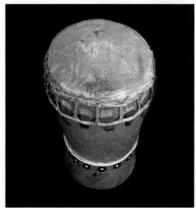

tifa, Ambon

tifa, Ambon

tifa, Ambon

tifa, Irian Jaya

anklung, Java and Sunda

Commentary on Individual Hymns

"Amen" (*STB* #107)

This amen response is by Paul Widyawan of Yamuger, a Roman Catholic center of liturgy and music in Yogyakarta. Widyawan is one of the main leaders at the center for composing and promoting hymns and anthems in Indonesian styles. The main melody uses the *pelog* tuning system, which has narrow intervals (similar to minor seconds) and gapped intervals (similar to major thirds). In this piece, the scale is an F = 5 four-tone scale (5 7 1 3). But the bass adds another pitch 4, and the melodic progression of the parts is typically Indonesian: 1-71/3--, 5 i̱7 5 i/7--, 3-4 4̲3̲4̲5̲/3. While the harmony is not traditionally Indonesian, the composer has avoided a Western chord at the end. This response can serve as an alternative to any existing three-fold amen chorus at the close of worship.

"Amin, Haleluya!" (*STB* #105)

This short prayer response was arranged by Sutarno according to a Javanese melodic motif and was first introduced at the sixth General Assembly of the World Council of Churches in Vancouver, in 1983.[45] Musically, it is in a Javanese style, in an E = 7 five-tone scale (7 1 3 4 5) with the final on 3. This is sung and accompanied in a basic gamelan style, in which the *kempul* (a medium suspended gong, marked with "P" in the score) is struck on the strong beat of every other measure while the largest gong (marked with "G") is only struck on the last beat of the cycle. Here, each measure is counted as two beats. If one regards the main melody as being played by *saron* (metallophones) with the *kempul* and gong, these instruments form the first three layers of the colotomic structure (for a detailed explanation, see the introductory part of this section). This piece is sung as a response to prayers of thanksgiving or praise. It also may be performed as a litany, with a response after each short statement of thanksgiving or praise. Since *kempul* and large gongs are not easily available, one can replace them with smaller gongs, but one should make sure that the sizes and tones are different and to play the lower tone at the end of the piece.

---

45   In Java, it is common for a person to have only one name. "Sutarno" is the full name of the arranger.

Ask your God" (*STB* #235)

(Indonesian: *Mintalah, mintalah*)

This is a paraphrase of Jesus' promise in Matthew 7:7, "Ask, and it will be given you; search, and you will find; knock, and the door will be opened for you." Subronto K. Atmodjo composed this hymn in a Western style, in a D = 5 six-tone scale (G = 1 2 3 4 5 7). The simplicity of style and form of a b (a') a c indicate that it was possibly intended for children. The b phrase is an answer of phrase a (5 3 1-) in the dominant (5 2 7-), but it concludes in the tonic; hence it is marked as a'. MINTALAH means "ask." This is a good hymn to use while teaching children about praying and simple trust in the merciful God.

"Bird call announces morning" (*STB* #305)

(Indonesian: *Burung murai telah bernyanyi riang*)

This unique hymn is from West Papua, formerly known as West Irian Jaya, an Indonesian province located on the western end of the island of New Guinea. The people of West Papua speak Indonesian, the national language, but their physical attributes and their culture are similar to those of other inhabitants of New Guinea. Like other New Guineans, the West Papuans are short, have dark skin, and have curly hair. Due to various geographical, ethnic, and cultural differences, they express a desire to be independent from Indonesia.

This is a very beautiful contextual hymn that metaphorically utilizes cultural and musical expressions to interpret the meaning of light and darkness and one's relationship with Christ. It uses many images to refer to Christ: "Morning Bird," "true Sun of heaven," "Earth's first born," "our Sunshine," etc. The second stanza picks up the bird motif to poetically describe the resurrection of Christ:

> Christ flew from death to new life before dawn,
> sang how your Spirit freed him, Earth's first born.

The entire hymn is a prayer for guidance.

The tune KUDO-KUDO (which might refer to the name of the original melody) is in a typical style of the Torres Straight region, in which the music is constructed melodically and harmonically with the major triad 1 3 5 (*do mi sol*). Jaap Kunst, the pioneer of ethnomusicology who extensively researched the music of Indonesia and this region, called this a "fanfare melody," alluding to the trumpet-like flourishes of medieval European courts. The ancient trumpets could only play the triad 1-3-5 and a high 2; when they played different pitches together, they formed a harmony or a chord. Songs of Irian Jaya are based on this harmonic practice; they are homophonic and parallel throughout, i.e., the melody and harmony have the same rhythm and move in the same direction. If all voices are placed in the same range, the tenor sings one tone higher than the main melody (creating a minor third, a major third, or a perfect fourth), and the bass or alto sings one tone lower (a perfect fourth, a major third, or a minor third). Here, the "one tone" means the neighboring tones between 5 1 3 5 i. There is only one exception; because the lowest tone of the scale is middle C (5), the lowest part of the harmony does not go down to lower A (3) but maintains 5-1 harmony. Singing this hymn, one could imagine playing trumpets in a fanfare to welcome Tuhan, Allah, Raja ("Lord, God, King") Jesus and to ask him to lead one to the new day. (trscr. & trsl. Hanock Tanatty; para. Jim Minchin)

"Come down, O Holy Spirit (*STB* #221)

(Indonesian: *Roh Kudus turunlah*)

Asking the Spirit to illuminate one's path and to inspire praise to the Savior, Subronto K. Atmodjo also prays for God's truth, love, grace, hope, and radiant faith so that one can serve the world.

The author composed this tune ROH KUDUS ("Holy Spirit") in a D = 7 *pelog* five-tone scale (G = 3 4 5 7 1), in a style similar to a German chorale in an E♭-major scale without 2 and 6; the melody moves along straight beats with quarter notes, except in the b section and the cadences. The piece is organized in a a' b a' form, and the accompaniment is mostly in Western four-part harmony. But one can see free progressions, part crossings, and imitations, all of which seem to demonstrate the composer's desire to depart from traditional Western chordal harmony and to create his own Indonesian style. (para. H.A. Pandopo)

"Dear God, how you love your creatures" (*STB* #180)

(Indonesian: *Dengan kasihMu, ya Tuhan*)

Iba Tahya's hymn affirms God's love for the nature and all creatures. Rudolf Pantou adds two more stanzas that thank God for providing one's needs and acknowledge Christ as this world's holy lover.

Pantou's tune MAKHLUK, meaning "creatures," is similar to medieval church chants in a Dorian mode: D = 2 3 4 5 6 7 1 2. The simple, flowing melody begins from the lower register, develops to a climax in the middle section, and returns to the initial motif to conclude the song. The harmony uses the double drone 2 and 6, with the tenor part moving slowly to create different colors and tension and release to good effect. (para. Jim Minchin)

"God's love is everlasting" (*STB* #115)

Paul Widyawan composed this paraphrase of Psalm 136:1 in a typical Indonesian *pelog* five-tone scale: D = 3 4 5 7 1 in a two-part canon. The melody begins with the lowest tone and goes up step-by-step according to this scale: 3 4 5 7 1 7 1 3. When the second voice enters, the melody comes down from the highest point: 5 4 3 1 7 5 4 3. After several repetitions, which may include a canon, all voices sing the third system in two parts. This is rather unusual for a canon, but it was the composer's intention.

This response may be sung after a reading of Psalm 136 or other thanksgiving psalms to affirm God's steadfast love. It may also be used as a response to a general prayer of thanksgiving. An interesting way to sing this is for members of the congregation to briefly share what they are thankful for, in just one or two sentences, and the congregation then responds with the first line of the music. The canonic singing may be done after the last prayer, at which time the entire song may be sung a few times as a climax, according to the direction.

"Have no fear, all you earth-lands" (*STB* #306)
(Indonesian: *Jangan takut, hai tanah*)

This is a paraphrase of Joel 2:21–24, in which the minor prophet assures the people of Judah in the South of God's care and blessing:

> Do not fear, O soil, be glad and rejoice,
> for the LORD has done great things! . . .
> For . . . he has poured down for you abundant rain . . .
> The threshing floors shall be full of grain . . .

The tune JANGAN TAKUT ("fear not") in an E = 2 six-tone scale (D = 1 2 4 5 6 7) was composed by the author S. Tarigan and M. B. Ginting in quite a different style. The song is constructed with two melodic motifs centered on the tone 5 (a: 24 52 45 / 5-5-; and b: 55 55 67/ 6 .5 5-) and the lower 1 only appears once near the end (5 41 2 2 /). The structure of the verse is a b a' c and the refrain is b' a" b' a'". Here the refrain is the reverse of the initial two phrases (a b) with only a slight difference, and both the text and the music are repeated, but with a very distinct cadence (a'"). Perhaps the repetitive musical phrases are to remind one of the unchanging love and blessings of God to all. (trsl. Tilly Lubis)

"Holy, holy, holy LORD" (*STB* #128)
(Indonesian: *Kudus, kudus, kuduslah Tuhan*)

This is the standard text of Sanctus and Benedictus, taken from MISA SUNDA of the Catholic Mass in Indonesia. The music, composed by Sukamto, is in a D = 5 five-tone scale (B = 3 4 5 7 1). It is in a Sundanese style (from the western part of Java) that is melismatic and very lively. A prominent feature is the joyful praise of "Hosana in the highest" expressed with the repetitive saw-tooth motifs, 57 57 57 and 13 13 13, that lead to the climax. This fast rhythmic feature reminds one of the medieval European description of the angels' flapping wings while they sang joyful praises and Alleluias to the shepherds. Since the text is probably familiar to most people, and the Indonesian is not very difficult to pronounce, the congregation can try singing in the original language. Liturgically, this is usually sung during the Holy Communion as part of the Great Thanksgiving. But it may also be used at various occasions for praising God.

"In fields of Ephrathah" (*STB* #137)

(Indonesian: *Di ladang Efrata para gembala*)

Ephrathah is not mentioned in the Gospels but is referred to in Micah 5:2 ("But you, O Bethlehem of Ephrathah, who are one of the little clans of Judah, from you shall come forth for me one who is to rule in Israel . . ."). Except for this detail, the author Waldemar Simamora recounts the nativity story with familiar features: the angels, the shepherds, David's Bethlehem, the Messiah, the straw manger, and, most important of all, the kingdom of God restored and peoples' dream of new life fulfilled.

Simamora composed this tune EFRATA (the older name of the small city of Bethlehem) in an anhemitonic penta scale, E♭ = 1 2 3 5 6, which is popular with the Batak in northern Sumatra. All six phrases are rhythmically the same, except the last two, which have almost identical melodies and exhibit the typical Batak style of approaching cadences: 2 2321 /2. (para. Jim Minchin)

"Jesus Christ, the life of the world" (*STB* #210)

(Indonesian: *Yesus Kristus kehidupan dunia*)

The author A. Lumentut expresses simple yet intimate relations with Jesus Christ, affirming that human beings depend on his saving love and eternal hope and requesting that the church witness to his truth in order to accomplish its mission. Lumentut also asks for forgiveness of sins, for guidance in the narrow path, and for reconciliation between peoples and nations.

Liberty Manik composed this tune KEHIDUPAN (meaning "life") in a D = 5 five-tone scale (5 6 1 2 3) with the final on 1. The music matches the text's structure perfectly, in that the musical phrase a b a' b' corresponds to the respective text setting. Since the first and third lines have the same text, the third phrase (a': 32/ 1 1 65 61/ 2--) musically imitates the first phrase (a: 56/ 1 1 21 23/ 3--) from an opposite direction and ends at a lower level. The same technique also applies to the second and fourth lines: b' answers and repeats b by the interval of a fourth lower and continues the idea of b with a full cadence. The composer exhibits genius in his treatment of text and melody, as seen in these passages: from 56/1... 23 /3-- to 32/1... 61/2-- and from 65 /32 ... 53/2-- to 32 /16 ... 12/1--. (para. H. A. Pandopo)

"Kyrie Eleison" (*STB* #119)

(Indonesian: *Tuhan, Kasihani*)

This Ambonese Kyrie composed by Christian I. Tamaela utilizes the motif of a Moluccan melody. According to Tamaela, the original melody was sung in front of a huge rock that symbolizes the presence of the ancestor spirit. A legend says that a woman and her children were so poor and suffered so much that they came to the rock and pleaded for it to eat them up or crush them to death, so that they could be relieved from the miseries of life. Tamaela took that story, contextualized it, and reinterpreted it as a symbol of one's sinfulness or helplessness as one approaches the rock of our salvation, Jesus Christ, praying for mercy, forgiveness, and deliverance. The original song has a sad tone, full of sorrow and anguish, and thus fits the mood of a contrite heart praying for the Lord's mercy.

The music BATU BADAONG ("ancestor's rock") is in a G = 2 five-tone scale (E = 7 1 2 3 4). The glides away from the tones, marked with downward strokes, are important for performing the style and creating the mood. "Kyrie eleison" is Greek, meaning "Lord, have mercy," but the Latin transliteration has been used in Western liturgies. This Kyrie is suitable as a response to prayers of confession, petition, and intercession. It should be sung either in the original language or in Greek.

In the notation for the *tifa* (drum) accompaniment, the notes with downward stems indicate a stronger, deeper, and more open sound produced by the right hand striking the center of the drum. The notes with upward stems denote a high-pitched sound produced by striking the rim of the drumhead with the fingertips while the left palm presses the drumhead. This technique is applicable to most drum patterns in Asian music. (para. Roland S. Tinio)

"LILIES OF THE FIELD"
("Lord Jesus spoke in parables," *STB* # 201)

(Balinese: *Bunga Bakung di Tegale / Mang yeng sab dan Sang Hyang Yesus*)

This hymn is a paraphrase of Jesus' teaching in Matthew 6:25–34, about God's love and care for the birds of the air and the lilies of the fields. It admonishes people not to be anxious about tomorrow, for God knows all needs. The most important task is to seek first the kingdom of God and his righteousness, and all the rest will be given.

The text was written by Wayan Mastra, the Bishop of the Protestant Church in Bali. In June 1988, I went to Bali to record material for a collection of new Balinese hymns, with the assistance of Bishop Mastra and I Nyoman Darsane (who were mentioned in the introduction for this chapter). Wishing to contribute to the project,

Bishop Mastra recalled from his childhood a traditional folksong from northeast Bali, which gave advice and encouraged young people to strive to reach their goals, no matter how high or how hard. Mastra chose one of Jesus' teachings (Matthew 6:25–34) and paraphrased it for this melody. However, he could not remember the entire song, which he had not sung for more than thirty years. I helped him to make a few rhythmic adjustments and reconstructed the song according to the original style. It was later presented to Darsane, who knew a slightly different version of this melody. But all agreed to accept the new version. I added the fourth stanza, which is the conclusion of Jesus' teaching (Matthew 6:31–34), after the recording and hence is without the original Balinese text (Loh 1988, 16–18 and 38). The original hymn seemed incomplete without this conclusion.

BUNGA BAKUNG, meaning "lilies," is in a B = 7 five-tone scale (E = 3 4 5 7 1). The beginning motive 71/3- 4 54 /3-1 31 /7--- is repeated at the ending. The rest of the phrases form the development, and the climax is at the end of the third system. There is no standard pitch in the Balinese gamelan, and all intervals in the scales are also slightly different from one another. So if this song were accompanied by another gamelan, the tune would sound different although the rhythm and melodic shape would be exactly the same, and they would be regarded as the same melody. This situation was evident at the recording of this song in 1988. The original plan was to record it with the gamelan accompaniment, the tuning of which was quite different, but Darsane changed his mind. When the gamelan was removed, the choir members immediately switched to a familiar scale in Western tuning. Although some of the singers in the recording sang the 4 (F) slightly sharper than notated, this would probably not happen with choirs of other musical cultures. (para. Rolando S. Tinio)

"Lord Jesus spoke in parables"

(Balinese: *Bunga bakung di tegale*)
See "LILIES OF THE FIELD" (STB #201)

"My boat of life sails on an angry sea" (*STB* #50)

(Indonesian: *Suka dan duka dalam hidupku*)

In this hymn, Toga Rajagukguk allegorically reflects on life's situation. Life is like a sailboat with a broken rudder and a ripped sail on an angry sea with frequent storms. But at a crucial point, the poet suddenly hears Jesus' assurance that with Him as the pilot and guide, one no longer need fear the storms or the darkness.

The author composes the tune PRAHU, meaning "boat," in a D = 1 five-tone scale (1 2 3 5 6). The melody has eight phrases: a b c d e f e'd'. All of the phrases have identical rhythmic patterns, except the syncopation that occurs twice in d and d'.

The last two phrases are variations of e and d , respectively. The composer has used as many possible combinations of pitches and shapes as one could imagine. When singing this hymn, one may wonder why it is so syllabically and rhythmically active and why the first six phrases are through-composed. And although the rhythm and melodic materials are similar, why do they all feel different? Perhaps it is the composer's way of depicting treacherous currents and storming waves. The melodic similarities between d and d' coincide with the text's assurance of Jesus, the pilot, in the second stanza, "I'll help you when everything goes wrong," and the confidence of the sailor, "It's all right, the Lord will be with me." One interpretation is that these phrases express a cause (assurance) and its consequence (trust). (para. Rolando S. Tinio)

"My God, why have you forsaken me?" (*STB* #274A, 274B)

(Indonesian: *Tuhanku, mengapa kautinggalkan aku?*)

The bitter cry of Christ on the cross in #274A, "My God, my God, why have you forsaken me?" (Matthew 27:46 and Mark 15:34; Jesus quotes from Psalm 22:1a), is expanded to a longer text in #274B. Fridolin Ukur reflects this cry as it resounds through every age and nation, including present human agonies, sorrows, and sufferings. Ukur affirms that the cry is intimate, sweet, gentle, tender, full of energies of life and hope, and full of trusting love that restores peace and justice.

The Filipino composer Francisco F. Feliciano set this text in a simple congregational hymn in a D = 6 seven-tone minor scale (6 7 1 2 3 4 #5). Four other languages (Tamil, Tagalog, Mandarin, and English) have been added for international gatherings.

The choral setting in #274B is a complex expression of this deeply moving text. A four-part chorus sings the main text like an ostinato or cantus firmus ("fixed melody") while a soloist adds a florid voice to convey the added textual reflections. Musicians should be able to analyze and trace the compositional techniques in the song, namely: counterpoint; chord progressions; dissonances; incidents of anticipation, suspension, and release; modulations; tone paintings; and climaxes. This is one of Feliciano's masterpieces, in which he portrays his faith and understanding of the meaning of Christ's suffering on the cross and how it is related to all today.

The tune ANTAMOK premiered in Manila in 1990 in one of Feliciano's musicals. Concerning this tune, he writes:

> About "Antamok," that's the name of a road in Baguio. A friend of mine owns a house on that road, and on one of our vacations, I spent some time there, writing "My God, Why Have You Forsaken Me?"[46]

---

46   From correspondence with the author, April 17, 2007.

Feliciano's performance suggestions are:

1. Congregation sings the ostinato (#274A) as a response to prayers, litanies, and intercessions. Multi-language simultaneous singing is recommended for international and ecumenical gatherings.
2. The congregation's part (#274A) may be repeated *n* times with choir adding voices one by one (#274B).
3. Full version for congregation, choir, and soloist: in the absence of a good soloist, the solo part can be recited on top of the music. (para. Jim Minchin)

"My shepherd Lord with flute so true of tone" (*STB* #291)

(Indonesian: *Gembala baik bersuling nan merdu*)

The author/composer C. Akwan relates the story behind this lovely hymn and his creative process[47]:

The image of the Good Shepherd came to me in 1971 when I took a bus for the first time from Salatiga to Magelang, a town in Central Java. What intrigued me most was the beauty of the landscape. From the window of the bus, I saw terraced rice fields along the slopes of the mountains and rice fields in the valley—gold and freshly green rice fields with blue mountains farther away and a clear blue sky. In the rice fields, I saw one Javanese boy of about twelve, wearing only shorts and sitting on the back of a water buffalo. I could only see him from the back. The scene looked peculiarly beautiful and peaceful. The boy was playing a bamboo flute. I could not hear the tune he was playing, but I imagined it to be peaceful and melodious. All of these images made an impression on me. In my mind, something heavenly was captured during these moments, an inner discovery.

In 1984, the Indonesian Institute for Sacred Music (Yayasan Musik Gereja) sought Christian songs from Indonesian composers. Perhaps for political or ecumenical reasons, it needed songs from Irian Jaya [now West Papua] to ensure its collections covered the whole of Indonesia—from Sabang in the most western tip of Sumatra to Merauke, the most eastern town in South Irian Jaya. As a result, I was requested to contribute at least one song.

I began composing the melody of the song that would later be known as "Gembala Baik." As usual, I first let the notes flow freely from my imagination and feelings, and rapturous moments of new discovery kept occurring. These moments would later guide me to enhance the composition of the melody.

When the flow of inspiration ended, I applied rules of composition to give the melody form, balance, and appeal, revising it more than once. It became a sixteen-bar song using the AABB form: eight bars for the AA and eight bars for the BB form. The last is also the refrain of the song. I imagined the tempo to be slow,

---

47   From the author's communication with Akwan, through Yamuger, March 31, 2005.

similar to the relaxed walking pace of an adult male. Originally, I used the key of E major for the melody. The Institute for Sacred Music raised it to F major. The scale used is pentatonic, of the CDEGA [1 2 3 5 6] type. This traditional scale is dominant in Irian Jaya, especially among the coastal people. Interestingly, it is also a widely used scale in the music of other peoples in various parts of the world.

Now that a large part of the music was shaped, what words would be appropriate for the melody? I recalled the image of the twelve-year-old boy playing the bamboo flute on the back of the water buffalo in 1971. The opening phrase of the lyrics became "Gembala baik bersuling nan merdu" ("The good shepherd who plays the flute melodiously/sweetly"). After this opening phrase, what should come next? I heard a voice from within me whispering softly and repeatedly, "Psalm 23, Psalm 23, Psalm 23." I had heard this inner voice many times when I tried to find the right words for other melodies. These moments of guidance were filled with intense emotions, with "explosions" or "flashes" of words and sounds. They formed a complex inner experience comparable to rapture or joy. After this lyrical inspiration, I applied rules of meter, rhyme, and other kinds of prosody to mold the lyrics and revised them more than once.

I gave the score to the Reverend H. A. van Dop, a Dutch minister and church-music expert who was one of the backbones of the Institute of Sacred Music. He immediately went to an organ and played the tune. Because I forgot to note the appropriate tempo, he played it much faster than I intended, which should be similar to that of "How Great Thou Art." He slowed the tempo and changed part of the melodic phrase in bar 14. The original notes were C A F A F (5 3. 1 3 1) in the key of F major; Van Dop changed the last three notes, making C A A C A (5 3. 3 5 3). Years later, I realized that the three verses of the song did not encompass the whole text of Psalm 23. Someday, I would like to add other verses.

The author composed the tune GEMBALA, meaning "shepherd," in a C = 5 five-tone scale (F = 1 2 3 5 6) in a b a b' c d c d' form with almost identical rhythmic patterns. The refrain of the song features *sol* and *la* (5 and 6) prominently (135/6 .6 6656/5 3.). This characteristic is also shown in the second half of Liberty Manik's hymn (*STB* #256), "When you travel far" (55/6 .5 6 16/ 5.). In both songs, the similar features are also repeated at the same structural points. Perhaps this indicates a favorite Batak style of melodic construction. (trsl. Tilly Lubis)

"Now at dawn we wait to see"
(Indonesian: *Di relung gunung gunung*)
See "THE HOLY LIGHT" (STB #154)

"Now come, O Holy Spirit" (*STB* #10)
(Indonesian: *O Roh Kudus Ilahi*)

In this prayer, E. P. Ginting asks the Holy Spirit to come and inspire one's soul, to ignite heavenly fire, to renew one's heart to unite with the Spirit, and to spread the gospel to the ends of the earth.

The tune O ROH KUDUS, meaning "O Holy Spirit," was composed by Ginting in an E♭ = 1 six-tone scale (C = 6 7 1 2 3 5) with the final on 6. It is through-composed with all four phrases having the same rhythmic pattern: 12/3 21 6 12/ 3 3-. (trsl. Tilly Lubis)

"O come quickly, Holy Spirit" (*STB* #7)
(Indonesian: *O datanglah ya Roh Kudus*)

This invocation to the Holy Spirit is in a call-and-response style. The soloist begins and ends with dramatic calls to the Spirit. When desired, an experienced soloist may either improvise the call freely or sing the version provided. After the soloist states the reason for invoking the Spirit, the congregation responds to the call with "O Holy Spirit" in harmony, which emphasizes the earnest plea. Because of early-sixteenth-century Portuguese influence, people in the Ambon area like to harmonize their songs, but they do not follow all the rules of Western theory, as shown in the unidiomatic progression in the bass part.

DATANGLAH ("O come") is in a D = 5 five-tone scale (G = 1 2 3 5 6), but the harmony has the tone 4 (C) as well. It was adapted from a traditional melody of Seram Island and harmonized by Christian I. Tamaela, who also composed the text. The *tifa* (drum) accompaniment is very important in this piece. For the drum pattern and playing method, see "Praise the LORD" (*STB* #104) for instructions. (para. I. L. & J. M.)

"O God, our Father" (*STB* #18)
(Indonesian: *Ya Allah Bapa*)

This prayer praises God's glory and gives thanks for his love, grace, and forgiveness of sins. "As Jesus taught, we call you Abba . . . we intercede through Jesus, our high priest . . . we pay him homage, the universe's King."

The music ALLAH BAPA ("God Father") was composed by the author Subronto K. Atmodjo in an F = 2 five-tone scale (C = 6 1 2 3 5) with the final on 6. This song is through-composed without any repetition, and all the phrases begin on the second beat. Atmodjo's use of a double duet is interesting, in that the song only has two voices in counterpoint, but the main melody is doubled by the tenor, and the counterpoint is provided by the alto and bass. This free harmonic treatment with counterpoint has preserved the natural flow of the main melody. (para. H. A. Pandopo)

"O God our Father" (*STB* #287)

(Indonesian: *Ya Allah Bapa*)

This hymn, with the same title as *STB* #18, prays to the Trinity: to God the Father for blessings and hope, to Jesus for inspiring one to live with forgiveness, and to the Holy Spirit for purifying one's heart to worship God and teaching one to pray for the world. In the refrain, the author Waldemar Simamora affirms that God alone bestows faithful love on those who embrace new life from God.

The tune, also with the name ALLAH BAPA ("God Father"), was composed by the author in an E♭ = 5 five-tone scale (5 6 1 2 3) with the final on 1 in a very orderly form: a a' b b' c c'. Except for the refrain, all of the phrases start on the same pitch that ends the previous phrase. This makes the song flow very smoothly and the singing very easy. (trsl. Toga P. L. Rajagukguk; para. Jim Minchin)

"O Lᴏʀᴅ God, set my feet on the way" (*STB* #67)

(Indonesian: *Oh Tuhan pimpin lah langkahku*)

This anonymous song has been popular among young people in Indonesia, Malaysia, and Singapore. The hymn is a prayer that is spoken at the beginning of a journey; it asks for God's guidance, that one may be a torch in the dark, leading those who have strayed from God's right path. This can be effectively used as a closing hymn or as a prayer response after benediction.

The melody is in a familiar Western style in an F♯ = 3 seven-tone D-major scale (D = 1 2 3 4 5 6 7); a raised ♯4 briefly modulates the tonality to A major. A guitar or other instrument may accompany this tune. However, it should not be too complicated, lest the simplicity be destroyed. The tune name OBOR means "torch." (para. Jim Minchin)

"O Lᴏʀᴅ, my God" (*STB* #126)

(Balinese: *O duh Aji*)

This is a Balinese version of a Kyrie Eleison ("Lord, have mercy") composed by Bishop Mastra after a folk motif. It may be sung three times, according to the liturgical tradition. The melody is formed within a typical Balinese *silesir* scale: E = 3 4 5 7 1. The feeling of three beats is not typical of Balinese rhythm, but the rhythmic flow of the text calls for a triple time. However, one need not emphasize the first beats; simply let the melody flow as one prays. It is suggested that a large gong be struck on the last note, with the syllable "tiang." This Kyrie is suitable for prayers of confession, petition, or intercession. Individuals may take turns praying in short phrases, with the group responding with this Kyrie.

"O Lord, our God" (*STB* #123)

(Indonesian: *Ya Tuhanku*)

This Kyrie is set to a Javanese melodic idiom by Sutarno in an F = 1 five-tone scale (E = 7 1 3 4 5) with the final on 7. It is suitable for prayers of confession and intercession. Having the congregation sing this together helps them to participate in the prayers more actively and makes the contents of the prayers more meaningful.

The *kempul* (suspended gong) is struck to mark the halfway point in the music while the large gong concludes the prayer in the last measure. Make sure that the two-quarter-note figures are counted as one beat. This Kyrie was first introduced to the ecumenical circle during the sixth General Assembly of the WCC in Vancouver, in 1983. (See *STB* #105, "Amin Haleluya," for more information on the style.)

"O worship the King" (*STB* #24)

(Indonesian: *Hai mari sembah*)

This well-known British hymn by Robert Grant (1779–1838) depicts the majesty and power of the almighty King. It has been translated into Indonesian and set to music in an Indonesian *pelog* tuning, a D = 3 five-tone scale (3 4 5 7 1). Although the Indonesian setting follows the original rhythm of the tune HANOVER (5/112/3-5'/127/1-) except at two points, the Indonesian melody's scale and lyrical, melancholy mood portray a God of grace and love rather than a glorious king. Here one sees how the musical setting can change the character of the hymn.

Some may feel that the Indonesian setting is more appropriate for the last two stanzas (except the last phrase). However, both musical interpretations are appropriate in their cultural contexts; singing the same texts with two different styles may reveal something about the mysterious attributes of God and one's relations with God. It might be interesting, therefore, to sing the first three stanzas with the HANOVER tune, with the proper modulation of style and mood, and then sing the next two stanzas with the MEDAN tune in unison, without any harmony—the two tunes and styles are appropriate for the different moods of the stanzas. The tune name MEDAN refers to one of the major cities in northern Sumatra, where the composer Daud Kosasih resides. (trsl. YAMUGER, the Church Music Center of the Roman Catholic Church in Yogyakarta)

"Oh, the cabbage price is falling" (*STB* #313)

(Indonesian: *Sayur kubis jatuh harga*)

S. Tarigan's contextual hymn is inspired by Habakkuk 3:17–19. Despite economic problems and deteriorating living conditions caused by poor harvests and cattle diseases, he praises God and sings for joy because he trusts that the LORD will not forsake his people.

The tune SAYUR KUBIS, meaning "cabbages," was composed by Tarigan in an $E = 3$ six-tone scale (3 4 6 7 1 2) in two sections, both of which are repeated. It is almost through-composed; only the first phrase of the second section is repeated. Care must be taken to differentiate the two cadences, <u>43</u> <u>36</u> /6-6- and <u>63</u> <u>46</u> 6-, at the end of the respective sections. It would be interesting to compare this tune with that of a hymn from the Paiwan tribe of Taiwan, "My heavenly father loves me" (*STB* #182), which has a similar text. (trsl. Tilly Lubis)

"Praise the Lᴏʀᴅ" (STB #104)
(Indonesian: *Haleluya, Puji Tuhan*)

This short praise response by Christian I. Tamaela is an adaptation of a traditional melody from Seram Island, in the northeastern Maluku Islands of Indonesia, which preserves certain qualities of the sixteenth-century Portuguese musical heritage. The main melody is in the bass in a $D = 5$ five-tone scale (5 6 1 2 3). The harmonization of the higher voice adds a sixth tone 4 and shows a departure from Western harmonic rules, making it sound more indigenous. The gliding tones and the *tifa* (drum) accompaniment are of the local style. This hymn should be sung with vigor. It can be used as response to prayers of praise and thanksgiving. For the drum accompaniment, the notes with downward stems indicate stronger, deeper, and more open sounds produced by the right hand striking the center of the drum. The upward stems denote high-pitched sounds produced by striking the rim of the drumhead with the fingertips while applying pressure to the drumhead with the left palm. Care should be taken for the different drumming pattern at the end of the piece.

"Sing the Lᴏʀᴅ a new song" (*STB* #100)
(Indonesian: *Nyanyikanlah nyanyian baru*)

The exuberant praise of Psalm 148 is paraphrased here with a joyful traditional Batak melody from Lake Toba in northern Sumatra. This psalm is an invitation to all creation and all creatures to join in the praise of their maker. The first three stanzas belong to the first section that summons the heavenly choirs, including the angels, heavenly host, sun, moon, stars, and cosmic waters. The second section includes the earthly choirs: thunders, mountains, rivers, flowers, woods, kings, princes, rulers, men and women, young and old. The two sections of the original psalm end with "Let them praise with the name of the Lᴏʀᴅ," but in this paraphrase, Tilly Lubis ends the stanzas with slightly different ideas: "Great is his name, sing his praise and rejoice; great is your maker . . . great is your king, glory be his domain." In the remaining stanzas, Lubis calls the forms of nature to clap their hands, and people to offer thanks, and finally for all to "Sing alleluia, rejoice in our King!"

It is a mark of Lubis's genius that this adaptation of a Batak folk melody matches the mood of both the texts and the wording. Many Batak songs are built on a pentachord—the melody is constructed within the interval of a fifth (1 2 3 4 5); the tone 6 occasionally appears but is not very prominent. In this song, however, the importance of 6 can be seen from the very beginning with an F = 1 five-tone scale (1 2 3 5 6). The melody is characterized by lively rhythms with syncopations, and the phrases are organized in a simple a a' bb form. The second phrase a' begins with a pick-up from the fourth beat to connect the two phrases, and the two b phrases together equal the length of one a phrase. The tune name NYANYIKANLAH means "let's sing." (para. Rolando S. Tinio)

"Soft the master's love song" (*STB* #203)

(Indonesian: *Lirih terdengar lagu kasih yang merdu*)

This is a paraphrase of Jesus' call, "Come to me, all you that are weary and are carrying heavy burdens, and I will give you rest . . ." (Matthew 11:28). The author Rudolf R. Pantou calls this the "Master's love song," so "beautiful to hear." The third stanza is one's response to Jesus, which affirms one's willingness to turn to him, for his love has no end.

The music LAGU KASIH, meaning "love song," was composed in an Indonesian style, in a G = 3 five-tone scale (C = 6 7 1 3 4), in a a' b form. The guitar accompaniment is an imitation of the Indonesian *celempung* (plucked board zither) style, which plays similar musical figures (6676 4676) with a haunting effect. Pantou suggests a match stick be placed between the guitar strings near the bridge to produce a gong-like sound. When played on a keyboard, the first note of each four-eighth-note figure may be doubled with the lower octave and held for two beats, to also produce a gong effect. (para. Jim Minchin)

"SURRENDERING TO GOD"
("Now let us follow Jesus Christ," *STB* # 77)

(Balinese: *Jalan, jalan jani*)

This hymn resulted from I Nyoman Darsane's participation in the recording of Balinese hymns by the Asian Institute for Liturgy and Music (AILM) in 1988. According to Darsane, he already had the melody in his mind, but when he heard the reconstruction of Bishop Mastra's "Lilies of the Field" (see the commentary on *STB* #201), he was inspired to write the text to this tune. This can be detected from the phrase "The God who tests us secretly will know our every need." The hymn urges people to follow Christ and surrender their lives to God. Like *STB* #201, this hymn was taught to the female choir members just a few minutes before the recording on June 15, 1988; they quickly learned the piece through rote and memory, without any written text or music (Loh 1988, 18).

The tune PENYERAHAN, meaning "to surrender" or "to commit," is in a C = 1 five-tone scale (E = 3 4 5 7 1). It is in a a' b c form; the first three phrases have the same rhythmic pattern. The final on 3 is a typical cadence in Balinese song. (para. I-to Loh)

"Thank you for the day you give us" (*STB* #236)

(Indonesian: *T'rima kasih ya Tuhanku*)

This is a hymn of discipleship and stewardship, giving thanks for God's tender mercy each day and for granting the time to learn about the perfect love of God. From the third stanza, the author/composer Jerry Taringan Silangit changes the subject to the first person to plead to be an obedient faithful steward to serve others according to Jesus' word and examples.

The tune TERIMA KASIH, meaning "thank you," is in a C = 5 four-tone scale (F = 1 2 3 5) with two ideas (a: 5 5 $\underline{21}$ $\underline{23}$/ 5-5 and b: $\underline{32}$/ 1 1 $\underline{21}$ $\underline{23}$/ 1-1) organized in a six-phrase form, a b a' a'' b b. Silangit's simple yet lovely composition follows the Batak pentachordal style: the melody is constructed within the interval of a fifth (1–5). This hymn is especially suitable for children. (trsl. Daud Kosasih; para. Rolando S. Tinio)

"The Church that is one" (*STB* #239)

(Indonesian: *Bersatu teguh*)

This is a short doctrinal hymn, explaining the nature of the Church. A. K. Saragih writes that there is only one true, committed "Church that is one in love of the Son." He also prays that those estranged would repent and return for unity.

The tune BERSATU TEGUH (meaning "united firmly") was composed in a C = 3 five-tone scale (3 4 6 7 1). The author/composer uses a repeated ascending motif (3 6 $\underline{71}$ 3') to begin the song and builds to a climax at the end of the first system. The second system is the reverse, a repeated descending motif (3' 1' $\underline{76}$ 7) concluding on the reiterated 6 6 /6-. This and some other songs by Saragih were composed during a composition workshop led by the late Liberty Manik in early 1980s, which produced many new hymns (for more information, see the biography of Liberty Manik). (para. Jim Minchin)

"THE HOLY LIGHT"
("Now at dawn we wait to see," *STB* #154)

(Indonesian: *Cahaya suci / Di relung gunung gunung*)

Using the image of dawn, waiting for the early sunlight, Paul Widyawan writes, "O holy Son, we receive your light, fill us with love . . . your love will hallow this and every day."

The author composed the tune CAHAYA SUCI ("holy light") in an Indonesian *pelog* five-tone scale, B = 3 4 5 7 1. But in the third system, he introduces 6, the "enemy tone,"[48] which is theoretically avoided unless it is needed for modulation or a special reason. Here the author asks, "Shall our clouds of sin overcome fire of

---

48 According to gamelan theory, the tone avoided in a particular scale or *patet* is called the "enemy tone"; it
    may be understood as a tone "foreign" to that particular scale.

love?" This introduces a new thought in the prayer and is a transition to an entirely new musical idea for the B section. So, it is logical that Widyawan borrows the "enemy tone" to lead to a new dimension of the prayer. The tune of the A section is very melodious and rhythmical and has lively contrasts between dotted quarter notes, sixteenth notes, and triplets. It sounds like an Indonesian *suling* (duct flute) melody, with the typical cadence 4343/3.

The B section is characterized by long, rhythmic reciting tones. The composer set the A and B sections with strong contrasts that create a good canonic effect. Rather than simply enjoy singing this beautiful song, the congregation should sing this as a prayer for Christ's guidance of a new day. If canonic singing is desired, the congregation as well as the choir should be divided into two parts each, so that the choir may properly lead their respective congregational parts. Probably the easiest way is for all to sing A and B once through in unison, then to divide the parts into a two-part canon, and to sing the coda in unison at the end. To be theologically consistent, the "O LORD" in the last phrase should address Jesus (O Lord), not God. (para. Colin A. Gibson)

"The Lord's Prayer" (*STB* #116)

This Lord's Prayer was reset for the 2000 edition of *Sound the Bamboo* by Christian Izaac Tamaela according to a Javanese song motive, which is in a *pelog* five-tone scale: E = 3 4 5 7 1. Tamaela divides the prayer into five sections, all ending with a gong, which is the gamelan style of signaling the completion of a phrase or section of a piece (*gongen*). Musically, the first, second, and fourth *gongen* are exactly the same. The third *gongen*, "Give us today" is a new petition, so the music changes from the initial 3 43 3 to a higher and new shape 5 75 4. This is imitated with a slight variation for "forgive us our sins," but the cadential phrase 31 71 1- is identical in all four *gongen*. The fifth *gongen* is a totally different musical idea (34 5 57 17 7-) because it conveys the climax of the Lord's Prayer ("for the kingdom, the power and the glory are yours now and forever"); the music builds to the highest point on "forever," and it descends gradually to conclude on the gong tone on the second syllable of "Amen."

It would be good to have a gong to mark the endings of each section. A deeper gong tone is better for creating a solemn mood. According to traditional aesthetics, the final gong stroke should be slightly delayed. This piece does not need any other instrumental accompaniment. However, for the sake of leading the congregation, one could use a melodic instrument with a mellow tone (such as a recorder, flute, or cello) to double the melody but not create harmony.

Liturgically, this is a prayer, not a hymn or an anthem; although a choir may lead or pray on behalf of the congregation with this piece, this is a prayer to God that Jesus taught. Therefore, it is important that the congregation is ready to pray/sing, following the liturgist who may say, "Let us pray to God, with the prayer that our Lord Jesus Christ has taught us." The organist then plays the first four notes (3 43 3-) and all join in the prayer.

"Tonight we see the light of the world" (*STB* #136)

(Indonesian: *Ai domma tubuh saborngin on*)

In this Christmas carol, the author/composer A. K. Saragih does not tell the nativity story as found in most carols but describes the light of the world coming from the tiny Child, illuminating the human scene. Saragih urges all to receive the light and to be like the shepherds leading their flocks to heed God's word, as sung by the angels, and to go see "the parent's" and "the whole world's" baby, who has come to restore hope to all humble people. The paraphraser Jim Minchin has carefully crafted the poem in a similar pattern, making it easy to see the beauty of the poem and to grasp its meanings.

The tune NGOLU NI PORTIBI is composed in an E♭ = 5 six-tone scale (A♭ = 1 2 3 4 5 6) in two sections with four phrases each— a b c d and e f e d'—in which the pair a b and c d are rhythmically the same. The second section shows contrast by repeating the e phrase and giving f a distinct feature (five straight ascending notes, 3, 5, 1 2 4) not found in other phrases. Another contrast may be seen from the two cadences in the respective sections. The d phrase approaches the cadence from high (5/5 1 3) and the d' approaches from below (3/ 5, 1 3), and both lead to the same cadence (212/ 1-). These similarities and differences make the song an interesting one to sing. (para. Jim Minchin)

"When you travel far" (*STB* #256)

(Indonesian: *Bila kau pergi ke tempat yang jauh*)

This is an assurance of Jesus' companionship, protection, consolation, and guidance when one travels far or is leaving home. Liberty Manik admonishes people to count on Jesus and to lean on his helping hand, and the journey's end will be in peace. The text is based on Psalm 121, and Manik replaced "the LORD" with "Jesus," similar to the way that Isaac Watts Christianized Psalm 72: "Jesus shall reign where e'er the sun."

Manik's tune PERJALANAN, meaning "on the way," uses a typical five-tone scale (E♭ = 1 2 3 5 6) in a b c b form. The two fragments of the c phrase only differ in their cadences. The melody is simple and full of warmth and melancholy. Manik has adopted traditional Western four-part harmony for its familiarity among Christians; this is probably why this hymn is so touching and is loved by many. This hymn has been sung at a few international gatherings as a farewell blessing, and many people have been moved to tears by the rich sonority of the harmony. Although anhemitonic penta scales—five-tone scales without half steps—are popular all over Asia (and in the southern United States and Scotland), the characteristic melodic shapes, rhythmic patterns, and cadential formulas of each culture has created distinct styles. Some musical cultures have maintained their unique identities while others have either lost their particular features or assimilated to new identities. In this song, the cadential phrase 53/ 2.1 21 32/1--- seems to exhibit strongest Indonesian folk character. (para. Rolando S. Tinio)

Before concluding, I would like to show how Pak Soenardi, the gamelan teacher at the Asian Institute for Liturgy and Music, has used Joseph Mohr's text. "Silent Night" to compose the hymn "Malam Kudas" in a Javanses gamelan style with the accompaniment of ten musical layers plus the drum.[49]

49   This piece was recorded by students of the Asian Institute for Liturgy and Music and published in *A Festival of Asian Christmas Music* (Loh 1984, 53).

Conclusion

In conclusion, the national slogan of Indonesia, "Unity in Diversity," is evident from the variety of musical styles of the country's hymns in *Sound the Bamboo*.

1. Scales: Although most Indonesian tunes use anhemitonic penta scales—1 2 3 5 6 or 6 1 2 3 5 (see *STB* #7, 18, 50, 100, 137, 210, 256, 287, 291)—occasionally the 4 (*STB* #136) or the 7 (*STB* #10) is added to the scale, or a variation 1 2 4 5 6 7 (*STB* #306) appears. The Batak in Sumatra focus their melodies within the pentachord, 1 2 3 4 5 (*STB* #236). However, many composers from Sumatra, Java, Bali, and Ambon utilize the typical Indonesian *pelog* tuning system, i.e., the combination of narrow and gapped intervals, either 3 4 5 7 1 or 1 3 4 5 7 (*STB* #24, 77, 115, 116, 126, 128, 201, 221). According to gamelan theory, the "enemy tone" 6 that is traditionally avoided only appears in particular instances with special functions (see the discussion of *STB* #154). Variations are the five-tone scale 6 7 1 3 4 (*STB* #203) or the six-tone scale 3 4 6 7 1 2 (*STB* #313). Western scales and the Dorian mode (*STB* #180) are also found. Only music from Irian Jaya (*STB* #305) is distinct from all other parts of Indonesia, in that it uses the 1-3-5 "fanfare melody" with its natural harmony.

2. Harmony: The contributors from Indonesia have mostly refrained from copying Western traditional harmony, except in *STB* #256. Since Ambon was colonized by the Portuguese, compositions from that area have utilized certain Western chords but have their own variations (*STB* #7, 104). Some Javanese hymns have been treated with a polyphonic texture but freely or in a double duet style (*STB* #235, 18). Other composers exercise more freedom, adapting indigenous accompaniment styles to haunting effect (*STB* #203) or employing a guitar accompaniment (*STB* #98).

3. Generally, compositions do not yet reflect the gamelan or other traditional folk styles of accompaniment, except the *tifa* drum (*STB* #7, 103, 104, 119) and gongs (*STB* #116, 123); a non-Indonesian composer experimented with the gamelan concept in *STB* #202 and *STB* #144. Since Indonesia has such a wide variety of ethnic groups and musical traditions, it is hoped that more church musicians will devote more of their energy and scholarship to the study of their diverse traditional music. Just as the gamelan has influenced the world of music, more innovative Indonesian church music can play a larger role in the ecumenical world.

Filipino Hymns

The Nation, People, and Cultures

The Philippines is the only Christian country in Asia, the result of its long history as a colony: Spain ruled it for 377 years (1521–1898) and the United States did for forty-eight years (1898–1946, which was interrupted by four years of Japanese occupation from 1942 to 1945). Ralph Tolliver, an American missionary, insightfully described the outcome of these long-term cultural and religious relations, saying that the Philippines are like an onion. The thin, outside skin of this onion is American (its technology, products, and language) and the next layer underneath is Spanish, in its "religion, music, social customs, commercial systems of telling time, counting money, and weighing vegetables." But when one peels away the Spanish layer, "the hard and durable core of Filipino life is Malayo-Indonesian. Proverbs and values, the family system, and personal relationships—the real game of life—is played by ancient tribal rules." A typical Filipino city-dweller "functions during office hours as an American, goes to mass on Sunday morning like a Spaniard, and rules his home like a traditional Filipino. He is a mixture of East and West, old and new" (Hoke 1975, 525f, for all preceding quotations). Although these comments were made more than twenty-five years ago, the core of Filipino life and society in urban and rural areas remains similar.

The Philippines is an archipelago of approximately 7,100 islands, with a total area of 300,000 square kilometers (about 115,831 square miles) and a population of 88.57 million.[50] There are eighty-one provinces grouped in seventeen regions, including the Cordillera Autonomous Region in the north, the Muslim Mindanao in the south, and the National Capital Region in metropolitan Manila. The religious beliefs of the people may be divided into three main categories: Christian (Roman Catholic 83%, Protestant 9%), Muslim (4%), and indigenous religions. Christians are concentrated in the lowlands of Luzon and the Visayas islands; Muslims mostly live in Mindanao and the Sulu islands and Palawan. Those who subscribe to folk or indigenous religions are mostly located in upland northern Luzon, Mindanao, and Palawan (Garland 4:839).

There are two official languages, Filipino and English, and seven other major dialects: Cebuano, Ilocano, Ilonggo, Bicol, Waray, Pampango, and Pangasinese. In Cordillera of northern Luzon, approximately one million people speak the related languages of Bontok, Ibaloy, Ifugao, Ilonggot, Isneg, Kalinga, Kankanay, Tinggian, as well as lesser-known ones (Garland 4:914).

---

50 National Statistics Office, Republic of the Philippines, August 2007, http://www.census.gov.ph/ (accessed February 7, 2009).

A Brief History of Christian Mission

In 1565, forty-four years after Ferdinand Magellan arrived in the Philippines in 1521, Miguel Lopez de Legazpi and about 380 men landed in Cebu; they were Augustinians. The Franciscans followed in 1577, the Jesuits in 1581, the Dominicans in 1587, and the Augustinian Recollects in 1606. The Jesuits founded the College of Manila in 1596 and the College of San Jose in 1601. The Dominicans established the College of Santo Tomas in 1619. The colleges of Manila and Santo Tomas became universities in 1623; the latter endures today (Athyal 1996, 177f). These educational institutions played important roles in the intellectual as well as spiritual life of the Filipino people.

During the American rule of the Philippines, many Protestant denominations entered the country and divided their missions by regions, including Presbyterians, Bible societies, Methodists, Northern Baptists, United Brethren, Disciples of Christ, Congregationalists, and the Christian and Missionary Alliance; the Protestant Episcopals and the Seventh-Day Adventists did not limit themselves to regions (Hoke 1975, 543f). Indigenous churches and sects also developed. The first one, the Philippine Independent Church (PIC) was a Roman Catholic faction; the founder was a Filipino priest, Gregorio Aglipay. He was one who revolted against the Spanish near the end of their rule and was excommunicated by the Vatican in 1899, prompted by Archbishop Nozaleda. He was later consecrated "First Supreme Bishop" by a council of priests. This denomination was later accepted by the American Episcopal Church in 1948; it is now regarded as a Protestant church, and it constitutes one of the largest denominations in the Philippines (Hoke 1975, 549f).

Another indigenous development was the Iglesia ni Cristo ("Church of Christ"), founded by Felix Manalo in 1914. He was influenced by Seventh-Day Adventists, Unitarians, and Jehovah's Witnesses. Manalo concluded that Christ was only a man and regarded himself as the "angel ascending from the east" (Revelations 7:2). This church is "syncretistic, simplistic, Unitarian, and nationalistic" (Hoke 1975, 549); hence, it gained strong support from the people. It is believed that the late dictator President Marcos belonged to or at least supported this church.

Many denominations—mainly evangelical, charismatic, Pentecostal, and other parachurch organizations—entered the Philippines following the Second World War. These churches have emphasized evangelism and church planting while the traditional mainline churches, including the Roman Catholic Church, focus on social justice and ecumenical cooperation. All have gained converts and supporters, but they also show certain weaknesses. Some positive signs of cooperation in the mission of the church were: the organization in 1948 of the United Church of Christ in the Philippines (UCCP), which includes all mainline Protestant denominations; the 1963 establishment of the National Council of Churches in the Philippines (NCCP, which includes UCCP, United Methodist Church, the Philippine Episcopal Church, and the Philippine Independent Church); and the most recent Philippine

Council of Evangelical Churches (PCEC) (Athyal 1996, 183–185). As Lorenzo C. Bautista says, "They all must deal with perennial tensions between tradition and modernity, faith and the social question, earthly life and eschatological vision and between charism and institution" (Athyal 1996, 194).

Some Philippine musical instruments in the collection of I-to Loh:

Maguindanao *kulintang*

Mindanao *kubing* (jaw harp)

Maranao *kulintang* (*sarunay*)

Kalinga *balingbing* (bamboo buzzer)

kubing (jaw harp; longer ones are from Mindanao, shorter ones are from northern Luzon): *ulibao, giwong, onnat*

Nose flute

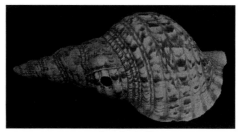

Conch shell

Early Christian Influences on Filipino Music

The Roman Catholic Church began its educational ministry as part of its mission. The Franciscan Father Juan de Santa Marta (born 1578) was in charge of a seminary program in Lumbang, Laguna, in 1606, where 400 boys were trained to sing and play the organ, flute, and other instruments; upon completion of their training, they returned to their villages to teach others. Other orders of Jesuits and Augustinians also emphasized the importance of music education for the sake of liturgies (Garland 4:841f). Daily exposure to and training in European music had a lasting effect, in the form of national styles of Spanish-influenced liturgical and folk music. In the contemporary church and secular repertoire, one can hear these influences: triple rhythms, frequently with the accent shifted to the second beat; compositions in a minor mode, but with a sudden modulation to the tonic major; and guitar accompaniment.

The *Pasyon*

Filipino composers have produced many Christmas carols, Lenten *pasyon* ("passion"), and other hymns and liturgical music. The first Filipino *pasyon* writer was Father Gaspar Aquino de Belen, who in 1703 printed his *pasyon* in Tagalog: *Holy Passion of Jesus Christ Our Lord* (Garland 4:843). A popular text of *Pasyon Kasaysayan ng Pasyon Mahal* by Mariano Pilapil consists of 2,660 stanzas, each with five eight-syllable lines; it contains sixty-eight intervening episodes, which insert twenty moral lessons or sermons. The *pasyon* has a basic melodic formula based on traditional, chant-like melodies or Westernized folk songs. Chanting the entire *pasyon* may take sixteen to twenty hours (Garland 4:843–45). In the Manila area, singing the Passion story according to the Gospels begins on Thursday afternoon and ends at Friday noon. The songs are frequently sung in two parts harmonized in thirds and sixths; they are broadcast through loud speakers so that all people around the area can hear them.

Some Filipino dramas and songs related to the Lenten and Easter stories have been developed in Catholic missions and are performed outdoors. Many of them have evolved into secular forms that are separate from Christian liturgy or faith.

The Wake

The Filipinos show their love for the deceased by holding wakes that vary in duration: three days for a young person and nine days for an adult. Friends and relatives join the grieving family by singing favorite hymns and praying. They keep awake all night by guessing riddles and playing games (Garland 4:851). In Bontok, men and women take turns on successive nights singing for the deceased, who is seated upright and tied to a chair. This ritual is meant to honor important persons before their burial (Garland 4:920).

Traditional Music of the Philippines

The North

Flat gongs are the principal instruments in the Cordillera. They are important for rice harvesting celebrations, weddings, and pacts of peace. The instrument is also associated with headhunting. There are many styles of playing gongs: with one's palms or with sticks, as an accompaniment for dances or as an ensemble. In the Southern Kalinga language, the *gangsa topayya* consists of six gongs. Four gongs play the same pattern, one beat behind the other, while the fifth one plays the ostinato, and the sixth one plays a more elaborate, improvised rhythm, making the music very exciting.

There are diverse types of bamboo instruments in both the south and the north: nose flutes (*tongali*), notched flutes (*palendag, suling*), buzzers (*balingbing*), clappers (*tagutok*), scrapers, reeds, lutes (*kudyapiq*), tubes (*tongatong*), tube zithers (*kolitong, kulibit*), jaw harps (*ulibao, giwong, onnat, awaedeng, kubing*), and slit drums (*agung a bentong*) (Garland 4:919, 924).

Kalinga Singing

The Kalinga people live in the Mountain Province of northern Luzon. Many of the Kalinga songs are in anhemitonic penta scales (five tones without half steps). They are short songs with simple or vigorous rhythms and non-lexical syllables, such as "ay-ay-sa-li-dum-may" or "dong-dong-ay-si-dong-i-lay" (see *STB* #92, 102, and 257). The songs are very popular and are frequently related to mountain life. Many have been set with Christian texts and are widely sung in worship services.[51]

Music of the Islamic Peoples

In the southern Philippines, the Islamic communities of Mindanao and the Sulu Archipelago have preserved certain pre-Islamic musical instruments. Most notable is the Maguindanao *kulingtang*, a set of five to eight horizontal-bossed gongs sitting on two strings tied to a wooden frame. This instrument is usually accompanied by two or three *agungs* (large suspended, bossed gong), two pairs of *gandingan* (gongs with lower boss), a *babandil* (a smaller gong), and a *dabakan* (drum). *Kulintang* have an important social value: they can be priceless heirlooms, and they are played to entertain guests at weddings, baptisms, or other formal rites (Garland 4:891f).

The vocal music of the Islamic community includes the five daily calls for prayer, the reading of the Quran, and the singing of religious songs and prayers on Friday noon services or other festivities commemorating Mohammad's life. Epic stories and classical narrative forms are also important in the training of musicians.

---

51   For further information, see Ronald Walcott, ed., *The Mountains Ring Out Their Joy*, AILM Collection of Asian Church Music No. 7 (Manila: Asian Institute for Liturgy and Music, 1987).

Rondalla

A *rondalla* is an ensemble of eight or as many as thirty instruments: *bandurria* (pear-shaped plucked lute with fourteen strings), laud, *octavina*, six-stringed *gitara*, and bass guitar. These ensembles were very popular during the early 1900s (Garland 4:854f). Many schools and companies still have *rondalla* ensembles.

Kundiman

This word refers to Spanish-Filipino love songs that have been popular since the 1800s. They are in a Western idiom and usually begin in a minor mode and shift to a tonic major at the second half (Garland 4:855). The *kundiman* style can also be seen in many contemporary hymns (see *STB* #263) and patriotic songs.

New Music

The diverse ethnic musical traditions in the Philippines attracted many anthropologists and ethnomusicologists in the early twentieth century. But it was not until Jose Maceda (1917–2004) abandoned his career as a concert pianist to become an ethnomusicologist that the study of traditional music and the development of modern music in the Philippines took a new direction.[52] Educated in France, Maceda was familiar with *musique concrète* and utilized many native ideas, instruments, and rituals in new compositions. For example, the works *Ugnayan* ("Atmospheres," 1974) and *Udlot-Udlot* ("Hesitations," 1975) use an environment of sounds created by hundreds of people. Maceda's *Pagsamba* ("Worship," 1968) is a monumental work for two hundred performers, which utilizes "the acoustical space of a round chapel in which choirs of singers and reciters, gongs, and bamboo instruments created masses of sounds that traveled around the circular space" (Garland 4:875f). Ramon Pagayon Santos (born 1941), a professor of composition at the University of Philippines, has also contributed to the repertoire of new music with Filipino and Asian musical elements, as shown in his *Ba-Dw Sa Kapoon-An* ("Divinity *Badiw*") from 1987 (Garland 4:877f). Another composer whose works have utilized Filipino elements and who has gained an international reputation is Francisco F. Feliciano (born 1941), who co-founded with Father Ellsworth Chandlee (1916–1981) the Asian Institute for Liturgy and Music in 1980. Feliciano is the only master composer in the Philippines who has made a significant contribution to church music. More information about his works can be found in the commentaries on his hymns and in his biography in this volume.

---

52   Maceda earned a PhD in ethnomusicology from University of California, Los Angeles, in 1954.

Commentary on Individual Hymns

"A BOY'S PRAYER"
("While I am asleep," *STB* #160)

(Filipino: *Panalangin ni totoy / Sa aking pagtulog*)

This is a very moving prayer by a boy, not only for himself but also for his parents. It reflects tragedies and injustices in the Filipino society, where many a father's wages are insufficient to feed his family. Many parents are working so hard to meet their families' needs that they are unable to take care of their children; hence, this boy prays to God not to let him go astray, so that he can also learn to earn a living. The text was written by Rody Vera, who was in his early twenties, for the Asian Institute for Liturgy and Music.[53] It was also a response to the WCC theme of the time, "Justice, Peace and Integrity of Creation," reflecting social problems such as poverty, militarization, and political oppression in the Philippines as well as other parts of the Third World.

The tune TOTOY, meaning "boy," was composed by Jonas Baes in an E♭ = 4 five-tone scale (4 5 7 1 3), which comes from the Indonesian *pelog* scale 3 4 5 7 1. Baes omitted the lower 3 for the accompaniment and placed it on the higher octave as a climax. The guitar accompaniment is very economical and offers room for one to imagine the boy's prayer. Notice how the opening and closing "chords" (D-B♭-E♭) convey a sense of insecurity, uncertainty, and loneliness. In the absence of a guitar, a keyboard may be used. For best results, one should train a boy to sing this in the service, especially for mission Sundays or when caring for children or those in poor countries. It is vital that the texts be translated into the local language and printed on the bulletin. (para. Rolando S. Tinio)

"Ay, Ay Salidummay, let us give thanks" (*STB* #113)

The Kalinga people in northern Luzon are fond of singing in non-lexical syllables such as "Ay, ay, sa-li-dum-may." Although the syllables do not have specific meanings, they are not without meaning. This phrase is frequently sung to express the mood of joy, but it can also express other feelings. One evening in early 1990, I heard a group of students having party in a neighbor's home. Every few minutes they burst into this one-phrase song, "Ay, ay salidummay, salidummay chiway," accompanied by clapping. They must have been having a good time, sharing their love, friendship, and joy together as a family of God. I transformed the song into a prayer of thanksgiving. The song has been well received in many groups of students and others.

---

53   Published in *Masdan, O Yahweh* ("Turn your gaze, O LORD"), AILM Collection of Asian Church Music No. 15 (Manila: Asian Institute for Liturgy and Music, 1990).

The melody is in a B♭ = 5 five-tone scale (E♭ = 1 2 3 5 6). The song may be used as a response to prayers of thanksgiving, especially in family or small group gatherings. Let the participants take turns sharing what they are thankful for, and the whole group can respond to share and own the thanksgiving prayer. A series of short, spontaneous thanksgiving prayers would make worship services contextually meaningful to all participants. See "Sing a song to the LORD," *STB* #92, for further information and accompaniment.

"Bear the weight of the cross" (*STB* #280)

(Filipino: *Pasanin mo ang krus*)

This is a brave and triumphant hymn about bearing the cross and needing strong faith and trust in order to be victorious over the powers of death and evil. This hymn is the work of two brothers, Aloysius and Jonas Baes, written for the AILM. The music, written in D natural minor (D = 6 7 1 2 3 4 5) with a simple motif 12/333/ 4-, is powerful, triumphant, and vigorous, especially when joined by the chorus in the third system. With moving reiterated drones and dissonance, the harmony is very effective in creating a resolute mood. The composer indicates that a soloist should sing the first two phrases, and the second voice should join the first in the ninth measure. Encouraging people to bear their cross for Christ, this hymn is suitable for Good Friday worship, especially in the form of a drama. However, it would be more meaningful if it were sung during an Easter service/ drama, as a commitment to carry the cross and to bear witness for Christ's victory. It is suggested that for the last repetition, the congregation should sing the main melody (the first three systems) while the sopranos sing the descant provided. The last phrase of the descant is quite thought-provoking: "We will climb up the hill of sorrows, there we'll uncrucify our freedom." The tune name PASANIN means "to carry." (para. Rolando S. Tinio)

"Behold the man we nailed on the cross" (*STB* #149)

(Filipino: *Tingnan, masdan ang tao sa krus*)

Catholicism in the Philippines emphasizes the cross as the symbol of Christ's suffering and also the suffering of the great majority of the people who live in severe poverty. The cross gives them hope in the midst of their suffering. Albert E. Alejo's passion hymn urges one to adore Christ. It is a powerful interpretation of Jesus' parable of the grain of wheat dying on the ground (John 12:24), the description of Jesus' blood on the cross that flows "like rain from heaven in drought, making the desert bloom," and Jesus' plea, "Father, forgive them all" (Luke 23:34). Alejo concludes with an affirmation that the cross is the way to reach God's promised citadel.

The music KRUS ("cross") by Eduardo P. Hontiveros is in a B = 3 E-minor seven-tone scale (E = 6 7 1 2 3 4 ♯5). It begins with a refrain and is through-composed. The meditative music flows with two counts per measure and should not be sung too forcefully or quickly.

"Blest be God who forever lives" (*STB* #264)

DANDANSOY is a popular folksong in the central Visayas region of the Philippines. It has features of the typical Spanish-Filipino *kundiman* style: a G-minor scale (G = 6 7 1 2 3 4 ♯5), a sudden modulation to its tonic major, (G = 1, with B♮ or the original 1 [B♭] sharpened, ♯1 [B]), triple time, phrases that begin from the second beat (creating the effect of an accented beat), and a guitar accompaniment. Salvador T. Martinez, the former Theological Secretary of the Christian Conference of Asia, wrote this text that reflects the spirit of Mary's Magnificat, praising God who is merciful and just, uplifting the lowly and the oppressed, and praying that God will be with those who trust Him. The phrases are isorhythmic (i.e. with the same rhythmic pattern) throughout. One may use a guitar accompaniment to enhance the folk style of this hymn.

"CHRIST OUR PEACE"
("Lift up the Cross, lift up our hearts," *STB* #261)

This is a powerful hymn by Rolando S. Tinio, calling all to be like Simon Cyrene, to "Carry the Cross to Calvary." Evil shall die; peace and justice shall reign, for Christ shall part the gloom of sin. The refrain "Lift up the Cross, lift up our hearts, Christ is the King who died for peace," is the central theme of this hymn that celebrates Christ's victory over evil, sin, and death. Singing it strengthens one's commitment to take up the cross for Christ.

The music PANATA, meaning "sacred vow," by Francisco F. Feliciano, is in a B = 3 seven-tone scale (E = 6 7 1 2 3 ♯4 5). The whole piece is based on a short motif, 322 3., with strong dance rhythms and an ostinato (i66 733) in different forms throughout. The accompaniment is a skillful treatment of this motif that appears in every measure in imitation, echoes, or other variations. The five measures of the refrain have exactly the same accompaniment, and the two accented beats in 6/8 time are carried through the song. When accompanying this hymn, it is important to play the accents in the bass clef, especially the repeated Ds and Bs in the tenor.

The composer provides performance notes: "Drums, tambourines, and other percussion instruments used in the locality and sitar (Indian plucked lute) when available may be used. The keyboard guide is very minimal so as to give much room for improvisation. To end the song, repeat the last bar of the refrain (on the word "peace") *n* times, then fade."

"DANCE OF LIGHT"
("This is our fiesta!" *STB* #278)

(Filipino: *Pandanggo sa ilaw / Kung pista sa nayon*)

PANDANGGO SA ILAW ("Dance of Light") is one of the most popular and beautiful folk dances of the Filipino folk festivals. Derived from the Castilian and Andalucian word "fandango," the Filipino *pandanggo* is performed in a fast triple time. This particular *pandanggo* originated in Mindoro in the Visayas region and employs lighted candles. Each dancer in the group balances a candle on his or her head and holds candles in both hands, swinging and skipping and forming tapestries of movement and light, all with coordinated skill so that the candles do not fall or fade. This dance is usually accompanied by *bandurrias* (Filipino mandolins) and guitars, and the surrounding people clap the triple rhythm. Francisco F. Feliciano took the original text of the *pandanggo* folk song and added a few Christian interpretations. For example, the first stanza summarizes the dance's movements and concludes with "praise to God who shows the way with such a bright gift of dance." In the second stanza, Feliciano asks God to "teach us how to pray as we leap and sway, when we've caught the Spirit's flame, there is no end to the light."

The tune shows typical remnants of Spanish musical style: a D-minor seven-tone scale (6 7 1 2 3 4 #5, plus #1 for modulation and #2 as an accidental), triple time with repetitive tones and accents on the second beat (0 3333/ 3 21 2/2), and a sudden modulation to the tonic major (D = 1) at the second half. All of these features fit the Spanish-Filipino *kundiman* style. The melody has many repetitions and sequences, which makes it easy to learn and to sing. It has a very fast, lively rhythm; a quarter note equals about 132. To follow the musical style, one may clap on the second and third beat but never on the first beat. Although the song ends on a D-major chord, one should ensure that the guitarists or instrumentalists play a D-minor chord (D-F-A) in the last incomplete measure, so that the congregation will be aurally prepared to sing the F in a minor mode at the beginning of the second stanza. (para. Rolando S. Tinio)

"Death steals like a thief" (*STB* #170)

(Filipino: *Dahil sa pagpanaw ng mahal sa buhay*)

This hymn, by Cirilo A. Rigos, affirms that one grieving for the loss of loved ones can find comfort and strength from God. It prays for God to let our eyes see the stars in the darkness and to dry up our tears, and when our time is up, God will grant us his mercy and promise of eternal rest.

The tune PAGYAO, meaning "departure" or "leaving," is in an E = 3 major scale (C = 1 2 3 4 5 6 7) with a raised #2 and #5; except the cadences of the first, the third, and the last phrases, most of the piece is harmonized in a minor mode and with chromaticism (altered chords and half-tone progressions). The composer Jerry Dadap treated the first phrase with a drone effect: the alto and bass repeat C throughout. From the second phrase, the music begins to develop in sequence; at times, the accents switch to the second beat, which is a favorite Spanish-influenced Filipino style. This phrase is longer and builds to the climax very effectively at the beginning of the third system, calling for "God our Father" (in Filipino only; the second and third stanza in English addresses "you, loving God" or "your tender care"). The melody fades gradually toward the end, with a feeling of repose and peace on a major chord.   (para. Rolando S. Tinio & J.M.)

"Deep in the human heart" (STB #248)

See the commentary in the section for New Zealand.

"EVENING SONG"
("When twilight comes and the sun sets," *STB* #161)

(Filipino: *Awit sa Dapit Hapon / Ngayong nagda dapit hapon*)

This is an evening hymn that associates God's love with the image of a mother hen sheltering her brood under her wings. The author, Moises Andrade, a Catholic priest, wrote this beautiful hymn to reflect the joy, peace, and contentment of being with the LORD. Andrade cites how Christ at the Last Supper invited his disciples to "receive his servant care." The hymn concludes by expressing the joy in praying together as a family "by a mother's love embraced in the blessed Trinity."

The music DAPIT HAPON, meaning "twilight" or "dusk," was composed by Francisco F. Feliciano in an E = 6 natural minor scale (6 7 1 2 3 4 5). It is through-composed without any repetition of phrases, but there are certain imitations, especially at the end. The composer specifies two guitars for accompaniment: one plucking the chords, another strumming. This hymn is appropriate for a family or community evening prayer/devotion. (para. Jim Minchin)

"Everywhere sorrow on Calvary's hill" (*STB* #148)

(Filipino: *Ang kalbaryo, sagisag ng lumbay*)

In the refrain, Vicente Mar. Aguila questions why the Father had to pay such a high price to crucify his own Son. The verses explore God's plan, from Calvary to glory, from death to resurrection, from darkness to light, and from despair to hope to resurrection!

The music KALBARYO (the Filipino word for Calvary) was written by one of the most important composers of the Philippines, Eliseo M. Pajaro, in an E-minor seven-tone scale (6 7 1 2 3 4 5) with two raised tones, ♯1 and ♯5. The style reflects the country's Spanish heritage: it is in triple time, especially with an accent on the second beat in the refrain, and consecutive thirds dominate the piece. The piece is rather long, consisting of eight phrases without exact repetition but with similar patterns and slight variations. The extended use of G♯ in the second to last phrase of the refrain marks a high point, modulating from E major (which is the tonic major of E minor) to a new tonal center in A minor at the climax, and the tune concludes in E minor. (para. Rolando S. Tinio)

"Far beyond our mind's grasp"
See "WHAT A GREAT MYSTERY" *(STB #82)*

"FRIEND TO FRIEND"
("Let us now as God's own people," *STB* #244)

This hymn is popular among young Filipinos. The text and music are by the Roman Catholic poet-composer Eduardo P. Hontiveros, who has written hundreds of songs in a similar style. The text is about Jesus' teaching: that we as his followers should love one another, feed the hungry, clothe the naked, and give drink to those who thirst. The music is in an F♯ = 3 D major scale (D = 1) with guitar accompaniment. The refrain is a duet of thirds and sixths and is very easy to sing. It would be good to sing this hymn at the conclusion of worship, with the congregation forming a circle or, if it is arranged in rows, holding hands as a symbol and commitment of loving and caring for one another.

"Give praise to the God of all earth" (*STB* #30)
(Filipino: *Purihin ang Panginoon*)

F. Ll. Ramirez summons people to utilize their musical instruments to praise God, to seek Jesus' comforting words and protection from our foes, and to bear our burdens. He also calls for all to obey God's commandments and proclaim God's deeds to the world.

The tune PURIHIN, meaning "give praises," is in an A = 5 D-major scale (D = 1) with a lively triple time. The music is in a two-part form. The phrase structure of part A is a a' b c d, in which the a' is a higher sequence of a; d and a have the same cadence and thus balance part A. Part B is the verse, with the phrases e e e' f, in which e begins with an A-minor seventh chord, which functions almost like a dominant seventh chord (Am7) of D, but e' modulates to D minor, which is a reverse of the typical Filipino style. A traditional Spanish tune begins in a minor key and modulates to its tonic major, but here it is the opposite, beginning in D major and modulating to D minor. The author/composer Ramirez provides a series of extended A-major chords at the end (A4–A–A9–A7) as preparation for the return to the refrain in D major; this follows the conventional method. As indicated, this song requires a guitar accompaniment to communicate the mood of praise. (para. Beath Nacion-Puyot)

"Holy God, holy mighty"
See "TRISAGION" (*STB* #122)

"How deep your love, O Master" (*STB* #147)
(Filipino: *Purihin ka, O Kristo*)

This hymn is about revering the cross of Christ, being thankful for God's love and redemption in Christ, and committing to carry Christ's cross. Influenced by almost four hundred years of Spanish rule and Roman Catholicism, reverence for the cross is one of the most sacred actions of devotion for Christians in the Philippines. During Holy Week, some Filipinos volunteer to be literally nailed on the cross as a sign of repentance or a wish for certain blessings from God. In the city of Manila, the cross of the Black Nazarene is carried along the streets, and those who touch the cross receive a special blessing. This hymn is sung on Good Friday as congregants enter the sanctuary and the cross is carried in procession around the church. The composer suggests that moods of repentance, gratitude, and, most of all, the mystery of salvation can be established by the soprano and the congregation singing the main melody a few times; gradually the alto, tenor, and bass join in, singing in two, three, and four parts.

Francisco F. Feliciano, a Roman Catholic who has taught in an Anglican seminary for most of his life and understands liturgy and theology, captured the mood and spirit of this sacred action with this text and tune. Whether we carry the cross or not, we can still sing this in worship to meditate on the mystery of God's salvation. The music is almost like an ostinato (i.e. the same material repeated) in C minor (C = 6 1 2 3 4 5 ♯5, plus ♯2) but with rich harmonic variations. It is not easy to sing well, but with diligent practice, it will be worth the effort. BANAHAW is the name of a mountain that is considered sacred by the Tagalog people.

"In great thanksgiving" (*STB* #31)

This is a hymn of thanksgiving for God's love and the forgiveness of sins, a plea to serve the Lord by seeking the lost, feeding the hungry, and teaching his way of peace and justice. It was written by a husband-and-wife team, Dick Melchizedek M. Solis and Mutya Lopez. Originally, the text "new life here" at the end of the first stanza referred to the dreams of Filipino and other Asian immigrants in the United States searching for prosperity, freedom, and opportunities. But it has been reinterpreted as a celebration of new life in Christ. This hymn, written in the 1970s for the Filipino communities in Salinas in northern California, was collected and recommended by the Filipino Caucus of the United Methodist Church for inclusion in the 1983 Asian American hymnal, *Hymns from the Four Winds*.

The tune name MALATE refers to an old district in Manila where the Methodist Church was located and where the Solises had served prior to their immigration to the United States. It was written by Mutya in an A = 3 D-minor scale (D = 6 7 1 2 3 4 6) with a flattened 7. Although the tune is in 4/4 time, the rhythmic pattern of the opening of each phrase and the modulation to G minor at the appearance of the high E♭ (from D = 333 4 3- to D = 666♭7 6-) are reminiscent of the music's Spanish influence. The accompaniment is in a romantic style. The hymn may be sung as a soprano and alto duet. Be careful of the cross-relationship between F♮ and F♯. The prelude is for introduction only. Sufficient time for breathing is needed at the end of each stanza.

"In the heavens shone a star" (*STB* #131)

The Kalinga people living in northern Luzon sing in pentatonic scales. Named after the tribe, the tune KALINGA is in a G♯ = 3 five-tone scale (E = 1 2 3 5 6). The text by Jonathan Malicsi and Ellsworth Chandlee portrays the nativity scene of stars, angels, shepherds, manger, the Christ child, the wise men, and the Lord and King. To make a Christmas service more meaningful after singing this lovely carol, it would be good to involve the congregation in performing symbolic acts that express their ways of adoring the Holy Child. The music is in a simple a a b b c form with a three-note coda (2 3 1-). Edgard Macapili has provided the guitar accompaniment, which is mostly in E9 chords that sound more contemporary. Macapili, a gifted singer, composer, conductor, and guitar player, is a graduate of AILM and Southern Methodist University; he married a Taiwanese woman, Siok-koan Ban, and currently teaches at Tainan Theological College and Seminary.

"In the lands of Asia" (*STB* #263)

In this hymn, Salvador T. Martinez alludes to the political and economic injustices of Asian societies that affect men, women, and children and prays to God for visions to heal the suffering and struggling.

The tune was composed by the author; hence, it is named MARTINEZ. It is in the favored Spanish-Filipino *kundiman* minor-key style, using an F = 1 D-minor scale (D = 6), which in the refrain modulates to its tonic major (D = 1) and is sung faster. In order to make a smooth transition back to a slower tempo and the minor, one should slowly strum a D-minor chord on the guitar before beginning the next stanza. The author has indicated that, should this hymn be sung in other parts of the world, the initial texts of the second and third stanzas may be changed to "in the global village" and "everywhere around us" or other words appropriate for the various contexts.

"Let us even now go" (*STB* #146)
(Cebuano: *Manglakat na kita*)

Angel Sotto wrote this text of the nativity scene, inviting us to go to Bethlehem to worship the newborn King and to spread the news so that the world may know God's love. The second and third stanzas were added by Lois F. Bello.

Sotto's tune MANGLAKAT, meaning "let's go," is in a B♭ = 1 seven-tone major scale (1 2 3 4 5 6 7). The triple time reflects the Spanish influence, as does beginning with the stressed second beat. The music is well organized in a b a' b' form with a coda. Notice that in a', the second portion begins after an eighth rest instead of a quarter rest. The tempo is rather fast, with one beat per measure. The melody and arrangement with guitar chords are by Elena G. Maquiso, who first introduced and included this hymn in her Cebuano hymnal. Cebuano is one of the major languages in the southern Philippines.

The sanctuary of the Chapel of Dumaguete Divinity School, where Elena G. Maquiso taught.
(Photo taken February 2005.)

"Lift up the Cross, lift up our hearts"
See "CHRIST OUR PEACE" (*STB* #261)

"LORD, your hands have formed this world"
See "THE EARTH IS THE LORD'S" (*STB* #178)

"MARY'S SALIDUMMAY"
("My soul magnifies the Lord," *STB* #102)

Henry W. Kiley of St. Andrew's Theological Seminary in Manila adapted Mary's Magnificat (Luke 1:46–55) using Kalinga non-lexical syllables: "Ay-ay, sa-li-dum-may, in-si-na-li-du-mi-way." While these are without particular meanings, the Kalinga tend to use these syllables to express a mood of joy, as seen from "Sing a Song to the Lord" (*STB* #92) and "Let us give thanks to God" (*STB* #13). In a wider application, non-lexical syllables may gain meanings from the song's title, the occasion, or the texts sung prior to or after them (see *STB* #244, "From this time onwards" in the Taiwan section). When singing these syllables, one can imagine blessed Mary's adoration: "My soul magnifies the Lord, and my heart exults." Because the contents of each stanza vary slightly, the mood of the non-lexical syllables also changes accordingly.

The tune MARY'S SALIDUMMAY is Kiley's adaptation of the Kalinga *salidummay* motive, which is usually in a five-tone scale without a half step. This one is in a G = 3 scale (E♭ = 1 2 3 5 6), it is through-composed, and the last stanza has a coda. The composer suggests that this hymn may be sung antiphonally, with the women singing the first two phrases and the men or the entire congregation singing the rest. One can also use bamboo buzzers (*balingbing*) to accompany the hymn. For more information, see the commentary on *STB* #92, "Sing a song to the Lord."

"Now the day is ending" (*STB* #159)
(Cebuano: *Salup na ang adlaw*)

In this beautiful evening prayer, using images of birds feeding and protecting their young, Elena G. Maquiso asks for God's loving care. She pleads for God's forgiveness if we have failed him, offended others, hurt others, or neglected to help the needy, and she asks God to grant us restful slumber and renewed energy in the morning.

The text and melody MONING (a female name) are by Maquiso, a well-known musician and Christian educator in Dumaguete, in the southern Philippines. The tune is in an A = 3 major scale (F = 1 2 3 4 5 6 7) plus ♯1. It is almost through-composed with isorhythmic phrases, i.e., all using the same rhythm: 3 5, 6, 1 3-3-. The setting is in a Western harmonic language with a romantic touch; there are altered chords in a few places, creating a very attractive mood in this hymn. One has feelings of intimate warmth, relaxation, and peacefulness when singing this hymn. (trsl: 1–2 by Cirilo A. Rigos & Ellsworth Chandlee)

"O Lᴏʀᴅ, who made all the heavens" (*STB* #76)

(Filipino: *Panginoon ng kalangitan at karagatan*)

In J. M. C. Francisco's hymn, the "faithful poor" offer to God their lives, sweat, and tears, and pray for God to enlighten their ways. The music is by Eduardo P. Hontiveros; hence, the tune is named ʜᴏɴᴛɪᴠᴇʀᴏs. It is in D major (D = 1), beginning with A = 5, in a two-part form (A = a a b c; B = d e d' f) in which e is a sequence of d that begins one tone lower. The use of hemiola (a rhythmic alteration in which six equal notes may be heard as two groups of three or three groups of two) makes this song more interesting. The song displays Hontiveros's typical harmonic style of consecutive thirds, except near the end of both sections. (para. Rolando S. Tinio)

"O many people of all lands" (*STB* #21)

Acknowledging the diversity of people of all cultures who gather to praise God, Natty G. Barranda's hymn gives thanks for God's providence for supplying all our needs and commits to share God's love and gifts in substance, deeds, and forms. This hymn was written in 1980 for the Asian American hymnal project and first appeared in *Hymns from the Four Winds* in 1983.

The tune ᴍᴀᴛᴇʀɴɪᴅᴀᴅ ("motherhood") was composed by Lois F. Bello, who was on the editorial committee of the Filipino Caucus for the hymnal project. It is in a C = 3, F = 6 minor scale; although not indicated clearly, it is in triple time, except the sixth and seventh syllables, "of all" (7 1), are in two. For the sixth and seventh syllables of the second system, "praise our" (2 3-), the accent also shifts from the first to the second beat on "our." Note the sudden modulation to the tonic major at the beginning of the second system (F major: 5 5 4 3-1). These are typical characteristics of the Spanish-Filipino *kundiman* style that most contemporary Filipinos enjoy (see *STB* #82, #146, #264, and #278). This hymn should be sung joyfully with one count per measure and a guitar accompaniment. It is suitable as a hymn of gathering at the beginning of worship; in this case, the fifth stanza, which is appropriate before dismissal, may be left out.

"Our souls are full of praises" (*STB* #29)

(Filipino: *Kadakilaan mo, O Diyos*)

This is a hymn of praise and thanksgiving for God's wondrous gifts of love, the natural beauty of God's creation, and for God's eternal care and never-failing love. The author Serafin E. Ruperto pledges to tell of God's deeds "to all the world."

Bernardino F. Custodio's tune is in a D = 3 G-minor scale (G = 6 7 1 2 3 4 5 ♯5) in a through-composed form, with all except the opening and closing phrases in the same rhythmic pattern. It is in traditional Western four-part harmony with a good counterpoint. The music modulates to its relative major (B♭, G = 57123-) at the end of the third system, which leads to the climax with another temporary modulation to C minor (3 to 4, i.e. G7 to C minor). The tune closes with a descending sequence (4217, 3176). The tune name ROSEWOOD is the name of a Filipino church in Los Angeles, where this hymn was frequently sung. The text was translated for the Asian American hymn project. (para. Romeo del Rosario & Jim Minchin)

"PRAISE THE LOVING GOD"
("Praise to you, O God," *STB* #98)
(Filipino: *Awit ng Pagpapasalamat / O Dakilang Diyos*)

This Muslim melody, MAMAYUG AKUN (meaning "My dear Mamayug") from the southern Philippines, was adapted by Francisco F. Feliciano to the text of Psalm 136: "O give thanks to the LORD, for he is good, for his steadfast love endures forever." But unlike the original call-and-response form in the psalm, this hymn omits the congregational responses. The hymn gives thanks for God's creation and tells of God's setting Jacob's children free, leading them through the desert, and giving them land to settle, so that they could hold their heads up high and feed on the food of life.

The melody is built on an F = 1 five-tone scale (1 2 3 5 6) in a chanting style and with a a' b form. Rudolf R. Pantou, a former composition student of Francisco F. Feliciano at AILM, created an interesting guitar accompaniment with a few rhythmic patterns; the percussive effect transforms this chant into to a lively song of praise. The end of each stanza should have a fermata (pause) so that the congregation has sufficient time to breathe before singing the next stanza.

"Praise to you, O God"
See "PRAISE THE LOVING GOD" (*STB* #98)

"She dances 'mid the city lights"
See "THREE WOMEN" (*STB* #186)

"Sing a song to the LORD" (*STB* #92)

Here, Francisco F. Feliciano's paraphrase of Psalm 96 is set to the exciting SALIDUMMAY tune by Ben Pangosban. As previously mentioned, the non-lexical syllables of the Kalinga have been adapted by Christians to express the mood of joy. Pangosban's setting captures the spirit of the melody and greatly enhances the telling about the mighty acts of God that are beyond one's comprehension. God's wondrous works are full of surprises, and so are the irregular rhythms of this hymn. The half-measure marks are provided for easier conducting, but all of the beats are equally strong, as seen from the suggested accompaniment. Two pairs of bamboo buzzers (*balingbing*) play in an interlocking manner, with closed (+ = covering the hole, thus lower) or open (o = higher) sounds. This pattern of two equally strong beats provides a vigorous rhythm with which to proclaim the greatness of God and his judgment to the world. A *balingbing* is made of a split bamboo tube with a hole to be covered by a thumb; it creates a buzzing sound when hit by the palm.

balingbing

"Sing to God, dance to God"
See "SING WITH HEARTS" (*STB* #33)

"SING WITH HEARTS"
("Sing to God, dance to God," *STB* #33)

Calling all to praise God with songs and dances, this interesting hymn is set to an F = 1 major scale that combines two musical styles in three sections. The initial section is a refrain, as an invitation to praise, with a fast (quarter note = 100) and vigorous Kalinga dance rhythm, ending on 6. The verses asking God to grant us wisdom and to inspire us with dance have a lyrical melody (quarter note = 69) in a b a b form. The third part is a coda ("with joyful hearts, with soul and body offer we our arts") ending with the second half of the b motif. Jonathan Malicsi skillfully provided the text to this INTAKO melody. "In," "ta," and "ko" were the original non-lexical syllables for the refrain. In section one, 4 (B♭) is not used, and sometimes the 7 (E) is sung slightly lower, which indicates that the melody is closer to the older Kalinga tradition. In the last section, the 6 (D) is absent, and the melodic idiom in the last two sections is closer to a Western one. This is an interesting example of cultural infusion or the cross-fertilization of East and West. Observing the tempo changes will help to express the spirit and style of this hymn.

"Sleep through the night, beloved child" (*STB* #277)
(Filipino: *Matulog pa, bunsong mahal*)

In this lullaby, a mother tells a baby that his father would be happy to see him when he returns, but he might be hiding in the mountains from a storm. She heard that his father was coming home, but he might not hold him or smile when she kisses him in greeting. Finally she tells the baby that she must stay beside his father for "insects may swirl in the slumber of his vacant gaze": the father is dead. If one were this mother, how would one feel, how would it be possible to tell an innocent baby the truth, and how could he understand the tragedy of the adult world? Under such difficult conditions, one could only pray for God's mercy. This was what the author and composer did. While the female parts sing the lullaby, the male choir sings prayers (stanzas 3 and 5) to the LORD to console the widow and the orphaned boy, to dry their tears, and to find final joy in the LORD.

This hymn vividly describes the frequent suffering in the Philippines during Marcos's twenty-year dictatorship. Roland S. Tinio conveys tragedy in this poem, which Francisco F. Feliciano has woven into a lovely lullaby with a sonorous five- to six-part chorus, including a female solo and descant and a three- to four-part male chorus. The music is constructed with a simple five-tone scale, D = 6 1 2 3 5. The motif consists of two sets of figures composed of four tones (in chorus 3/3 2 5.) and five tones (in solo and descant 121. 2/1.), the movement of each evoking a rocking cradle, with a rich harmony of all tonal combinations. This hymn premiered in 1990 in a musical drama portraying the condition of the Philippines during the Marcos regime (see further discussion under "A BOY'S PRAYER," *STB* #160). The music was deeply moving; many who heard the singing were in tears! The tune TAGULAYLAY, meaning "lamentation," is definitely not an ordinary hymn to be sung in worship. But it expresses how Christians can and should extend their love, sympathy, and care for those in the deepest pain and loss and should cry with those who weep. This song would have a powerful effect in a drama.

"Still, I search for my God" (*STB* #176)

This is an example of the innovative use of imagery to guide the development of a musical motif. It is a meditative hymn, searching for God and marveling at his creation—its beauty, diversity, harmony, and perfection. Instead of providing a definitive answer to the source of such a mystery, the author/composer Francisco F. Feliciano takes a more Asian approach, asking indirectly, "Who else could it be?" He gives the answer in the third stanza, breathing in the presence of God and singing, praising, and worshiping God with joy. This hymn faithfully reflects the words of I Peter 1:8, "Although you have not seen him, you love him; and even though you do not see him now, you believe in him and rejoice with an indescribable and glorious joy."

This tune WASDIN PANG IPAAD (meaning "each one does his part") utilizes a visual image as a metaphor for sound. The composer says that when one casts a small stone into a calm lake, it stirs ripples, at first small and then bigger and wider, and these gradually fade away. The melodic construction evolved from this image. The tonal movements describe the expanding ripples (3- 34323. 3 /6644/323.), building up to the climax (3/6 6 6/ 767.), and then gradually fading (6/ 76 643/ 22. 2242/3-). Feliciano innovatively employs two guitars, one playing only four tones

(3- 4- 6- 7-) and the other playing the accompaniment in dissonant arpeggios. It is important to sing this hymn slowly and "with utmost simplicity," adding nothing to the score. Let the music lead to the mystery. In a worship service expressing God's love through his creation, it would be effective to have a soloist sing the first two stanzas and to have the congregation join in the third stanza to evoke the mystery and joy of God's love.

"THE APOSTLES' CREED"
("I believe in God the Father," *STB* #117)

The Apostles' Creed is set by Francisco F. Feliciano with a *salidummay* motif from the Kalinga in northern Luzon. The tune BANAWE is named for a place famous for its hundreds of terraced rice fields. Built into the high mountain slopes by the genius and skills of farmers in order to grow rice in abundance, Banawe's rice terraces are referred to as the eighth wonder of the world.

The Kalinga melodic construction of this hymn seems to reflect these terraces: from low C = 5 (55 1), going up (11 5 5 /6 i), and coming down (i6 5. 3 /1 5, 1 11/ 21 5, 5--). One can see the three climaxes (6 i6) are set to texts on God the Father, Jesus Christ, and the Holy Ghost. These three phrases are the most important affirmations of faith. But when Feliciano states the same words again ("the Father Almighty"; "in Jesus Christ, his only Son our Lord"; "in the Holy Spirit"), he makes the music descend to the lowest notes (1 11 21 5, 5-), as if the almighty God has incarnated himself in human form, dwelling lowly with us. The rest of the creed is set in reiterated tones (1 11 11, 22 22, or 33 33, etc.) like the different levels of the rice fields. Also, the text "the Holy Catholic Church" is set on the lower level (1 1 21215,5-), seemingly acknowledging the reality of the church being on earth. The composer seems to suggest that only the three of the triune God deserve the highest exaltation. Whether or not the composer had this in mind when he set the text to this tune, one can find inspiration for theological interpretation in these musical elements. This setting shows one function of the art of music, expressing possible implications and hidden meanings behind the sound. When asked why the melody goes beyond the reach of most singers in the general public (to a high f), the composer replied that the effort to reach high notes would highlight or strengthen people's intentions of confessing their faith.

One of the composer's suggestions is that the congregation only sings the three passages marked "I believe, I believe…" and adds their confessions between them. Or the congregation may only sing these three phrases and recite the rest of the Creed or allow the choir to recite it. The final Amen should be sung as suggested in four parts, repeating the final measure a number of times to reaffirm one's faith.

"THE EARTH IS THE LORD'S"
("Lord, your hands have formed this world," *STB* #178)
(Ikalahan: *Imegmoy pitak ay yay*)

Acknowledging the love and sovereignty of God in the world, the husband-and-wife team Ramon and Sario Oliano composed this hymn to affirm that all of nature and everything growing—including plants, animals, and human beings—are the signs of God making all things new everyday. They also apply this principle to spiritual matters and ask God to uproot sins and provide "homes for Christ." The Ikalahan people are farmers living in the mountains. This hymn expresses God's blessings in an Ikalahan context:

> Sweet potatoes fill our bags, when the garden yields its due.
> Chickens run, and pigs grow pump, children too:
> Your bounty's signs that you make all things new.

The music GAYOM NI HIGAMI, meaning "Your loving care of us," is an Ikalahan traditional melody with a B♭ = 5 five-tone scale (E♭ = 1 2 3 5 6). The music has five short phrases (a b a' c a''), of which the first three have eight counts each; a' is a variation of a one octave higher. The c phrase has only seven counts; it repeats two-thirds of phrase a (1. 6 1 65 5) from the fourth note onward, and the last note of the phrase (5) becomes the first note of the last phrase (1 65 /5 6 1), a kind of contraction. The organization of this short form is very interesting. The surprising, concluding contraction expresses well the newness of God's creation. (trsl. Delert Rice; para. Jim Minchin)

"THE GREAT THANKSGIVING"
("The merciful goodness of the Lord," *STB* #42)

The prayer of thanksgiving during the Eucharist is one of the most important prayers in the liturgical tradition. This prayer is said or sung before the Sanctus ("Holy, Holy. Holy Lord, Heaven and earth are full of your glory . . ."). This melody is adapted from the Ilocano Passion chant. Every year beginning on Maundy Thursday, the Ilocano people sing the passion stories (see the introduction of this chapter) of the Gospels until the noon of Good Friday. The hours around noon are the most sacred time of the year in the Philippines. Even in Manila, the streets are empty because most people are in church, praying. These chants are frequently sung in parallel thirds. Hence, the smaller notes are optional for the second voice. This chant (in an F = 6 four-tone scale, E = ♯5 6 7 1) should be sung responsively as specified, and the harmony is only added in the congregational response. The reciting tone should not be rushed. (trsc. Father Foster)

"The merciful goodness of the Lᴏʀᴅ"

See "The GREAT THANKSGIVING" (*STB* #42)

"The Lᴏʀᴅ is my shepherd" (*STB* #88)

(Filipino: *Si Yahweh ang aking pastol*)

Psalm 23 is here sung in a Gregorian chant style; an antiphon is written polyphonically in four parts, and the bass doubles the soprano. It is in a D = 6 five-tone scale (6 1 2 3 5). For nearly three decades, Francisco F. Feliciano has been the director of music at the Episcopalian St. Andrew's Theological Seminary in Manila, and he has written and composed innumerable psalms in similar styles; this is one of the most popular. The antiphon may be sung in the original language. It is important that the chant has a natural tempo of recitation; the clarity of the text is emphasized and should not be rushed.

"This land of beauty has been given" (*STB* #266)

The Philippines is rich in natural resources, and its land is very fertile. Yet there is an enormous gap between the wealthy and the poor. A small number of the affluent own much of the land, but the majority of the poor have little or nothing. There have been land reform policies, but they were not successful. This prompted Elena G. Maquiso to write this hymn in the late 1960s, to implore the rich to share their lands with their tenants, because the mercy of God is for everyone. Maquiso uses plain, daily language to present the facts and state the problems.

The music is in a C = 3 F-minor scale (F = 6 7 1 2 3 4 ♯5) in a syllabic form. Singing this as a solo with a guitar accompaniment is the best way to communicate the message, and the congregation can join in at the last stanza. Dᴜᴍᴀɢᴜᴇᴛᴇ is the name of the city in Negros Oriental, in the central part of the Philippines, where Maquiso lived and taught at the Divinity School of Silliman University. I recorded this hymn at Maquiso's home in 1970, with her singing, and it was first published in *New Songs of Asian Cities* in 1972.

"THREE WOMEN"
("She dances 'mid the city lights," *STB* #186)

Tom Maddela's hymn depicts the circumstances of three kinds of women in contemporary Manila and compares them to three women in the Bible and their encounters with Christ. The messages of the Biblical women are clear. Mary the Magdalene exclaims: "The Lord is risen; come with me and listen." The Samaritan woman witnesses: "Christ is here to help us." To the third woman who represents all the Marthas of this world, Christ says: "There's time for work, there's time to tarry. Behold your sister Mary."

Francisco F. Feliciano composed this tune in an E = 6 minor scale (6 7 1 2 3 #4 5). It is very syllabic and in a a b c form; the c ends with the cadence of a. Note that the unusual #4 (C#) appears only once for the most important words of the stanzas: respectively, "risen," "tells us," and "tarry." Care should be taken to treat the value of all the eighth notes equally in both 2/4 time and 6/8 time. The tune name ERMITA is the red-light district in Manila, where many women struggle to make a living.

"TRISAGION"
("Holy God, holy mighty," *STB* #122)

Francisco F. Feliciano imitates the Orthodox tradition of singing the Trisagion in D major (D = 1) with parallel chords: all three parts move in parallel motion, except the penultimate note in the tenor and bass. The TRISAGION, meaning "three holies," is usually sung during the Eucharist as a part of the Great Thanksgiving. It should be sung slowly, solemnly, and in harmony but without accompaniment. This beautiful harmonic progression creates a sense of mystery that evokes the presence of God and one's contrite heart begging for God's mercy. It should be sung a number of times to establish the mood.

"We believe: Maranatha, light of the day" (*STB* #45)

This is a response to the affirmation of faith. It was originally written during the 1987 Asian Workshop on Liturgy and Music in Makiling, Manila. This is an affirmation of faith to God for his creation, to Christ for his redemption and resurrection, and to the Spirit and Truth for love, joy, and hope. This response should be sung after each section of confession of faith, as printed. After the leader's intonation, the congregation responds in harmony. The second part is a canon imitating the first part, and the third part is a drone; the penultimate note creates tension, delaying the resolution of the final cadence.

The confession of faith may vary in different churches and on different occasions. Each community is encouraged to write its own confession of faith for a particular purpose. No matter the content, one can use this as a powerful response to strengthen one's faith and to own one's confession. If the congregation has difficulty singing in parts, it is fine to simply repeat the leader's part in unison. If the leader is unable to sing, the choir may take his/her place.

"WHAT A GREAT MYSTERY"
("Far beyond our mind's grasp," *STB* #82)
(Filipino: *Kay Laking Hiwaga / Hindi ko maisip*)

Although most Protestants would not emphasize this, partaking of the body of Christ is always a mystery. The author Francisco F. Feliciano, a Roman Catholic, states this clearly in this Communion hymn. He writes that in this celebration of the mystery of Christ's suffering and redemption, God is calling us through the veil. We are not worthy to receive the elements, yet it is God's free gift for life. So we should thank God for the divine feast of fellowship and pray:

> May our lives be altars glowing with your Spirit
> To light the lamps of those who also seek your face.

Feliciano's adaptation of the Bicol folksong CATUROG NA NONOY for this hymn is interesting. Originally, the tune was a lullaby from Bicol, in the southern Philippines. The melody is in an A = 5, D = 1 major scale, but the triple rhythm with frequent accents on the second beats reflects its Spanish heritage. The guitar accompaniment further strengthens its folk spirit. If no guitars are available, one can also use a keyboard to play the accompaniment as written, lest the style be corrupted.

The beautiful song seems a perfect setting for the text. One wonders about the composer's reason for choosing a lullaby melody for this Communion hymn. Does he imply that God's love is like a mother's never-ending love and tender care for her own baby, willing to sacrifice her life in order to give life to her child? The music provides room for imagination and theologizing.

This hymn is suitable for any Holy Communion service and is especially appropriate for use during Holy Week. However, the fourth stanza would be more meaningful and effective if sung after the Communion or prior to the dismissal.

"When my troubles arose" (*STB* #97)
(Filipino: *Nang ako'y manganib*)

Psalm 120 is the first of fifteen Songs of Ascents (Psalms 120–134); they are sung on pilgrimages to Jerusalem or in processionals during annual festivals. Psalm 120:7 expresses longing for Jerusalem's peace. Like the psalmist, the composer Judith Laoyan felt that the faithful are frequently afflicted, so she employed the psalm text that expresses the "hopefulness and wholesomeness of life" (Mays 1994, 385–388). After giving thanks, the psalmist cries out for deliverance "from all those lying lips" and for peace. This is further supported by the bass ostinato harmonized by Francsco F. Feliciano, which repeatedly encourages, "Dig-dig-wi" (here meaning "go forth") "and seek the peace of the Lord." "Dig-dig-wi" also belongs to the category of non-lexical syllables, i.e, it does not have a specific meaning but may gain meanings through the context or function of the text.

The music CORDILLERA (the name of a region in the northern part of Luzon, where the Kankanay word *digdigwi* comes from) is in a G = 1 six-tone scale (B = 3 #5 6 7 1, but with a raised #2) with the final on 6. The song is based on two related motifs (6 6 #5 6- and 6 6 7 1-) with repetitions and sequential development (7 7 1 1 #2 3-). One should be careful when singing the augmented second (1–#2, which sounds like a minor third). There are seven counts per phrase—the rhythmic structure being 2+3+2 on the melody—while the ostinato is 3+2+2 but two counts behind. In the last system, however, the rhythmic patterns change.

"Who will set us free?" (*STB* #130)

This simple text by Bernardo Maria Perez was written for youths and young seminarians at the St. Andrew's Seminary in Manila, where Francisco F. Feliciano was the organist and choir director for many years. The text expresses simple yet important questions to Jesus: "Who will set us free? Who will clear our sight? Who will be our light? Who will give us life?" In this modern era full of temptations, confusions, restlessness, hardships, and doubts, one can understand how young people demand realistic answers. So they ask Jesus not to let their hopes be futile. Feliciano captured this mood in this simple hymn. It is in an A = 3 five-tone scale (D = 6 1 2 3 5). The song was quickly adopted, and it meant a lot to those at the seminary; hence, the tune was named ST. ANDREW'S. A guitar accompaniment is natural for this style, but one may improvise with other styles. The composer suggests that the last phrase of the last stanza be repeated many times and then fade.

"With the grace of this day's food" (*STB* #164)
(Filipino: *Sa harap ng pagkaing dulot mo*)

Rolando S. Tinio wrote this table grace, not only thanking God for daily food but also asking God to bestow spiritual nourishment so that we can grow in wisdom and be deserving of God's bounty.

The tune LATOK is named for a traditional Filipino low table, just a few inches tall, at which families have their meals. The music is by Francisco F. Feliciano in E minor (E = 6). It develops from a simple motif (67 /1 7 1/ 7 3) with repetitions and variations and leads to a powerful climax in the third system ("bestow on us LORD"). The hymn is arranged like a three-part chorale with beautiful counterpoint, a wide range, and individual part progressions and crossings. The composer admits that he prefers three-part settings because they offer more space in which the different voices can move. If sung in parts, this table grace becomes a beautiful choral thanksgiving.

"You have made us from above" (*STB* #197)

(Ikalahan: *Amamin wad nangkayang*)

This prayer by Ramon Oliano asks Jesus to set us free to become his disciples. Oliano cites St. Paul's conversion and Jesus' ministries in Galilee—feeding the crowd, healing the sick, and teaching the truth—and asks Jesus to draw from us what we can be.

The music TOOAK NI ABOH, meaning "I am only human," is a Kalinga traditional melody. Kalinga songs are frequently in a five-tone scale (1 2 3 5 6) and in a simple form (see *STB* #178, "THE EARTH IS THE LORD'S"). This tune has five phrases of eight counts each (a b c c d) with almost identical rhythms. The text was translated by the Reverend Delbert Rice, an American United Methodist missionary, who has spent most of his life in an Ikalahan community in Imugan, in Nueva Viscaya. There he not only serves as a pastor but also works on developing the vocational skills and improving the life conditions of the Ikalahan, teaching them to read and write their own language and preserving their culture. Ramon Oliano is one of Rice's colleagues. (trsl. Delbert Rice; para. Jim Minchin)

Conclusion

1. Having been colonized by Spain and the United States for more than four hundred years, the Philippines has absorbed aspects of the Spanish and American cultures, especially in the areas of music, art, and language. Today, Ralph Tolliver's allegory of a Filipino being like an onion (a term that is not meant to be derogatory) is still evident in all aspects of life and Christian expression, except the outer, American layer has probably become much thicker over the past quarter century.

2. Because more women and men have had opportunities to receive advanced Western educations, there are many distinguished Filipino lawyers, scholars, artists, musicians, composers, and poets. Many have made a significant impact on the Church and society; Filipinos contributed the largest number of hymns to *Sound the Bamboo*.

3. Some of the ancient traditions and music of the Philippines' diverse ethnic cultures are still active today. Once this heritage is systematically studied and encouraged in the educational curriculum, the people of the Philippines will have more confidence in proclaiming their identities and can transform the "onion" complex.

South Asian Subcontinent

The South Asian subcontinent includes Bangladesh, India, Nepal, Pakistan, and Sri Lanka. The ethnic groups of these countries are distinct, but they have similar musical styles based on the Indian musical system, which features ragas, microtones, embellishments, drones, and complex rhythmic cycles.

Bengali Hymns

The Country and Its People

The British Empire colonized India from 1858 to 1947. India and Pakistan gained independence in 1947, and Pakistan was divided into East and West Pakistan. East Pakistan was originally East Bengal; West Bengal (with Calcutta as its center) remained a state of India. East Pakistan fought for independence and became the independent country of Bangladesh in 1971, which Pakistan did not recognize until 1974 (Garland 5:15f). The major languages in Bangladesh are Bengali and English (Garland 5:5).

Agriculture accounts for about half of the country's gross domestic product, and the annual per capita income of the country is only US$160. Bangladesh has a total area of 144,000 square kilometers (about 55,599 square miles) and a population of 153,546,896,[54] of which 87% is Muslim, and less than 0.5% is Christian (Athyal 1996, 361f).

A Brief History of Christian Mission

According to Simon Sircar, Jesuit missionaries entered the Indian region of Bengal in 1576 with the Portuguese explorations. Protestants entered two hundred years later, with William Carey working in Bengal from 1793 with the Baptist Missionary Society (Athyal 1996, 362). Many Protestant missions entered Bangladesh after 1900. Today, there are twenty Christian denominations in Bangladesh, of which Roman Catholic is the largest with 225,000 members; others include the Bangladesh Baptist Sangha (25,000 members), the Garo Baptist Convention (15,000 members), the Church of Bangladesh (Anglican, 12,000 members), and smaller denominations with members numbering 1,000 to 9,000 (Athyal 1996, 368f).

Rabindranath Tagore

Rabindranath Tagore (1861–1941) won the Nobel Prize in 1913 for his book of poems, *Gitanjali* ("Song Offerings"). Among the poet's 2,500 songs, those that were composed during his third phase of his work (1921–41) are considered emblematic of the "Tagore musical style," in which he combined folk idioms and classical melodies. They represent the culmination of Tagore's experiences and experiments during the previous forty years (Garland 5:850). Tagore classified his songs into four major categories (worship, homeland, nature, and love) and two

---

54   CIA, "The World Factbook, Bangladesh," July 2008 estimate, https://www.cia.gov/library/publications/the-world-factbook/geos/bg.html (accessed February 18, 2009).

minor categories (variety and ceremonial). In the worship category, he wrote 650 songs, also known as "Brahma songs."

> They are mostly in *dhrupad* style, and their combined lyricism and music make the essence of allegiance to God universally inspiring . . . His experimentation of these devotional songs gave new direction to Bengali urban music (Garland 5:850).

Tagore's song "My golden Bengal, I love you" became the national anthem of Bangladesh. His compositional style is modeled on the four-movement structure of the *dhrupad*. He said there were two elements in *dhrupad*: vastness/depth and control/symmetry. Tagore composed all the music for his songs and treated poetry and music equally. This is another area of research for church musicians and ethnomusicologists to pursue. The following quote from the website of Visva-Bharati, the school Tagore founded, expresses his approach to composing music:

Rabindranath Tagore
(after Visva-Bharati website
(http://www.visva-bharati.ac.in/at_a_
glance/at_a_glance.htm)

In fact Rabindranath did not attempt creation of new forms in abstract music. What he did was to bring it down from its heights and make it keep pace with the popular idiom of musical expression. In the second place, his own music is so inextricably blended with the poetry of words that it is almost impossible to separate the mood from the words and the words from the tune. Each expresses and reinforces the other. Hence his songs have not the same appeal outside the Bengali-speaking zone as they have in his native Bengal.[55]

Bengali Music

Baul songs form the richest stream of Bengali music, and Tagore was strongly influenced by them. Bauls are members of a mystical sect that follows a spiritual and philosophical discipline through songs (Garland 5:859). It is believed that Baul song, with its enriched lyricism and music, has greatly influenced the development of Bengali urban music (Garland 5:859f).

Although Bangladesh also has its own varieties of folk musical styles, Bengali music in general is similar to Indian music. Bart Shaha says:

---

55 "Rabindranath Tagore: The Founder," http://www.visva-bharati.ac.in/Rabindranath/Contents Rabindranath Contents.htm?f=../Contents/Music.htm (accessed February 18, 2009).

> For millenniums, our music came from the bards, mystics, *rishis* (those *shadhu* and *sannayasis* who heard the birds in the woods, the flow of the springs, etc., and developed the raga system which is common in the entire subcontinent).[56]

Hence, Bengali music shares features with Hindustani music of northern India, including microtones, embellishments, ragas, rhythmic cycles, drones, and accompaniment with harmonium (small, pumped reed organ), *talam* (finger cymbals), and tabla (drums).

Commentary on Individual Hymns

"Come, Lord Jesus Christ" (*STB* #8)

(Bengali: *Esho hae Probhu*)

This is an earnest prayer for union with Christ or for Christ's deliverance. It is like the prayer of a prisoner in a solitary cell, who stares at the only small window, high on the wall, and waits all night for the sun to shine in. The author assures us that Christ is our only trust and hope. Bart Shaha composed this song in a C♯ = 3 seven-tone scale (3 4 5 6 7 1 2), similar to the Western Phrygian mode. The composer created a tone painting with a long descending line to symbolize Christ coming down from heaven to dwell with mortals. For the text that asks Christ to set us free, the music begins at the bottom and gradually ascends to reach the climax that states, "Our trust is in you!" This phrase allows one to burst out with a loud cry to show helplessness and total trust in Jesus. Gliding tones are important in all Bengali songs, especially in this one when approaching and departing the climax.

ESHO HAE PROBHU are the Bengali words for "Come, O Lord." For an accompaniment, one can use a pair of concussion bells to strike once at the beginning of every four beats. This is one of the most popular hymns sung during the Advent season in Bangladesh today. It may also be sung at the beginning of worship, as an invocation for the presence of Christ, or as a response to prayers of petition or intercession. (para. J. M. & I. L.)

"Glory be to you, O God" (*STB* #19)

(Bengali: *Joy Probhu tomari joy*)

Indian *bhajans* are simple songs with simple texts that feature different key words in various stanzas. A *bhajan* is a spiritual song, praising the attributes of God. This is a Bengali version of a *bhajan*, which praises the God of love, salvation, deliverance from bondage, joy, and happiness. The tune name JOY means "glory" or "victory" in Bengali, similar to the Hindi word *jeye* (see *STB* #39). Bart Shaha

---

56   From the author's correspondence with Bart Shaha, February 28, 2007.

wrote this in a B♭ = 1 seven-tone scale (1 2 3 ♯4 5 6 7) with a raised fourth (♯4). The music reaches the climax toward the end to give glory to God. Since the verses are mostly the same, it would be easy to sing this *bhajan* in Bengali. This song may be sung as part of a litany of thanksgiving for God's love, salvation, deliverance, and joy. Members of the congregation can boldly speak of what God has done in their daily lives, and the whole congregation can respond with one of the stanzas appropriate for the context or by singing the first stanza. (para. J. M. & I. L.)

"Jesus, come dwell within our yearning hearts" (*STB* #70)
(Bengali: *Jishu esho amar antore*)

This devotional hymn is in a C = 5 seven-tone scale (5 6 7 1 2 3 4) similar to the Western Mixolydian mode, with plenty of gliding tones and ornaments that are typical of the Bengali style. Samar Das's text and tune express our yearning for Jesus to come into our hearts. Because Jesus is in heaven, we may find heavenly joy and peace in him. The hymn should be sung as a prayer with a soft and lyrical voice. The melody is soloistic and has plenty of embellishments, so it would be best sung as a solo, but the congregation can join in the A section like a refrain, which has to be repeated. If possible, the refrain should be sung in the original language to enhance the mystery of devotion. This is appropriate as an opening hymn for morning or evening prayer or at any retreat where peace and tranquility are desired. The tune name JISHU ESHO means "Jesus, come." (para. Colin A. Gibson)

"Joy, O Jesus, crown of all" (*STB* #28)

This hymn of praise to Jesus—the "crown of all" and "sweetest Lord"—is by Bindunath Sarker. It says that the birth of Christ brought forth love and peace to the world and glory in heaven; it also urges all people to play drums and zithers praising Jesus' power and to welcome him with hallelujahs and hosannas. The images in the text relate to Jesus' birth and triumphant entry to Jerusalem; hence, this hymn may be appropriate for Advent, Christmas, and Palm Sunday.

Samar Das adapted a Bengali song for the tune SAMAR. It is in a G = 7 seven-tone scale (A♭ = 1 2 3 4 5 6 7), beginning with the seventh degree of the A♭ scale and ending on 1; these features are not uncommon in Bengali music. A six-beat rhythmic pattern is popular in Bengali songs, and gliding tones and embellishments are also important features of the folk tradition. Traditionally, each line of the text and tune are repeated. Because the hymn is fairly long, the repeat signs have been omitted and singers may decide whether they wish to repeat the lines. The word *joy* in Bengali means "glory" or "victory," similar to *jeye* in Hindi (see *STB* #39, #204, #284). In Father Jim Minchin's excellent paraphrase of this hymn, he purposefully retained this key word. (trsl. Martin Adhikary; para. Jim Minchin)

"Lᴏʀᴅ, we did not live up to your teachings" (*STB* #43)

(Bengali: *Amra tomar adesh rupe*)

Silent meditation is important in many Asian cultures. In this prayer of confession, Bart Shaha purposefully wrote two intervals of total silence in the score, and each occurs after three repetitions of two phrases: "Lᴏʀᴅ, forgive us" in the A section and "Christ, forgive us" in the B section. According to the Indian system of rhythmic cycles, each phrase should have two measures or twelve counts; in this piece, the music should lead to another cycle of twelve counts after the text's three pleas for forgiveness. But the composer allows for only six counts of silence, thus interrupting the rhythmic cycle. What does it mean? This may be interpreted in two ways.

1. The composer may intend the silence as a space to allow one to reflect on one's shortcomings and to plead more earnestly for God's forgiveness. The silence also invites "the still small voice" to awaken one's conscience so that one might see one's true sinful self and to examine one's relationship with God. As expressed by Madeleine L'Engle, "the deepest communion with God is beyond words, on the other side of silence" (L'Engle 1980, 128).

2. One is reminded of Jesus' parable of the tax collector's attitude when praying in the temple: "But the tax collector, standing far off, would not even look up to heaven, but was beating his breast and saying, 'God, be merciful to me, a sinner!'" (Luke 18:13). The silence of six counts interrupts the musical flow and alters the rhythmic cycle from twelve to six, which is quite uncomfortable to people familiar with the musical tradition. Perhaps the compositional decision illustrates the tax collector's agony, contrite heart, and hesitation: he silently, humbly waited for God's forgiveness, but he was restless and (in the middle of the rhythmic cycle) begged again. Thus, the cycle is broken for another earnest plea for mercy.

The music, mood, silence, and irregular rhythmic cycle of this prayer enable us to feel the powerful presence of God.

The melody is in a B = 6 seven-tone scale (6 7 1 2 3 ♯4 5), which is similar to the Aeolian mode, but the raised ♯4 also occurs in the descending order (5 ♯4 3). Musically, the B section builds to a climax, the plea to Christ for forgiveness, where gliding tones and ornaments are vital to the spirit of this prayer. The best way to sing this part is to imagine the attitude of the tax collector's prayer in Luke 18:13. This response may be sung after prayers of confession. It is important to sing it according to the form //Ref. A//Ref. B// Ref. A// and observe the absolute silence for six counts at the end of sections A and B.

Sᴀɴɢᴇᴇᴛᴀ means "music." It is also the name of Shaha's eldest daughter, who at a very young age began to learn singing and dancing. "Sangeet Guru" is also a title of respect for a master musician in Bangladesh. (para. I. L.)

"This world is so full of rhythm" (*STB* #172)

(Bengali: *Chandae bhora tomar gora*)

This hymn praises the wondrous works of God in the cosmos, the beauty of rhythm and music, the sky, wind, streams, sea, fresh air, birds, new day, and new tunes—all have inspired the author to give thanks. The melody is in an F♯ = 3 seven-tone scale (D = 1 2 3 4 5 6 7) plus accidentals on ♯2, ♯5, and ♯6, with a very wide range (equaling a thirteenth, from A to high e). The poet/composer Bart Shaha uses many four-syllable phrases in triplets, with mostly isorhythmic (repeated rhythm) patterns to develop musical ideas and to gradually and effectively build to the climax before the last system. The repeated pattern of triplets should be carefully executed. Since the music is rather complicated, and the triplets and gliding tones are also quite demanding, it is suggested that this hymn be sung as a solo. In a worship context, it would be ideal to read a passage of a Psalm (e.g., 19:1–6, 92:1–4, or 148), have the soloist sing a stanza as an interlude to praise the beauty of God's marvelous creation, then read another passage, and sing again.

The tune name AMAR KACHE means "to me." Shirley Murray did a very good job in paraphrasing this hymn. Notice the form: refrain, A, refrain, B, refrain. Only section A and the second half of section B are not repeated.

Conclusion

The Bengali hymns represented here feature a variety of scales. Although half of them are major scales, the unconventional use of 7 (*si*) as the initial (in *STB* #28), and the use of the Phrygian mode (*STB* #8), the Mixolydian mode (*STB* #70), and the Aeolian mode (*STB* #43), as well as gliding tones and ornaments foreign to Western idioms, have strengthened the identities of these tunes and contributed to the diverse musical styles of Bengali hymns.

 **Indian Hymns**

The Country, Its People, and Its Religions

South Asia constitutes over one-third of the Asian population; peoples in this area live mostly in agricultural villages and small towns, each preserving certain cultural and musical traditions and with particular regional and national identities (Garland 5:5). India's relations with Great Britain began in 1608 when the East India Company was established in Surat, Gujarat. The British Empire finally colonized India in 1858; India gained independence in 1947.

India has an area of 3,287,590 square kilometers (about 1,269,346 square miles) with a population of 1,147,995,904.[57] According to a 1991 survey, there are 4,635 distinct ethnic groups; in northern and central India, 75.3% speak Indo-Aryan languages, which include ninety-four main languages, and 22.5% speak Dravidian languages, which include twenty-three main languages (Johnstone 2001, 309).

The Dravidian culture was one of the most important indigenous civilizations of India before the migration of the Indo-Aryans. Although there are no written records of it, the areas of Tamilnadu, Kerala, and Karnataka are culturally connected to the ancient Dravidians, who developed foundational ideas of religion and philosophy, including Hinduism. The Indo-Aryans who migrated from 2000 to 1500 BCE through the northern Hindu Kush were authors of the Vedic literature and were skilled in agriculture and warfare, to which they introduced horse-drawn chariots (Duncan 1999, 102–04).

Languages

India has twenty-five union states and seven union territories. English and Hindi are the official languages of India. Scholars believe that there are approximately 500 languages (and as many as 1,652 dialects) in the country, of which fifteen are major languages within the two main divisions:

Indo-Aryan languages: Hindi (spoken by forty percent of the population), Urdu, Bengali, Punjabi, Marathi, Gujarati, Oriya, Assamese, Kashmiri, Sanskrit, Sindhi

Dravidian languages: Telegu (mostly spoken in Andhra Pradesh), Tamil (in Tamilnadu), Malayalam (in Kerala), Kannada (in Karnataka) (Athyal 1996, 395f)

---

57 CIA, "The World Factbook, India," July 2008 estimate, https://www.cia.gov/library/publications/the-world-factbook/geos/in.html (accessed February 19, 2009).

Because of the complexity of Indian languages and the lack of uniformity in transliteration systems, a system of compromise was employed for *Sound the Bamboo*, as explained in the general introduction of this volume. To preserve the transliterations by the authors of the reference materials, the presence of different spellings was inevitable. For instance, "Tamil" is spelled "Thamilz," referring to the text or language in the *Sound the Bamboo* hymnal, but not in other places.

Religions

Approximately eleven percent of India's population practices Islam, which entered India during the eighth century. Other religions include Sikhism, Buddhism (active since the sixth century BCE), Jainism, Zoroastrianism, Bahai, and animism.

Four-fifths of India's population is Hindu. In 1977, the Supreme Court of India defined Hinduism thus:

> Hinduism incorporates all forms of belief and worship without necessitating the selection or elimination of any. The Hindu is inclined to revere the divine in every manifestation, whatever it may be, and is doctrinally tolerant, leaving others—whatever creed and worship practices suit them best . . . The core religion does not even depend on the existence or nonexistence of God or on whether here [*sic*] is one god or many (Sumithra 1990, 13).

Sumithra affirms Hinduism as "an ocean of different and conflicting philosophies and logics, religions and cultures, social and ethical systems" (Sumithra 1990, 13).

The two most important concepts in Hinduism are of karma and the caste system. The concept of karma is that:

> . . . individual souls exist everlastingly, passing from body to body in continuous rebirth, the condition and circumstances of each being determined in every detail by the merit or demerit of the works (karma) that the individual has previously done (Athyal 1996, 398).

This doctrine justifies the caste system. One belongs to a certain caste because of one's karma in the previous life.

Hinduism, which does not have set doctrines, has acquired many popular divinities and sacred literatures, such as the *Vedas*, *Brahmanas*, *Upanishads*, and *Punas* ("ancient stories"). The most popular stories, which have traveled to Thailand and Indonesia, are the epic tales of the *Mahabharata* and the *Ramayana*, which are performed with dance, drama, and music. These stories have inspired many generations of poets and musicians to compose devotional songs called *bhajan* in Hindu worship (Garland 5:11). These songs have been popularized by the Indian film industry. The Christian church has also utilized them, identifying them as spiritual songs in praise of the attributes of God (see *STB* #15, #17, #26, #281, #284, and #309).

Hinduism and Indian Society

Since 1500 BCE, Indian society has recognized a hierarchy of classes (*varna*) and caste (*jati*), each of which has its own dharma, which are associated behavior patterns, duties, and obligations toward the larger society. The ancient laws of the Indo-Aryans identified five classes, ranging from the upper classes, whose duties were to study and to sacrifice, to the lower classes, whose duties were to serve the upper classes:

1. *brahmins*: professional priests and teachers
2. *kshatriyas*: rulers, warriors, and protectors
3. *vaishyas*: merchants and traders
4. *shudras*: artisans, musicians
5. *panchamas*: the outcasts excluded from the Hindu society, whose duties include sweeping, tanning leather, and cremating corpses. They are known as "untouchables." (Garland 5:9)

A Brief Introduction to Indian Music Theories

One of the most important ancient documents on music is Bharata's *Natyasastra* (dating from about 200 BCE to 200 CE). It gives instruction on learning music and chanting hymns of the *Samaveda* (Garland 5:25, 110). Most of the historical studies and theories for modern musical practices are derived from this source.

Indian musical culture is normally divided into two traditions. The Hindustani culture in the north has more Aryan, Arabic, and Muslim influences, and the Carnatic (also spelled Karnatak) culture in the south is more Dravidian and considered a more indigenous tradition. It is beyond the scope of this section to deal with these musical cultures in great detail, but a brief explanation of their common features and major differences will be helpful to the reader unfamiliar with them.

Raga

The concept of raga is very complicated. A raga may be understood through the analysis of scale, mode, melodic shape, tonal center, ascending and descending orders, initial and final, etc. A raga has associations with moods, times of day, and seasons. One of the most famous musicians, Ali Akbar Khan, says simply that raga "is some combination of notes which charms the mind and produces the moods of love, joy, pathos, heroism, and peace" (Garland 5:64). Another definition says that a raga is like a map that musicians follow in their performances: "a catalogue of melodic movements that the artist unfolds, details, and expands while following a traditional performance format that has been passed down from teacher to students" (Garland 5:66).

Both Hindustani and Carnatic explanations of raga contain the following broad concepts:

1. Extra-musical associations: spiritual and cosmic understanding of music, religious verses, color, time and emotions (mood), natural cosmologies, poetic and visual images suggested by music
2. Scales and functional tones: scale patterns, pitch organizations, tonal centers, initial and final, principal movements
3. Pragmatic dimension, as seen through performance styles
4. Traditional transmission through teacher to student, essential in understanding the ethos and balance of the first three ideas
5. Tonic and dominant drones, ornaments and microtonal inflections (more prominent in South India) (Garland 5:66, 89–91)

Some scholars have characterized the quasi-emotional effect of a raga in nine *rasa* ("juice," "flavor," or "essence"):

> Love, heroism, disgust, anger, mirth, terror, compassion, wonder, peace— and one more is added sometimes: devotion (*bhakti*). But scholars also believe that these are all very subjective; they are not systematized (Garland 5:69).

Sruti, Svara, Vadi, Samvadi

The smallest perceptible increment of pitch in Indian classical music is a microtone called a *sruti*. The ancient theories indicate that there are three sizes of *sruti*: twenty-two cents, seventy cents, and ninety cents (Malm 1977, 96). The octave in Indian music is theoretically divided into twenty-two *srutis*, and there are seven scale-degrees (*swaras*) to the octave. *Swara* means the "selected pitches" (each of which consists of one to four *srutis*) from which scales, ragas, and melodies are constructed. The scale (*that* in Hindi) of a raga is identified by the pitches (*swara*) used, which may differ in ascending and descending contexts. There are two important tones in a raga: the tonic (*vadi*, "speaker") and the dominant, a fifth or fourth below the *vadi* (*samvadi*, "co-speaker, consonant"). One (the tonic) or both (the tonic with the dominant) of these important tones are played as drones.

Often used in Carnatic music, the *sruti* box is a tiny harmonium that produces drones to accompany singing. Carnatic musicians also emphasize ornamentations or embellishments (*gamaka*) in personal ways. *Gamaka* may be described as oscillations or shakes (*kampita*) between two tones, comprising two to fifteen oscillations. The second type of *gamaka* includes accents, slides (*jaru*), and glottal stops. These *gamakas* are important factors in expressing the "flavor" of ragas (Garland 5:92f). I feel that *gamakas* are the soul of Indian music; without them, many Indian songs today would sound much like Western songs.

The names of the seven degrees (*swara*) are Sadja (short name: Sa), Rsabha (Hindustani: Re; or Carnatic: Ri), Gandhara (Ga), Madhyama (Ma), Pancama (Pa), Dhaivata (Dha or Da), and Nisada (Ni). The abbreviated syllables are used for solmization. Sa is the tonic, and Pa is the dominant; both are stable and do not change although sometimes Pa is not used in a raga. The other tones (Re, Ga, Ma, Dha, and Ni) all have two possibilities in Hindustani music, i.e., re1 (D♭) and Re2 (D), ga1 (E♭) and Ga2 (E), ma1 (F) and Ma2 (F♯), dha1 (A♭) and Dha2 (A), ni1 (B♭) and Ni2 (B). The tone labeled with a lowercase letter and the numeral "1" (e.g. "ma1") indicates that the interval between this note and the preceding one (e.g. "Ga2") is approximately a minor second while an uppercase letter and the numeral "2" (e.g. "Ma2") represent a tone approximately a major second (above Ga2, in this example).

Hindustani Scales and Ragas

The following is a Hindustani *bhairav* raga, which is associated with the dawn; it is shown with the typical ascending and descending melodic progression in two *sargam* notations, Western letter notation, and cipher notation (Garland 5:80):

Sa	re	Ga	ma	Pa	dha	Ni	Sa'	Sa'	Ni	dha	Pa	Pa	dha	Pa	ma	Ga	ma	Pa	Ga	ma	re	Sa
S	r1	G2	m1	P	d1	N2	S'	S'	N2	d1	P	P	d1	P	m1	G2	m1	P	G2	m1	r1	S
C	D♭	E	F	G	A♭	B	c	c	B	A♭	G	G	A♭	G	F	E	F	G	E	F	D♭	C
3	4	♯5	6	7	1'	♯2'	3'	3'	♯2'	1'	7	7	1'	7	6	♯5	6	7	♯5	6	4	3

Notice how the descending line features the characteristics of the raga by decorating the tones up and down between the dominant (7) and the tonic (3): 7176♯5, 67♯5643.

A *hemant* raga, associated with evening (Garland 5:80):

Sa	Ga	ma	Dha	Ni	Sa'	Sa'	Ni	Dha	Pa	Dha	Ni	Pa	Dha	ma	Pa	Ga	Ga	ma	Re	Sa
C	E	F	A	B	c	c	B	A	G	A	B	G	A	F	G	E	E	F	D	C
1	3	4	6	7	1'	1'	7	6	5	6	7	5	6	4	5	3	3	4	2	1

The ascending scale has only five tones (C = 1 3 4 6 7 1), but the descending line keeps going up and down and adds another two tones, (5) and (2):

$$1\,7\,6\,5,\ 6\,7\,5\,6\,4\,5\,3,\ 3\,4\,2\,1.$$

Carnatic Scales and Ragas

The Carnatic view of raga is more complicated, in that it "encompasses the concepts of scale, mode, tonal system, melodic motifs and themes, microtones, ornaments, and improvisation within a three octave range" (Garland 5:89). "Raga" also means "color." The form expresses "wide ranges of emotion: feelings, intensity, passion, love and beauty" (Garland 5:90).

A Carnatic octave is theoretically divided into twenty-two *srutis*, and it has a number of possibilities. Whereas Sa and Pa remain constant without change, Ri, Ga, Ma, Da, and Ni all have four possibilities: R1 R2 R3 R4, G1 G2 G3 G4, etc. However, in actual practice, they only use three possibilities for Ri, Ga, Da, and Ni, and only two for Ma, as follows:

C	♭	D	♯	E	F	♯	G	♭	A	♯	B	C
Sa		Ri		Ga	Ma		Pa		Da		Ni	Sa'
	R1	2	3		M1	2		D1	2	3		
		G3	1	2					N3	1	2	

The following illustration gives the embellishment of a Carnatic *sankarabharana* raga, which looks like a Western major scale but, with the ascending and descending embellishments, it sounds very Indian. (after Garland 5:94)

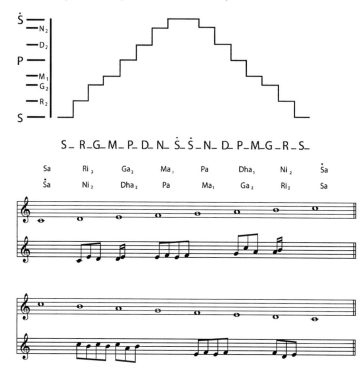

Ascending and descending scale of *rāga sankārabbara na*: in graphic representation and in Indian solfège, showing interval structure with subscripts; the ornamentation (*gamaka*) integral to the scale pitches is shown in Western notation.

Tala

Tala (or *tal* or *taal*) refers to the Indian rhythm and metric cycle. As early as 1240, scholars had classified 120 *talas* (Garland 5:111). One *tala* can be as short as two beats or, in South India, as long as twenty-nine beats, which lasts for forty-five seconds (Garland 5:138). In ordinary practice, a *tala* ranges from five to twelve beats, and *talas* are grouped in threes and twos; for example, a *rupak tala* in northern India is seven beats, organized as $3 + 2 + 2$. The first beat of the first group is called *sam*, marked with a circled X; the next first beat in the subsequent division is a clap (*tali*) followed by a hand-wave (*khali*), marked with a circled 0.

In South India, the poet/saint Purandara Dasa (1484–1564) codified the theory of *tala* by three hand gestures (*anga*) (Garland 5:111–12):

Laghu: clap + counting fingers on additional number of beats   1n

Drutam: clap and wave, 2 beats (like *khali*)   0

Anudrutam: a solitary clap, one beat   U

The three-beat *laghu triputa tala* (equaling seven beats: 3-beat *laghu* plus 2 *drutam*, i.e., $3 + 2 + 2$) may be demonstrated by this *anga*:

13				0			0	
1	2	3	+	1	2	+	1	2
Clap	pinkie	ring		clap	wave		clap	wave

The four-beat *laghu adi tala* (equaling eight beats) is as follows:

14				0		0	
1	2	3	4	5	6	7	8
Clap	pinkie	ring	middle	clap	wave	clap	wave

The following chart illustrates four types of South Indian *tala* in common practice today.

caturaśra (quadratic 4) tiśra (triple) 3		miśra (mixed) 7	khaṇḍa (broken) 5
ādi madhyâdī	rūpaka (2 +4)	triputa	'ara jhampā'
deśādī	tiśra (1 + 2)	miśra cāpu (3 =4)	khaṇḍa cāpu (2 +3)
	(tiśra laghu)	(miśra laghu)	

(after NGDI, 9:120)

Musical Structure

The main Carnatic compositional form is called *kriti,* which has three sections: *pallavi, anupallavi*, and *charanam*. *Pallavi*, the first section, may adorn the composition and is short, having two to four or five *tala* cycles (Sharma 1999, 265). *Anupallavi*, the second section, has the same length, but it normally ends with a passage of text or *solfege* in double tempo. *Charanam* (also spelled *caranam*) is the last section of composition (Sharma 1999, 222); it is the longest, echoing the melody of the *pallavi* toward its end and repeating its double-time passage (Garland 5:145). Many Indian Christian lyrics are composed according to this form, but it is simplified and usually called *kirtana* (which will be discussed later).

Devotional Songs and Light Classical Music

Since ancient times, many sages and poets have composed *bhajans,* devotional poems sung by groups for daily Hindu worship in temples or homes. They include songs and dances in praise of the principal Hindu deities. They are generally based on a raga, and the chorus repeats after the leader, line by line. In contemporary practice, professional musicians set Purandara Dasa's songs to classical Carnatic and Hindustani ragas and perform them (along with amateurs) in formal concerts and in non-classical music gatherings (Garland 5:104–06). A new genre influenced by film music has entered the contemporary scene: light classical music. These devotional hymns are sung to ragas borrowed from classical Hindustani devotional poetry or traditional compositions with romantic texts. "Light music" also refers to ensemble performances of devotional music in traditional ragas and *talas* with the accompaniment of violin, *vina*, flute, sitar, guitar, and *mridangam* (Garland 5:107). This style of performance has been utilized by many Christian communication centers that have produced many popular cassettes, CDs, and videos.

Bhajans are spiritual songs; the word comes from *bhakti* ("devotion") and *bhagavan* (also spelled *bhagawan* or *bhagwan*, "god"). The Sanskrit word *bhaj* means "to share" or "to partake of" (Garland 5:254). So the original meaning of *bhajan* is "shared praise," which repeats six Indian titles of gods: Divine Light, Ray of Life, Form of Radiance, Lamp of our Path, Essence of Love, Dweller in the Soul (Lott 1986, 13f). While the traditional style of religious music required men and women to be seated separately, the informal *bhajan* does not. *Bhajan* sessions begin with the incantation "om," which is considered a mystical sound of ancient origin, combining the three sounds A-U-M, symbolizing the beginning, the middle, and the end of life (cf. Tirabassi and Eddy 1995, 74). *Bhajans* range from complex to simple litanies, singing names, and refrains. Tempos are usually fast, avoiding the slower *talas.* The most popular rhythm is the eight-beat *kaharva tala* or the sixteen-beat *tintal tala.* The song repertoire draws mostly from medieval saintly compositions but also includes simplified and newer compositions (Garland 5:255). Many Christians have adapted the *bhajan* form and style to compose spiritual songs for praising the attributes of God (see *STB* #9, #15, and #47).

The Harmonium and Indian Lyrics

Indian Christians have been composing their own hymns for centuries. But they identify these hymns as lyrics, referring to their own style of hymn texts and tunes as against hymns of Western origin. Many of these lyrics and other contemporary devotional songs (*bhajans*) no longer follow the classical raga concept. Many are written in major and natural minor tonalities and with Western chordal harmony. While some Christian broadcasting institutions have the funds to accompany these lyrics in light music styles with Indian and Western musical instruments, local churches often can only afford a small harmonium, with or without a drum (tabla), for accompanying and leading the congregational singing.

The harmonium, which is like an accordion, may have been introduced to India by missionaries. Instead of being carried on the shoulders, the harmonium is placed on the floor. The player sits on the floor; the right hand plays the keyboard while the left hand pumps the wind box. Due to the keyboard's definite pitch, the ornaments and microtonal embellishments that are typical of classical Indian singing cannot be properly played on the harmonium, which can only play the skeleton of a melody performed by an experienced singer.

I have discovered an unwritten rule of common practice for accompanying a lyric or a *bhajan*. At the end of a phrase, or on notes of long duration, the harmonium player plays that note and adds a chord to it, using that note as the root of the chord (say CEG or CE♭G), or its third for the root (E♭A♭C or EAC), or its fifth (FAC or FA♭C); the chord is major or minor depending on the scale (raga) of the piece or the pleasure of the player. Musicians also add Western harmony at random; this technique must have been influenced by Western hymns. In village churches, the *bhajans* and lyrics are accompanied by *talam* (a pair of concussion bells) and tabla (a pair of tuned drums), or *mridangam* (a double-headed drum) in the south. *Manjira or talam* refers to very thin finger cymbals or a pair of concussion bells, which are struck with an open sound (marked "o" in the score) on the strong beat and a closed sound ("+") on the weak beat. This accompaniment is popularly used with folk songs and *bhajans*.

Vocal Music

Carnatic vocal production is unique. "Women sing in an unmixed chest voice with high larynx, to produce a strong, focused tone capable of very rapid note passages"; the voice can be very "sweet" (Garland 5:231). Men's voices are more flexible and use a relaxed larynx. Head voice and falsetto are taboo in Carnatic music. But the soul or spirit of Indian vocal music relies on the ability of the singer to decorate the melody with microtonal ornaments (*gamaka*), without which many contemporary Indian songs would sound like Western songs.

Musical Instruments

There are many traditional Indian musical instruments. The more prominent are introduced here.

Idiophones

Manjira / talam: finger cymbals or a pair of concussion bells, which are most important for the accompaniment of singing (indicated in the score by o = strong and + = weak).

Chordophones

Violins: Western violins, most popular as accompaniment of singing or in ensemble but held with a lowered left arm

Tamboora (or *tambura*): four-stringed plucked lute, tuned Pa-Sa'-Sa'-Sa (lower octave); the first string may be tuned to Ma. This provides the effect of continuous drone and is the "most important point of concentration for the musician" (Sharma 1999, 444).

Sitar: long tube-necked plucked lute with gourd resonator, with movable brass frets, five main metal strings, two drone strings, and eleven to seventeen sympathetic strings. The most important Hindustani solo instrument.

Veena (or *vina*): a generic name for more than two-dozen stringed instruments. The *rudra veena* or *been*, the most important instrument in Hindustani music, is a lute-type zither, with two gourd resonators on both ends of the bamboo tubes with frets, four main strings, and three drone strings (Sharma 1999, 457).

Sarod: a plucked lute (with wooden pick), with steel fingerboard, resonator covered with skin, three principal strings, four subsidiary strings, and a dozen sympathetic strings

Sarangi: bowed lute with three main strings, twenty-seven sympathetic strings, with innumerable types.

Membranophones

Tabla: a pair of drums for Hindustani classical music, with metal bowl-shaped bodies and a dough paste on the skins. The right drum (*dahina*) is tuned at middle Sa, and the left side drum (*bayan*) is tuned at lower Sa.

Mridangam: double-headed barrel drum of South India, with dough paste on the left side to produce a deep sound

Aerophones

Many kinds of flutes

Nagaswaram: similar to an oboe

Some Indian instruments from the personal collection of I-to Loh:

talam, concussion bells

poor man's *tambura*

tambura

harmonium, reed organ

sitar

tabla: *dahina* (left) and *bayan* (right)

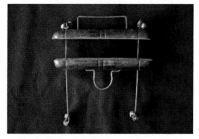

clappers

A Brief History of the Mission of the Christian Church

St. Thomas and the Indian Church

Regarding the history of Christian mission, Rajendra Prasad, the President of India from 1952 to 1962, said:

> Remember, St. Thomas came to India when many of the countries of Europe had not yet become Christian, and so those Indians who trace their Christianity to him have a longer history and a higher ancestry than that of Christians of many of the European countries. And it is really a matter of pride to us that it so happened.[58]

---

58   Quoted in S. G. Pothan, "The Syrian Christians on Kerala," in Moffett 1998, 24.

Samuel H. Moffett says:

> "One of the oldest and strongest traditions in church history is that Thomas the apostle carried the gospel to India not long after the resurrection and ascension of Jesus Christ" (Moffett 1998, 25).

After examining documents and traditions, Moffett further asks:

> Can we say with any certainty that Thomas was in truth the planter of the church in India? Few have dared to answer that question with an unequivocal yes or no. Given the difficulty of proving a negative answer and an equal hesitation to accept unwritten traditions without some reservation, most opinions range from "possible" to "probable," with a discernible trend toward the latter position since the discovery of the Gundaphar evidence and the renewal of interest in oral tradition as a source of history (Moffett 1998, 35).

There are many legends about St. Thomas, including his martyrdom on what is known as St. Thomas Mount in Mylapore outside Madras; today, there is cathedral with a tomb and a monument there. During my first trip to India in the summer of 1971, I had the privilege of visiting that sacred place. I felt awe standing in front of the monument, touching the tomb and contemplating the ministry of St. Thomas.

The photos on the right were taken during my second visit to St. Thomas Mount on January 21, 2006.

St. Thomas Mount

The cave where St. Thomas
was said to have hidden.

Historical Connections of Churches in India

Athyal (1996, 400–07) summarizes the historical connections of the churches in India:

1. Syrian Christians: 345 CE–1500. The liturgy and the Bible of the Thomas Church were in Syriac.
2. Roman Catholics: 1500–1700. Portuguese Catholics attempted to convert the St. Thomas Christians.
   Francis Xavier arrived in Goa in 1542. In 1653, the St. Thomas Christians revolted against the Catholics and became independent.
3. The Mar Thoma Church separated from the Syrian Orthodox Church in 1879.
4. British colonization: 1700–1947. Danish Royal Mission in Tranquebar in 1706. William Carey arrived in Bengal in 1793; he went to the Serampore area in 1800 and established Serampore College in 1818, with a strong theological department. The king of Denmark gave permission to confer the degree of Arts and Divinity in 1827.

German Lutherans have worked in India since the eighteenth century, British and American Protestants arrived during the nineteenth century, and Pentecostals and other denominations arrived in recent years.

In 1947, Protestant churches joined together and formed the Church of South India (CSI). As of 2007, India has over twenty-five million Christians, which is approximately three percent of the entire population. Eighty percent of these Christians are in Andhra Pradesh, Tamilnadu (with three million) Karnataka, and Kerala, and fifteen percent are in northeastern India: Assam, Arunachal Pradesh, Mizoram, Nagaland, etc. The approximate numbers of Christians in the major denominations are:

- Roman Catholic: a little above 50%
- Church of South India: 1.6 million
- Council of Baptist Churches in Northeast India: 1.1 million
- Methodist Church of India: 900,000
- Lutheran: 800,000
- Church of North India: 600,000
- Presbyterian Church of India (based in the northeast): 300,000
- Syrian Christians: 3 million (Syrian Roman Catholic: 1.4 million; Syrian Orthodox: 1.4 million)
- Mar Thoma Syrian Church: 400,000   (Athyal 1996, 419)

Because of the long-term connections to and the influences of the Western churches, Tamil Christians acquired three hymn traditions: Western hymns sung in English, those translated into local languages, and some indigenous compositions in Indian as well as Western styles. There are strong cultural and sociological factors that contribute to the use of Western hymns:

Due to the influence of missionaries . . . lower-caste people have strongly identified with Western education and Victorian Puritanism in order to raise themselves from their former status. Singing hymns in English symbolizes their new cultural identity (Garland 5:922).

Indian Christians began translating hymns and the Bible into Tamil in the seventeenth century. However, they were unable to preserve the linguistic character and classic poetic structure of the hymns, which became almost meaningless when sung in Tamil. Today, two systems or traditions co-exist: that of the Church of South India (CSI), whose members are mostly middle-class and lower-class and sing translated Western hymns, and that of the Lutheran churches, which generally work among the poor, rural congregations and never use hymns from the West. Since the beginning of Lutheran mission, there has been a strong presence of contextual hymns (see *STB* #38, #133, #142, and #198).

The Roman Catholic Church has been very open to the adaptation of local idioms, music, philosophies, and ideas in the development of contextual music and liturgies. This may be seen from the architecture and interior decoration of the chapel of the National Biblical, Catechetical and Liturgical Center (NBCLC) in Bangalore.

The chapel of the Roman Catholic National Biblical, Catechetical and Liturgical Center (NBCLC), Bangalore. Photo: I-to Loh, January 28, 2006.

Inside the sanctuary of the NBCLC, Bangalore. Photo: I-to Loh, January 28, 2006.

Christian Carnatic Music

As early as the seventeenth century, missionaries began to use Carnatic devotional songs (*kirtana*).

The Italian Jesuit Robert de Nobili first composed Christian Carnatic music to attract potential Brahmin converts in the early seventeenth century. Upper-caste converts brought classical poetic and musical traditions of Hinduism to Indian Christianity . . . Until recently, they controlled positions of influence in the church as priests, bishops, pastorate committee members, theologians, and choirmasters. Consequently, they have had a tremendous impact on indigenized music and theology, particularly in promoting Carnatic music as the ideal indigenized style (Garland 5:923).

The most important collection of Indian Christian songs is *Tamil Church Hymnal and Christian Lyrics*, which contains more than 400 Christian *kirtana*, many of them composed in the eighteenth and nineteenth centuries by upper-class poets, such as Vedanayagam Sastriar (1774–1864; see *STB* #282, with the name spelled "Veedhenayegam Sasthriyar") and H. A. Krishna Pillai. The *Tamil Church Hymnal* was published by the American Congregational missionary Edward Webb in 1853 (Garland 5:923).

Two lyrics in *Sound the Bamboo* (#214, "I sing praise to your holy name," and #276, "Blest are the poor folks") seem to be composed in the Christian *kirtana* form. This prompted me to contact Santosh Kumar, a PhD candidate in the field of Indian music in Australia, to verify this classification. These are Santosh Kumar's comments on *kirtana*:[59]

> Is it O.K. to call hymns 214 and 276 *kirtanas*? Yes, it is perfectly all right in our hymn books to mention them as *kirtanas* because the word *kirtana* is being used by the many churches in South India for the indigenous hymns, and they will not feel any difficulty.
>
> But I think that equating the three parts of a Karnatic *kirtana (pallavi, anupallavi,* and *charanam*) to the ABC parts that we have in hymns 214 and 276 and considering them as in the form of *kirtana* or calling them *kirtana* will present the following difficulties for **non-Christians**, who will not be able to see the relationship between these two, because:
>
> 1. These Christian *kirtanas* are far behind in musical quality and complexity when compared to **any** Carnatic *kirtana*. (The Christian *kirtanas* are like light music next to the real *kirtanas*.)
> 2. The aspect of *sangati* is missing from Christian *kirtanas*. The *pallavi* (and sometimes *anupallavi* and *charanam*, too) of a Carnatic *kirtana* will normally have only one or two lines of text, but it will have many *sangatis* (the same lines will be improvised and made more complex,

---

59   From the author's correspondence with Santosh Kumar in 2004.

one after another)—that is the beauty of the Carnatic *kirtanas*, which is totally missing from our Christian *kirtanas*.

3. Christian *kirtanas* normally have more than one *charanam*, but Carnatic *kirtanas* have normally only one *charanam*.

4. Compared to the Carnatic *kirtanas*, indigenous Christian *kirtanas* are very short. For example, it would take a minimum of ten minutes to properly finish singing one Carnatic *kirtana* (which is the time allowed for a candidate to sing a *kirtana* in Carnatic music competitions conducted by government in schools and colleges).

To further clarify the concept of *kirtana,* Thomas Thangaraj offered his responses.

Three things to be noted in Santosh Kumar's comments:[60]

First, when Tamil Christians use the term *keerthanai* [*sic*, different spellings] they do not think of *keertana* in the classical mode. Their popular use of the term simply means hymns or songs. The *Kiristava Keerthanaigal* has all kinds of genres of lyrical form within it. Kumar is right in saying that hymns 214 and 276 are not *keertana* only if we compare them with classical *keerthana.*

Second, the aspect of *sangati* is intentionally left out in Christian *keerthanai* because of the business of corporate singing in the church. One cannot afford to have *sangati* when people are singing together in worship.

Third, Christian *keerthanaigal* have the additional job of offering religious education to the singers and therefore they are bound to have many verses covering the various areas of the topic addressed.

From these statements, it is understood that "Carnatic Christian lyrics" only generally refers to hymns or lyrics written by an Indian. These do not belong in the strict, classical *kirtana* category, which is soloistic and not congregational. Identifying *STB* #214 and #279 and other similar pieces as specifically Christian *kirtana,* however, is acceptable because they are congregational, are shorter in duration, have multiple stanzas for *charanam*, and do not have the *sangati* improvisation.

As reported by Thomas Thangaraj in his "Toward a Singable Theology" (Francis 1992, 170), the Tamilnadu Theological Seminary (TTS) in Madurai has been the

---

60 From the author's correspondence with Thomas Thangaraj, April 14, 2007.

leading force behind contextualizing their lyrics since 1971, when Dayanandan Francis and Thangaraj joined the faculty. They tried to incorporate classical Indian musical styles into Western-sounding melodies and to employ popular musical styles with theological messages. Thangaraj states:

> [These new lyrics are] making a theological statement that piety, devotion, and faith are all communicatarian categories and not just individual matters. By singing together we affirm that God is not a God of the individual but a God of the community of faith. In this we are surrounded by a cloud of witnesses both within the Christian tradition and within the *bhakti* traditional of Hinduism. (Francis 1992, 170)

According to Thangaraj, there are four traditions of Tamil Indian church music:

1. Western hymns in English and German
2. Indigenous hymns with Tamil lyrics and classical Indian music
3. Tamil folk melodies (e.g., *kummi, kollattam*) from the oral tradition
4. Pentecostal and revival songs, hybrids of popular and Indian classical music, and film music, often with guitar accompaniments. These convey more evangelical and conservative theologies.

Dayanandan Francis's *Christian Lyrics and Songs of New Life* (published by the Christian Literature Society in 1988) includes one hundred songs, of which seventy-one are by TTS faculty and students (Francis 1992, 163f and 172). V. P. K. Sundaram (see *STB* #84) and Theophilus Appavoo were also involved in this effort of contextualizing music and liturgy. In 1994, the Reverend Appavoo composed the first liturgy with a folk-music style, utilizing *kummi* (a women's circle dance), *oyilattam* (a men's line dance), *temmangu pattu* (a duet with alternating vocal lines), and laments. In order to bring the message closer to the majority of the people, Appavoo portrays Jesus as a farmer "who removes the weeds and *nerinji* thorns from the fields of his people's hearts"; Appavoo even encouraged his students and villagers to adapt his songs to fit their contexts (Garland 5:925–27). I had the privilege of meeting these four musicians/scholars/theologians during my visits in 1984 and 1989. But by the time of my last visit in January 2006, Sundaram and Appavoo had passed away and Dayanandan Francis was ill. I was able to witness the spirit of contextual liturgy and music in the daily morning worship of the Tamilnadu Theological Seminary, where students gather every week to enthusiastically learn new lyrics accompanied by the harmonium, tabla, and *talam*. The illustration on the following page is from Appavoo's setting of the Lord's Prayer.

The liturgical music of Mar Thoma Church is somewhat different from that in the Church of South India or other denominations. It is a compendium of West Syriac chants, Anglican hymns, and Malayalam compositions in the Carnatic style.

Many Protestant churches in India continue to sing Western hymns with organ or piano accompaniment, and their choirs also sing anthems in polyphonic settings.

Opening lines of setting of the Lord's Prayer by Appavoo.

(after Garland 5:926)

Commentary on Individual Hymns

"All sisters, all brothers, all of the earth" (*STB* #84)

(Thamilz: *Buumiyin maandheriir kuudivaariir*)

This is a free paraphrase of a portion of Psalm 100 in an Indian cultural context. The hymn summons all people to come and offer songs and flowers of joyful praise to worship God; it also relates the sharing of bread and wine at the table as the nourishment of our faith. The lyrics conclude with the confidence that God's goodness and faithfulness will always meet the needs of God's children.

The text and tune BUUMIYIN MAANDHERIIR ("all people of the earth") were written by V. P. K. Sundaram, a well-known Carnatic musician/composer/poet, who taught the Thamilz language at the Tamilnadu Theological Seminary in Madurai. Although the melody is based on an E♭ = 1 five-tone scale (1 2 3 4 5), the lively rhythm with plenty of skips and ornaments makes this a joyful song in an Indian style. If desired, one may play B♭ and E♭ as drones throughout, with variations of the two notes and their octaves, like playing a *tambura*. (trsl. John Barathi; para. Ronald Walcott)

"Blest are the poor folks" (*STB* #276)

(Thamilz: *Eliyavarku sontham intha ulgam endru*)

The Thamilz text and the melody were composed by M. Thomas Thangaraj, a former member of faculty at Tamilnadu Theological Seminary in Madurai. The refrain (*pallavi*) is built on two leading texts from the Gospels, namely, "Blessed are the meek, for they will inherit the earth" (Matthew 5:5) and "Blessed are you who are poor, for yours is the kingdom of God" (Luke 6:20). The words expresses anguish about the situation of the poor in today's world and longs for the day when the poor will inherit the earth. It has the character of a lament and a plea. The imagery of a house with many rooms comes from another biblical text, "In my Father's house there are many dwelling places" (John 14:2a). The main goal of the song is to invite Christians to be proactive in working toward economic justice in the world. The text is constructed as *pallavi*, *anupallavi*, and *charanam* sections, which is similar to the *kirtana* form. James Minchin provided the English paraphrase.[61]

Most of Thangaraj's compositions belong to the "light music" tradition of Tamil Christianity (see the earlier discussion in the introduction). This particular piece is set in F minor, and the Indian character of the hymn lies in the rhythm of seven beats per bar. The scale is a C = 3 F-minor seven-tone scale (6 7 1 2 3 4 ♯5) with the final on 6. It features a three-beat *triputa tala*: 3+2+2. The order of singing the full text is: Verse 3x, Form: //:A:// BA //: CA:// BA//.

---

61   The preceding comments are from the author's correspondence with Thomas Thangaraj, April 14, 2007.

"Christ is all to me" (*STB* #55)

(Thamilz: *Yellaam Yesuvee*)

Speaking and singing all of Jesus' names express our trust in him. It is said that Y. Gnanamani from South India wrote both the text and tune YELLAAM YESUVEE ("everything is Jesus") while he was suffering from a painful illness. In spite of this, he acknowledged that "Christ is all to me." Like a *bhajan* (a spiritual song), the lyrics provide a long list of names for Christ: Shepherd, Comforter, Friend, Father, Brother, Source of Joy, Healer, Teacher, Way, Life, Truth, Bread, Milk, Honey, Wine, and Water from the Well of Graces. It is important for us to reflect on the meanings of these names and how they may be related to Indians as well as to our daily lives; in this way, singing these hymns may become spiritual nourishments to all. The original paraphrase by D. T. Niles, which first appeared in the *EACC Hymnal* of 1963 with a four-part harmony, was altered by Rolando S. Tinio for the trial edition of the *Sound the Bamboo* in 1990.

The melody is in a D = 1 seven-tone scale (1 2 3 4 5 6 7) with a raised fourth (#4). This version was transcribed from a recording of the experienced organist/ singer William Manoharan, who taught at Tamilnadu Theological Seminary. It preserves some of the ornaments and hence is more interesting than the popular version. Congregations are encouraged to sing the ornaments so that the beauty of the Indian style may be manifested.

"Come now, and lift up your hearts" (*STB* #91)

This is one of the most popular hymn melodies in India. It has been the setting for many different texts, such as Psalms 23 and 95 and "Send us with your blessing" by E. Soundararajan (see *STB* #251 and his biography in this volume). This anonymous paraphrase of Psalm 95:1–8 summons people to make joyful noises to the LORD, the almighty God, the great Creator. It also urges people to hearken and heed God's word.

When I first heard this song in 1972, I did not feel that it was originally Indian, yet I did not dare argue with so many Indians who claimed it to be so. In 1989, however, when I was invited to present a paper at the Societas Liturgica Congress in York, England, I found the answer to the puzzle. In a discussion of folk hymnody with a young musician from Finland, I cited this melody as an example that lacked the characteristics of an Indian folk song. To my surprise, this young man said that it was a Finnish folk song! He sent me the score, which was called "Nyt Kevat on" and was composed by Carl Michael Bellman from Sweden. The melodic lines and structures of the Indian and the Swedish tunes are the same, except the ornaments and a few other details. It is likely that some earlier Swedish or European missionaries introduced the song to South India, and it became so popular that it became a Carnatic hymn melody.[62]

---

62   The author originally wrote the preceding account in 2003.

During many moves between the Philippines and Taiwan, I had misplaced the sheet of music sent by the young Finn. A good friend and colleague, the Reverend Per Harling, a Swedish member of the Global Praise Working Group, kindly sent another score of this "Swedish melody." To my surprise, it originated from France! The score is reproduced here.

Fredman's Epistel N:o 48

This is Per Harling's explanation:[63]

> I have been looking at the Indian Carnatic hymn melody and, yes, there is a resemblance to an old well-known Swedish song by Carl Michael Bellman. He is still one of the most known and loved troubadours of Sweden, even if he lived a long time ago, at the end of the eighteenth century. He wrote many songs called "Fredmans epistlar," which were sung commentaries on the life in Stockholm at that time. I recognize #91 in *Sound the Bamboo* as Fredmans epistel #48, called "Solen glimmar blank och trind." I have checked the internet to find out if it really is Bellman who wrote the music. You know, sometimes he composed his own music, and sometimes he put words to other—more or less known—melodies from his time. I found out that this particular tune is not by Bellman! It is a tune that has a French origin.

About the title "Nyt Kevat on," provided by my Finnish friend, Per answered:

> The name you have given the melody sounds very Finnish! Probably it is a Finnish translation of the original Swedish text. Unfortunately I do not understand a word of Finnish. The words in Swedish mean "The sun— being bright and round—glitters."[64]

Thus, this melody has two identities, French-Swedish and Indian (Carnatic). The two melodies sound quite different, but they share a melodic contour, and their structures are very similar. South Indians had so internalized the French melody that they changed the initials and cadences, added ornaments and variations, and eventually turned it into a Carnatic melody of their own!

In late 1989, I felt uneasy and was somewhat apologetic: because of my ethnomusicological curiosity, I had, on the one hand, found and proved the identity of this melody but, on the other hand, unintentionally hurt the Indians' pride for claiming the song. However, after a few years of reflection, I feel that the discovery of its true identity does not change the Indian ownership of this hymn. The fact that the Indians changed the initials and inserted typical embellishments, and that there are as many different versions as different regions of India, is proof that the tune acquired the status of an Indian folk tradition, a part of the public domain. Another setting of this melody, with the Reverend Elisha Soundararajan's text, is illustrated here:

---

63   From the author's correspondence with Per Harling, February 21, 2007.
64   From the author's correspondence with Per Harling, February 22, 2007.

I - rai - va A - se Than - tha-nup - pum
Send us with your bless - ing, Lord, on our way.

Sel - vom Um pu - gal Pa - rap - pi - du - vom
We will praise you by night and break of day.

Na - tti - am Na - da - gam Nal - li - sai - yal
Moved to pro - claim you in all ways we can.

A - vi Un - mai - yai tholu - thi - du - vom:
Sing - ing and danc - ing, each wom - an, child child and man.

(after *Thuma Mina* 1995, no. 190)

I created the tune name SWEINDIA as a contraction of "Sweden" and "India" (given the newer discovery, it should probably be changed to "Franco-Sweindia" to acknowledge the multinational links in this melody). This setting is a replica of a *tambura* (plucked lute) accompaniment; it follows the Indian tradition of accompanying the voice with a *tambura*, playing the dominant and tonic of the *sankarabarenam* raga seen in the hymn.

"Dear friends, walk with me, let us go" (*STB* #198)

(Mundari: *Sene sakinge seneme*)

Daud Dayal Singh Horo wrote the text and tune of this hymn, inviting friends to follow the Savior who has already gone and prepared the way. Horo assures us that Christ's grace will always shine brightly in all circumstances; we need to be renewed daily by Christ's love until we reach his throne. This hymn is appropriate as a sending forth before or after the benediction.

The music SENE SAKINGE (like *STB* #142, HALA HALA, and #38, SIRMA APOM) is in an anhemitonic penta (five tones without a half step) scale (5 6 1 2 3), but this one adds a lower C = 2. The descending and ascending fourth (5-2, 2-5) are prominent features of this tune that centers on 5. The style is also very different from either Hindustani music in the north or Carnatic in the south. This reflects either the ethnic style of the Munda people in Ranchi or the composer's personal style. This hymn, and *STB* #142 and #38, were taught and translated by Bishop Hans in Ranchi in 1984. His son, the Reverend Cyril Hans, kindly explained the tune's name:

"Sen" is "to walk" and "sene" is the poetic form. "Saking" is a friend, a bosom friend, or a dear friend, also used poetically.[65]

So the first line of the hymn, "Dear friends, walk with me," is a good translation. (para. Rolando S. Tinio)

Ever and always be praise (*STB* #95)
(Thamilz: *Ennaallume thudhippaai*)

This is a hymn of praise for God's mercy, redemption, healing, and forgiveness. The last two stanzas acknowledge that one's life is like grass that easily decays, but God's faithfulness never changes. Finally, the hymn blesses the eternal God in the throne and praises the Savior.This is D. T. Niles's paraphrase of "Ennaallume thudhippaai," a text based on Psalm 103 by S. Paramaanandham, which first appeared in the 1963 *EACC Hymnal* under Niles's name. The structure is similar to the *kirtana* form—the first two systems compose the *pallavi*, the middle section repeats as the *anupallavi*, and last two systems form the *charanam* (see explanations of these terms in the general introduction to this chapter)—but the poetic structure has been changed. This melody is also popularly set to the text of KANNGELLEI (meaning "eyes"; see *STB* #56, "I lift my eyes to the LORD"); hence, the tune has the same name. The melody was transcribed from a recording of an experienced singer, and thus it retains the ornaments that were missing from the other publication. The hymn is in an E = 3 seven-tone scale (C = 1 2 3 4 5 6 7) with a raised fourth (#4), a style that is quite popular in Christian light music. The last phrase is exactly the same as the initial phrase, which confirms the Christian *kirtana* form.

---

65   From the author's correspondence with Cyril Hans, February 22, 2007.

"Following Jesus, Savior and Master" (*STB* #227)

(Hindi: *Yesu ke piche jayenge ham sab*)

A *bhajan* is a simple spiritual song praising the attributes of God. However, the theme and focus of this song are statements or affirmations of the followers of Jesus, the Christ. To establish the mood, the melody begins with the vocable "ah"; it then describes the duties of a pilgrim life: we are to wear the servant's robe, to light our candles bright, and to seek the way of peace. It is appropriate to sing this *bhajan* as a response to a sermon or as a commitment before entering the world.

YESU KE PICHE, meaning "following Jesus," is in an A = 3 seven-tone scale (F = 1 2 3 4 5 6 7) with two raised tones (♯2 and ♯1) as lower auxiliary tones to their respective higher neighbors (3 ♯2 3 and 2 ♯1 2) and with six-beat patterns. Both the text and tune were composed by Anto Amarnad, a multitalented Indian Catholic priest. Since the original Hindi text is easy to pronounce, the congregation is encouraged to sing in the original language, but one should ensure that the meanings of the text are explained. Notice that the first system is for an introduction only. All stanzas begin at the second system following the refrain. (para. Colin A. Gibson)

"From the unreal, lead me to the real" (*STB* #281)

(Sanskrit: *Asa tomaa sathgamayaa*)

This *bhajan* is taken from one of the most famous Sanskrit poems in the well-known ancient Hindu scripture, the *Upanishad*. Since this prayer does not name the deity, some Christians have adopted it as a *bhajan* to pray to God. According to John 14:6, Jesus says, "I am the way, and the truth, and the life." If the Sanskrit poem is interpreted as "From falsehood, lead me to the Truth; from darkness, lead me to your Light; from death, lead me to eternal Life. Let peace prevail," it offers common ground for Christian theologization. What may be debatable is the "om," the mystic syllable of ancient origin. According to Indian tradition:

> The mystic sound OM is chanted in a long drawn-out note, beginning with a deep-throated tone and gradually transposing to the nasal hum. This is another ancient Indian symbol with diverse meanings. Being properly comprised of three letters (A-U-M) it can mean the three worlds, the three primary scriptures, the beginning, middle and end of life ... We chant this ancient mystic sound ... attuning ourselves to the "eternal sound" of our cosmic life (Lott 1986, 13).

Could this "om" be allegorically compared to the concepts of Alpha and Omega? This *bhajan*, therefore, is controversial among some churches and theologians in India. Some churches are willing to accept this adaptation, and others are hesitant or even resistant. In due time, one hopes that Indian theologians will develop more convincing theories to eliminate the fear of Hindu influences.

The music is in an E = 6 five-tone scale (6 7 1 2 3) with gliding tones and ornaments. It should be sung slowly and solemnly as a petition prayer for God's guidance. According to the tradition, the leader sings a phrase, which the congregation repeats. It would be best to sing this in Sanskrit to feel the original spirit of the prayer. *Shanthii* (or *shanti*) means "peace." Playing *talam* (finger cymbals) on the first beat of the first three phrases and on the first beat of each *shanthii* will sound like a traditional accompaniment. This hymn may be sung as a meditation on Christ's salvation, as a response to the reading of the Word, as a confession of faith or trust, or as a prayer for guidance after the benediction. (para. Jim Minchin)

"Give us Light" (*STB* #58)
(Hindi: *Jyothi dho Prabhu*)

This typical *bhajan* from northern India prays to the LORD for giving light, life, peace, salvation, and grace. It is the Indian tradition to repeat important words and phrases many times. The tune JYOTHI DHO, meaning "give light," is in a C = 6 seven-tone scale (6 7 1 2 3 4 5), with the melody undulating and gradually building to the climax at the third repetition of the same words and returning slowly to recapitulate the second phrase at the end of the song. Both the text and music by Charles Vas are constructed in A B A' form. This *bhajan* is suitable for singing after a reading of the Word or as a prayer for guidance after the sermon or the benediction. It can also be sung as individual responses to prayers for light, life, peace, salvation, and grace, respectively. A *talam* (finger cymbals) accompaniment on the first beat of each measure is best.

"Glory to God" (*STB* #127)
(Kurukh: *Ara hehelnu kulehe dhau*)

This is a short form of the Gloria, the song of the angels in Luke 2:14. When I visited the prolific composer Justin Ekka in 1984, he had already written over 4,000 songs in five languages. Ekka originated from the eastern region of India, and his style of music is quite different from North or South Indian songs. Ekka works for All India Radio, a capacity that requires him to be versatile in many musical styles and languages. This Gloria in a C = 1 five-tone scale (1 2 3 5 6) is a short liturgical response and is best sung after a reading of the Gospel or the New Testament or after the forgiveness of sins. Singing this in the original language is recommended. (para. I. L.)

"Hala, hear our Christmas song" (*STB* #142)

(Mundari: *Hala, rasi kath the dho*)

This is a lovely Christmas carol in Mundari, greeting the Christ Child with joy. After telling the nativity story, it concludes with a pledge of trust and obedience and a prayer for peace. Both the text and tune HALA HALA were written by Daud Dayal Singh Horo, who belongs to the Munda tribe in the Ranchi area. The music is quite different from Hindustani or Carnatic styles: it is in a D = 5 five-tone scale (5 6 1 2 3) without half steps or ornaments. It is suitable for children. According to the Reverend Cyril Hans, the son of Bishop Hans, who taught this song:

> "Hala" is a word of praise in the Mundari language, not much used in conversation, but only in literary or poetic form. It means "Praise."[66]

(trsl. Bishop Hans; para. J. M. & I. L.)

"I have come to you to take your touch" (*STB* #157)

This is one of the poems by Rabindranath Tagore that has been sung in Christian churches. It is a morning devotion to the Divine, yearning for a touch by this Friend, so that His eyes would become our eyes and to accompany us and lead our way. With an imaginative metaphor, the climax is on the word "kiss" in the C section: "Let your love's sunshine kiss, kiss the peaks of my thoughts and linger in my life's valley, where harvest ripens." This gives much room for philosophically and theologically minded persons to interpret or imagine possible implications.

There has been some concern about whether Tagore is a Christian. Bengali-speaking churches in Kolkata (or Calcutta) and Bangladesh have been singing many of Tagore's lyrics and have been spiritually nourished. If one believes that God is the Creator of the universe and all human beings, then He does not reveal Himself only to Christians but can also shed new light on His truth through great poets and artists. Whether or not Tagore is a Christian is immaterial. Sometimes theological debates do not solve our problems and we have to admit that there will not be absolutely correct answers until we all see God, face to face. As written in St. Paul's Epistles to the Corinthians (I Corinthians 13:12): "For now we see in a mirror, dimly, but then we will see face to face. Now I know only in part; then I will know fully. Even as I have been fully known." Liturgically, this hymn would be suitable as a morning prayer, either sung by one person or as a congregational prayer.

The music TAGORE is in a D = 6 seven-tone scale (6 7 1 2 3 #4 5), but the sixth degree (#4) appears only once at the most crucial point: the only triplet (#4 3 2), describing the "desert of noise." This appearance of #4 breaks the rule

---

66   From the author's correspondence with Cyril Hans, February 22, 2007.

of the Dorian mode, which makes it sound more Indian in style. Incidentally, I learned the explanation for this correction from B♭ to B♮ only in January 2006. It was also later suggested that the beginning of the coda at the end of the sixth system should begin with a quarter note on G, and thus the eighth rest should be discarded.

The composer Sharada Schaffter relates the background of this song:[67]

> It was at an Asia-Region WACC conference in Manila in 1990 that I heard the choir of the Asian Institute of Liturgy and Music sing at the morning devotions. Inspired by this, I put down on paper, for the first time, a tune I had composed earlier for one of Rabindranath Tagore's poems and spontaneously offered it to Dr. Francisco Feliciano, the director of the choir. After it found a place in *Sound the Bamboo*, a composer-friend, Dr. Randall Giles (Director, Department of Music and Liturgy, Church of South India, Madras Diocese), arranged it for the keyboard. Subsequently, another musician-friend, Augustine Paul, added an obligato for the flute. An ensemble of a drone on the tonic, a tenor recorder, and a flute adds color to the melody, for a change. Interestingly, Paul finds that the tune, which is in the Dorian mode, is based on the raga *karaharapriya*, one of the seventy-two *melakarthas* in the South Indian classical (Carnatic) system of music; I have had no exposure to this highly developed art, much less its finer nuances!

Musically, the song is divided into four sections, each of which returns to the initial phrase as a refrain. The second half of the refrain also functions as the coda in augmentation (doubling the note values). It is at the final cadence that a second voice suddenly appears, obviously of Western influence. The setting by Giles was unavailable at the time of editing, so only the original version is included in *Sound the Bamboo*.

Tagore is believed to have composed over 2,500 songs (both text and tunes); unfortunately, none of them are available in Western notation. For more information about Tagore's poems and music, see his biography at the end of this volume.

"I lift my eyes to the Lord" (*STB* #56)
(Thamilz: *Kanngellei eereduppeen*)

Originally this was a Thamilz text of Psalm 121, "I lift up my eyes to the hills—from where will my help come?" written by T. Aiyaathurai Baagavedhar of South India, and it was paraphrased into English by D. T. Niles in the 1963 *EACC Hymnal*. Because some of the wordings were rather difficult to sing, Beth Nacion-Puyot

---

67   From the author's interview and correspondence with Schaffter, February 8, 2006.

was asked to do some alterations for the 1990 edition of *Sound the Bamboo*. The text emphasizes that people of faith will have God's protection because God is a sanctuary. This hymn is suitable as a prayer of trust in the LORD.

The composer of the tune KANNGELLEI (meaning "eyes") is anonymous. It is in an E = 3 seven-tone scale (C = 1 2 3 4 5 6 7), with a ♯4 between two 5s. The B section begins in a high register, forming a wide range of a tenth (from middle C to e). The ornaments for the descending line in the fourth system make this tune more Carnatic in style. The music was transcribed from the singing of the late William Manoharan, who was studying at Asian Institute for Liturgy and Music when *Sound the Bamboo* was being edited (see "Slaves of Christ," *STB* #249). The text and music were written in a form similar to the Carnatic *kirtana* (see the discussion in the introduction). Each stanza should be sung following the refrain.

"I sing praise to your holy name" (*STB* #214)

(Malayalam: *Enyesuvin sannidhiyil*)

The form of this melody is close to the traditional Indian *kirtana* poem, which includes three sections: *pallavi, anupallavi,* and *charanam.*

> *Pallavi*: a short chorus or refrain with two to four or five *tala* cycles.

> *Anupallavi*: a sub-chorus of the same length as the *pallavi* but ending with a passage of text or *sangait* (improvised and with solfege) in double tempo, with instrumental accompaniment.

> *Charanam*: the verse, the longest section, which toward the end echoes the melody of the *pallavi* and repeats its double-time passage.
> (Cf. Garland 5:145)

The form of the lyrics of *STB* #214:

> *Pallavi*: (A, refrain)
> I sing praise to your holy name,
> > Jesus Christ, Lord of sweetness and light.
> *Anupallavi*: (B, repeated, but without the aforementioned characteristics)
> > He's the one who will wipe all our sorrows and tears,
> > And will turn all our sadness to joy.
> *Charanam*: (C, verses)
> 1. He has ransomed us from captivity,
>   So that we may live with him and be free. (2 lines repeated)
>   He's the Son of the Father in heaven (with music of B section)
>   Who has giv'n us a share in a land of hope and dreams. (continue to A)

2. Though we walk through the darkness of the night,
   We shall never lose our way, he's our guide. (2 lines repeated)
   In submitting to his loving reign, (with music of B section)
   We will gain all the freedom the world can never give.   (continue to A)

Many Indian lyrics are composed with this form. This Malayalam text shows some of the characteristics of the *kirtana*; the *charanam* actually ends with the melody of *pallavi*. However, the *anupallavi* does not end with a passage of text or solfege in double tempo, as is the practice in classical *kirtana*. This is why Santosh Kumar indicated that the use of the term *kirtana* is problematic for classical Indian musicians (see the chapter introduction for further discussion).

The tune ENYESUVIN SANNIDHIYIL (Malayalam for "In the presence of my Jesus") loosely follows the *kirtana* form in three sections, A, B, and C. The melody is in a C = 5 seven-tone scale (F = 1 2 3 4 5 6 7) with the final on 1. The A section has two phrases and is self-contained with a full cadence. The B section is organized by the development of sequences, such as 35 4 43 2/ 24 3 32 1 (the ornaments are not transcribed here). The first two phrases of section C are also in sequence, and the last two phrases are exactly the same as section B. For performance, the form is A B A C A (following the indicated repeats). The hymn is appropriate for praising and expressing trust in God on any occasion. (trsc. I-to Loh; para. Rolando S. Tinio)

"Jesus, Jesus, how we adore you" (*STB* #41)
(Hindi: *Jei jei Yesu*)

Praising and adoring Jesus for his love and salvation, this hymn states what Jesus has done for all humankind as the giver of life, peace, and joy. It concludes with a summons that all, great and small, tell Jesus' story.

The tune JEI JEI YESU ("glory to Jesus") is a traditional Hindustani melody set to a text written by C. Jadra and translated by the missionary C. D. Rocky; there is little information about either contributor. I discovered this hymn as a worn mimeographed copy while working on the Asian American hymnbook project (which resulted in *Hymns from the Four Winds* in 1983). After returning to Asia, I was able to find someone who knew this melody and re-transcribed it accordingly. It is in a G = 5 six-tone scale (C = 1 2 3 5 6 7), but it has a very wide range, equaling a thirteenth (from low G to e). As is common in folk traditions, there are a number of versions to this melody; a simpler one was chosen for this collection. This hymn of praise should be sung energetically and joyfully. According to the tradition, the verse is repeated, and the singer continues to the refrain in the second system. The first system, however, is only sung once as an introduction. (para. Jim Minchin)

"Jesus, Savior Lord, lo to you I fly" (*STB* #59)

(Thamilz: *Yesu raajenin thiruvediku*)

This lyric is D. T. Niles's paraphrase of Psalm 61 that first appeared in the 1963 *EACC Hymnal* and was included with four-part harmony in a few Western hymnals. It is one of the most popular South Asian hymns, and both Pakistanis and Indians proudly claim ownership of it. Like Isaac Watts, who Christianized the Psalms with the message of the gospel, Niles also addresses "Jesus, Savior Lord" in this psalm. The word *sarennam* means "I take refuge" or "surrender." The multiple repetitions of *sarennam* is the main feature of this prayer to Jesus, the Rock and Refuge, which asks for a dwelling place in his tent and for his faithfulness, so that one can eternally praise his name. This may be sung as an opening hymn or as a response to the altar call.

This version of the tune SARENNAM ("surrender") is a transcription of the singing of William Manoharan, an organist from Tamilnadu Theological Seminary in Madurai. It is in an E♭ = 1 seven-tone scale (1 2 3 4 5 6 7) with a sharpened ♯2, ♯4, and ♯5, all of which function as ornaments of their respective higher auxiliary tones (3 ♯2 3; 5 ♯4 5; 6 ♯5 6). With these ornaments or altered tones, this version may not be easy to sing; nonetheless, it preserves more authentic Indian/Pakistani styles. Furthermore, because of its popularity in AABB' form, many different versions may be found. Although it would be difficult to say which version is the correct one, there are certainly wrong versions. Experienced Indian/Pakistani singers or people who know the tradition can make the distinction. In this case, people may choose their preferred version. An accompaniment of tabla drums and concussion bells would add to the liveliness of this hymn.

"Joy abounds, dear Lord" (*STB* #309)

(Hindi: *Mero man lago*)

This Hindi *bhajan* expresses the joy of contemplating the Lord Jesus because no one can match his grace; he gave his life to save us, and he never turns away those who seek him. It concludes with a prayer for wisdom. The melody is in an A = 1 six-tone scale (1 2 3 5 6 7); it uses many sequences of repeated eighth notes from weak to strong beats, going up or down (32 21 16 61). Both the text and tune are anonymous. The tune name MERO MAN LAGO means "my mind is filled with joy." According to Roger Gaikwad (Director of the Extension Program, Senate Center for Extension and Pastoral Theological Research, Kolkata), the text is not pure Hindi but a mixture of certain dialects of Hindi. Notice that the single consonant at the end of a syllable is voiced, i.e., a schwa "ə" is added. For instance, "man" and "prem" are sung as two syllables, i.e., "ma-nə" and "pre-mə." But for "shan," the "n" closes at the end of the note as one syllable: "shan" not "sha-nə." One can sing this as a hymn of trust or prayer for guidance. (para. Jim Minchin)

"Syriac Kyrie"
("Kurie laison," *STB* #301)

Coming from the Mar Thoma Church of South India, this Kyrie ("Lord, have mercy") is from an ancient Syriac liturgy. History and legends reveal that St. Thomas, one of the disciples of Jesus, was the first one to bring the gospel to South India (see the introduction of this section for further discussion). How much the Syrian Orthodox or Mar Thoma Church of today preserves the Christian tradition of the first century is of interest to many scholars. But the notion that Indian Christians received the gospel directly from one of Jesus' own disciples is a fascinating thought, and it is certainly a source of pride for Indian Christians.

This Kyrie, in an E = 6 four-tone scale (6 7 1 2), may be sung at any time as a response to prayers of confession or intersession. It was taught to me by a young priest/musician who had studied at AILM, the Reverend Ninan Geroge from the Mar Thoma Church.

"O come to us, pastor of the flock" (*STB* #162)
(Thamilz: *Vaarum aiyaa podhegeree*)

Indian families often light a small copper oil lamp (*kuthu villeku*) at home, especially at night. The sacred flame (*aarti*) of this lamp can symbolize the presence of God, Jesus Christ, the Light of the world, the Word of God, or the presence of the Holy Spirit. This beautiful text is an evening hymn, sung as a grace before supper to invite the Noble One to partake of the meal. The hymn refers to Luke 24:13–35, which describes two disciples on the road to Emmaus. Not recognizing a stranger as the risen Lord, they invited him to dine with them. It was not until the Lord had broken the bread that they recognized him. Hence, the hymn's invitation to the Lord to dine has a special meaning. The text also refers to John 10:11, "I am the good shepherd. The good shepherd lays down his life for the sheep."

Both the text and the tune VAARUM AIYAA ("come, master") were written by Veedhenayegam Baagavedhar, an important poet/composer of South India. The music is in an E♭ = 1 seven-tone scale (1 2 3 4 5 6 7); the ornaments and melisma (in which one syllable is stretched over several notes) show strong South Indian characteristics. Since the third phrase is repeated, there are many different variations. This hymn may be sung as a family gathers for evening meals or devotion or during Holy Communion. A pair of concussion bells or *talam* (finger cymbals) may be struck on the first beat of each measure to accompany this hymn. (para. Jim Minchin)

"O Father God, you're merciful" (*STB* #38)

(Mundari: Sirma apom saya dana)

In this prayer of thanksgiving for the mercy of the Parent God, the author expresses his joy in worshiping God, listening to God's Word, and walking with God in righteousness.

Both the text and tune SIRMA APOM were written by Daud Dayal Singh Horo. The music is in an E = 6 pentatonic scale (6 1 2 3 5) that always ends on 5 (see *STB* #142, HALA HALA, and #198, SENE SAKINGHE). The rhythm is quite simple, and its style must reflect that of the Munda tribe in the Ranchi area. Regarding the tune name, the Reverend Cyril Hans gives this explanation:

> *Sirma* is "Heaven" and *apum* is "your Father." *Apu* is "Father." Often in singing the word is distorted and also said or sung as "Sirima."[68]

So the tune name means "Your heavenly Father." (para. J. M. & I. L.)

"O God, highest God" (*STB* #270)

(Mizo: *Aw lalpa chungnung*)

This hymn was written to celebrate the emancipation of the people of Mizoram in upper northeast India in the 1920s. The Mizo tribe had a long history of slavery. The poor, oppressed, or marginalized had to submit to the authority of the tribe's chief for protection and in time became his slaves. A Welsh Presbyterian medical missionary, the Reverend Fraser, saw this injustice and decided to take the slavery issue to the courts. He insisted that human beings are created equal and that the mission of Jesus and the meaning of the gospel are "to bring good news to the poor . . . to proclaim release to the captives . . . to let the oppressed go free" (Luke 4:18). Unfortunately, neither the Mizo leaders nor the occupying British officers were sympathetic, preferring to maintain the status quo and enjoy their privileged status. Fraser lost the case, but the British Parliament sensed the importance of the issue and took up the matter, eventually abolishing slavery for the Mizo. According to the Reverend Roger Gaikwad (Director of the Extension Program, Senate Center for Extension and Pastoral Theological Research, Kolkata)—who told me the above story in February 2006—Fraser was not able to stay in Mizoram since his views were rejected by both the Mizo and local British authorities. This was the price he paid for his "preferential option to the poor" and "speaking the truth in love" (Ephesians 4:15).

The emancipation led Thanga (his full name) to write this important hymn in a doctrinal context. In the first stanza, Thanga praises God for choosing to be with the poor and enslaved and to empower them. In the second, he praises God for

---

68   From the author's correspondence with Cyril Hans, February 22, 2007.

answering prayers and not forsaking them. The third stanza is a prayer for God's grace to those who would oppose God and that God would touch them and redeem them. Stanza 4 gives God the highest praise for setting people free and filling the whole earth with peace. It concludes with the summary of the Lord's Prayer.

The tune MIZO was adapted from a Mizo melody. The most peculiar feature of this music is the use of neutral thirds above and below G. The interval of a neutral third (approximately 350 cents) is slightly larger than a minor third (300 cents) but smaller than a major third (400 cents). The key signature is not an F; it is a half-flat "p" which is slightly higher than B♭ but lower than B♮. For convenience, I have used the initial D = 5 (5 6 1 2 3), with 6 (Ep [E half-flat]) and 3 (Bp) approximately 50 cents lower. In the first system, the small arrows pointing down indicate approximately a quarter tone (one-fourth of a tone, i.e., a microtone [50 cents]) lower than E♮; thus, the G is a center tone, with two neutral thirds above (Bp) and below (Ep). It is not easy to sing this hymn "correctly," but a willingness to try would greatly encourage our Mizo sisters and brothers. This would be an excellent hymn for the United Nations Human Rights Day on December 10 or for other services or occasions dealing with human rights issues.

This song was recorded at the United Theological College in 1989, when students from Mizo sang it for me. The eighteenth revised edition of the Mizo hymnal *Kristian Hla Bu* (published in 2005) has a four-part setting of this hymn in tonic *sol-fa* notation (*Kristian Hla Bu* #434), which is quite different from what the Mizo sang. Apparently, this hymn is still enslaved by Western musical theory and needs to be emancipated! This hymn is a great witness to the love of God that has set people free from slavery of any kind. This song may be accompanied with a frame drum, playing on every beat with the same strength throughout. (para. Ronald Hines)

"O God of love" (*STB* #63)

This is a devotional song, praying for the God of love and truth to protect us from evil powers, so that we might witness and live for his love. Both the text and tune are by the prolific writer/composer B. M. J. Dhyriam; hence, the tune is named DHYRIAM. The melody is in a G = 3 seven-tone scale (E♭ = 1 2 3 4 5 6 7) with raised ♯1 and ♯2, plenty of gliding tones, and a six-beat cycle. All of these features exhibit the popular Indian light-music style of today.

"O Jesus, we would praise you" (*STB* #282)
(Thamilz: *Siir Yesu nadhenukku*)

This hymn of praise to Jesus, the eternal Trinity, was composed by one of the most famous Carnatic poets, Veedhenayegam Sasthriyar (also spelled Vedanayagam Sastriar). The poetic form of this text is quite different from the ordinary *bhajan*. It also praises the attributes of Christ as the "Lord of all people," "Teacher of the

Way," "our hymn forever," the "Word of God," "great Presence of the world," "Light of Justice," "breath of Spirit," and "guest of honor." This hymn fuses two genres of songs: the contents of a *bhajan* with the structure (text and musical form) of a *kirtana* in three sections—*pallavi*, *anupallavi*, and *charanam* (for more information, see the general introduction of this section). This hymn is appropriate for praise, thanksgiving, and the affirmation of God.

The tune SIIR YESU (meaning "perfect Jesus") is in a B♭ = 1 seven-tone scale (1 2 3 4 5 6 7). It begins with a triplet (counted as two beats) that is repeated at the beginning of each section, but the second stanza of the Thamilz has an extra syllable and should be rendered carefully. The second system uses the sequence three times (4654, 3543, 2432), and there is a different cadence for the second stanza, which is only for the Thamilz language. One should ignore the asterisks when singing in English. (trsl. Samson Prabhakar: para. Shirley Murray)

"O praise the Lᴏʀᴅ" (*STB* #15)
(Hindi: *Om Bhagawan*)

This *bhajan* by Bishop Azariah of South India, who taught it in the Ecumenical Workshop on Music and Liturgy in Manila 1980, was the first *bhajan* that I learned. As previously mentioned, "om," a mystical syllable of ancient origin, is the combination of three sounds, A-U-M, symbolizing the beginning, the middle, and the end of life (cf. Tirabassi and Eddy 1995, 74). BHAGAWAN, one of the Hindu terms for a god, has been adopted as a name for the Christian God, a practice that is not widely accepted.

In the form of a typical *bhajan*, this spiritual song praises the Father ("Fount of love"), the Son ("our Savior"), and the Holy Spirit ("Comforter"), and the English version adds another praise, to the Trinity. Although the many ornaments in this *bhajan*, which are essential to the spirit and the style, are rather complicated, congregations are encouraged to attempt singing them. The willingness to try and to honor the tradition is more important than the authenticity of the style, which varies according to regions and personal preferences. The multiple ornaments may be simplified by singing the one closest to the primary note.

According to the *bhajan* tradition, all phrases (marked by double measure lines) are sung by the leader and repeated by the congregation. The melody is in an E = 6 six-tone scale (6 7 1 2 3 5) with plenty of embellishments. It begins slowly and solemnly and gradually increases in tempo from the second stanza, but it slows down at the last stanza. The coda should be sung very slowly and softly as an internalization of praise, audible only to oneself. This is the way the great majority of *bhajans* are sung. A pair of concussion bells or *talam* (finger cymbals) may be played on the first of every four beats to accompany this song.

4x

Performance form: //:AAB://A//:Coda://
(trsc. & para. I. L.)

"On the night of Christmas" (*STB* #133)

(Kurukh: *Hare inna makha*)

The theme of this Christmas carol is the shining star that drives away all darkness, dispels every form of death, and leads to heaven's light.

The culture of the Kurukh-speaking people, who belong to neither northern (Hindustani) nor southern (Carnatic) traditions, is demonstrated in this Christmas carol, PUNA BINKO (meaning "shining star"). It is in an E = 6 five-tone scale (6 1 2 3 5). The repeated triplets of the voice alternating with or echoed by the drum pattern plus the harmony with the intervals of thirds and fourths are distinct characteristics of the Kurukh folk tradition in the Chotanagpur region of India. The author/arranger Picas Khess is a young pastor in the Lutheran church who studied at AILM in 1983 and taught this song to the students. The accompaniment of drum, jingles, and gong also reflects the song's regional style (see the explanation in the hymnal regarding the playing method). This carol was first recorded and published in 1984, in the first volume of the AILM Collection of Asian Church Music, entitled *A Festival of Asian Christmas Carols*. (para. Rolando Tinio)

"Praise God from whom all blessings flow" (*STB* #36)

(Thamilz: *Thandhaanei thudhippoomee*)

This lyric is by one of the most famous Carnatic poet/composers, V. Maasilaamanni. The original text had five stanzas, but it was paraphrased and reduced to four stanzas and introduced to ecumenical circles by D. T. Niles through the *EACC Hymnal* of 1963. The first line is borrowed from the British hymn writer Thomas Ken's famous doxology, "Praise God from whom all blessings flow" (1674). The content of this lyric, however, is quite distinct. The images of Psalm 24:7–10, "Lift up your heads, O gates . . . that the King of glory may come in," have been changed; this hymn calls directly, "Zion! your Savior," "your Bridegroom," and "your Master comes to you." Here, as in his other lyrics (see *STB* #249, "Slaves of Christ"), Niles exhibits his poetic craftsmanship:

> His the cup so drink it,
> His the yoke—why shrink it?
> His the sword, so wear it,
> His the load, so bear it.

Niles concludes the stanzas with the same opening phrase and melody.

Maasilaamanni's melody THUDHI (meaning "praise") is in a C = 5 seven-tone scale (F = 1 2 3 4 5 6 7). It is in two sections: the phrase structure of the A section is a b a , and the B section consists of a series of sequences (5 5 5 55 65, 4 4 4 44 54, etc.). This version of the melody sounds quite different from the popular version now known in the ecumenical circle because it was transcribed from a performance by a trained Carnatic singer. In this respect, it is closer to the Carnatic style. It is unfortunate that the English and Thamilz texts are inconsistent in many places; this shows the difficulty of translation. The traditional Western harmonization of the popular version has been purposefully ignored. Leaders are reminded to respect the hymn's cultural roots and to sing it without superimposing Western harmony.

"Praise to you, Jesus" (*STB* #17)
(Bengali: *Joy Probhu Jishu*)

Bhajans, or Hindu spiritual or devotional songs, have a long history. Although some Christians deny their value and function in the church, Christian *bhajans* have already found a place in worship. The simplicity, repetitive nature, and call-and-response style of the *bhajan* fit contemporary practices. Usually, *bhajans* praise the attributes of the triune God, but this one centers on Jesus, calling him Emmanuel our God, who gave up his glory to save all people and showered upon us great and wonderful things beyond our understanding, so that thousands of tongues will acknowledge his Gospel truth. This hymn is suitable for praising and thanking God in a variety of worship settings.

JOY PROBHU, meaning "glory to Lord," is in an A = 1 seven-tone scale (1 2 3 4 5 6 7), but it begins with the seventh degree of the scale (7 on G♯). The melodic material is constructed with repetition, variation, and repeated cadences (7 5 67 1-), making this hymn very easy to sing. The translator Kalyan Banerjee, who introduced this song, is a teacher and church musician in Kolkata (Calcutta). (para. Shirley Murray & J. M.)

"Sarennam, O the divine light" (*STB* #47)
(Telegu: *Sarennam, Dhivya jyothi*)

Sarennam is one of the most common words in Indian worship, meaning we "take refuge" in God (Psalm 46:1) or we "surrender" ourselves to God. The word *sarennam* has a few different spellings and pronunciations according to different regions, but they all denote the same idea. In this typical *bhajan* (spiritual song), the singer addresses God and takes refuge in the "Divine Light," "Life Giver," "Fount of Love," "the Compassionate," "Word of mercy," and the "Holy Spirit." The music DHIVYA JYOTHI (meaning "divine light") is in a B = 3 five-tone scale (E = 6 1 2 3 5) with two altered tones ♯1 (G♯) and ♯2 (A♯). The melody has many sixteenth-note ornaments that are characteristic of Indian melodies. One should take note of the repetitions, which are important in the performance of Indian repertoire. For the beauty and authenticity of the style, harmony should not be added, except the drones on E and B. This hymn may be accompanied by a pair of concussion bells (*talam*), with an open sound (indicated by a small "o" in the score) on the first strong beat of the four-beat cycle.

Both the text and music were written by the Right Reverend Govada Dyvasirvadam, who since 2002 has been the Bishop of Krishna-Godavari Diocese in Andhra Pradesh, which is part of the Church of South India. Some Indian friends have expressed their doubts about the authorship of this *bhajan* due to its resemblance to certain other *bhajans*. I trust Bishop Dyvasirvadam's claim as the author/composer, but I recognize that it shares some features with other *bhajans*. This *bhajan* is appropriate for the beginning of worship, for expressing our yearning for union with God, for listening to God's word, or for praying for God's mercy.

"Seasons come, seasons go" (*STB* #26)
(Kannada: *Ella kaladollu*)

Kannada is one of the four major languages in South India and is spoken in the state of Karnataka. This anonymous *bhajan* praises the living God, who is our "Father," "Mother," "Kindred Spirit," "Alpha," "Omega," "true Light," "our joy, our delight and bliss." Although the melody is basically in a D = 3 five-tone scale (B♭ = 1 2 3 5 7), the main motif is constructed on an ascending minor third, 3-5 and 7-2. After series of sequences, the ascending motif is enlarged to a fourth and a fifth (5-1, 5-2) that build to the climax. The singing style has gliding tones and ornaments that further strengthen the South Indian character, making this a superb *bhajan* of praise. The tune name THANDHEYU NII NE means "You are the Father." (para. Ronald Hines)

"Slaves of Christ, his mercy we remember" (*STB* #249)
(Thamilz: *Dhaaseree yith therenniyei anbaai*)

As one of the most popular lyrics by the South Indian poet/composer V. Santiago, this hymn is widely known with the paraphrase and alteration by D. T. Niles, who included this in the 1963 *EACC Hymnal*. As previously discussed, this publication is monumental in the history of Christian hymnody, since it was the first Asian hymnal to include many indigenous tunes and texts as well as standard ecumenical hymns (see the general introduction of this volume for further discussion).

While there are only two stanzas in D. T. Niles's paraphrase, the original text has five. The refrain is a call to all "slaves of Christ" to fulfill their duty. Here, one can appreciate Niles's rhyming skills:

> . . . our witness we shall bear,
> for all his brethren care,
> and his communion share
> in all our work and prayer.

A similar technique is also exhibited in the second stanza, where the author states that the Savior expects his followers to accomplish his mission, so that:

> his peace may shatter human pride,
> the right from wrong divide,
> the widow's cause decide,
> injustice set aside.

The euphonic beauty of the rhymes also reflects the original structure of the Thamilz text, as one can see in the score. From this, one can appreciate how artists have exercised their poetic gifts from God to the utmost, to communicate the truth and thus "participate in the continuing creation of God," as I frequently emphasize.

The melody of DHAASEREE (meaning "slave" or "servant") is in a G = 1 seven-tone scale (1 2 3 4 5 6 7) with two identical sections. Beginning with the third phrase is a series of sequences: 6543 4, 5432 3, 4321 2, 3217 1. Since this tune is also a very popular melody, there are many versions, and some have been arranged and harmonized in Western four-part harmony. The *Sound the Bamboo* version, however, is a transcription from the singing of the late William Manoharam, an experienced organist from Madurai. With all the *gamakas* (ornaments and gliding tones), the song sounds more Carnatic in style. Manoharam had an opportunity to study at AILM for a year. It was then that I was able to record his singing of some of the Carnatic lyrics in *Sound the Bamboo*.

"So be it" (*STB* #109)

(Kurukh: *Ennem manan neka*)

This is a short response "amen" or "so be it" by Justin Ekka. It is in an E = 1 five-tone scale (1 2 3 5 6). The best way to use this piece is as a way for the congregation to own their prayers wholeheartedly, by singing it at the conclusion of their prayers. If desired, it can also be sung as an "amen chorus" to conclude worship. In this case, the congregation should be prepared so that all are ready to join in the response after the initial tonal cue.

"Thousands and thousands of songs" (*STB* #37)

(Thamilz: *Aayirem, aayirem padelgellei*)

This is one of the most popular songs in Tamilnadu today, and it has found a place in most of the hymnals published by charismatic preachers and Pentecostal groups in addition to its presence in the mainline ones. The text's heartfelt praise of God and the easy-to-learn, joyful melody have contributed to the hymn's popularity. The text was written by T. Dayanandan Francis, a former faculty member at Tamilnadu Theological Seminary, in Madurai, and a former General Secretary of the Christian Literature Society, in Chennai. Francis is a Thamilz-language scholar, and the text reflects his poetic imagination and splendid use of Tamil imagery and rhyme. His rhyme of *allelillai* ("no more sorrow") with *alleluia* is creativity at its best. Francis incorporates various texts of praise from the Bible; some of the texts include "Sing to the Lord a new song" (Psalms 149:1) and "Come to Zion with singing" (Isaiah 35:10).

The melody was composed by M. Thomas Thangaraj, Francis's colleague at Tamilnadu Theological Seminary. Together, Francis and Thangaraj worked on several hymns of this kind during the 1970s for the Teaching Mission program of the Seminary. Here, Thangaraj's primary concern was to craft a melody in the light-music tradition, which is easy to learn and even easier to sing.[69] The melody is set in an F-major scale and works well with a guitar accompaniment.

"We bow before you, O great and holy" (*STB* #39)

(Hindi: *Jeye ho, Theeree sam nee*)

JEYE HO, meaning "victory be to you" or "glory be to you," is the most common phrase for praising God in the Indian subcontinent, with only slight variations. The phrase "Humbly at your feet we bow in quiet reverence" is a contextual expression of utmost reverence in front of the Holy One. The second stanza asks God for forgiveness, vision, and protection. The verses are enclosed in a joyful chorus of praise. Liturgically, this may be sung as an opening hymn, calling people to join in praise and adoration and asking for forgiveness.

This tune is adapted from a traditional Hindi melody. It is in a Bb = 1 six-tone scale (1 2 3 5 6 b7); the b7 is very important and should be rendered carefully. This hymn was originally arranged by Victor Sherring into a four-part chorus at the "echo" section, where the tenor and alto form parallel sixths/thirds (3 33 32 1 with 5 55 54 3). Concerning this setting, Carlton Young said:

> I first heard this hymn when the Indian Methodist Centenary Choir toured the US in 1955–56. It was a favorite of Bliss Wiant, who often used it in his workshops. Obviously at that point in time, the settings were intentionally very Western, for Western ears and pocketbooks! . . . In 1992, Sherring wrote me: the hymn was first included in *Jaya Ho*, a 1956 collection of songs in Indian and Western musical notation published in Lucknow by the Centenary Music Committee; and in *Joyful Songs of India* (1955–56), a collection of translated songs.[70]

Since Indian music uses only drones, I took the liberty of simplifying Sherring's arrangement, maintaining the double drones (tonic and dominant) and letting the alto echo the main melody. The beginning section with the bass singing the

---

69   From the author's correspondence with Thomas Thangaraj, April 14, 2007.
70   From the author's communication with Young, October 23, 2007.

ostinato/drone (11 1) establishes the joyful mood for praising God. It is important to sing the ornaments, and all should join in unison in the third system to end the refrain. Since the verses express quiet reverence before the holy God and ask for forgiveness, the mood should be more solemn and the singing should be softer than in the previous section. Men should not forget to sing the last "jeye ho" in the last measure, so that all parts can begin the song again. One may use drums and concussion bells or finger cymbals (*talam*) for accompaniment; the "o" indicates a strong and open sound, and "+" signifies a weak and closed sound.

"Why, O Lord, why?" (*STB* #251)
(Thamilz: *Een aandevenee?*)

This hymn is an honest quest for answers to the problems created by human beings. The author Elisha Soundararajan, a village pastor in a Madras suburb, asks God why some people erect barriers to divide the world of God's creation. Why do children of Adam and Eve engage in wars and not live in peace? Why are there natural disasters? Why can only a few enjoy the wealth beneath the earth? After expressing his doubts to God, Soundararajan asks whether these conditions have been caused by our sin of greed. The author urges us to lose our selfishness and pray for God's kingdom to reign. This hymn would have a powerful effect if sung on Human Rights Day or other occasions concerned with social justice.

The tune EEN, meaning "why," was composed by the author's son, S. John Barathi. (In the South Indian tradition, children do not carry the family name. But Barathi added the initial "S" to identify with his father, Soundararajan.) Barathi was a student at AILM as a composition major. He wrote this tune in an F♯ = 3 seven-tone scale (D = 1 2 3 4 5 6 7) with a raised 4 and ornaments and gliding tones that characterize the Carnatic style. Notice that the ♯4 only goes up to 5 and never in a descending progression. Although the music may appear difficult, the imitative sequences of a few motifs (72 2; 3543; 35 4; etc.) make this hymn easy to sing. When asked to what raga this song belonged, Barathi confessed that he did not have any particular raga in mind. This may indicate that contemporary composers are not constrained by the theory of raga. This marks a point of liberation from tradition, but it also poses the danger of falling into the trap of Western styles if one is careless or not familiar with one's tradition. (trsl. S. John Barathi; para. Rolando S. Tinio)

"Worship and praise we give" (*STB* #25)
(Thamilz: *Un paadhem pannin dheen enaallum thudhiye*)

For the most part, Christians in Singapore are either Chinese descendents or from South India. This Thamilz lyric, praising Jesus for his love and mercy, which I recorded in Singapore in 1988, was considered anonymous. But recently the Methodist Bishop Robert Solomon of Singapore said that this text had been written by Sarah Nowroji from Chennai, India, in 1969, and the tune was written by Sathy Victor, who was from the same town. It was translated by the late professor C. R. W. David of Tamilnadu Theological Seminary in Madurai and paraphrased by Rolando S. Tinio of the Philippines. The structure of the lyric resembles the traditional Carnatic, three-part *kirtana* form. The first stanza is like a *bhajan* naming Jesus' attributes as the reason for our singing. The second stanza asks Jesus to be our guide and give us strength as a heavenly blessing. The third stanza presents our hardships with the belief that Jesus will help us overcome. The last stanza presents the imagery of Psalm 23: that the Lord leads us in the path of righteousness; his rod and staff will free us from fear and give us peace, comfort, and joy. Since it contains a variety of themes, this lyric can be sung at various stages of the liturgy. One may also choose particular stanzas for appropriate contexts.

The tune PANNIN DHEEN (meaning "bowed down") is in a D = 1 seven-tone scale (B = 6 7 1 2 3 4 5) with a raised 5. The lively rhythm, skips, sequences, ornaments, and the wide range equaling an eleventh (from low B to e) make this a very interesting song in an Indian style. A tabla and concussion bells accompaniment would add life and spirit to this lyric.

"You are full of light, Lord Jesus" (*STB* #298)

(Malayalam: *Velivu niranjor Iisho*)

This short liturgical prayer is from the ancient Syriac tradition. It is believed to be from the Liturgy of St. James and has been in continuous use among the Mar Thoma churches in South India.[71] The Mar Thoma Christians believe their church was established during the first century CE by St. Thomas, one of the apostles of Jesus Christ. This hymn, which is only sung during the Eucharist (Holy Communion), is a prayer to Jesus, acknowledging him to be the "Light of the whole universe," asking him to "open our inner eyes . . . let your Light show some glimpse of you." In churches of other denominations, this hymn could be sung as a prayer for illumination before or after the reading of the Word. The melody is in a B = 3 five-tone scale (E = 6 7 1 2 3). It was taught by the Reverend Ninan George of the Mar Thoma church, who had studied at AILM. This hymn should be sung without accompaniment. (para. J. M. & I. L.)

---

71   M. M. Ninan, "Liturgical Tradition of the Malnakara Syrian Christians: The Liturgy of Saint James of Jerusalem," *Prof. M. M. Ninan's Biblical & Apologetic Studies*, http://www.acns.com/~mm9n/liturgy/liturgy.htm (accessed March 1, 2009): "Liturgy of St. James the Just. James was the Bishop of Jerusalem soon after the formation of the Church on the Pentecost. James was the brother of Jesus who was not a believer during Jesus' lifetime and to whom Jesus appeared after his resurrection. But he evidently had been a scholar in the scripture and had a prestige as a rationalist and righteous man according to the law. Jacobaya Liturgy is said to have been written by James."

Conclusion

Of the thirty-nine Indian compositions in *Sound the Bamboo*, twenty-three have melodies constructed in major or minor scales with a tonal center or final on 1 (*do*), twelve on 6 (*la*), and four on 5 (*sol*). Retaining the ornaments in some of the melodies has kept alive the Indian musical spirit; without the ornaments, many of the hymns would sound like Western songs. This may indicate that nearly two-thirds of the tunes are of more recent vintage and possibly contain Western influences, although some Indians argue that songs in major scales are part of their traditional ragas. One may conclude that most Christians in India enjoy singing or composing in *do* (a major/diatonic scale), and less than one third of them like songs in natural minor scales, with the final on *la*. Indian composers should remember that there are thousands of ragas that can be utilized. Are other ragas too remote from modern life to be meaningful to today's Indians? Have Indian Christian composers researched their rich musical heritage? Both Hindustani and Carnatic secular music of today utilize a greater variety of ragas, modes (I use this term simply for convenience), rhythmic cycles, and other traditional musical instruments, thus exhibiting the unique features and beauty of Indian music.

Shoki Coe's approach, the "double wrestling" of faith and culture, can enhance the efforts of Indian theologians, poets, and musicians to reflect their Christian faith through an Indian context (Coe 1994, 268). Because many Indian Christian artists have already contributed so much to help the world to read the Bible through Asian eyes (see Takenaka and O'Grady 1991), one envisions that the next generation of Indian Christian poets and composers will be inspired to create new works of Indian heritage to proclaim the Good News.

Nepalese Hymns

The Nation, the People, and Their Music

Nepal is a small country between China and India, with a total area of 147,181 square kilometers (about 56,827 square miles) and a population of 29,519,114.[72] Fifty-five percent of the population speaks Nepali, the national language; other languages include Newari, Tibetan, and Tibeto-Burman dialects (Garland 5:5). There are seventy different tribes in this primarily Hindu state. The 1962 constitution declared religious freedom but "has prohibited anyone from converting someone else. Together with this no one, even by his own will, can change his religion" (Athyal 1996, 380). However, the 1991 rewritten constitution is silent on the issue of personal choice, indicating that there is some possibility for it. Over the years, this constitutional contradiction has made evangelism quite difficult. Although Jesuit priests entered Nepal in 1628, and the Capuchin friars worked successfully in the early eighteenth century, it was not until the 1950s that other denominations began evangelistic and educational missions. After the 1990 revolution, the new Nepalese constitution stated, "Each religious group will have the right, within the law, to maintain its identity; and preserve and protect its religious sites and trusts" (Athyal 1996, 386). The liberal interpretation of this clause has given hope and encouragement for Christian mission. According to Ramesh Khatry's 1990 report, 45% of Nepal's population is Buddhist, 3.5% is Muslim, and about 0.3% is Christian, with approximately 100,000 members (Athyal 1996, 380). At the time of this writing, the latest figures indicated that the population of Christians has exceeded 700,000.

Nepalese Music

Indian court musicians migrated to Nepal as early as the seventeenth century. More recently, the influx of northern Indian light-classical music and film music has further weakened the Nepalese musical tradition. The caste system was legalized in 1854 and abolished in 1951, yet it is still in practice today. Nepalese musicians and types of music are not free from the caste system. There are three castes of musicians:

> *Damai*: Provide entertainment at auspicious functions that mark the life cycle, such as births, funerals, and weddings. Accompanying instruments include kettledrums, cymbals, and natural horns or trumpets.

---

72 CIA, "The World Factbook, Nepal," July 2008 estimate, https://www.cia.gov/library/publications/the-world-factbook/geos/np.html (accessed February 28, 2009).

Gaine: Singers of texts that are improvised with current events, messages, stories, and myths. The primary instrument is the *sarangi* (an Indian bowed lute with three main strings and twenty-seven sympathetic strings; there are innumerable types) (Garland 5:696–708).

Badi: Traditionally nomadic musicians and dancers hired by upper castes as entertainers; more recently associated with the sex trade.

Some Nepalese musical instruments from the personal collection of I-to Loh:

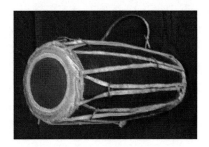

madal

concussion bells

Nepalese flute

trumpet

Commentary on Individual Hymns

"Christmas is here" (*STB* #304)
(Nepali*: Hera dajai*)

This song was composed in the typical Nepalese folk style, in which the music is sung in turn by girls and boys. It is a popular Christmas carol and has become a favorite Nepalese dance piece. In this lively and joyful carol, Loknath Manaen says that what happened long ago to the shepherds is now happening to all of us today: those who adore the Child will gain power to walk God's way. Manaen says "Old superstitions claimed to give guidance: they left us empty, downcast." He proclaims Christ entered our darkness to give us new life and stresses that this Child, who created the world, will sacrifice himself on the cross for saving and healing our deepest pain.

The time signature of HERA DAJAI (meaning "Look, brothers") combines the 3/4 and 6/8 times. It is in an F =1 seven-tone scale (1 2 3 4 5 6, with a flattened seventh, ♭7), making it different from other hymns. One could also sing this in a B♭-scale, from F = 5 (5 7 1 2). The hymn is quite long; the musical ideas repeat with variations and build naturally to the climax. The *madal* (double-headed drum) accompaniment supports the three- and two-beat rhythms (of 3/4 and 6/8 time). In the accompaniment score, the directions of the stems indicate the higher or lower pitch of the drum, which should be played without accents. This makes the singing more interesting. The music will flow smoothly if one conducts the whole hymn in 6/8 time (two counts per measure). This carol was collected in 1989 in Kathmandu, and the author/composer kindly provided the translations, but they were not ready for the 1990 edition of *Sound the Bamboo*. Thankfully, Father James Minchin paraphrased this for the 2000 version.

"Friends, listen humbly" (*STB* #208)
(Nepali: *Lau suna sathi satya ko bani*)

A powerful sermon or evangelism, this hymn is a personal witness that no other enticements or religions can satisfy our hearts except the sacrificial redemption of Christ. The author encourages people not to trust blindly the gurus or idols but to turn to Christ, our captain who is the Way, Truth, and Life.

KHALING is the family name of the author/composer. It is composed in a B = 3 eight-tone scale (G = 1 2 3 4 ♯4 5 6, with a flattened seventh, ♭7); it has a long refrain and two verses. Musically, the second half of the verse is the same as the refrain, making an A B A form. The text is contemplative, and the melody is very lyrical. Important features of this song are the three-beat reiterated tone pattern with the accent falling on the second beat, the gliding tones, and the ornaments. It may be more suitable for a soloist to sing the verses so that the congregation can listen carefully to the messages in the hymn and then join at the refrain. This hymn could be sung as part of a sermon or after the sermon. (trsl. Loknath Manaen: para. Jim Minchin)

"O give praise to Jesus" (*STB* #204)
(Nepali: *Jaya hos Yishu raja ko*)

This hymn gives praise to Christ our King, who died on the cross to set us free. The text of the second stanza is a decision to follow in his footsteps. The tune JAYA HOS YISHU (meaning "O give praise to Jesus, the King") is in an F = 1 seven-tone scale (1 2 3 4 5 6 7). It is in ABB'A form and belongs to the contemporary style that has Western influences, but the ornaments add the Nepalese musical flavor. The author/composer Dona Rongong wrote this hymn in 1976 for Vacation Bible School. Rongong has composed between forty and fifty songs; many of them, such as *Charai auney chan Yeshu raja*, *Uthi hera akashai ma*, and *Pratidhwani hoina*, are popular with Nepalese Christians. (trsl. Loknath Manaen: para. Shirley Murray)

"Oh! What a lovely day" (*STB* #138)

(Nepali: *A ho ka ti ramai lo*)

The structure of this Nepali hymn is similar to the Indian *kirtana* form (see the explanation in the India section), i.e., it is divided into three sections. The first four measures form the *pallavi*, the next six measures form the *anupallavi*, and the verse for eight measures forms the main part, the *charanam*. Except the first two phrases, all sections are repeated. This hymn is a Christmas carol, reflecting on the joy of and praising the birth of Jesus, who has come to be king in our hearts. The verse describes the small crying baby on the manger bed and expresses our willingness to offer our hearts to be ruled by him.

The tune KHRIST RAJA, meaning "Christ King," belongs to a contemporary Nepali style, i.e., semi-classical light music in a lively rhythm. In the F = 1 seven-tone scale (1 2 3 4 5 6 7), #4 appears only once. The author/composer John Dick Khawas, who is vision impaired, relates the background of this hymn:

> The song was composed in 1968 when I was in a hostel for a month of winter vacation. I was thinking of how to spend this long holiday. In that time, I received an invitation from one pastor: he wanted me to spend Christmas with him. I was so happy for this opportunity. I was pondering the love [of] God in the Christmas season, and my heart was filled with joy, so I composed this song *Aho Katee Ramailo Khushi ko din aayeo*.[73]

Khawas has produced one album called *Sakshi Ka Githaru* ("Song of Testimonies"), which contains fifty songs. He has composed Christian songs since 1962 and is revered as the foremost composer of Nepali devotional songs. (trsl. Loknath Manaen: para. Shirley Murray)

"Sun has gone, night has arrived" (*STB* #134)

(Nepali: *Bheri goth chharda ni chharda*)

This short Christmas carol by H. M. Lama uses a third person to ask the shepherds about their routine duties of tending their sheep and their startling encounter. Then the voice suddenly becomes that of the angels, telling them the good news, and urging them to go to Bethlehem to "see God cradled there, a baby!"

The melody COWSHED is in a B = 3 six-tone scale (3 5 6 7 1 2); it has two long phrases and ends on 5. The lovely melody, with childlike melancholy, is isorhythmic (repeating the same rhythmic pattern), except at the cadences. (trsl. Loknath Manaen: para. Jim Minchin)

---

73   From the author's correspondence with Khawas, March 27, 2006.

Conclusion

The analysis of five hymns cannot justify a conclusion about Nepal's musical style. However, while most of these songs are more recent in style and tend to use Western major scales, they exhibit distinctly Nepalese characteristics. Two long hymns are unique: "Christmas is here" (*STB* #304), which combines 3/4 time and 6/8 time with lots of excitement, and "Friends, listen humbly" (*STB* #208) is lyrical and full of ornaments. The Nepalese musical features of these two hymns overshadow their Western-influenced major tonality and thus make evident a Nepalese identity.

 # Pakistani Hymns

The Nation and Its People

Pakistan, which means "Land of the Pure" in Urdu, was created in 1947 from the partition of the British-controlled Indian subcontinent. The official name of the country became the Islamic Republic of Pakistan in 1956 (Athyal 1996, 467). Pakistan has an area of 803,940 square kilometers (about 310,403 square miles) and is bordered by India to the east, the People's Republic of China in the far northeast, Afghanistan and Iran to the west, and the Arabian Sea to the south. It is the sixth most populous country in the world, with an estimated population of 172,800,048,[74] and it is the second most populous country with a Muslim majority. Urdu is the national language, but Punjabi, Sindhi, Pashto, Balochi, and English are also spoken (Garland 5:5). Pakistan's identity as a Muslim country can be seen in the social, cultural, and religious aspects of daily life (Garland 5:744).

Pakistan is primarily a Muslim country, and the Islamic orthodoxy disapproves of music. However, the segregation of religious recitation (chanting of the Qur'an) leaves room for its development into art music. The founding of the National Institute for Folk Heritage in Islamabad has greatly enhanced the preservation, study, and development of Pakistani music. Further, political Islamization during the 1980s also helped the "Arabization" of music (Garland 5:745–747). During the past few decades, the mass distribution of cassette recordings spread the standard Islamic recitations cultivated in Egypt, and, since the 1990s, Western pop has had a stronger influence on music, especially in the use of electronic instruments (which is a worldwide phenomenon).

The region of Punjab, meaning "Land of Five Rivers," is split between India and Pakistan. With the 1947 partition, the region was divided into Indian East Punjab and Pakistani West Punjab, and hundreds of Muslim musicians in the east migrated to West Punjab. (Both provinces are now named Punjab by their respective countries.) Today, Punjabi musicians belong to low-status occupational groups (Garland 5:762). The *ghazal* is a form of romantic love poetry introduced to Punjab in the twelfth century from Persia (now Iran). It is performed to light classical music, emphasizing the supremacy of the text and the subservient role of the music (Garland 5:766).

---

74 CIA, "The World Factbook, Pakistan," July 2008 estimate, https://www.cia.gov/library/publications/the-world-factbook/geos/pk.html (accessed March 1, 2009).

The Psalms of the Pakistani Church

The Church of Pakistan was formed on November 1, 1970, taking the ancient Taxila Cross (related to the region's St. Thomas mission) as a symbolic emblem. The Church is a union of the Anglican Church of India, Pakistan, Burma, and Ceylon; the United Methodist Church in Pakistan; the United Church in Pakistan (Scottish Presbyterian); and the Pakistan Lutheran Church, with a total membership of 200,000 (Athyal 1996, 474).

Christians in Pakistan began composing hymns during the eighteenth century. According to Farhana Nazir,[75] the official hymnal for today's Pakistani mainline churches (including Catholic ones) is *Geet Ki Kitab* ("Book of Religious Songs"), and the other main source of hymns is the *Zabur*, the Book of Psalms. The term *zabur* means "song" or "music" and usually refers to a Punjabi psalm. According to Bishop John Samuel, the former General Secretary of CCA, Shahbaz was a Presbyterian pastor who was born in the latter half of the 1800s and died in the early 1900s. He was a talented musician, and he adapted many classical ragas and set Punjabi words to the music.

From the very beginning of the CCA's search for Asian hymns, contact with Pakistan has been limited. This resulted in the small number of hymns included in the 1990 edition of *Sound the Bamboo*. In 1992, at the Ecumenical Seminar on Liturgy and Music in Manila, Pakistani representatives introduced a few more hymns. All but two Pakistani selections in *Sound the Bamboo* (#73 and #120) are settings of psalms. Apparently, psalm singing has been very strong in the history of Pakistani churches, and most of these texts were set to traditional or folk melodies. This points to the possibility of a huge repertoire of contextualized psalmody in Pakistan that awaits further investigation.

Commentary on Individual Hymns

"Be joyful in the Lord, all lands" (*STB* #94)
(Punjabi: *Ae sab zamiinde loko*)

Punjabi is the common language of the historical Punjab region, which was split between India and Pakistan. Punjabi songs and hymns have thus originated from both countries, although some of them are no longer known as Punjabi songs. Psalms set to these songs are especially popular, and this selection is one example. The original Punjabi text had six stanzas; these were condensed in the English version into four stanzas by Francisco F. Feliciano. Psalm 100 is one of the most read and sung psalms in the Bible. It calls God's people to make joyful noises to the Lord and to enter God's house with thanksgiving, for the love and faithfulness of the Lord endures forever.

---

75   Nazir received a Master of Theology degree in 2004 from Princeton Theological Seminary.

The tune KHUSHI RAHO (meaning "live joyfully") is a traditional melody in an F = 1 seven-tone scale (1 2 3 4 5 6 7) with a lively 6/8 time. The Punjabi psalms (*zabur*) are very popular with their Punjabi melodies. This tune has five phrases in the form a b c b a': after the third phrase (c), the form reverses; the second phrase (b) is joined by the initial phrase (a) to conclude the song. The sixth measure (phrase c) is sometimes rendered as /6 - 54 4 - 4/ instead of /6 - 54 3 - 3/. This shows the dynamic of the oral tradition: both versions are acceptable. (trsl. Sherazi Almoos Hizqial)

"Blest be God, praised forever" (*STB* #40)

(Punjabi: *Rab ki hove sanaa hameshaa*)

This lively song of praise was recorded in Lahore in 1989. It is the paraphrase of a part of Psalm 150 and utilizes all musical instruments, including the tabla (a pair of drums common in northern India and Pakistan), to praise God. The second stanza suddenly switches from an Old Testament to a New Testament voice to praise Jesus as our Savior and Shepherd. The sixth stanza states "cymbals clash! drive out bad spirits and killjoys." Singing this hymn can replace a responsive reading of Psalm 150.

The tune SANAA ("praise") is apparently a contemporary melody in a C = 5, F = 1 seven-tone scale (1 2 3 4 5 6 7). In Pakistan, this type of hymn melody is a *geet* (religious song), not a *zabur*, which is more like a classical psalm. The ornaments and gliding tones, therefore, are important in bringing out the Punjabi characteristics. After singing the verse, one should sing the refrain again but proceed to the second ending without repeating. According to the folk tradition, there are two ways of singing the initial phrase: 61 1 and 51 1. The first version appeared in the 1990 edition of *Sound the Bamboo*. However, according to another entry in system four, 51 1 seems to be the style. It is recommended that the congregation sing the refrain in Punjabi. *Rab* is pronounced as two syllables: "ra-bə" ("ə" is a schwa, a neutral vowel). In fact, all of the final consonants in Punjabi (such as "s," "m," and "d") are voiced, i.e., one adds a schwa: "sə," "mə," "də." An improvised accompaniment of concussion bells (marked by "o" and "+" in the score), drum, and/or other Indian and Pakistani instruments is encouraged. (trsl. Samuel Paul: para Jim Minchin)

"Come soon, LORD, save me" (*STB* #86)

(Punjabi: *Yad Yahaovaa di sab karange*)

Based on Psalm 22:22–31, this prayer asks God not to turn his face from us but to pity our plight. Knowing that God's rescue is near, the author shifts from pleading to praise at the repetition of the refrain. The first stanza summons all nations and creations to praise God, who reigns. Stanza 2 points to the fact that all must die, so the author urges all to seek God, the source of life and hope. The last two stanzas remind future generations to make known God's faithfulness, mighty acts, and deliverance, even to people yet unborn.

This tune was recorded at a church in Lahore in 1989; hence, the tune is named LAHORE. This melody comes from the Pakistani psalm collection *Zabur*. It is a lively melody in a Phrygian scale (3 4 5 6 7 1 2). The music is in A B A form. The large skip at the beginning (<u>33</u> 1) and the repeated notes in the B section (<u>6666</u> <u>3333</u>) are special features of this song. Since the two stanzas in the Punjabi version are sung differently, the transcription appears complicated. But Ronald Hines's good paraphrase eliminates some of the syllables for easier rendering in English. When singing this hymn, one should add a schwa ("ə") to all of the final consonants that take a syllable, as described in the preceding commentary.

"Have mercy on us, LORD" (*STB* #120)
(Urdu: *Khudaayaa, raeham kar*)

Among the Asian Kyries, this one is the longest. I visited Pakistan in 1989 for the first time, looking for Pakistani hymns. I went to one of the Catholic centers in Karachi and was allowed to browse the library. After going through many piles of books, I found a handwritten manuscript with notations, which included this "Khudaayaa raeham kar." I was overwhelmed by the beauty and spiritual depth of this Kyrie. The signature of the composer, R. F. Liberius, was on the manuscript; I learned later that he was an Italian Roman Catholic priest serving in Pakistan. After returning to AILM, I felt that it was a pity that this beautiful tune lacked the typical embellishments. I added ornaments at crucial points, and a few Indian and Pakistani friends checked it for accuracy. Since then, I have introduced this Kyrie in the ecumenical meetings (WCC, CCA, WARC, LWF, etc.).

The melody of KHUDAAYAA (meaning "O God") is in an A = 3 natural minor scale (D = 6 7 1 2 3 4 5), and it is well organized. As is the case for most Kyries, it has three sections, A B A, each with three phrases. The musical and text organization are as follows:

Structural form:	A	B	A
Musical phrases*:	a b a	b c a	a b a
Text:	Lord	Christ	Lord
	have mercy	have mercy	have mercy

*Phrase cadences: a: closed b: open c: to climax and open

The climax occurs at phrase c: a big jump to the highest point, with the textual cry to the Messiah (*masii*) for mercy, and a slow glide down to the word *kar*. It is as if one's heart is torn because of the earnest plea for mercy. This is an excellent example of a piece of music perfectly matching the original text; it is also a powerful theological statement of one's deepest quest for and total reliance on God's mercy. The pronunciation of the syllable "khu" is like a guttural "hoo" with strong air in the throat. The word *raeham* should be pronounced "rah," as in "hat," and "hәm" with a schwa, a neutral vowel; the "m" sound should be closed and prolonged like a hum for the whole length of the note.

This song of prayer is so powerful that it has moved many people in worship services.

During the 1992 "Justice, Peace, and Integrity of Creation" Conference of the World Council of Churches in Seoul, Korea, the animateurs led the singing in the late-morning sessions, when most of the participants were still fiercely debating and were not enthusiastic about singing. When it was my turn to lead, I went to the podium and began to sing this song with the accompaniment of a pair of small concussion bells. Before the end of the first phrase, the hall was quiet, and all of the participants joined from the second phrase to pray for God's mercy. Later, some expressed how they were moved by the piece. Its spiritual quality captures the hearts of the people and compels one to kneel humbly before God. I thank the Lord for the gift of this Kyrie to the ecumenical world.

"I'll teach and instruct you the way you should go" (*STB* #89)
(Punjabi: *Sikhavañ ga thenuñ vikhavañ ga rah*)

This is a short paraphrase of Psalm 32:8–11, admonishing people not to be like a horse or a mule without comprehension but to put their trust in God and rejoice as God's children. The music SIKHAVAÑ (meaning "teaching") is in an Eb = 1 seven-tone scale (1 2 3 4 5 6 7) with ABA' form. The reiterated tone motif at the beginning of the respective sections (1/ 1 11 1, 5 /5 55 5) is the major characteristic of this song. This psalm comes from the Reverend Shahbaz's *Zabur* collection. (trsc. & trsl. Sherazi Almoos Hizqial; para. Jim Minchin)

"Jesus, Savior Lord, lo to you I fly" (*STB* #59)
(Thamilz: *Yesu raajenin thiruvediku*)
See the commentary in the India section.

"My people, bless the name of God Messiah" (*STB* #34)
(Punjabi: *Rahe gaa naam sadaa tiker ma sih daa*)

This is a hymn of praise to the holy name of God, the Messiah, taken from the Reverend Shahbaz's *Zabur*. The main text is adapted from Psalm 72:17–19, but the author Christianized the psalm, as did the Englishman Isaac Watts (1674–1748), by calling nations to turn to Christ for peace and guidance. The literal translation of the original first stanza reads:

The name of the Messiah remains forever;
He will remain as long as you see the sun.

The tune PAK NAAM (meaning "pure name") is in an F = 1 seven-tone scale (1 2 3 4 5 6 7); it has only two phrases of three measures each. The melismatic ending of the first phrase (with several notes to one syllable) and the other ornaments may seem difficult, but they are the soul of this tune and should not be left out. Simply treat the ornaments like very short and light "shakes" or appoggiatura, and they will come out naturally. (trsl. Sherzi A. Hizqial; para. Jim Minchin)

"O Lᴏʀᴅ, God in heaven and powerful Creator" (*STB* #293)

(Punjabi: *Khudaa vandha thuñ lashkarañ*)

This is a Punjabi paraphrase of Psalm 84, verses 1, 2, and 4: "Our hearts are longing to dwell in God's temple and sing God's praise." The Punjabi melody KHUDAA VANDHA (meaning "O God") is taken from the Reverend Shahbaz's *Zabur* collection; it is in a G = 6 six-tone scale (6 7 1 2 3 5). Musically, it is in an ABA form. The B section is a strong contrast from A, with a higher melody expressing a longing for and the joy of dwelling in God's house. Since the text varies upon repeating the refrain, note the lowercase letters at the beginning of the text, which indicate the order for singing the stanza, such as: a, b, verse (with the second system repeated, followed by the third system), c. The original first phrase reads: "O God, you are God of all peoples." (para. Jim Minchin)

"O Lord Jesus, enfold me in your arms" (*STB* #73)

(Urdu: *Prabhu lele mujhee tuñ baahoñ meñ*)

A prayer to Jesus to enfold one and to never part, this hymn was written by a young musician named Samuel Paul. It is a commitment to follow Christ, to bring the lost to discover joy, and to witness truth.

The tune PRABHU LELE (meaning "Lord, hold me") was composed by the author. It is in an A = 6 seven-tone scale (6 7 1 2 3 4 5) plus a sharpened 2, with the final on 3. When the composer taught this song during the 1987 Asian Workshop on Liturgy and Music in Makiling, Philippines, he sometimes sang the A (7*6 7) and G (7*5 6, both marked with *) higher, either as sharps or higher microtones, thus making the melody seem more romantic in style. (para. Shirley Murray)

"Praise the Lord, to God give praises" (*STB* #295)

(Punjabi: *Karo Rab dhi hun vadhyai*)

This is a simplified Punjabi paraphrase of Psalm 148, summoning all creatures, dancing angels, hosts of heaven, sun, moon, and constellations to praise God, venerate their Maker, and sing God's glory. The original Punjabi text has only three stanzas while the English has five.

The tune name KARO RAB comes from the first two words of the first phrase. *Rab* means God. The two original Punjabi lines read: "God be praised now, and be exalted as high as the heavens." This hymn is taken from the Reverend Shahbaz's *Zabur*. All the tunes in that psalm collection are attributed to Shahbaz, but they are popularly known as Punjabi melodies. The tune is in an E♭ = 1 six-tone scale (1 2 3 4 5 6) with a simple a a b b' form, but it is syllabic in setting (with one syllable per note). (trsl. Sherazi A. Hizqial; para. Jim Minchin)

"Restless, I wait in prayer for you" (*STB* #294)

(Punjabi: *Theri najath dhe shouk dhe wich*)

The power and glories of God's law have always been the dream of poems and the hope of the distressed. This paraphrase of Psalm 119:81–88 is a cry to God: "When will you come to save me? . . . How long before you comfort me?" God's Word and the Torah are the sources of hope, as the poet concludes:

> My foes have nearly sapped my strength:
> I refused to let your precepts go.
> Spare my life, show your steadfast love,
> Then I will keep your mouth's decrees.

The tune THERI NAJATH ("your salvation") is taken from the Reverend Shahbaz's *Zabur* collection; it was possibly composed by Shahbaz but is known as a Punjabi melody. The melodic construction is rather complicated. If it is described as a G scale (G = 1 2 3 4 5 6 7), then one should add a sharp on the fourth tone (♯4, C♯) and flatten the seventh degree (♭7, F), i.e., 1 2 3 ♯4 5 6 ♭7. Thus the melody would be sung as 3 2 3 1 2 6 ♭7 6 5. If it is a D scale (D = 1), then the third tone (3) should be flattened (♭3, F♮), i.e., 1 2 ♭3 4 5 6 7; thus it should be sung as 6 5 6 4 5 2 ♭3 2 1. People are free to choose whichever scale seems easier. The melodic idiom is Punjabi in style, with 6/8 time, and it is very rhythmic. The A B A phrase structure makes it easier to sing. Since the repetitions of text and music are slightly different, follow the lowercase letters: the order should be a, b, verse, c (see *STB* #293, "O Lord, God in heaven and powerful Creator" for further explanation). (para. Jim Minchin)

Conclusion

From the analyses of these hymns, one realizes that psalm singing is characteristic of the Pakistani church. The psalm settings are mostly in ABA form (*STB* #86, #89, #293, #294). In other settings, some of the phrases are repeated (e.g., *STB* #94: a b c b a ; #295: a a b b), and none of them are through-composed. This indicates that the composers have clear ideas of composition. Among the eleven Pakistani hymns, seven of them have their final or tonal center on 1 (*do*), i.e., melodies are constructed in major scales. Two hymns (*STB* #120 and #293) are in minor scales with the tonal center on 6 (*la*), and two hymns (#73 and #86) are centered on 3 (*mi, similar* to the Phrygian scale). Although some of the melodic progressions may reflect similarities with those of the West, which might indicate Western influence, the composers have mostly retained the traditional idioms and typical ornaments and thus preserved the tunes' Punjabi and national identities.

Sri Lankan Hymns

The Nation, Its People, and Their Religions

"Lanka" or "island" was the name of this land in the Indian epics, and "Sri" is an honorific title meaning "sacred." Sri Lanka's civilization began over 2500 years ago. The island was colonized by the Portuguese in the sixteenth century and the Dutch in the seventeenth century. It became known as Ceylon when the British gained control in 1796, and it became a crown colony in 1802. Affiliations with the British crown ended in 1948, and the country's name was restored in 1972, when the new constitutional republic was formed. Sri Lanka has an area of approximately 65,610 square kilometers (about 25,332 square miles), located about thirty-nine kilometers (or about twenty-four miles) from the southern tip of India (Garland 5:954).It has a population of 21,128,772, of which Sinhalese constitute 73.8%, Sri Lankan Tamil 3.9%, Indian Tamil 4.6%, and Sri Lankan Moors 7.2%; other and unspecified groups form 10.5%.[1] The Sinhalese (an Indo-Aryan people) migrated in the sixth or fifth century BCE from India, and Buddhism was introduced in the third century BCE. A great civilization developed around the cities of Anuradhapura (from about 200 BCE to about 1000 CE) and Polonnaruwa (from about 1070 to 1200). The Indian Tamils established a kingdom during the thirteenth century (Athyal 1996, 435).

Buddhists compose about 69% of the population, Hindus 15%, and Christians and Muslims each make up 7.6%. Christian communities were formed in Sri Lanka as early as the sixth century. Roman Catholicism arrived with the Portuguese in 1505; Dutch Protestant missions began in 1602. The London Missionary Society sent its representatives to the island in 1805, followed by many other denominations. The medical or educational missions of these churches have gained respect and recognition from local communities[76] (Athyal 1996, 436–42).

After 450 years under colonial rule, the recently independent country has regained its identity through the restoration of two languages, Sinhalese (or Sinhala) and Thamilz, and Buddhism. In the eyes of most Sri Lankans, Christianity is associated with Western imperialism and should have been eliminated after the country's liberation; in turn, Buddhist education is encouraged, and all public ceremonies are conducted with Buddhist rituals (Hoke 1975, 593f). It is encouraging to see that more Christians are involved in nation building and in working for justice, human rights, and labor welfare. Christian support of the labor unions is important, especially as demonstrated in the Workers' Mass celebrated on May Day (see *STB* hymns #9, #191, and #229). Sri Lankan Christians utilize contextual signs, symbolic acts, and music to express their faith, love, and care for their country and people.

---

76   CIA, "The World Factbook, Sri Lanka," July 2008 population estimate and 2001 census provisional data, https://www.cia.gov/library/publications/the-world-factbook/geos/ce.html (accessed March 3, 2009).

Traditional Music

It was once understood that there were three genres of Sri Lankan music:

1) intoned recitation: a narrow three-tone scale for reciting Vedic and other chants
2) Indian Buddhist music: of the Theravada tradition, which has coexisted and competed with Islamic music and music of older religions
3) Islamic, non-Indian music (Garland 5:956f)

However, more recent studies indicate a long tradition of Sinhalese music without a written theory and transmitted orally from teacher to pupil. The most popular Sinhala drum is called *gata bera* (a double-headed barrel drum, played by both hands), which can be seen in festivals and folk performances. Probably due to Sri Lanka's long duration under colonial rule and Western influence, the contemporary music is like "light music" in India: the melodies are syllabic and have reiterated tones, stepwise progressions, and major tonalities. Tabla drums, guitars, flutes, and violins are used for accompaniment.

The enduring conflict between the Sinhalese and the Tamils has resulted in many tragedies. The following modern psalm by Rex Joseph offers one account of the situation.[77]

"How Can I Sing to Thee, Oh Lord?"

1. My soul Oh God wishes to praise thee
   but when I look round and the suffering see
   it loses all the zealous fervour
   to sing to thee Oh my Creator.

2. Children have become helpless orphans.
   Parents have lost their teen-age sons,
   Wives have lost their handsome husbands.
   They've been killed by soldiers and militants.

3. Blood flows around me like spiteful rivers.
   Cries of pain jar right into my ears.
   Dead human bodies stink on the way side
   People watch them and go on to the other side.

4. The rich here sit on banquets every day;

---

77   *Asia Journal of Theology* 5, no. 1 (April 1991): 130f.

the poor on the other hand eat only once a day.
The price of food is as high as the mountain
For the poor; even bread is like the fruit forbidden.

5.   Thugs march out in vociferous demonstrations
the citizens hide inside houses with trepidation
Frauds have taken the reins of the nation
The just person is but a matter of derision.

6.   Children suffer today without proper education
Abels die in plenty by Cain's assassinations.
A silky sweet flower lies crushed on the track[78]
The hearts of her parents and brothers into pieces crack.

7.   The good and the righteous suffer in life
while evil doers thrive like hive.
Even the dog howls at the righteous with indignation
And the heavens too hail the might with celebration.

8.   Can I fiddle and strum when my house burns to consumption
or rhyme and dance when my nation plunges into deterioration.
When will poor and oppressed have favourable life situation,
Then will to thee a hymn of praise ring loud in unison.

Commentary on Individual Hymns

"Calvary's work is complete" (*STB* #275)
(Sinhala: *Kalvari yanavä*)

This hymn, written by E. Walter Marasinghe, is like talking to the risen Christ, relating that he dined with his disciples following his resurrection and commissioned them to scatter the good news of love. Then the author calls singers to be Christ's true followers and tell his stories in song. The refrain is a praise and prayer to Christ to "breathe your peace on the world." This hymn is appropriate for singing after a sermon or before sending forth by the choir. Let the congregation join at the refrain as a prayer to Christ.

---

78   This line refers to the author's only daughter, who was eleven years old when she was run over by an Indian military vehicle while returning home after Sunday worship.

The tune KALVARI YANAVA, meaning "going to Calvary," was composed by a vision-impaired scholar/poet/composer, D. P. M. Weerakkody. The musical form is somewhat complicated. After the introduction and refrain, both of which are in an Eb = 1 seven-tone scale (1 2 3 #4 5 6 7) and repeated (with the first interlude in between), the verse begins in the B section, which is to be sung by a soloist. Not only does the music change to an eight-tone scale with two sharpened tones (Eb = 1 2 #2 3 #4 5 6 7), it also ascends to a series of high Fs with an ornate melody, coinciding with lyrics about Christ seated at the table with the disciples. After the second interlude, the contrasting C section follows in a lower register (Bb = 5 6 b7 1 2 3) with reciting tones and the introduction of b7. The similar endings of the three sections unify this song. The complex nature of this piece makes it difficult for a congregation to sing. Therefore, the composer suggests that the congregation sing only the introduction and refrain (A section) and that the choir or soloists sing the rest. Notice the performance form, with repetitions as indicated: Introduction – Refrain – Introduction – Interlude I – B – Interlude II – C – Refrain – Interlude I – B –Interlude II – C – Refrain. (para. Jim Minchin)

"Cold is the edge of the night wind" (*STB* #272)

This carol by E. Walter Marasinghe is a poetic and imaginative reflection of the birth of Christ. For instance, the first stanza reads:

> Star to say "Here is no creature:
> lying below is a baby,
> in him the full divine nature."

The second stanza describes the context:

> Tinkle of cowbell in stable,
> echoes the heavenly ringing.

The third stanza poses the critical question:

> Where, Lord, the key of his Kingdom,
> opening the gate to your city?
> Only the child-like can find it,
> held in the hands of your pity.

The meditative nature of the text makes this a good hymn to be sung by the choir as a sermon or after a sermon on the meaning of the birth of Jesus. The congregation responds by singing the second half of the hymn.

The author also composed the tune SISILA SULANGA, which means "cool wind." The melody uses a seven-tone scale (C = 1 2 3 4 5 6 7), but 4 only appears once near the beginning, and 7 appears twice. The hymn begins with a low-key, recitative style (C = 1 3 3 3 3 43 2 3-) for a soloist to tell the story; the congregation then sings the important message in the second section (the second time with harmony) and, with more vitality, the last two systems, where the most important messages are stated. The flute prelude and interlude are important for creating the mood. The simple two-part harmony, although not indigenous, utilizes a variation of the drone in Indian and Sri Lankan traditional music, which does not hinder the style. The ornaments in the second to last system demonstrate the beauty of Sri Lankan singing. Although the song is in a major scale, the final ending on 3 (*mi*) makes this song somewhat exotic.

"Draw near, God of grace, we pray" (*STB* #74)
(Sinhala: *Vaa vaa arul arasee*)

This is a prayer for God to dwell with us, "your Church, your Bride," and to help us seek God's will. It also says "we will follow you through pain and strife . . . so that we bear others' grief." This hymn may be sung as a prayer for guidance near the conclusion of the service.

The melody THEVARAM, meaning "invocation [to God]," was first taught by the Reverend D. S. Dharmapalan in the United States. He also set a different text that appeared in the 1990 edition of *Sound the Bamboo*:

> Come, O gracious Lord, O come; let your presence us refine.
> Give your blessings, Lord, we pray; holy and righteous one, O come.
>
> May your graciousness attend, that our prayers to you ascend.
> Lend yourself to us, we pray; with your mercies us array.

Dharmapalan's text is an opening hymn, to be sung by the choir or congregation as an invocation. In one of the workshops in Manila, I found a Sri Lankan participant who knew the original text of this hymn. She provided the new text for paraphrasing by Jim Minchin.

The E♭ = 1 seven-tone scale (1 2 3 4 5 6 ♭7), the embellishments and the ♭7 are important features of this melodious song, which can be accompanied with concussion bells on the first beat of each measure.

"Full of wondrous beauty are God's artful ways"
See "THE GRANDEUR OF GOD" (*STB* #179)

"God's own light came to earth" (*STB* #271)

(Sinhala: *A lōkaya āvā*)

E. Walter Marasinghe interprets the birth of Christ as the coming of God's own light to the earth. This light will "warm every corner of the universe," will "awaken the happiness of . . . people abandoned into slavery," and will shine everywhere "with beauty and joy to the end of all the centuries."

Marasinghe also composed the setting for this unusual Christmas hymn. The tune name ALOKAYA AVA means "the light has come." The composer uses a G = 3 eight-tone scale (C = 6 7 1 #1 2 3 #4 5), in which #1 appears twice and #4 only once. The main motif (3 5 6 75 6-) and the sequences of motivic imitations (11 66 22 11 and 61 71, 35 3 6) carry the lively melody to its climax before returning to the theme to conclude the song. Although the song may look complicated, it is not very difficult to sing. One suggestion is for a soloist to sing the verse, and the congregation can join in the refrain. This hymn may be sung in services on the theme of Jesus being the light of the world or relating to his ministry and salvation.

"In the coldness of night" (*STB* #273)

(Sinhala: *Sithala ra yame*)

This hymn tells the story of the nativity of Christ. It does not romanticize the beauty of the event but describes the "little master," who empathizes with suffering children:

> Huddled in their huts and clinging to their mothers' breast,
> rags they wear against the cold and cannot hope for rest.

The author E. Walter Marasinghe even tells the baby Jesus what his future sufferings will be: "You will bear our load of sorrow, all our sin and shame." Since the verse is a conversation with the Christ Child, a soloist or a unison choir can sing it as a part of a sermon or a response to a sermon, and the congregation can join at the refrain.

Marasinghe's tune SITHALA RA YAME, meaning "in the coolness of the moonlight," is similar in style to his other compositions: it is in a major scale, has a fast rhythm with repeated tones in a recitative style, and uses sequences (21 76, 76 55, 6532 1-). The form is simple: prelude – refrain – verses – refrain. (para. Jonathan Malicsi & Jim Minchin)

"LORD, have mercy" (*STB* #300)

(Sinhala: *Swamin wahanse*)

This short Kyrie was taught by a young man attending the CCA Training Program in Seoul in 1993. The rhythm and embellishments are important for conveying the earnest prayer for mercy. Make sure that the first line is repeated after the second line. For congregations unfamiliar with the style, they can repeat after the worship leader. It is recommended to sing this hymn in Sinhala. The last syllables of *wahanse* and *manawa* are pronounced with a schwa ("ə," a neutral vowel). For accompaniment, a pair of concussion bells may be played at the first and the last note of each phrase. This Kyrie is appropriate as the congregation's response to short prayers of confession, intercession, and petition. Make sure that the congregation is ready to respond immediately after each prayer. (trsc. I. L.)

"My soul doth magnify the Lord" (*STB* #103)

As paraphrased by the Sri Lankan theologian/poet D. T. Niles, and matched to an Indonesian folk song from Maluku, this Magnificat shows the global and ecumenical aspect of magnifying the Lord for the good news of salvation. The hymn acknowledges the power of the Holy Spirit turning the world upside down. This is what Christians should look for and expect to happen in the world today. Liturgically, the Magnificat is often sung at evening services, but it can also be used for any occasion as a thanksgiving, praise, response, or commitment to God's redeeming love.

The tune GUNUNG NONA, meaning "Miss Mountain," is a folk song from eastern Indonesia, with a C = 5 six-tone scale (F = 1 2 3 4 5 6) in a lively 6/8 time. When the Maluku people climb the beautiful mountain on Ambon Island for recreation, they sing this song, moving their bodies in a slow yet joyful rhythm. According to Christian Tamaela, the original text of this song is "Naik-naik ke Gunun Nona." It is not clear who adapted this tune or when it was adapted for Christian usage. D. T. Niles's text first appeared with this tune in the *EACC Hymnal* in 1963. It has become one of the most popular hymns in ecumenical gatherings, not only in Asia but also in other parts of the world.

It is common for Indonesian men to improvise harmony with thirds or sixths to sound more "contemporary." The rhythm of this hymn's drum accompaniment is important for portraying an authentic style. The upward stems denote high pitches, produced by striking the rim of the *tifa* drum with the fingertips of the right hand while the fingers of the left hand presses on the drumhead. The downward stems denote deeper and more open sounds produced by the right hand striking the center of the drumhead. Make sure that the triplets are on the strong first and fourth beats of the six-beat pattern. A guitar accompaniment is also popular with this song.

The original text and translation are:

NAIK-NAIK KE GUNUNG NONA
(Climb up, Climb up the Miss Mountain)[4]
(*Naik* = "climb up"; *ke* = "to")

Naik-naik ke Gunung Nona (Climb up, climb up the Miss Mountain)
Kusu - kusu melulu (The green grass are covering the mountain)
Balik muka, kanan dan kiri (Turn around the face, right and left)
Laut biru melulu (I see the blue sea around me)
Meski cinta, tinggal cinta (Even though there is love, and keep in love)
Mama panggil pulang dulu e (Mother is calling me to go home)
Meski cinta, tinggal cinta (Even though there is love, and keep in love)
Mama panggil pulang e (Mother is calling me to go home)

(trsl. Christian I. Tamaela, 12/19/06)

"O Father God, we give you praise" (*STB* #16)
(Sinhala: *Deviyani obatai*)

This simple yet solemn song by Nirmal Mendis praises the triune God by repeating one word, the title of the tune, PRASANGSA, meaning "praise." This hymn was taught by the same young Sri Lankan who introduced the Kyrie (*STB* #300) in Seoul, Korea, in 1993. The music begins in the lowest register, using a minor-third ascending motif ($\underline{6}$ /1 $\underline{1}$ 1-) and moving upward in sequence. In the second system, the motif is reversed, with a descending major third ($\underline{6}$ /4 $\underline{4}$ 4-). The second half of the song begins with a major motif ($\underline{1}$/ 3- 3-. $\underline{3}$/5 - 5-.), reaches the climax ($\underline{5}$ /i - i -.), and returns to the initial motif to conclude. Care should be taken to observe the time changes between three and four counts in each measure. A pair of concussion bells may accompany this hymn; strike them once on each strong beat. Notice that the syllable "pra" is pronounced "prə." This hymn is appropriate as a song of praise at the beginning of worship. It may also be used effectively at evening prayer, with a soft but wholehearted spirit of thanksgiving and praise. (para. I. L. & J. M.)

"O most holy, O most holy" (*STB* #286)
(Sinhala: *Athi shudha, athi shudha*)

This is an anonymous hymn of prayer: people gathering in God's name, addressing the holy Trinity to send blessings for our understanding of God's great love. The author acknowledges that our hope is in Jesus' mercy and pleads for the Spirit to give us strength to see God's will done. This hymn is appropriate as a prayer of trust and for guidance.

The tune ATHI SHUDHA, meaning "most holy" is in a C = 5 seven-tone scale (F = 1 2 3 4 5 6 7). It uses a prominent motif ($\underline{71}$ 2 2) and repeated tones ($\underline{11}$ 1 1, $\underline{55}$ 5 5) and develops in sequential phrases ($\underline{34}$ 5 5 , $\underline{23}$ 4 4 , $\underline{12}$ 3 3) through the song. This simple song is a children's favorite, which I recorded in Colombo during a Sunday school session in 1996. (para. Shirley Murray)

"Son of the Father" (*STB* #191)

(Sinhala: *Jesuni devputh rajathumane*)

This hymn, written by Edmund Sydney Waragoda, is taken from the Sri Lankan Workers' Mass. Sri Lankan Christians have been very active in upholding justice and human rights. The Workers' Mass is a part of the May Day Celebration of the Laborers. The text of this hymn addresses Jesus as "Son of the Father . . . Lord and slave, . . . worker's friend . . . author of our faith." He is the "Seed of the Father . . . lover of the soil, man of earth, son of toil." The fifth stanza concludes the prayer: Lift our spirit, guide our wills, steer our hands, use our skills;

> Lord, we worship you with hand and mind.

Asia has many manual laborers and agrarian workers, and this last phrase sums up the most important theology of Asian Christians today: We worship God with hand and mind. In other words, worship and life, faith and deeds, evangelism and social service, and love and justice are inseparable. This is also one of the emphases of the mission of WCC and CCA.

The name of the anonymous tune is RAJATHUMANE, which is an honorific for "king." It is in an A = 5 seven-tone scale (D = 1 2 3 4 5 6 7); it is syllabic (with one syllable per eighth note) and should be sung at a moderate tempo (approximately eighty-eight beats per minute). The second half of the song begins with a skipping motif (51 11), which is imitated in downward sequences (57 7, 46 6, 35 5). To describe Jesus' birth as a human being, the melody stays within a narrow range of the middle register; when portraying Jesus as one with God, the pitches jump upward. To illustrate Jesus' humbling himself and shunning wealth, the music moves downward in a sequence. In the final phrase, the music rises again (11 34 55 67 1-), to signify our worshiping and praising the Lord on high. Thus, the song describes the meaning of Jesus' incarnation as well as our adoration of Him.

Jeffrey Abayasekera taught me this hymn in Hong Kong in 1968, after we attended a seminar sponsored by the Urban and Rural Mission Committee of CCA in the Kyoto Kwansei Christian Seminar House. This experience marked the beginning of my journey to collect new Asian hymns for CCA. In early 1972, Fred Kaan was invited to the editorial meeting with Masao Takcnaka and me in Jakarta, and he paraphrased this hymn to the present form. It is not a direct translation. This hymn first appeared in the 1972 *New Songs of Asian Cities* and was subsequently included in the 1980 full-harmony edition of *Cantate Domino*, the WCC hymnal. The superimposed Western harmonic setting in that publication seemed to imply that the Sri Lankan workers had to wear Western suits and ties in their worship.

"Sun and moon and stars above" (*STB* #283)

(Sinhala: *Hiru sandu tharu* ["*Hiru sandawa tharu*" is a mistake.])

Describing the wonder and beauty of God's creation in the universe and on earth, this hymn summons all parents, brothers, sisters, friends, and neighbors, who are all children of our loving Father, to come and praise the King and accept the Lord. It also acknowledges joy in worshiping God and safety in God's care. It is a prayer for making us pure in heart and filling our lives with peace and joy.

Similar to other Sri Lankan songs, the tune DEV PASASUM ("praise to God") is syllabic, with reiterated tones and a stepwise progression (55 56 54 32 1) in a major scale. This hymn was recorded as sung by a group of Sunday school children in Colombo, after the 1996 CCA General Assembly. A lively rhythm and constantly moving melody make this a joyful song of praise. (para. Shirley Murray)

"THE GRANDEUR OF GOD"
("Full of wondrous beauty are God's artful ways," *STB* #179)

Describing the beauty of the universe, E. Walter Marasinghe helps us to comprehend the wisdom of God and the wonders and functions of God's creation. Words are inadequate to tell of God's worth, so Marasinghe concludes:

All we can do is to rest in God's arms,
captured by one Name, Love, and its sweet charms.

Father James Minchin skillfully paraphrased this hymn with beautiful inner rhymes on every fourth syllable, as seen from the second line of each stanza.

First stanza: "listen, my friends, Spirit descend,"
Second stanza: "rivers flow down rifts in the ground;"
Third stanza: "lion's warning growl, wolves' cruel howl;"
Fourth stanza: "moon's lustrous light hallows the night;"
Fifth stanza: "heaven and earth tell of God's worth."

The tune DEV TUMA MAV, meaning "the whole world that the LORD has made," was also composed by the author. It is in a G = 3 E♭ major scale (1 2 3 4 5 6 7). The second half begins from a high note and comes down gradually, with descending three-tone motifs in sequence (1 65, 6 53, 5 31), making the melodic progression very logical and easy to sing. The repetition of the last two measures creates a sense of serenity. This is a good hymn of praise for God's creation. It can also be a calm and introspective meditation on the wonder of God's love.

"This is the story" (*STB* #199)

(Sinhala: *Natha thithee nathi soka biya*)

This hymn retells the story of the lost sheep with an emphasis on the shepherd's resolve to overcome all hardships to search for and rescue the lamb. The last stanza asks the Lord why his body is bruised, torn, and bleeding. The author alludes to Christ's redeeming act, quoting Jesus: "This is my blood I have poured out for your sake." Thus, the lost sheep is equated with each one of us. Musically, the last two phrases of each stanza contrast the foolishness of the lost sheep against the love of the shepherd, as reflected in the text: "Step after step, he went wand'ring far away" against "Though it grows dark, I must go and search for him" and "His loving feet found their way home to the lamb" against "This is my blood I have poured out for your sake."

The composer of NATHA THITHEE is anonymous. The tune, in an E = 3 C-major scale (C = 1 2 3 4 5 6 7), also features the popular style: a major scale with sequential development (5 55 6--, 6 66 7--, 7 77 1) near the end. This hymn was also collected from a recording of Sunday school children in Colombo in 1996.

The first line of the hymn can also appear as "Nada didee nathi soka biya." (para. Shirley Murray)

"We worship you, Creator God" (*STB* #9)

(Sinhala: *Namo namo mavunkarun*)

This is one of the most beautiful and authentic indigenous hymns in *Sound the Bamboo*. It was taught by Jeffrey Abayasekera in 1968. The hymn pays reverent homage to God the Trinity. The content is similar to the Indian *bhajans* that praise the attributes of God, from whom we find solace, peace, grace, and joy. It concludes with a plea to this "Source of Being . . . Word of Light, incarnate Love, the Way to bliss . . . Breath of peace" to come into our midst as we worship.

The tune NAMO NAMO, meaning "worship," is in a D = 3 #5 6 7 1 #1 2 3 eight-tone scale with a speech-like rhythm; it frequently uses #5 6 for the cadences. The melody develops slowly until the climax in the third phrase, which introduces a new pitch (#1). The melody then returns to the second half of the first phrase and ends on 7. This final tone is unusual according to Western practice, but it is familiar to people in Sri Lanka and Indonesia. It seems to create an unfinished feeling, implying that worship should continue in daily life, without end. When singing this hymn, the congregation should repeat each phrase after the leader. If possible, the first stanza should be sung in the original language to acquire the spirit of the tune. This hymn may be sung at the beginning of worship or at anytime one desires to pay homage to God. One should respect the integrity of the song by singing it without any harmony. (para. J. M.)

"Worship the Lord, worship the Father" (*STB* #229)

This hymn, like *STB* #191, "Son of the Father," was taught by Jeffrey Abayasekera in 1968 in Hong Kong. It is excerpted from the Offertory Hymn (of the Elements for Holy Communion as well as other gifts) in the May Day service (see the commentary on *STB* #191). The text states that worshiping the Triune God means offering to serve humanity, to risk and sacrifice, and to be united as a true community through the bread and wine on the table. It concludes with a prayer for a just and healing society. Only by so doing can worship and work become one. Fred Kaan composed a free paraphrase of this anonymous hymn for the 1972 *New Songs of Asian Cities*. It was then included in the full-music edition of the 1980 WCC hymnal, *Cantate Domino*, edited by Erik Routley. The Sixth General Assembly of the WCC in 1983 opened with this hymn; since then, it has been popular in many ecumenical functions.

The tune is named PIYADEVI, meaning "God the Father." The melody is in a major scale and was originally a carpenter's song. The setting is syllabic and rhythmic and has sequences (133 333 343 217, 122 222 232 176) and repeated figures (565 565). Thanks to Kaan's craft in paraphrasing, the hymn is not difficult to sing, but it should not be sung too fast. With the 6/8 time, the first and fourth eighth notes should be sung with slight accents so that the music flows. While the hymn is intended as an offertory in the service of Holy Communion, it may be used for the general offering or as an opening hymn.

Conclusion

Sri Lanka has produced indigenous Sinhala music, but there are some Indian influences, such as the use of violin, guitar, sitar, harmonium, and tabla accompaniment. Sri Lankan texts are interesting and have theological depth, and the music is mostly lively and syllabic. As a likely result of the country's long colonial status, Sri Lankan composers have internalized Western musical idioms. Nearly one third of these eleven hymns use major scales and end on 1; two hymns end on 6. Only two lyrics have peculiar features: *STB* #9 begins with 3 but ends with 7, and *STB* #16 uses 6 as the initial but 1 as the final. Sinhala Christians should reclaim their traditional musical heritage and develop new styles to strengthen their Sri Lankan musical identity.

THE SOUTHWEST PACIFIC OCEAN

The Southwest Pacific Ocean region includes Australia, New Zealand, and Papua New Guinea.

 # Australian Hymns

The Nation, Its People, Its Music Cultures

Australia, situated in the southern Pacific, has an area of 7,686,850 square kilometers (about 2,967,909 square miles) and a population of 21,007,310.[79] The continent's earliest inhabitants migrated at least forty thousand years ago from what is now Southeast Asia; indigenous Australians constitute about 2.6% of the current population. These people speak 111 indigenous languages, reduced from more than 260 languages extant two hundred years ago (Johnstone 2001, 83). Australia's modern history began in 1788 when the British government established a settlement at Port Jackson, in the present Sydney, for convicts and soldiers (Garland 9:408). Today, Christians constitute approximately 67.5% of the population, but rapid Asian immigration and increasing numbers of non-religious people are lowering this figure. Of the Christian population, Roman Catholics represent 25.21%, Anglicans 20.23%, and Protestants 12.83% (Johnstone 2001, 83). Historically, as the number of European immigrants increased, so also did their contact with indigenous Australians. For example, indigenous people were invited to perform their music and dances for immigrant audiences, and musical styles brought by the European immigrants have affected indigenous musical styles.

Australia has two indigenous traditions: the Aboriginal Australian and the Torres Strait Islander (Garland 9:410). In central Australia, Aboriginal men sing songs to the accompaniment of clapsticks, but women accompany themselves by beating rhythms on their bodies. In Arnhem Land in northern Australia, solo singing is accompanied by clapsticks; the most important musical instrument is the *didjeridu*. The *didjeridu* is a kind of wooden trumpet measuring about one to one and one-half meters (about three to five feet) long, which is blown with loose lips to produce the fundamental tone as a drone. Overtones, such as a tenth or eleventh above, may be produced through overblowing (Garland 9:393–95). The rich harmonic tones, pulsations, and rhythmic patterns that a good performer can produce with a *didjeridu* led to the instrument's popularity during the last few decades of the twentieth century, and it has become a national symbol of Aboriginal Australian music.

Australian *didjeridu* (made in Bali)

---

79   CIA, "The World Factbook, Australia," July 2008 estimate, https://www.cia.gov/library/publications/the-world-factbook/geos/as.html (accessed March 4, 2009).

The music of the Torres Strait Islands is known for the rhythmic singing of fanfare melodies, as Jaap Kunst has described; these are sung with the harmonic series 1 3 5 (*do mi sol*) or doubled thirds, melodically and harmonically (Kunst 1967, 102). Also, the music has been influenced by Polynesian and Melanesian religious workers, supported by the London Missionary Society since the mid-1800s. The result was a new style of music that combines Protestant hymnody with a Polynesian tradition (Garland 9:412).

Commentary on Individual Hymns

"A SONG OF COSMIC PRAISE"
("Sing a new song," *STB* #35)

This hymn is a majestic song praising the whole creation of God. It reflects Psalm 148, in which all creation, stars, mountains, waters, plants, creatures, and peoples are summoned to praise God. To this text, James McAuley adds more contemporary expressions—such as universal energies, magnitudes of space and time, diatoms, and human beings with their artistic talents, wisdom, and will for truth and justice—all joining to praise and reflect the grandeur, the bounty, the wonder, the beauty, the wisdom, and the glory of Christ.

Richard Connolly's tune COSMIC PRAISE matches the content, style, and spirit of the text. Although it is in a D = 2 A-natural-minor scale (A = 6 7 1 2 3 4 5) with the final on 3, both the initial on 2 and the final on 3 are unusual. But the melodic development and the harmonic treatment have a contemporary sound.

Concerning this hymn, Shirley Murray says:

> In 1956, James McAuley asked Richard Connolly to set one of his hymns to music, and a fruitful collaboration resulted in their first collection, *We Offer the Mass* (1959). This was so successful that they were commissioned to continue their work in two more collections. Hymns from these collections have appeared in hymnals in Australia, England, and North America.[80]

I collected this hymn in 1971 at Richard Connolly's office, on behalf of the Urban and Rural Committee of the Christian Conference of Asia, and it first appeared in the 1972 *New Songs of Asian Cities*.

---

80   From the author's communication with Shirley Murray, January 27, 2007.

"Comfort, comfort all my people" (*STB* #184)

Using Isaiah 40:1–2 ("Comfort all my people . . . all your sins are taken away") as an introduction and refrain, Robin Mann develops this theme. The first three phrases of each verse describe conditions of tears and sorrows while the next three assure of God's responses to ease the suffering. But they are all set to the same melody.

The author composed the tune DOROTHY with many repeated tones (in chords) and a triadic accompaniment. The tune is in a B = 5 six-tone major scale (E = 1 2 3 4 5 6, without 7), featuring 5, which is also the final. The homophonic chordal progression in the treble voices and basses conveys a calm and steady feeling against the lively broken chords or arpeggios of the tenor. Wesley Milgate comments on the background of this hymn:

> Mr. Mann's song was written about three days after the birth of his twin sons in July 1975, for his wife Dorothy, who was experiencing depression at the time; the words and music began forming as he was driving home after visiting the hospital. (Milgate 2000, 48)

"Father welcomes all his children" (*STB* #168)

This baptismal hymn uses Jesus' call—"Let the little children come to me . . . for it is to such as these that the kingdom of heaven belongs" (Matthew 19:14)—as the foundation of the refrain and the first stanza. The author Robin Mann states the doctrine of baptism is to "die to sin" through the water and the Word, to rise with Christ, and to live in the peace of God.

Mann composed this lively tune KRISTIN in F major (F = 1) with a series of sequences (<u>34</u> 5 5 2, <u>12</u> 3 3 7; 5 <u>54</u> 3 1, 4 <u>43</u> 2 , 3 <u>32</u> 1), which makes this hymn easy to sing for everyone, especially children. According to Wesley Milgate, this text and tune were written in July 1973, after the birth of the author's first child, Kristin, for her baptism (Milgate 2000, 56). This hymn was first published in *Songs for the People of God.*[81]

"In faith and hope and love" (*STB* #230)

At the beginning of this hymn of discipleship, James Philip McAuley quotes the three most important words in St. Paul's letter (I Corinthians 13:13)—faith, hope, and love—and continues: "with joyful trust, we move towards our Father's home above." The verse lists a number of names for and descriptions of Christ: star, map, bread, rescue, shelter, friend, beginning, end, hope, reward, redeemer, and Lord.

Richard Connolly's tune ARALUEN has an irregular meter and begins with three descending lines, which should be sung in 2/2 and 3/2. Although the tune is in D major (D = 1), the refreshing flattened seventh (C♮) changes the character of the

---

81   Rodney M. Boucher, *Songs for the People of God* (Adelaide, South Australia: Rodan Publications, 1974).

melody. Notice that the composer has provided an instruction: "A cantor or small group may sing first the refrain, and then each verse, the congregation responding with the refrain in each case."

"Lᴏʀᴅ of life" (*STB* #267)

This is an affirmation of faith that the Lᴏʀᴅ of life and of nations is our only hope to provide justice, peace, and unity through Christ. In stanza 2, the author Anthony Kelly insightfully delineates God's love in four dimensions: its lengths are beyond all measure, its heights call, its breadth has room for all, and its depths hide the treasure. Kelly concludes, "Through Christ, our Way, we find true peace," a new vision, a new heaven, a new earth, and a healed world. According to Wesley Milgate, this hymn was commissioned in 1986 by the Papal Visit Committee. The text draws from Ephesians 2:14–22; John 11:52, 14:27, 17:22–23; Colossians 3:15; I Corinthians 12:13; Ezekiel 11:19, 36:26; Matthew 6:10 (Luke 11:2); Ephesians 3:17–19; John 14:6; Colossians 1:20; Psalms 85:8; Revelations 21:1–2, 22:2. Originally there were four stanzas, but the third stanza was omitted from the approved setting by Christopher Willcock (Milgate 2000, 85).

The tune GOD OF PEACE was composed by Willcock as an attractive melody in G major (G = 1) with figures and sequences (17 6, 21 7, 43 2. 5 /32 1). It is easy to follow and remember.

"MARRIAGE SONG"
("Take each other's hands," *STB* #169)

This hymn is like a sermon or teaching to newlyweds-to-be, advising them to let their faith become their prayers. The second stanza stresses the importance of sharing and mutual support: "you may offer, by your kiss, hope in travail, taste of bliss." The last stanza reminds the couple to face the reality of pain and joy and to realize they also have to live for others: "light your hearth to warm the poor."

James Minchin composed the words and music. The tune CANA TUESDAY, which is very modern, uses only one motif (D = 6; 67 1 2 /3-), the partial reversal of it (56 3 2/3-), and other variations. Beginning with measure 9, Minchin uses the 67 1 motif six times, from F = 671 to 71 2, gradually rising to G = 67 1, 71 2 to reach the climax (12 3) with the words "you have found." The three-note motifs (67 1) change intervals each time, from major second and minor second (67 1) to minor second and major second (71 2) and vice versa, until the climax is formed by two major seconds (12 3), which illustrates the couple's goal of uniting in harmony and equality. This careful crafting of major and minor intervals could be interpreted as expressing the behaviors—showing mutual respect and support, giving and taking, and meeting each other's needs—whereby the marriage will be successful. Non-musicians may find it easier to understand the composition if offered this simple analysis using the movable *do* system. Since the poet/composer is a jazz pianist, the hymn would sound better with a jazzy piano accompaniment.

"May the grace of Christ" (*STB* #81)

This Trinitarian Benediction by the British poet John Newton (1725–1807) was set by the Australian composer Colin Brumby in a four-part canon titled NEWTON in F major (F = 1). The congregation may be divided into two to four groups to sing the canon, and members of the choir may be assigned to assist each group so that the four-part harmony will be complete. The eight-measure melody may be repeated any number of times before proceeding to the final Amen in four-part harmony. This benediction was part of the "Short Hymns" in *Olney Hymns 1779* (Milgate 2000, 89). It begins with a reference to 2 Corinthians 13:14, and it is popular when sung at marriage ceremonies.

"Sing a new song and wait upon the promise of the LORD"
See "A SONG OF COSMIC PRAISE" (*STB* #35)

"Your coming, Lord" (*STB* #187)

This hymn is about the incarnation and sacrifice of Christ, which offer salvation, and about our joy and peace, which are often enslaved by evil. The author asks Christ to come and give us light as he did to his disciples during his ministry and following his resurrection. Then the author prays for Christ's presence as we share the Communion Elements, which enable us to understand his perfect love. The last stanza acknowledges that Christ will come again in glory to judge and to claim his own. This hymn may be sung at a Communion service.

The tune GRACE by the editor of the *Australian Hymnal*, Canon Lawrence F. Bartlett, is in E major and begins with B = 5. The melody is fast and syllabic with repetitions and imitations, which makes it easy to sing. The accompaniment is simple but contrapuntal. Take note that the full cadence only occurs at the end of the last stanza.

Conclusion

Regretfully, no hymns or songs from the Aboriginal Australian churches were included in this collection. However, it is not surprising that the language and musical styles of the Australian churches are reminiscent of their roots in the United Kingdom. One hopes that the music of the indigenous Australians will someday inspire Westerners to identify with native people and develop new styles of church music.

 # New Zealand/Aotearoa Hymns

The Nation, the People, and Their Music

New Zealand, or Aotearoa in Maori, is situated about 2000 kilometers (1250 miles) southeast of Australia and consists of two mountainous main islands and numerous smaller islands, forming a total area of 268,680 square kilometers (about 103,738 square miles). Polynesian people migrated to Aotearoa before 1000 CE; over time, they developed into the Maori culture. Europeans arrived in the nineteenth century, mainly the Scots (now centered in Dunedin), English (in Canterbury), and the Dalmatians (in the Northland region) (Garland 9:928). New Zealand has a population of 4,173,460;[82] 77% is European, 18.2% is Polynesian (including 510,000 Maori and 193,000 Pacific Islanders, from Samoa, Tonga, Cook Island, Niue, etc.), and 4.3% is Asian (Johnstone 2001, 497). The British signed a treaty with the Maori people in 1840, which claimed sovereignty, but disputes still remain about the terms. New Zealand became an independent dominion in 1907 and a fully independent nation in 1947, as a constitutional monarchy with a parliamentary democracy; the British monarch is the symbolic head of state. New Zealanders are primarily Christian: Anglican 14.9%, Roman Catholic 12.4%, Presbyterian 10.9%, Methodist 2.9%, Pentecostal 1.7%, Baptist 1.3%, other Christian 9.4%, others 3.3%, unspecified 17.2%, non-religious 26%.[83]

Maori Music and *Moteatea*

Traditional Maori songs were sung only in unison because singing in harmony was considered a bad omen. The melodies usually had narrow ranges and stepped progressions, and large skips were rare (Garland 9:933). However, singing songs is important to the Maori because it keeps them in touch with their cultural roots: "The vanished would materialize, and visions of ancestors pass before our eyes; for a moment, times merge, and the present and past are one" (Garland 9:933f). Two important instruments are the *koauau,* a stumpy wooden or bone flute with three holes, and a trumpet/flute called *putorino.*

Moteatea is the traditional Maori musical poetry with multiple compositional and performance functions. *Moteatea* can be "trivial and profound, sacred and profane, instructive and amusing":

> Songs were composed in connection with every known feeling, with every human activity. The Maori broke into song to express joy, sadness,

---

82 CIA, "The World Factbook, New Zealand," July 2008 estimate, https://www.cia.gov/library/publications/the-world-factbook/geos/nz.html (accessed March 5, 2009).
83 CIA, "The World Factbook, New Zealand," 2001 census, https://www.cia.gov/library/publications/the-world-factbook/geos/nz.html (accessed March 5, 2009).

love, hatred, contempt, ridicule, mirth, and the whole range of emotions known to man. He sang himself into a fight, and out of it. He sang to avenge an insult or a trifling sight; he sang when a relative died, and also when he lost a fish hook. He sang when he was short of food and in days of plenty. He sang his prophetic visions and his dreams. (Garland 9:938)

The Maori people sing their genealogies, through which their history and philosophies of religion and life are transmitted. They conceive "the universe as completely spirit, the ultimate reality of the Maori culture" (Garland 9:939). One of the spiritual forms is *whe*, the primordial element, which is manifested in the physical world as sounds. Genealogies also describe "the creation of the physical realm represented in the sky father (Ranginui) and the earth mother (Papatuanuku), who, having been bound together for aeons, were separated by their children. The universe as we know it then came into existence" (Garland 9:939). Maori further believe that all generations (of gods, winds, sea, birds, etc.) received their voices and were drawn from the primordial *whe*.

Into this system, humanity was created, and it too received a voice created through the *whe*. As this voice evolved into words and phrases, the compositional constructions of language developed (Garland 9:939).

Western-style hymn singing has changed the practice of Maori song, as seen from their adoption of part-singing in gospel songs and Victorian hymns. The basic harmonic structure of hymn tunes and the tonic/subdominant/dominant/tonic progression have been integrated into Maori songs. Also present, however, are the contrapuntal male voices, a feature that is traditional in the Pacific region. Today's choral competitions and festivals further demonstrate the Maori enthusiasm for choral singing.

Commentary on Individual Hymns

"A HYMN FOR CHURCH UNITY"
("Jesus, Savior, Spirit, Sun!" *STB* #314)

This is a prayer of confession and petition for Jesus to "melt us, fuse us . . . mould us to your heart's desire." The author Shirley Murray confesses, "We have gone seeking crosses of our own, building churches not the Church . . . stubborn walls of human pride built to keep the Christ outside," and she prays for Christ to consume our shame and make us one. This is an excellent hymn for a congregation, a nation, ethnic groups, or ecumenical gatherings.

The tune SOON EE by the Singaporean composer Swee Hong Lim was named after his second child and means "pure will (of God)" in the Teochew dialect. It is composed in a D = 5 five-tone scale (5 6 1 2 3) with a simple melody in an a b a' b' form. The eight-measure motif adopts an ascending orientation that emphasizes significant words with high notes, as found in the fourth and twelfth measures. The accompaniment utilizes Western chords with stylized figures to break from traditional Western four-part harmony. However, the composer encourages people to improvise freely.

When Murray learned Lim was interested in creating congregational songs, she gave him a set of hymn texts, leading to this setting of her 1985 text.

"Carol our Christmas"

See "UPSIDE DOWN CHRISTMAS" (*STB* #143)

"Child of Christmas story" (*STB* #141)

In this hymn, Shirley Murray conveys a mother's perspective in her vivid description of a baby's behavior. With the lovely image of the Christ Child's finger curled around ours, Murray prays, "Come to melt our hearts, and come to change the world." She also asks this Child to tell us his name, how to love him, to teach us what we lack, and to be our hope again. The words are direct and simple yet profound and realistic. In the midst of commercialized holiday celebrations, singing this hymn during a Christmas service will encourage the congregation to meditate on how to love the Christ Child along with the suffering babies in the world and to take concrete actions.

The tune name IXTHUS is the Greek word for "fish," which is an ancient acronym for "Jesus Christ, God's Son, Savior" in Greek. This was the symbol that early Christians used during their persecution by the Roman Empire to secretly reveal their identities to other Christians. The text asks the Child to tell us his name; the tune name answers that question and inspires people to reconsider what they are celebrating. As the composer, I employed engaging yet mysterious musical expressions for this very unusual text. The motif of the melody, built in the triad of D7 (D = 5 -7- 2- 4), comes from a Nepalese melodic idiom, which can be seen in HERA DAJAI (*STB* #304). The two different endings (4 5 75 7 1- and 4 5 75 7 5-) are also important features. The simple drum patterns add to the moods of loneliness (the Child in the cold stable) and mystery (who is he?). The downward stems indicate lower pitches produced by striking the larger head of the Nepalese *madal* (a conical double-headed drum), and the upward stems denote higher pitches produced by the smaller head. No other accompaniment is necessary.

"Christ is our peace" (*STB* #262)

This text was written for the ninth General Assembly of the Christian Conference of Asia (CCA) held in Manila in 1990, with the theme "Christ, Our Peace, Building a Just Society." I was responsible for directing the music and worship during the assembly. At my request, Shirley Murray wrote this "down to earth" interpretation of peace: Peace is not a concept or ideal far from our reach; it is in your mouth and in your hands. But there is a price to pay: "Those who would go with Christ also must bleed." Murray concludes, "Peace will flow on through the hearts that believe: this may we know, thus may we live." Regarding the original inspiration of this hymn, she said, "The rather spare lines of this text come from the influence of Celtic prayers and songs, which I have always loved, and which have a strength in their simplicity."[84]

This hymn, one of the theme songs during the CCA Assembly, was published in *Sound the Bamboo* in 1990. At that time, I composed a different setting for the gamelan, an Indonesian gong-chime orchestra. The students of the Asian Institute for Liturgy and Music performed that setting as a prelude for a morning service in which this hymn was sung.

The music in an E = 6 six-tone scale (B = 3 5 6 7 1 2). It is quite different from my usual style: its 3/4 time and guitar chords are foreign to traditional Taiwanese music. The tone 7 (set to the word "peace") appears in the fourth system and changes the feeling of the five-tone scale (6 1 2 3 5). Further, the music concludes on 2 instead of 6 as one might expect. All of these changes are intended to portray one idea: peace is breaking new ground.

The tune name SAM-KIAP is a small town (also known as Sanxia) near Taipei where my father, the Reverend Sian-chhun Loh, had been a pastor. In that town, my family experienced hardship during World War II: constant harassment by the Japanese secret police, the imprisonment of my father (for "speaking the truth in love" against the government), the constant fear and dodging of bombs from American B-24s and B-29s, the scarcity of food. It was a great joy when the war finally ended in August 1945. One day in early 1946, a very tall soldier in an American uniform (perhaps one of the former "enemies" who bombed our neighborhood?) entered my church in Sam-kiap. He removed his hat and knelt in front of the Communion Table and prayed. It was a moving sight for me, a nine-year-old boy; I sensed for the first time that the war had ended and peace had arrived. So, I named this tune after the town to commemorate the peace that I had experienced over a half-century ago.

"Come to this Christmas singing" (*STB* #145)

Regarding the writing of this hymn in 1983, Shirley Murray said:

> This was an early experiment, for me, in contextualization. "Making this child our own" was the intention, with the use of imagery New Zealanders recognize, when the season was high summer, and the wealth of our islands' resources seemed to contrast with much of the rest of the world. At this time, too, New Zealand was moving towards declaring our country

---

84   From the author's correspondence with Shirley Murray, May 18, 2004.

"Nuclear-Free." "Aroha" is the Maori concept of warm, all-embracing love.[85]

The main message in this Christmas carol, therefore, is not singing but bringing gifts of New Zealand's treasures—beautiful shell and stone, traditional wisdom, the laughter of the young, love—and, most important of all, "making this child our own." Murray contextualizes Christmas by offering the nation's wealth of land and water and its cultural riches as gold and incense for Christ. She concludes with an image of Christ born in poverty and in the cold as a reminder for all to share their wealth, love, and peace.

There are two tunes written for this text. The first tune, AROHA (meaning "love," *STB* #145A), was composed by Douglas Mews in F major (F = 1) in 6/8 time, with a lively rhythm and an interesting harmony. The second system modulates to A minor (A = 6), and the third system moves to the dominant of G minor (D-major chord), which reaches the tonic of G minor at the beginning of the fourth system. Here, the composer has skillfully brought together the various tonalities like gifts, matching the spirit of the text.

The second tune, GERALDINE (*STB* #145B), is in E major (E = 1) and was composed by Colin A. Gibson. Since he is a poet as well as a composer, Gibson sensitively treats the tune according to the structure of the poetry. Murray's poem uses a unique metrical structure and a complicated rhyme scheme, and Gibson's musical phrase structure follows these.

The poetical meter and accents have two identical structures: 7 7 7 6, 7 7 7 6.
(> = accented; . = unaccented)

7	7	7	6
>..>.>.	>..>.>.	>..>.>.	>..>.>

The rhyme scheme of the eight-line poem (the same letter means the same rhyme):

a	a	b	c
d	d	e	c

Gibson's musical phrases correspond to the poetic structure (the same letter denotes the same melody):

a	a	b	c (half cadence, open)
d	d	e	c' (full cadence, closed)

---

85   From the author's correspondence with Shirley Murray, May 18, 2004.

When the rhyme scheme changes from a to b, the music also changes, with a flattened seventh degree of the scale (D without the ♯). The same also applies to the second part of the song: G♯ is changed to G at phrase e. This is a good example of structural unity between text and tune.

For people around the world, this is a wonderful Christmas carol; it expresses difference from European Christmas carols and, most of all, it prompts one to consider what cultural gifts can be brought to Christ.

"Deep in the human heart" (*STB* #248)

The core of the gospel is the redemption of both body and soul, as proclaimed by Jesus at the temple when he launched his ministry (Luke 4:18–19). This hymn by Bill Wallace reflects the burning fire for justice in the human heart. Only when the world is full of love, sharing, freedom, and truth and free from hunger and fear can there be justice and peace. Wallace urges all to work with Christ as part of a community, to bring new hope and abundant life to all humanity.

Wallace reflects:

> [This text] is an affirmation that within each human being there is a sense of justice. However, it appears that only a minority of the rich and powerful are prepared to be in touch with this. If they were, it would necessitate that they share their wealth and their power. Injustice is not just a product of individual selfishness but of institutional oppression. The call to Christians is to take our stand with the poor and the oppressed.[86]

The tune PATATAG is the title of a musical that depicts Christian involvement in the struggle for human rights and democracy in the Philippines. The composer Francisco F. Feliciano uses a scale similar to the Indonesian *pelog* tuning: an E = 7 six-tone scale (7 1 3 4 5 6) plus 2, which only appears once. The melody should be sung with vigor and should begin on an upbeat. Each beat should have two quarter notes, and each count should be accented in order to communicate the spirit of the text. Since there is no harmonic structure indicated, one may use percussive instruments to support this song. This powerful hymn can be sung as a commitment to social justice near or at the end of a service.

"For the man and for the woman" (*STB* #238)

Colin A. Gibson wrote this hymn of thanks and praise in a peculiar way. The first three stanzas are lists of many things that one can be thankful for: man and woman, body and soul, mind and spirit, labor and prayer, harmony of nations, sounds of many lands; rock and flower, earth and air; rhythm and chanting, sound and silence,

---

86   From the author's correspondence with Bill Wallace, August 10, 2004.

color and design, etc. In the second half of the fourth stanza, Gibson finally uses four verbs to state the purpose of naming all these items: "We will praise you, great Creator . . . make us one and make us many, your delight is our desire."

The tune was named MAKILING after the venue for the 1987 Asian Workshop on Liturgy and Music, sponsored by WCC and CCA. The Philippine National Arts Center is a beautiful resort on Mount Makiling, near Manila. Gibson was invited to participate in this workshop, and he wrote this text and tune for the closing worship. The melody is in a C = 3 six-tone scale (F = 6 7 1 2 3 5) with largely the same rhythmic pattern (33 /6 6) throughout, and the 7 only appears twice. The tune was composed as a canon, but Gibson subsequently provided the harmony. People are encouraged to add melodic and percussive improvisations in any style to add excitement to this song of praise. Because of its extensive coverage of many subjects, this hymn would be appropriate for any large events for thanksgiving.

"God of the Bible, God in the Gospel" (*STB* #255)

This hymn was featured in the tenth General Assembly of the Christian Conference of Asia (CCA) in Colombo, Sri Lanka, in 1996, on the theme of "Hope in God in a Changing Asia." The text was woven from six Bible studies, and there is one verse for each day of the assembly; these affirm the faithfulness of an unchanging God but urge the world and its people to change. Shirley Murray describes how God abides with humankind through Christ, whose suffering empowers them to be fearless and faithful, even facing the cross. This is the only hope for the world to change. The refrain is from Lamentations 3:22–23 (from the *Good News Bible*).

Murray comments:

My favorite image is the "small paper lanterns" which, though seemingly ineffectual, flicker through the darkness of the world and give us hope to keep going.[87]

The tune COLOMBO includes elements of Indian music because Colombo is the capital of Sri Lanka, and Sri Lankan music is similar to Indian music. As the tune's composer, I felt that the idea of change could best be expressed through an Indian musical language. The framework of the tune is structured in 8/8 time: each measure has eight counts, which are constant and never changing, symbolizing God's faithfulness no matter how other factors change. The additive rhythms within this framework of eight are shown in two patterns—A (3+2+3) and B (3+3+2)—that express the necessity for human beings to change. Like an Indian drone, pattern A in the bass is unchanged for three measures, but in the fourth measure, the drone (on D) begins to change and move. This leads to pattern B in the fifth measure, in which the pattern switches from 3+2+3 to 3+3+2. The bass'

---

87   From the author's correspondence with Shirley Murray, May 18, 2004.

higher drone (A, a fifth above the original drone) turns into a descending melodic line in the seventh measure while the tenor assumes the drone, a big change. The eighth measure features another change to pattern A; the bass resumes the drone while the tenor makes its most active move to end the section.

The refrain begins with pattern B, which has changed again with a fresh drone on G; it continues with variations for two measures, but it concludes with pattern A. The concept of change is also conveyed in the scales. The original scale of the melody is D = 3 4 5 ♭7 1 for the first A pattern, but it changes to B♭ = 1 3 4 5 7 in pattern B and ends with pattern A, i.e., the change occurs between ♭7 and 7. The refrain uses the scale of pattern B but finally returns to pattern A in scale and rhythm. The final surprise, a D-minor chord (D-F-A), does not follow Asian or Indian music theories, but it was intended as another sign of the necessity for people to change.

These complicated changes in scales, rhythmic patterns, drones, and other figures were arranged to describe the mystery of the faithful, unchanging God and the need for change in human beings. An accompaniment of drum (with patterns as notated), concussion bells (o + + following A and B patterns), and keyboard (which is not Indian) will make the changes easier for the singers. Despite the seeming complexity of this piece, it was sung without problems during the assembly's daily morning worship.

Since this hymn has philosophical and theological content, it is appropriate for interpreting the "breadth, length, height, and depth of the love, mystery, and faithfulness of God" (Ephesians 3:18). If the rhythm and scale are too difficult for the general congregation, a trained choir should sing the hymn for the first few stanzas, and the congregation should join at the refrain after the third stanza. This would be a good hymn to sing when contemplating the faithfulness of God and our human weaknesses and total reliance on God.

"God of the galaxies spinning in space"
See "HONOR THE EARTH" (*STB* #269)

"God, receive our prayer" (*STB* #111)

This prayer response was written by Janet Gibbs. As in any kind of intercessory prayer, the prayers need not be long, only a brief sentence or two, after which the leader says, "This is our prayer," and the congregation responds by singing, "God, receive our prayer." Then the next person says another short prayer. Prayers can also be said by one person. One suggestion is to divide the prayers into sections or according to topics, allowing members of the congregation to share prayers, with the group responding as above. The leader leads the response with or without accompaniment. If cues are necessary, it should be sufficient to play E and G♯ simultaneously, so that the congregation can match these notes.

"He came singing love" (*STB* #205)

This simple yet profound hymn uses the word "singing" to symbolize the ministry or the mission of Jesus in his birth, death, and resurrection. The hymn says that he came, lived, and died singing love, faith, hope, and peace, but he arose in silence; for the love, faith, hope, and peace to continue, we must be the singers. The genius of the author/composer Colin A. Gibson is shown in his treatment of text and music: the singers stop after the word "silence." The rest with fermata creates a space, during which singers can contemplate the implication of the word they have just sung as well as how one might fulfill Christ's mission of love, faith, hope, and peace.

The melody of SINGING LOVE is in a B♭ = 5, E♭ = 1 major scale, supported by a simple accompaniment. For this song to be effective, a leader should conduct the congregation, stopping singers after the word "silence" and for increasingly longer periods at the same spot in successive stanzas. This will enable the congregation to ponder the meanings of silence and their thoughts or resolutions about carrying on the mission of Jesus. I have introduced this hymn to great effect in several ecumenical assemblies with thousands singers. This is an excellent hymn after a benediction and/or before sending forth.

"HONOR THE EARTH"
("God of the galaxies spinning in space," *STB* #269)

In this hymn, Shirley Murray contrasts the greatness of God and his beautiful creation with the covetous greed of human beings. She points our attention to the ravaged lands and polluted air and urges us to keep our life whole by caring for God's garden and honoring the earth. Regarding the writing of this hymn, Murray comments:

> This was one of my first efforts to grapple with the theme of environmental disaster and our care of the planet. It was first printed in [the 1990 edition of] *Sound the Bamboo* and its reception encouraged me to continue writing "green" hymns, especially in view of New Zealand's sensitivity to environmental matters. It has been said that our true spirituality is rooted in our land and its landscape.[88]

The tune HONOR THE EARTH was composed by Douglas Mews in descending and ascending lines in E♭ major (E♭ = 1), which are repeated before modulating to F minor (F = 6) and to its relative A♭ major (A♭ = 1) at the end of the third system. Mews carefully builds to the climax on the most crucial word of this hymn, "care," with the longest count (four beats). This is a powerful hymn for ecology Sundays or any time one wishes to emphasize the importance of caring for God's creation.

---

88   From the author's correspondence with Shirley Murray, May 18, 2004.

"HUNGER CAROL"
("Child of joy and peace," *STB* #144)

Shirley Murray wrote this extraordinary carol in 1987 as a response to celebrations of Christmas that do not consider the meaning of the humble birth of the Christ Child: while the angels proclaimed the good news, Mary and Jesus struggled to rest in a filthy barn, too poor to stay in an inn. A recent fact is that a child dies every forty-eight seconds. Statistics from more than a decade ago showed that 1500 children died every hour, due to the lack of food or related problems around the world. While the name Bethlehem means "house of bread," Murray warns that if we only celebrate the birth of Jesus by beautifully decorating Christmas trees and joyfully exchanging presents, our neglect of the hungry and starving babies is akin to crucifying the newborn Child on the Christmas Tree. What a terrifying warning!

To depict the mystery of God's gift, and the irony of having the wrong mood and attitude for celebrating Christmas, I used my favorite Indonesian *pelog* scale (C = 3 4 5 7 1). The scale might pose problems for people unfamiliar with this style of music. It may help the congregation to learn the scale, ascending and descending (C = 3 4 5 7 1 3 1 7 5 4 3), a few times before actually singing the song. The accompaniment was inspired by Indonesian gamelan music, in which the kettle gongs anticipate, imitate, decorate, or double the main melody while the larger and lower gongs punctuate it at different intervals. In this setting, to assist the congregation, the main melody may be doubled by a flute throughout. However, the decorative tones in groups of threes and fours should be articulated to maintain the pseudo-Indonesian style.

SMOKEY MOUNTAIN is a huge garbage dump in the outskirts of the city of Manila. It is estimated that more than fifty thousand people scavenge through the waste to make a living. This is a tragedy, and the enormous socio-economic contrast is grossly unjust: the rich live like kings in palaces with plenty of servants and throw away tons of waste while the poor, including many starving children, search in filthy garbage to fill their hungry stomachs. This Christmas carol is definitely not joyful, but it challenges us to reconsider the decorations on the Christmas tree! One suggestion is for the choir, congregation, men, and women to alternate in singing the stanzas, in order for the larger group to concentrate on listening to the words sung to this sad and mysterious tune. The hymn's effect would be even more powerful if concrete actions were taken after singing it, such as offering food or gifts to the needy, especially to children. This hymn will also remind people why they decorate Christmas trees. As Murray commented:

> "Hunger Carol" was written [in 1987] as a protest of our consumer society, its excesses and heartlessness. This carol has been used for the annual appeal of Christian World Service, and set in various modes, but the tune,

with its associations of the place "Smokey Mountain" gives a unique dimension to the feeling of the hymn.[89]

"In nature as in Jesus" (*STB* #233)

Environmental disasters became a worldwide concern in the last half of the twentieth century. Bill Wallace points out:

> The espoused dualism between nature and human beings lies at the root of our current ecological crisis. Unfortunately, most Christian worship is basically anthropocentric and hence reinforces this dualism. This hymn is an attempt to give an ecological perspective within the Christian setting.[90]

He expresses this concern in these lines from the first stanza:

> "In nature as in Jesus, all life is truly one, but we divide Christ's mantle and drown creation's song."

This is a provocative idea concerning our relationships with nature, Jesus, and other human beings. Unfortunately, as Wallace writes, "People break this network for lust, for wealth, for power, and senseless pain and killing mark nature's darkest hour." It is time that we ask for God's forgiveness, so that the idea of protecting God's creation and conserving natural resources may grow within us "in heart, and hands, and head." The last stanza is a celebration of the unity of all life in God. I feel, however, that the hymn leader should omit the last stanza unless one has committed to change. Or the leader may let the congregation sing this stanza after a period of reflection on how it is easier to sing about change than to actually change. The last stanza may also be sung after a prayer of confession.

KHOAN-PO is Taiwanese for "environmental protection." As the composer, I set Wallace's meaningful text to this tune for *New Songs of Asian Cities* in 1972. It was intended for young people and the general public and has a semi-narrative style with a guitar accompaniment. Although the tune is in D-natural minor (D = 6 7 1 2 3 4 5), the B♮ (♯4) breaks the tonality, reflecting with a bit of tone painting how we "drown creation's song."

"Jesus, Savior, Spirit, Sun!"
See "A HYMN FOR CHURCH UNITY" (*STB* #314)

"Jesus the Lord stands with the poor"
See "LIVING IN CHRIST WITH PEOPLE" (*STB* #202)

89　From the author's correspondence with Shirley Murray, May 18, 2004.
90　From the author's correspondence with Bill Wallace, August 10, 2004.

"LIVING IN CHRIST WITH PEOPLE"
("Jesus the Lord stands with the poor," *STB* #202)

"Living in Christ with People" was the theme of the seventh General Assembly of the Christian Conference of Asia in Kuala Lumpur, in 1981. The CCA sponsored a workshop for liturgy and music in Manila in December 1980 to study the theme, prepare liturgies, and compose new hymns. This hymn was written by the Associate General Secretary of CCA, the Reverend Ron O'Grady. It portrays Jesus as an Asian who is poor, hungry, thirsty, oppressed, unemployed, an outcast, a slave, and a beggar, suffering insults and bearing all the agony. The hymn concludes with a prayer to Jesus to strengthen our wills, to fight against injustice, and to live with the people.

I was invited to the 1980 workshop and was touched by this text. It reminded me of my first visit to Jakarta, Indonesia, in 1970, when I encountered so many suffering people: squatters using cardboard for shelter, mothers bathing their babies in filthy ditches, beggars and starving children begging for food. It was nearly impossible to set such a sad text to music. During that trip, I learned a Balinese song, "Meon meon," which had a melody that sounded a little "sad"; I adapted the first phrase and developed it into this hymn after the Manila workshop. It uses an Indonesian *pelog* scale, C = 3 4 5 7 1. I had learned to play the Javanese gamelan, and I simplified the complex polyphonic strata of the gamelan into voice, *saron*, and *bonang* parts (for more information, see the discussion of gamelan in the Indonesian section). A *saron* is a metallophone and here plays the fixed melody, which is the simplified outline of the main vocal melody. A *bonang* is a kettle gong, which here accompanies the melody by doubling, anticipating, imitating, or decorating it. In this setting, the *bonang* plays a G at the end of the first measure, anticipating the vocal G at the beginning of the second measure, and this principle continues throughout the piece, with slight variations.

Tondo is the poorest region in Manila, where the garbage dump called Smokey Mountain is situated (for further discussion, see the commentary on "Hunger Carol," *STB* #144). It is suggested that a soloist or choir sing the first three stanzas of this hymn so that the congregation can listen to and feel the impact of the text. However, the fourth stanza should be sung by all, as a prayer and commitment to live "with people in every deed." Singing this hymn will help congregations to understand the hardships of life and suffering and will remind them of the price we have to pay to be called followers of Christ.

"Loving Spirit" (*STB* #220)

My favorite tunes are inspired by the texts of Shirley Murray, who is considered one of the world's best writers of English hymns. She has a feminine touch and motherly perspective that are not present in works by men. Her hymns are tender, neat, imaginative, unconventional, provocative, surprising, and deeply moving. While the concept of the Holy Spirit may be mysterious, Murray portrays the Spirit as within us—"chosen me to be." She uses various metaphors to describe one's relationship with the Spirit:

> Like a mother, you enfold me, hold my life within your own, feed me
>   with your very body, form me of your flesh and bone.
> Like a father, you protect me, teach me the discerning eye, hoist me
>   up upon your shoulder, let me see the world from high.
> Friend and lover . . . I am known and held and blessed: in your promise
>   is my comfort, in your presence I may rest.

Few hymn writers have drawn analogies between one's relationship with the Holy Spirit and the intimate human relationships of the family.

I was impressed and deeply moved by this beautiful text and pondered how to express the mysterious yet intimate relations with the Holy Spirit in music. I have always been fascinated by the so-called "gypsy scale" that likely originated in India, which combines a variety of small (minor second) and large (augmented second) intervals, and I decided to explore the possibilities of these combinations. In cipher notation, the gypsy scale is: C♯ = 3 4 ♯5 6, 7 1 ♯2 3; the South Indian name for this scale and tone formation is *mayamalava gowla* raga, which is within the family of *bhairav* raga. It is organized in two tetrachords, each consisting of a minor second (3-4), augmented second (4-♯5), and another minor second (♯5-6). The two disjunct tetrachords are separated by another major second (6-7). With these various intervallic relations and progressions, the music evokes different feelings. I utilized the Indian additive rhythm of 3 + 2 + 2, called three-*laghu triputa tala*, which also suggests mystery (see further discussion in the Indian section). The rhythm seems to be irregular and constantly moving, yet, after a while, one can predict its regularity. The melody begins from the lowest note of the scale (C♯ = 3) and ascends and descends stepwise. The motif gradually expands to a wider range and finally reaches the climax at the first beat of the third system. Melodic embellishments are most important for the Indian style of singing—they are the life and soul of the music—so the ornaments should not be left out.

To make the tune more interesting, an Indian drone supports the melody. The tonic (C♯, foundation) and the fifth (G♯, dominant) constitute the double drones. The fifth slowly develops to a more complex inner melodic line while the bass line also builds, leading to the climax with the inner melody to express the "wonder" of the Spirit near the end of the tune and gradually returning to the original point. An accompaniment of drum and concussion bells according to the notation will add to the distinct style of this piece. This tune was completed in 1990, in time to be sent to Geneva for the preparation of the seventh General Assembly of WCC in Canberra, in 1991.

I was satisfied in giving this text a different life with an unusual musical style. I had thought that the tune was too exotic and difficult for most people, but, surprisingly, it was the theme song at the WCC Assembly, where I was privileged to teach it in a sing-along session. And, to my amazement, the first female bishop in Australia chose this hymn to be sung at her consecration. The tune name CHHUN-BIN combines the names of my parents, Loh Sian-chhun and Ang Bin, and pays grateful homage to them for giving me life and nourishing me to follow their footsteps in serving God. (My father had already joined the heavenly chorus in 1984, but my mother was eighty-three when I wrote the music.)

In teaching this hymn, one should try singing the tetrachord a few times to become familiar with the scale: 3 4 #5 6, then reversed. Then try to connect to the higher tetrachord: 7 1 #2 3 and the reverse. Practice the rhythm and conducting by counting the *triputa tala*: "one two three, one two one two" (1 2 3 +1 2 +1 2) as in a triangular three-beat pattern. The first beat has three counts, and the second and third beats each have two counts. The drum pattern is played throughout the hymn. When concussion bells are used, the pattern should be o (open, 1 2 3) / + (closed, 1 2) / + (closed, 1 2) and should not be rushed. At the end of each stanza, it is advisable to play an interlude of the first two measures of the accompaniment before continuing to the next stanza.

"MIND-SET OF CHRIST"
("This is the mind-set of one who has come," *STB* #310)

On the request of the preparation committee of the Asian Mission Conference in 1994, Shirley Murray wrote this interpretation of Philippians 2:5–11 on kenosis (Jesus humbling himself) for the theme "Call to Witness Together Amid Asian Plurality." Murray avoids Christ's name in the first four stanzas of the verse, only stating either "the mind-set of one who" or "the mind-set that," and then lists his servant attributes that side with the poor and the oppressed. Then Murray says that this one turns all values upside down and is nailed to a cross. After presenting the features of the one who has emptied himself, Murray finally states in the fifth stanza "This is the mind-set of Christ for our time." In the refrain, Christ appears:

> Turn around all our thought, all our mind
>   to the will and the way of Christ Jesus!

Cipanas is a small city near Jakarta, the capital of Indonesia, and was the venue of the Asian Mission Conference. I served as the director of music for the event, and I wrote this as the theme song; hence, the tune is named CIPANAS and composed in an Indonesian style. The melody is in a *pelog* tuning, B = 3 five-tone scale (3 4 5 7 1). The first phrase of the ascending and descending scale provides the overall shape and structure of the song. The motif of the refrain (43 1-, set to the words "turn around") is the same as the third system, with the lyrics "washing the footsore," "bending to burdens," "tempted and tortured," etc. The intention is to musically stress that to "turn around" is to follow the example of Christ by emptying oneself to serve others. Only when one is willing to empty oneself to wash other's feet can the words "turn around" be meaningful. Further, the music of the last phrase of the refrain (34 5 7-, 57 1 3) imitates the same melodic idea in the second system, where the text says "servant and helper," "grasping no glory," "one with the outcast," etc. Only by following these examples to serve and help can we witness that we have turned our mind "to the will and the way of Christ Jesus." Thus the two musical ideas and theology of the hymn are purposefully matched and integrated. The song builds to a climax on the final words "Christ Jesus," who is our highest model.

The song should be accompanied by a zither-type plucked instrument (*celempung*) to recreate an Indonesian style. The repetitive figures of three or four notes also reflect the characteristics of Balinese gamelan instrumentation. Therefore, the groupings and phrasings are important. This text is one of the best exegeses on kenosis (Philippians 2:1–5) in a contemporary Asian context, so it is a good model to sing this hymn as part of the sermon or as a response to a call to discipleship.

"Son of God, whose heart is peace" (*STB* #60)
(Maori: *Tama ngakau marie*)

This hymn is a prayer asking God for love, forgiveness, and release from evil, so that one can be safe and warm in Jesus' arms. It is a traditional hymn of the Maori, the original inhabitants of New Zealand. Set in G major (B = 3, G = 1), it is simple, sincere, and passionate.

The native peoples in the Pacific are known for their open-throat singing style, which is light and lyrical and evokes flowing water or spring breezes. Harmonically, their songs reflect traditional practices that are skillfully integrated with idioms learned from Western missionaries. Thus, four-part harmonic singing is popular anywhere in the Pacific nations. In addition to the Western tonic (1-3-5), dominant (5-7-2), and sub-dominant (4-6-1) chords, other tones that do not belong to the chords are added at times. In other songs, tenors and basses may create their typical counter-melodies with strong chest voices.

Because the Maori language is easy to pronounce, all are encouraged to sing at least one stanza of this hymn in the original language to feel the song's original flavor. According to some Pacific traditions, the hymn may be sung softly without clear breaks between phrases. Thus, members of the congregation or choir may take turns breathing at different points but not at the end of any phrase. It would also be good to accompany this hymn with a guitar playing broken chords. One can imagine singing this hymn at dusk, near the beach of a Pacific island, admiring the beauty of the golden sunset and the roaring waves and feeling the caresses of the cool breezes . . . while remembering God's love and praying for mercy.

"SONG TO THE SPIRIT"
("Spirit who broods," *STB* #222)

Shirley Murray wrote this text in 1989 at the WCC Pacific Workshop of Liturgy and Music in Melbourne. It relates to the theme "Come, Holy Spirit, Renew the Face of the Earth" of the seventh General Assembly of the WCC, in 1991. Utilizing modern expressions, the poet prays to the Spirit who broods as a mothering bird with peace in her wings, to the Spirit of truth who is like a laser searching "the right," to the Spirit of love who is quick to forgive and keeps no score, and to the Spirit of hope who is never subdued. It is only when we embody and learn to express this four-dimensional Spirit that the face of the earth can and will be renewed.

I composed the tune KENG-SIN, meaning "renewal" in Taiwanese, in 1990. Featuring a lively rhythm, the music is in a B = 3, E-minor scale (E = 6 7 1 2 3 4 $\sharp$5) with two altered tones, $\sharp$1 and $\sharp$2, that reinforce the tune's Middle Eastern folk style. One should feel free to dance, clap in any pattern, and use any instrument to improvise or harmonize the tune in any style and tempo that the Spirit inspires.

"The God of us all" (*STB* #181)

Limitations of language and understanding can lead to misinterpretations of the Bible and the concept of God. Descriptions of a differently gendered God have caused much unnecessary dispute and division in the Church. During the 1980 Ecumenical Seminar on Music and Worship in Manila, the Reverend Ron O'Grady wrote this hymn, affirming that God is our Father and Mother, and it touched many hearts. What is most impressive is O'Grady's description of God as a mother who "teaches us her truth and beauty" and "shows us a love beyond duty." It is difficult to understand why some faithful Christians object to descriptions of the motherly nature of God.

SANTA MESA is the name of the Manila district where the 1980 workshop took place. As the composer, I interpreted the text with a scale (C$\sharp$ = 3 4 6 7 1 3) that is similar to the Japanese *in* scale (3 4 6 7 2 3 1 7) to portray the tender femininity of the character of God. It was my first attempt to adapt a scale from a foreign culture. In Chinese and Japanese philosophy, *in* (or *yin*) refers to the negative or feminine, and *yang* is the positive or masculine. This scale portrays the gracefulness, intimacy, and loving eyes of a mother patiently watching her children grow and meet her expectations. The simple accompaniment is intended for the *koto* (Japanese long zither); hence, running figures fill in different spaces. Bringing out the counterpoint will underscore the beauty of the tune's Japanese style. One may use a cello for accompaniment. Psalm 103:13 may be added to the Scriptural reference: "As a father has compassion for his children, so the LORD has compassion for those who fear him." This hymn is appropriate for sermons on the attributes and loving kindness of God, parental responsibilities, or gender equality; it can also be sung on Mother's Day or other occasions that celebrate the Christian family.

"The grain is ripe: the harvest comes" (*STB* #268)

With the opening lines, "The harvest comes . . . your time is now," Shirley Murray invites all to heed God's call for justice: "God comes in truth the sharpest laser to scan the earth, to take our measure." Nothing can be hidden, and no one can escape the responsibilities of feeding the hungry and making peace. Murray concludes, "The harvest comes from love's good seeding."

The tune GREENSBOROUGH by Philip Nunn of Australia is in a D = 6 natural minor scale (6 7 1 2 3 4 5). The sharpened 4 (♯4) at the repetition reinforces the statement that the "time is now." Nunn uses tone painting to communicate the phrases "justice will stream from hill and river, more than you dream and running over": to the word "running," he sets a melismatic melody (with many notes for one syllable of text) in quarter notes (7 1 2 1 7 6 7 5), like a stream flowing to the end of the tune. In addition to traditional counterpoint, chordal progressions, discords, and some surprises, Nunn extensively employs parallel thirds and fifths to good effect.

Regarding the setting, Shirley Murray writes:

At the WCC Pacific Workshop on Liturgy and Worship in Melbourne [1989], I met Australian composer Philip Nunn. He set this hymn on the spot and named it after the parish church we were working in at that time, to prepare a televised worship event for the whole of Australia at Pentecost. The theme addresses a sub-section on justice and peace: "the harvest comes from love's good seeding."[91]

"This is the mind-set of one who has come"
See "MIND-SET OF CHRIST" (*STB* #310)

"UPSIDE DOWN CHRISTMAS"
("Carol our Christmas," *STB* #143)

The celebration of Christmas in New Zealand, and elsewhere in the southern hemisphere, is in the summer, which may seem upside down to those with Western perspectives. Sheep outnumber people in New Zealand, so there are plenty of shepherds and musterers. The author Shirley Murray states that during Christmas, these shepherds find "not angels but sheep to be shorn" and that wise ones searching for signs of truth are not limited by the seasons. She expresses an important message: Christmas is not a season and is not limited to the supposed day of Christ's birth. Murray has commented:

---

91   From the author's correspondence with Shirley Murray, May 18, 2004.

This is not the first New Zealand carol to describe a Southern Hemisphere summer at Christmas time, since we have had to throw away images of snow and holly long ago. But, helped by my longtime friend and collaborator, Colin Gibson, with his engaging tune, this carol has become the title piece for a collection of New Zealand carols and was part of a movement to express our own context, while trying to create a theology for our part of the world.[92]

Murray's central theme is found in the fourth stanza:

Right side up Christmas belongs to the universe,
made in the moment a woman gives birth;
hope is the Jesus gift, love is the offering,
everywhere anywhere, here on earth.

Thus, the real meaning of Christmas is God's offering of hope and love in Jesus Christ!

The tune REVERSI was composed by Colin A. Gibson in F major (F = 1) in a waltz-like rhythm in a a'a b form. This hymn should be sung at a very fast tempo (quarter note = 176–192), with one beat for each measure.

"Why have you forsaken me?" (*STB* #189)

Quoting the bitter cry of Christ on the cross, "My God, my God, why have you forsaken me?" Bill Wallace states that we will conquer fears only if we trust in God's love. This hymn shows the mystery of God's love through Christ, in his weeping at the death of Lazarus and his deepest pain and agony of being forgotten, and we are assured that we are always in God's care.

SHIMPI is the Japanese word for "mystery." Taihei Satō composed this tune after meeting Wallace at the Ecumenical Workshop on Music and Liturgy in Manila in 1980, when all participants encouraged one another to utilize their musical talents to serve God. Satō uses a Japanese *in* scale (E = 3 4 6 7 2) to portray the agony of Jesus; simple textures add color to the music, which is very Japanese in style. The tritone (an augmented fourth, 4-7) between F and B is difficult to sing and should be taught carefully. Satō comments:

The note *mi* is the fifth in A minor: the dominant note. My idea is that it means we're subordinate to the earth, to this world. That's why the note is so important as to appear ten times in this tune. To go half up and down between *mi* and *fa* (also *ti* and *la*, *mi* and *re*) expresses our wish and wavers. But it more reveals the waver of Jesus; he directly called for God

---

92   From the author's correspondence with Shirley Murray, May 18, 2004.

and cried, wept, and prayed, and Jesus committed himself on the cross at last. I realised that *ti—re—re—ti* in the last phrase is the last breath, the last word, the thanksgiving, the prayer for forgiveness, of all the living. And then I think the last *la* leads to the salvation we are supposed to reach with Jesus. Thus I wish to sing this *la* (the main tone in A minor) as the final goal of the ten-times-repeated dominant *mi*.[93]

Since its publication in a 1981 hymnal,[94] this hymn has become very popular in North America, appearing in seven major denominational hymnals and supplements (Satō, however, said that it has appeared in fourteen hymnals worldwide). Wallace says:

> Its success is due to the fact that it was one of the first hymns on Christ's cry of dereliction from the cross and as such helped people to acknowledge that the feeling of being abandoned by God is a normal part of the grieving process.[95]

"Within your heart and mind, O Christ" (*STB* #188)

The Reverend Bill Wallace wrote this hymn to help us understand and accept the "trilogy of inner health." He directs our attention to the example of Christ, "the man who spoke with prophet's fire, showed mother-love, and child-like fun," to encourage people, especially men, to free themselves from the bondage of gender stereotypes and to share their power with women. This is a revision of a hymn published in the 1990 edition of *Sound the Bamboo*. The earlier text was:

> Although a man, yes Mary's son, your life affirmed the womanly—
> You claimed your sisters, dearest Christ, as equals in your company.
>
> You free us all to laugh and cry, to know when others need our touch,
> To nurture Earth, her children too, through God who mothers us so much.
>
> Entrenched control of wealth and power remains within the rule of men—
> Let us who share the flesh of Christ share power and be new born again.
>
> God, help us each to be at ease with both our strength and tenderness,
> That male and female in our heart may be as one in graciousness.

---

93   From the author's correspondence with Taihei Satō, January 15, 2007.
94   Bill Wallace, *Something to Sing About: Hymns and Reflections in Search of a Contemporary Spirituality* (Melbourne: The Joint Board of Christian Education of Australia and New Zealand, 1981).
95   From the author's correspondence with Bill Wallace, August 10, 2004.

As the composer, I used a D = 6 five-tone scale (6 7 1 3 4) to establish a feminine and graceful quality. The arpeggio figures in the accompaniment form a counterpoint that suggests interaction and mutual dependency. Care should be taken at the final cadence, which is a major third (4-6), not the usual fourth (3-6). The tune ESPAÑA was named after the street in Quezon City (part of metropolitan Manila) where I wrote this tune. España Boulevard is one of the busiest in Manila; it is used by millions of men and women who commute everyday on crowded Jeepnies (mass transportation vehicles converted from American military Jeeps). On this street, one can observe all sorts of interactions between women and men. This hymn is appropriate for emphasizing women's liberation and gender equality.

Conclusion

From this selection of hymns, it is clear that there is no shortage of competent New Zealand composers. But one might wonder why the composers of so many tunes are other Asians, including Japanese, Filipino, Singaporean, and Taiwanese. The answer is complex. Firstly, during the Ecumenical Seminars on Music and Worship in 1980, 1987, and 1989, many of these texts were written or introduced to Asian participants, who found them beautiful. Secondly, Shirley Murray's poems have a special power that touches Asians so deeply that they want to complement her gift with their artistic spirituality. Thirdly, some Asian countries lack good hymn-text writers. On the whole, although white New Zealanders are Caucasians, their thinking has an affinity with that of Asians; hence, their poems have inspired other Asians to develop their creativity in composing new music. It is a good sign and witness of the embrace of the people from this remote, southern Pacific island into the fold of the Asian community of faith. *Soli Deo gloria.*

 # Papua New Guinean Hymns

The Nation and Its People

Papua New Guinea is situated east of Indonesia, between the Coral Sea and the South Pacific Ocean. It occupies the eastern half of the island of New Guinea, which is considered the second largest in the world (the western half of New Guinea is occupied by the Indonesian provinces of Papua and West Papua, formerly known as Irian Jaya). Papua New Guinea has a total area of 462,840 square kilometers (about 178,704 square miles), and the estimated population is 5,931,769.[96] Archeological evidence indicates the first inhabitants may have come from Southeast Asia nearly 50,000 years ago; it is believed that a major migration of Austronesian-speaking peoples settled the island's coastal regions roughly 2,500 years ago.[97] The large number of ethnicities in Papua New Guinea includes Melanesian, Papuan, Negrito, Micronesian, and Polynesian peoples; there are 820 indigenous languages, but Tok Pisin or Melanesian Pidgin serves as the lingua franca; other languages are English (spoken by one to two percent of the population) and Motu (spoken in the Papua region in the south).[98]

In 1885, Papua New Guinea was colonized by Germany (in the north) and the United Kingdom (in the south); in 1902, control was transferred to Australia, which administered the country until its independence in 1975.[99]

A Brief History of Church Mission

In 1871, the London Missionary Society sent its first representative to New Guinea, and other missionaries followed. From the 2000 census, the religious distribution in Papua New Guinea is: Roman Catholic 27%, Evangelical Lutheran 19.5%, United Church 11.5%, Seventh-Day Adventist 10%, Pentecostal 8.6%, Evangelical Alliance 5.2%, Anglican 3.2%, Baptist 2.5%, other Protestant 8.9%, Bahai 0.3%, indigenous beliefs and other 3.3%.[100] From the very beginning of Christian mission, hymns have played an important role in the missionaries' work. For example, the

---

96   CIA, "The World Factbook, Papua New Guinea," July 2008 estimate, https://www.cia.gov/library/publica-tions/the-world-factbook/geos/pp.html (accessed March 8, 2009).

97   Wikipedia, "Papua New Guinea," http://en.wikipedia.org/wiki/Papua_New_Guinea (accessed March 8, 2009).

98   CIA, "The World Factbook, Papua New Guinea," https://www.cia.gov/library/publications/the-world-fact-book/geos/pp.html (accessed March 8, 2009).

99   CIA, "The World Factbook, Papua New Guinea," https://www.cia.gov/library/publications/the-world-fact-book/geos/pp.html (accessed March 8, 2009).

100   CIA, "The World Factbook, Papua New Guinea," https://www.cia.gov/library/publications/the-world-fact-book/geos/pp.html (accessed March 8, 2009).

Lutheran mission introduced German hymns to New Guinea. From 1898 to 1984, according to Ann M. Gee, the Lutherans printed nearly forty hymnals, mostly with Western hymns and some indigenous texts in the Gedaged (or Graged) and Jabem languages. Other missions and the languages employed were: Wesleyan (Dobu, Kuaua), Anglican (Binandere, Wedau), Kwati (Suau), London Missionary Society (Hiri Motu, Kiwai, Toaripi), and Unevangelized Field Mission (Gogodala); after the late 1950s, when English became the national language of education, the religious importance of these languages declined (Garland 9:193).

Gee also classifies the impact of the long process of indigenization in New Guinea on its music in the following ways:

A. Existing Western music, printed in hymnal
B. Music composed in a Western style by an indigenous person
C. Music using indigenous musical material, adapted by an indigenous person
D. As in C, but adapted by a Westerner
E. Music composed by a Polynesian, as in *peroveta* [Polynesian hymns in two parts sung by choirs, with texts about prophets]
F. Music composed by an indigenous person in a traditional style
G. "Popular" Western style, as in gospel songs
H. Traditional percussion: *kundu* [single-head hourglass, cylindrical, conical, or goblet drum], *garmut* reed, or *kundu* with *garmut*
I. Conch trumpets
J. Rattles and other traditional instruments
K. Western instruments, like organ
L. Guitars, ukuleles

(Garland 9:194f)

Textual indigenization includes the following:

M. Existing Western texts, printed in hymnal
N. New Western texts (as in M), but translated into an indigenous language
O. Composed by an indigenous person in English or German, based on Western theology
P. Composed by an indigenous person in an indigenous language, based on Western theology
Q. Composed by an indigenous person in an indigenous language, based on New Guinean theology
R. Western (as in M), but translated into Tok Pisin
S. Composed in Tok Pisin by an indigenous person
T. Composed in Tok Pisin by a Polynesian

(Garland 9:195)

I agree with Gee that the categories A, M, and N are not true examples of indigenization since they were only translations of Western hymns. The approaches described in items E, F, Q, S, T, and the use of native musical instruments are the ideal results of maturity in contextualized music and theology.

Conch Bands

The Reverend Heinrich Zahn (1902–1932), a Lutheran missionary in New Guinea, formed a band in 1925, which contained nineteen conchs to accompany singing in four-part harmony. The shells were of gastropods, with holes drilled through the apex or the side. Zahn used cipher notation (1 2 3 4 5 6 7); *5 indicated one half step below 5, i.e., #4. Incidentally, Ambonese Christians in Indonesia have the same tradition; it is not known whether they learned it from New Guinea or vice versa. Zahn's conch-shell hymnal contained eighty-three hymns, some with titles in English, German, and Jabem (Garland 9:195f).

Following its independence in 1975, Papua New Guinea increased indigenization efforts, including the use of more indigenous music and instruments. During the 1990s, the distribution of musical styles in rural areas may have been 10% English hymns with translations (of hymn texts, not musical styles), 10% choruses with guitar accompaniment, and 80% indigenous music with drums (*kundu*). But the proportion in urban parishes would have been approximately 45%, 45%, and 10%, respectively (Garland 9:197).

kundu drum

A conch from the Moluccas.

Commentary on Individual Hymns

"O come, all you people" (*STB* #4)
(New Guinean: *Aso, aso, aso ngane*)

The Lord Jesus, via the leader, calls people to worship, and the congregation responds, "Let's all go now." The language is Manu, one of the 820 indigenous languages in Papua New Guinea. The music is in an $F = 1$ three-tone scale (1 2 3) with the final on 2 and a free rhythm with no regular beat or meter. When singing this hymn, count the eighth note at the beginning of each phrase as one and let the melody flow with the text. If the leader has difficulty singing alone, some of the choir may sing the leader's part, and others may help the congregation to respond. This song should be repeated a few times to establish the mood of an invitation to worship. I learned this song from a New Guinean pastor who participated in one of the CCA conferences.

"We gather, Father God" (*STB* #6)
(Melanesian Pidgin/Tok Pisin: *Mi pela i bung papa God*)

This simple hymn expresses one's desire to worship God. It was composed in a pidgin, a language that mixes simple English words with local vocabularies and grammar; pidgins developed and are widely used in non-English-speaking countries that trade with or were colonized by English-speaking countries. One may be able to figure out the approximate meaning of the pidgin in this hymn through the sound of the syllables. Properly translated, it reads:

> We are gathered here, Father God, to honor you, and to thank you truly.
> We your people seek to be united with you in worship.

This song was taught to me by a Catholic priest who attended one of the CCA meetings in Manila in the mid-1980s. It is in a $G = 5$ six-tone scale ($C = 1\ 2\ 3\ 5\ 6\ 7$). According to Ann M. Gee's analysis, this hymn would belong to the B and S categories introduced above, i.e., an indigenous person composed this in a Western style with the Tok Pisin language. A suggestion is to sing this hymn in the original language to experience fellowship with the native people in worship and unity in Christ. The drum accompaniment provides another indigenous characteristic. Although the hymn sounds like a C-major song, one should respect the integrity of the style by avoiding any chords or complicated harmony.

Conclusion

These two very short songs provide a glimpse of the music of Papua New Guinea, which features a short range and irregular rhythms. These hymns also highlight the importance of developing contextual music in order to prevent the loss of indigenous musical identities through the imitation of Western styles.

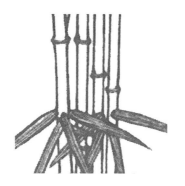

Part Three

Biographies of Authors, Translators, Paraphrasers, Composers, and Arrangers

Abbreviations

AILM: Asian Institute for Liturgy and Music
CCA: Christian Conference of Asia
CCPE: *CCP Encyclopedia of Philippine Art*
CUMH: *Companion to United Methodist Hymnal*, 1993
DAC: *A Dictionary of Asian Christianity*, 2001
NSAC: *New Songs of Asian Cities*, 1972
SRKII: *Sambika Dainihen Ryakkai* ("Companion to *Sambika II*"), 1980
SRK21: *Sambika 21 Ryakkai* ("Companion to *Sambika 21*"), 1997
STB: *Sound the Bamboo: CCA Hymnal 2000*
ZMSS: *Zanmeishi (xinbian) Shihua* ("Companion to the *New Songs of Praise*"), 1993
WCC: World Council of Churches

Adams, Raymond

Born in England, 11 January 1949, Raymond Adams is a member of the United Reformed Church (UK), Adams earned a BA with honors in music from Southampton University, did further theological studies at Westminster College, Cambridge, and received a certificate in pastoral theology (Cambridge Federation of Theological Colleges) and an MA in practical and contextual theology from Oxford Brookes University. He served in local ministry in the United Reformed Church in London (1973–78) and was a missionary to Taiwan, serving as the head of the Department of Church Music, Tainan Theological College and Seminary (1979–86), and he assisted in producing the *Hymnal Supplement I* (1985). Upon returning to England, Adams served a local parish in Surrey (1986–94) and was elected moderator of the South Western Synod of the United Reformed Church (1994–2002). His current post is the deputy general secretary of the United Reformed Church (from 2002). His works include: harmonization of the hymn tunes, "Lam-sin" and "Yang Kuan San Tieh"; hymn and song settings to texts by Cecily Taylor in *Hymns and Congregational Songs*, vol. 1, no. 3 (Stainer and Bell, 1989); *Reflecting Praise* (Stainer and Bell and Women in Theology, 1993); *Supplement 96* (Hope Publishing Company, 1996); *Sound Bytes: Ninety-four Songs of the Twenty-first Century for Children to Share with Everyone*, (Stainer and Bell, 1999).

Composer: GO-SUN-CHEH (*STB* #152).

Adhikary, Martin

Born in Orissa, India, in the 1950s, Martin Adhikary serves a parish in the Orissa area. He is a talented musician who sings and composes. He studied at AILM for one year during the late 1980s.

Translator: "Joy, O Jesus, crown of all" (*STB* #28).

Aguila, Vincent Mar

Born in the southern part of Luzon, the largest island of the Philippines, Vincent Mar Aguila was a pastor and a poet and wrote many hymns. He died in Luzon.

Author: "Everywhere sorrow on Calvary's hill" (*STB* #148).

Akwan, Celsius

Born in Indonesia in the 1950s, Celsius Akwan graduated from Satya Wacana Christian University in Salatiga Central Java (majoring in English, 1979) and Sekolah Menengah Atas Gabungan (Catholic and Protestant Senior High School) in Jayapura (1967). Akwan served as a senior English instructor at Canadian and American oil and gas companies (June 1992–January 2002); a life-insurance trainer for Niaga Bank in Jakarta and Surabaya (January 1992–April 1992); and an English instructor in Jakarta (1980–91) and East Kalimantan (1985). Akwan also served on the editorial staff of *Topchords*, a pop-music magazine published in Salatiga (1977–80), and *Serikat*, a monthly magazine published by GKI Irja, Jayapura (1967–70). He retired from Gulf Resources in January 2002 and has been involved in publishing and English-teaching businesses in Jakarta. Akwan has been active in many different denominations: Evangelical Christian Church in Irian Jaya, until 1970; Western Indonesia Protestant Church, GPIB, until 1987; and Indonesia Christian Church of Central Java in Bekasi, West Java, GKI Jateng, since 1987. Since January 2002, Akwan has been the choir director of the mixed choir at GKI Bekasi, West Java; of Satya Wacana mixcd students choir (1977–80); of Christian Youth of GKI Hamadi, Jayapura (1967–70); of Protestant male students at SMA Gabungan in Hamadi (1964–67); and the male youth choir of GPIB Salatiga (1971–80). He is the composer of "For the Peace of the World" (arranged for four parts by the Reverend H. van Dop from Yamuger), a "hymn" for students from Satya Wacana and Kwansei Gakuin University in Osaka, in a cultural exchange program (which began in 1979). Akwan is an active member (1975–85) of Yayasan Musik Gereja (Institute for Sacred Music), the publisher of Kidung Jemaat in Jakarta, in which his compositions "Tuhan, Datang Segera"

(1981) and "Gembala Baik Bersuling nan Merdu" (1984) appeared. He is known for his skill in choral singing techniques and has won a number of first prizes in national competitions.[101]

Author/composer: "My shepherd Lord," GEMBALA (*STB* #291).

Alejo, Albert E.

Albert E. Alejo is Filipino and has collaborated with Eduardo P. Hontiveros, a famous Roman Catholic composer/priest, in songwriting.

Author: "Behold the man we nailed on the cross" (*STB* #149).

Almoos, Sherazi Hizqial

Born in Faisalabad, Pakistan, 4 September 1963, Sherazi Hizqial Almoos, usually known to his friends as Sherazi (Hizqial being his father's name), graduated from high school in 1979 and in 1984 received a Diploma of Associate Engineer degree after three years of study at the Government College of Technology. Because of his talent in music, Almoos received a full scholarship to study at Asian Institute for Liturgy and Music, Manila, and received his BCM in 1994. He is a good composer as well as a player of tabla (paired north Indian drums). Since returning to Pakistan, Almoos has used his music and poetry to disseminate the message of peace, unity, and tolerance inside and outside of churches. He has produced some works for television and for children in the Beacon House School, including "Dove of Peace" and "Dreams of Life and Hope for Children." He has also organized a touring music group performing contemporary church music and many of his own compositions.

Translator: "My people, bless the name of God Messiah" (*STB* #34); "Be joyful in the Lord, all lands" (*STB* #94); "Praise the Lord, to God give praises" (*STB* #295).
Transcriber: SIKHAVAN (*STB* #89).

---

101 Information in this entry is derived from the author's communication with Yamuger, March 30, 2005.

Amarnad, Anto

Born in Trichur, Kerala, India, 19 January 1956, Father Anto Amarnad is a Roman Catholic priest. He was invited to attend the Asian Workshop on Liturgy and Music in Makiling, the Philippines, in 1987. He is a Carmelite Religious Priest, ordained in 1985. During his studies at the University of Sagar, Amarnad received a bachelor's degree in Hindustani music, psychology, and Hindi literature. He has produced more than thirty audiocassettes in Hindi, Malayalam, and Sanskrit. After his ordination, Amarnad did his postgraduate studies in theology in Bangalore and received a diploma in pastoral counseling in the Philippines. He was then a lecturer at Ashta Theological Seminary. After three years of teaching, Father Amarnad went to Rome for further studies in theology, receiving a licentiate and doctorate from Salesian University, Rome, with a specialization in catechetics and youth pastoral ministry. Currently he is a professor of theology and the dean at Samanvaya Theological College. Amarnad also teaches classes in several theological and religious institutes of higher learning in and outside of Madhya Pradesh. He has composed more than 250 songs, which are used in the Churches of North and South India. He has written a few books, several articles, poems, and stories in several magazines.[102]

Author/composer: "Following Jesus, Savior and Master" (*STB* #227).

Anderson, Boris

Boris Anderson was born in Hull, Yorkshire, England, 11 August 1918, of an Anglo-Scottish father, a Presbyterian minister, and an Anglo-Welsh mother, an artist and musician. Anderson was educated at the Royal Grammar School, Newcastle upon Tyne, and Oxford University, earning an MA degree in theology. Anderson married Clare Porteous (see the following entry), and they went to Taiwan as missionaries. They had two children, Jane and Robin. Anderson served as the vice principal of Tainan Theological College and Seminary (TTCS) of the Presbyterian Church in Taiwan (PCT) and was a professor of New Testament, Church History and Western Philosophy (1948–63). After returning to England, he served as the secretary of the Overseas Mission Committee, Presbyterian Church of England (1964–72), and subsequently as secretary of the World Church and Mission Department, United Reformed Church (1972–83). Anderson is very interested in music and frequently plays the flute; his wife Clare often accompanied him on the piano. He was on the hymnal committee of the PCT that produced the official hymnal in 1964. He was the author of "The Future of Taiwan" (1972) and the editor of Shoki Coe's

---

102 Information in this entry is derived from the author's interview and correspondence with Amarnad, February 12, 2006.

Recollection and Reflections (1994). He was also the author, under the pseudonym "Anne Ming," of "Taiwanese Voice" (1981), published by the British Council of Churches. With his wife Clare, Anderson translated two hymns for the 1963 *EACC Hymnal*; they revised them in 1981, and these versions are included in *Sound the Bamboo*. In recognition for his contributions to theological education in Taiwan, TTCS awarded him an honorary Doctor of Divinity degree in 1987.

Co-translator: "God created heaven and earth" (*STB* #173); "God, the LORD in love and might" (*STB* #175).

Anderson, Clare (née Porteous)

Boris and Clare Anderson

Clare Porteous was born in Islington, London, England, 21 June 1923, of Anglo-Scottish parents. Her father was a Presbyterian minister and the traveling secretary for Fellowship of Reconciliation (F.O.R.), and her mother was a teacher and musician. She married Boris Anderson (see the above entry) and they had two children, Jane and Robin; Robin died in July 1976. Clare Anderson was educated at Nottingham High School and King Edward VI Birmingham and Newnham College, Cambridge, earning an MA degree in Classics. She was a lecturer in New Testament Greek at Tainan Theological College (1948–63) and a lecturer in Greek and Latin literature in English translation at Cheng-Kung University, Tainan. She also taught her children together with other foreign children according to the British private tutoring system. Anderson taught classic literature in London (1963–76), participated in the new translation of *Domesday Book* from Latin (1977–83), and worked with Ghanaian and Chinese communities in London. She was a good pianist and frequently accompanied her husband Boris, who plays the flute. In 1999, she published a collection of her poems, entitled *Sad, Mad, Good, Bad*. She died in 2008.

Co-translator: "God created heaven and earth" (*STB* #173); "God, the LORD in love and might" (*STB* #175).

Andrade, Moises

Born in Santa Cruz, Manila, the Philippines, 23 September 1948, Moises Andrade is a Tagalog from a Roman Catholic family. He received a Master of Science degree in chemistry from Far Eastern University (1978), a Doctor of Theology degree from University of Santo Tomas, the Philippines (1975), and a Licentiate in Sacred Liturgy from Pontificio Instituto Liturgico, Rome (1994). Andrade is currently a priest ministering a parish in Valenzuela, the Philippines. He taught part-time at the Asian Institute for Liturgy and Music and has written many hymn texts.

Author: "When twilight comes and the sun sets" (*STB* #161).

Aragaki, Tsugutoshi

Born in 1938 in Iloilo, Banay, the Philippines, to a Catholic family originally from Okinawa, Japan, Tsugutoshi Aragaki studied composition at Kunitachi University and is currently a professor at the Shirayuri Women's University and at a Catholic seminary in Tokyo. Aragaki is a prolific composer; his works include many operas (e.g., *The Twenty-Sin Martyrs*), cantatas (e.g., *Foot Prints on the Sand*), and organ pieces (e.g., *Memorial 40, Transfiguration* according to themes from *Etenraku*). Aragaki's works in church music are widely used among both Catholic and Protestant churches (cf. *SRK21*, 23, 66).

Author/composer: "Gathering round the table of the LORD," MARANATHA (*STB* #83).

Arai, Toshi

Born in Japan, 7 January 1933, Toshi Arai is a graduate of Aoyama College (BA, 1955), Tufts University (MDiv, Christian Education, 1958), Harvard University, Hartford Seminary (STM, History, 1960), and the Pacific School of Religion and Graduate Theological Union (CAPS, 1969). He served as a chaplain of the International Christian University in Tokyo, director of the Christian Academy, education secretary of CCA, and director of the Subcommittee on Renewal and Congregational Life, WCC. Arai is a great fundraiser and promoter of music and worship; under his sponsorship, the WCC was able to hold many Ecumenical Seminars on Liturgy and Music around the world from 1984 to 2000. Arai initiated and supervised the WCC Worship Resource Center. After returning to Asia, he became the Associate General Secretary of the CCA until his retirement. He was a sponsor, recruiter, and advisor for the Asian Institute for Liturgy and Music in Manila and a strong supporter of the editing and publishing of *Sound the Bamboo: CCA Hymnal 2000*. Arai was instrumental in producing the Japanese electronic "Hymn Player." He retired in 2001. A highly respected gentleman, Arai is a soft-spoken man of action. He speaks and reads Japanese, English, German, and French, and reads Latin, Greek, and Chinese. He is the editor of the following publications: *Children of Asia*, (1979), *Church and Education in Asia* (1981), and *World Christian Encyclopedia*, Japanese edition (1986).

Translator: "In the world abound," stanzas 3 and 4 (*STB* #216).

Atmodjo, Subronto Kusumo

Born in Desa Margomulyo, Tayu, Pati, Jawa Tengah, Indonesia, 12 October 1929, Subronto Kusumo Atmodjo was a talented musician and was sent by the Ministry of Culture and Education to study music and choral conducting at Musikhochschule "Hans Eisler" in Germany. He also studied ensemble music in Berlin. Upon returning to Indonesia, Atmodjo served at the Ministry of Culture and Education as a staff member at the Cultural Inspection Office in Jakarta. A gifted composer and musician, Atmodjo wrote many hymns that exhibit a Javanese style. His wife, Titi Subronto Kusumo Atmodjo, quoted him as saying, "[All sacred songs] should represent Javanese melody to enrich hymns in the purpose of exalting God."[103] Atmodjo has been regarded as one of the best hymn writers in Indonesia; his compositions have been widely used by both Roman Catholic and Protestant churches. He was, unfortunately, suspected by the government of being a Communist sympathizer and was imprisoned for more than twenty years. Upon his release, the Communication Department of the National Council of Churches in Indonesia published a few of his compositions as a gesture of support to the respected poet/composer. He died several years ago.

Author/composer: "O God, our Father," ALLAH BAPA (*STB* #18); "Come down, O Holy Spirit," ROH KUDUS (*STB* #221).
Composer: MINTALAH (*STB* #235).

Baagavedhar, T. Aiyaathurai

T. Aiyaathurai Baagavedhar is from the southern state of Tamilnadu in India.

Author: "I lift up my eyes to the LORD" (*STB* #56).

Baagavedhar, Veedhenayegam

Born in August 1885 in Tamilnadu, India, a member of the fourth generation of the famous Veedhenayegam family (see the entry for Sasthriyar, Veedhenayegam), Baagavedhar was a talented composer, poet, and evangelist (or "Sasthriyar," a title that equaled a doctorate in Tamilnadu). He began his ministry at the age of eighteen. He had seven children; his grandson Durai Raj Veedhenayegam Sasthriyar (modern spelling: Vedanayagam Sastriar) is the sixth generation that has faithfully continued the family vocation of poet/musician/evangelist (the history of this family may be seen online at http://www.sastriars.org). Legend says there was a king who liked the beautiful Christian songs, so he invited one Baagavedhar (there were several in the family) to perform in return for payment. Not wanting to be paid to sing, Baagavedhar rejected the invitation. At the time, refusing a

---

103   From the author's correspondence with Mrs. Titi Subronto Kusumo Atmodjo, March 31, 2005.

king's invitation meant the death penalty, but Baagavedhar said he would be a martyr, that he was an evangelist singer to spread the gospel, not to gain profit. His refusal made the king even more curious about his singing. So Baagavedhar was summoned to the palace, and he bravely sang all the Christian lyrics, which were so beautiful and moving to the king that Baagavedhar became the king's official singer, and the seeds of the gospel were sowed.

Author/composer: "O come to us, Pastor of the flock," VAARUM AIYAA (*STB* #162).

Durai Raj Veedhenayegam Sasthriyar, grandson of Baagavedhar

Baes, Aloysius

Born in Los Banos, Laguna, the Philippines, 28 July 1948, Aloysius Baes is Tagalog and belongs to the Roman Catholic Church. Baes earned his PhD in physical chemistry at the University of Minnesota in the United States. He is currently a professor at the University of the Philippines, Los Banos campus. He is the elder brother of Jonas Baes (see the following entry).

Author: "Bear the weight of the cross" (*STB* #280).

Baes, Jonas

Born in Los Banos, Laguna, the Philippines, 14 March 1961, Jonas Baes is Tagalog and belongs to the Roman Catholic Church, and he is a younger brother of Aloysius (see above entry). Jonas Baes graduated from the University of the Philippines (BA, Composition, 1982) and did his graduate studies in ethnomusicology at the University of the Philippines (1985). He received a diploma in composition from Aufbaustudium Komposition Freburg Musikhochschule, Germany (1994), and a PhD in Philippine Studies from the University of the Philippines (2004). Since the late 1980s, he has been teaching at the Asian Institute for Liturgy and Music as well as the University of the Philippines, and he has done field research on Filipino folk music.

Composer: TOTOY (*STB* #160); PASANIN (*STB* #280).

Ban, Byong-sop

Born in 1924 in Chungbuk, Korea, and raised in Manchuria, China, Ban Byong-sop studied at Hanshin Theological Seminary, Dōshisha University in Japan, and Lutheran Theological Seminary in Chicago. He received a PhD degree from San Francisco Theological Seminary. Ban is a famous scholar in the fields of Christian literature and hymnology; one of his early contributions was his essay on Sijo literature and imagery. He has written more than one hundred hymns, one of which appeared in the 1967 edition of the interdenominational hymnal *Chansongga* (#303, "Every heart beats like the ocean"). Ban has received an American Hymn Society award for his contributions to church music. He has published many collections of sermons and poems and translated many books. Ban is a Presbyterian and was a member of the Korean Hymnal Committee.

Author: "Gather here, believers in Christ" (*STB* #243).

Banerjee, Caleb (Kalyan)

Born in Kolkata, India, 15 January 1955, Caleb Banerjee is a graduate of Rabindra Bharati University (MMus, Indian Vocal Music, 1976) and was awarded the Anil Memorial Shield for receiving the highest marks in Bengali song. Banerjee has been a teacher of Indian music at schools and Bengali Bible College in Kolkata. Since 1978, he has been the music director of the Assembly of God Church School and has been conducting and training choirs at the Future Foundation School, Tollygunge, Kolkata. Since 1984, he has been the director and composer of the Rahales Little Theatre and has composed more than 200 songs for their programs. He is also a poet and a singer whose songs have been broadcast over television and radio; he was invited to perform in Bangladesh (1981, 1984, and 1987) and the United States and Canada (1987). He was invited to sing a tribute to Mother Teresa at her funeral. Banerjee was also chosen to arrange two choir pieces for the visit of Pope John Paul II to Kolkata in 1986. For more than fifteen years, he has directed Kolkata's most prestigious shows, "Songs of the Season" and "The Sound and Light Program," at the Assembly of God. Banerjee can play harmonium, tabla (paired drums), *tambura* (plucked lute), piano, and sitar (plucked lute with sympathetic strings). He was a judge for the All India Singing Contests. He was invited to the 1987 Asian Workshop on Liturgy and Music in Manila, and he assisted I-to Loh with coordinating the recording of Indian *bhajans* for the CCA Communication Desk in 1996.

Translator: "Praise to you Jesus" (*STB* #17).

Barathi, Soundararajan John

Born in Tirukolur, India, 12 July 1960, Soundararajan John Barathi is the eldest son of the late Reverend Eliazer Soundararajan (see entry for E. Soundararajan). Barathi studied Western Music Theory, Grade V (1985) and Classical Guitar, Grade VIII (1986) at a local program sponsored by and affiliated with the Trinity College of Music in London. He also learned sitar privately for two years, along with Carnatic and Hindustani music. After graduating from a college in Madras (BA, Psychology), Barathi was accepted at the Asian Institute for Liturgy and Music (AILM) and earned a Bachelor of Church Music degree in composition (1991). He also received an MA in church music composition (2001) from the Graduate Division of the Department of Church Music, Tainan Theological College and Seminary. Barathi developed his skills while composing about twenty-five choral anthems in Indian and contemporary international styles, some of which have been published by AILM and performed in Europe. He has also composed many children songs,

school songs, and recently has composed and directed a three-hour Passion play written by his late father, E. Soundararajan, which involved hundreds of performers and singers. Barathi has been invited to be part of music and worship teams for a number of WCC and CCA conferences. Since returning to India in 2001, he was appointed the director of music and liturgy at the Diocese of Madras, Church of South India, he has conducted numerous workshops for liturgy and music, and he has served as a resource person for contemporary

John Barathi (on the far left) and his recorder group

liturgy for the National Council of Churches in India and United Evangelical Churches in India. He taught music at Saraswathi Vidhyalaya, a private school, for three years and served as a lecturer of church music at Trinity Theological College in Nagaland in northeast India for two years. Currently, Barathi is also a private teacher of classical guitar, piano, recorder, and Western music theory. He is married to Evelin Priscilla Vasanthi, who has earned the equivalent of a master's degree in Indian vocal music. They have a son, Jasperraj Samuel Barathi (eleven years old and learning to play tabla), a daughter named Jenita Caren Rajakumari (nine years old), and have recently adopted a girl who was orphaned by the December 2004 tsunami.

Translator: "All sisters, all brothers, all of the earth" (*STB* #84); "Why, O LORD, why" (*STB* #251).

Composer: EEN (*STB* #251).

Barranda, Natty G.

Born in 1940 in the Philippines, Natty G. Barranda graduated from a law school and practiced law before immigrating to the United States. She taught at Wilberforce University, Ohio, for more than two decades until her death about 1990.

Author: "O many people of all lands" (*STB* #21).

Bartlett, Lawrence Francis

Born in 1933 in Mosman, Sydney, Australia, Lawrence Francis Bartlett graduated from Sydney Conservatory of Music (1953) and Ridley College, Melbourne (ThL, Theology, 1963). He was the assistant director of music at the King's School, Parramatta (1952–57), and was a tutor in church music at Ridley College (1958–60). Ordained as an Anglican priest in 1961, Bartlett became the curate of Holy Trinity, Williamstown, and of St. Stephen's Willoughby (1962) and was appointed the precentor of St. Andrew's Cathedral (1962–68) as well as the cathedral organist (1965). He became the rector of St. Thomas's, Enfield (1968), and of St. Michael's, Vaucluse, and finally the canon of St. Andrew's Cathedral. Bartlett taught church music at the Sydney Conservatorium and has composed many hymn tunes. In 1973, he was the executive secretary of the committee that initially prepared the Australian hymnbook, *With One Voice*. He became the secretary of the Australian Hymn Book Company, served as the chair of the editorial committee that compiled *Sing Alleluia*, and has made significant contributions to the hymnody of Australia (cf. Milgate 2000, 31).

Composer: GRACE (*STB* #187).

Befu, Nobuo

Born in 1913, in Takachi County, Japan, Nobuo Befu was baptized in 1934 in Yokohama at Shiro Church. He taught in a high school for thirty years and showed much interest in children's work; he has been a member of the Association of Children's Culture since 1937. He began writing hymns in the 1970s, especially ones for children. He is currently teaching Hebrew at Tokyo Union Theological Seminary and is a member of the Ginza Church (cf. *SRKII*, 51).

Author: "In old Galilee when sweet breezes blew" (*STB* #195).

Bello, Lois Florendo

Born in Bawang, La Union, in the northern Philippines, 13 March 1920, Lois Florendo Bello was the first Filipina to graduate from Westminster Choir College,

Princeton, New Jersey, and was considered the best soprano in the Philippines in the 1960s. She received two bachelor's degrees in music and English education from the University of the Philippines (1946); she earned her second BM from Westminster Choir College and a Master of Arts degree from the same school, majoring in choral conducting. Bello taught church music at the Union Theological Seminary in Cavite and served as the head of the Department of Sacred Music for fourteen years, where she taught choral conducting, hymnology, and voice. She later served for four years as the head of the Department of Music at Philippines Christian College. She also served as a choir director for Ellinwood Malate Church, Holy Trinity Episcopal Church, and Union Church of Manila. She founded the Manila Concert Choir, which she conducted for twenty years; this was the first choral group appointed by the President of the Philippines to be ambassadors of goodwill to Taiwan. This group was also the first in the Philippines to adopt choreography as a visual interpretation in its performances. Lois Florendo married an American, Victor Bello, and immigrated to the United States. There, she served as a choirmaster at Rosewood United Methodist Church, Bethany Presbyterian Church, and Lutheran Church of Our Redeemer. She founded DBP Choir of Greater Los Angeles and the Philippine Concert Chorale, which toured nationally and performed at Lincoln Center, the Kennedy Center, and Ahmanson Theater. She also organized the singing groups Belles of Harmony and Leisure Village Chorale. Bello was the chairperson of the Filipino sub-committee for the Asian American hymnbook project of the National Federation of Asian American United Methodists, which produced *Hymns from the Four Winds* in 1983. Because of her contributions in the field of church music, the Union Seminary of the Philippines in Cavite awarded Bello an honorary Doctor of Divinity degree in 1997. She has also received awards of distinction from the Mayor of Los Angeles, the Philippine Consul General, and the Filipino American community of Los Angeles. In recognition of her golden anniversary of ministry in choral conducting, Bello was asked to conduct a choir of one hundred voices to sing Handel's *Messiah*, as an offering to the Union Theological Seminary of the Philippines.[104]

Composer: MATERNIDAD (*STB* #21).

Boriputt, Naga

Naga Boriputt is a Thai composer.

Composer: MAHACHAI (*STB* #151).

---

104 Information in this entry is derived from the author's interviews and correspondences with Lois Bello and Lilies M. Kapili, March 3, 2005.

Brumby, Colin James

Born in Melbourne, Australia, 18 June 1933, Colin James Brumby was educated at the University of Melbourne Conservatorium of Music (BM, 1957). He also studied in London with Alexander Goehr and John Carewe while working as the head of the music department at Greenford Grammar School (1963–64). Brumby earned a Doctor of Music degree and a Diploma in Education. At the University of Queensland, he served as a lecturer in music (1964–66), as a senior lecturer (1967–76), as the head of the Department of Music (1976–79), as a Reader in Music (1977), and as an associate professor. As one of the most prolific composers in Australia, Brumby has published more than one hundred compositions, including songs, choral music, concertos, and orchestral works, and he has written a book, *The Art of Prolonging the Musical Tone*. His *Four Australian Christmas Carols* was published in 1985. He was the 1981 recipient of the Advance Australia Award (cf. Milgate 2000, 24).

Composer: NEWTON (*STB* #81).

Bunya, Tomoaki

Tomoaki Bunya was born in 1942 in northeast China to a pastor of the Holiness Church. His family returned to Osaka, Japan, after the Second World War. Bunya received a degree in music from Osaka Educational University. Two of his compositions, written while he was a student at the University, were accepted in *Sambika Dainihen* (1967); one of them is included in *Sound the Bamboo*. Bunya has published many hymns, choral pieces, and religious songs. He currently teaches at Osaka Christian University and is a member of Osaka Kibōgaoka Church (cf. *SRK21*, 312).

Composer: INORI NO ZA (*STB* #158).

Carroll, Ewing W.

A United Methodist missionary under the auspices of the General Board of Global Ministry (GBGM), Ewing W. Carroll went to Taiwan in the late 1960s and later to Hong Kong. For a number of years, Carroll was the Asia Secretary for the GBGM. Most recently, he was the representative of US churches for the Amity Foundation, which prints the Bible and other religious books in China.

Translator: "Winter has past, the rain is o'er" (*STB* #71).

Chandlee, Ellsworth

Born in Harrisburg, Pennsylvania, USA, 6 November 1916, Ellsworth Chandlee was an American Episcopal missionary to the Episcopal Church in the Philippines. He taught liturgy at St. Andrew's Theological Seminary in Manila for many years until his death (8 December 1981) of severe heart failure. Chandlee trained specialists in the field of liturgy and was the co-founder with Francisco F. Feliciano of the Asian Institute for Liturgy and Music in Manila in 1980, which later was renamed Samba Likhaan. The official announcement of Chandlee's death from St. Andrew's Seminary said: "His faith was in the sure and certain hope of the resurrection of Christ and of all flesh and, accordingly, his funeral was full of Easter hymns and strong in joy and hope." He wished to be cremated and his ashes interred in the seminary chapel and so he rests before the High Altar where he had stood so often in the years since it was built. A plate marks the spot.

Author: "In the heavens shone a star" (*STB* #131).
Co-translator: "Now the day is ending" (*STB* #159).

Chang, Hsiang-chi (Zhang Xiangqi)

Born in the early 1970s in southern Taiwan, Chang Hsiang-chi is a graduate of the Junior College of Home Economics, which is being expanded to the Tainan Women's Institute of Arts.

Composer: O-LO (*STB* #5).

Chao, Tzu-chen (Zhao Zichen)

Born in 1887 or 1888 in Zhejiang Province, China, Chao Tzu-chen came from a small business family, graduated from Methodist Dongwu University, and went to the United States and earned a master's degree from Vanderbilt University. After receiving a bachelor's degree in theology (1917), he returned to Dongwu University to teach sociology. Chao was the head of the religion department as well as the chaplain of Yanjing University (1925–51). He was ordained by the Reverend Minghua He as a priest in the Zhonghua Shenggonghui (Chinese Anglican Church) in 1941. He was imprisoned the same year by the Japanese military police on 8 December, when Japan started the Pacific war. Chao resumed his church position after the war and began teaching Chinese literature and the poetry of Du Fu, with emphasis on religious thoughts. At the 200th anniversary of the founding of Princeton University in 1947, Chao was awarded an honorary doctorate (cf. Wang 1993, 61–64). He was a delegate to International Mission Council conferences in Jerusalem (1929), Madras (1938), and Whittby, Canada (1947). During the first General Assembly of the World Council of Churches (WCC) in Amsterdam in 1948, Chao was elected as one of six presidents. Because of his opposition to the Korean

War, he resigned from the position in 1951. Chao was against the Kuomintang regime's persecution of progressive students, and he played a significant role in the liberation of the people. As a result, he was invited as a delegate to the First Political Consultation of the Chinese People and eventually became an executive committee member of the same organization in Beijing. Chao was well versed in Western philosophy and Chinese classics, with a particular interest in poetry, drama, calligraphy, and art. He was also critical of Reinhold Niebuhr's theology. Among Chao publications are: *Jidujiao Zhexue* ("Christian Theology," 1925), *Yesu Zhuan* ("The Life of Jesus," 1926), *Minzhong Shengeji* ("Hymns of the People," 1932), *Jidujiao Jianjie* ("Introduction to Christianity," 1948), and many scholarly essays in English appearing in the journals *Chinese Recorder* and *International Review of Mission*. Chao was a strong promoter for contextualizing theologies in China; he insisted that although Christianity had come from the West, he had his own interpretations of the gospel and did not need to rely on those from the West. He even stated that Westerners were expecting Asian interpretations and contributions. Before Chao was released from prison, he expressed that he would help the church to achieve a state of "self-reliance, self-support, self-propagation, and self-rule, so that the Church of China could be indigenized, without relying on foreigners" (cf. Xi Yue Ji quoted in Wang 1993, 63f). In 1956, Chao was accused of siding with the American mission boards that were regarded as imperialists by China, and he was forced to resign from his professorship and the position of dean at the School of Religion, Yanjing University. Toward the end of his life, after seeing the condition of the new government as well as the inability of the church to practice its theology, Chao said that Christianity was no longer relevant for him (*DAC* 2001, 932f). Because of his concern for the welfare of the people, especially the poor and the farmers, he wrote many hymns, utilizing simple folk melodies to convey Christian messages. The new *Zanmeishi* includes eleven hymns (*Zanmeishi* #30, #31, #43, #59, #101, #130, #138, #148, #184, #202, and #204) from his collection *Hymns of the People* (of 1931 or 1932); six of the texts are in *Sound the Bamboo*. Chao died in 1979.

Author: "God, we praise you for this LORD's day" (*STB* #13); "Golden breaks the dawn" (*STB* #155); "Praise our God above" (*STB* #165); "Great are your mercies, heavenly Father" (*STB* #174); "Jesus loved each little child" (*STB* #200); "May the Holy Spirit's sword" (*STB* #223).

Chelliah, Calvin

Born in the late 1960s in Peninsular Malaysia to a Tamil Indian Lutheran pastor (see the following entry), Calvin Chelliah is a talented musician, a graduate of Lutheran Seminary in Malaysia, and the first graduate of the Asian Institute for Liturgy and Music in 1984 (BCM, Composition). Upon returning to Malaysia, he helped to edit the first Malaysian hymnal supplement with indigenous compositions. He became a language teacher and has been active in language societies.

Translator: "Your word will be a lamp to guide our feet" (*STB* #46).

Chelliah, D. A.

The father of Calvin Chelliah, D. A. is a famous and respected Lutheran pastor of Tamil Indian origin in Kuala Lumpur, in Peninsular Malaysia. He is a poet and a musician and has written many lyrics and tunes.

Author/composer: "This is the God beyond all gods," KARTHAAR (*STB* #139).

Chen, Pen-li

"Chen Pen-li" is a pen name of I-to Loh (see the entry for Loh, I-to).

Arranger: P'U-TO (*STB* #13); JIA-OU (*STB* #71); MEI-HUA SAN-NONG (*STB* #93); HUAN-SHA-XI (*STB* #135); SHENG-YE JING (*STB* #140); QING-CHEN (*STB* #156); CECILIA (*STB* #200); SIBU (*STB* #240).

Chen, Shih

Chen Shi (Kawamura) before graduating from Taipei Teachers Training School
(after Lin & Su, 2003).

Born in 1901 in Zhiben, Katipol, Taidong County, Taiwan, Chen Shih (original name: Panter; Japanese name: Kawamura Jitsu) was one of the most important composers of the Pinuyumayan (formerly Puyuma) tribe from the southeast coast of Taiwan. He attended the Taipei Teachers Training School, where he received a Western education, including music studies. He played the violin, piano, and reed organ. According to his son, Mingren, Chen's teacher was so impressed with his musical talent that he wanted to send him to study music in Germany but could not do so because Chen's father objected. Chen's education in Taipei must have influenced his style of composition. He was the first Pinuyumayan to become a principal of a school, and he was also elected a council member of Taidong County. In 1960, he led his tribe to erect a monument between Sanhe and Huayuan villages to commemorate the original place of their ancestors. Chen was a respected leader and considered himself a good person who did not need to become a Christian. The Reverend Sian-chhun Loh spent many years guiding Chen to understand the Christian gospel; on one occasion, after more than six hours of uninterrupted conversation, Chen finally accepted Christ and eventually became a deacon in the church (Cheng 1984, 448). According to Mingren, Chen composed more than 200 songs, but most of them are in the oral tradition as folksongs of the people and are in the public domain (Lin & Su 2003). I-to Loh's recordings of Chen singing in 1972 may be the only documents of the authentic versions of these songs. He died in Zhiben in 1973.

Composer: KATIPOL (*STB* #96).

Chen, Zemin

Born in China, 15 October 1917, the Reverend Chen Zemin graduated from Hujiang University in Shanghai (1941) and Jinling Seminary (1944). He was a professor of theology as well as the academic dean at Jinling Theological Seminary. He is also a musician and a composer. He served in Zhejiang Shaoxing in a Christian hospital as the head of the Religious Service Department, during which time he wrote a devotional book, *Pillar of Cloud and Pillar of Fire.* Chen has been teaching at Jinling Seminary since 1950 and has been an enthusiastic supporter and promoter of contextual church music. Since he plays the classical *qin* (plucked zither), he has adapted a few hymns from the *qin* repertoire with great success. In 1981, he arranged a *qin* piece, *Pingsha Luoyan*, as an anthem for Easter (cf. Wang 1993, 298f). I-to Loh visited Jinling Seminary in 1987, and Chen conducted the seminary choir performing this piece. In China, he is indeed one of a kind, as a theologian, composer, musician, and administrator.

Adapter: MEI-HUA SAN-NONG (*STB* #93).

Chiu, Teng Kiat

Born and educated in Fujian Province, China, Chiu Teng Kiat became a home missionary in Fujian as well as Kunming. He earned an MTh degree from Princeton Theological Seminary. For many years, he served Chinese-speaking congregations in Toronto, Philadelphia, San Francisco, and Oakland (cf. Loh, 1984a, 4). Chiu also worked in the Christian Study Center at Tao Feng Shan, Hong Kong, a place originally established to study Christian strategies for mission to Buddhists, Buddhist monks, and inter-religious dialogues. Until recently, converted monks or artists stayed there to create Chinese-style porcelains, calligraphy, paintings, and artifacts with Christian content. About a decade ago, this center was converted into a Lutheran seminary. The Reverend Chiu retired from the American Presbyterian Church and currently resides in Westminster Gardens, Duarte, California.

Paraphraser: "In all the seasons seeking God" (*STB* #237).

Chong, Julia (née Nga Chee Wu)

Born in Guangzhou, China, 14 August 1926, Julia Chong was a pianist, a piano teacher, and a composer of hymns, songs, operettas, and orchestral works. She learned to play the piano from missionary teachers in China and served as an organist since her teenage years. Chong moved from Guangzhou to Penang, Malaysia, with her parents during World War II. She subsequently studied at Trinity Teacher's Training College, Singapore (1949–52), and received a Licentiate of the Royal School of Music in piano performance (1951); she also received a Licentiate of the Trinity College of Music, London (1959–61), she attended the Cardiff College of Music and Drama (1958–59), and she was a Fellow of the Trinity College of Music (1961). Chong also studied at Peabody Conservatory in the United States (1964–65) and Kyung Hee University, Korea (MA, Composition, 1973–75). She married a medical doctor, Datuk Chun Hian Chong, in 1952 and traveled with him to England, the United States, and Korea. She studied music, raised three daughters, taught students, and served faithfully as an organist at her Chin Fu Methodist Church in Kuching, Sarawak, East Malaysia, until several months before her death. For her musical contributions to Malaysia, Chong received several awards, including the Sijil Kehormatan Negara (1968) and Johan Bintang Kenyalang (1988). She was the Honorary Curator of the Sarawak Museum. She died 4 November 2001 in Kuching.

Composer: KUCHING (*STB* #211).

Clark, Douglas L.

Born 25 June, 194 in Walthman, Massachusetts, Douglas L. Clark graduated from Princeton University (BA magna cum lauda, 1967) and Indiana University (MA, 1969), both with major in Germanic Languages and Literatures. He also earned theological degrees from Bangor Theological Seminary (MDiv, 1974) and Boston College Chestnut Hill (MA in Theology, 1978.) Rev. Clark served as an interim pastor in many local churches and was a pastor at the United Church of Christ in Lenox, MA (1989–1996), and a Senior Minister at First Congregational Church, UCC Riverside, CA (1996–1996), and a Senior Minister at First congregational Church, UCC Riverside, CA (1996–2000). He also taught at a few colleges. Received a Teaching Excellence Award for 1986–1987 in Boston college Chestnut Hill, and was an Adjunct Faculty at Wesley Theologically Seminary, Washington DC (2005–2007). His publications include: "'How the Breath Comes to the Bones' (Ecclesiastes 11:5, NRSV): A Progressive Christian Ethical and Theological Perspective on Human Embryonic Stem Cell Research," presented at the 2006 AAR/SBL Mid-Alantic Regional Meeting, Baltimore, MD; "Sarah's Dilemma:

An Ecumenical Assessment of Assisted Reproduction," presented at the Northeast Regional Meeting of the Assisted Religion, Wellesley College, 1987.

Author: "Hope for the children" (*STB* #260).

Compain, Alice

Originally a member of the China Inland Mission (CIM), Alice Compain was a missionary in Thailand, but she has been working among the Khmer in Cambodia. She plays the violin well, and she has encouraged native Christians to compose new hymns. Compain helped with the editing of the Khmer hymnal. (For her photo, see the entry for Songsan Prasopsin.)

Translator: "Oh! Jesus Christ is the true God" (*STB* #206).

Connolly, Richard

Born in 1927 in Sydney, Australia, Richard Connolly was educated in Christian Brothers and Marist Brothers schools and studied organ with Father Joseph Muset; Connolly also studied theology and music in Rome. Upon returning to Australia, he attended the University of Sydney and earned a BA in 1956. Since then, he has been on the staff of the Australian Broadcasting Commission in Sydney and is currently the Director of Radio Drama and Features. He has composed much incidental music for theater, television, and films, as well as hymns; many of his tunes are developed in collaboration with James Philip McAuley (such as "Songs of the People of God," 1982).[105]

Composer: COSMIC PRAISE (*STB* #35); ARALUEN (*STB* #230).

Custodio, Bernardino Feliciano

Born in Manila, the Philippines, 26 May 1911, Bernardino Feliciano Custodio was a famous conductor, composer, and teacher. He received a bachelor's degree in piano performance from the University of the Philippines (1939) and a master's degree from the University of Santo Tomas. He taught at the University of the Philippines right after his graduation, and he received a Fulbright Grant in 1947. In the early 1950s, Custodio led a group of teachers from the University of the Philippines to join the newly established Conservatory of Music at the University of Santo Tomas; he was its director from 1958 to 1961. He served as the associate conductor of the Manila Symphony Orchestra and conducted the 1946 inauguration concert of the Philippine Republic's first president, Manuel A. Roxas. Custodio

---

105 Information in this entry is derived from the author's correspondence with Shirley Murray, January 27, 2007.

wrote a number of pieces for piano, for orchestra (such as *Malayan Suite*, 1932) and for chamber ensembles (such as *Serenade for violin, cello, and piano*, 1932) (cf. *CCPE* 6, 308).

Composer: ROSEWOOD (*STB* #29).

Dadap, Jerry (Jeremiah Amper)

Born in Hinunangan, Leyte, the Philippines, 5 November 1935, to a musical family of thirteen siblings, Jerry Dadap initially studied theology at Silliman University in 1954. He also received musical training under Priscilla Magdamo and obtained his bachelor's degree from the Conservatory of Music at the University of the Philippines in 1964. Dadap also studied composition at Mannes School of Music in the United States in 1971 and earned a postgraduate diploma. Dadap was among the first to explore the symphonic potential of the *rondalla,* as seen from his *Philippine Symphonic Medley for Rondalla* (1967); he encouraged and popularized Filipino compositions by inaugurating the Lahi concert series; and he was the first Filipino to conduct a performance of his work in Carnegie Hall, New York, in 1971. Dadap teaches at Santa Isabel College and the University of Santo Tomas. He has written over fifty major works, including *Violin Concerto in Three Movements* (1965–66), as well as music for ballet and opera. He has also composed many choral anthems for his choirs; those published are *Choral Cycle No. 1* (1964) and *Choral Cycle No. 2* (1966) (cf. *CCPE* 6, 309).

Composer: PAGYAO (*STB* #170).

Darsane, I Nyoman

Born on a Friday about 1939 in Bali, Indonesia, I Nyoman Darsane is a graduate of the Fakultas Senirupa, the fine arts department of the University of Diponogoro Semarang in Central Java (BA, 1964). (In the Balinese tradition, "Nyoman" is the name for the third child in the family and "I" is the equivalent of "Mister.") Darsane became a Christian while attending the University. His girlfriend, who would later be his wife, introduced him to Christianity. By the third time he attended Salvation Army services, he had already read the Bible and had found faith in God. Through his positive Christian conduct and loving care, Darsane convinced his Hindu father to let him search for salvation in his way, and finally he led his father into the Christian faith as well. In order to qualify as a Balinese artist, one has to combine many skills: painting, dancing, poetry, puppeteering, composing, and performing music. As a young boy, Darsane was blessed with the opportunities to learn all these skills, but painting is his main career. He had his first art exhibition in 1974 through the help of a Singaporean friend; he has presented many exhibitions in Indonesia as well as Korea, Thailand, Germany, and other European countries. In 1980, in Chiang Mai, Thailand, Darsane experienced a turning point in his artistic career: he began to contextualize Christian art with Balinese styles. His motto for artistic expression may be summarized in the theological statement originally proposed by Bishop Wayan Mastra: "Christ is my Life, but Bali is my body." Among Darsane's favorite biblical themes are the prodigal son, new life in Christ, Mary and Martha, and the parables of the lost sheep and the ten virgins; he put many of these themes into dances, paintings, and musical compositions. He says that conflicts between good and evil, right and wrong, and light and darkness are constantly present in the struggle of daily life; therefore, these ideas are symbolically expressed through all his works. Darsane was featured in I-to Loh's *Kristus Sundaring Bali (Christ the Light to Bali)*, published by AILM in 1988. Recently, a book has been published in Germany concerning Darsane's life and work: *Bali ist mein Leib, Christus ist mein Leben: der Kunstler I Nyoman Darsane* (edited by Karl-Christoph Epting and published in 1999 by Hans Thoma Verlag).

Author/composer: "Surrendering to God," PENYERAHAN (*STB* #77).

Das, Samar

Born about 1930 in Bangladesh, Samar Das was one of the country's most famous composers/poets. Das was a member of the Baptist Church. After graduating from St. Paul's College, he studied at Lucknow Music College in India and received a Master of Music degree. He played the piano, accordion, and Hawaiian guitar. Das served as a chief music producer and a music director of radio and television in Dhaka and as the honorary principal of the Christian Center for Musicians. He composed the theme song for one of the South Asian Games in Bangladesh. Because of his involvement in and contributions to cultural events, he received many awards: the Southeast Asian International Music Conference Gold Medal (1979), the Dishari Padak award in Church Music, the International Film Music "Sequence Award," and a UNICEF award for "Best Bengali Children's Song." Das published LP records and cassettes, Bengali folk songs, dance music, and Christian lyrics (hymns), all of which were either in classical, traditional folk, Bengali, and Indian styles or were blended with Western and contemporary styles. Das considered his most important works to be his orchestration for the Bengali national anthem and the recording of *Bangladesher Ridaey Hote* for the liberation war of Bangladesh. He recently passed away.

Author/composer: "Jesus, come dwell within our yearning hearts," JISHU ESHO (*STB* #70).

David, C. R. W.

Born in Dindigul, Tamilnadu, India, 31 January 1932, C. R. W. David was a graduate of American College in Madurai and United Theological College in Bangalore. He also pursued advanced studies in Library Sciences at Northwestern University in the United States (1971); Interdisciplinary Human Studies at the University of Bradford, UK (postgraduate diploma, 1977); Communications at the University of Minnesota, US (MA, 1979); and Radio, T.V. & Video at Hatch End, UK (certificate). An expert in the field of communications, David introduced courses in Communications Studies and the MTh program in Communications at Serampore University, Kolkata. He also established the MS program in Communications at Madurai Kamaraj University. For his enormous contributions in communications, church and social institutions, Christian ministry, and theological education, David was awarded an honorary Doctor of Divinity degree by the Academy of Ecumenical Indian Theology and Church Administration, Chennai, on 5 September 1998. He served as a pastor at the Karnataka Diocese (1959–70) and taught and served as the vice principal at Tamilnadu Theological Seminary (1970–77). Upon retirement, he became the director of the Unemployed Young People's Association. He also served as the president of Inba Illam ("Home for the Old and Needy"), Madurai; the vice president of the Council of Management of the Christian Literature Society, Chennai; and the treasurer of the Tamilnadu Theological Book Club, Madurai, until the end of his life. He published many books and articles in English and Thamilz and also made many video and audio programs for Christian broadcasting. He died in 2001.

Translator: "Worship and praise we give" (*STB* #25); "Grant, LORD, that we may not faint" (*STB* #185).

Del Rosario, Romeo

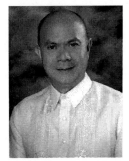

Born in Manila, the Philippines, 7 January 1949, Romeo Del Rosario received a BA in Psychology from Philippine Christian University (1968); a Master of Divinity degree from Candler School of Theology, Emory University, Atlanta, Georgia (1972); and a PhD in Theological and Religious Studies, majoring in Ecumenics and Mission from Boston University Graduate School (1981). He is a clergy member of the California-Pacific Annual Conference of the United Methodist Church. Del Rosario is a missionary of the General Board of Global Ministries of the United Methodist Church. He served as a pastor in California (1978–85); taught at Theological Hall in Freetown, Sierra Leone, West Africa, and directed its Theological Education by Extension program (1985–88); served as the United Methodist liaison pastor with the Middle East Council of Churches in Jerusalem (1989–92); and taught at Sabah Theological Seminary in Kota Kinabalu, Sabah, Malaysia, where he was also the academic dean for the Malay Department (1992–2001). After teaching theology and ecumenics at Union Theological Seminary in the Philippines for a few years, he was elected its president in 2005. He was appointed the Country Director for the United Methodist Mission in Cambodia and the District Superintendent of two provinces next to the Vietnam border. He teaches at the Cambodia Methodist Bible School and is the chairperson of the Theological Education Committee, which supervises the Bible School. He is the chairperson of the Board of Ordained Ministry, which oversees pastors-in-training and all ordained clergy.[106]

Paraphraser: "Our souls are full of praises" (*STB* #29).

Dhyriam, Benjamin Muthyam John

Born in South India, 26 September 1923, Benjamin Muthyam John Dhyriam is a member of South Andhra Lutheran Church. He received a BA from A. C. College, Andhra University. He is a prolific writer in Telegu, Thamilz, and English; as a composer, he is equally good in Carnatic as well as Hindustani classical styles. Not only does he play the harmonium, sitar (plucked lute), mandolin, guitar, and musical saw, he is also a talented artist and sculptor. Prior to 1984, Dhyriam composed nearly 3000 songs and recorded 1310 songs. His compositions combine classical, semi-classical, light music, and semi-Western styles. He was invited to attend the 1987 Asian Seminar on Liturgy and Music in Makiling, the Philippines. By January 2006, he had composed music for 4850 lyrics in Thamilz and Malayalam and written 460 lyrics in Thamilz, 1100 lyrics in Telegu, and twenty-five hymns in English. It is no wonder he has been felicitated forty-six times in Tamilnadu and Andhra Pradesh. Dhyriam has been awarded the titles Sangeetha Ratna, Sangeetha Sarathi, Sangeetha Vibhushan, Sangeetha Kala Praveena, Aadhunika Salrala Kavi, Arutkalaignar, and "King of Christian Music." In South India, he is also known as an orator, philosopher, philanthropist, psychologist, mythologist, theologist, artist, and a soul-stirring preacher. He was the editor and music director of the Christian Literature Society in Madras and the director of the recording company, His Master's Voice. He has conducted and directed many programs on television, radio, and the stage. Dhyriam also served for five years as the chief judge of All India Radio, Madras, the highest position in this field. Since his retirement, he has been engaged in setting Biblical texts to 1000 of 34,848 ragas, with the intention of bringing a younger generation to the Church with songs of praise to God via their rich Indian musical heritage.[107]

Author/composer: "O God of love," DHYRIAM (*STB* #63).

---

106 Information in this entry is derived from the author's communication with Del Rosario, March 16, 2009.
107 Information in this entry is derived from the author's interview with Dhyriam, January 19, 2006.

Dyvasirvadam, Govada

Born in India, 28 March 1951, Govada Dyvasirvadam is a gifted pastor and theologian and is active in the ecumenical movement and youth training. He has earned MA, MTh, and PhD degrees and was the general secretary of the Church of South India for a number of years before he was elected Bishop of Andhra Pradesh in 2002. He also serves as the chair of the Board of Trustees for the United Theological College, Bangalore. He and his wife, Ramani Ramya Krupa, have three grown sons and one daughter.

Author/composer: "Sarennam, O the Divine Light," DHIVYA JYOTHI (*STB* #47).

Eang, Chhun

Born in Kompong Cham, Cambodia, 20 December 1954, Chhun Eang grew up in a Buddhist family and studied nursing in 1972. Eang's youth was corrupted by immorality and gambling. On 20 June 1984, he encountered a former schoolmate reading the Bible. Eang assumed that it was a pornographic novel and wanted to borrow it, but he was told that it was the New Testament, about the love of God, Jesus Christ, and his Gospel. Somehow the Spirit was working in Eang: he confessed his sins and accepted Jesus as his Savior. At the time, churches, Bibles, and pastors were rare in Cambodia; Eang had to ride his bicycle thirty kilometers to another town to worship with friends and to study the Bible. Eang was baptized on 26 January 1988. In 1990, he enrolled in the Bible Correspondences Courses from Campus Crusade for Christ, and in 1989, he established the Bashac River Church near the Mekong River with only four members; it grew to more than one hundred members in 2007. In 1991, he established the Prektalong Church. Eang completed his medical training in 1994, but he wanted to dedicate his life to fulltime ministry and went to India for two months in 1995 to study the Bible and English. Upon his return, he established a church in his hometown. His church became associated with the Church of God in Singapore in 1998, and Eang was ordained as the pastor on 26 March 2000. He was a delegate to the tenth General Assembly of the Christian Conference of Asia in Colombo, Sri Lanka, in 1996. Eang believes that the ecumenical movement is a strong witness to the teaching of Christ. Although his church prohibited him from joining ecumenical organizations or activities, he became very active in CCA, to which he was elected a member of the Central Committee in 2006.

Author: "Now I know," stanza 2 (*STB* #289).
Translator: "Now my heart is sure that Jesus lives" (*STB* #312).

Ekka, Justin

Born in the 1930s in the Ranchi area of India, Justin Ekka is one of the most prolific composers and lyric writers in India. He works for All India Radio. Ekka is humble, sincere, and soft-spoken, yet he is full of energy and compassion for people. His love and sympathy have compelled him to work on the behalf of blind children, teaching them to find joy and happiness through songs and dances. I-to Loh says:

> When I visited him in 1984, he took me to the school for vision-impaired children where he was a volunteer teacher of singing and dancing. Following a whole day of teaching, we returned to his simple home for a dinner of rice and beans. After dinner, Ekka said he would play one song for me; he sat cross-legged on the floor with his eyes closed and played a very beautiful melody on his violin. I asked him when he composed it, and he said, "Today!" I was perplexed, for I had been with him the whole day: when did he find time to compose that song? He said, "I composed this song while I was accompanying the dancing and singing children." I was in awe: he could play one thing and simultaneously compose a totally unrelated song! I felt like a tiny ant admiring a giant elephant! I had never felt so humbled. To me, Justin Ekka is the richest person in the world.

Indeed, by that time, Ekka had already written more than 4,000 lyrics (hymns) in five different languages along with music. If he has been able to keep this pace of work, after almost twenty-five years, the number of his hymns must now exceed those of Charles Wesley (who wrote over 6000 hymns). As a person with meager possessions yet with a constant flow of new works, Ekka is the model of one who is "poor in things but rich in soul." This is the opposite of stanza 3 in Harry Emerson Fosdick's hymn "God of grace and God of glory," which says many of us are "rich in things and poor in soul."

Composer: "So be it" (*STB* #109); "LORD, have mercy" (*STB* #124); "Glory to God" (*STB* #127).

Endo, Masuko

Born in 1909 in Okayama Prefecture, Japan, Masuko Endo lost her father at the age of eight; she graduated from Wake Girl's High School in 1926. Endo became a Christian at the age of twenty-four. After marrying, she worked with her husband on their farm. During those years, she wrote and published many poems relating to her Christian faith and farm life. When her husband was very ill, Endo assumed all responsibilities of the family chores and farming; she persisted in her activities in the Christian community, even walking four kilometers to attend worship services and prayer meetings (cf. *SRKII*, 114f).

Author: "In the dawn of the morn" (*STB* #158).

Feliciano, Francisco F.

Born in Morong, Rizal, the Philippines, 19 February 1941, Francisco F. Feliciano received a Teacher's Diploma (1967) and Master of Music degree (Composition, 1972) from the University of the Philippines. He studied church music at BerlinerKirchenmusikschule,Berlin(1973–77),andreceived a Diploma in Music Composition from the Hochschule für Musik, West Berlin, Germany (1977); from Yale University, he received both an MA with distinction (1978) and a DMA (1984) in Composition. His teachers at the three schools came from various ethnic backgrounds: Eliseo Pajaro was Filipino, Isang Yun was Korean, and Krzysztof Penderecki was Polish. During college, Feliciano began his music career as an organist at St. Andrew's Theological Seminary. He was a professor of composition and music theory at the University of the Philippines, a resident conductor of the Philippine Philharmonic Orchestra (1982–92), a member of the League of Filipino Composers, an editor of *CCA Hymnal Supplement I* (1981), and one of three executive editors of the 1990 and 2000 editions of *Sound the Bamboo*. Most importantly, he and Father Ellsworth Chandlee co-founded the Asian Institute for Liturgy and Music (AILM); Feliciano became the director in 1980. The AILM has since expanded and is now called Samba Likhaan Foundation, for which Feliciano serves as the president. This is the first institution in Asia committed to the cultivation and development of Asian liturgy and music and has trained many talented students from India, Indonesia, Singapore, Malaysia, Taiwan, Thailand, Japan, and the Philippines. Feliciano is one of the best choral conductors in Asia; he is also known for his hymns, liturgical music, and choral and orchestral works. He has been awarded countless scholarships and has won many prizes for compositions. His doctoral dissertation was "Four Asian Contemporary Composers (Takemitsu, Chou Wen-chong, Isang Yun, and Jose Maceda): The Influence of Tradition in their Music." Feliciano's important compositions include: *Ayyuwan Chi Pita* ("Promise of the Earth," concerning human rights and environmental issues), 1993; the opera *La Loba Negra* ("The Black She-Wolf"), 1984; music for the ballet *Yerma*, 1982; the orchestral pieces *Transfiguration*, 1983, and *Die Verklacrung Christi*, 1976; *Isostasie III* for strings and woodwinds, 1981; the choral works *Pokpok Alimpako*, 1981 (which won an award for best contemporary composition in Arezzo, Italy), *Si Yahweh ang aking Pastol* (Psalm 23), 1981; *Umawit sa Kagalakan* (Psalm 100); *Te Deum*, 1981, and hundreds of hymns, canticles, and psalm settings.

Author/composer: "How deep your love, O Master," BANAHAW (*STB* #147); "Still, I search for my God," WASDIN PANG IPAAD (*STB* #176).
Author/arranger: "What a great mystery," CATUROG NA NONOY (*STB* #82).
Author: "Sing a song to the LORD" (*STB* #92); "Dance of light" (*STB* #278).

Composer: "We believe" (*STB* #45); BANAWE (*STB* #117); "Trisagion" (*STB* #122); ST. ANDREW'S (*STB* #130); DAPIT HAPON (*STB* #161); ERMITA (*STB* #186); PATATAG (*STB* #248); PANATA (*STB* #261); ANTAMOK (*STB* #274); TAGULAYLAY (*STB* #277).

Composer of ostinato: CORDILLERA (*STB* #97).

Adapter: MAMAYUG AKUN (*STB* #98).

Altered: KUCHING (*STB* #211).

Father Foster

Father Foster is a Catholic priest in the Philippines, possibly serving in the northern part of Luzon among the Ilocano.

Transcriber: "The great thanksgiving" (*STB* #4).

Fowler, J. Andrew

Born in Killeen, Texas, USA, 27 March 1935, J. Andrew Fowler is the son of a medical doctor, Joseph Anthony Fowler, who had prepared to be a medical missionary in the Belgium Congo in 1932 but was unable to leave the United States because of the Great Depression. Andrew Fowler graduated from Southwestern University in Georgetown, Texas (1957), and Southern Methodist University in Dallas (BD 1963, STM 1964, and DMin 1976). In 1957, the Board of Mission of the United Methodist Church sent him to Sarawak, Malaysia, as a missionary teacher. He married Monina Cepeda, a missionary nurse from the Philippines, in 1960 in Kapit, Malaysia. They have two children: Mananina, who was born in the Philippines, and Joseph Claude, who was born in Malaysia. In 1964, Fowler was ordained an Elder in the Sarawak Iban Provisional Annual Conference of the Methodist Church. He served for nineteen years in Sibu, Kapit, and Sarikel and six years in Kuala Lumpur as the vice principal of the new Seminari Theologi Malaysia, where he taught courses in missiology. Fowler and his family returned to the United States in 1985. He served as a mission interpreter, peace-with-justice educator, and local pastor; he retired in 2000, residing in Killeen. Fowler has written and published many articles, including "Accommodation in an Iban Church Today," in *Practical Anthropology* (Sept.–Oct. 1970); "Towards Wholeness in Ministry Among the Iban," in *Missiology* (July 1977); "Evangelism Without Imperialism Among the Iban," in *Southeast Asia Journal of Theology* (no. 2, 1978); "Building a Witness Model," in the *Church Development and Renewal* newsletter, General Board of Global Ministries, United Methodist Church (July 1978); "In Christ with the Iban," (Jan. 1981); "Coupling Personal Faith and Social Justice," in *Central Link* of the UMC Central Texas Conference (Dec. 2002–Jan. 2003).

Author: "The Rice of Life" (*STB* #190); "The LORD is pure unbounded love" (*STB* #211).

Francis, T. Dayanandan

T. Dayanandan Francis was born in Tamilnadu, India, 14 August 1932. His father, the late Reverend E. Tychicus, was the principal of Arcot Theological Seminary, Vellore, in South India. Francis is one of the most outstanding and influential theologians, scholars, and writers in India today. Influenced by the Christian Endeavor Movement as a high school student, he dedicated himself to Christian service in 1954 while he was an undergraduate student in Madras. He graduated from Madras University (MA, Tamil Language and Literature, 1958), Serampore University (United Theological College, Bangalore, BD, 1962), and University of Poona (PhD, Linguistics, 1974). He also did postdoctoral studies in philosophy and religion at King's College, University of London. The World University Round Table in Arizona awarded Francis with an honorary Doctor of Letters degree in 1981. Francis was ordained as a presbyter of Church of South India in 1972. He married Felicia Padmini, who worked in C. M. C. Hospital, Vellore, and taught at several schools in Bangalore. As a scholar and theologian, Francis has taught Biblical subjects at United Theological College, Bangalore (1962–66), and History of Religions, Hinduism and Indian Philosophy at Tamilnadu Theological Seminary, Madurai (1971–79); he also served as the Dean of Studies and Dean of Post-Graduate Studies at the same seminary (1977–79). Francis has served as the general secretary of the Christian Literature Society since 1979 and the chair of the National Association for Christian Communication of NCCI of India since 1984. He is a prolific writer; his publications include: *Christian Poets and Tamil Cultures* (1977); *New Approaches to Inter-faith Dialogue* (as editor; published by the Church of Sweden Mission); *Called to Communicate* (1987); *Aspects of Christian and Hindu Bhakti* (1987); *The Relevance of Hindu Ethos for Christian Presence: A Tamil Perspective*; *The Mission and Message of Ramalinga Swamy*; and many scholarly articles in academic journals. He has also published more than twenty books in Thamilz covering theological, devotional, inter-religious, and literary subjects and in the field of linguistics. Since 1964, Francis has been a member of the Interconfessional Thamilz Bible committee. He has translated four books from English to Thamilz; the most recent is *Christian Lyrics and Songs of New Life* (fifteenth edition, enlarged; Madras: Christian Literature Society, 1988).

Author: "Thousands and thousands of songs full of praise" (*STB* #37).

Francisco, Jose Mario C.

Born in Binan, Laguna, the Philippines, 19 January 1949, Jose Mario C. Francisco graduated from Ateneo de Manila University (BS, Chemistry, 1966; MA, Literature, 1973), Jesuit School of Theology at Berkeley (STL, 1986), and Graduate Theological Union (PhD, Philosophical Theology, 1986). He entered the Society of Jesus on 30 June 1968 and was ordained priest on 27 March 1977. He taught English, philosophy, and theology at Xavier University (1972–74),

Ateneo de Manila University (1975–78, 1986, 1993–present), Loyola School of Theology (1986–), East Asian Pastoral Institute (1996–present), and Jesuit School of Theology at Berkeley (2000–present). He has held various research and administrative positions at the above institutions, such as dean of the Loyola School of Theology (1989–92) and director of the East Asian Pastoral Institute (1996–present), and he is the co-founder and co-editor of *Pulong: Sources for Philippine Studies*. Francisco has actively participated in various social development services: he has served as the national chaplain and a trustee of Jesuit Volunteer Philippines (1993–present), as chair of the board of trustees, Emmaus Center for Formation (1999–present), and as convener, Coalition for Peace (1991–92). His scholarly publications include two books: *Living Theology: The Intersection of Theology, Culture and Spirituality* (as editor; Manila: Jesuit Conference of East Asia and Oceania, 2001) and *A Theoretical Program for Interpreting Religious Narrative: Listening to the Philippine Pasyon Tradition* (1986, PhD dissertation, Graduate Theological Union; in press). He has published dozens of essays, such as: "Christianity as Church and Story and the Birth of the Filipino Nation in the Nineteenth Century," in *History of Christianity*, vol. 8 (Cambridge: Cambridge University Press, forthcoming); "Roman Catholic Church" and "Friars and the Land Controversy" in the *Dictionary of Asian Christianity*, edited by Scott W. Sunquist (Grand Rapids, Michigan/Cambridge, UK: William B. Eermans Publishing Co., 2001); "Integrative or Divisive?: Christian Symbols and Rituals in Philippines Society," *Pulso*, Monograph 7 (June 1991), Institute for Church and Social Issues (ICSI).

Author: "O LORD, who made all the heavens" (*STB #76*).

Fukunaga, Sandra

Born in the United States as a *nisei* (second generation) Japanese American, Sandra Fukunaga still has a good command of the Japanese language. She is a member of the Japanese American United Methodist Church in Los Angeles, and she helped with the Asian American hymnal project, which published the 1983 *Hymns from the Four Winds*.

Translator: "Dawn and the light of sunrise" (*STB #54*).

Gibbs, Janet

Born in New Zealand, Janet Gibbs was the organist at a church called St. Andrew's on The Terrace, where John and Shirley Murray are members. Gibbs is a very talented musician, and the Reverend John Murray requested her to compose a short liturgical response for the church. She has since moved to Melbourne, Australia.

Composer: "God, receive our prayer" (*STB* #111).

Gibson, Colin Alexander

Born in New Zealand, 26 March 1933, Colin Alexander Gibson came from a Methodist family. He graduated from Christchurch Teachers College (1961) and the University of Otago (BA Hons, Latin and English; PhD, English). He also has an MA Dip Hons and Dip Teaching LTCL. He is versed in English, French, and Latin, and he is the organist and choirmaster at the Mornington Methodist Church, Dunedin, a position he has held for more than forty years.

Gibson was the Donald Collie Professor of English and head of the English department at the University of Otago; he is now an emeritus professor of English and still teaches and carries out administrative work. He is an internationally distinguished scholar with editions of Renaissance dramas published by the Clarendon Press, Cambridge University Press, Macmillan, and St. Martin's Press. Gibson has published numerous articles and essays and edited a variety of journals. He is currently the editor of *Word and Worship*, an ecumenical journal for lay leaders of worship. He takes a special interest in the visual arts as they relate to literature and religion. He has been writing church music, including hymns and hymn settings, for more than thirty years; his work is known internationally through published collections such as *Singing Love*, *Reading the Signature*, and *Songs for a Rainbow People*, and in national hymnbooks such as *With One Voice*, *Alleluia Aotearoa*, *New Zealand Praise*, *Carol our Christmas*, and the recent New Zealand Hymnbook Trust publication, *Faith Forever Singing*. His hymns and his settings of texts by Shirley Erena Murray, with whom he frequently collaborates, are published in more than forty international hymnbooks. Gibson is a long-standing member of the editorial board of the New Zealand Hymnbook Trust. He frequently writes about and lectures on hymns and hymn writing and has given workshops and presentations throughout New Zealand and in the United States, the Philippines, Australia, and Great Britain. In New Zealand, religious radio and television programs often feature his work. In addition to his writing and compositions for the Church, he has a body of songs (many of them for children), piano pieces, and extended choral works. His larger choral pieces for the Church include *Balaam and Balak*, *The Animals' Nativity*, and the cantata *The Spirit Within*, which has been performed in Auckland, Wellington, Palmerston North, Blenheim, and Kaikoura.

Gibson's wife, Jeanette, is a talented embroiderer and textile artist; four of her works grace the Mornington church. She has been commissioned to create stoles for ministers in New Zealand, Australia, and Samoa, and is currently completing a large memorial panel for a Christchurch Roman Catholic church. Jeanette and Colin have three children: Marcus, a computer expert, John, a professional musician, and Philippa, an executive officer for the Antiquarian Booksellers Association of Great Britain.[108] Gibson says that his music is "eclectic in style (Western classical in bias)." In textual writing, he is "for simplicity, for metaphor and symbol derived from the New Zealand environment and social experience." His theology is liberal and Christocentric. Regarding his work, Gibson writes:

> Much of my writing originates from a response to local need and personal experience among my congregation. I am becoming increasingly interested in exploring the relationship between religious experience, music, and my country's landscape and natural environment. If there are themes in my writing, they would include the joyful and comic elements in worship, freedom and openness (the freedom of Christ), and the response of Christian love and understanding to personal suffering and social disharmony.[109]

Author/composer: "He came singing love," SINGING LOVE (*STB* #205); "For the man and for the woman," MAKILING (*STB* #238).

Paraphraser: "Jesus, come dwell within our yearning hearts" (*STB* #70); "The Holy Light" (*STB* #154); "Following Jesus" (*STB* #227).

Composer: REVERSI (*STB* #143); GERALDINE (*STB* #145B).

Ginting, E. P.

Born in Medan, North Sumatra, Indonesia, E. P. Ginting is a pastor of the Batak Karo Protestant Church (GBKP). He earned a Doctor of Pastoral Studies degree from the Southeast Asia Graduate School of Theology (SEAGST) and has been teaching at the Theological Seminary in Abdi Sabda. He has written a number of books on theological issues and has served as the moderator of his church.

Author/composer: "Now come, O Holy Spirit," O ROH KUDUS (*STB* #10).

Ginting, M. B.

M. B. Ginting is an Indonesian composer.

Co-composer: JANGAN TAKUT (*STB* #306).

---

108   From the author's correspondence with Gibson, August 13, 2004.
109   Quoted from the registration form of Asian Workshop on Liturgy and Music, Manila, 1987.

Gish, George W., Jr.

Born near Glen Elder, Kansas, USA, 5 December 1936, George W. Gish, Jr., graduated from Emporia State University (BA, 1958) and University of Michigan (MA, Far Eastern Studies, 1967). He also studied Missionary Orientation Studies at Stony Point, New York, and Garrett Theological Seminary, Evanston, Illinois (1967–68), and he studied at Franciscan Japanese Language School, Sophia University, and Naganuma Japanese Language School, Tokyo (1968–70). Gish served first as a short-term, "J-3" Methodist Missionary in Nagoya Gakuin Boy's School, Nagoya Central Church, and Seto Eisen Church (1958–61) and was a lecturer in English at Nagoya University (1961–62). He served as an associate pastor in Pecatonica, Illinois (1962–64), before being assigned as a United Methodist missionary to Japan in 1968. He subsequently served as the Director of Creative Arts for the Audio-Visual Activities Commission (AVACO) of the National Christian Council of Japan (1970–73), the editor of the *Kyodan* newsletter, the audio-visual director of the United Church of Christ in Japan (1973–83), a United Methodist Church (UMC) Missionary Field Representative for Japan (1976–94), the United Methodist Diaconal Minister at the Detroit Conference (1983), and the associate pastor of Honda Kinen Church, Tokyo (1983–2003). At Aoyama Gakuin University, Tokyo, Gish was a professor of Japanese cultural history and the religious activities director (1976–79), the coordinator of Japanese arts courses in the International Division (1989–2003), and a lecturer in Japanese cultural and music history. After his retirement in April 2003, he has served as a UMC missionary individual volunteer, a professor emeritus at Aoyama Gakuin University, and a dean of the International Community Division, Edogawa City College of Life, Tokyo. In addition to his academic positions, Gish has served as the founder of the Society for the Spread and Promotion of Heike Biwa; he presently serves on the boards of Japan Biblical Theological Seminary, Christian Child Welfare Association (CCWA), and Research Action Institute for Koreans in Japan (RAIK). He is the executive director of the Society for Overseas Cultural Exchange and the executive vice-chairman of AVACO. Gish received music education from a young age and studied the *shakuhachi* (vertical flute) and *biwa* (plucked lute) after coming to Japan. His MA thesis concerned the origins of the *biwa*. His published articles include: "Watakushi to Nihon no biwa gaku," *Kokusai Bunka*, no. 194 (1970); "Religion as a World Phenomenon: Beyond Christian Ecumenism," *Japan Christian Quarterly,* vol. 37, no. 1, Kyo Bun Kwan, Tokyo (1971); "*Biwa*: Its Past and Presence," *An Asia Notebook,* no. 22, IMC, Tokyo (1971); "Japanese Artists Explore Christian Faith," *Japan Christian Quarterly*, vol. 42, no. 4, Kyo Bun Kwan, Tokyo (1976); "Japanese Christianity and the Emperor Myth," *The Christian Gospel and Its Ethical Implications For Japanese Society,* 21st Annual Hayama Missionary Seminar Papers, Tokyo (1980), and many other articles written in Japanese concerning Japanese culture, arts, music, and liturgy. Gish's other publications include: *The Biwa in History: Its Origins and Development in Japan* (MA thesis; Ann Arbor: University of Michigan, 1967); the chapter "History of Biwa" in *Orasho kikō* ("Accounts of Hidden Christian Chants"), ed. Minagawa Tatsuo (Tokyo: Nihon Kirisuto Kyōdan Shuppan, 1981); and *Wandafuru difarensu: nihon no subarashisa o shiranai nihonjin e* ("Wonderful Difference: to Japanese who don't know what is wonderful about Japan") (Tokyo: Gakken, 2004).[110]

Paraphraser: "Jesus built the Church" (*STB* #68); "In old Galilee when sweet breezes blew" (*STB* #195).

Gnanamani, Y.

Y. Gnanamani is from Aruppukkottai in South India.

Author/composer: "Christ is all to me," YELLAAM YESUVEE (*STB* #55).

Grant, Robert

Born in 1779 in Bengal, India, Robert Grant was a graduate of Magdalene College, Cambridge (1801 and 1804). He was a lawyer, a Member of Parliament, a judge advocate general, and a governor of Bombay (now Mumbai). He was knighted in 1834. Grant wrote a few hymns, which appeared in the *Christian Observer* (1806–15), H. V. Elliot's *Psalms and Hymns* (1835), and in *Sacred Poems* (published by Grant's brother Lord Glenelg in 1839) (cf. Young 1993, 757). He died in Dalpoorie, India, 9 July 1838.

Author: "O worship the King" (*STB* #24).

Green, Fred Pratt

Born in Roby, near Liverpool, England, 2 September 1903, Fred Pratt Green was a graduate of Didsbury College, Manchester. In 1928, he was ordained as a Methodist pastor and served many churches in England from 1927 to 1969. Encouraged by the poet Fallon Webb, Green published his poems in *The Unlikely Earth* (1952), *The Skating Parson* (1963), and *The Old Couple* (1976); some of them appeared in the *Oxford Book of Twentieth-Century English Verse*. In 1977, Green was appointed to co-edit an ecumenical collection for all-age worship, *Partners in Praise* (London: Stainer & Bell and Chester House Publications, 1979). In 1984, he set up The Pratt Green Trust, a charitable body for the furtherance of hymnody and church music, principally

---

110 Information in this entry is derived from the author's correspondence with Gish in 2004.

funded by the royalties from his hymn writing (for more information, see the website http://www.prattgreentrust.org.uk/Fred%20Pratt%20Green_pgt.htm). Green was a prolific writer of more than 300 hymns, many of which were included in supplements to the British Methodist *Hymns and Songs* (1969) and *Partners in Praise* (1979). He was the leader of the "hymn explosion" in England; Erik Routley considered Green the "most important hymnist in Methodism since Charles Wesley" (Young 1993, 758). Green was awarded an honorary doctorate in Humane Letters from Emory University (1982) and was made a Fellow in the Hymn Society of America and Canada. He died 22 October 2000 in Norwich, England.

Author: "God is here as we your people meet" (*STB* #49).

Hanaoka, Nobuaki

Born in the 1940s and raised in Japan, Nobuaki Hanaoka graduated from the Kanto Gakuin University School of Theology in Yokohama, Japan. He then traveled to the United States in 1970 to continue his theological education. He received an MDiv from the Colgate Rochester Crozer Divinity School and Bexley Hall. Upon graduation, he began his pastoral ministry in Seattle, Washington. In 1976, he moved to California to pursue his doctorate at the Graduate Theological Union in Berkeley. But Hanaoka discontinued his academic career; he was appointed to Buena Vista United Methodist Church in Alameda, Pine United Methodist Church (UMC) in San Francisco, Japanese UMC in Sacramento, and Epworth UMC in Berkeley. Currently, he coordinates urban ministries for the United Methodist congregations and agencies in the city of San Francisco as the executive director of San Francisco United Methodist Mission. Hanaoka and his wife Ayako have three grown children. He has been active in peace and justice ministry as well as music ministry in parish settings. Hanaoka was a member of the Japanese hymnal sub-committee for the Asian American hymnbook project that produced *Hymns from the Four Winds* in 1983. He has been active in promoting contextual theology, liturgy, and music.[111]

Author: "Praise the LORD" (*STB* #23).
Translator: "Now let us sing a new song to the LORD" (*STB* #27); "In the dawn of the morn" (*STB* #158); "Send your word, O LORD" (*STB* #218).

---

111   Information in this entry is derived from the author's correspondence with Hanaoka, August 26, 2004.

Hans, Sadanand Abinash Bishram Dilbar

Bishop Hans and his son, Rev. Cyril Hans

Born in Ramtoleya, Ranchi District, Bihar, India, 30 January 1910, Sadanand Abinash Bishram Dilbar Hans attended Church Lower Primary School in Ramtoleya, where he learned the Sadri, Mundari, and Hindi languages, and Church Middle English School in Kamdara, where he developed his command of English and was awarded the Dalton Scholarship. At St. Columba's Collegiate School, Hazaribagh, he was awarded the Cunningham Scholarship. Hans obtained a BA from Patna University and a diploma in secondary education from Patna Teachers' Training College. Instead of studying for a Master of Education degree, he went to Bishop's College, Kolkata, to study theology; his thesis on the relationship between Christianity and Munda culture and traditional religion entitled "Not Without Witness" was published by the Indian Society for Christian Knowledge (ISPCK), Delhi, in 1954. He began to serve as a deacon in 1944 and was consecrated Bishop of Chota Nagpur in 1957; he was the first Indian bishop of the Munda tribe in the Anglican Church. He attended the Lambeth Conferences in 1958 and 1968 and the Anglican Congress in Canada in 1963, when he was awarded the Doctor of Divinity (Honoris Causa) from the University of King's College, Halifax, Canada. Bishop Hans contributed the chapter entitled "Tribal Self-Identification" in *Tribal Awakening,* published by the Christian Institute for the Study of Religion and Society (CISRS), Bangalore, in 1964. Hans edited two editions (1942 and 1982) of *Munda Durang*, a collection of Mundari literary works. He twice edited revisions of the *New Testament of the Bible*, published by the Bible Society of India. For the Diocese of Chota Nagpur, he revised the *Mundari Book of Common Prayer* and hymnbook that contained locally composed Mundari lyrics. Hans was also the editor of the Mundari magazines *Samparting* and *Johar*; he was the founder and chairman of Horo Senra Samaiti ("Horo Cultural Society with the Government"). At Ranchi University, he served as a member of the senate and as a member of the academic board of the Tribal and Regional Languages Department. In 1985, he received the Guru Gomke Pandit Raghunath Murmu Award for promoting Adivasi language and literature. In 1989, he received a special certificate from Ranchi University for his service to Mundari culture, languages, and literature. He died 12 January 1993 in the Ranchi District.[112]

---

112 Information in this entry is derived from the author's correspondence with the Reverend T. S. Cyril Hans, March 17, 2006.

Translator: "O Father God, you're merciful" (*STB* #38); "Hala, hear our Christmas song" (*STB* #142); "Dear friends, walk with me, let us go" (*STB* #198).

Hayashi, Hikaru

Born in Japan in 1931, Hikaru Hayashi studied at Tokyo Arts University. Although he did not complete his academic degree, he has become a prolific composer of various genres, including songs, choruses, and operas. He also composes scores and themes for television drama productions.[113]

Arranger: ETENRAKU (*STB* #54).

Hawn, C. Michael

Born in Cape Girardeau, Missouri, 22 September 1948, C. Michael Hawn is a professor of sacred music and the director of the Master of Sacred Music program at Perkins School of Theology, Southern Methodist University (SMU), USA. Hawn holds Doctor of Musical Arts and Master of Church Music degrees from Southern Baptist Theological Seminary, Louisville, Kentucky, and a Bachelor of Music Education degree from Wheaton College, Illinois. In addition, he studied at Florida State University (Orff Certification), Oberlin College Baroque Performance Institute, and Aston Magna Baroque Performance Institute. A countertenor, Hawn studied with Russell Oberlin and René Jacobs. He is a life member of the Choristers Guild—having served as president of the board of directors (1990–92, 2001–03) and as interim executive director (2002–03)—and the Hymn Society in the United States and Canada. Prior to joining SMU in 1992, Hawn was a professor of church music at two Baptist seminaries for fifteen years. He has also served as a minister of music at churches in Kentucky, Georgia, North Carolina, and Texas. Hawn is a frequent contributor to church music periodicals in the areas of church music education and hymnology; he has published more than 250 articles. He has edited many books, including *For the Living of These Days: Resources for Enriching Worship* (Macon, GA: Smyth & Helwys, 1995) and a three-year children's choir resource, *Stepping Stones: An Ecumenical Children's Choir Curriculum* (Garland, TX: Choristers Guild, 1995, 1996, 1997). From September 2004, he has written a

---

113 Information in this entry is derived from the author's correspondence with the Reverend Sōji Kitamura, September 18, 2006.

weekly column for *The United Methodist Reporter* entitled "History of Hymns" and a feature on a global (non-Western) hymn in *Worship Arts*, a bi-monthly journal. He has led clinics on children's choirs and worship throughout the United States. Hawn founded and served as the chair of the board of directors for the Children's Chorus of Greater Dallas (1996–98). Hawn is also a promoter of global music and worship; he has done research and taught in Nigeria, Kenya, Cuba, Haiti, Mexico, Nicaragua, Singapore, Malaysia, Taiwan, the Philippines, Thailand, Hong Kong, Argentina, Brazil, South Africa, Zimbabwe, Japan, and Korea. His research results were published in *Halle Halle: We Sing the World Round* (Choristers Guild, 1999), *Gather into One: Praying and Singing Globally* (William. B. Eerdmans, 2003), and *One Bread, One Body: Exploring Cultural Diversity in Worship* (The Alban Institute, 2003). In February 2006, Hawn served as the music director of the ninth assembly of the World Council of Churches in Porto Alegre, Brazil. He has recently published four articles on Australian congregational song in *The Hymn: A Journal of Congregational Song* and has contributed eighteen articles on sub-Saharan African hymnody to the *Cambridge Dictionary of Hymnology* (2008). An edited volume in process, *New Songs of Celebration Render* (GIA Publications, anticipated 2010), explores the theological and musical developments in congregational song in North America since the Second Vatican Council. He was made a Fellow of the Hymn Society (FHS) in 2008. Michael Hawn is married to Collyn Sanderson Hawn, a school psychologist for the Richardson Independent School District. They have adult two children, M. Aaron Hawn and Lindsay Hawn.[114]

Altered: "O give thanks to the Lord" (*STB* #99).

Heber, Reginald

Born in Malpas, Cheshire, England, 21 April 1783, Reginald Heber was a clergyman who contributed two distinct hymns, "Holy, holy, holy, Lord God almighty" and the controversial "From Greenland's icy mountains." By the age of five, Heber had thoroughly read the Bible. During his studies at Brasenose College, Oxford, he won many prizes for both Latin and English poetry: the Latin Prize in 1803 for "Carmen Seculare"; the Best English Essay Prize in 1805 for "The Sense of Honor"; the English Prize in 1803 for "Palestine," a poem recited in the Oxford Theatre; "Europe: Line on the War" (1809); and "The Passage of the Red Sea." Heber was elected a fellow at All Souls College, Oxford (1804), and became vicar of the family estate of Hodnet, Shropshire (1807), where he served for sixteen years; he wrote

---

114 Information in this entry is derived from Hawn's curriculum vitae and the author's correspondence with Hawn, June 10, 2006.

all of his hymns during this time. In 1815, he was appointed Brampton lecturer at Oxford and was named preacher of Lincoln's Inn in 1822. In 1823, he was appointed Bishop of Calcutta; at the time, the position had jurisdiction over the whole of India, Ceylon (now Sri Lanka), and Australia. Heber was later awarded the DD degree from Oxford. After three years of intense missionary work, Heber died at the age of forty-two of a cerebral hemorrhage in Tiruchirappalli (called Trichinopoly by the British), India, on 3 April 1826. (For more information, see the website http://www.hymnsandcarolsofchristmas.com/Hymns_and_Carols/Biographies/reginald_heber.htm)

Author: "Lovely star in the sky" (*STB* #132).

Hibbard, Esther

Born in Tokyo, Japan, 23 September 1903, to an American missionary teacher working for the YMCA, Esther Hibbard arrived in the United States at the age of ten. She graduated from Mount Holyoke College, South Hadley, Massachusetts, and the University of Wisconsin (MA, English). She was sent by the Congregational Mission Board to teach at Dōshisha Christian High School for Girls in 1929 but was evacuated in 1941 due to the war. Hibbard obtained a doctorate in Asian civilization from the University of Michigan and returned to Japan in 1946 to teach at Dōshisha, which became a college of liberal arts in 1948. After her retirement in 1968, she remained in Japan to teach at Tohoku Gakuin and returned to the United States in 1973. She has translated a number of hymns from Japanese to English and has researched Ulysses motifs in Japanese literature (Fyock 1996, 555f).

Translator: "Lo, now ascends the morning sun" (*STB* #194); "In this world abound" (*STB* #216).

Hines, Ronald

Born in Dayton, Ohio, USA, 18 November 1944, Ronald Hines was raised in Colorado. His father was a pastor in the Evangelical United Brethren (EUB) Church; the EUB Church and the Methodist Church merged in 1968 to become the United Methodist Church. Ron received his BA (English major, philosophy minor, 1966) from Westmar College, Le Mars, Iowa. He attended United Theological Seminary, Dayton, Ohio (MDiv, 1970). While at seminary, he was a choir director for a Dayton congregation, which was predominantly African-American; he also served an internship in Philadelphia and Warminster, Pennsylvania, which linked an inner-city black congregation and a suburban white congregation. Hines pursued advanced studies at the School of

Theology at Claremont, California, and received a PhD in Personality and Religion (1976). After serving as the associate pastor at Seattle First United Methodist (1974–79) and as the pastor at Prosser, Washington (1979–83), he and his family were called to be missionaries for the World Division, General Board of Global Ministries, United Methodist Church. Although the Hineses learned the Indonesian language at Cornell University, they were never granted visas to enter Indonesia and were transferred to the Philippines for three terms (1984–94). Hines also served as a pastor of English services at Knox Memorial United Methodist Church (1984–87), as a visiting faculty member at Harris Memorial College (1984–85), and as an associate professor of Faith and Culture at Union Theological Seminary (1985–94), teaching courses in liturgy and many other subjects. He was also the pastor in charge of The University Church, an ecumenical congregation at the Philippine Christian Center for Learning (which combined Philippine Christian University and Union Theological Seminary). Since returning to the United States, Hines has served as the pastor at Tacoma Asbury (five years) and Puyallup First (two years) United Methodist churches, and he has been the superintendent of Seven Rivers District (and thus on the bishop's cabinet) for three years. For the summers of 2002 and 2003, he was a chaplain for the Jubilate worship workshops, which emphasize music. Hines was the choir director of his father's church during high school. While a student at Westmar College, he traveled with a male quartet each summer, singing in more than sixty churches and twelve church camps. Because of his long interest and experience in music, he is sensitive to hymn text treatments, as evident from his paraphrases for *Sound the Bamboo*. Hines and his wife Lois have two ecumenically and internationally minded grown children, who, after graduating from universities, have been traveling around the globe and actively serving different communities.[115]

Paraphraser: "Seasons come, seasons go" (*STB* #26); "Come, smell the scent of sweet wild flowers" (*STB* #52); "Come soon, LORD, save me" (*STB* #86); "Ohoradiya, in God's temple, praise the LORD, God" (*STB* #101); "All Christians must love one another" (*STB* #213); "O God, highest God" (*STB* #270).

---

115 Information in this entry is derived from the author's correspondence with Hines, August 12, 2004.

Hong, Junchol

Born in Korea, 20 June 1958, Junchol Hong is a member of the Anglican Church. He graduated from Sejong University with a Master of Music degree in choral conducting. He has been the conductor for the "Village in Music" choir for more than ten years and is currently a part-time professor of conducting at Seongkonghoi (Anglican) University. He also serves as the general secretary of the Korean National University of Arts Fund. He was a member of the revision committee of the 1990 hymnal of the Anglican Church of Korea.

Author: "Broken communion tore you apart" (*STB* #297).

Hontiveros, Eduardo Pardo

Born in Roxas City, the Philippines, 20 December 1923, Eduardo Pardo Hontiveros comes from an artistic and musical family. He entered San Jose Seminary in 1945 and later joined the Jesuit order. He graduated from Berchmans College, Cebu (MA, Philosophy, 1949), and Gregorian University in Rome (Doctor of Sacred Theology, 1958). He taught theology at San Jose Seminary and Loyola School of Theology (1958–89) and served as the president of the latter (1983–89); he later became the dean of St. John Vianney Seminary in Cagayan de Oro City. Hontiveros began conducting choirs at San Jose Seminary and arranged choral pieces in English, Latin, and Tagalog. He wrote pieces especially for the urban poor, such as *Misa ng Bayan sa Awit* ("The People's Mass in Song"), and he initiated an annual singing festival, which operated from 1971 to 1978. Hontiveros helped to organize the Jesuit Music Ministry in 1986, and he has published many audio recordings, including: *Luwalhati sa Diyos* ("Glory to God"), *Panunuluyan* ("In Search of an Inn"), *Aking Pastol* ("My Shepherd"), *Papuri't Pasasalamat* ("Praise and Thanks"), *Himig Heswita* ("Jesuit Hymns"), *Awiting Pansamba* ("Songs of Praise"), *Tugunan, Taon A* ("Responsorial Psalm, Year A," 1989), *Magsiawit sa Panginoon* ("Let's Sing to the Lord," an anthology, 1989), and *Pagsamba* ("Praise Book," 1991). For his contributions to music ministry, he received the Ateneo de Manila's Tanglaw ng Lahi Award in 1976 (cf. *CCPE* 6, 320).

Composer: HONTIVEROS (*STB* #76); KRUS (*STB* #149).
Author/composer: "Friend to friend," FRIEND (*STB* #244).

Horo, Daud Dayal Singh

Little is known of Daud Dayal Singh Horo's life, but his works have great influence in India. According to the Reverend Cyril Hans, a place of preeminence has to be claimed for Horo both for his compositions of Mundari song and for his excellence of singing. Horo was born in the village Deogami in the Ranchi district, and he died there as well. As a composer of Mundari songs and lyrics, he was quite a genius. He was at the zenith of his poetic powers while he was training for priesthood in the Anglican Church in Ranchi; he was eventually ordained in 1880. He could compose both in the Mundari and Sadri (Nagpuri) languages, and many of his songs feature perfect rhymes. He composed one hundred songs in Sadri, but they are not in print. Horo's songs are loved by both Munda and non-Munda people. One of his major works, based on *The Pilgrim's Progress* by John Bunyan, is now in print and entitled *Surud Salukid* ("The Lotus Flower Heart"). Divided into three parts, it features 123 of the 300 songs that he wrote under this title. Some of the songs have more than one tune. They are widely sung in churches of all traditions. This work has been published five times (in 1931, 1966, 1967, 1976, and 1989); the latest is the popular fourteenth edition of the Mundari Church Hymnal, which incorporates *Surud Salukid*.[116]

Author/composer: "O Father God, you're merciful," SIRMA APOM (STB #38); "Hala, hear our Christmas song, hala hala (STB #142); "Dear friends, walk with me, let us go," SENE SAKINGE (STB #198).

Hu, Te-ngai (Hu De-ai)

Born in China, probably in the early 1900s, Hu Te-ngai was a music student at Yanjing University, where Bliss Wiant taught during the 1930s (Wang 1993, 247).

Composer: LE PING (*STB* #155).

Im, Song-suk

Born in Kongju, Korea, 19 January 1933, Song-suk Im is a graduate of the College of Korean Language Education, Kongju National University. He published his first poem, "Parade," in 1967. He received the twenty-fifth Annual Prize on Modern Literature in 1980 and the sixth Annual Prize on Modern Poetry in 1985. Between 1970 and 1989, he published seven collections of poems.

Author: "To the high and kindly hills" (*STB* #53).

---

116   Information in this entry is derived from the author's correspondence with Cyril Hans, 2006.

Imakoma, Yasushige

Born in Tokyo in 1926, Yasushige Imakoma became acquainted with the Christian gospel after the Second World War, amid the chaos of Japan's defeat, and entered the Seminary for Rural Ministry in 1952. He subsequently studied at Japan Biblical Seminary. He first served in a Kawasaki church, but in 1968 he devoted his ministry to the blind and became the head of the Japanese Association of Christian Mission to the Blind. He returned to pastoral work in 1976 and served the Tokyo Toshimaoka Church until 1989. He is currently an associate pastor in a Shimizu church (*SRK21*, 51).

Author: "Send your Word, O Lord" (*STB* #218).

Ishida, Naoi

Born in Sapporo in 1935, Naoi Ishida was baptized at the age of nineteen. He currently works for a company and serves faithfully in an Eikō church in Kamakura (*SRK21*, 337).

Author: "Jesus built the church" (*STB* #68).

Ishiyama, Yukiko

Born in 1923 in Fukushima, Japan, Yukiko Ishiyama is a member of the Japan Anglican Church in Wakamatsu Seito Church. While teaching at a high school, she submitted her works for *Sambika Dainihen* (the second volume of *Sambika*), and they were accepted for publication.[117]

Author: "Here I am" (*STB* #44).

Jadra, C.

C. Jadra is from Karnataka in South India.

Author: "Jesus, Jesus, how we adore you" (*STB* #41).

---

117 Information in this entry is derived from the author's correspondence with the Reverend Sōji Kitamura, September 19, 2006.

Jiang, Puqi

Born in China, 6 September 1944, Jiang Puqi is a member of the Protestant Church in China. He graduated from Shanghai Conservatory of Music with a Diploma in violin and orchestra conducting (1968). He was a teaching assistant at his alma mater (1968–73) and was the conductor of the Jiangsu Provincial Song and Dance Ensemble (1973–present). In 1981, he began teaching music at the Nanjing Theological Seminary, and in 1984 he made the first recording of indigenous Christian hymns from China, "The First Fruits." For graduate studies, Jiang went to the Conservatory of Music of the University of Cincinnati in 1986, pursuing an MM degree in orchestra conducting. In 1987, he was invited by the World Council of Churches as a Chinese delegate at the Asian Seminar on Liturgy and Music in Makiling, Manila. He served as the president of the Chinese Students and Scholars Association at the University of Cincinnati (1990–91). He returned to China and has been the conductor of the Jiangsu Provincial Symphony Orchestra since 2005.

Arranger: "Amen" (*STB* #108).

Julkiree, Boonmee

Born in the 1930s in Thailand, Boonmee Julkiree is a talented lay leader of the Church of Christ in Thailand (CCT). She has represented women's groups at many ecumenical conferences and has made significant contributions in promoting the rights and equal opportunities of women in Thailand. Before retiring, she represented the CCT for more than ten years as the coordinator for missions among the Lao. (For her photo, see the entry for Terry MacArthur.)

Translator: "Day of joy, let us be glad" (*STB* #11); "Upon this day of peace" (*STB* #14).

Kaan, Frederik Herman

(Photo from Stainer & Bell, Ltd.)

Born in Haarlem, the Netherlands, 27 July 1929, Frederik Herman Kaan graduated from the University of Utrecht and then went to England. Upon receiving a BA (1954) from the University of Bristol, he began his ministry in England. He was ordained by the United Reformed Church and served several congregations in South Wales (1955–63) and Plymouth Church (1963–68), where he wrote hymns to accompany the themes of his sermons. Kaan was one of the pioneers of the 1960s "hymn explosion" in England. He served as the minister-secretary of the International Congregational Council, Geneva, Switzerland (1968–78)

431

and was the executive secretary of the World Alliance of Reformed Churches. Because of his poetic gifts and his dedication to social justice, Kaan was invited by the Urban and Rural Mission Committee of CCA to go to Jakarta, Indonesia, to assist I-to Loh in paraphrasing the Asian songs/hymns that Loh had collected from Asian countries, which resulted in the publication of *New Songs of Asian Cities* (1972). Kaan has since written many hymns on human rights and ecology issues. Because of his contributions to the ecumenical movement, the Reformed Seminary in Debrecen, Hungary, conferred Kaan an honorary ThD in 1978. He also earned a PhD from the Geneva Theological College in 1984 for his dissertation entitled "Emerging Language in Hymnody." He was on the Worship Committee of the sixth General Assembly of WCC in Vancouver, 1983. Carlton Young writes about Kaan: "His linguistic ability, ecumenical service, and fervent concern for the powerless are apparent in his hymns, numbering more than 200" (Young 1993, 779). Indeed, Kaan's hymns appear around the globe in more than a dozen languages. His published works include *Pilgrim Praise* (1972), *The Hymn Texts of Fred Kaan* (1985), *Planting Trees and Sowing Seeds* (1989), and *The Only Earth We Know* (1999). The most recent biography of Kaan is by Gillian R. Warson: *Healing the Nations: Fred Kaan, The Man and his Hymns* (2006).[118] Kaan died 4 October, 2009.

Paraphraser: "Son of the Father" (*STB* #191); "Worship the LORD, worship the Father" (*STB* #229).
Co-author: "We who bear the human name" (*STB* #258).

Kao, Chun-ming (Ko Chun-beng)

Kao Chun–ming and Le–tin Li

Born in Tainan, Taiwan, 6 June 1929, the twelfth of thirteen children, Kao Chun-ming came from a noble and affluent family. His grandfather, Kao Chang (Taiwanese: Ko Tiong), was the first Taiwanese convert (baptized on 12 August 1866) and the first Taiwanese preacher (active 1867–1912) (cf. Kao and Kao-Li 2001, 28 and 36). Kao Chun-ming is one of the most respected pastors in Taiwan. He attended a high school in Japan. After suffering during World War II, he realized the value of life and began to search for truth and Christian faith, influenced by the Japanese Christian scholar Kanzō Uchimura. Following his graduation from Tainan Theological College and Seminary (attended 1948–52), Kao volunteered to serve the underprivileged aborigines in Taiwan. He began

---

118 Information in this entry is derived from Stainer and Bell, "Fred Kaan," http://www.stainer.co.uk/kaan.html (accessed March 26, 2009).

teaching at the Yushan Theological College in 1957, and he married Le-tin Li in 1958. At Yushan, he served as the principal and established the model of physical labor for the faculty and students—planting trees, growing vegetables, and raising cattle to supplement the college's meager income and limited funds. During these years, Kao went to Japan to study rural ministries, and he later studied at Selly Oak College, England (1963–64). In 1970, in recognition of his Christ-like leadership, he was first elected the moderator and then the general secretary of the Presbyterian Church in Taiwan (PCT); he suffered a long period of political and religious persecution by the Nationalist Kuomintang government. Kao issued three PCT statements (in 1971, 1975, and 1977) against the dictatorship and its oppressive rule, urging the government to respect human rights, to hold national elections, to abolish martial law, and to declare Taiwan an independent country. Because he harbored a dissident in 1979, Kao was jailed from 1979 to 1984. Through all of this, the PCT expressed its faith by "speaking the truth in love" (Ephesians 4:15) and chose to "obey God rather than any human authority" (Acts 5:29), retaining Kao as the general secretary. In 1984, Knox College in Canada awarded him an honorary Doctor of Theology degree; earlier, in 1973, he received an honorary doctorate from McGill University and Presbyterian Seminary, Canada. The persecution from the government made the PCT stronger and more courageous in maintaining solidarity with the people and helping the victims and the families of political prisoners. Kao has been retired for more than ten years but still serves the church and the people in innumerable ways.

Author: "Watch the bush of thorns" (*STB* #252).

Keet, Malai Koet

Malai Koet Keet is a Thai poet.

Author: "All Christians must love one another" (*STB* #213).

Kelly, Anthony

Born in 1938 in Newcastle, New South Wales, Australia, Anthony Kelly, CSSR, graduated from Hamilton Marist Brother's College and St. Clement's College, Galong, New South Wales. He was ordained a priest of the Redemptorist Order in 1963 and pursued doctoral and postdoctoral studies in Rome, Toronto, and Paris. He was a lecturer in theology at Yarra Theological Union in Melbourne and served as its president for ten years. He also taught in the Philippines, Canada, and the United States and has published eight books, including *Seasons of Hope* (1986). He served as the president of the Australian Catholic Theological Association, he was the chair of the Forum of Australian Catholic Institutes of Theology, and he was head of the Sub-Faculty of Philosophy and Theology at Australian Catholic University from 1999 to 2004. Kelly's scholarly interest is in the liberating dimensions and artistic implications of the gospel; he has collaborated with the composer Father Christopher Willcock on many works (Milgate 1988, 85). In February 2004, Kelly was appointed by His Holiness Pope John Paul II to the International Theological Commission.[119]

Author: "LORD of life and LORD of nations" (*STB* #267).

Khaling, Dibya

Born in Darjeeling, West Bengal, India, 28 March 1952, Dibya Khaling was of the Kirat (Rai) ethnic group. His family, with three sons and one daughter, belongs to the Nepali Isai Mandali Church in Gyaneswar. Khaling studied at North Bengal University, India, and received a Bachelor of Arts degree. He was a famous composer of traditional, pop, and contemporary styles, with many hymns, cantatas, operas, documentaries, and incidental film music to his credit. He was also one of the most popular folk composers and singers in Kathmandu, Nepal. Khaling believed that his gift of music was intended for the glory of God; he consciously proclaimed the message of the gospel to his people through his music, singing and accompanying himself with a keyboard. He was also a respected poet. He died in Nepal in 2006.

Author/composer: "Friends, listen humbly," KHALING (*STB* #208).

Khawas, John Dick

Born in Nepal, 28 March 1937, to the Kalu Khawas family, John Dick Khawas is vision impaired but serves as a composer and teacher in Kalimpong, West Bengal, India.

Author/composer: "Oh! What a lovely day," KHRIST RAJA (*STB* #138).

Khess, Picas

Born in late 1950s in the Ranchi area of India, Picas Khess is a Lutheran pastor and a gifted composer in the Ranchi District. In 1984, he was granted a full scholarship to study for one year at the Asian Institute for Liturgy and Music, Manila.

Author/arranger: "On the night of Christmas," PUNA BINKO (*STB* #133).

---

119   "Anthony J. Kelly Homepage," http://dlibrary.acu.edu.au/staffhome/ankelly/ (accessed March 15, 2009).

Kiley, Henry Wilson Q.

Born in Sagada, Mountain Province, the Philippines, 26 September 1936, Henry Wilson Q. Kiley studied at the University of the Philippines (AB, History, 1960), St. Andrew's Theological Seminary (SATS) in Manila (BTh, 1961), and General Theological Seminary, New York (STB, 1962; STM, 1964), and he was a doctoral candidate at the University of St. Andrew's, Scotland (1971–73). Kiley began his teaching career immediately after graduation from his alma mater (SATS) and, except spending time studying abroad, he dedicated his life to theological education; he became the sub-dean in 1979 and served as dean from 1980 to 1994, when he retired. In appreciation of his contributions to theological education, Kiley was conferred an honorary DD from General Theological Seminary in 1981. He was the Philippine Episcopal Church (PEC) delegate to the Anglican Congress (Toronto, 1962) and attended the International Mission Consultation (Netherlands, 1972). He also served as the chairman of the Association for Theological Education in Southeast Asia (ATESEA; 1985–89) and was the chairman of the PEC Commission on Church Autonomy and Anglican Province of the PEC; he has been a member of the PEC Executive Council since 1980. His writings include: "The Primal Visions of the Sagada Igorots" (STM thesis); "Autonomy: Branter or Achieved?" (*PEC Journal of Ministry* 1, no. 1, May 1988); "On the Origin, Character and Experience of the Eucharist: A Response to the BEM Document" (*Asia Journal of Theology* 4, no. 1, 1990); and "The Eucharistic Church" (*Journal of Theology* 4, no. 2, 1990).

Paraphraser/composer: "Mary's Salidummay," MARY'S SALIDUMMAY (*STB* #102).

Kim, Doo Wan

Born in 1924 in Pyongannamdo, North Korea, Doo Wan Kim is a composer and choral conductor. He graduated from the Kunitachi Conservatory of Music in Japan in 1945 and the Kurohae Theological College in Korea in 1966. He also earned an MA in music from a college in Los Angeles, California, and a Doctor of Music degree from Linda Vista Theological Seminary. Kim served as a professor at Seoul Theological Seminary, the director of the Christian Philharmonic Orchestra, the president of the Korean Church Music Council, an advisor to the Korean Hymn Society, and the president of Agape Music Mission. He is a prolific composer of more than 4000 hymn tunes, nine collections of sacred solos, and five volumes of cantatas, including "Noel," "God comes to you," "We are waiting for Jesus," and "The first fruit of Resurrection." He has also published eight books on topics related to church music: history, education, aesthetics, music ministry, and choral conducting.

Composer: IMMANUEL (*STB* #192).

Kim, Hae Jong

Born in 1935 in Seoul, Korea, Hae Jong Kim became a Christian during the Korean War. At the age of seventeen, he served as a translator to a chaplain of the United States Marine Corps. Kim sensed the call to the ministry and entered Seoul Methodist Theological College. He went to the United States, graduated from Ohio Methodist Seminary (MDiv, 1964) and served as a pastor in northern New Jersey. He earned his PhD from Drew University in 1984. He was the first Korean superintendent of the United Methodist Church (UMC), was a delegate to the UMC General Assembly, and served as one of the directors of World Mission. Kim was elected a bishop of western New York in 1992. He was later appointed as a bishop of the Pittsburgh area. He also served as the president of the New Jersey Korean Church Council and the president of the National Federation of the Korean United Methodist Church. He contributed two hymns to the Korean-English Presbyterian hymnal, *Come Let Us Worship* (Geneva Press, 2001): "Let there be light" (no. 69) and "Dream on, dream on" (no. 383).

Translator: "Harvest thanksgiving" (*STB* #166).

Kim, Helen

Born in Inchon, Korea, 27 February 1899, Helen Kim was one of the most respected and influential educators in Korea. She was a 1918 graduate of Ewha College, Seoul, and she went to the United States to study at Ohio Wesleyan University and Boston University. She earned a PhD in 1931 from Teachers College of Columbia University, the first Korean woman to receive a doctorate in the United States. Returning to Ewha College, she became the dean in 1931 and the president in 1939. (The name of the college was changed to Ewha University in 1945, and the highest enrollment was about 8,000 in the 1970s.) She retired in 1961. Kim also served as the official spokeswoman for the South Korea government and was the founder and publisher of *The Korea Times,* an English newspaper. As a Methodist educator and church leader, she represented Korea at many international conferences, including the International Missionary Council and World Council of Churches. She also served as an ambassador-at-large to the United Nations and served on World Councils for the YWCA and the Red Cross (cf. Young 1993, 781). During a 1954 celebration for Columbia University's bicentennial in Seoul, the Korean alumni praised Kim "for perpetuating the traditional policy of free inquiry, free speech and free press."[120]

---

120   "Columbia250 celebrates Columbians ahead of their time, Helen Kim," http://c250.columbia.edu/c250_celebrates/remarkable_columbians/helen_kim.html (accessed March 15, 2009).

She died in Seoul, 10 February 1970.

Author: "Dark is the night" (*STB* #253).

Kim, Jung-joon

Born in 1914 in Korea, Jung-joon Kim was a theology graduate of Aoyama Gakuin, Japan, and Emmanuel Theological Seminary, Canada, as well as Hamburg Seminary, Germany. In 1949, he began to serve as a professor of Old Testament studies at Korea Theological Seminary (a Presbyterian institution), and he became its president in 1961. He also served as the chairman of the Northeast Asian Theological University. As an ordained Presbyterian pastor, Kim was one of the pioneers in the field of contextual theology and published several books, including *Understanding the Ecumenical Movement*, *Studies on Amos*, and *The Faith and Theology of the Israelites*. He translated Augustine's *Confessions*. He died in 1981.

Author: "This new morn, full of grace" (*STB* #153); "Endless grace" (*STB* #183).

Kim, Kook Jin

Born in Korea, 24 April 1930, Kook Jin Kim was an amateur composer who had trumpet and reed-organ lessons at a young age. He composed his first children's song in 1946. He graduated from high school in 1949 and entered Songhwa (Pyongyang) Theological College. He taught Sunday school classes. His mentor was an American missionary music professor, Dwight Malsbary, who asked why Kim only studied Western music, inspiring him to search for his Korean identity. As a result, although his compositions are in Western styles, they all reflect Korean elements. His published works include: *Piano Pieces for Korean Melodies* (1971), *Piano Sonatine Album* (1974), *Song Collections* (1978), "The Lord's Prayer," "Hallelujah, Symphony no. 2," "New Piano Sonatine" (1979), and *Piano Sonata Collection* (1983).

Composer: KEUN-LOH (*STB* #234).

Kim, Kyung-soo

Born in 1925 in Korea, Kyung-soo Kim was a poet. He went to the United States to study at the Graduate Program of Texas Christian University. As a Presbyterian minister, he served in Changhyen Church and Hosanna Church. He died in 2002.

Author: "Joy found in truth surely sets the world free" (*STB* #66).

Kim, Marion

Born in the United States, 2 June 1945, Marion Kennedy Kim is a graduate of Ohio State University, Columbus, Ohio (BS, music education, 1966; major instrument: oboe). Her graduate studies include: psychology at the New School for Social Research, New York (1967); anthropology of education, at Teachers College, Columbia University, New York (summer 1971); Chinese language studies at St. John's University, New York (1971); teaching English as a second language (1972) and journalism (1977) at Kent State University, Ohio. She also studied the Korean language at Myongdo Language Institute, Seoul, Korea (1969–70). Kim has twenty-eight years of experience as an English-language editor and eight years of experience as an English teacher. She is a competent Korean speaker and worked with Korean organizations for twenty-eight years. She began her career as an oboe player in local orchestras (1964–66) and became a computer programmer with American Telephone Co., White Plains, New York (1966–67). Subsequently she served as an elementary school music teacher in Elizabeth (1967–69) and Woodbridge (1970–71), New Jersey; she taught English conversation and composition at Women's Christian College, Tokyo (1973–75), and at Musashino Buddhist Women's Junior College, Tokyo (1975–76). She was the English editor for the National Council of Churches in Korea, Seoul (1978–80) and served as the English editor and occasional teacher of the Christian Broadcasting System in Korea, Seoul (1980–1989), and the editor of newsletter "NCCK Activity News" of the National Council of Churches in Korea, Seoul (1989–93). She was an instructor of English conversation and writing at Hanil University and Theological Seminary during the summers of 1991, 1992, and 1993; the editor of the "Civil Society" magazine of the Citizens' Coalition for Economic Justice, Seoul (1994–2001); the director of the International Department, Citizens' Coalition on Economic Justice, Seoul (1999–2001), in which post she edited English-language materials (reports, books, dissertations, project proposals, etc.); the editor of the quarterly English-language magazine *Sang Saeng* and other publications for UNESCO Asia-Pacific Centre of Education for International Understanding (2001–05); and a teacher of English for grades 3–6, Elementary School of Seoul National University of Education, Kyodae (2005–present). Kim has been a translator and interpreter from 1978 to 2006. She published *Once I Had a Dream,* a collection of Korean *minjung* ("grassroots") women's stories in 1992, and a Japanese translation of this was published in 1995. For about ten years, she served the Korean National YWCA as a member of the Environment Committee and the Special Policy Committee on University Y, and she is currently a member of the organization Women Making Peace.

Paraphraser: "This is my one, my lifelong wish" (*STB* #48); "Joy found in truth
    surely sets the world free" (*STB* #66); Lovely star in the sky" (*STB* #132);
    "This new morn, full of grace" (*STB* #153); "Endless grace" (*STB* #183).

Kim, Ok-youn

Born in Korea, 10 April 1959, Ok-youn Kim graduated from Presbyterian College and Theological Seminary, Seoul (BA, Christian education, 1981; MDiv 1992). She also earned a Certificate in Science in Library Studies at Sungkyunkwan University, Seoul, in 1984. She went to the United States to study at the Women's Theological Center, Boston, Massachusetts, receiving a Certificate in Theology in 1993, and she received her DMin from Chicago Theological Seminary in 1997. She volunteered for the Chicago-area organization Korean American Women In Need (KAN-WIN). Kim's interest in theology and music in an Asian context brought her to Taiwan; in 2000, she earned a certificate from the Council of World Mission Program at Tainan Theological College and Seminary, Tainan. From 1981 to 1997, she served as an evangelist, a Bible teacher, a religious educator, and a student advisor for six Korean churches and Soong Eui High School. She was also a pastor and education coordinator from 1997 to 1999. She also served as the Seoul Public Relations Coordinator from 2001 to 2004. She began teaching at Jangsin University and Theological Seminary and Kyung In Women's College in 2000. Since 2003, she has been a chaplain and a professor at Kyung In Women's College.

Translator: "Dark is the night, black the stars" (*STB* #253).

Kim, Seong Ho

Born in the 1930s in Korea, Seong Ho Kim is a minister of the Holiness Church. He actively promotes Korean hymns and has served as the general secretary of the Korean Hymnal Society since the 1980s.

Author: "Ogiyongcha, morning sunlight beams in splendor" (*STB* #225).

Koizumi, Isao

Born in 1907 in Osaka, Japan, Isao Koizumi graduated from the University of Commerce in Osaka and then taught at his alma mater. In 1942, he moved to Tokyo and served in many governmental or private trade institutions. He was very active in church music; he studied choral conducting with Hitoshi Nagai and composition and organ with Toraji Ōnaka. In 1951, he served as the choir director and organist at the United States Far East Air Force Chapel Center in Tokyo and in the Futaba Church (today the Higashi Nakano Church). From 1954, he was on the music editorial committee of *Sambika* ("Songs of Praise"). He was an early editor of the journal *Worship and Music* and was responsible for writing the music section of the companion to *Sambika* published in 1955. In addition to his devotion to hymnology, he also published a book on eighteenth-century orchestration (cf. *SRK21*, 239). He died in 1992.

Composer: KAMITAKATA (*STB* #27).
Arranger: TOKYO (*STB* #242).

Kosasih, Daud

Born in Medan, Sumatra, Indonesia, 10 April 1964, Daud Kosasih is the son of a Methodist minister and a talented composer and choral director. He initially studied at the Asian Institute for Liturgy and Music, majoring in composition and graduating with a BCM. He was sent to Germany to study with a prominent composer and later entered Tainan Theological College and Seminary, Taiwan, studying composition with Tsong-hsian Yang and earning his MACM in 2001. Currently, he teaches at a university in Medan and is very active in composing and conducting church choirs and choruses.

Composer: MEDAN (*STB* #24).
Translator: "Thank you for the day you give us" (*STB* #236).

Koyama, Shōzō

Born in 1930 in Japan, Shōzō Koyama heard Christian hymns for the first time as a student in a family worship service in Nakano Prefecture. He was baptized by Isamu Ōmura. After graduating from Kunitachi Music University, he became a lecturer at Tamagawa College. From 1959 to 1995, he was a professor at Kunitachi, and he maintains a presence at the school as an emeritus professor (cf. *SRK21*, 52).

Composer: CHRISTIAN HOME (*STB* #68); COME TO ME (*STB* #207); MIKOTOBA (*STB* #218).

Kumud, Mayaw

Born in Hualian, Taiwan, 25 August 1957, Mayaw Kumud is from the family of Pacidalan of the Ami tribe. He is married to a Tayal woman, Sayun Lohin; they have two sons, one daughter, and an adopted son. Mayaw, as he prefers to be called, graduated from Yushan Theological College and Seminary with a BTh in 1976; he continued to study theology at Tainan Theological College and Seminary for one year, but he graduated from Taiwan Theological Seminary in Taipei with an MDiv degree. He is one of the very few

Taiwanese who have participated in diverse leadership training sessions, including: WCC leadership training for multicultural mission in Jamaica, leadership training for laborers mission in Korea, basic and intermediate urban and rural leadership training in Taiwan, Amis Selal leadership training, Ketagalan leadership training, and NGO foreign mission training by the Government Foreign Affairs Office. Mayaw served a congregation in Hualian (1983–85) and in Anguang Church, where he was ordained as a Presbyterian pastor (1987–2000). He was elected the moderator of the western Ami synod. He has been very active in social justice and was the director of the Fishermen's Service Center in Kaohsiung (1985–87). He is a strong advocate for human rights for minority groups, for which the Kuomintang government imprisoned him for one year (1995). After the Progressive Democratic Party (DPP) won the national election in 1999, Mayaw served as an associate to the first Minister of Tribal Affairs, the Reverend Yohani (2000–02). Subsequently he was a senior agent for the DPP Central Committee (2002–04) and the deputy director of the Ethnic Affairs Office (2004–06). Currently he is a pastor in the Jilung area. He is also a talented musician and has adapted and set many traditional ethnic melodies to hymns.

Author/arranger: "Praise be to God," PAHEMEKEN (*STB* #32).

Kuptarat, Solot

Born in 1957 in Uttaradit, Thailand, Kuptarat received his first music lessons from his father. He received a BA in music from Payap University in 1979 and an MA in music from Mozarteum in Austria in 1981. He has been teaching music at Payap University since 1981. He is married and has two sons; his wife also teaches music at Dara Academy, a local girls' school.

Composer: PHAWANA (*STB* #296).
Arranger: NAAMPHAI (*STB* #303).

Kya Bing, George

Born in the 1930s in Myanmar, George Kya Bing was the general secretary of the YMCA in Myanmar. In this position, he represented Myanmar at many international conferences, spreading awareness about the difficulties of his country. He died in Myanmar.

Author/composer: "Gracious Father, love divine," CHITCHIN MYETA (*STB* #196).

La, Un-yung

Born in 1922 in Seoul, Korea, Un-yung La was the most prolific Korean composer of his time. He studied composition under Moro Isaburō at Tokyo Imperial College of Music. La began his teaching career at the age of twenty-three at the College of Music, Yonsei University, where he taught for twenty-one years and served as a dean. He also taught at Sejong University, Mukwon University, and Jonnan University. He was an advocate for studying and developing native Korean folk traditions, from which he gained insights for developing contemporary Korean styles. He pioneered a method for the modernizing of Korean music. One of his most memorable songs is his 1950s setting of Psalm 23, a soprano solo with piano accompaniment. He was credited with developing "La's New Harmonization." During more than forty-two years of teaching and composing, he published more than 1500 compositions, including thirteen symphonies, six concertos, four orchestral works, three operas, fourteen chamber pieces, eighteen art songs, nine cantatas, 1105 hymns, and 200 children's songs. He also wrote ten textbooks on music theory: *The Fundamentals of College Music, Harmony, Counterpoint, Musical Form, Choral Arranging, Orchestration, Musical Composition, Musical Analysis, Musical Expression,* and *Contemporary Harmony.* La served as the president of the Korean Hymn Society, the Korean chair of the International Society of Contemporary Music, the president of the Korean Modern Music Society, the chair of the Korean Hymnal Committee, and the choir conductor for Hosanna Church and Seoul Songnam Church for thirty years. Because of his contributions, Portland University conferred on La an honorary doctorate in liberal arts in 1974, and, upon his death in 1993, the Korean government awarded him the Kum-kwan Arts Medal, the highest artistic honor in Korea.

Composer: SO-WON (*STB* #48); JIN-LI (*STB* #66); HON-SHIN (*STB* #75); HANURE BINNANUN (*STB* #132); NEW MORN (*STB* #153); UN-CH'ONG (*STB* #183); HAN GA JOK (*STB* #243); CHOO-SOO (*STB* #245).

Lai, Vuluk

Born in Pingtung, Taiwan, 7 July 1959, Vuluk Lai (Han name: Zhaocai Lai) is a pastor from the Paiwan tribe. After graduating from Yushan Theological Seminary, he went to Manila to study church music at the Asian Institute for Liturgy and Music; at the same time, he was enrolled in La Salle University to study Christian education. After receiving his BCM and MA degrees, he returned to his hometown to serve his people. He received an MTh in the areas of music, liturgy, and the arts at Tainan Theological Seminary, which is a consortium of seminaries under the Southeast Asia Graduate School of Theology (SEAGST). His MTh thesis concerns the issues of contextual art and church architecture. He is equally gifted in writing poetry, composing, singing, painting, and doing theologies with these disciplines. He designed the front covers of the 1990 and 2000 editions of *Sound the Bamboo*. His wife Uping, from the Ami tribe, is also a graduate of AILM with a BCM in voice. In addition to his parish ministry, Lai teaches courses in music and tribal cultures, part-time, at two colleges. He hopes to pursue a ThD study in liturgy and the arts at the Southeast Asia Graduate School of Theology in Tainan.

Author: "My heavenly Father loves me" (*STB* #182).

Lama, H. M.

H. M. Lama is Nepalese.

Author/composer: "Sun has gone, night has arrived," COWSHED (*STB* #134).

Laoyan, Judith

Born in Baguio City, the Philippines, 6 November 1966, of Ibaloi ethnic origin, Judith Laoyan belongs to the Episcopal Church in the Philippines (PEC) and is married to an Episcopalian priest, the Reverend Mosomos. She graduated from St. Louis University, Baguio (BS, psychology), and from the Asian Institute for Liturgy and Music (AILM: Bachelor of Church Music, 1991). She served on the staff of AILM until 2002, when she received a full scholarship to study at Southern Methodist University, Dallas, Texas, for a Master in Sacred Music degree. She earned the degree in 2005 and returned to the Philippines. She was one of the editors of the new hymnal of the PEC and is currently teaching at the Methodist School of Music in Singapore.

Composer: CORDILLERA (*STB* #97).

Law, Daniel

Born in 1946 in Hong Kong, Daniel Ping-Liang Law graduated from the Chinese University of Hong Kong (CUHK: BA, music, 1970) and Northwestern University, USA (PhD, theory and composition, 1979); he also earned a diploma from the Royal School of Church Music (1981). An outstanding student, he won many prizes and awards from all the schools he attended. He is a talented musicologist, composer, conductor, and hymnologist and a devoted Christian. Law taught at China Graduate School of Theology from 1975 to 1976. Since 1976, he has served at CUHK as a lecturer, a professor, and a member of the Board of Trustees; since 2001, he has been the dean of the Faculty of Arts and a professor of music. He was a visiting scholar at Harvard University (1984–85) and Stanford University (1992–93), where he also taught. Many of his students have followed in his footsteps and have become good musicians serving their churches in Hong Kong. Law is a humble and soft-spoken scholar. His writings and publications about theology, worship, church music, and hymnology contain some of the most thought-provoking articles in Chinese. According to I-to Loh, there is in China or in the Chinese-speaking world not a better church-music scholar than Law. Aside from conducting many choirs and orchestras, Law has researched contemporary music theory, history of music theory, liturgical music, hymnology, and electronic music. His most important church music publication is the three-volume *Shengyue Zonglun* ("Essays on Sacred Music"). He has edited three hymnals: *Shengming Shengshi* ("Hymns of Life"), *Huaren Shengsong* ("A Collection of Hymns by Chinese-Speaking Composers/Authors," 1992), and *Sound of Grace*. He has written many scholarly articles about music education, church music, and musicology, and he is writing a book on Chinese hymnody. More than forty of Law's commissioned compositions have been performed in local and international venues and been released as CD recordings. Among his important compositions are eight major orchestral works and more than a dozen chamber music and instrumental solo pieces. His works for church music include: "Alleluia, with verse 'The Holy Child'" (1979), a setting of Psalm 33 (1980), a setting of Psalm 100 (1989), the anthem "God be in my head" (1994), and "Christmas Suite" (1996). He was the chief editor for the eight volumes of *Hong Kong Vocal Music Collection* (1999, published by the Hong Kong Association of Choral Societies and Chinese Christian Literature Society).

Composer: SZE LING (*STB* #49).

Lee, Dong Hoon

Born in 1922 in Korea, Dong Hoon Lee graduated from the Tokyo Imperial College of Music. He was a violinist, a composer, and the conductor of the Pilgrim Choir in Seoul. He died in 1975.

Composer: BAI (*STB* #253).

Lee, Geonyong

Born in Daedong, South Pyongan Province, Korea, 30 September 1947, Geonyong Lee is a renowned composer and professor of composition. He graduated from Seoul Arts High School (major in composition, 1965) and the College of Music of Seoul National University (BM, composition, 1974; MM, 1976); he earned a diploma in composition from the Frankfurter Musikhochschule, Germany (1978), and diplomas in composition and musicology from Johann Wolfgang Goethe University, Germany (1979). He also enrolled in the doctoral program at the Department of Aesthetics, Seoul National University (1983–86). Lee has held various professional positions: president of the Korean National University of Arts (KNUA; 2002–06), dean of the School of Music, KNUA (2001–02), commissioner of the Operation Committee, KBS Korean Traditional Orchestra (2001–present), commissioner of the Evaluation Committee of Performance at the Seoul Arts Center (2000–present), commissioner of the Operation Committee of the KBS Symphony Orchestra (1998–present), the directing commissioner of the Korean Federation of Environmental Movement (1997–present), dean of academic affairs, KNUA (1992–97), professor of composition, KNUA (1992–present), president of Min-Um-Yeon (a society for the study of Korean music, 1989–99), professor of music at Seoul National University (1983–92), and professor of music at Hyosung Women's University (1979–83). Lee has actively promoted contextualized church music in Korea and was a visiting professor of composition at the Asian Institute for Liturgy and Music, Manila. He has successfully combined Korean traditional music with Western styles. He has written many choral works, including: *Music of 100ᵗʰ Anniversary of Mission* (1985), *Psalms of Anger* (1985), and *Hallelujah Sangsadiya* (for choir and traditional Korean orchestra, 1986).

Author/composer: "Come now, O Prince of Peace," ososo (*STB* #241).

Composer: SASUMI (*STB* #62); JONGUIGA KKOTPINUN (*STB* #90); OHORADIYA (*STB* #101); SHIPCHAGA (*STB* #150); OGIYONGCHA (*STB* #225); YANG SHIK (*STB* #290); KALAJIN APUMUL (*STB* #297); CHUYO ULIRUL ("O LORD, please have mercy on us," *STB* #299).

Lee, Hyun-chu

Born in 1944 in Chunju, Korea, Hyun-chu Lee is a graduate of Methodist Theological Seminary. He won his first poetry competition with the poem *Man-yok* ("Night Rain," sponsored by *Choson Daily News* in 1964), and he published his "Modern Children's Fables" in 2006. He translated the book *The Dalai Lama's Study of the Mind*, and he has written around a dozen books that cross disciplines, including *The Bible and Folk Stories*.

Author: "O God of great love" (*STB* #64).

Lee, Ke Joon

Born in 1932 in Korea, Ke Joon Lee graduated from Methodist Theological Seminary (earning a BA), Boston University, and Emory University. He has served as the chaplain of Yonsei University.

Author: "Jesus, our true Lord of love" (*STB* #192).

Lee, Song-chon

Born in 1936 in Korea, Song-chon Lee studied medicine at Korean National University. He gave up his medical practice to earn a Master of Music degree from the Graduate School of Seoul National University; he later earned a PhD in cultural philosophy at Seongkyunkan University. He was a professor at Seoul National University and served as the president of the National Traditional Music Academy. His compositions include works for solo instruments, vocal ensembles, and symphony orchestras, and more than 300 songs. He died in 2003.

Composer: NAUI DOUM (*STB* #53).

Lee, Tong-il Tom

Born in the early 1930s in Korea, Tom Lee was first Korean to graduate from Westminster Choir College, Princeton, in the 1950s, earning a degree in choral conducting. He taught church music in Korea for many years and immigrated to the United States in the 1960s. He is an ordained pastor of the United Methodist Church, and he helped the Korean Caucus of the National Federation of Asian American United Methodists to compile *Hymns from the Four Winds* (1983).

Translator: "To the one Creator of all" (*STB* #75); "Jesus Christ, workers' Lord" (*STB* #234).

Lee, Yong-cho

Born in Korea, 17 April 1943, Yong-cho (Young-jo) Lee received his bachelor's and master's degrees from Yonsei University in Seoul. He continued his studies with Carl Orff and Wilhelm Killmayer at the Hochschule für Musik in Munchen, Germany. Later, Lee entered the American Conservatory of Music in Chicago and earned his DMA; he subsequently taught there and became the chairman of the theory and composition department from 1989 to 1994. He was then invited to teach at the Korean National University of Arts as a professor of composition, and he became the dean of the School of Music. Lee's music is characterized by a strong Asian sensibility combined with a German theoretical influence. He has composed countless works, including chamber music, orchestral works, and choral music; many of them have been performed and well received in Asia and the United States. One of his operas, *Whang-Jinie*, has been performed in Beijing (2000), Tokyo (2001), Los Angeles (2002), Moscow (2003), and Hanoi (2004). He has arranged more than eighty pieces for church choirs. Currently he is the director of the Korean National Institute for the Gifted in Arts.

Composer: KIDO (*STB* #64).

Leung, C. W.

C. W. Leung is Chinese and lives in Hong Kong.

Co-translator: "God is here as we your people meet" (*STB* #49).

Li, Dong

Born in Szechuan, China, Li Dong graduated from Trinity Theological College with MDiv (1994) and MTh (1996) degrees. At present, he is the vice-principal of Szechuan Theological Seminary. He has been the chairman of Szechuan China Christian Council (CCC) since 2002.

Paraphraser: "May the love of the LORD" (*STB* #315).

Li, Pao-chen (Li Baozhen)

 Born in Baoding, Hebei Province, China, 18 July 1907, Li Pao-chen was a famous linguist, composer, and choral conductor. He graduated from Oberlin College (1935–37) with a degree in music. Upon returning to China, he became the head of the National Academy of Music (1941–44). He served on the editorial committee of the Chinese hymnal, *Putian Songzan* ("Hymns of Universal Praise," 1936). He was one of the pioneers of composing and singing in colloquial Chinese. His motto was "Singing according to the way of speaking" (Zhao 2004, 2–3). In 1941, Li organized and conducted a chorus of one thousand youths to stimulate their patriotic spirits to fight against the Japanese invasion and colonization of China. His concern for developing Chinese traditional music was evident in his transcriptions of five classical *qin* pieces played by the master Fu-xi Cha: *Xiao-xiang shui-yun*, *Ou-lu wang ji*, *Pu an zou*, *Kai gu yin*, and *Mei-hua san-nong* (Zhao 2004, 6). He immigrated to the United States and earned his DMusEd in 1948 from Columbia University, New York. He taught Chinese language courses at Yale University, American Military Academy, and University of Iowa (1944–71). He was a frequent visitor to Taiwan, invited from 1957 by the Nationalist government to promote choral singing and education, and he conducted workshops and choral concerts around the island and in many universities. Upon his retirement in 1972, he resided in Taiwan until his death, 8 April 1979. He translated and introduced famous Western choral pieces and composed and arranged numerous choruses, many of which were patriotic in character and exemplified Chinese styles. He also composed a few church anthems, which, according to him, were the impetus that led him to his musical career.

Composer: WEN TI (*STB* #80).

Liang, Jifang

Born in China, Liang Jifang was a talented music student at Yanjing University during the 1930s.

Composer: HUAN-SHA-XI (*STB* #135); CHENG CHING TSAN (*STB* #167).

Liberius, R. F.

Born in Italy, R. F. Liberius went to Pakistan as a priest serving the Multan Diocese of the Roman Catholic Church. According to Bishop John Samuel of Pakistan, Liberius was a wonderful person; he was interested in creating new liturgies and composing new lyrics. He played the organ and conducted choirs, and he participated in many ecumenical activities.

Composer: KHUDAAYAA (*STB* #120).

Liew, Samuel

Born in Singapore, 28 August 1942. A graduate of Trinity Theological College, Singapore, the Reverend Samuel Liew was an ordained pastor in the Trinity Annual Conference of the Methodist Church of Malaya (prior to the separation of Singapore from Malaysia in 1965). Liew is a talented poet and musician, and he was concerned about the relevance of the Christian gospel to the time. He frequently summarized his sermons into hymns, set them to original music, and sang and accompanied himself with the guitar. Hence, in the 1960s, he and three other Methodist ministers—including the Reverend Ho Chee Sin, who became the Bishop of the Methodist Church in Singapore—organized Christone, a male quartet with guitar accompaniment; they sang in nightclubs and traveled throughout the region as musical evangelists. It was a pioneering effort to bring the gospel to non-Christians, but it was met with strong objections from the church authority. Liew immigrated to the United States in 1991 and settled in Denver, Colorado. His wife Jane works at the Denver Newspaper Agency, and his married daughter, Li-Anne, is a research scientist at the National Institute of Standards and Technology (NIST) of the United States Department of Commerce, in Boulder, Colorado. Liew works part-time as the choir director and minister of music of the Centennial Lutheran Church in Englewood, Colorado. He still arranges and composes new music using folk tunes from Singapore, Malaysia, and Indonesia.[121] According to Yip Kok Choong, the general secretary of the Asia Pacific Alliance of YMCAs, Liew—who used to pastor his church in Kampar, Malaysia—wrote several songs (including "Call me by my name," *STB* #265) on afternoons when pouring rain kept the church youths indoors.

Author/composer: "Call me by my name," MY NAMES (*STB* #265).
Author/adapter: "Now let us tell of your victory," RASA SAYANG (*STB* #22).

Lim, Ok In

Born in Kilju, Korea, 1 June 1915, Ok In Lim graduated from Nora Teacher's College, Japan; she began writing in 1940. Especially interested in and concerned about women's issues, she wrote the books *Stories of Second Wives* and *Stories of Ex-Wives*. Lim was a professor of literature and a dean of home economics at Keonkook University; she was active in serving communities and was elected a president of YWCA. Since the 1960s, she published many essays and novels on Christian life, including a book titled *Crossing the South After the War.* She was the recipient of the Asian Freedom and Korean Women's Literature award (cf. Young 1993, 786). She died in 1995.

Author: "Harvest thanksgiving" (*STB* #166).

---

121 Information in this entry is derived from the author's correspondence with Samuel Liew, February 7, 2007.

Lim, Swee Hong

Born in Singapore, 11 June 1963, Swee Hong Lim obtained his Bachelor of Church Music degree in composition from the Asian Institute for Liturgy and Music, the Philippines (magna cum laude, 1989). He received a Master of Sacred Music degree in 1995 from the Perkins School of Theology, Southern Methodist University, Dallas, Texas. For several years in Singapore, he served as the director of Worship and Music Ministries at Wesley Methodist Church and Paya Lebar Methodist Church. In 2006, he earned his PhD in Liturgical Studies from Drew University, New Jersey (with a thesis titled "Giving Voice to Asian Christians: An Appraisal of the Pioneering Work of I-to Loh in the Area of Congregational Song"). He also served as a local pastor of the Greater New Jersey Annual Conference of the United Methodist Church. He is currently teaching at Trinity Theological College and the Methodist School of Music in Singapore. His numerous compositions and articles have appeared in various publications, including *Chalice Hymnal*, *New Century Hymnal Companion*, *The Faith We Sing* (a United Methodist hymnal supplement), and the *Global Praise* series. He is married to Maria Ling (see her entry below), and they have three children.

Author/composer: "Lord, have mercy," SINGAPURA (*STB* #118).
Composer: SOON TI (*STB* #315).

Lin, Sein

Born in the late 1940s in Myanmar, U Lin Sein graduated from the Myanmar Institute of Theology with a Bachelor of Theology degree. As a student, he demonstrated his musical talent. He had a special interest in working with children and introduced concepts of early childhood development to churches. He composed children's songs and published several cassette tapes and videos of children's songs for Christian educational programs. For a number of years, he served as the secretary for Christian education at the Myanmar Council of Churches (MCC), and he is currently the director of the education and communication department of MCC. He has been involved with Christian education and has actively incorporated media as a means of communicating the gospel.[122]

Author/composer: "Mighty God, power over heaven and earth," HP'YA SHIN (*STB* #57); "Happy are those following Jesus Christ," NAUH LAIH THU MYA (*STB* #226).

---

122   Information in this entry is derived from the author's correspondence with Anna May, January 4, 2007.

Lin, Shengben

Born in 1927 in Guangdong, China, Lin Shengben is from a musical family. He entered Baptist Seminary in Guangzhou and the Church Music Department of the Baptist Seminary in Shanghai, under the tutorship of Geshun Ma. After graduating from Jinling Union Theological Seminary, Nanjing, Lin led a Cantonese-speaking congregation in a Shanghai parish. After his ordination in 1980, he served Jinling Church, Shanghai; he also taught church music at the Jinling Theological Seminary. He was a member of the committee that edited the new hymnal, *Zanmeishi Xinbian* (1985), and he has composed many hymns and choral arrangements. He was also instrumental in publishing many choral anthems for the church. After retiring, he spends most of his time running workshops that promote music ministries in different parts of the country.

Composer: JIA-OU (*STB* #71).

Ling, Maria

Born in Singapore, 26 April 1961, Maria Ling obtained her Bachelor of Theology degree from Trinity Theological College, Singapore (1986) and graduated from Perkins School of Theology, Southern Methodist University, Dallas, Texas (Master of Theological Studies, 1995). For ten years, she served at Wesley Methodist Church, Singapore, working on a variety of concerns, including youth and family life. During that time, she also initiated various ministry groups at Wesley, including one for foreign workers in Singapore and a fellowship group for overseas graduates re-entering the Singaporean culture; these groups continue to flourish. Subsequently, Ling served as a Christian ministry worker within the Singapore Methodist school system. In 2001, she was made a pastor of the Greater New Jersey Annual Conference of the United Methodist Church and appointed to Quakertown United Methodist Church. She is married to Swee Hong Lim, and they have three children. (For her photo, see the entry for Lim, Swee Hong.)

Author: "May the love of the LORD" (*STB* #315).
Paraphraser: "We all believe in one God of love" (*STB* #51); "Come one and all, let's follow Christ, our Lord" (*STB* #78); "Happy are those following Jesus Christ" (*STB* #226).

Ling, Tiing Chang

Ling Tiing Chang was born in China, 12 May 1925, and immigrated to Sibu, East Malaysia. He served as a schoolteacher and principal in a primary school in East Malaysia. During the 1970s, he received special training in education and music at Birmingham University, England. Ling was an amateur poet versed in the Chinese classics, and he was a successful businessman, a dynamic church leader, and a strong supporter of music ministry. He wrote more than one hundred songs. In February 1987, he was invited to attend the Asian Workshop on Liturgy and Music in Manila; he stayed for an additional half-year as a Poet-in-Residence at the Asian Institute for Liturgy and Music to write hymns and to study with I-to Loh. There, he wrote twenty-one hymns/poems in Chinese, which were later published by the Chinese Christian Association in the Philippines under the title *Christian of the Time*. That same year, he won the first prize in the Sarawak Open Composition Contest. He was instrumental in establishing the Sibu Chinese Music Club. He was a lay preacher until his death on 2 December 2002, and he served for a number of years as the chairman of the Board of Laity and the secretary of the Sarawak Chinese Annual Conference and the Methodist Church in Malaysia.[123]

Author/composer: "God has formed the church to be," SIBU (*STB* #240).

Liu, Tingfang

Born in 1891 in Zhejiang, China, Liu Tingfang was first educated in China then in the United States, earning a BB from Yale University and an MA and PhD from Columbia University. He also studied at Union Theological Seminary, New York. After returning to China, he taught in many schools and universities. A leading writer and educator, he was the editorial chair of *Putian Songzan* ("Hymns of Universal Praise," 1936), he translated many hymns into Chinese, and he was a co-editor of the "Union Book of Common Prayer." He served as a delegate to the World Council of Churches. Politically, he was a member of the Chinese legislative body. He moved to the United States in 1941 and taught at the University of New Mexico, Albuquerque, until his death on 5 August 1947 (cf. Young 1993, 785).

Translator: "For the beauty of the earth" (*STB* #171).

---

123   Information in this entry is derived from the author's correspondence with Lu Chen Tiong, November
      2004.

Loh, I-to

Born in Tamsui, Taiwan, 28 September 1936, I-to Loh is the author of this volume. He graduated from Tainan Theological College and Seminary (TTCS: MDiv, 1963), Union Theological Seminary, New York (SMM, composition, 1966), and the University of California at Los Angeles (UCLA: PhD, music/ethnomusicology, 1982). He has taught at his alma mater, TTCS, and served as the head of the Department of Church Music for many years; he also served as the president of the seminary from 1995 until his retirement in 2002. He was sent as a United Methodist missionary to teach at the Asian Institute for Liturgy and Music (AILM; 1982–94); in this capacity, he traveled and promoted contextual Asian church music and liturgy in many member churches of the Christian Conference of Asia (CCA), and he edited the 1990 and 2000 editions of *Sound the Bamboo: CCA Hymnal*. Loh was a consultant and animateur to three General Assemblies of WCC (1983, 1991, and 1998), and he was the director of music at five General Assemblies of CCA (1985, 1990, 1995, 2000, and 2006), the ninth General Assembly of LWF (Lutheran World Federation, 1997), the twenty-third Congress of WARC (World Association of Reformed Church, 1997, co-director), the World Alliances of YMCAs (1984, animateur), and the Asian Alliance of YMCAs (1987 and 1989). He has lectured in numerous Ecumenical Workshops on Liturgy and Music, sponsored by WCC and CCA around the globe, and he has taught at Taiwan Theological College and Seminary, Tunghai University, Soochow University, and Tainan Teacher's College. He has published twenty-one books and collections of hymns/songs from Asia and Africa, including: *New Songs of Asian Cities* (1972), *A Festival of Asian Christmas Carols* (1984), *Let the Hills Sing* (1986), *African Songs of Worship* (1986), *Sing a New Song to the Lord* (1987), *Christ the Light to Bali* (1987), *Hakka Songs of Worship* (1987), *The Love of God Sets Us Free* (1988), *Thousands and Thousands of Songs Full of Praise* (audiocassette, 1990), *All Peoples Praise* (1995), and *Jyothi Do Prabhu* (recordings of *bhajans* and lyrics from India, 1996). In addition to writing dozens of academic papers, he published the monograph *Teach Us to Praise* (1992, revised 2002). Loh has translated more than 300 hymns from English and other languages to Taiwanese or Mandarin, and he has published more than one hundred hymns, liturgical responses, and acclamations in Asia and North America. He is the editor of the official hymnal of the Presbyterian Church in Taiwan, *Seng-si* (2009). For his contributions to hymnology, he was named a Fellow of the Hymn Society of North America and Canada in 1995. On 14 July 2006, he received the

2006 Distinguished Service Award from the Global Consultation on Music and Missions. Also in 2006, Loh's first CD, *Originality*, a collection of his choral compositions, won the award for the best production of classical composition at the seventeenth Golden Music Prizes of the Bureau of News and Information of the Taiwan Government. His wife, Hui-chin (MDiv, TTCS; MRE, Princeton Theological Seminary), is a specialist in Christian education and has helped with all of his publications; they have three children and six grandchildren.

Author: "Let us come to worship God" (*STB* #3); "Praise Lord Jesus," stanzas 2 and 3 (*STB* #20); "This is the God beyond all gods," stanza 3 (*STB* #139); "LORD, we thank you for this food" (*STB* #163); "Lilies of the Field," stanza 4 (*STB* #201); "Strive and toil for God," stanza 3 (*STB* #246); "May the LORD bless you with joy," stanza 2 (*STB* #288).

Adapter: "Let us come to worship God," HI-A-O-HO-I-AN (*STB* #3); "Let all nations come, praise the LORD," KATIPOL (*STB* #96); "O give thanks to the LORD," MIHAMEK (*STB* #99).

Author/adapter: "Green the wild fields, blue the sky," LOK-HNG (*STB* #257).

Author/composer: "Jesus Christ sets free to serve," SEOUL (*STB* #247); "Find from nature proof of God's grace," HUI-HIONG (*STB* #308).

Composer: BENG-LI (*STB* #85); "Come Holy Spirit, renew the face of the earth" (*STB* #114); IXTHUS (*STB* #141); SMOKEY MOUNTAIN (*STB* #144); SANTA MESA (*STB* #181); ESPANA (*STB* #188); BI-NIU (*STB* #190); TONDO (*STB* #202); CHHUN BIN (*STB* #220); KENG-SIN (*STB* #222); CHHI-PHE (*STB* #252); SU-KONG-PAN (*STB* #254); COLOMBO (*STB* #255); BKL (*STB* #260); SAM-KIAP (*STB* #262); CIPANAS (*STB* #310).

Arranger: MAN-JIANG-HONG (*STB* #65); JU-MENG-LING (*STB* #223).

Transcriber/composer of drone accompaniment: SWEINDIA (*STB* #91).

Adapter: WEN-TI (*STB* #80); "LORD, have mercy on us" (*STB* #121); MO-LI-HUA (*STB* #171).

Translator: "May the LORD, gracious God" (*STB* #80); "You have come, Lord Jesus" (*STB* #193).

Lubis-Nainggolan, Tilly

Born in Batusangkar, West Sumatra, Indonesia, 4 February 1925, Tilly Lubis graduated from the Hogere Burger School, Medan (1947); the Gymnasium Amersfoort, Belanda (majoring in Latin and Greek, 1949); the Rijksuniversiteit Groningen, Belanda (1949–50); the University of Indonesia (1968); and HKBP Nommensen University (1978–81). She began piano studies at the age of seven and continued to take lessons for more than seventeen years from various masters from Indonesia and the Netherlands. She taught at various schools, including

SMA Katolik Budi Mulia (1961–70) and SMP Taman Asuhan (1976–81), both in Pematangsiantar. She was a lecturer of English at Krisnadwipayana University, Jakarta (1982–84), and she taught music and English at Institut Agama Kristen, Jakarta (1984–86). From 1979 to 2002, Lubis served as a manager of Employment and Management Training, PT Union Carbide Indonesia, and in other positions in Singapore and Australia. In 1990, she began to serve at Yamuger (Institute of Sacred Music) in Jakarta; she was the secretary from 1991 to 1995. She has directed or headed the following choirs or musical groups: Suara Sektor VIII GPIB Paulus (1994–2000), Yamuger (1995–2000), Women's Chorus HKBP Menteng, Jalan Jambu (1996–99), Suara Lansia HKBP Menteng, and Jalan Jambu (1999–2002). She was a member of Yamuger and Yayasan Serafica (2000–02). She died 17 August 2002 in Jakarta.

Author: "Sing the LORD a new song" (*STB* #100).
Translator: "Now come, O Holy Spirit" (*STB* #10); "My shepherd LORD" (*STB* #291); "Have no fear, all you earth-lands" (*STB* #306); "Oh, the cabbage price is falling" (*STB* #313).

Lumentut, A.

The Indonesian author A. Lumentut was likely a participant of the workshop led by Liberty Manik during the early 1980s.

Author: "Jesus Christ, the life of the world" (*STB* #210).

Maasilaamanni, V.

Born in 1853 in Silukuvarpatti, in South India, V. Maasilaamani was the elder brother of V. Santiago (see entry for Santiago, V.). Maasilaamani was a violinist and a preacher; in 1890, he began to assist American missionaries in Tirukoilur. He was ordained in 1901 in Madurai American Mission and was appointed in 1906 to teach catechism. He served as a parish pastor in Tiruvannamalai (1915–17) and published eleven lyrics with tunes, all widely sung today. He died in 1932.

Author/composer: "Praise God from whom all blessings flow," THUDHI (*STB* #36).

MacArthur, Terry

Born in Alpena, Michigan, USA, 8 September 1949, Terry MacArthur received an MDiv from Methodist Theological School in Delaware, Ohio. He returned to rural Michigan to serve for seven years as a United Methodist pastor. After receiving an STM from Union Theological Seminary in New York, he served as the organist and choir director at Zion Lutheran Church in Brooklyn. At the same time, he worked on the General Board of Global Ministries. From 1988 until 2000, he was a United Methodist missionary in Geneva, serving as the Worship Consultant for the World Council of Churches. During this time, he coordinated worship teams for the Canberra (1991) and Harare (1998) General Assemblies of the WCC, as well as other ecumenical meetings and numerous Ecumenical Workshops on Liturgy and Music around the world. In 1999, MacArthur was a visiting professor of music and worship at Tainan Theological College and Seminary for the graduate program in church music. From 2000 to 2003, he was the music and worship minister for both the English-speaking congregation of the Lutheran Church of Geneva and the Latin American community of the United Methodist Church of Geneva. Today, he continues his work with the Lutheran Church as well as other activities related to church music around the world. He is a sensitive, creative, and talented musician and liturgiologist; his knowledge and experience of the world of ecumenical liturgies and music is matchless.

Paraphraser: "In this world abound," stanzas 3 and 4 (*STB* #216); "Dark is the night" (*STB* #253).

From left to right, John Barathi, Inchai Srisuwan, I-to Loh, and Terry MacArthur, rehearsing a Thai hymn before JPIC Worship, Seoul, Korea, 1991. Boonmee Julkiree can be seen in the upper right corner of the photo (see *STB* #11 and #14).

Maddela, Tomas Silvino Sinnung

 Born in Manila, 31 December 1958, of the Ibanag people, Tomas Silvino Sinnung Maddela studied at Trinity College of Quezon City (Associate in Arts, classical music, 1977), St. Andrew's Theological Seminary (SATS: BTh, cum laude, 1982; MDiv, cum laude, 1989), and Pontificio Instituto Liturgico, Roma (Licentiate in Sacred Liturgy, magna cum laude, 1988). He is a candidate for a Doctor of Sacred Theology degree in liturgy. Since 1988, he has taught liturgics at SATS, Asian Institute for Liturgy and Music (AILM), Maryhill School of Theology (1989–present), Aglipay Central Theological Seminary (1993–96), and St. Louis University (1998–present). He has served as the dean of studies at AILM (1995–96), the academic coordinator and registrar (1994–present) and dean (2001–present) at SATS, the academic coordinator (1994–2008) and dean (2001–08) of the Southeast Asia Graduate School of Theology (SEAGST, Philippines area), and the secretary of the Philippine Theological Society (1999–2008). Since 1991, Maddela has held ecclesiastical posts: as a chaplain of the Episcopal Church Ministry for Prison (1991–93), as a member of the National Commission for Liturgy and Church Architecture, Episcopal Church in the Philippines (PEC, 1989–93), and as a member of the National Commission for Liturgy and Christian Education, PEC (1994–present). He was the project coordinator of the Book of Common Prayer and Hymnal Project, PEC (1997–2002); the registrar of the synod, PEC (1996–present); the vice-chairman of the Board of Trustees, Christian Literature Society of the Philippines of New Day Publishers (1998–2000); a representative of the Ecumenical Dialogue on Baptism (NCCP-CBCP, 1998–2000); the PEC Representative (1999–present) and a member of the Steering Committee (2001–05) of the International Liturgical Anglican Consultation. Maddela has attended numerous workshops, seminars, and conferences, including the Lutheran World Federation Conference on Liturgical Inculturation (Hong Kong, 1996), three meetings of the International Anglican Liturgical Consultation (Kerala, India, 1999; Berkeley, California, 2001; Oxford, 2003), and the WCC Faith and Order Conference (Prague, Czech Republic, 2000). He has written articles and edited various publications for SATS and PEC. In addition to English, he also speaks Spanish and Italian, he has a reading knowledge of Latin, Greek, and French, and he is fluent in seven Filipino dialects.

Author: "Three women" ("She dances 'mid the city lights," *STB* #186).

Maita, Shōko

Born in 1935 in Manchuria, Shōko Maita was baptized in 1953 by a Roman Catholic priest at the Peace Memorial Chapel in Hiroshima. He was a graduate of Elizabeth Music University, where he majored in composition and church music. Later, he studied composition at Kunitachi Music University. He was a music professor at Tōhō College until March 1997 (cf. *SRK21*, 51).

Composer: GARIRAYA NO KAZE (*STB* #195).

Malicsi, Jonathan

Born in Olongapor City, the Philippines, 26 April 1947, Jonathan Malicsi obtained a BA in English (1966), an MA in linguistics, and a PhD in anthropology and sociology (1981) from the University of the Philippines (UP); he also studied linguistics at the State University of New York (1980). Malicsi began to study music in 1974 and was tutored by Herbert Brauer (at Berlin Conservatory), Mercedes Santiago, and Kathy Sternberg. He also studied with visiting artists from the Metropolitan Opera, Curtis Institute, and Salzburg Mozarteum. He received his Bachelor of Music degree from UP in 1984. Malicsi has taught English, comparative literature, and linguistics at UP, and he was a professor and the chair of the linguistics department. He began performing in 1965, singing with the UP Madrigal Singers and UP Concert Chorus. He was a tenor soloist for Rossini's *Messe Solenelle,* Handel's *Messiah*, Mozart's *Coronation Mass*, and Britten's *War Requiem*. He also played major roles in M. Pajaro's opera *Balagtas at Selya*, Jerry Dadap's *Andres Bonifacio: Ang Dakilang Anakpawis* ("The Great Plebeian"), the Filipino adaptation of *The Little Prince* by Rolando de la Cruz and Lucrecia Kasilag, and Mozart's *Magic Flute* and *The Marriage of Figaro*. He won the Ulo Ng Apo Award for cultural development from the Olongapo City government (cf. *CCPE* 6, 336f).

Author: "Sing with hearts" (*STB* #33).
Co-author: "In the heavens shone a star" (*STB* #131).
Co-paraphraser: "In the coldness of night" (*STB* #273).

Mam, Barnabas

Barnabas Mam is Cambodian.

Author: "Now I know" (*STB* #289).

Manaen, Loknath

Born in Darjeeling, India, 28 February 1947, Loknath Manaen is Nepali. He studied history, philosophy, English, and Nepali, and he earned a Bachelor of Arts degree. Manaen founded the Bible Society in Nepal in 1977 and served the organization for eighteen years. During his last eight years in office, he coordinated the first Nepali translation of the Bible in Nepal by Nepali scholars. From 1979, he worked for twenty-five years to ensure the availability of a hymnal for the Nepali church. He was involved in publishing Bible study books and editing early Nepali Christian magazines. He works full-time on writing and music ministry, and he has published secular and Christian novels, stories, and essays. Nepali singers regularly obtain songs from Manaen for their albums. He is keenly involved in "Back to the Bible" radio and film-related ministries. He and his wife have two daughters, and the family belongs to the Indigenous Church of Nepal. Manaen is currently in Virginia, United States, editing a translation (from English to simple Nepali) of Old Testament study material. He translated all of the Nepali hymns in *Sound the Bamboo*; his assistance was most valuable.

Author/composer: "Christmas is here," HERA DAJAI (*STB* #304).

Translator: "Sun has gone, night has arrived" (*STB* #134); "Oh! What a lovely day" (*STB* #138); "O Give praise to Jesus, the King" (*STB* #204); "Friends, listen humbly" (*STB* #208).

Manik, Liberty

Born in the early 1930s in northern Sumatra, Indonesia, Liberty Manik is one of the most important Indonesian church musicians. He studied church music and musicology in Germany for twenty years and obtained a PhD in music. He returned to Indonesia and taught at various seminaries and universities. In the early 1980s, he was a visiting professor at the Asian Institute for Liturgy and Music, Manila. Manik was commissioned by the Indonesian Council of Churches to conduct research and workshops for creating and promoting contextual hymns, from which a number of hymns were published. His reputation as a scholar and composer is evidenced by his composition of "Padamu Negeri," one of the national songs frequently sung in official ceremonies. Manik remained single, dedicating his energies to education. Upon his death, his personal collection and music library were moved for preservation to the Department of Church Music at Jakarta Theological Seminary (STT Jakarta).

Author/composer: "When you travel far," PERJALANAN (*STB* #256).
Composer: KEHIDUPAN (*STB* #210).

Mann, Robin

Born in Murray Bridge, in the state of South Australia, 26 July 1949, Robin Mann was educated at Immanuel College, Adelaide, and the University of Adelaide (BA, DipEd). He taught at a high school for three years, served as a parish worker at St. Stephen's Lutheran Church for five years, and worked among college students. In 1971, Mann founded the interdenominational group, Kinderkrist, which employed contemporary music for worship and produced three music collections: *Even Stones Can Sing* (1978), *All Together Now* (1980, with audiocassette), and *All Together Again* (1983, with audiocassette). He also composed music for *Outback Christmas* (a Christmas pageant in an Australian setting), which has been performed almost every year since 1981 (cf. Milgate 2000, 48).

Author/composer: "Father welcomes all his children," KRISTIN (*STB* #168); "Comfort, comfort all my people," DOROTHY (*STB* #184).

Maquiso, Elena Granada

Born in Guindulman, Bohol, in the southern Philippines, 9 July 1914, Elena Granada Maquiso was first educated at Silliman University, Cebu, the Philippines (BA, 1948; Bachelor of Christian Education, 1949). At Hartford Theological Foundation, she received an MA in 1951 and a Doctor of Religious Education degree in 1960. She also studied at the School of Sacred Music, Union Theological Seminary, New York (1951–52); in 1958, she received an Advanced Certificate in Advanced Religious Studies from the same institution. From 1952, excepting leaves of absence for research and study, she taught at Silliman University in the fields of church music and Christian education; she also served as a professor of Christian education, as the acting dean and coordinator of the Religious Literature Center of the Divinity School, and as the director of the Ulahingan Research Project that led to her in-depth studies of the oral traditions of ancient epics, myths, and legends.

The interior of Maquiso's bamboo house.

She also taught in Southern Mindanao Institute (now Southern Mindanao College) and Farmers Institute, two schools related to the Church. One of Maquiso's greatest contributions was the editing and publishing of the Cebuano hymnal, *Awitan sa Pagtoo* (1973), which includes many of her original compositions and hymn texts and is widely used among Cebuano-speaking congregations. She also published *Mga Sugilanon Sa Negros* (1980) and five volumes of *Ulahingan: Epic of the Southern Philippines* (1992; originally planned as ten volumes). She was a co-editor of a children's hymnbook in Cebuano, and she wrote a chapter on native rites and celebrations for a book to be published by the Commission on Christian Education and Literature, National Council of Churches. She also wrote many articles on the cultural heritage and native resources of Filipinos in the Church. Maquiso's love for and understanding of Southern Filipino and Indonesian cultures led her to design and build her house entirely with bamboo (1977–78), which won a special prize from the government. She also received the Bahay Filipino Award, the Outstanding Achievement Ministry (Northern Annual Conference) Didache Award, the Outstanding Silliman Award, the Outstanding Year of 1988, and the Guintong Buhay Lifetime Achievement Award. Silliman University named her Professor Emeritus of Christian Education and recently dedicated the Hall of the Department of Liturgy and Music in her honor. Not only was Maquiso an enthusiastic professor, she was also a champion of issues of justice, as seen from her hymn DUMAGUETE (*STB* #266) (cf. her 1966 dissertation for Hartford Seminary Foundation, "A Study of Indigenous Hymns in the Evangelical Church in the Philippines: Implications for Christian Education."). She died 17 June 1995, in Dumaguete.

Author/composer: "Now the day is ending," MONING (*STB* #159); "This land of beauty has been given," DUMAGUETE (*STB* #266).
Arranger: MANGLAKAT (*STB* #146).

Marasinghe, Eugene Walter

Walter Marasinghe on sitar and Banerjee Kalyan on tabla, 1987.

Born in Sri Lanka, 8 November 1933, Eugene Walter Marasinghe belongs to the Church of Ceylon (the former name of Sri Lanka). He was the librarian at University of Peradeniya, where he also was a professor of Sanskrit. He graduated from the University of London with a BA with honors, and he received a PhD from the University of Calcutta in 1968. He also studied music, especially playing the sitar (plucked lute) at Shantiniketan in India. He is also a dramatist and is equally skilled in English, Sinhala, Sanskrit, and Peli. He is a specialist in northern Indian music and composes in its classical styles as well as in traditional Sri Lankan folk styles; hence, he has contributed a great deal to the development of Sinhala hymnody. He was invited in 1980 and 1987 to the Ecumenical Workshops on Liturgy and Music in Manila.

Author/composer: "Grandeur of God," DEV TUMA MAV (*STB* #179); "God's own light came to earth," ALOKAYA AVA (*STB* #271); "Cold is the edge of the night wind," SISILA SULANGA (*STB* #272); "In the coldness of night," SITHALA RA YAME (*STB* #273).

Author: "Calvary's work is complete," (*STB* #275).

Martinez, Salvador T.

Born in 1939 in Manila, the Philippines, Salvador T. Martinez is a minister of the United Church of Christ in the Philippines. He served as a professor of religion and philosophy and as the dean of the College of Arts and Sciences of Silliman University, Dumaguete, the Philippines. He also served as the executive secretary of the Commission on Theological Concerns of the Christian Conference of Asia. He is presently an international associate of the Common Global Ministries Board of the United Church of Christ and the Christian Church (Disciples of Christ), serving in Chiang Mai, Thailand, as a professor of theology and ethics and the director of the international MDiv program of McGilvary Faculty of Theology, Payap University. Martinez is also a poet, an amateur painter, and a musician.

Author/composer: "In the lands of Asia," MARTINEZ (*STB* #263).
Author: "Blest be God who forever lives" (*STB* #264).

Mastra, I Wayan

Born in Bali, Indonesia, 16 October 1931, I Wayan Mastra was the first graduate of the high school in Bali. He grew up in a Hindu family, but while at boarding school at the age of twenty-one, he had an unusual religious experience and became a Christian. He responded to a call from God to be an evangelist to his people, and he entered Jakarta Theological Seminary. Upon graduation, he pursued further studies at Dubuque University, United States, and received a PhD in theology with a dissertation entitled "Salvation of the Non-believers" (1971). He returned to Bali and began his difficult ministry among the Hindus, who compose ninety-eight percent of the population. He was elected the moderator of the Protestant Church in Bali (1971–88); at the time, the position held the title of Bishop. Mastra's motto for his ministry is "Christ is my life, but Bali is my body." He is behind many efforts for contextualizing theology, music, and worship. With I Nyoman Darsane (see the entry for Darsane, I Nyoman), he established the Foundation of Art and Communication in 1984, which trained young artists in dance and music to communicate the gospel. Mastra developed a holistic approach to evangelism: the good news of Jesus Christ also applies to the physical needs of the people. He believes that Christians should be the agents for bringing blessings to their people. Thus, he founded the Dhyana Pura Hotel in Kuta as a moderately priced resort for tourists and for church retreats and conferences as well as a school for hotel management training, which has played an important role in improving the quality of service in Bali's tourism industry. He was elected for a second term as Bishop (1992–2002), and he has contributed significantly toward bringing the Church to a state of independence. His interpretation of and writings on Balinese contextual theologies and arts are embraced by Indonesians as well as theological communities in Asia and Europe. Now retired, he lives in Kuta but is still actively engaged in lecturing and dialoguing with Hindus. He feels joy and honor that one of his daughters is following in his footsteps, dedicating her life to bringing the gospel to her people.

Author: "Lilies of the Field" (*STB* #201).
Author/composer: "O Lord, my God" (*STB* #126).

Mendis, Nirmal

Born in Sri Lanka, Nirmal Mendis was a priest of the Diocese of Colombo for many years. He also served in a parish in Quebec, Canada. He did postgraduate studies in Buddhism and Pali and is now a teacher in a state school in Amparai, Sri Lanka.[124]

Author: "O Father God, we give you praise" (*STB* #16).

McAuley, James Philipp

Born in Lakemba, Sydney, Australia, 12 October 1917, James Philipp McAuley graduated from Fort Street Boys' High School. He was a choirboy and server at St. Anne's Anglican Church, Strathfield, and studied organ with G. Faunce Allman at St. James's Church, Sydney. Later he studied at the University of Sydney, earning BA and MA degrees. After receiving a diploma in education from the Sydney Teachers' College, he taught in state secondary schools and served in the Army

---

[124] Information in this entry is derived from the author's correspondence with Chitra Fernando, April 12, 2007.

Directorate of Research and Civil Affairs, mainly in New Guinea, during World War II. In 1946, he was appointed a lecturer in government administration at the Australian School of Pacific Administration, Sydney, a position he held until 1960. In 1944, he and Harold Stewart wrote poems as the fictitious Ern Malley to criticize current trends in modernist verse, an exercise that had tragicomic repercussions beyond the hoaxers' intentions. McAuley made his mark as a poet with a collection of verses called *Under Aldebaran* (1946). He was received into the Roman Catholic Church in 1951; a few years later, he began writing hymns with Richard Connolly, which were published from 1959 to 1966. McAuley was invited to do the preliminary translation of the "Song of Songs" from French for the Jerusalem Bible. In 1955, he published a second book of poems; in 1956, he became the founding editor of the periodical *Quadrant*. He was appointed a Reader in poetry at the University of Tasmania in 1960 and was a professor of English at the school from 1961 to 1976. In 1969, he was elected a Fellow of the Australian Academy of the Humanities. McAuley was a good musician; as a young man, he considered making a career as a pianist. He concentrated on the organ and for most of his life played regularly for church services, with occasional forays as a jazz pianist and a player of Renaissance and Baroque virginals. His interests embraced philosophy, anthropology, comparative religion, history, ornithology, and literature, and his central preoccupation was the erosion of traditions, customs, and beliefs. He usually subjected his lyrics to a few dozen drafts in a meticulous search for perfection.[125]

Author: "A song of cosmic praise" (*STB* #35); "In faith and hope and love" (*STB* #230).

McKinney, L. G.

Born in the United States, L. G. McKinney was a missionary of the Southern Baptist Church. His field of study was hymnology. According to the Reverend Gabriel C. S. Chi, who was the co-editor of the *Baptist Hymnal*, McKinney was sent to Hong Kong with the purpose of editing the hymnal. He also taught church music at a Baptist seminary, conducted choirs, and was the bass soloist for a number of choral concerts. He returned to the United States when he retired.

Harmonizer: SI-SHI (*STB* #237).

Mews, Douglas Kelson

Born in St John's, Newfoundland, 22 September 1918, Douglas Kelson Mews immigrated to New Zealand in 1969, where he married and had three children.

---

125 Information in this entry is derived from the author's correspondence with Shirley Murray, January 27, 2007.

He was awarded numerous accolades from the Trinity College of Music, London: he was named an Honorary Fellow in 1956 and received a doctorate in music in 1961. From 1974 to 1984, he was an associate professor of music at Auckland University and gave frequent recitals and lectures, often broadcast on the radio. He composed song cycles, liturgical music, and numerous pieces for choir, orchestra, and chamber ensemble, including three Biblical operas and a Maori opera. A Roman Catholic, he was the director of music at St. Patrick's Cathedral, Auckland, from 1970 to 1982. He was also a music editor with the New Zealand Hymnbook Trust and wrote hymn, carol, and liturgical settings. He died in 1993.[126]

Composer: AROHA (*STB* #145A); HONOR THE EARTH (*STB* #269).

Milgate, Wesley

Born in 1916 in Australia, Wesley Milgate is a hymnologist and the author of *A Companion to Sing Alleluia* (Sydney: The Australian Hymnbook Pty. Ltd., 2000).

Author: "Your coming, Lord" (*STB* #187).

Minchin, James Blundell

Born in Victoria, Australia, 29 November 1942, Father James Blundell Minchin is an Anglican vicar and a former Diocesan Consultant in the Diocese of Melbourne, Australia. He graduated from the University of Melbourne (BA, classics, 1965; MA, politics, 1980) and the Australian College of Theology (Licentiate of Theology, 1965). He is fluent in English, Latin, and Greek, and he also reads and speaks French and Malay. Minchin's classical language skills provided unexpected assistance when he paraphrased texts for the 1990 and 2000 editions of *Sound the Bamboo*, allowing him to maintain the meters of the original lyrics and music. In fact, Minchin was the most important poet working on the majority of the paraphrases and translations for *Sound the Bamboo*. He devoted much time to traveling to Manila or Taiwan for editorial meetings or concentrating on the difficult task of paraphrasing. Benefiting from his broad theological mind, imagination, creativity, and mastery of poetic devices, many of the simple songs or rough translations of Asian hymns in *Sound the Bamboo* were transformed into beautiful hymns.

For a number of years, Minchin was a missionary to Singapore, teaching liturgics at Trinity Theological College. He served as a parish priest for Urban and

---

126   Information in this entry is derived from the author's correspondence with Shirley Murray, December 13, 2006.

Rural Australia, as a chaplain at Corpus Christi College in Oxford, as a consultant to the Australian Anglican Liturgical Commission, and as a member of the National Ecumenical Church Music Committee. He is not only a preacher, broadcaster, and writer but also a talented musician, composer, and player of piano and organ. He plays and composes in folk and jazz idioms, and he is well versed in Anglican liturgy and theology, especially within Catholic and radical traditions. Among his publications are *No Man Is an Island: A Study of Singapore's Lee Kuan Yew* (1986); *Jazz in the Church*, vols. 1–3 (1968–70); two long plays of music, *Move Two Mix* (1968) and *Seven Whole Days* (1970); and several articles for journals of theology, music, and political science.

Author/composer: "Marriage song" (*STB* #169).

Co-author: "We believe: Maranatha" (*STB* #45).

Paraphraser: "We worship you, Creator God" (*STB* #9); "Upon this day of peace" (*STB* #14); "O praise the LORD" (*STB* #15); "Joy, O Jesus, crown of all" (*STB* #28); "My people, bless the name of God Messiah" (*STB* #34); "Thousands and thousands of songs" (*STB* #37); "Blessed be God, praised forever" (*STB* #40); "To the high and kindly hills" (*STB* #53); "God of region and of world" (*STB* #61); "O God of great love" (*STB* #64); "Released by love to share new life" (*STB* #72); "Draw near, God of grace, we pray" (*STB* #74); "What a Great Mystery" (*STB* #82); "I'll teach and instruct you the way you should go" (*STB* #89); "In fields of Ephrathah" (*STB* #137); "How deep your love, O Master" (*STB* #147); "I sing a song of victory" (*STB* #151); "Evening Song" (*STB* #161); "Harvest thanksgiving" (*STB* #166); "The Earth is the LORD'S" (*STB* #178); "Grandeur of God" (*STB* #179); "Dear God, how you love your creatures" (*STB* #180); "You have made us from above" (*STB* #197); "Soft the Master's love song" (*STB* #203); "From the Bible we learn God's will" (*STB* # 217); "To everyone a call comes" (*STB* #228); "Ask your God" (*STB* #235); "The Church that is one" (*STB* #239); "God has formed the Church to be" (*STB* #240); "Watch the bush of thorns" (*STB* #252); "Green the wild fields, blue the sky" (*STB* #257); "God's own light came to earth" (*STB* #271); "Cold is the edge of the night wind" (*STB* #272); "My God, why have you forsaken me?" (*STB* #274); "Calvary's work is complete" (*STB* #275); "Blest are the poor folks" (*STB* #276); "Dance of Light" (*STB* #278); "From the unreal, lead to the real" (*STB* #281); "O LORD, God in heaven and powerful creator" (*STB* #293); "Restless, I wait in prayer for You" (*STB* #294); "Praise the LORD, to God give praises" (*STB* #295); "As the incense goes up" (*STB* #296); "Broken communion tore you apart" (*STB* #297); "Christmas is here" (*STB* #304); " Bird call announces morning" (*STB* #305); "Find from nature proof of God's grace" (*STB* #308); "Joy abounds, dear Lord" (*STB* #309).

Co-paraphraser: "Day of joy, let us be glad" (*STB* #11); "I lift my eyes to the Lord" (*STB* #56); "On the night of Christmas" (*STB* #133); "Everywhere sorrow on Calvary's hill" (*STB* #148); "Behold the man we nailed on the cross" (*STB* #149); "The Holy Light" (*STB* #154); "Death stills like a thief" (*STB* #170);

"Grant, LORD, that we may not faint" (*STB* #185); "Gracious Father, love divine" (*STB* #196); "Dear friends, walk with me, let us go" (*STB* #198); "Come children, men and women all" (*STB* #209); "He rules over all" (*STB* #212); "Holy are the Bible's many books" (*STB* #219); "Come down, O Holy Spirit" (*STB* #221); "There was once a time" (*STB* #232); "Strive and toil for God" (*STB* #246); "In the coldness of night" (*STB* #273).

Mizuno, Genzō

Born in 1937 in Nagano Prefecture, Japan, Genzō Mizuno suffered from dysentery with severe diarrhea and high fever at the age of nine, which led to the paralysis of his whole body. At thirteen, he was baptized. He was unable to move or speak; he could only blink his eyes. With his mother's patient and loving care, he was able to communicate ideas by working through the fifty Japanese phonetic symbols that she put on the wall; she pointed at each sound symbol until he blinked his eyes, confirming the selection. Through this arduous process, Mizuno became known as "The Blinking Poet." He wrote innumerable *tanka* (thirty-one-syllable poems with 5-7-5-7-7 structure) and haiku (with seventeen syllables and 5-7-5 structure) and hymns, such as "The love of Christ," which have touched and encouraged many people. He died 6 February 1984.

Author: "Why am I living?" (*STB* #250).

Moody, Kathleen

Born in London, England, 26 June 1920, to an Anglican family, Kathleen Moody graduated from London University in Sociology (1941) and Selly Oak College in Theology (1948), and she studied music at Trinity College of Music (1959–60) and Guildhall School of Music and Drama (1962–65). During World War II, she served as a social worker in the London area, but she was called to be a missionary to Taiwan in 1948. She taught English, sociology, and music at Chang-jung Girls High School and Tainan Seminary. She also promoted classical music, choral music, and mainline church music, and she eventually founded the first college-level church music program at the Tainan Theological College and Seminary in 1959. She was on the Church Music Committee of the General Assembly of the Presbyterian Church in Taiwan for the entire thirty-eight years of her service. She has had an enduring influence on church music and church music education in Taiwan. I-to Loh credits her for his career in church music. Moody retired in 1985 and returned to Great Britain; she lives in Chichester, West Sussex, England, where she joined a nearby Roman Catholic Church. Until the age of eighty-five, she actively joined choirs or folk dancing groups.

Paraphraser: "Gathering round the table of the Lord" (*STB* #83); "Holy night, blessed night" (*STB* #140); "Holy Spirit, Pentecost gift" (*STB* #152).

Murray, Shirley Erena

Born in 1931 in Invercargill, New Zealand, Shirley Erena Murray studied music as an undergraduate but received a master's degree (with honors) in classics and French from Otago University. Her upbringing was Methodist, but she became a Presbyterian when she married the Reverend John Stewart Murray, who was a moderator of the Presbyterian Church of New Zealand. Shirley began her career as a teacher of languages, but she became more active in Amnesty International, and for eight years she served the Labor Party Research Unit of Parliament. Her involvement in these organizations has enriched her writing of hymns, which address human rights, women's concerns, justice, peace, the integrity of creation, and the unity of the church. Many of her hymns have been performed in CCA and WCC assemblies. In recognition for her service as a writer of hymns, the New Zealand government honored her as a Member of the New Zealand Order of Merit on the Queen's birthday on 3 June 2001. Through Hope Publishing House, Murray has published three collections of her hymns: *In Every Corner Sing* (eighty-four hymns, 1992), *Everyday in Your Spirit* (forty-one hymns, 1996), and *Faith Makes the Song* (fifty hymns, 2002). The New Zealand Hymnbook Trust, for which she worked for a long time, has also published many of her texts (cf. back cover, *Faith Makes the Song*). In 2009, Otaga University conferred on her an honorary doctorate in literature for her contribution to the art of hymn writing.

Author: "Child of Christmas story" (*STB* #141); "Upside down Christmas" (*STB* #143); "Hunger Carol" (*STB* #144); "Come to this Christmas singing" (*STB* #145); "Loving Spirit" (*STB* #220); "Song to the Spirit" (*STB* #222); "God of the Bible, God in the Gospel" (*STB* #255); "Christ is our peace" (*STB* #262); "The grain is ripe: the harvest comes" (*STB* #268); "Honor the earth" (*STB* #269); "Mind-set of Christ" (*STB* #310); "A hymn for church unity" (*STB* #314).

Paraphraser: "Praise to you Jesus" (*STB* #17); "Son of God, whose heart is peace" (*STB* #60); "O Lord Jesus, enfold me" (*STB* #73); "This world is so full of rhythm" (*STB* #172; "This is the story" (*STB* #199); "O give praise to Jesus, the King" (*STB* #204); "O Jesus, we would praise you" (*STB* #282); "Sun and moon and stars above" (*STB* #283); "O most holy, O most holy" (*STB* #286); "This is the day of joy and peace" (*STB* #303); "Now my heart is sure that Jesus lives" (*STB* #312).

Co-paraphraser: "Food for pilgrim people" (*STB* #290).

Co-translator: "Oh! What a lovely day" (*STB* #138).

Nacion-Puyot, Beth (Mary Ann Lilibeth)

 Born in Quezon City, the Philippines, 31 July 1961, of the Ilocano people, Beth Nacion-Puyot belongs to the Iglesia Filipina Independiente (Philippine Independent Church). Multi-talented, with skills in organization, administration, and writing, she was the executive director of the Samba-Likhaan Foundation and, from 1987, a faculty member of the Asian Institute for Liturgy and Music (AILM). In addition to her administrative responsibilities, she is also a writer, a commentator, and a radio announcer for DWWW in Manila, a role she performs early every morning with ease and joy.

Paraphraser: "Give praise to the God of all earth" (*STB* #30).
Co-paraphraser: "I lift my eyes to the LORD" (*STB* #56).

Nagasaka, Kanjirō

Born in 1871 in Takasaki City, Japan, Kanjirō Nagasaka was a graduate of the Theology Division of Dōshisha College. He was a pastor of the Congregational Church and served in a few local congregations before assuming positions as a professor at Kōbe Women's College, as the principal of Kōbe Women's Theological College, and as the head of the Theology Division at Seiwa Women's College. He assisted the missionary Clara Brown in editing, writing, and translating *Yuki Bira* (1911), which is considered the first indigenous Japanese children's hymnal (cf. *SRK21*, 275). During the last years of his life, Nagasaka lived in Kyoto and was still active in evangelism. He died in 1952.

Author: "Plodding on with weary footsteps" (*STB* #207).

Nakaseko, Kazu

Born in 1908 in Japan, Kazu Nakaseko was a composer and theorist. He contributed an article entitled "Symbolism in Ancient Chinese Music Theory," to the *Journal of Music Theory* (vol. 1, 1957, published by Yale University). He died in 1973.

Arranger: MOSO (*STB* #216).

Newton, John

Born in London, England, 24 July 1725, John Newton was educated at Stratford, Essex, where he learned some Latin. At the age of eleven, he went to sea with his father and subsequently had an adventurous career as a sailor. During his wandering life, he had lost his Christian faith but was awakened by a storm and had a strong conversion experience. He educated himself, mastering the first six books of Euclid by drawing the figures on the sand. He taught himself Latin, Greek, Hebrew, and Syriac; he read Virgil, Terence, Livy, and Erasmus and learned Horace by heart. He studied the Bible with devotion and adopted Calvinist views of theology. While he was a captain of slave ships, he would read the liturgy with the crew twice each Sunday. He was ordained a priest in 1764, and he became the curate of Olney, Buckinghamshire. In the same year, he published *The Authentic Narrative*, an account of his life at sea and of his religious experiences. During his residence at Olney, Newton published a volume of *Olney Sermons* (1767) and the *Review of Ecclesiastical History*. In 1779, he issued the *Olney Hymns*, containing sixty-eight pieces by William Cowper and 280 by Newton, including "How sweet the name of Jesus sounds"; the book was greatly and enduringly popular. In 1781, he published his most considerable work, *Cardiphonia*, a selection of his religious correspondence. In 1792, the University of New Jersey presented him an honorary Doctor of Divinity degree. Newton continued to preach until the last year of his life, when he was almost too blind to see his text. He died of consumption on 11 July 1807. Along with *Olney Hymns* (1779, with editions in 1781, 1783, 1787, 1792, 1795, 1797, etc.), another major work by Newton is *Messiah: Fifty...Discourses on the...Scriptural Passages...of the...Oratorio of Handel* (1786). Posthumous works: *The Works of Rev. John Newton* (6 vols., 1808; new edition, 12 vols., 1821) and *The Works of Rev. John Newton* (1 vol., with memoir by R. Cecil, 1827).[127]

Author: "May the grace of Christ" (*STB* #81).

Ng, Alison

Born in Tawau, Sabah, Malaysia, 1 February 1954, Alison Ng worked for three years after high school, responding to the call for full-time ministry. After receiving a Diploma in Theology from Singapore Bible College (SBC), she returned to serve the Anglican Church. Feeling the need for the development of church music, she went back to SBC in June 1983 as a member of the first group of church music students. Graduating with a BCM in July 1987, she served as a music minister at the Basel Christian Church of

127 Information in this entry is abridged from Wholesome Words, Christian Biography Resources, http://wholesomewords.org/biography/bnewton2.html (accessed March 19, 2009).

Malaysia and as a music lecturer at Sabah Theological Seminary. She has been a full-time staff member of the seminary from 1990 to the present.

Translator: "We all believe in one God of love" (*STB* #51); "Come one and all, let's follow Christ, our Lord" (*STB* #78).

Niles, Daniel Thambyrajah (D. T.)

Born in Tellipallai, Sri Lanka, 8 May 1908, Daniel Thambyrajah Niles was the son of a famous lawyer and grandson of a pastor/poet. He graduated from United Theological College, Bangalore (1929–33), and became a Methodist minister in Jaffna (1936). He served as the general secretary of the National Christian Council of Sri Lanka (1941–45), as the principal of Jaffna Central College (1953–61), as the chairman of the Methodist Conference of Northern Sri Lanka (1954–64), as the chairman of the Northern District Synod (1964–68), and finally as the president of the Sri Lanka Methodist Conference from 1968 until his death. Niles was active in ecumenical organizations and attended the 1938 International Missionary Council conference at Tambaram, where he began a close friendship with Hendrik Kraemer, the famed Dutch theologian. Niles preached at the opening service of the WCC organizing session in Amsterdam in 1948 as well as the assembly in Uppsala in 1968. He served as the chairman of the WCC Youth Department (1953–59) and was elected one of the six presidents of WCC in 1968; he also served as the executive secretary of its Department of Evangelism. One of the founding members of the East Asia Christian Conference (EACC, later renamed Christian Conference of Asia, or CCA) in 1957, Niles also served as its first general secretary (1957–68) and as a chairman (1968–70). One of his major contributions was the editing of the first *EACC Hymnal* in 1963, to which he contributed as many as thirty-five paraphrases of hymns from other countries and ten of his original hymns. Concerning the *EACC Hymnal*, he said:

> In 1959, when the EACC Assembly met in Kuala Lumpur, the hymns we sang were from one of the Western collections of hymns. Soon after, the decision was taken to put out a collection which included a substantial number of Asian tunes. The EACC hymnal was published in 1963 for use at the Bangkok Assembly of the EACC held in 1964.[128]

---

128 From D. T. Niles's autobiography, quoted by his son, Preman, in correspondence with the author, December 8, 2006.

Niles's son, Preman, says:

> "In the preface to that hymnal, [D. T.] refers to his grandfather, who was a Tamil poet who expressed almost all of his theology in his poetry, and that in some ways [D. T.] wanted to emulate his grandfather."[129]

Niles was not only a poet, eloquent speaker, and efficient administrator but also a powerful preacher, evangelist, teacher, and theologian. His publications included *Buddhism and the Claims of Christ* (1967), *That They May Have Life* (1952), and *Upon the Earth* (1962), which was regarded the best statement on mission theology and strategy. His last work was *A Testament of Faith* (1972). Niles was awarded honorary doctorates of divinity from Budapest University, Hungary, and Serampore College, India. He died 17 July 1970 in Vellore, India.[130]

Author: "My soul doth magnify the LORD" (*STB* #103).
Paraphraser: "Praise God from whom all blessings flow" (*STB* #36); "Christ is all to me" (*STB* #55); "I lift my eyes to the LORD" (*STB* #56); "Jesus, Savior Lord, lo to you I fly" (*STB* #59); "Ever and always be praise" (*STB* #95); "Slaves of Christ, his mercy we remember" (*STB* #249).

Nowroji, Sarah

Born in 1969 in Chennai (formerly Madras), India, Sarah Nowroji came from an orthodox Hindu background. Her father was a violinist, a disciple of Mysore T. Chowdaiya.

Author: "Worship and praise we give" (*STB* #25).

Nunn, Philip

Philip Nunn was born in Australia. In 1989, he was invited to the Ecumenical Workshop on Liturgy and Music in Melbourne for the preparation of the seventh WCC Assembly to be held in 1991. There, Nunn composed the tune "Greensborough" for Shirley Murray. Following the workshop, he joined a religious order.[131]

Composer: GREENSBOROUGH (*STB* #268).

---

129   From the author's correspondence with Preman Niles, December 8, 2006.
130   Information in this entry is abridged from *DAC*, 606.
131   Information in this entry is derived from the author's correspondence with Shirley Murray, December 13, 2006.

O'Grady, Ron

Born in Wellington, New Zealand, 14 May 1930, Ron O'Grady is a founder of ECPAT International, which aims to end child prostitution, child pornography, and the trafficking of children for sexual purposes. He was the CEO of ECPAT International from its founding until 1997. He then served a term as the chairman; on retirement from that position, he became the first honorary president. He has written numerous articles and his four books (*The Child and the Tourist*, *The Rape of the Innocent*, *The ECPAT Story*, and *The Hidden Shame of the Church*) have been translated into more than a dozen languages. For eight years from 1974, he was the associate general secretary of the Christian Conference of Asia, based in Singapore; he was later a director of overseas aid for the Australian Churches. O'Grady's interest in the arts led him to join Masao Takenaka in founding the Asian Christian Art Association in 1978. He has written and edited a number of books on art, including *The Bible Through Asian Eyes* (co-written with Takenaka; Auckland: Pace Publishing, 1991) and *Christ for All People: A Millennium of Christian Art* (2001), and fifteen books on meditation, human rights, and tourism. He is a recipient of the Bronze Medal of Save the Children Canada and was appointed an Officer of the New Zealand Order of Merit (ONZM) by Her Majesty Queen Elizabeth of England. An ordained minister of the Associated Churches of Christ in New Zealand, O'Grady and his wife Alison have three children and three grandsons.

Author: "The God of us all" (*STB* #181); "Living in Christ with people" (*STB* #202).

Oh, Byong Soo

Born in 1916 in Korea, Byong Soo Oh was a pastor and poet. He served as the president of the Mokyang Literature Society.

Author: "Jesus Christ, workers' Lord" (*STB* #234).

Oliano, Ramon

Born in Imugan, northern Luzon, the Philippines, Ramon Oliano came from a prominent family. His grandfather, Bassit Oliano, was the most respected elder in the Ikalahan community in northern Luzon and was always called to settle disputes. Bassit wisely allowed a girl to study at the Methodist high school; this girl later married Bassit's second son, Inway Oliano. Like his father, Inway was a ritual leader and good reconciler and, although he never became a Christian, he helped the Reverend Delbert Rice to translate many Ilocano hymns. Ramon Oliano is Inway's younger brother. Ramon is very creative; although he only attended primary school, he has a broad knowledge of the traditional culture, and he has written from twenty to thirty hymns and a few books, some of which are unpublished. He is Rice's colleague, working together to translate hymns and argue cultural and Biblical interpretations. Ramon Oliano was about sixty-five years of age in 2005.[132]

Author: "You have made us from above" (*STB* #197).
Co-author: "The earth is the LORD's" (*STB* #178).

Oliano, Sario

Born in 1946 in Imugan, northern Luzon, the Philippines, Sario Oliano attended an Ikalahan elementary school and had two years of high school education. Sario is the grandson of Bassit Oliano, the eldest son of Inway, and the nephew of Ramon (see the above entry). Sario provided Delbert Rice's first introduction to the Ikalahan culture. He accompanied Rice to Bible Society translation seminars, where he learned the techniques and methods to analyze poems and translations. He has translated many poems, ritual songs, and hymns and has a wide knowledge of Ikalahan culture. He is greatly respected by his people and is the chairman of the 58,000 hectares of ancestral land that was returned by the government.[133]

Co-author: "The earth is the LORD's" (*STB* #178).

Pajaro, Eliseo M.

Born in Badoc, Ilocos Norte, the Philippines, 21 March 1915, Eliseo M. Pajaro was one of the most important composers and conductors in the Philippines. He earned a diploma in music (1947) at the University of the Philippines (UP) and a master's degree in music (1951) and a PhD in composition (1953) at Eastman School of Music, University of Rochester. In 1947, he began teaching music theory and composition at UP; he became an associate professor in 1962 and a professor in 1969. He also taught various musical subjects at National Teachers College (1939–41, 1946–47), Philippine Women's University (1953–54), and Santa Isabel College (1964–67). At UP, he was the Francisco Santiago Chair in Composition (1973), the

---

132 Information in this entry is derived from the author's conversation with the Reverend Delbert Rice, January 28, 2005.
133 Information in this entry is derived from the author's conversation with the Reverend Delbert Rice, January 28, 2005.

Special Assistant for Cultural Affairs (1969), and the chairman of the Committee on Cultural Presentations, Office of the President (1974). Pajaro also held a number of administrative positions at UP: director, Department of Cultural Affairs (1961–64); chairman, Department of Humanities (1966–67); executive director, UP President's Committee on Culture (1964–68); acting director, Conservatory of Music (1967–68); and acting dean, College of Music (1968–69). He was a conductor of the UP Male Glee Club, the University Symphony Orchestra, and the National Symphony Orchestra. He received innumerable fellowships, awards, and honors, including a Guggenheim Foundation Fellowship, Presidential Medal of Merit Award, Republic Cultural Heritage Award in Music, International Who's Who of Intellectuals, and Who's Who in the World. Pajaro held membership in many cultural and professional organizations. His commissioned works include *Prayer for Peace* (1951), *Philippine Symphony No. 2* (1953), *Concerto no. 1 for Violin and Orchestra* (1959), the opera *Binhi Ng Kalayaan* ("Seed of Freedom," 1961), *The Dawn of a New Day* (the inaugural hymn of the Constitutional Convention, 1971), and *Marilag Fantasy* (for the inauguration of the National Arts Center, 1976). He wrote more than one hundred compositions in all forms. His major choral compositions include "Our Savior's birth," "The soul that trusted God," "Be exalted, O God," "Songs of thanksgiving," "Great is the mystery," "How excellent is Thy name," "Mass for the Lady of the Cenacle," and two volumes of *Himig Pilipino* (comprising fifty-five songs). Upon his retirement from UP in 1980, Pajaro was appointed Professor Emeritus. He died 6 October 1984.

Composer: KALBARYO (*STB* #148).

Pandopo, H. A. (Hermanus Arie Van Dop)

Born in Utrecht, the Netherlands, 28 May 1935, Hermanus Arie Van Dop studied music as a child, learning the piano and organ, which was common for a pastor's son at the time. He graduated in 1964 from the University of Utrecht with a "doctorandus" (the equivalent of a master's degree) in theology. After studying at a school for mission (1964–67), he was sent as a missionary to Indonesia in 1967 with the purpose of raising the standard of church music ministry. "Pandopo" is his Indonesian name. Initially, he worked four and one-half years at Malino and Makassar as a pastor of the Church of South Sulawesi (GKSS). In 1972, he moved to Jakarta to serve the Protestant Church of Western Indonesia (GPIB) as a pastor; he also began to work for the Indonesian Institute for Sacred Music (Yamuger) and taught at Jakarta Theological Seminary (STT Jakarta). Because of Van Dop's interest in music, he did extensive field research of the indigenous music of various ethnic groups in Indonesia. He also mastered the language of Bahasa Indonesia, and he wrote many hymns, composed tunes, and translated hymns from other languages to Indonesian. He translated and edited the entire Genevan Psalter and composed litanies, liturgical responses, and many short songs. He was the major force behind the work of Yamuger, and he was one of the editors of *Kidung Jemaat*, the major interdenominational hymnal in Indonesia, as well as the *Kidung Ceria* ("Hymnal for Children"). He harmonized most of the new Indonesian hymns under Yamuger. He is the author of *Menggubah Nyanyian Jemaat* ("Composing Congregational Hymns"), and he has written countless articles on church music, liturgy, art, and church architecture. He also taught at STT Cipanas and the Jakarta Art Institute during the 1980s. Being an organist, Van Dop designed and supervised the construction of eight bamboo pipe organs (two large ones and six smaller ones), four of which are now housed in Belgium, the Netherlands, England, and Japan. He is an excellent choral conductor and a good educator; he is very strict yet humble and loving, and he especially cares for ordinary people and children. He retired in September 2004 and returned to the Netherlands. After serving thirty-seven years in Indonesia, he is greatly missed by his students and colleagues, who regard him as the "Father of Indonesian Church Music."

Paraphraser: "O God, our Father" (*STB* #18); "Jesus Christ, the Life of the world" (*STB* #210).
Co-paraphraser: "Come down, O Holy Spirit" (*STB* #221).

Bamboo organ built by H. A. Van Dop, at STT Jakarta.

Pangosban, Ben

Born about the 1940s in northern Luzon, the Philippines, Ben Pangosban was a talented Kalinga poet, composer, musician, and dancer. He participated in many cultural events, promoting Kalinga culture and arts. I-to Loh felt privileged to know Pangosban and to see him dance in 1980. Perhaps the best example of his work is his setting of Psalm 96 in the Kalinga style with a strong rhythm (*STB* #92). He passed away in the 1980s.

Composer: SALIDUMMAY (*STB* #92).

Pantou, Rudolf R.

Born in Java, Indonesia, 11 July 1957, Rudolf R. Pantou studied at the Asian Institute for Liturgy and Music (AILM) as a composition major; he was a quiet yet gifted composer and guitar player. While studying at AILM, he married an Indonesian minister. Upon returning to Indonesia, he taught part time at Jakarta Theological Seminary (STT Jakarta). He later moved with his wife to Sulawesi.

Author/composer: "Dear God, how you love your creatures," stanzas 2 and 3, MAKHLUK (*STB* #180); "Soft the Master's love song," LAGU KASIH (*STB* #203). Arranger: MAMAYUG AKUN (*STB* #98).

Park, Jae Hoon

Born in 1922 in Kimhwa, Korea, Jae Hoon Park is a conductor and composer and one of the most beloved church musicians in the history of the Korean Church. He came from a Christian family, with three minister brothers. He graduated from a mission high school and moved to Japan. After entering the Tokyo Imperial Music College, he was drafted to serve in the army, but he managed to escape and returned to Korea. He taught at a primary school and served as a choir conductor at Yongrak Presbyterian Church. After Korea's liberation from Japan in 1945, Park published a collection of his compositions of children's songs, which became very popular in the schools. During the Korean War (1950–53), he served in the music department of the Korean Navy. At the age of thirty-seven, he went to study church music at Westminster Choir College in New Jersey (1959–60); he then went to Theological College in Indianapolis and earned an MA in church music (1960–63). After returning to Korea, he initiated the journal *Church and Music* (1964–66), for which he contributed numerous articles promoting church music. Park was the conductor of the Sonmyonghoi Children's Choir (1964–66), taught composition and choral conducting at Hanyang University (1967–73), and was one of the founders of the Korean Church Music Society. In 1982, he was ordained a pastor to a Korean Presbyterian church in the United States. He composed two operas, including *Esther* (1971), and two oratorios, including *St. Mark's Passion*. He published six volumes of his compositions, entitled *Chanmi* ("Praise," 1947–54), which initiated the use of Korean compositions in Korean churches. Park's compositions are mostly in Western styles; from 1964, he has employed Korean melodic idioms but retains Western chordal harmony and occasionally uses parallel fourths. A few of his famous hymn tunes appeared in the *Korean Hymnal* (1967): "O, Come home" (no. 317), "God's great grace it is has [sic] brought us," (no. 460), and "Lift your eyes and look to heaven" (no. 256). Park was the editor of the *Korean-English Hymn Book* (1983), *Hands in Hands* (1983), and the *Korean-Russian Hymnal* (1992).

Composer: KAM-SAH (*STB* #166).

Paul, Samuel Stephen

Born in Lahore, Pakistan, 27 February 1963, Samuel Stephen Paul is a member of Brethren Fellowship in Lahore. (Because some ethnic groups in India and Pakistan do not use family names, Christian converts traditionally adopt a Christian name as their family name.) Paul graduated from Dyal Singh College, served as a Sunday school teacher, and is an assistant editor in a Christian publishing house. He is an amateur poet/composer; he plays the guitar and accordion and has written fifteen songs in Urdu. He was invited to participate in the Asian Workshop on Liturgy and Music in Manila in 1987 and has since been promoting and developing Pakistani church music.

Author/composer: "O Lord Jesus, enfold me," PRABHU LELE (*STB* #73).
Translator: "Blest be God, praised for ever" (*STB* #40).

Perez, Bernardo Maria

Born in Manila, the Philippines, 2 June 1933, Father Bernardo Maria Perez is a Benedictine monk (OSB). He graduated from University of Santo Tomas (BS, architecture) and San Beda College (BS, philosophy), and he studied theology at the Loyola House of Studies. He was ordained on 21 December 1969 and has served at San Beda College (1971–74, 1977–83, and 1986–2001). Perez is a specialist in architecture, and he has written many essays in this field, which have been published by GCF Books.

Author: "Who will set us free?" (*STB* #130).

Pierpoint, Folliot Sandford

Born in Bath, Somersetshire, England, 7 October 1835, Folliot Sandford Pierpoint studied at Queen's College, Cambridge, and was a classical master at Somersetshire College. As a gifted poet, he contributed works to *Lyra Eucharistica* and *The Hymnal Noted*, and he published a few volumes of poems (cf. Young 1993, 813). He died 10 March 1917 in Newport, England.

Author: "For the beauty of the earth" (*STB* #171).

Poitras, Genell

Genell Poitras was an American missionary of the United Methodist Church to Korea.

Translator: "Gather here, believers in Christ" (*STB* #243).

478

Pongnoi, Sook

Sook Pongnoi is a Thai Christian.

Author: "Come children, men and women all" (*STB* #209).

Pope, Marion

Marion Pope was a missionary of the United Church of Canada to Korea. While serving in Korea, she earned a doctorate in nursing from Yonsei University. She mastered the Korean language and has translated many Korean hymns into English. Several years ago, she retired and returned to Canada.

Translator: "Cross of Christ, you stand above us" (*STB* #150); "Jesus, our true
    Lord of love" (*STB* #192).
Paraphraser: "Ŏgiyŏngcha, Morning sunlight beams in splendor" (*STB* #225);
    "Come now, O Prince of Peace" (*STB* #241).
Co-paraphraser: "Food for pilgrim people" (*STB* #290).

Prabhakar, Samson

 Born in South India, 14 October 1948, Samson Prabhakar was raised in a devout Christian family; his father was John Christabhakta, a Hindu convert, and his mother was Hilda Hebsiba. Prabhakar received a secular education in Puttur, a small town in southern Karnataka, and a theological education at the United Theological College, Bangalore, where he became a professor of Christian education and taught in the Department of Christian Ministry from 1980 to 2001. He earned his doctorate from the University of Bern, Switzerland (1985–88); his dissertation concerned Indian-Christian religious education, with a focus on young people. He is an ordained presbyter of the Church of South India (CSI), which was formed from a union of four Protestant churches in 1947, and he spent several years in the pastoral ministry in Mumbai (formerly Bombay). Prabhakar is trained in both Indian and Western music and has composed a number of Indian lyrics and songs that are used in his church. He has contributed to the worship and liturgy of the Church of South India, particularly ecumenical institutions and schools, by composing liturgies for special occasions and festivals that emphasize inculturation. His writings on Christian worship have appeared in *So We Believe, So We Pray* (1995, published by the World Council of Churches); a recent article was included in the *Oxford History of Christian Worship* (2006, edited by Geoffrey Wainwright and Karen B. W. Tucker). As of 2006, Prabhakar was the director of the doctoral program of the Board of Theological Education of

the Senate of Serampore College (BTESSC) and South Asia Theological Research Institute (SATHRI).[134]

Translator: "O Jesus, we would praise you" (*STB* #282).

Prasopsin, Songsan

Born in Thailand, 29 September 1932, Songsan Prasopsin was an ordained pastor of the Morrison Church in Evangelical Fellowship of Thailand. He was a professional folk singer, musician, and actor. After becoming a Christian, he dedicated his life to evangelism. He taught at a Bible college in Payao Province and recorded radio programs with the group "Voice of Peace," with which he visited Denmark in 1981. He was a professional *ranat ek* (wooden xylophone) player and used it to accompany Thai hymns. He contributed twenty hymns to the Thai hymnal. Along with Inchai and Ruth Srisuwan (see their separate entries), Prasopsin was a powerful force and inspiration in the development of contextual Thai hymns. He died in the early 2000s.

Author: "Day of joy, let us be glad" (*STB* #11); "Upon this day of peace" (*STB* #14).
Author/composer: "Holy are the Bible's many books," HOLY WORD (*STB* #219).

Songsan Prasopsin accompanied by Alice Compain on the violin.

Price, Frank W.

Born in 1895 in China, Frank W. Price was a graduate of Davidson College and Yale Divinity School. He also studied at Columbia University and Yale University. Upon his ordination in 1922, he was sent as a missionary to China; he taught at Nanjing Theological Seminary and Hangzhou Christian College. He was detained

---

134   Information in this entry is derived from the author's interview with Prabhakar, January 29, 2006.

for three years by the Communist regime, was released in 1952, and returned to the United States. Price was elected the moderator of the Presbyterian Church in the United States (1953–54). He also taught at Union Theological Seminary, New York, and was the director of its Mission Research Library for ten years, until his retirement. He published two books entitled *Chinese Christian Hymns* (1953) and *Marx Meets Christ* (1957) (cf. Fyock 1996, 633; Glover 1994, 2:572f). Price translated twenty-three Chinese hymns from the *Putian Songzan* ("Hymns of Universal Praise," 1936) into English, some of which became popular with English-speaking congregations. He died in 1974 in Lexington, Virginia.

Translator: "Fount of Love, our Savior God" (*STB* #65); "May the Holy Spirit's sword" (*STB* #223).

Paraphraser: "God, we praise you for this LORD's day" (*STB* #13); "Golden breaks the dawn" (*STB* #155); "Praise our God above" (*STB* #165); "Great are your mercies, Heavenly Father" (*STB* #174); "Jesus loved each little child" (*STB* #200).

Ra, Won Yong

Won Yong Ra is Korean.

Author: "To the One Creator of all" (*STB* #75).

Rajagukguk, Toga P. L.

Born in the 1960s in northern Sumatra, Indonesia, Toga P. L. Rajagukguk is a pastor of the Batak Protestant Christian Church (HKBP). He is a gifted poet and musician and studied at the Asian Institute for Liturgy and Music in Manila during the early 1990s. After the disastrous 2004 tsunami, he was appointed to serve in Banda Aceh in northwest Sumatra, where countless numbers of residents disappeared.

Author/composer: "My boat of life sails on an angry sea," PRAHU (*STB* #50).
Translator: "O God our Father" (*STB* #287).

Ramirez, F. Ll.

F. Ll. Ramirez is Filipino.

Author/composer: "Give praise to the God of all earth," PURIHIN (*STB* #30).

Rice, Delbert

Born in Corvallis, Oregon, USA, 24 January 1928, Delbert Rice attended Oregon State University (OSU) and earned his BS in electrical engineering (1950); he received a BD (MDiv) from Western Evangelical Seminary (formerly George Fox Evangelical Seminary) in 1955. In 1950, he was married to Esther R. Bernham (BS, home economics, OSU); they have four sons, one daughter, eleven grandchildren, and one great-grandson, and a few adopted children. Rice initially served as a pastor in a few local churches. He went to the Philippines with his wife and two children as missionaries, worked in the lowlands for ten years, and moved to the mountains to serve the Imugan communities in Nueva Viscaya. Wanting to understand the local cultures, he enrolled at Silliman University to study anthropology and completed his MA thesis on the Ikalahan culture in 1972. Rice taught at Missionary Orientation Center in New York (1967), Silliman University (1969, 1971), and Shalom Bible College, which he founded (1980–2000); he has done anthropological research on Negrito society (1970, 1978, 1985), Cordillera church viability (1971), Poleg resource development (1997–98), Ikalahan history and prehistory (1994), and Kalahan biodiversity (1995). Currently, he is the educational consultant to the Kalahan Educational Foundation, which he established and has served since 1972. He is an adjunct faculty member at the University of the Philippines, Los Banos, a board member of the Upland NGO Assistance Committee, and a chairman of the Upland Marketing Foundation.

Rice's approach to mission is unique. He casually introduces the living Christ to the Ikalahan according to their lifestyle and culture, systematically working his way through the Bible, dramatizing the stories, and letting the people apply them to their contexts. In 1966, Rice revived the traditional music that the Ikalahan had been reluctant to admit, taping their songs, transcribing them, and encouraging the people to set new Christian texts. He was fascinated by their use of songs for social indoctrination, in order to educate the young about traditional values and social norms. Rice attended traditional rituals and recorded, transcribed, and analyzed them to better understand and apply the elements; in various rituals, an unnamed god was worshiped and working among the people. Rice founded a high school to train the young Ikalahan to understand their history and culture; he also established the Shalom Bible College to train pastors, who could pursue inductive Bible studies with cultural approaches. Since his arrival in the region, the number of churches has increased from two to forty-five, and they are strong and self-supporting. Rice and his wife adopted a few Ikalahan children; their natural children are married to locals. They have not only planted the seeds of the gospel but also revived the native cultures and brought prosperity to the community as well as abundance to their daily lives. Rice is a scholar of Ikalahan languages, history, poems, and rituals and is producing a book of more than 150 Ikalahan rituals with original texts and

English translations, which will be important for pastors and theologians pursuing liturgical studies and contextual theologies.

Among Rice's publications are numerous articles on missions, indigenization, theology, music, and culture in the magazine *Practical Anthropology*; "Developing Indigenous Church Music," *Silliman Journal* XVI, 4 (1969): 339–59; "Democratization of Resources," *Our Threatened Heritage* (Solidarity Press); "Indigenous Peoples in the Philippines," Baguio Religious Acculturation Conference journal; "Ikalahan Livelihood," *Bayani* magazine; "Ecosystems and the Christian Mission," *Riding the Third Wave*, ed. Richard Schwenk; *Mission Notes*, co-written with Alex Grant; *The Quiet Ones Speak* (New Day Publishers, 2001); and *Walking with a Trouble Maker* (New Day, 2002). Rice has given more than twenty-four addresses to national and international conventions on topics related to anthropology, forestry, ecology, politics, economics, and Biblical or non-Biblical revelation. He has received many awards, including: Philippine Band of Mercy (for service to the handicapped), Commission on National Integration (for service to minorities), Outstanding Sillimanian (from Silliman University), Outstanding Alumnus (from Western Evangelical Seminary), Likas Yaman Award (from the Philippines President Corazon Aquino), Golden Award (from the International Research and Communication Center).[135]

Translator: "The Earth is the LORD's" (*STB* #178); "You have made us from above" (*STB* #197).

Ricketson, Bettie A.

Bettie A. Ricketson was probably a missionary to China or Hong Kong.

Translator: "We assemble with joy and praise" (*STB* #167).

Rigos, Cirilo A.

Born in 1932 in Mauban, Quezon Province, the Philippines, Cirilo A. Rigos graduated from the Union Theological Seminary, Manila, and was an ordained minister of the United Church of Christ in the Philippines. For many years, he served as the pastor of the Cosmopolitan Church and the Ellinwood United Church of Christ in the Philippines (UCCP). He also served as the general secretary of the UCCP from 1968 to 1972 and the general secretary of the United Bible Societies in London. He was a human rights activist who was outspoken against the excesses of the Marcos regime of martial law. He was a co-founder of the Wednesday Forum and Kilosbayan, where issues of grievances were openly aired. He died from cancer in 1996.[136]

---

135 Information in this entry is derived from the author's correspondence and interview with Rice, January 28, 2005.

136 Information in this entry is derived from the author's correspondence with Salvador T. Martinez, February 6, 2005.

Author: "Death steals like a thief" (*STB* #170).
Co-translator: "Now the day is ending" (*STB* #159).

Rockey, C. D.

C. D. Rockey may have been a Western missionary in northern India.

Translator: "Jesus, Jesus, how we adore you" (*STB* #41).

Rohrbough, Katherine R.

Born in Hunter, New York, USA, 9 July 1896, Katherine R. Rohrbough was a graduate of Wellesley College and Boston University School of Theology. With her husband, Lynn, she founded the Cooperative Recreation Service, in Delaware, Ohio, and published church games and songbooks, many of which were the major resources for church camping and recreational ministries from the end of World War II to the 1970s. According to Carlton Young (1993, 820), many Third World songs and hymns became available in English translations through these publications. She died 21 October 1932 in Delaware, Ohio.

Translator: "We bow before you, O great and holy" (*STB* #39).

Rongong, Dona

Born in 1955 in Kalimpong, West Bengal, India, Dona Rongong is Nepalese and the son of the late A. C. Rongong.

Author/composer: "O give praise to Jesus, the King," JAYA HOS YISHU (*STB* #204).

Rossman, Vern

Born in 1927 in Colorado, USA, Vern Rossman grew up in Oklahoma. He is a graduate of Phillips University (BA, 1948), Yale Divinity School in New Haven (BD, cum laude, 1952), Union Theological Seminary in New York (STM, 1960), and the Naganuma School of Japanese Language and Culture in Tokyo (diploma); his major subjects were Bible studies, sociology, Christian ethics, theology, and Japanese language and culture. He served as a missionary to Japan for ten years and was a director in the social action department of the Disciples of Christ. He then served seven years as the executive director of Intermedia, the overseas literacy and communications program of the National Council of Churches, which took him to thirty countries. He was arrested in Greenwood, Mississippi, during the civil rights struggles of the 1960s and as one of the seven protesters in the Griffiss Plowshares; he served twenty months in federal prison for that action at Griffiss

Air Force Base in 1983. Rossman began two prison ministries, which continue in Indiana and New Jersey. He has written one book and two plays, and for four years he was the editor of a social action newsletter. Now retired, he lives in Garber, Oklahoma, where he continues to write and engage in social activism.[137]

Translator: "Distracted by the world's concerns" (*STB* #69); "Plodding on with weary footsteps" (*STB* #207).

Routley, Erik Reginald

Erik Routley in 1978 (after Carlton Young, *Duty & Delight: Routley Remembered, A Memorial Tribute to Erik Routley, 1917–1982* [Carol Stream, IL: Hope Publishing Company, 1985] 50f).

Born in Brighton, Sussex, England, 31 October 1917, Erik Reginald Routley graduated from Lancing College in Sussex (1931), Magdalen College in Oxford (BA, 1936), Mansfield College in Oxford (1939), and Oxford University (BA, 1940; BD, 1946; PhD, 1952), and was ordained as a Congregational minister in 1943. He began teaching at Mansfield College after serving two parishes and was a lecturer in church history, a chaplain, a librarian, and a director of music (1948–59). After entering pastoral work, he was elected the president of the Congregational Church in England and Wales (1970–71) and was appointed the first chair of the Doctrine and Worship Committee of the new United Reformed Church. In 1975, he was invited as a visiting professor and director of music at Princeton Theological Seminary, and he later was a professor of church music and director of the chapel (1978) at Westminster Choir College, New Jersey. Routley was a prolific writer, hymnologist, hymn critic, organist, and composer. He was also one of I-to Loh's idols; while Loh was a student, he read all of Routley's early books and corresponded with Routley a few times concerning hymn styles. They first met in 1966; when they met again in 1980 at Princeton Seminary, they had a good discussion about ethnic hymns. According to Carlton Young (1993, 821f), Routley was the most influential hymnologist of his generation. He wrote more than fifty books and several hundred articles. Among his most important publications are: *The Church and Music* (1950), *The English Carol* (1958), *Church Music and Theology* (1959), *Music, Sacred and Profane* (1960), *Hymns Today and Tomorrow* (1964), *Exploring the Psalms* (1975), and *Christian Hymns Observed* (1982). He was the editor of *Bulletin: The Hymn Society of Great Britain and Ireland* (1948–74), and he co-edited *Hymns for Celebration* (1974), *Ecumenical Praise* (1977), and *Companion to Congregational Praise* (1953). He was the editorial consultant of *Cantate Domino* (third edition, 1974) and the editor of *Rejoice in the*

---

137 Information in this entry is derived from the author's correspondence with Rossman, 2004.

Lord (1985). He died 8 October 1982 in Nashville, Tennessee, USA.

Fred Pratt Green composed this memorial following Routley's death:

> He was, of all of us, the most alive.
> He lived his life *allegro*, let us say,
> Even *con brio*; yet he could contrive,
> In his untiring and warm-hearted way,
> To play it *con amore*. To each friend
> He was most loyal, lovable, and kind;
> As author, teacher, his exciting mind
> Instructed us how wit and wisdom blend.
>
> His many gifts made debtors of us all:
> His love of hymnody, his dedication.
> But, as God's servant, was he apt to be,
> In giving of himself, too prodigal?
> Be sure of this: he needs no threnody;
> What he deserves of us is celebration.[138]

Paraphraser: "Happy is he who walks in God's wise way" (*STB* #87); "Light of the world, salt of the earth" (*STB* #254).

Ruperto, Serafin E.

Serafin E. Ruperto lived in Anabu, Imus, Cavite, the Philippines. He belonged to the United Evangelical Church of Christ (Iglesia Evangelica Unida de Kristo).

Author: "Our souls are full of praises" (*STB* #29).

Sang, Maung

Born in the late 1960s in Myanmar, Sang Maung was originally trained as a lawyer and is a talented musician. He studied at the Asian Institute of Liturgy and Music, Manila, and obtained a BCM in composition. Upon completion of his studies, he went to the United States to study theology.

Translator: "Mighty God, power over heaven and earth" (*STB* #57); "Glory be to the Father" (*STB* #106); "Gracious Father, love divine" (*STB* #196); "Happy are those following Jesus" (*STB* #226); "There was once a time" (*STB* #232).
Author/transcriber/adapter: "God of region and of world," FALAM CHIN (*STB* #61).

---

138   Quoted from Young 1993, 822.

Santiago, V.

V. Santiago was born in 1869 in South India. His father served as a British soldier, was a Roman Catholic, had six children (four became pastors—see the entry for V. Maasilaamanni), and later converted to the Protestant Church. Santiago was a mathematics professor at the American College in Madurai. He helped the Basel Mission for two years, he was pastor at Vathulagundu in 1908, and he became a presbyter in 1911. He was chosen as the president of the Church of South India in 1917 and served as the moderator from 1919 to 1921. Due to health problems, Santiago stopped working in 1920, but he was the first Indian to be appointed the leader of the Madurai Church Union. Coming from a musical family, he translated many Western hymns, including "When I survey the wondrous cross," and "Nearer my God to Thee," and he wrote twenty-two lyrics, including both text and music. He died in 1929 in southern India.

Author/composer: "Slaves of Christ, his mercy we remember," DHAASEREE (*STB* #249).

Saragih, Absalom K.

Born in Pematangsiantar, North Sumatra, Indonesia, 11 March 1936, Absalom K. Saragih is a retired government officer. He is a well-known composer of hymns and choruses in native styles, with more than one hundred pieces to his credit. He belongs to the Simalungun Protestant Christian Church (GKPS) and serves as a church elder.

Author/composer: "Tonight we see the Light of the world," NGOLU NI PORTIBI (*STB* #136); "The Church that is one," BERSATU TEGUH (*STB* #239).

Sarker, Bindunath

Bindunath Sarker is Bengali.

Author: "Joy, O Jesus, crown of all" (*STB* #28).

Sasthriyar, Veedhenayegam

Born in 1774 in South India, Veedhenayegam Sasthriyar belonged to a famous and important musical family that used their multiple artistic gifts solely to proclaim the gospel. (The modern spelling of the name is Vedanayagam Sastriar.) According to Durai Raj Veedhenayegam Sasthriyar (see the entry for Baagavedhar, Veedhenayegam), a member of the sixth generation of the family, the title "Sasthriyar" was the equivalent of a doctorate—Christians honored pastors who were versed in the Bible, Tamil poetry, music, and literature—and a special term for an evangelist who preached through singing, a tradition that continues in the Sasthriyar family. Veedhenayegam Sasthriyar's father was born in 1735 to a devout Hindu who, at the age of twenty-five, converted to Christianity and was cast out of his community. He learned Latin and the Scriptures and became a catechist. His son, Veedhenayegam Sasthriyar, received an education in literature and mathematics at the age of five. A missionary named Schwartz visited Tirunelveli in 1786 and was impressed by the intelligence of the twelve-year-old boy and decided to educate him further in Thanjavur. Veedhenayegam's interest in the Psalms led him to become the sweet singer of Tamil Christians. He also studied at Lutheran Theological Seminary; he became versed in Lutheran liturgy and theology, and at the age of nineteen, he was a class teacher in the mission school, at which he later became the headmaster. By the age of forty, he had already written eighty books and many verses. He was frequently invited to the courts to preach the gospel and became known as "the king among evangelical poets." In 1830, Veedhenayegam was excommunicated by the Thanjavur Church and began collecting data on history and teaching the Tamil language. He continued daily worship in the family, and he died after a worship service on 24 January 1864. He wrote approximately fifty-two books on Biblical themes, and his evangelism through songs is known even today. Chandran D. S. Devanesen comments:

> Vedanayagam was an artistic, temperamental poet and thoroughly human. But the depth of his devotion to his Bethalem Nathar, Christ, makes him great Baktha of the Lord. Vedanayagam is an inspiring example of the complete identification that we need as Christians with our own people and culture . . . Vedanayagam helps us to communicate, to promote understanding, to gain appreciation for the creative flow of Christ and His message with Tamil literature and culture contributing to harmony and tolerance.[139]

Author: "O Jesus, we would praise you" (*STB* #282).

Satō, Taihei

Born in 1936 in Miyagi Prefecture, Japan, Taihei Satō was baptized at Sendai Higashi Sambancho Church as a high school student. After graduating with a degree in music from Tōhoku University, he taught at a women's junior college and then went to the School of Sacred Music, Union Theological Seminary, New York, and earned his Master in Sacred Music degree, majoring in composition.

---

139   Cf. http://www.sastriars.org. See also the entry for Baagavedhar, Veedhenayegam.

Upon returning to Japan, he conducted choirs and composed in the Sendai area. He later moved to Tokyo, and he is currently teaching at Rikkyō Women's Junior College. In addition to being a choral conductor and a children's music educator, he is known as a specialist in the work of the author Kenji Miyazawa, who also composed music. This led Satō to dedicate his life to the restoration and revival of reed organs; he became the president of the Japan Association of Reed Organs (cf. *SRK21*, 339f). More than 700 reed organs have been restored because of his work. He has published a few collections of organ works, such as *Remembrance* (compact disc, 2001), and has given concert tours with *shō* (mouth organ) players in Japan as well as the United States and England.[140]

Composer: SHIMPI (*STB* #189); NAN NO TAME (*STB* #250).

Saw Si Hae

Saw Si Hae and his family

Born in Myanmar, Si Hae is one of the most gifted composers of church music in his country. ("Saw" is a Burmese title of respect for men, the equivalent of "Mister" in English.) He worked for the late Bishop Gregory of the Anglican Church in Myanmar, promoting church music around the country. Currently, he is the director of Youth for Christ in Yangon (Rangoon). He and his wife are dedicated to working on the behalf of orphans and have helped many homeless children.

Author/composer: "There was once a time," ACHIÑ (*STB* #232); "To you, O LORD, I lift my soul," YANGON (*STB* #292).

Saw Gideon Tun Shwe

Born in Pathein, northern Myanmar, 21 October 1941, of the Karen (Kayin) people, Saw Gideon Tun Shwe attended the Ko Tha Byu high school. He majored in science for two years at the Intermediate College of Yangon (Rangoon) University, and he completed his Bachelor of Science degree in botany at Yangon University. Gideon studied at the Burmese Institute of Theology, which was later renamed the Myanmar Institute of Theology, earning a bachelor's degree in religious education. Upon graduation in 1971, he began his ministry with the Student Christian Movement as the secretary of the group. Because of his interest in music, he began writing

---

140 Information in this entry is derived from the author's correspondence with Satō, January 15, 2007.

songs for university students. He retired from this work in 1992, but he is still involved in church music. He was appointed by the Self Supporting Karen Baptist Mission Society to translate and edit their hymnal in 2000, for the celebration of the twenty-fifth anniversary of the Myanmar Blind Christian Fellowship, and he has contributed a few hymns, including a setting of Psalm 121. Gideon is married and has two daughters; one of them recently received her master's degree in gender studies from the Myanmar Institute of Technology.

Author/composer: "Come, O come, let us praise parent God," LAJAHLE (*STB* #1).

Saw Tun Meh

Born in Kayin Jyi, Myanmar, one hundred miles north of Yangon, 13 January 1933, Saw Tun Meh graduated from a mission high school. He entered Burma Divinity School and graduated in 1959. (This school's name has changed many times, from Burma Baptist Divinity School to Burma Divinity School to Karen Baptist Theological Institute, which indicated the 1965 merger of two institutions: Karen Women's Bible School and Karen Theological Seminary (for men). Its current name is Myanmar Institute of Theology in Insein.) Tun Meh also studied at the Bossey Ecumenical Institute, Geneva, in 1988. For many years, he served as the general secretary of one of the seventeen Baptist associations; he was the director of mission and evangelism of the Baptist Convention for ten years. He was appointed as the principal of the Karen Baptist Theological Institute in 1986, and he taught courses in mission and evangelism until his retirement in 1998; he still serves as an advisor. Tun Meh came from a non-Christian family and was the first convert. His familiarity with the practice of animism among the Karen people enabled him to publish a book, *Remember I* (2000), dealing with Karen oral traditions, religious practices, ancient proverbs, and idioms. It became so popular and was in such demand that the second volume was published in October 2004. He also edited a Karen-Burmese-English dictionary, released at the same time. As one of the pioneers of indigenous theology, Tun Meh has attended and made contributions to many international and ecumenical conferences.

Translator: "Hear and heed the angel's words" (*STB* #307).

Say Pa, Anna May Chain

Born in Myanmar, 29 March 1942, Anna May Chain ("Say Pa" is her husband's last name) was educated at Yangon University (BA), Myanmar Institute of Theology (BRE), Southeast Asia Graduate School of Theology (MTh), and Princeton Seminary, New Jersey (PhD in Old Testament studies). She was the first woman in the Myanmar church to earn such a high academic degree. From 1964, she taught the Old Testament at Myanmar Institute of Theology until 1979, and she was a professor of Old Testament and feminist theology from 1989 to the present. She served as the vice-principal from 1990 to 1998 and became the principal in 1998. She has been an active leader in the Myanmar Baptist Convention, serving as the vice-president and the chair of Leadership Development. She was also the vice-president of the Myanmar Council of Churches and a member of the Central Committee of the WCC. She retired in 2008.

Translator: "May the LORD bless you with joy" (*STB* #288).

Schaffter, Sharada J.

 Born to a musical family in India, 24 April 1928, Sharada J. Schaffter has been singing in choirs and playing the piano since she was nine years old. She has been an organist since she was thirteen. Beginning in her early twenties, she (and her husband Surender, who is a flutist) served as an organist and choirmaster in churches in Chennai for several decades. She conducted a men's choir for several years while her husband was absent. She was the conductor of the Madras Philharmonic and Choral Society for six years and is now the director of the Handel Manuel Chorus. Schaffter graduated from the University of Madras and was a mathematics teacher for a while. Seeing the low condition of women in Indian society, she gave up her teaching career and became a social activist, working as a volunteer with the Women's Forum for Social Action at the Institute for Development Education, Chennai. She studied Development and Group Communication and Management in Rural Reconstruction at the International Institution in the Philippines; afterward, she worked with women in villages near Chennai. Because of her expertise and dedication, she has been invited as speaker or workshop leader on the subject of "Women and the Media" at conferences in Hong Kong, Sri Lanka, Madhya Pradesh, Karnataka, Kerala, and Tamilnadu. She is currently a member of the Asian Network of Women in Communication, Manila, which is part of the World Association for Christian Communication, which is headquartered in London and has offices in thirteen Asian countries. Schaffter is also the honorary director of a service organization, Seva Trust. Recently she published the book *Privileging the Privileged: Gender in Indian Advertising* (New Delhi and Chicago: Promilla & Co. Publishers, in association with Bibliophile South Asia, 2005).[141]

Composer: TAGORE (*STB* #157).

---

141   Information in this entry is derived from the author's interview with Schaffter, January 28, 2006.

Shaha, Bartholomew

Born to a Roman Catholic family in Bangladesh, 14 June 1946, Bartholomew Shaha is a graduate of Notre Dame College (BA, 1968), Christ the King Seminary (1973) and the University of Portland (MA, communications, 1980). In 2004, he obtained a PhD in social sciences from the University of Hong Kong. For almost thirty years, Shaha has had a distinguished and extensive YMCA career at the local, national, regional, and global levels. He is now serving as the secretary general of the World Alliance of YMCAs, based in Geneva, Switzerland. He began his YMCA career in 1973 as the first general secretary of the Chittagong YMCA, a position he held until 1981 when he was appointed as the executive secretary for leadership development of the former Asia Alliance of YMCAs, based in Hong Kong. In 1988, he returned to Bangladesh as the national general secretary of Bangladesh YMCAs. From 1992 to 1995, he served as the executive secretary for global programs and communications at the World Alliance of YMCAs. In 1996, he was appointed the general secretary of the Asia and Pacific Alliance of YMCAs, which comprises YMCAs in twenty-seven countries of the Asia and Pacific region. He has also developed and successfully implemented plans for the extension and strengthening of YMCA movements in the region.

Shaha studied Bengali music and Indian classical music under Sushi Baroi, Prioda Ranjan Sengupta, Rita Boucher, and Ustad P. C. Gomes. He writes his own music in *swaralipi* (Bengali notation). He is also a gifted writer and poet; he has edited and published writings, composed hymns and songs, and written poems that reflect contemporary issues and express a vision of a new society of justice and peace. Among his published works are "Seeking Abundant Life For All" and "Leaders We Want." Thirty-five of his songs are included in *Geetaboli*, the Bengali Catholic hymnal. *Jagoroni* ("Songs of Awakening and Hope") is a popular collection of his songs and hymns, available on audiocassette. His book *Tomakei Daki* (published in 1977 in Chittagong) includes texts and music widely used in liturgy and prayer. Several of Shaha's articles, poems, and songs have been published by *Pratibeshi*, *Bangladesh Observer*, *Far Eastern Economic Review*, the publication of the Asian Institute of Liturgy and Music, and many other national and international reviews and magazines. The compact disc *We Come with Hope*, produced by the Asia and Pacific Alliance of YMCAs in Hong Kong, features several of Shaha's songs now widely sung by international choirs. He also produced a compact disc in 2003 entitled *Amar Bhashar Jonneye* ("For My Mother Language") with fourteen Bengali songs on various themes. In addition to music, Shaha also has broad interests in painting, calligraphy, poetry writing, worship, and liturgical experimentation. His publication of Bengali liturgical and devotional songs, entitled *Tumi Nayoban Probhu* ("You are just, Lord"), was at press at the time of this writing.[142]

142　Information in this entry is derived from the author's correspondence with Bart Shaha, 2006 and February 28, 2007.

Author/composer: "Come, Lord Jesus Christ," ESHO HAE PROBHU (*STB* #8); "Glory be to you, O God," JOY (*STB* #19); "LORD, we did not live up to your teachings," SANGEETA (*STB* #43); "This world is so full of rhythm," AMAR KACHE (*STB* #172).

Sherring, Victor C.

Born in Kanpur, Uttar Pradesh, India, 9 July 1919, Victor C. Sherring was raised in the Methodist schools in Mathura, Uttar Pradesh. He graduated from Southwestern College, Winfield, Kansas (AB, 1941) and Garrett Biblical Institute, Illinois (MA, 1945). He has been teaching at the Howard Plested Girls' Intermediate College, Meerut, Uttar Pradesh, where he serves as the superintendent. He is known for arranging and popularizing Indian songs. In 1955 and 1956, he led concert tours of the India Centenary Choir throughout India and in seventy cities in the United States (cf. Young 1993, 830).

Arranger: JEYE HO (*STB* #39).

Shi, Qigui

Qigui Shi was born in 1929 in Suzhou. His father Rangzai Shi was a professor and a member of the editorial committee that produced *Putian Songzan* ("Hymns of Universal Praise," 1936). Qigui entered Jinling Seminary in 1949; upon his graduation in 1953, he served parishes in Shanghai. He was ordained in 1955, became the chief pastor at the Muen Church in Shanghai, and was involved in editing their new hymnal in 1980. In 1992, he was elected an executive member of the China Christian Council. He contributed six hymn tunes (nos. 9, 79, 127, 193, 358) and two texts (nos. 103, 127) in *Zanmeishi (xinbian)* ("Hymns of Praise," new edition, 1985). He also composed a few anthems for choirs (Wang 1993, 16–17).

Composer: SHENG-YE JING (*STB* #140).

Shoemaker, Elise

Born in the United States, Elise Shoemaker was on the staff of the Worship Desk of the General Board of Global Ministry, United Methodist Church, during the early 1980s. She is gifted in music and poetry, and she contributed some paraphrases for the Asian American hymnbook project then associated with her position. She organized many workshops on music and liturgy among different ethnic groups of the United Methodist Church.

Paraphraser: "To the one Creator of all" (*STB* #75); "Jesus Christ, workers' Lord" (*STB* #234).

Silangit, Jeramin (Jerry)

 Born in Kabanjahe, North Sumatra, Indonesia, 12 July 1948, Jeramin Silangit graduated in 1968 from the teachers training program in the German language at Nommensen University, Pematangsiantar, North Sumatra. He studied music at the Hochschule für Kirchenmusik der Evanglishen Kirche von Westfalen, Herford, Germany (1968–72), and received further music training at the Rijksuniversiteit in Utrecht, the Netherlands, (1977–79). He is known for his compositions and skills in choral conducting. Since 1975, Silangit has conducted Glorius Choir (GKI), Serfim Choir (GBKP), Youth Music Ensemble, and Kusuma Santi Choir, all in Jakarta. More recently, he was the director of Gita Paramita Choir, Bahana Rohani Choir (GKJ Nehemia), Male Chorus Gracia (GKI Pondok Indah), Perpulungan Choir (GBKP Bekasi), and the Student Choir of the Christian University of Indonesia (UKI). He has composed, arranged, and published nearly eighty hymns, choral anthems, and folksong arrangements as well as many choral works by European composers, many of them for male choruses. In 1997, Silangit was invited to attend the Ecumenical Seminar on Music and Liturgy in Tainan, Taiwan; after this experience, his interests and views on church music expanded to embrace global perspectives. He currently teaches in a music school in Jakarta. Silangit is married; his wife is a teacher of English, and they have a daughter studying in the university.

Author/composer: "Thank you for the day you give us," TERIMA KASIH (*STB* #236).

Simamora, Waldemar

Born in the 1940s in Pematangsiantar, North Sumatra, Indonesia, Waldemar Simamora is a pastor of the Batak Protestant Christian Church (HKBP) and is gifted in music and poetry. In 1984, he studied one year at the Asian Institute for Liturgy and Music in Manila and began to compose hymns in both Javanese and northern Sumatra styles. Pastor Simamora has been teaching at the Theological Seminary of the HKBP (STT HKBP) in Pematangsiantar.

Author/composer: "In fields of Ephrathah," EFRATA (STB #137); "O God our Father," ALLAH BAPA (STB #287).

Solis, Melchizedek Maraon

Born in the Visayas region of the Philippines, 13 July 1929, Melchizedek "Dick" Maraon Solis is from an artistic family. He received his AB degree in English. He belongs to the Presbyterian Church and dedicated himself to the ministry after graduating from a seminary. He also received a Doctor of Ministry degree in the

United States. He and his wife, Mutya Lopez, immigrated to the United States and have been serving the Filipino community in Salinas, California. Solis is a talented writer, speaker, and community organizer. Among his publications are *Link: A Novel About Real Power* (Salinas, CA: SRMNK Publishers, 1997) and *Pilipinas A to Z: A Barangay Activity Book* (Quezon City: Giraffe Books, 1997). He has written a number of hymns, such as "Come, Holy Spirit," and has published a compact disc, *Global Songs of Peace: Kapayapaan*. He is retired but still actively writes and serves various communities.

Author: "In great thanksgiving" (*STB* #31).

Solis, Mutya Lopez

Born to a musical family in the Visayas region of the Philippines, 11 May 1930, Mutya Lopez Solis is the wife of Melchizedek (see the entry above). She received her initial music training at Silliman University, earning an AB in music, with a major in piano. She subsequently earned her master's degree in music education from Philippine Women's University, Manila. In parish ministry, she is a strong partner with her husband, and she has set his texts to music in Filipino styles. She is a piano teacher, and she edited the publication *Itugyan: Original Compositions, Transcriptions for Violin, Choral Arrangements by Prof. Zoe Radriguez Lopez* (Salinas, CA: SRMNK Publishers, 1998).

Composer: MALATE (*STB* #31).

Sotto, Angel

Born in 1885 in Cebu City, the Philippines, Angel Sotto was a reporter at his uncle's newspaper. In the predominantly Roman Catholic Philippines, Sotto was likely one of the earliest Protestant converts in his region in the early 1900s. He dedicated his life to the ministry and studied at Manila Theological School. He became a popular and controversial speaker, writer, and publisher, and he established seven churches during his life. Sotto was also the first Filipino to have composed original hymns (both texts and tunes) and translated Spanish songs into Cebuano-Visayan dialects. He published the first Visayan hymnal, *Mga Alawiton* (cf. *Companion to the New Century Hymnal* [Pilgrim Press, 1998]). He died in 1976 at the age of ninety-one.

Co-author/composer: "Let us even now go to Bethlehem," MANGLAKAT (*STB* #146).

Soundararajan, Eliazer

Born in Cuddalore, Tamilnadu, South India, 26 September 1932, Eliazer Soundararajan first served as a drawing teacher at St. Andrew's High School, Arakonam. After graduating from Tamilnadu Theological College, Thirumaraiyur, Madurai, in 1966, he became a deacon in the Church of South India. In 1968, he was ordained as a presbyter by Bishop Newbegin. The following year he became the presbyter-in-charge, and in 1975, he was appointed as the religious drama advisor to the Madras Diocese. Soundararajan received a BD from Serampore University in 1979. He was a prolific poet and playwright, with as many as 500 lyrics and tunes and seventy-five plays to his credit. Most of the plays, especially the passion plays, were performed under his direction. Because of his contributions, Soundararajan received awards from the World Christian Tamil Academy; he was a delegate to the United Kingdom for an assembly in 1984. In 1997, he passed away in Chennai due to heart failure. He is survived by his wife and five children; his eldest son is a composer (see the entry for Barathi, John).

Author: "Why, O LORD, why?" (*STB* #251).

Srisuwan, Inchai

Born in northern Thailand, 10 January 1950, Inchai Srisuwan graduated from Thailand Theological Seminary in Chiang Mai in 1976 with a diploma in church music, majoring in trombone and conducting. He is a talented composer and instrument maker. He and his wife Ruth (see the entry below) served at the Center for Church Planting and Church Growth in Northeast of Thailand, a project of the Evangelical Covenant Church of America in the Isaan community. As the director of music, Srisuwan composed hymns with the accompaniment of the local instruments, such as *khaen* (mouth organ), *ranat ek* (xylophone), *klui* (flute), *phin* (plucked lute), *ching-chap* (concussion bells), *thong* (drum), etc. He also organized and taught small *khaen* ensembles in the family churches, and the worship services featured original compositions and local instruments. He later studied at the Asian Institute for Liturgy and Music and obtained his Bachelor of Church Music degree, majoring in composition and ethnomusicology. He has done extensive research on the music of northeast Thailand and has improved the techniques of instrument making. Srisuwan was invited to assist I-to Loh in the music leadership of the ecumenical conferences of the WCC and CCA as well as the Asian Alliance of YMCAs. Recently, he has worked in the slums of Bangkok, evangelizing and educating children in traditional Thai music ensembles. Frequently, he and his wife are invited to perform in Finland, Denmark, and the United States. Both are considered the pioneers of indigenous Thai church music. Among his publications are textbooks about traditional Thai instruments, which he also makes: *khaen*, *phin*, *saw* (lute), *pong lang* (suspended xylophone), *klui*, *wode* (panpipes).

Composer: NA-MAT-SA KAAN (*STB* #2); CHIIWIT (*STB* #72); PHRA-KHAM-PHII (*STB* #217).

Srisuwan, Ruth

Born in Thailand, 18 October 1951, Ruth Srisuwan graduated from Payap University (BA with honors, voice, 1978) and Thailand Theological Seminary (diploma in church music and conducting, 1978). Srisuwan is a talented poet, singer, and dancer. She is able to sing both in the Thai traditional style as well as the Western bel canto style. She and her husband Inchai (see above entry) served at the Center for Church Planting and Church Growth in Northeast Thailand, established by the Evangelical Covenant Church of America. She was the head of the drama, song, and dance department, and she was the choreographer and poet of the Center. At the Center, after the daily Bible study, Srisuwan summarized the content of the passage and wrote a hymn, which her husband set to music in a traditional Isaan style and taught to the staff; the hymns were then taught to the family churches. The Isaan church prospered through the musical and artistic contributions of the Srisuwans. They now work in the Bangkok slums and are frequently invited to assist in ecumenical services. Srisuwan has researched the folk music of northeast Thailand and has written textbooks about Christian dance and vocal training. In 1986, she published her first songbook. Along with her husband, she is a pioneer of indigenous Thai church music.

Author: "Come and worship God with songs of praise" (*STB* #2); "Released by love to share new life" (*STB* #72); "From the Bible we learn God's will" (*STB* #217).

Stowe, Everett M.

Everett M. Stowe was a Methodist missionary in Japan.
Translator: "Here O LORD, your servants meet" (*STB* #242).

Sukamto

Sukamto is Javanese and a Roman Catholic.
Author: MISA SUNDA (*STB* #128).

Sundaram, V. P. K.

Born in 1915 in Madurai, South India, V. P. K. Sundaram first learned music from his father, V. Paramasivam, who was Hindu but had a vision of Jesus saying, "Follow me," and converted to Christianity. He founded the first girls' school in South India. Sundaram studied at a village school in Bodinayakanur and became a teacher in a model school in Pasumalai; in 1935, he became the headmaster of the school. He also studied music with Shankara Sivanar, a court poet under the king of Ramanathapuram. Sundaram earned a doctorate from the University of Madras with a dissertation entitled "Musicology in Ancient Tamil Literature." His highly respected scholarship encompassed Tamil literature, music, and drama. At the age of thirty-five, he composed a song to teach the story of the Prodigal Son to children, and he taught at American College in Madurai from 1959 to 1969. He was a close friend of the Reverend Larbeer, an American missionary with whom Sundaram wrote a three-hour passion play (drama with music), which has been performed regularly during Lenten season for more than thirty years. Sundaram taught courses in Tamil language and literature at Tamilnadu Theological Seminary (1969–79) and was a research scholar and professor emeritus at the South Indian Institute of Tamilology, Bharathidasan University (1979–83). He published the important *Tamil Lexicon on Musicology*, which asserted that Tamil music was an independent system and did not derive from that of the Sanskrit. Sundaram was not only a sportsman, musician, and artist but also a poet; his monumental book *Arulkural* contains 1200 couplets of Biblical stories and teachings. He wrote many books and musical compositions, he helped with the inter-confessional translation of the Bible, and he served as a Tamil advisor to the Bible Society. In 1989, I-to Loh was privileged to visit Sundaram and learn some Indian lyrics from him. Sundaram's most famous lyrics are his settings of Psalm 42, "My soul longs for you, O LORD," and Psalm 128, "Happy is everyone who fears the LORD," which is the most popular wedding song in India; it has been sung even by non-Christians in their matrimony services. Sundaram died in 2003.

Author/composer: "All sisters, all brothers, all of the earth," BUUMIYIN MAANDHERIIR (*STB* #84).

Sutarno

Born in Java, Indonesia, Sutarno is a theologian and a former president of Satia Wacana Christian University. (In Java, a person frequently uses only one name.) He served as a member of the Central Committee of the World Council of Churches, and he contributed two short liturgical pieces for the General Assembly of the WCC in Vancouver (1983); these are included in *Sound the Bamboo*. He was a pastor of the Javanese church and served as the director of a Christian newspaper and as the chairman of the Communion of Churches in Indonesia.

Arranger: "Amin, Haleluya" (*STB* #105); "O LORD, our God" ("Ya Tuhanku, kasihanilah daku," *STB* #123).

Sutisno, Nj

"Nj" is an Indonesian honorific title for a woman, similar to "Mrs." in English. Sutisno is a famous folk composer, and her composition "Becak" is one of the most popular songs in Indonesia.

Composer: BECAK (*STB* #258).

Tagore, Rabindranath

Born in 1861 in Bengal, northeast India, Rabindranath Tagore won the Nobel Prize in 1913 for his book of poems, *Gitanjali* ("Song offerings"). Tagore composed about 2,500 songs; those written during his third compositional phase (1921–41) are characteristic of the "Tagore musical style," in which he combined folk idioms with classical melodies and genres, representing the culmination of experiences and experiments over the course of forty years (Garland 5:850). Tagore classified his songs into four major categories worship, homeland, nature, and love and two minor categories variety and ceremonial. In the worship category, he wrote 650 songs, also known as "Brahma songs." Mostly in the *dhrupad* style (consisting of four movements), their combined lyricism and music make the essence of allegiance to God universally inspiring; his experimentation of these devotional songs gave new direction to Bengali urban music (Garland 5:850). His song "My golden Bengal, I love you," became the national anthem of Bangladesh. Tagore said there were two elements in *dhrupad*: vastness/depth and control/symmetry. He composed all the music for his songs, treating poetry and music equally. He died in 1941.

Author: "I have come to you to take your touch" (*STB* #157).

Tahya, Iba

Iba Tahya is an Indonesian poet.

Co-author: "Dear God, how you love your creatures" (*STB* #180).

Tai, Nai-chen (Dai Naichen)

 Born in Teng-san, Tainan, southern Taiwan, 2 February 1963, Tai Nai-chen was raised by devoted parents. He studied church music, majoring in trumpet at Taiwan Theological College and Seminary, Taipei. He sensed the call to ministry and entered Tainan Theological College and Seminary and graduated in 1992; his MDiv thesis dealt with the phenomena of praise choruses in the church. Tai and his classmate, Cai Zheng-dao, co-composed a few hymns that were included in the PCT Hymnal, *Seng-si*. Tai worked in a parish in Taipei City, moved to Tainan, and relocated again to the north.

Composer: TENG-SAN (*STB* #112).

Takano, Kikuo

Born in 1927 in Sado, Niigata Prefecture, Japan, Kikuo Takano began writing poems while working as a high school teacher. Some of his poems were set to music by Saburō Takada, such as "Mizu no inochi" ("The Life of Water") and "Watashi no negai" ("My Wish"). These choral pieces have become well known in Japanese musical circles. Takano died in 2006.[143]

Author: "To everyone a call comes" (*STB* #228).

Takata, Saburō

Born in 1913 in Japan, Saburō Takata is one of the most important contemporary composers in Japan. He was a composition graduate from the Tokyo University of the Arts, and he was a professor at the Kunitachi Music University from 1953 to 1979, earning emeritus status when he retired. He is a devoted Christian; he was first a Protestant, but he joined his wife in the Catholic Church. Consequently, he has composed for both Catholic and Protestant churches. After the Second Vatican Council (1962–65), the Catholic Church encouraged the use of ethnic art, music, and liturgies. Takata was the first to accept the challenge to compose Psalm and liturgical settings for the Mass. He brought the Protestant vigor of singing hymns to the Catholic Church. His numerous choral works and short compositions include "The life of water," "Aoki ōkami," "Musei dōkoku," "Hitori no taiwa," "Kuina wa tobazu ni," "Koshikata," and many other choral pieces, which have become part of the standard concert repertoire. He has been the president of Japan Association of Modern Music (*SRK21*, 98).

Composer: STILL SMALL VOICE (*STB* #228).

---

143 Information in this entry is derived from the author's correspondence with Sōji Kitamura, September 19, 2006.

Takenaka, Masao

Masao Takenaka (right) and Ron O'Grady (left)

Born in northern China, 6 September 1925, Masao Takenaka was a graduate of Kyoto University (MA, 1948), Dōshisha University (BD, 1950), and Yale University (BD, STM, PhD, 1954). He belonged to the United Church of Christ in Japan. Takenaka was a professor of theology and Christian ethics at Dōshisha University until his retirement, and he was a visiting professor at Yale University. He was not only a theologian, educator, and artist but also a pioneer of urban and rural mission in WCC as well as CCA. With Takenaka's encouragement and assistance, I-to Loh traveled to many Asian countries to collect songs, which resulted in the publication of *New Songs of Asian Cities* in 1972. Takenaka was the founder and the first chairperson of the Asian Christian Art Association. He was also on the board of trustees of the Asian Institute for Liturgy and Music in Manila, and he was a co-founder and chairperson of the Program on Theology and Culture in Asia (PTCA), which trains young scholars in doing theology with Asian cultures and resources. His publications include *Reconciliation and Renewal in Japan* (1967), *Christian Art in Asia* (1975), *God is Rice* (1986), *That All May Be One* (1987), *The Bible Through Asian Eyes* (1991, co-written with Ron O'Grady), *The Place Where God Dwells* (1995), and *Mi to Shinjitzu: Kindai Nihon no Bijitsu to Kirisutokyō* ("Beauty and Truth: Recent Japanese Arts and Christianity," 2006). Takenaka died in Kyoto, Japan, 17 August 2006. His death was a profound loss for I-to Loh, who had intended to ask Takenaka to write the foreword for this volume.

Co-author: "We who bear the human name" (*STB #258*).

Tamaela, Christian Izaac

Born in Soahuku, Seram Island, Indonesia, 17 September 1957, Christian Izaac Tamaela is a graduate of the Theological Seminary of Ambon, Moluccas (MDiv); the Asian Institute for Liturgy and Music, Manila (BCM); and Tainan Theological College and Seminary, Taiwan (MTh, liturgy and music, under the Southeast Asia Graduate School of Theology, 2000). He is now studying in a PhD program at Vrije Universiteit, Amsterdam. Tamaela has taught at the Faculty of Theology, Christian University in Moluccas (UKM). A talented musician, artist, theologian, and liturgist, he assisted I-to Loh at a few WCC and CCA assemblies as a co-animateur, and he has attended other ecumenical seminars on liturgy and music.

Tamaela at CCA Assembly, 2000

Tamaela is a good composer; many of his songs have been used in ecumenical circles. He has written a number of choral anthems, including "Toki gong," and a collection of Moluccan songs, *Kapata-kapata Rohani* ("Spiritual Songs from Central Moluccas," published in 1991, AILM Collection of Asian Church Music, no. 19).

Author/adapter: "O Come quickly, Holy Spirit," DATANGLAH (*STB* #7).
Adapter: "Praise the LORD" (*STB* #104).
Composer: "The Lord's Prayer" (*STB* #116); BATU BADAONG (*STB* #119).

Tan, Timothy

"Timothy Tan" is a pen name of I-to Loh (see the entry for Loh, I-to).

Author: "LORD, we give you heartfelt praise" (*STB* #112).

Tanaka, Akira

Born in 1947 in Tokyo, Japan, Akira Tanaka graduated from Seijō University and studied organ at Senzoku Gakuen. During the early 1970s, he was a teacher at Tenenchōfu.[144]

Composer: MIKOKORO (*STB* #44).

Tanatty, Hanoch

Born in the late 1960s in Irian Jaya (now West Papua), Indonesia, Hanoch Tanatty is an excellent tenor with a crystalline, light tone. He received a BCM from the Asian Institute for Liturgy and Music and now teaches church music at the seminary in his hometown.

Translator/transcriber: "Bird call announces morning," KUDO-KUDO (*STB* #305).

---

144 Information in this entry is derived from the author's correspondence with Sōji Kitamura, September 19, 2006.

Tang, Baimei

Born in 1962 in a Paiwan village in Taiwan, Baimei Tang is a graduate of Yushan Theological College and Seminary. She adapted the hymn "Hear now, God's own people" while she was still a student. It was very popular among the seminary students and was first included in the collection *Let the Hills Sing* (1986). Tang's husband is also Paiwan; they currently serve a parish in the Paiwan Presbytery of the Presbyterian Church of Taiwan.

Adapter: "Hear now, God's own people" (*STB* #215).

Tarigan, S.

S. Tarigan is Indonesian.

Author/co-composer: "Have no fear, all you earth-lands," JANGAN TAKUT (*STB* #306).
Author/composer: "Oh, the cabbage price is falling," SAYUR KUBIS (*STB* #313

Teng, Philip

Philip Teng is Chinese.

Co-translator: "God is here as we your people meet" (*STB* #49).

Thanga

Born in 1883 in Mizoram, northeast India, Thanga was a member of the first generation of Christians in Mizoram to receive higher education. (In the Mizo culture, a person uses only one name.) Thanga was a well-known lyricist who contributed sixteen translations of Western hymns and three original lyrics to *Kristian Hla Bu* ("Mizo Christian Hymnal," eighteenth revised edition, 2005; nos. 328, 434, 573). His daughter was the first Mizo in this region to earn BA and BD degrees. Thanga contributed to the Church as well as to society his lyric for the emancipation of slavery in Mizoram; it is included in *Sound the Bamboo*. He died in 1957.

Author: "O God, highest God" (*STB* #270).

Thangaraj, M. Thomas

M. Thomas Thangaraj was born in Srivilliputhur, Tamilnadu, South India, 7 September 1942. His father, the Reverend M. A. Melechizedec, was the pastor of the town's St. Thomas's Church. Thangaraj is the D. W. and Ruth Brooks Associate Professor of World Christianity at the Candler School of Theology, Emory University, Atlanta, Georgia, USA. Before joining Emory University, Thangaraj was a minister in the Church of South India in the Tirunelveli area and taught at the Tamilnadu Theological Seminary, Madurai, from 1971 to 1988. He was educated at the graduate and postgraduate level at St. John's College, Palayamkottai; Madras Christian College, Madras; Serampore College, Serampore, West Bengal; and United Theological College, Bangalore. He earned his Doctor of Theology degree from Harvard University. His doctoral research concerned the relationship between Saiva Siddhanta (a Hindu philosophical tradition from southern India) and Christianity, especially around the concept of the guru.

Thangaraj has given lectures in the United Kingdom, the Philippines, Japan, Sweden, Denmark, Norway, Germany, Myanmar (Burma), Taiwan, India, and the United States. He has been actively involved in programs of inter-religious dialogue at national and international levels. While teaching at the Tamilnadu Theological Seminary, Thangaraj was also a part-time professor in the Department of Religion, Philosophy, and Sociology of the American College and a lecturer in the Department of Gandhian Studies of Madurai-Kamaraj University, especially in the programs on inter-religious dialogue. He worked with the Sub-unit on Dialogue with People of Other Faiths of the WCC in Geneva, Switzerland. He has published widely, both in English and in Tamil, and his most recent publications include *The Crucified Guru: An Experiment in Cross-Cultural Christology* (Abingdon Press, 1994), *Relating to People of Other Religions: What Every Christian Needs to Know* (Abingdon Press, 1997), and *The Common Task: A Theology of Christian Mission* (Abingdon Press, 1999).

Apart from his academic interests, Thangaraj is keenly interested in South Indian music, both classical and popular, and also in the art of hymnody in Tamil. Twenty of his hymns are now incorporated in the official hymnbook of the churches in Tamilnadu. A few of his hymns in English are published in the United States, Sweden, Germany, and Denmark. He served on the Assembly Worship Planning Committee for the eighth Assembly of the WCC held in Harare, Zimbabwe, in 1998. He is a 2001–2002 recipient of the Lilly Theological Research Grant of the Association of Theological Schools. He was a William Paton Fellow at Selly Oak Colleges, Selly Oak, United Kingdom (autumn 2001), and a visiting professor at Tainan Theological College and Seminary, Tainan, Taiwan (spring 2002). His current research concerns the theological themes that emerge in Indian Christians' encounters with religious pluralism. He was a member of "Thinking Together," a group of theologians of various faiths that gather annually for three years, sponsored by the Office of Inter-Religious Relations, WCC. Currently, Thangaraj teaches at Emory during spring semesters and works at the Bishop Stephen Neill Research and Study Centre, Tirunelveli, India, during fall semesters.[145]

Author/composer: "Blest are the poor folks," THIS EARTH (*STB* #276).
Composer: AAYIREM (*STB* #37).

Thompson, J. O.

Author: "The call for reapers" (*STB* #245).

Tin, John Jyigiokk (Ji-giok Tiⁿ)

John Jyigiokk Tin was born in Taiwan, 27 June 1922. ("Ji-giok Tiⁿ" is the Taiwanese spelling of his name.) Tin converted to Christianity while he was a college student. In 1946, he graduated from Dōshisha College in Kyoto, Japan, in the fields of theology and modern Western thought. Upon his return to Taiwan in 1949, he was appointed to serve in a small Presbyterian church in Po'-te, a fishing village. He went to Chicago and earned an MTh from McCormick Theological Seminary (1958) and did further studies at the Graduate School of Ecumenical Studies (1959) and the Evangelisch-theologische Fakultaet, Hamburg (1975). In the early 1960s, he taught at Tainan Theological College in the fields of church history, history of doctrines, ecumenism, and church and society.

With an American missionary, the Reverend George Todd, Tin educated Taiwanese church congregations to be involved in social transformation. He founded the Christian Academy to engage more lay people and church leaders in dialogue. He participated in the small group that drafted the first appeal of the Presbyterian Church in Taiwan (PCT) to the repressive Kuomintang government on December 29, 1971, urging the latter to reform and to hold national elections. It was also an appeal to the world, especially to the US president Richard Nixon (who was going to visit China for the first time since that country was opened to relations with the West) not to betray Taiwan. Tin also played a significant role in drafting the Confession of Faith of the PCT in 1985. In 1989, he retired

---

145   Information in this entry is derived from the author's correspondence with Thangaraj, November 2004.

from teaching and became an emeritus professor, but he founded the Institute of Social Transformation and continued to facilitate dialogues between the Church and society. In recognition for his contributions, Tainan Theological College and Seminary awarded Tin an honorary Doctor of Divinity degree in 1997. Since 1994, he has taught Romanized Taiwanese to the general public, with the idea of preserving and developing Taiwanese culture and identity.

Tin is an amateur poet. He has written many hymns and poems; one of them, "Tai-oan chhui-chhi," won an international prize. His love for Taiwan and Taiwanese culture is reflected in his writings. He retired for the second time in 2002 and celebrated his golden anniversary of marriage with his wife Chhun-leng, who has been the strongest supporter and unacknowledged assistant behind Tin's career and success. His publications include *[The Complete Book of] Taiwanese Metrical Psalms for Responsive Reading* and *Tai-oan Chhui-chhi* (a collection of hymns/songs related to Christian faith and the democratic movement in Taiwan, edited by Jin-sek Go, 2002).

Author: "Holy Spirit, Pentecost gift" (*STB* #152); "Light of the world, salt of the earth" (*STB* #254).

Tinio, Rolando Santos

Born in Gagalangin, Tondo, Manila, the Philippines, 5 March 1937, Rolando Santos Tinio was a graduate of the University of Santo Tomas (Bachelor of Philosophy, 1955) and the State University of Iowa (Master of Fine Arts, 1958); in 1968, he took a non-degree course in theater arts through a British Council scholarship at Bristol University. From 1958 to 1975, he taught English, Filipino, and theater arts at Ateneo de Manila University and subsequently headed the English department and later the department of Filipino. He wrote poetry first in English and then in Tagalog; four of his published collections are: *Sitsit sa Kuliglig* ("Whistling at Cicadas," 1972); *Dunung-Dunungan* ("Pedantry," 1975); *Kristal na Uniberso* ("Crystal Universe," 1989); and *Trick of Mirrors* (1993). Tinio's contribution to the theater arts may be seen from his masterful translations of Western works into Tagalog: *The Glass Menagerie* (1966), *Death of a Salesman* (1966), *Waiting for Godot* (1967), and *Miss Julie* (1967). He also founded and directed the Teatro Pilipino (1975–92) and translated the major plays of William Shakespeare, Anton Chekhov, Albert Camus, Oscar Wilde, and Eugene Ionesco. He was an innovative and imaginative director of traditional and modern plays and operas. He also wrote plays and appeared as an actor in many productions. His essays on language are collected in *A Matter of Language, Where English Fails* (1990). With all his multiple talents and contributions, Tinio won several Don Carlos Palanca Memorial Awards for literature and was named one of the "Ten Outstanding Young Men" in 1967; he also received the Gantimpalang Quezon sa Panitikan award in 1977 and the Gawad CCP Para Sa Sining award for theater in 1993 (cf. *CCPE* 7: 412f). Tinio was one of the major paraphrasers for the hymns in *Sound the Bamboo*. He died 7 July 1997.

Author: "With the grace of this day's food" (*STB* #164); "Christ our peace" (*STB* #261); "Sleep through the night, beloved child" (*STB* #277).

Paraphraser: "Worship and praise we give" (*STB* #25); "Praise be to God" (*STB* #32); "My boat of life sails on an angry sea" (*STB* #50); "Mighty God, power over heaven and earth" (*STB* #57); "O Lord who made all the heavens" (*STB* #76); "Lord, as the earth welcomes showers of rain" (*STB* #90); "When my troubles arose" (*STB* #97); "Sing the Lord a new song" (*STB* #100); "My Heavenly Father loves me" (*STB* #182); "Three women" (*STB* #186); "You have come, Lord Christ" (*STB* #193); "Lilies of the field" (*STB* #201); "I sing praise to your holy name" (*STB* #214); "Thank you for the day you give us" (*STB* #236); "Why, O Lord, why?" (*STB* #251); "When you travel far" (*STB* #256); "Bear the weight of the cross" (*STB* #280).

Co-paraphraser: "Day of joy, let us be glad" (*STB* #11); "On the night of Christmas" (*STB* #133); "Everywhere sorrow on Calvary's hill" (*STB* #148); "Behold the man we nailed on the cross" (*STB* #149); "Death steals like a thief" (*STB* #170); "Grant, Lord, that we may not faint" (*STB* #185); "Gracious Father, love divine" (*STB* #196); "Dear friends, walk with me, let us go" (*STB* #198); "Come children, men and women all" (*STB* #209); "He rules over all" (*STB* #212); "Holy are the Bible's many books" (*STB* #219); "There was once a time" (*STB* #232).

Alterer: "Christ is all to me" (*STB* #55).

Translator: "A boy's prayer" (*STB* #160).

Tong, Chunfa

Born in Pintong, Taiwan, 16 August 1946, Chunfa Tong, whose original Paiwan tribal name is Masegseg, is a graduate of Tainan Theological College and Seminary (MDiv, 1976), Princeton Theological Seminary (MTh, New Testament, 1983), Fuller Theological Seminary (MTh, missiology, 1984), and Tokyo International Christian University (PhD, comparative culture, 1995). A talented musician, New Testament scholar, and expert in tribal culture, Masegseg was a professor of New Testament at Yushan Theological College and Seminary, which is the Presbyterian seminary for training tribal pastors in Taiwan; there, he also served as the dean of students and the head of the music department, and he conducted the seminary choir and the Tribal Chorus. After earning his doctorate, he was the president of Yushan Seminary for four years and was subsequently called to serve as the dean of the College of Aboriginal Studies at Donghua University, Hualien. From when he was a student, Masegseg showed his talent and interest in indigenous music, and he adapted a number of indigenous songs for Christian purposes. As an ordained pastor serving in a secular university, he continues to be a leader in shaping tribal esteem. In this way, he has contributed significantly to the Church and to society. In 2008, he was appointed the director of the National Museum of Prehistory in Taitung.

Co-author: "Praise Lord Jesus" (*STB* #20).

Torii, Chugorō

Born in 1898 in Hokkaidō, Japan, Chugorō Torii was one of the early Japanese church musicians who contributed tremendously to the hymnody of Japan. After graduating from a music school in Tokyo (majoring in voice), he dedicated his life to music education. He taught at Aoyama Teacher's College in Tokyo, at Tamagawa University, and at the Church-related Seitoku Gakuin Women's Junior College. He also served as a choir director for Reinanzaka Church and Nagahara Church. He was on the hymnal committees for the 1931 and 1954 editions of *Sambika*. He was also on the editorial committee of the Sunday School Hymnal as well as the children's *Sambika* (*SRK21*, 166). He died in 1986.

Composer: CHRISTMAS DAY (*STB* #194).

Tsugawa, Shūichi

Born in 1896 in Aichi Prefecture, Japan, Shūichi Tsugawa was a pastor's son and a graduate of the theology division of Kwansei College. After serving the church for a few years, he decided to give up his pastoral work and began teaching music and choral conducting, which he had enjoyed since he was a student. He subsequently taught at Jiyū College and Keizen Women's College. Tsugawa arranged and edited many choral music collections and wrote a book on hymn authors and composers. He was a president of the Japan Association for Choral Music. At Kwansei College, he was a classmate of Kō Yuki, with whom he co-wrote a few hymn tunes (*SRK21*, 310). He died in 1971.

Composer: UCHI NARU MIYA (*STB* #69).

Ukur, Fridolin

Born in Indonesia, Fridolin Ukur was a talented artist, poet, and pastor. He belonged to the Evangelical Church in Kalimantan. He earned a doctoral degree in theology and was known as a powerful leader. Ukur served as the director of the Institute of Research of the Communion of Churches in Indonesia, for which he was also the general secretary in the late 1980s. He died in Indonesia.

Author: "My God, why have you forsaken me?" (*STB* #274A); "Jesus, your last cry on the cross" (*STB* #274B).

Vang, Cher Lue

Cher Lue Vang belongs to the Mong tribe in Thailand.

Translator: "Come children, men and women all" (*STB* #209).

Vas, Charles

Charles Vas is an Indian Roman Catholic priest. He has composed many lyrics and *bhajans*.

Author/composer: "Give us light," JYOTHI DHO (*STB* #58).

Vera, Rody (Rodolfo)

Born in Makati, in metropolitan Manila, the Philippines, 5 December 1960, Rody Vera is a playwright, singer, performer, stage actor, television and film scriptwriter, theater director, and acting teacher. Vera earned an AB in Philippines Studies from the University of the Philippines (UP). He has written nineteen original works for local stages and eleven works for performance abroad, translated Shakespeare's *The Tempest* and *Anthony and Cleopatra* and Goethe's *Faust*, and adapted a dozen works. He has been the director or coordinator for more than fifty workshops of theater, music performance, and playwriting in the Philippines and other Asian countries, Australia, North America, and Europe. He has received many grants and awards, including a Rockefeller Foundation grant and the Carlos Palanca Award for Literature, which he won six times. Vera has written a few lyrics for plays, such as *Masdan O Yahweh* (1990) for the performing group Patatag, sponsored by the Asian Institute for Liturgy and Music. Vera is currently a member of the Artistic Committee of the Philippine Educational Theater Association, and he constantly travels locally or abroad for workshops and performances.

Author: "A boy's prayer" (*STB* #160).

Victor, Sathy

Sathay Victor was born in Chennai (formerly Madras), India.

Composer: PANNIN DHEEN (*STB* #25).

Walcott, Ronald

Born in the late 1930s in the United States, Ronald Walcott is an American composer and ethnomusicologist. He received a PhD in music from the University of California at Los Angeles (UCLA). He has done extensive fieldwork in Sri Lanka and the Philippines. While in the Philippines, he studied the music of the Kalinga people; he has published a collection of Kalinga "salidummay" songs for the Asian Institute for Liturgy and Music. Walcott was I-to Loh's schoolmate at UCLA and kindly assisted in paraphrasing some of the songs for *Sound the Bamboo* in 1989.

Paraphraser: "All sisters, all brothers, all of the earth" (*STB* #84).
Co-paraphraser: "Strive and toil for God" (*STB* #246).

Wallace, William (Bill) Livingston

Born in Christchurch, New Zealand, 9 April 1933, to Anglo-Celtic parents, Bill Wallace has a BA and a diploma in education. He is currently a minister of the Methodist Church of New Zealand, is married, and has four children and two grandchildren. Aside from being a parish minister for thirty-four years, Wallace has also been a hymn selector for the "Praise Be" television program in New Zealand, the founding chairman of the New Zealand Chapter of the World Conference on Religion and Peace, a part-time coordinator of the Hornby Community Care Center, and the chair of Contemporary Hymns, New Zealand. His poems seem to pierce one's heart; many of his hymns are included in major denominational or ecumenical hymnals in North America, Europe, and Asia. Wallace has published five collections of hymns: *Something to Sing About* (hymns and reflections in search of a contemporary spirituality); three volumes of *Singing the Circle* (*Sacred Earth, Holy Darkness, Darkness and Light*, and *Broken Bread, Broken Chains*); and *The Mystery Telling: Hymns and Songs for the New Millennium* (vol.1). He has also composed about one hundred hymn tunes; many of them have been harmonized by other composers and published. He is currently working on a third volume of hymns and books of songs for children and for teens.

Author: "Within your heart and mind, O Christ" (*STB* #188); "Why have you forsaken me?" (*STB* #189); "In nature as in Jesus" (*STB* #233); "Deep in the human heart" (*STB* #248).

Wang, Dawei

Wang Dawei's birth in 1951 in Shandong, China, seemed a miracle. According to Wang, his mother had a serious illness that was assumed to cause infertility. After she married and became a Christian, she and her husband prayed earnestly for children, despite the doctor's opinion that it was impossible. At the age of forty-three, she gave birth to Dawei (David); the parents dedicated their only child to God. But Wang was a junior high school student during the Cultural Revolution (1966–76): he experienced hardship and was unable to keep his Christian faith. He worked in a chemical factory, and he was later promoted to head its warehouse department. Before Wang's father passed away in 1981, he encouraged Wang to return to his Christian faith. This changed his life, and he began to serve in his church as an organist (cf. Wang 1933, 251f). (For more information, see the commentary of *STB* #156 in the Chinese hymns section.)

Author/composer: "God be praised at early morn," QING-CHEN (*STB* #156).

Wang, Mingdao

Born in 1900 in China, the Reverend Mingdao Wang was one of the most influential preachers in China. He was one of the leaders who established an indigenous church with the Three-Self principles: self-propagation, self-government, and self-support (see the introduction to the section on Chinese hymns). His Bible study group in Beijing was the foundation of his Christian Tabernacle in 1937; membership increased to 570 in 1949. Wang rejected any liturgy, rituals, or celebrations not found in the Bible. Believing that the Bible and the Holy Spirit were sufficient for one to become a servant of God, he never received any formal theological training. He was also against any secular and political involvement. He refused to participate in the Three-Self Patriotic Movement (TSPM) and was imprisoned in 1955. Although he signed a confession recanting his stand the following year and was released, he felt guilty for betraying the Lord; he revoked his confession and was imprisoned again until 1979. Wang's basic theological stand was "regeneration in Christ." He believed that a person could change society only if he was changed through rebirth in Christ (*DAC* 2001, 886f). He died 28 July 1991.

Author: "We assemble with joy and praise" (*STB* #167).

Wang, Weifan

Born in 1927 in Taizhou, Jiangsu Province, China, Wang Weifan studied at Zhongyang University as well as Nanjing University. He graduated from Jinling Seminary, Beijing, and served there as a professor for a long time. He has written books on Bible studies and theological reflections, such as *Li-wei Ji* (a commentary on the book of Leviticus). He is equally skilled in Christian liturgy, poetry, Chinese literature, and singing. During the Cultural Revolution (1966–76), he was persecuted and banished to the frontier to perform hard labor. Wang possessed a most admirable faith and noble character; even with his suffering, he never complained. He accepted all tribulations with faith and perseverance. I-to Loh was privileged to visit Wang in 1987 and was deeply touched by his sincerity and spirituality. Some of Wang's meditations appear in his book *Shizijia pang de xishui: Shengri moxiang Jidu* ("The Streams beside the Cross: Meditating on Christ on Sacred Days," Hong Kong: Christian Communications International Ltd., 2005).

Author: "Winter has passed, the rain is o'er" (*STB* #71).

Weerakkody, D. P. M.

Born in Sri Lanka, D. P. M. Weerakkody is a scholar, poet, and musician. Although he is vision impaired, he received a doctorate in classics and has been a lecturer of Western classics at the University of Peradeniya. I-to Loh was privileged to listen to Weerakkody playing the accordion and singing his composition KALVARI YANAVA in 1984.

Composer: KALVARI YANAVA (*STB* #275).

Weragoda, Edmund Sydney

Born in Sri Lanka, Canon Sydney Weragoda (also spelled Waragoda) was an Anglican priest who served in the Diocese of Kurunegala in Sri Lanka. He was chiefly responsible for the Sinhala version of the "Hymn for Sri Lanka" composed in English by the Reverend W. S. Senior and set to a classical Sinhala tune. He was one of the leaders and writers of the Workers' Mass for the Christian Workers Fellowship, which upholds human dignity and laborers' rights. The texts and music of this Mass are strong examples of contextual theology and music; they are good models for other Asian churches. Weragoda and his family immigrated to Australia.

Author: "Son of the Father" (*STB* #191).

512

Wesley, Charles

Born in Lincolnshire, England, 18 December 1707, Charles Wesley was probably the greatest hymn writer in the Western world. He went to Westminster School at the age of nine and became a King's Scholar in 1721, which meant free room and board for the duration of his stay. In 1729, he received his first degree at Christ Church, Oxford, and became a college tutor. He was one of the first "Oxford Methodists." After a short stay in the country of Georgia in 1737, he came under the influence of Count Zinzendorf and the Moravians. His work was identified with that of his brother John Wesley, and Charles was an indefatigable itinerant and field preacher. It is said that he wrote no fewer than 6500 hymns. He wrote hymns for every occasion, including hymns for little children. Some of his best-known hymns are: "Christ, the Lord, is risen today," "Hail the day that sees him rise," "Hark! The herald angels sing," "Christ! Whose glory fills the skies," "Jesus, Lover of my soul!" "Oh! For a thousand tongues to sing," "Our Lord is risen from the dead," "Come, thou long-expected Jesus!" "Light of those whose dreary dwelling," "Ye servants of God! Your Master proclaim," "Love divine, all loves excelling!" "Soldiers of Christ! Arise," "Blow ye the trumpet, blow," "Lo! He comes, with clouds descending," "Come, let us join our friends above," "A charge to keep I have." Some of Wesley's texts have recently been set by Asian composers.[146] He died 29 March 1788 in London.

Author: "Gentle Jesus, meek and mild" (*STB* #231).

Wiant, Bliss

Bliss Wiant was a pioneer of contextualized Chinese church music. Born in Dalton, Ohio, 1 February 1895, he was raised in a minister's family of eleven children. Educated at Wesleyan University (BA, 1920), Boston University (MA, 1936), Peabody College (PhD, 1946), Harvard University, and Union Theological Seminary, Wiant was ordained a deacon in the Methodist Episcopal Church in 1923. The same year, he and his wife Mildred (see the entry below) went to China as missionaries and taught at Yanjing University. During his twenty-eight-year tenure, Wiant returned to the United States a few times for further studies and received his doctorate with the dissertation "Character and Function of Music in Chinese Culture." He became a specialist in Chinese music and published scholarly articles, such as "Possible Polyphonic Treatment of Chinese Melodies." He was a professor of choral music and the piano, and he was the organist for the state funeral of the founding father of the Chinese republic, Dr. Sun Yat-sen. Wiant conducted the Yanjing University Chorus to perform Handel's *Messiah*, Haydn's *Creation*, Brahm's *German Requiem*, and Mendelssohn's *Elijah*. He was the music editor for *Putian Songzan* ("Songs of Universal Praise," 1936), to which he contributed

---

146   Cf. *A Dictionary of Hymnology,* ed. John Julian (New York: Charles Scribner's Sons, 1892).

forty-seven arrangements. In the new *Zanmei Shi*, six of his arrangements (nos. 31, 69, 130, 202, 204, 370) have been retained. Wiant returned to the United States in 1951. He served as the pastor of St. Paul's Church, Delaware, Ohio; as the minister of music at Mahoning Methodist Church, Youngstown; and as the executive director of the National Fellowship of Methodist Musicians from 1957 to 1961. He was the director of music at Scarritt College and for the Ohio Council of Churches. He went to Hong Kong between 1963 and 1965 to assist with editing the new *Putian Songzan*, and he was a professor of music at Chung Chi College, Chinese University of Hong Kong (Young 1993, 858; Wang 1993, 65f). He died 1 October 1975 in Delaware, Ohio.

Harmonizer: HUAN-SHA-XI (*STB* #135).
Arranger: LE P'ING (*STB* #155).

Wiant, Mildred Kathryn Artz

Born in Lancaster, Ohio, 8 June 1898, Mildred Wiant was a graduate of Ohio Wesleyan University; she was a singer and educator. After marrying Bliss Wiant (see above entry), she went to China. She was an associate professor of voice at Yanjing University. After returning to the United States, she served at Scarritt College. In the 1960s, she taught at Chung Chi College, Chinese University of Hong Kong. She translated about fifty Chinese hymns into English, included in *Worship Materials from the Chinese* (1969).

Translator: "Midnight stars make bright the sky" (*STB* #135).
Co-paraphraser: "In all the seasons seeking God" (*STB* #237).

Widyawan, Paul

Born in Yogyakarta, Indonesia, 18 January 1945, Paul Widyawan studied music at Albert Greiner Singschule, a department of Leopold Mozart Conservatory in Augsburg, Germany. Widyawan's interests are not limited to music; he is also active in painting and choreography. He plays the *kulintang,* piano, organ, guitar, and gamelan, and he has published many choral arrangements of folk songs and Christmas carols. He has been the leader of the Vocalista Sonora choir since 1964; he conducted this choir on tours in 1976, 1981, 1984, 1988, and 1992 to the Netherlands, Belgium, Germany, Austria, Italy, and Switzerland. He teaches church music at the Center for Liturgical Music in Yogyakarta; he also taught music at Sanata Dharma University Yogyakarta from 1971 until 1996. Widyawan has collected many ethnic songs and arranged them in publications such as *Bolelebo, Mutiara Samudra, Kambanglah Bungo, Domidow,*

Dami Piranta, and *Folksong*, all published by the Center for Liturgical Music in Yogyakarta. He has participated in forty-five workshops on music composition and has guided courses for choir leaders in Sumatra, Nias, Mentawai, Kalimantan, Celebes, Flores, Timor, Sumba, Alor, Rote, the Moluccas, Papua, and Java. In 1987, he was invited to attend the Ecumenical Seminar on Music and Liturgy in Manila, and in 2004, he attended the International Jesuit-Congress on Liturgy in Bangkok. He was honored to perform two Masses with Vocalista Sonora for Pope John Paul II: in 1988 in Castel Gandolfo, Italy, and in 1989 during the pope's visit to Yogyakarta. Widyawan was the director and producer of the operas *Zar und Zimmermann* by Albert Lorzing, *Prodana Navesta* by Friedrich Smetana, *Der Freischütz* by Carl Maria von Weber, and *Aida* by Guiseppe Verdi. He has been invited to jury many National Choir Festivals. On 30 October 2004, he conducted a concert for the fortieth anniversary of Vocalista Sonora in Yogyakarta.[147]

Composer: "Amen" (*STB* #107); "God's love is everlasting" (*STB* #115).
Author/composer: "The holy light," CAHAYA SUCI (*STB* #154).

Willcock, Christopher John

Born in Australia, 8 February 1947, Christopher John Willcock studied at the Conservatorium of Music in Sydney (Associate in Music, theory, 1963; piano, 1964), University of Sydney (BM with honors, composition, 1974), Melbourne College of Divinity (BD, 1978), the Institut Catholique in Paris (master's degree, sacramental theology, 1982), and he continued to pursue his doctorate. On 1 March 1969, he entered the Society of Jesus and was ordained as a priest on 17 December 1977. Willcock taught in a number of schools, such as St. Aloysius' College (1973–74) and United Faculty of Theology (1983–86), and directed choirs at various churches. His compositions include Masses, anthems, Psalm settings, and songs, some of which were commissioned by the International Committee on English in the Liturgy (ICEL), to which he was a consultant to the music subcommittee (1976), the Psalter subcommittee (1979), and the advisory committee (1982). He was also a member of the World Council of Churches liturgical working group (1979–81). Willcock served the Melbourne Archdiocesan Liturgical Committee from 1984 and the National Liturgical Committee from 1985 (Milgate 2000, 50f).

Composer: GOD OF PEACE (*STB* #267).

---

147 Information in this entry is derived from the author's interview with Widyawan and correspondence with Father Karl Prier, April 7, 2005.

Wong, Heyward Wing Hee

Born in 1917 in Hankou, Hubei Province, China, Wing Hee Wong moved to Shanghai at the age of three. He was a composer, music educator, choral conductor, and a successful architect. He was the editor of the new *Putian Songzan* ("Hymns of Universal Praise"), which was published in English and Chinese editions in Hong Kong in 1977; he contributed a large number of translations, harmonizations, and original compositions to the hymnal. Wong began his music career in Shanghai, where he served as the associate conductor of the Chinese Music Drama Company; he also conducted the Shanghai Municipal Symphony Orchestra. He studied at Columbia University under Theodore Urbach, V. Saricheff, Pierre Monteux, Fritz Mahler, and Adolf Schmitt, and he earned a doctorate in music and music education. He composed many art songs that are often performed by Chinese artists. He went to Hong Kong in 1967 and became a prominent figure in the musical scene, especially as the conductor for the Hong Kong Oratorio Society for more than two decades. Since the founding of the World Association of Chinese Church Music in 1972, Wong was its president for more than a decade. After his retirement, he returned to Hong Kong several times to assist with Bible translation and to conduct the Hong Kong Oratorio Society. He played a significant role in the leadership and development of church music among Chinese and Chinese-speaking churches around the world. He died in 2003 in the United States.

Arranger: XUAN PING (*STB* #165).

Wu, Jingren

While he was a student at Tongwu University, Wu Jingren became a Christian upon listening to a sermon by Suqing Li. Wu taught at the YMCA high school in Shanghai, and he later was the principal of Tongwu high school in Wuxi. Wu co-wrote with Weiyu Zhu the Christmas carol, "Holy night, blessed night." He passed away in the 1930s (Wang 1993, 143).

Co-author: "Holy night, blessed night" (*STB* #140).

Wu, Rense (Jen-se)

Born to a Presbyterian minister's family in Tainan, Taiwan, 23 March 1961, Wu Rense graduated from the Junior College of Home Economics in Tainan. She was sent by the Tainan Theological College and Seminary to study organ with Karl Hochreither at Musik Hochschule in West Germany for four years, where she received her diploma in organ performance. She teaches organ part-time at Tainan

Theological College and Seminary and is currently directing a few church choirs in Tainan; she was also the editor of *Siong-im-jip*, published by the Presbyterian Church in Taiwan (PCT). Wu actively promotes Taiwanese Romanization, serving as the general secretary of the Association of Taiwanese Romanization, and she has published a number of articles relating to hymns and the Taiwanese language. She is the editor of the "Series of Classical Composers," a program of educational DVDs produced by the Chimei Museum. Wu promotes organ music and performs recitals for charities at different churches and organizations.

Composer: "Lamb of God" (*STB* #129).

Wu, Wendong (Wen-tung)

Born in the 1970s in Taiwan, Wendong Wu was a member of the Heavenly Melody Choir, which had a weekly television show. As a young composer, Wu knew it was important to capture the hearts of the listeners by speaking in their language. Although most of the choir's earlier compositions and choral settings were in traditional Western styles, Wu gradually developed a style of his own: adapting folk idioms and treating them with the popular Western harmony. This strategy successfully attracted audiences, and the Heavenly Melody Choir paved the way for the later development of praise choruses in Taiwan.

Composer: YE-DI DI HUA (*STB* #177).

Xu, Lujia

Born to a minister's family in June 1931 in Nanchang, Jiangxi Province, China, Lujia Xu graduated from the Luxun College of Arts in piano performance. In 1953 and 1954, he won prizes in national competitions. While he was a college student, his teacher was a distinguished Russian professor who studied under the pianist and composer Sergei Rachmaninoff. Xu also studied with a Polish professor who was a specialist of Chopin, who conferred on Xu the honorary title "The Eleventh Heir of the Chopin Legacy" as well as "The Piano Poet of China." Xu was a professor of piano at the National Conservatory in Beijing. Because of his Christian faith, he was tortured during the Cultural Revolution (1966–76). He was invited to teach at the Asian Institute for Liturgy and Music, Manila, in 1989 and was subsequently requested to contribute a few arrangements of Chinese compositions to *Sound the Bamboo*. Xu's wife, who was a professor of voice, joined him in the Philippines and also taught voice at AILM; she passed away there. Xu immigrated to Canada in the late 1990s. On 1 December 2004, he visited Hong Kong and presented a lecture/recital and testimony of his life in Christ at the Sen Lok Christian Church.

Harmonizer: CHENG CHING TSAN (*STB* #167).
Arranger: CHU-TOU-GE (*STB* #174); SINIM (*STB* #231).

Yamaguchi, Tokuo

Born in 1900 in Nagasaki, Japan, Yamaguchi Tokuo was baptized when he was a student at a Christian college. After graduating from the theology division of Aoyama College, he became a Methodist pastor and served in many areas of Japan, including Hokkaidō. From 1937 until his death in 1995, he served at Toyohashi Church (*SRK21*, 262).

Author: "Here, O Lord, your servants meet" (*STB* #242).

Yanagida, Tomotsune

Born in 1908 in Japan, Tomotsune Yanagida was a scholar formerly associated with the professor Kanzō Uchimura. He published a few books on Japanese literature and served as the president of Kinjo University. He died about 1997.

Author: "Dawn and the light of sunrise" (*STB* #54).

Yang, Chen-chang (Zhenchang)

Yang Chen-chang is Chinese.

Author: "In all the seasons seeking God" (*STB* #237).

Yang, Ernest Yinliu

Born in Wuxi, Jiangsu Province, China, 10 November 1899, Ernest Yinliu Yang was one of the most important church musicians, ethnomusicologists, hymn composers, and writers in China. He graduated from St. John's University in Shanghai and Guanghua University. He was well versed in Chinese classics, poetry, and history, and he began his musical career during college. He studied the Chinese instruments *xiao* (notched flute), *sheng* (mouth organ), *di* (bamboo flute), and *erhu* (bowed lute) with monks; he learned *kunqu* (Kun opera), *pipa* (plucked pear-shaped lute), and *sanxian* (three-stringed plucked lute) from Wu Wanqing; and he studied English, piano, music theory, composition, and hymnology with missionaries. Yang was on the editorial committee of the 1936 edition of *Putian Songzan* ("Hymns of Universal Praise"). His interest in Chinese traditional music and folk music led to extensive research of ancient musical history and theories as well as folk operas such as *kunqu* (the forerunner of Peking opera). He taught at the national conservatories in Nanjing and Chongqing, and he served as a professor and head at the Central Conservatory. Yang published countless scholarly books and articles and two volumes of Chinese music history (*Zhongguo gudai yinyue shigang*, 1981). His contributions to Chinese hymnody are comparable to that of Ralph Vaughan Williams in modern English hymnody. He died 25 February 1984.

Author/adapter: "Fount of love, our Savior God," MAN-JIANG-HONG (*STB* #65).

Yang, Jiaren (Chia-jen)

Born in the 1910s in China, Yang Jiaren was the first Chinese musician to earn a Master of Music degree in the United States. While he was a university student, he studied piano with an Italian master who had won first prize in a worldwide piano competition. By the late 1930s, when he went to study in the United States, Yang was already an accomplished pianist and served as a teaching assistant. He returned to China about 1941. He taught at the Shanghai Conservatory of Music and served as the head of choral conducting. Since he was a devout Christian, he volunteered to teach at Jinling Seminary (then in Shanghai). He was equally skilled at piano, voice, and conducting and conducted many major oratorios and Masses. The famous pianist Fu Cong was his student. Because of his successful career in music, Yang and his wife, who was also an accomplished musician, were persecuted during the Cultural Revolution (1966–76). They could not bear the disgrace and suffering, and they eventually committed suicide. It is a shame that the Chinese Church lost its first musician in this way.[148]

Composer: SI-SHI (*STB* #237).

Yang, Jingqiu

Born in Wujin, Jiangsu Province, China, Jingqiu Yang was a schoolteacher before his conversion to Christianity. After graduating from Jinling Seminary, he became a Methodist pastor, and he served many congregations in Shanghai and Suzhou, where he became a district superintendent. He joined the Three-Self Patriotic Movement (TSPM) early in his ministry, with the conviction that once the Lord had opened the door of opportunity, no one could close it. In 1954, he was elected one of the TSPM committee members during its first national conference. Since his youth, Yang was industrious and had a good command of Chinese classics and literature. In 1929, one of his hymns won first prize from the hymnal committee of the Chinese Anglican Church; this hymn was one of three that was included in the 1936 edition of *Putian Songzan* (cf. Wang 1993, 121–23).

Author: "Midnight stars make bright the sky" (*STB* #135).

---

148 Information in this entry is derived from the author's conversation with the Reverend Gabriel Chi, December 13, 2006

Yang, Warren

Warren Yang is Chinese.

Co-translator: "We assemble with joy and praise" (*STB* #167).

Yang, Wangshun

Born in Taiwan, 21 November 1932, Yang Wangshun is the only professional composer in Taiwan who has dedicated the past thirty years to writing music for the church. He graduated from the Academy of Arts in Taipei as a composition major, and he taught high schools for many years until he decided to devote his time to composing. He has published thirty volumes of anthems (more than 600 pieces) in Taiwanese and Mandarin and with Taiwanese and Western musical styles. He has also published two cantatas, *Kiu-chu Kang-seng* ("Nativity of the Savior") and *Ki-tok Koh-oah* ("Christ Has Risen"), as well as one LP record, five audiocassettes, four compact discs, and two video compact discs. He was the choir director for Ji-nan Presbyterian Church in Taipei for more than twenty years; the choir's many concert tours have introduced Yang's works to the public. He has been invited many times to train and to conduct choirs and to perform his works in Singapore and Kuala Lumpur and Sibu in Malaysia.

Composer: SU-HOK (*STB* #79).

Yeh, Wei-hsin (Weixin)

Wei-hsin Yeh is a prolific author for the Heavenly Melody Choir and the Christian Gospel Broadcasting Corporation, founded by Doris Braughan (for more information, see the commentary on *STB* #177 in the section on Taiwanese hymns). Yeh's command of the Chinese language and her sensitivity to the needs and concerns of the younger generation enable her to write many hymns and choral arrangements that speak to today's young people.

Author: "Flower of the field" (*STB* #177).

Yokosaka, Yasuhiko

Born in 1956 to two ministers of the United Church of Christ in Japan (UCCJ), Yasuhiko Yokosaka graduated from Baker University (BM), Yale Institute of Sacred Music (MM), and Columbia University (Doctor of Education). While he was a student at Yale, he received the Hugh Porter Scholar award. Yokosaka has a special interest in hymnology; while he studied in New York, he assisted Raymond Glover in editing the Episcopalian Hymnal (1982). In 1997, he was invited to attend WCC Seminar on Liturgy and Music in Taiwan, and he was a consultant for the 2000 edition of *Sound the Bamboo*. Through Yokosaka's efforts, many Asian hymns have been included in *Sambika 21*. He is currently a professor of musicology and arts management at the University of Niigata, where he plans concerts of such artists as Emmanuel Pahud of the Berlin Philharmonic Orchestra. Yokosaka has also given lectures and workshops on hymnody in Europe, the United States, and various countries in Asia. He has published more than thirty books, such as *Atarashii sambika sakka tachi* ("Authors of New Hymns," 1999) and numerous papers, such as those in *The Companion to The Hymnal 21* and *Christian Hymnody: Its History and Background*.[149]

Translator: "Here I am" (*STB* #44).

Yokota, Seiei

Born in Okinawa, Japan, Seiei Yokota is a Baptist minister in Okinawa. He has written a number of hymns using the Okinawan language, which is quite different from Japanese. Yokota is committed to the contextualization of Christian faith and has assisted in the publication of the *Okinawa Sambika* hymnal, which includes a few traditional melodies.

Author/adapter: "Come, smell the scent of sweet wild flowers," TINSAGU NO HANA (*STB* #52).

Yuki, Kō

Born in 1896 in Japan, Kō Yuki was the leading hymnologist and mentor for today's *Sambika* scholars. Yuki began writing hymns from his third year in high school; he wrote and translated many hymns, and many people appreciate their high quality. Yuki was a graduate of the theology division of Kwansei College. He served two churches in the Tokyo area, including the present Higashi Nakano Church, which he pastored for fifty years. During that time, he not only served on the editorial committees of the 1931 and 1954 editions of *Sambika* but also taught hymnology, worship, and Christianity in the theology division of Aoyama College, the Women's University of Tokyo, and other junior colleges. After the end of the Second World War, Yuki was on the executive committee of the National Council of Churches in Japan, and he was the chairman of the *Sambika* committee for many years. He published many books, including *Collection of Hymns, Harps,*

---

149 Information in this entry is derived from the author's correspondence with Yokosaka, January 10, 2007.

Life of Jesus through Poems and Paintings, Introduction to Christian Worship, Companion to Sambika (text), *Poems and Music for Praise,* and *Collection of Sermons* (cf. *SRK21*, 20f). He died in 1985.

Author: "Distracted by the world's concerns" (*STB* #69).

Yuya, Saichirō

Born in 1864 in Hyōgoken, Japan, Saichirō Yuya studied medicine at Tokyo Imperial University, but he felt the Lord calling and gave up his medical studies to attend Dōshisha Divinity School. After graduation, he worked in parish ministry and switched to teaching. He was one of the editorial committee members of the 1903 *Sambika*, and he contributed a few hymns. He died in 1941.[150]

Author: "In this world abound" (*STB* #216).

Zhu, Weiyu

Born in 1890 in China, Weiyu Zhu grew up in a poor family. When he was young, he could only afford three years of private tutoring. As an adult, he converted to Christianity, gave up his business, and became a preacher. He was ordained by the Methodist Church and worked in many parishes in Suzhou and Shanghai, and he was the superintendent of two districts. He was a strong supporter of the Three-Self Patriotic Movement (for more information, see the section on Chinese hymns). When the church was having financial difficulties, Zhu relinquished his own pension to those who were more needy. He was a talented poet and preacher, and he published five volumes of his sermons (Wang 1993, 143). He died in 1986.

Co-author: "Holy night, blessed night" (*STB* #140).

---

150 Information in this entry is derived from the author's correspondence with Sōji Kitamura, September 19, 2006.

Afterword

This book has been infused by an agenda, which is also a dream: that my Asian colleagues will reclaim what God has given to them through their own cultures, share what God has revealed to them from ancient times, and interpret what the Good News of Jesus Christ means to them and their people today. The following is intended to help my colleagues and future generations to pursue the inexhaustible task of contextualizing church music in Asia.

1. The pride in ethnic identity and treasuring the ethnic styles

Asian churches employ three broad musical styles, illustrated by the diagram of a continuum below: (1) music that exhibits indigenous and traditional styles; (2) music in Western styles or with strong Western influences; and (3) inculturated or contextualized music that exists between the first two examples. Although some composers preserve and develop their own styles, i.e., stay on the left side of the continuum, many tend to be pulled toward Western styles, the right side of the continuum.

$$\leftarrow \text{ in between } \rightarrow$$

Indigenous ← _____ → Western

One can see from the hymn analyses and commentaries in this volume that some Asians utilize their heritage to express their newly acquired Christian faith, others struggle to maintain their indigenous musical identities, but the majority embraces the musical languages of the West. To use the symbol of a rainbow: if multiple ethnic groups in a country maintain their respective musical styles, the effect is as if many small rainbows are formed. However, if all groups move toward the right side of the above continuum, i.e., toward adaptation and imitation of Western styles, the small rainbows disappear. Looking at regions and at Asia as a whole, one can see larger rainbows composed of multicolored national and ethnic music. Adopting a global perspective, one can say that the continents and oceans of the world constitute the largest, most beautiful rainbow; if any one of the colors—Asian, Pacific, African, Latin American, Middle Eastern, Eastern European, North American, or Western European—is missing, the beauty of the rainbow is impaired; the rainbow might even disappear. All peoples of the world have the right and duty to preserve and develop their colors in the rainbow—God's emblems of beauty and God's gifts—that are also global signs of our unity in diversity through music.

2.   The need for theological depth and proper interpretations

Some hymns and music that exemplify local or Asian realities with poetic beauty, theological depth, and indigenous or contextual musical expressions are unknown or not yet translated into other languages; often, these musical styles cannot be reproduced by non-natives without proper instrumentation and performance techniques. Therefore, there is a need for sharing theological ideas, for liturgical experiments, and for musical innovations to lead to mutual learning and cross-fertilization. In many cases, the imagery and particular connotations of words or expressions cannot be adequately translated. It is difficult to reproduce in translation the meanings, feelings, intimate text-tune relations, and artistic beauty of the original material. However, competent poets and composers are doing theology with their artistic skills, using text, music, and liturgy to communicate their Christian faith, an endeavor that calls for serious dialogues between poets, musicians, artists, liturgiologists, and theologians.

3.   The importance of the integration of music and liturgy in theological education

I have concentrated the past two decades of my professional career on educating and promoting contextual and global songs in ecumenical liturgies. In an ideal situation, pastors would know the proper use of music in liturgical contexts. Since most theological curricula cannot adequately educate theological students in the fields of liturgy and music, one alternative is to train church musicians in the fields of liturgy and theology. I have attempted to do this with the cooperation and contributions of many prominent international scholars, theologians, and musicians at Tainan Theological College and at the Southeast Asia Graduate School of Theology. All students in the Master of Arts in Church Music program must have sufficient courses in theology and liturgy, and candidates for Master or Doctor of Theology degrees in Liturgy and Music should also have sufficient courses in Asian and global music and ecumenical liturgy. Theological and liturgical practices can be learned through books, but world music and its application to liturgy require practical experience—to sing and thus internalize musical styles and spirit. Since specific musical instruments may be difficult to obtain, instrumental substitutes and/or simplification of performance is encouraged.

The purpose of singing Asian and global hymns is to acknowledge that God is revealed to humankind in different artistic forms; sharing these hymns enhances a deeper understanding of the meanings of Christian faith and is a witness of our unity in diversity. One may not be able to sing and reproduce hymns as they originally were created, but a willingness to try is the first step toward accepting each other and is a new way to see the marvelous deeds and wonders of God's

524

glory. Eileen M. Johnson's phrase, "but on Sunday morning, I-to Loh isn't there—*you* are," encourages one to sing other people's songs as circumstance allows; authenticity, while ideal, is not the purpose, and even I cannot reproduce indigenous hymns to precisely match the original styles.[151] What is most important is that the motivation for churches to enter the unknown—to "put out into the deep water and let down your nets for a catch" (Luke 5:4)—should not be hindered by an inability to "authentically" teach new songs; the alternative is to restrict a congregation's repertoire of Christian expression to Western sources.

4. The urgent task for ethnomusicological research

It is vital for all Asian churches, through their universities, schools, and colleges, to pursue ethnomusicological research, i.e., the study of traditional musical forms. This may save these forms from extinction and also lay a foundation for studying and developing new songs of worship. It is important for churches to understand the cultures' aesthetic views, theories, philosophies, idioms, features, singing styles, instrumentation, and multipart practices when applicable. In this way, more people can appreciate their indigenous music and composers will have the basic knowledge and tools for linking the past to the present, transforming the old, and developing new and innovative Christian works. This task has become more urgent because modern media and mass communication hasten the decay of traditional art forms and values.

5. The potential for developing Asian Christian art music

I challenge Asian church musicians to develop our church music by composing more hymns and liturgical responses in indigenous styles for worship, mission, and spiritual nourishment. Like the European Baroque and Classical periods, when creativity in church music laid the foundation of art music for concert halls, Asian musicians could develop art music (such as larger choral works, cantatas, oratorios, and musical dramas) that would become concert pieces for the masses. Christian messages could be communicated to believers and nonbelievers alike. Innovative and indigenous Christian art music should be part of the cultural heritage that Asian musicians use to demonstrate their artistic achievements; the people of a country or region can then feel pride in these works that reflect their heritage.

With modern, contextual, and innovative artistic efforts, Christian art music can again provide for all people a glimpse of God's glory. In those moments, all are invited to shout, as in Psalm 150:6:

"Let everything that breathes praise the LORD!
Praise the LORD!"

---

151 See Eileen M. Johnson, "Hymn Performance: I-to Loh Isn't There," *The Hymn, A Journal of Congregational Song* 57, no. 2 (Spring 2006): 33–35.

I-to and Hui-chin Loh at I-to's retirement farewell party, June 18, 2002.

Appendix

Resources of Asian Music, Worship, and Arts

(First compiled in 1986, revised and enlarged 2007)

Over the past century, some Asian churches have developed excellent resources of music, worship, and the arts, but most are unknown or unavailable to outsiders. Many hymns or art works were created for particular worship celebrations but have since been forgotten or discarded, and most have never been published. Since 1968, I have had the privilege of visiting many Asian countries and churches and have come across many valuable resources. The materials listed here are those that I have collected during the past three to four decades, and they are now mostly housed in the Hiong-im Gak-hong (Center for the Study and Promotion of Taiwanese Church Music) at Tainan Theological College and Seminary.* Hymnals of different countries and denominations are included in this list if they feature a substantial number of indigenous or contextual hymns. Since most of the official prayer books or liturgies in Asia are translations and are not very different from those of their respective mother churches in the West, they are omitted. I have chosen to include only published works that are either in English or in original languages, that exhibit native musical styles, and that are in staff or cipher notation. Countries such as India and Sri Lanka have extensive materials, but these are mostly without notation and would be unintelligible to most and hence omitted.

The resources are listed by country and year of publication.

I. Collections of Hymns
(and some anthems or choral arrangements)

PAN-ASIAN (multiple countries of origin)

East Asia Christian Conference (EACC) Hymnal, ed. John Milton Kelly and Daniel Thambyrajah Niles (Kyoto: East Asia Christian Conference, 1963).
- 103 Western and 97 Asian hymns, mostly in traditional Western styles and harmony

New Songs of Asian Cities, ed. I-to Loh (Urban Industrial Mission Committee of the Christian Conference of Asia, 1972).
- 62 songs of social concern
- 49 songs from 15 Asian countries
- with audiocassette
- out of print

CCA Hymnal Supplement I, ed. Francisco F. Feliciano (Singapore: Christian Conference of Asia [CCA], 1981).
- 32 hymns from various countries in Asia
- in English only

Hymns from the Four Winds, ed. I-to Loh (Nashville, TN: Abingdon Press, 1983).
- 125 hymns in English by Asians and Asian Americans

A Festival of Asian Christmas Music, ed. I-to Loh (Manila: Asian Institute for Liturgy and Music [AILM]; Quezon City: New Day Publishers, 1984).
- 16 Christmas carols and anthems from the Philippines, India, Malaysia, Hong Kong, Taiwan, and Indonesia
- in original languages and English translation
- with notes on composers and their music
- Chinese edition (1985) available from Taiwan Church Press
- with audiocassette and songbook

CCA Hymnal Supplement II, ed. I-to Loh (Singapore: CCA, 1985).
- 22 hymns from Malaysia, the Philippines, and Indonesia
- original languages and English translations

Songs of Our People, ed. I-to Loh (Hong Kong: Asia Alliance of YMCAs, 1987).
- 37 songs from Asia
- in original languages and English translations
- revised and enlarged in 1991: 75 hymns

Asian Songs of Worship, ed. I-to Loh (World Council of Churches [WCC] / AILM, 1988).
- 47 hymns and responses from Asia
- in original languages and English

Bungkos: A Collection of Choral Pieces by AILM Composers (Manila: AILM, 1990).
- nine choral pieces by students and graduates of AILM, performed by AILM Chorale, directed by Joey Navaro
- featuring diverse Asian styles from India, Myanmar, Thailand, Singapore, Indonesia, and the Philippines
- audiocassette only

Sound the Bamboo: CCA Hymnal 1990, ed. I-to Loh (Manila: AILM, 1990).
- co-editors: Francisco F. Feliciano, James Minchin
- 280 hymns from 22 Asian countries
- in 38 languages with English translations
- supercedes all previous CCA and AILM hymn publications
- audiocassette: *Thousands of Songs Full of Praise*, featuring 20 songs from the Indian subcontinent, dubbed from field recordings

We Come with Hope: Songs of Prayer and Social Commitment (Hong Kong: Asia Alliance of YMCAs, 1997).
- CD with 16 songs from Asian countries
- in different languages and English

Sound the Bamboo: CCA Hymnal 2000, ed. I-to Loh (CCA / Taiwan Church Press, 2000).
- co-editors: Francisco F. Feliciano, James Minchin
- revised and enlarged edition
- 315 hymns from 22 countries
- 44 languages with English translation
- 2006 edition published by GIA Publications, Inc., Chicago, IL

BANGLADESH

Songs of Awakening and Hope, 1984.
- 15 songs by Bart Shaha, in Bengali
- with interpreted translations
- with audiocassette

CAMBODIA

"Khmer Hymns," ed. Sam Sarim (Bangkok: Kanok Bannasan [OMF Publishers], 1985).
- 206 Khmer hymns
- original compositions and adaptations from folk melodies

CHINA

Zanmeishi (xinbian) ("New Hymns of Praise") (Shanghai: Three-Self Patriotic Movement Committee of Protestant Churches, 1985).
- 400 hymns, including 102 original Chinese compositions
- all Western traditional harmony
- with audiocassette (containing only some hymns)
- 1998 English-Chinese edition

Shipian Songzan Quanji ("The Whole Book of the Psalms of Praise") (Anhui, China: Anhui Theological Seminary, 1998, 2005).
- contains 150 Psalms in Mandarin, in prose form, with one to three different tunes each, either adapted from folk melodies or composed in cipher notation
- with three additional songs for wedding occasions and sending off

HONG KONG

Putian Songzan ("Hymns of Universal Praise") (Hong Kong: Chinese Christian Literature Council, 1977).
- in Chinese and in English (separate volumes)
- 678 hymns and liturgical responses
- 62 by Chinese authors

Huaren Shengsong ("Chinese Praise"), ed. Daniel Law (Hong Kong: Christian Communications Ltd., 1992).
- coordinated by the World Association for Chinese Church Music.
- 123 hymns by Chinese, Taiwanese, and overseas Chinese authors
- features a mixture of Chinese and Western styles

Putian Songzan ("Hymns of Universal Praise"), ed. Angela Tam (Hong Kong: Chinese Christian Literature Council, 2006).
- more than 900 hymns; new bilingual edition in Mandarin and English
- includes the majority of Psalms with many settings: responsive reading, antiphons, and chanting styles

- prayers, acclamations, and readings
- contains many important twentieth- and twenty-first-century Western hymns
- features some hymns from the Third World
- also contains more than 100 descants by Hong Kong Chinese composers

INDIA

Sacred Hymns in Marathi, music edition, comp. E. R. Bissell (Poona: Bombay Tract and Book Co., 1930).
- 682 hymns in staff notation, from Marathi and European sources
- preface and indices in English

Tune Book to Tamil Christian Lyrics, ed. H. A. Popley (Madras, Allahabad, Colombo: The Christian Literature Society for India, 1932).
- 100 hymns in Tamil
- with staff and Tamil *sargam* notations
- with introduction in English

Masihi Sangeet ("Christian Lyrics of India") (Bangalore: The United Theological College Library, 1961).
- specially prepared for the Third Assembly of WCC, 1961
- 37 Indian lyrics (hymns) in different Indian languages with English text, not singable
- in Western staff notation

Bhajans (Bangalore: National Biblical Catechetical and Liturgical Centre, 1977).
- a collection of songs of praise in various languages used at the National Biblical Catechetical and Liturgical Centre (NBCLC)
- 63 songs in praise of the attributes of God
- with English translations, not singable

INDONESIA

Madah Bakti (Indonesian Roman Catholic Hymnal) (Yogyakarta: Pusat Musik Liturgi, 1982).
- 600 hymns and liturgical pieces, the majority of Indonesian origin
- features full piano and vocal score and guitar chords
- 3 volumes, with audiocassettes

Kidung Jemaat (Jakarta: Yayasan Musik Gereja (Yamuger), 1984).
- 478 hymns
- includes 100 Indonesian original compositions
- in cipher notation

Kristus Sundaring Bali ("Christ the Light to Bali"), AILM Collection of Asian Church Music, no. 12, ed. I-to Loh (Manila: AILM, 1988).
- a collection of new Balinese hymns recorded by I-to Loh
- 13 songs and hymns by I Nyoman Darsane and Bishop Wayan Mastra
- with Balinese gamelan accompaniment
- in Balinese, some with singable English translations
- with information about cultural, liturgical, and musical context and detailed transcriptions and analyses
- with audiocassette and photos

Kapata-Kapata Rohani, AILM Collection of Asian Church Music, no. 19, ed. Felicidad Prudente (Manila: AILM, 1991).
- spiritual songs from the central Moluccas
- 20 songs/liturgical responses collected, adapted, and arranged by Christian I. Tamaela
- Western and cipher notations
- some have singable English translations
- with photos and background information

Nyanikanlah Kidung Baru (Jakarta: Gereja Kristen Indonesia, 1991).
- 230 Indonesian hymns in cipher notation
- some written by Indonesians and Asians

Mazmur dan Kidung Jemaat (Jakarta: Yamuger, 1995).
- builds on *Kidung Jemaat*'s 478 hymns with the addition of 150 Psalms, many by Louis Bourgeois
- in cipher notation

Pelengkap Kidung Jemaat, Yamuger Cetakan ke 4 (Jakarta: Yamuger, 2004).
- 308 hymns in cipher notation
- 68 entries by Indonesian authors/composers

JAPAN

Japanese Hymns in English, ed. P. S. McAlpine (Nagoya: Tsunubue Sha, 1965).
- 50 hymns by Japanese poets and composers
- with some Western tunes
- including historical notes and biographical sketches on authors and composers

Tomo ni Utaō (Tokyo: Sambika Committee, 1976).
- 50 hymns, 24 by Japanese authors
- in staff notation

Ryukyu Sambika, ed. Furugen (Okinawa: Central Baptist Church, 1992).
- 70 hymns, mostly translations from the West, and 35 hymns of Okinawa origin
- in staff notation and in Okinawan language

Sambika 21 (Tokyo: Sambika Committee, 1997).
- 580 hymns and liturgical responses, mostly of European origins
- combines hymns from earlier editions of *Sambika* (1954, 1967), *Tomo ni Utaō* (1976), and children's *Sambika* (1987)
- features many new hymns by Japanese and other nationalities
- 15 hymns from Asia but harmonized by the editors
- with companion, *Sambika 21 Ryakkai* (1997).

KOREA

A Collection of Korean Hymns (Korean Hymnal Committee, 1984).
- 22 new hymns in Korean
- with English translations, mostly not singable

100 Selection of Korean Hymns: vol.1, 1985; vol. 2, 1986; vol. 3, 1991.
- 300 original compositions by La Un-yung, the most famous and prolific composer in Korea
- melodies in Korean styles with four-part harmony
- texts in Korean with titles in English

New Korean Hymns, ed. Chay Shiwohn (Seoul: Korean Christian Academy, 1985).
- 12 new hymns and anthems in Korean and English translations; with notes
- with audiocassette

Songs of the Minjung: Jesus Christ Sets Free to Serve (Ecumenical Youth Council in Korea, 1985).
- 26 songs in English, concerning contemporary social problems, justice, and freedom
- with notes on political struggles in history

Contextualized Korean Hymns, vol. 1 (Seoul: Korea Traditional Music Mission, 1986).
- 100 new hymns in Korean composed by Sungmo Moon
- melodies in Korean styles, with four-part Western traditional harmony
- with an essay in Korean and English

Chanyong Chanyong ("Praise, Praise"), ed. Hung Chong-soo (Seoul: Church Music Research Center, Presbyterian Theological University, 1991).
- 140 new hymns by Koreans
- some in Korean styles, all with Western harmony

Heenyonul Uihan Norae ("Songs for Jubilee"), AILM Collection of Asian Church Music, no. 18 (Manila: AILM, 1991).
- 15 original hymns, anthems, some with singable English translations
- texts by Goh Jung-hee, music by Lee Geonyong
- all in Korean styles, contemporary

Korean English Hymnal (Seoul: Agape Publishing Co., 1997).
- 558 hymns and liturgical responses, in Korean and English
- with 42 entries by Korean authors and composers

Kogak Chansongga (Hyangrin Kogak Chansongga Editorial Committee, 2008).
- 236 hymns written by Korean poets and composers
- mostly in Korean styles, some with four-part harmony or guitar chords
- appendix with a few liturgies with a few Western hymns

LAOS

Laotian Hymns, 1985.
- in Laotian, with Western notation
- available via Alice Compain, O.M.F., 239 Soi Hutayon, Susan Phlu, Bangkok, 10120, Thailand

MALAYSIA

C.C.M. Hymnal No. 1, ed. Calvin Chelliah (Petaling Jaya, West Malaysia: Malaysian Council of Churches, 1986).
- 24 new Malaysian hymns and liturgical responses by Tamil, Malay, and Chinese composers in Malaysia
- in original languages and English
- with audiocassette (M$6.00)

PHILIPPINES

Alawiton Sapagtao, ed. Elena Maquiso, (Dumaguete City: Silliman University Press, for United Church of Christ in the Philippines, 1974).
- 355 hymns and service music in Cebuano language, the majority by Filipino authors, 130 by the editor
- 179 Psalms and responsive readings

Buksan Mo Ang Aming Mgal Labi, ed. Francisco Feliciano (Manila: AILM; Quezon City: New Day Publishers, 1982).
- 11 new Filipino anthems in Tagalog
- 4–6 parts for singers at an intermediate level and above
- with songbook, LP record, and audiocassette

Kanta ni Piyantayo (Quezon City: New Day Publishers, 1982).
- over 200 original hymns in Kalahan, Kankanai, Ibaloy, and Ilocano
- some with tonic *sol-fa* notation
- with a few translations of Western hymns

Ang Pilipino Himnal (Manila: National Council of Churches in the Philippines, 1985).
- about 130 original hymns, including a large number by the late Eliseo Pajaro
- appendix features 50 Western hymns translated to Tagalog

O Senor Tagbalay, ed. Felicidad Prudente (Manila: AILM, 1986).
- Christmas songs from Cuyo Island, Palawan, Philippines
- with native instrument accompaniments
- without scores
- audiocassette, brief notes, texts, and translations

The Mountains Ring Out With Their Joy, AILM Collection of Asian Church Music, no. 7 (Manila: AILM, 1987).
- recorded and edited by Ronald H. Walcott
- 25 hymns/songs from Kalinga-Apayao, Abra, Mountain Province, and Ifugao
- fully transcribed with original texts and translations
- with field data, notes, and commentary
- photos

Mulla Sa Labing Mga Musmos, AILM Collection of Asian Church Music, no. 13 (Quezon City: New Day Publishers, 1989).
- 10 simple anthems by Lucy C. Uy (poet) and Jerry Dadap (composer)
- in Pilipino, with English translations at the back

Imnaryong Pilipino ("Filipino Hymnal"), ed. Anders Salomonsson et al. (Bacoor, Cavite: Iglesia Filipina Independiente, 1990).
- 106 hymns and liturgical music in Pilipino
- mostly in Filipino style, with guitar chords
- only a few pieces from Asia and the West
- with a complete Mass and other worship resources

Masdan, O Yahweh, AILM Collection of Asian Church Music, no. 15 (Manila: AILM, 1990).
- a collection of songs for peace and freedom, by the group Patatag
- 10 original compositions, from unison to six-part chorus
- in Tagalog, some with singable English translations
- available in audiocassette and VHS video

Hymnal of a Faith Journey (Quezon City: United Church of Christ in the Philippines, 2002).
- official hymnal of the United Church of Christ in the Philippines (UCCP); project coordinator: Grace Roble-Tabada
- contents follow the UCCP Statement of Faith
- progressive, contextual, and global in perspective
- contains 394 hymns and 67 prayers, litanies, and worship resources
- in English; Filipino compositions are mostly bilingual
- with guitar chords guide
- nearly 50% hymns by Filipinos
- 40% classical Western hymns
- 6% Asian hymns
- 4% international and contemporary hymns

The AILM Collection: Hymns, Psalms and Songs for Worship, vol. 1, ed. Francisco F. Feliciano (Manila: AILM, 2005).
- contains 97 songs and hymns, 18 Psalms, 5 canticles, 16 service music pieces
- mostly composed by Francisco Feliciano
- many reprinted from *Sound the Bamboo: CCA Hymnal 1900*
- with a few works by other Asian composers
- all in English; many texts adapted or written by Lillibeth Nacion Puyot

TAIWAN

Le-pai Gak-chiong ("Liturgical Music"), 1973.
- 36 original hymns and liturgical responses composed by I-to Loh
- in Taiwanese (Hokkien) and Mandarin

Le-pai Gak-chiong II ("Liturgical Music II"), ed. I-to Loh (Tainan: Taiwan Church Press, 1984).
- 34 hymns and liturgical responses from Asia, Europe, and Africa
- in Taiwanese, Mandarin, and English

Ke-yu Sheng-ge ji, ed. Chen Chien-chung (Hakka Missions, 1985).
- 80 Hakka hymns, arrangements, and hymn anthems of Han and Hakka origins

- in Hakka language (characters)
- in staff notation and with audiocassette

Qun Shan Huan Chang ("Let the Hills Sing"), ed. I-to Loh, AILM Collection of Asian Church Music, no. 4 (Tainan: Taiwan Church Press, 1986).
- 25 hymns from six Taiwanese tribes: Ami, Bunun, Puyuma (Pinuyumayan), Paiwan, Tayal, and Yami (Tao)
- in original languages and English translations
- fully transcribed with notes on tribal music and individual pieces
- with audiocassette and songbook

Hakka Songs of Praise, ed. I-to Loh and Chen Chien-chung, AILM Collection of Asian Church Music, no. 6 (Tainan: Taiwan Church Press, 1987).
- 17 new hymns and anthems from the Hakka people of Taiwan
- in Romanized Hakka, Chinese characters, and English translation
- accompanied by Hakka instruments
- notes and cultural information in Chinese and English
- with audiocassette

Ho-peng Sin-koa ("New Songs of Peace") (Taipei: Mennonite Church in Taiwan, 1987).
- 29 new hymns and 2 anthems by Taiwanese and Chinese authors
- in Romanized Taiwanese and characters

Xiang Yehehua Chang Xinge ("Sing a New Song to the Lord"), ed. I-to Loh, AILM Collection of Asian Church Music, no. 9 (Tainan: Tainan Theological Seminary; Manila: AILM, 1987).
- 16 anthems, representing the best of contextual works by composers from Taiwan, Hong Kong, the Philippines, and China
- in Mandarin, Taiwanese, and some in English
- with translations and notes in Chinese and English
- with audiocassette

Ban-chok Chan-bi ("All Nations Praise"), ed. I-to Loh (Tainan: Taiwan Church Press, 1988).
- 60 songs/liturgical responses from 22 countries around the world, more than half from Asian countries
- in Taiwanese and English; some in original languages

Ban-chok Chan-bi II ("All Nations Praise, vol. 2"), ed. I-to Loh (Tainan: Tainan Theological Seminary / Taiwan Church Press, 1991).
- 57 songs and liturgical responses from 27 countries around the world
- 39 from Asian countries
- in Taiwanese, English, and original languages

Hoan-lok Ko-siong I ("Rejoice and Sing, vol. 1"), ed. I-to Loh (Tainan: Taiwan Church Press, 1992).
- 39 songs and anthems from Asia, Africa, and Latin America
- in Taiwanese, Mandarin, and original languages
- with notes in Mandarin

Sapahemek to Tapang, 1992.
- hymn collection of the Western Ami Presbytery
- 200 hymns, 40 adapted from Ami melodies or newly composed
- 4 composed by other tribes
- Romanized and in cipher notation
- some with Ami multipart settings

Senai Tua Cemas (Taipei: Paiwan Presbytery of the Presbyterian Church of Taiwan, 1993).
- 410 hymns in the Paiwan language
- 80 hymns adapted from tribal songs or newly composed
- Western hymns in staff notation; tribal songs in cipher notation

Suyang Uyas, ed. Tien Hsin-te and Hayu Udaw Chuang (Taipei: Truku Presbytery of the Presbyterian Church of Taiwan, 1994).
- 330 hymns in the Truku language
- 36 works from Truku folk origin or newly composed
- in Western and cipher notations

Ban-bin Siong-chan ("All Peoples Praise"), ed. I-to Loh (Tainan: Tainan Theological College and Seminary, 1995).
- 157 hymns and responses from 36 countries (some previously published)
- more than 60 original compositions by the editor
- in original languages and Taiwanese; some in English
- with notes in Chinese

Shan-hai Huan-chang ("Mountains and Oceans Sing with Joy"), 1996.
- special album for the fiftieth anniversary of Yu-shan Theological Seminary, Shou-feng, Hua-lien; recorded under the direction of Rev. Hayu Yudaw Chuang
- CD with 12 aboriginal songs/hymns and arrangements by Hayu Yudaw

Hakka Hymns (Taipei: Presbyterian Church of Taiwan, 1999).
- 350 hymns in Romanized Hakka and Chinese characters
- 71 tunes by Taiwanese: 30 new compositions, 25 adapted from Hakka folk melodies, 16 from tribal or newly composed melodies

Se-ki Sin Seng-si ("Century New Hymnal"), ed. I-to Loh (Taipei: Presbyterian Church in Taiwan, 2002).
- supplement to PCT hymnal
-130 hymns and liturgical responses from 35 countries
- more than 50 entries by Taiwanese
- with CD
- with a companion volume (2003), written by I-to Loh and Yi-juan Lin
- English-Taiwanese and Mandarin editions, in press

Logos: To chia jiok-the ti Tai-oan, Taiwan Church Anthems Series 1, ed. Tony Liu, I-to Loh, and Yajing Hwang, 2006.
- supported by The Rev. and Mrs. Sian-chhun Loh Memorial Fund for Church Music Education, and Tainan Seminary Foundation
- 10 anthems, from unison to four-part choruses
- in Romanized Taiwanese and Chinese characters; a few works in Mandarin
- composed by faculty and students of Tainan Theological College and Seminary

Seng-si, ed. I-to Loh, assoc. ed. Hui-chin Loh, 2009.
- official hymnal of the Presbyterian Church in Taiwan
- with 650 classical and contemporary hymns from 73 countries, plus 78 prayers (28 by Taiwanese) and 81 line drawings (by Taiwanese artists)
- approximate distribution of hymns: 50% from the West, 25% from Taiwan, 25% from the Third World
- in Romanized Taiwanese and Chinese characters; some hymns with original languages
- with 20 indexes

THAILAND

Traditional Thai Hymns (Bangkok: Kanok Bannasan [OMF Publishers], 1984).
- 27 hymns in Thai
- with audiocassette

Rak Phrajao Rao Pen Thai ("The Love of God Sets Us Free"), ed. I-to Loh, AILM Collection of Asian Church Music, no. 14 (Manila: AILM, 1989).
- 9 new hymns from the Isaan area of northern Thailand and two *piphat* ensemble pieces
- features compositions by Ruth and Inchai Srisuwan
- accompanied by *khaen* ensemble
- with a 23-page essay with cultural background, contextual liturgies, musical analyses, and notes on authors and hymns
- with audiocassette

Cassettes and Compact Discs

There are innumerable audiocassettes and compact discs of music from different countries that vary in content, style, and quality. Since most of them are in native languages, the information may be inconsistent. Here are only a few examples. Contact information is provided for those interested in obtaining recordings.

HONG KONG

Xixun Fuin Yuequ ("Good News Cantonese Gospel Music") (5 CDs)
- composed, adapted, or arranged from traditional Cantonese music or folk tunes
- arranged by Lin Jing Tian

    Zhenzheng Chuanbo Youxian Gonsi
    Zhungyi Hengsheng Zhungxin, Room 1203
    71 Kuifang Huogui Matou Road, New Territory, Hong Kong

Email: info@gnci.org.hk; website: www.goodnewscom.org

INDONESIA

Madah Bakti 2000 (2) PML 1022
- 22 new compositions using different styles from 12 ethnic groups

    Roman Catholic Pusat Musik Liturgi, Yogyakarta
    Jln. Ahmad Jazuli 2 – Yogyakarta 55224

Email: pml@idola.net.id

    Yamuger (Indonesia Institute for Sacred Music)
    Jl. Wisma Jaya No. 11, Rawamangun, Jakarta 13220, Indonesia

Email: yamuger@bit.net.id; Fax 021-4720129

    Sekolah Tinggi Theologica
    Duta Wacana
    Jl. Dr. Wahidin 17
    Yogyakarta

INDIA

Bhajans: Kannada, Malayalam, Tamil and Telegu (4 CDs)
 - composed and recorded by faculty and students of The United Theological
   College, Bangalore

   Email: proutc@rediffmail.com

Christmas: The Light of Hope. (CD)
 - composed and recorded by Kalyan Banerjee

   Baptist Church, Midnapore
   P.O. and Dist. Midnapore (West) Pin-721101

Everlasting Songs
 - 12 Bengali devotional songs, sung by Kalyan Banerjee

   22/12, Biren Roy Road (West) Kolkata – 34

PHILIPPINES

Missa Mysterium (CD)
 - composed and conducted by Francisco F. Feliciano, 1997

   For this and many other recordings, contact:
   Asian Institute for Liturgy and Music
   P.O. Box 3167, 1099 Manila, Philippines
   Email: fffsamba@pacific.net.ph
   Fax: +63-2-722-1490

THAILAND

   Overseas Missionary Fellowship
   239 Soi Hutayon
   Suan Phli, Bangkok, 10120

II. Worship Resources

A Handbook for Christian Worship Celebration, comp. Lydia N. Niguidula (Quezon City: New Day Publishers, 1975).
- intended for use by all the denominations of the National Council of Churches in the Philippines
- material is largely drawn from traditional Protestant liturgies
- each section is introduced with brief historical background and Biblical foundation

Your Kingdom Come (Singapore: Christian Conference of Asia, 1980).
- one month of meditation on the Lord's Prayer by Masao Takenaka (art), Ron O'Grady (text), and T. K. Thomas (text)

Worship Handbook, Seventh Assembly of CCA, Bangalore, 1981 (Singapore: Christian Conference of Asia, 1981).
- four complete liturgies with 15 hymns of international origins
- 32 from *CCA Hymnal Supplement I*

Your Will Be Done, ed. Alison O'Grady (Singapore: CCA Youth, 1984).
- reflective writings, prayers, and hymns related to the discerning of God's will for our lives
- with art works, photos, and 33 songs
- mostly of Asian origin and drawn from existing publications

Worship Resources, Eighth Assembly of CCA, Seoul, 1985 (Singapore: Christian Conference of Asia, 1985).
- 7 complete liturgies
- 28 Asian hymns and 6 responses
- 4 of Western origin
- with audiocassette (produced by the Korean Christian Broadcasting System)

Report of the 1987 Asian Workshop on Liturgy and Music (February 10–22, 1987, Makiling, Philippines), ed. Felicidad Prudente (Manila: AILM, 1987).
- contains details of daily proceedings
- 20 complete liturgies and songs from Asia
- transcriptions of nearly 100 songs/responses
- 7 papers and a list of resources
- photos and a list of participants
- with two audiocassettes

Worship Resources: Mission of God in the Context of the Suffering and Struggling People of Asia (Asia Mission Conference, September 21–27, 1989, Cipanas, Indonesia), ed. Tomas Maddela (Singapore: CCA, 1989).
- 5 complete liturgies and other resources
- 31 hymns and responses

Worship Resources, Ninth General Assembly, Manila, 1990, ed. Pura P. Calo and Maryssa J.R. Mapanao (Singapore: CCA, 1990).
- 8 complete liturgies
- 25 hymns and responses
- keynote address
- with a discussion of music and instruments in the liturgies
- photos of musical instruments used

Conference Papers: 2002 Asia Pacific Conference on Music and Worship, ed. Lillibeth Nacion Puyot (Quezon City, Philippines: Asian Institute for Liturgy and Music, 2002).
- full texts of keynote speech and three papers
- outlines of 7 presentations
- three workshop outlines
- list of participants

In the Circle of Faith, Worship Resource Book, 2002 Asia Pacific Conference on Music and Worship, ed. Lillibeth Nacion Puyot (Quezon City, Philippines: Asian Institute for Liturgy and Music, 2002).
- 17 liturgies with full texts
- lists of sources of music, participants, and planners of each liturgy

III. Periodicals on Church Music and Liturgy

Reihai to Ongaku
- worship and music quarterly, in Japanese

2-3-18 Nishi- Waseda, Shinjuku-ku, Tokyo

Shengyue Jikan
- sacred music quarterly, in Chinese

Hong Kong Baptist Press, 322 Prince Edward Road, W. Kowloon, Hong Kong

"Church Music" quarterly, in Korean, Seoul

IV. Arts

Christian Art in Asia, ed. Masao Takenaka (Kyobun Sha / CCA, 1975).
 - 120 plates from Asian artists, with brief biographies

Christian Art in India, ed. Herbert E. Hoefer (Madras: Gurukul Lutheran Theological College Research Institute, 1982).
 - essays and paintings
 - 36 artists and their works

Ajiya Kokusai Kirisutokyo Bijitsu Ten, 1986.
 - catalogue of Asian International Christian Art Exhibition, October 2–7, 1986, Kyoto
 - 82 plates by Asian artists, the majority by Japanese artists
 - with notes in Japanese

Consider the Flowers: Meditations in Ikebana, ed. Masao Takenaka (Kyo Bun Kwan, 1990).
 - 8 plates of Japanese flower arrangements with meditations

Masao Takenaka and Ron O'Grady, *The Bible Through Asian Eyes* (Auckland: Pace Publishing, in association with Asian Christian Art Association, 1991).
 - paintings by 87 artists
 - with essays, Biblical reflections, poems, and music
 - in English

Beberapa Wajah Seni Rupa Kristani Indonesia ("Many Faces of Christian Art in Indonesia"), ed. Endang Wilandari Supardan et al. (Jakarta: Persekutuan Gereja-gereja di Indonesia, 1993).
 - 79 paintings by Indonesian artists
 - with essays, interpretations, and comments in Indonesian and English
 - photos and biographical notes of the artists

Naomi Wray, *Frank Wesley: Exploring Faith with a Brush* (Auckland: Pace Publishing, 1993).
 - a study and interpretation of the paintings of the northern Indian artist Frank Wesley, now residing in Australia
 - with a glossary of Indian words and a dictionary of the artist's symbols

Masao Takenaka, *The Place Where God Dwells: An Introduction to Church Architecture in Asia* (Hong Kong: Christian Conference of Asia, 1995).
 - photos of church buildings and internal designs of 49 churches in Asia
 - with introduction, notes, and comments

Bali ist mein Leib, Christus ist mein Leben: der Künstler I Nyoman Darsane,
  ed. Karl-Christoph Epting (Karlsruhe: Hans Thoma Verlag, 1999).
  - more than 40 plates of Darsane's paintings and sketches of Biblical women
    with comments and an essay by Bishop I Wayan Mastra

Masao Takenaka, *Bi to Shinjitsu: Kindai Nihon no Bijitsu do Kiristokyō* ("Beauty
  and Truth: Recent Japanese arts and Christianity") (Tokyo: Shinkyō
  Shuppansha, 2006).
  - 15 chapters, color and black-and-white plates, 339 pp.
  - introduces 49 artists and analyses and comments on their works

Image: Christ and Art in Asia
  - quarterly publication by the Asian Christian Art Association
  - subscription fee: US$10–30

        The Asian Christian Art Association
        25-D Malaambing Street, UP Village
        Quezon City, Philippines

Online subscription: www.asianchristianart.org
Bank transfer: mail.acaa@gmail.com (for bank information)

* Hiong-im Gak-hong ("Center for the Study and Promotion of Taiwanese Church
Music") was founded in 1994, when I-to Loh donated his archive to Tainan
Theological College and Seminary (TTCS). This collection of Asian church music
and ethnomusicology materials includes:
  - a large number of hymnals from Asian countries
  - hymnals from mainline churches in the West
  - original hymns and compositions by Asian composers
  - books on church music, liturgy, and music
  - books on ethnomusicology and music of Asian countries
  - LP records, audiocassettes, and compact discs of folk music around the
    world
  - original field recordings since 1968 of Han and tribal music of Taiwan
  - original field recordings since 1969 of songs and hymns from Asian countries
    (Japan, Korea, China, Hong Kong, Thailand, Myanmar, Bangladesh,
    Nepal, India, Pakistan, Sri Lanka, Malaysia, Singapore, Indonesia, New
    Zealand, Australia, the Philippines, and Taiwan)
  - Christian arts of Asia
  - manuscripts and scores of I-to Loh's original compositions
  - musical instruments: Taiwanese ensemble, northern Thai ensemble, Balinese
    gamelan anklung
  - many other instruments from Taiwan, Asia, Africa, and Latin America
    (See: http://www.globalchurchmusic.org/docs/index.php)

The Center has also been enriched by the donation of Carlton Young's collection of church music, including thousands of scores, choral anthems, records, hymnals and books on Western church music. Mary Oyer has also contributed some books and videos of African music and African musical instruments. Hiong-im Gak-hong, therefore, has become a resource center for global church music.

The Center recently relocated to the main library of the Tainan Theological College and Seminary. The Program of Theology and Culture in Asia (PTCA) also transferred its collection of theological books to this library. Hence, it has become the best library in Asia for research on Asian theology, music, and worship.

Bibliography

ABBREVIATIONS

ATESEA Handbook: Association for Theological Education in South East Asia *Handbook.*

DAC: *A Dictionary of Asian Christianity.*

CCPE: *Cultural Center of the Philippines Encyclopedia of Philippine Art.*

Garland 4–9: *The Garland Encyclopedia of World Music*, vols. 4–9.

NGDI: *The New Grove Dictionary of Music and Musicians*, 1980.

NGDII: *The New Grove Dictionary of Music and Musicians*, second edition, 2001.

SRK1955: *Sambika Ryakkai.*

SRKII: *Sambika Dainihen Ryakkai.*

SRK21: *Sambika 21 Ryakkai.*

ENCYCLOPEDIAS, DICTIONARIES, AND OTHER RESOURCES

The Church Hymnary. 1973. 3rd ed. Oxford University Press.

Cultural Center of the Philippines Encyclopedia of Philippine Art. 1994. Vol. VI, *Philippine Music.* Eds. Nicanor G. Tiongsaon and Joi Barrios. Manila: Cultural Center of the Philippines.

A Dictionary of Asian Christianity. 2001. Eds. Scott W. Sunquist, David Wu Chu Sing, and John Chew Hiang Chea. Grand Rapids, Michigan: William B. Eerdmans Publishing Company.

The Garland Encyclopedia of World Music. 1998–2002. New York: Garland Publishing, Inc. / Routledge.

Vol. 4, *Southeast Asia.* 1998. Eds. Terry E. Miller and Sean Williams.

Vol. 5, *South Asia: The Indian Subcontinent.* 2000. Ed. Alison Arnold.

Vol. 7, *East Asia: China, Korea and Japan.* 2002. Eds. Robert C. Provine, Yoshiko Tokumaru, and J. Lawrence Witzleben.

Vol. 9, *Australia and the Pacific Islands.* 1998. Eds. Adrienne L. Kaeppler and Wainwright Love.

Global Praise 2: Songs for Worship and Witness. 2000. Eds. S. T. Kimbrough, Jr., and Carlton R. Young. New York: General Board of Global Ministries, The United Methodist Church.

Gugak Chonchip. 1981. Seoul: Guklip Umak Won ("National Music Academy").

The Hymnal 1982. 1985. New York: Church Hymnal Corporation.

Hymns of Universal Praise. 1986. Hong Kong: Chinese Christian Literature Council.

Korean Year Book 1992

The New Grove Dictionary of Music and Musicians. 1980. Ed. Stanley Sadie. London: Macmillan Publishers. 20 vols.

The New Grove Dictionary of Music and Musicians, second edition. 2001. Ed. Stanley Sadie. London: Macmillan Publishers. 29 vols.

The Oxford Companion to Music. 1955. Ed. Percy A. Scholes. 9th ed. London: Oxford University Press.

Taiwan Church Report. 2003. Ed. Zu Sancai. Taichung: Christian Resource Center.

Thuma Mina: International Ecumenical Hymnbook. 1995. Ed. Dieter Trautwein et al. Munchen: Strube Verlag GmbH; Basel: Basileia-Verlag GmbH.

Zhongguo Yinyue Cidian. 1986. Ed. Danqing Yicong Editorial Committee. Taiwan: Danqing Book Co.

BOOKS AND ARTICLES

Association for Theological Education in South East Asia (ATESEA). 2000–2001. *Handbook*. Ed. Choo Lak Yeow. Manila: Troika Press / South East Asia Graduate School of Theology.

ATESEA Occasional Papers. Eds. Choo Lak Yeow and John C. England. Singapore: ATESEA/PTCA.
1988. No. 6, *Doing Theology with Cultures of Asia*.
1989. No. 8, *Doing Theology with People's Symbols and Images*.

Athyal, Saphir, ed. 1996. *Church in Asia Today: Challenges And Opportunities*. Singapore: The Asia Lausanne Committee for World Evangelization.

Beckett, Jeremy, and Trevor Jones. 1981. *Traditional Music of the Torres Strait*. Canberra: Australian Institute of Aboriginal Studies.

Brailoiu, Constantin. *1955*. Un probleme de tonalite (la *metabole* pentatonique). *Melanges d'histoire et d'esthetique musicales* 1: *63–75*.

Butocan, Aga Mayo. 1987. *Palabunibunyan*: *A Repertoire of Musical Pieces for the Maguindanaon Kulintangan*. Manila: Philippine Women's University.

Chay, Shihwohn, ed. 1985. *Korean Church Music*. Seoul: Korea Christian Academy and AILM.

Chen, Shanqing. 1985. Introducing a Treasury of Material on Early Christian Music. *Music and Art* (Hong Kong) 5 (June): 44–46.

Cheng, Lian Ming, ed. 1984. *A Centennial History of the Presbyterian Church of Formosa 1865–1965*. 2ⁿᵈ ed. Tainan: Taiwan Church Press.

Chiung, Wi-vun Taiffalo. 2005. *Gi-gian, Gin-tong kap, Khi-sit-bin* ("Language, Identity, and Decolonization"). Tainan: National Cheng Kung University.

Cho, Gene Jinsiong. 2003. *The Discovery of Musical Equal Temperament in China and Europe in the Sixteenth Century*. Lewiston, NY: The Edwin Mellen Press.

Christian Conference of Asia. 1990. *Peoples of Asia, People of God: A Report of the Asia Mission Conference* 1989. Ed. Salvador T. Martinez. Singapore: Christian Conference of Asia.

Christian Conference of Asia, Urban Rural Mission. 1977. *Towards a Theology of People* 1. Singapore: Christian Conference of Asia.

Chun, In-pyong. 1984. *Goryo Umak*. Korea: Choson Akpo Publisher.

Chupungco, Anscar J. 1981. *Cultural Adaptation of the Liturgy*. New York: Paulist Press.

Church of South India. 2000. *Book of Common Worship*. Chennai: Church of South India Centre.

Coe, Shoki (alias Ng Chiong-hui or Chang-hui Hwang). 1973. Contextualization as the Way Toward Reform. *Theological Education* 9 (4, Summer): 233–43.

———. 1994. *Recollections and Reflections*. Ed. Boris Anderson. Tainan: Formosa Christians for Self Determination.

Duncan, Stephen F. 1999. *A Genre in Hindusthani Music (Bhajans) As Used in the Roman Catholic Church*. Lewiston, NY: The Edwin Mellen Press.

Francis, T. Dayanandan. 1988. *Christian Lyrics and Songs of New Life*. Madras: Christian Literature Society.

Francis, T. Dayanandan, and F. J. Balasundaram, eds. 1992. *Asian Expressions of Christian Commitment: A Reader in Asian Theology*. Madras: The Christian Literature Society.

Fyock, Joan A. 1996. *Hymnal Companion. Prepared by Churches in the Believers Church Tradition*. Ed. Lani Wright. Elgin, IL: Brethren Press.

Garfias, Robert. 1975. *Music of a Thousand Autumns*. Berkeley: University of California Press.

———. 1981. Speech and Melodic Contour Interdependence in Burmese Music. *College Music Symposium* 21 (1): 33–39.

Glover, Raymond F., ed. 1990. *The Hymnal 1982 Companion*. Vol. I. New York: Church Hymnal Corporation.

———. 1994. *The Hymnal 1982 Companion*. Vols. II, IIIA–B. New York: Church Hymnal Corporation.

Grimes, Barbara F., ed. 1984. *Languages of the World: Ethnologue*. Dallas: Wycliffe Bible Translators.

Grout, Donald J. 1973. *A History of Western Music*. Rev. ed. New York: W. W. Norton.

Hahn, Man-young. 1974. *Survey of Korean Arts: Folk Arts*. Seoul: National Academy of Arts.

———. 1990. *Kugak: Studies in Korean Traditional Music*. Tr. and ed. Inok Paek and Keith Howard. Seoul: Tangu Dang.

Hawn, Michael C. 2003. *Gather into One: Praying and Singing Globally*. Grand Rapids, Michigan: William B. Eerdemans Publishing Company.

Hoke, Donald E., ed. 1974. *The Church in Asia*. Chicago: Moody Press.

Hood, Mantle. 1954. *The Nuclear Theme as a Determinant of Patet in Javanese Music.* Groningen/Djakarta: J. B. Wolters.

————. 1971. *The Ethnomusicologist.* New York: McGraw-Hill.

Hood, Mantle, and Hardja Susilo. 1967. *Music of the Venerable Dark Cloud. The Javanese Gamelan Khjai Mendung.* Los Angeles: Institute of Ethnomusicology, University of California, Los Angeles.

Howard, Keith. 1995. *Korean Musical Instruments.* London: Oxford University Press.

Huang, Yi-ping. 1998. The Parting of the Way: Three Generations of Ch'in Performance Practice. PhD diss., University of Maryland, Baltimore.

Jang, Yeonok (Chang Yonok). 2000. Development and Change in Korean Narrative Song P'ansori. PhD diss., School of Oriental and African Studies, University of London.

Jiang, Yu-ling. 2001. Shengshixue chuantong de bijiao yanjiu: yi 16 shiji Ouzhou yinwen shipian fazhan wei li. *Zongjiao yinyue xueshu yantaohui lunwen ji.* Foguangshan Wenjiao jijinhui (May 2001): 217–36.

Johnson, Eileen M. 2006. Hymn Performance: I-to Loh Isn't There. *The Hymn, A Journal of Congregational Song* 57 (2, Spring): 33–35.

Johnson, Y. Gnana Chandra. 2003. *Kiristhanve Kiirtheni Kaveingnergall* ("Christian Lyric Poets").

Johnstone, Patrick, and Jason Mandryk. 2000. *Operation World: When We Pray God Works. 21st Century Edition.* Cumbria, UK: Paternoster Publishing.

Kao, Chun-ming, and Li-chen Kao-Li. 2001. *Shi-zi-jia zhi lu: Kao Chun-ming mu-shi hui-yi- lu* ("The Way of the Cross: Memoir of the Rev. C. M. Kao"). Ed. Hui-ling Hu. Taipei: Wang Chun-feng Wen-hua.

Kim, Seongdae. 1999. Inculturation in Korean Protestant Hymnody. PhD diss., Drew University.

Kim, Yong Bock. 1992. *Messiah and Minjung: Christ's Solidarity with the People for New Life.* Singapore: Urban Rural Mission, Christian Conference of Asia.

Kishibe, Shigeo. 1984. *The Traditional Music of Japan.* Tokyo: Ongaku no Tomo sha.

Koizumi, Fumio. 1958. *Nihon dento ongaku no kenkyu 1* ("Studies on Traditional Music of Japan, vol. 1."). Tokyo: Ongaku no Tomosha.
————, ed. 1976. *Asian Music in an Asian Perspective: Report of Asian Traditional Performing Arts.* Tokyo: Heibonsha.

————. 1981. *Nihon dento ongaku no kenkyu 2: Rizumu* ("Studies on Traditional Music of Japan, vol. 2: Rhythm"). Tokyo: Ongaku no Tomosha.

Koyama, Kosuke. 1999. *Water Buffalo Theology. Twenty-Fifth Anniversary edition, Revised and Expanded.* Maryknoll, New York: Orbis Books.

Kunst, Jaap. 1949. *Music in Java.* Tr. Emil von Loo. 2nd rev. ed. 2 vols. The Hague: Martinus Njihoff.

————. 1967. *Music in New Guinea.* The Hague: Martinus Nijhoff.

Lee, Hye-Ku. 1981. *Essays on Traditional Korean Music.* Tr. and ed. Robert C. Provine. Seoul: Royal Asiatic Society, Korea Branch.

L'Engle, Madeleine. 1980. *Walking on Water: Reflections on Faith & Art.* Wheaton, Illinois: Harold Shaw Publishers.

Liang, Ming-yue. 1985. *Music of the Billion: An Introduction to Chinese Musical Culture.* New York: Heinrichshofen.

Lim, Swee Hong. 2006. Giving Voice to Asian Christians: An Appraisal of the Pioneering Work of I-to Loh in the Area of Congregational Song. PhD diss., Drew University. Published by VDM Verlag Dr. Mueller, 2008.

Lin, Song-en and Su Liang-yi, eds. 2003. *Haiyang hoaiyan: Hui-yi fu-qin de ge, 1.* Taidong: National Museum of Prehistory.

Liu, Te-yi. 1991. *Ling ni jinru yinyue diantang.* Taipei: Youshi Wenhua Shiye.

Loh, I-to. 1972. *New Songs of Asian Cities.* Singapore: Christian Conference of Asia, Urban Rural Mission; Tainan: Taiwan Church Press.

————. 1982. Tribal Music of Taiwan: with Special Reference to the Ami and Puyuma Styles. PhD diss., University of California, Los Angeles.

————. 1983. *Hymns From the Four Winds.* Nashville: Abingdon.

————. 1984a. *Mini Companion to Hymns from the Four Winds.* National Federation of Asian Americans, United Methodist Church. Mimeograph.

554

———. 1984b. *Festivals of Asian Christmas Music.* Manila: Asian Institute for Liturgy and Music.

———. 1985. *Festivals of Asian Christmas Music.* Chinese edition. Tainan: Taiwan Church Press.

———. 1986. *Let the Hills Sing.* Manila: Asian Institute for Liturgy and Music; Tainan: Taiwan Church Press.

———. 1987. A Glimpse at the Multipart Practices in Traditional Asian Music. *Report of the 1987 Asian Workshop on Liturgy and Music.* Ed. Felicidas A. Prudente. 258–73. Manila: Asian Institute for Liturgy and Music.

———. 1988. *Kristus Sundaring Bali* ("Christ the Light to Bali"). Manila: Asian Institute for Liturgy and Music.

———. 1989. *Rak Phra Jao, Rao Pen Thai* ("The Love of God Sets Us Free"). Manila: Asian Institute for Liturgy and Music.

———. 1991a. Toward Contextualization of Church Music in Asia. *Hymnology Annual: An International Forum on the Hymn and Worship* 1: 89–114.

———. 1991b. Worshiping with Incarnated Music: My Mission. [In Chinese.] *Lam-sin Sin-hak* 2 (1): 113–32.

———. 1992. *Teach Us to Praise: In Search for Contextual Church Music.* [In Chinese.] Tainan: Tainan Theological Seminary Press. Rev. ed., Tainan: Taiwan Church Press, 2002.

———. 1993a. Contemporary Issues in Inculturation, Arts, and Liturgy: Music. *Hymnology Annual* 3: 47–56.

———. 1993b. A Survey of Texts and Musical Styles in *Sound the Bamboo: CCA Hymnal 1990. Hymnology Annual* 4.

———. 1994a. Asian Worship. In *The Complete Library of Christian Worship, vol.7: The Ministries of Christian Worship*, ed. Robert Webber, 217–21. Nashville: Star Song Publishing Group.

———. 1994b. Transmitting Cultural Traditions in Hymnody. *Church Music Workshop* 4 (4, September–December 1994): 1–11.

———. 1995. *Ban-Bin Siong-Chan* ("All Peoples Praise"). Tainan: Tainan Theological College and Seminary.

———. 1996. *Music and Musical Styles*. New York: General Board of Global Ministries, The United Methodist Church.

———. 1997. Resources on Asian Music, Worship and the Arts. *Theology and the Church* 22 (2): 59–81.

———. 2000. *Sound the Bamboo: CCA Hymnal 2000*. Tainan: Taiwan Church Press; Chiang Mai: Christian Conference of Asia.

———. 2001. Music, Asian Christian. In *A Dictionary of Asian Christianity*, ed. Scott W. Sunquist, 569–74. Grand Rapids, Michigan: William B. Eerdmanns Publishing Co.

———. 2002. Doing Theology with Music: Using "Welcome the New Year with the Spring Wind" as an Example. [In Chinese.] *Theology and the Church* 27 (2): 209–15.

———. 2003a. A Preliminary Dialogue between Music, Worship and Theology. [In Chinese.] *Theology and the Church* 28 (1): 157–75.

———. 2003b. Symbols and Symbolic Acts in Asian Worship [In Chinese.] *Theology and the Church* 28 (2): 271–83.

———. 2005a. Revisiting Ways of Contextualization of Church Music in Asia. *Theology and the Church* 30 (2): 450–74.

———. 2005b. In Search for Asian Identities in Asian Hymns: An Overview of Texts and Musical Styles in *Sound the Bamboo*. *Cultural Encounters: A Journal for the Theology of Culture* (Multnormah Bible College and Seminary) 1 (2): 89–110.

———. 2005c. Contextualization Versus Globalization: A Glimpse of Sounds and Symbols in Asian Worship. *Colloquium: Music, Worship, Arts* (Yale Institute of Sacred Music): 125–39.

———. 2007a. The Development of Contextual Church Music (Hymns) and the Post-colonial Taiwan. [In Chinese.] In *Shoki Coe Memorial Lectures*. Tainan: Tainan Theological College and Seminary.

———. 2007b. *Worship in Dialogue with Culture: Probing from Liturgical and Musical Dimensions*. [In Chinese.] Hong Kong: Jiandao Theological Seminary.

————. 2007c. Ideal and Practicality: Challenges for Editing the New Hymnal of the Presbyterian Church in Taiwan. [In Chinese.] *The New Messenger* 102: 12–19.

————. 2008a. Contextualization of Asian Liturgy and Music: from AILM to Global Contexts. A Personal Recollection, Reflection and Vision. Paper presented at AILM Colloquium, Manila, Philippines, August 9, 2008.

————. 2008b. Taiwan jiaohui qingjinghua liyi yu inyue fazhan zhi guocheng yu jiantao ("Reflection on the development of contextualization of liturgy and music in Taiwan"). Paper presented at Chung Chi Divinity School, Chinese University of Hong Kong, October 21, 2008.

Lott, Eric J., ed. 1986. *Worship in an Indian Context.* Bangalore: United Theological College.

Lui, Tsun-yuen. 1968. A Short Guide to Ch'in. *Selected Report* (UCLA Institute of Ethnomusicology) 1 (2): 179–204.

Maceda, Jose. 1963. The Music of the Maguidanao in the Philippines. PhD diss., University of California, Los Angeles.

————, ed. 1971. *Musics of Asia.* Manila: National Music Council of the Philippines and UNESCO.

————. 1990. In Search of a Source of Pentatonic Hemitonic and Anhemitonic Scales in Southeast Asia. *Acta Musicologica* 72 (2–3): 192–223.

Malm, William P. 1958. *Japanese Music and Musical Instruments.* Tokyo: Charles E. Tuttle.

————. 1977. *Music Cultures of the Pacific, the Near East and Asia.* Englewood Cliffs, NJ: Prentice-Hall.

Mastra, Wayan. 1985. Putting the Gospel in Its Context. In *Lion Handbook of Christianity: A World Faith*, ed. Robin Keeley, n.p. Oxford: Lion Publishing.

Mays, James Luther. 1994. *Psalms.* Interpretation: A Biblical Commentary for Teaching and Preaching. Louisville: John Knox Press.

McPhee, Colin. 1966. *Music in Bali.* New Haven: Yale University Press.

Milgate, Wesley. 1999. *A Companion to Sing Alleluia.* Sydney: The Australian Hymn Book Pty. Ltd.

Miller, Terry E. 1990. The Theory and Practice of Thai Musical Notation. *Ethnomusicology* 36 (2): 197–222.

Miller, Terry E., and Andrew Shahriani. 2005. *World Music: A Global Journey.* New York: Routledge.

Moffett, Samuel Hugh. 1998. *A History of Christianity in Asia.* Vol. 1, *Beginnings to 1500.* Maryknoll, NY: Orbis Books.

Morton, David. 1968. *The Traditional Music of Thailand.* Los Angeles: Institute of Ethnomusicology, University of California, Los Angeles.

———. 1976. *The Traditional Music of Thailand.* Berkeley: University of California Press.

Myers, Helen, ed. 1992. *Ethnomusicology: Historical and Regional Studies.* London: Macmillan.

Nacion-Puyot, Lillibeth, ed. 2000. *The Circle of Faith: Worship Resource Book. 2000 Asia Pacific Conference on Music and Worship.* Quezon City: Asian Institute for Liturgy and Music.

———. 2002b. *Asia Pacific Conference on Music and Worship Conference Papers.* Quezon City: Asian Institute for Liturgy and Music.

National Center for Korean Traditional Performing Arts. 1996. *A Study of Musical Instruments in Korean Traditional Music.* Seoul: National Center for Korean Traditional Performing Arts.

Park, Seong-Won. 2000. Worship in the Presbyterian Church in Korea. In *Christian Worship in Reformed Churches Past and Present,* ed. Lukas Vischer, 194–207. Grand Rapids, MI: William B. Eerdmans Publishing Co.

Prabhakar, David. *Kristava Kerthanai Kalangiam* ("Christian Lyric Poets"). Chennai: Vivi Publishers.

Prudente, Felicidad A., ed. 1987. *Report of the 1987 Asian Workshop on Liturgy and Music.* 258–73. Manila: Asian Institute for Liturgy and Music.

———. 2000. Musical Process in the Gasumbi Epic of the Buwaya Kalinga People of Northern Luzon. PhD diss., University of Michigan.

Rice, Delbert. 1999. *Quiet Ones Speak: Testimonies Concerning Christian Beginnings.* Quezon City: New Day Publishers.

Ross, I. 1979. Ritual and Music in South India: Syrian Christian Liturgical Music in Kerala. *Asian Music* 11 (1): 80–98.

Routley, Erik. 1981. *Music of Christian Hymns.* Chicago: GIA Publications, Inc.

Sambika Iinkai, Nihon Kirisuto Kyodan, ed. 1955. *Sambika Ryakkai.* Part II, music section. 9th ed., 1981. Nihon Kirisuto Kyodan Syuppan Kyoku.

———. 1974. *Sambika Dainihen Ryakkai.* 2nd ed., 1980. Nihon Kirisuto Kyodan Syuppan Kyoku.

———. 1977. *Sambika 21 Ryakkai.* Nihon Kirisuto Kyodan Syuppan Kyoku.

Sharma, Manorama. 1999. *Music India.* New Delhi: A.P.H. Publishing Corporation.

Sherinian, Z. 1998. The Indigenization of Tamil Christian Music: Folk Music as a Liberative Transmission System. PhD diss., Wesleyan University.

Shorter, Aylward. 1988. *Toward a Theology of Inculturation.* Maryknoll, NY: Orbis Books.

Sumithra, S. 1990. *Christian Theology from an Indian Perspective.* Bangalore: Theological Book Trust.

Takenaka, Masao. 1985. *God Is Rice: Asian Culture and Christian Faith.* Risk Book Series. Geneva: World Council of Churches.

———. 1995. *The Place Where God Dwells: An Introduction to Church Architecture in Asia.* Christian Conference of Asia and Asian Christian Art association Pace Publishing.

Takenaka, Masao, and Ron O'Grady. 1991. *The Bible Through Asian Eyes.* Auckland: Pace Publishing /Asian Christian Art Association.

Thangaraj, M. Thomas. 1992. Toward a Singable Theology: Venturing into Life: The Story of the Tamilnadu Theological Seminary. In *Asian Expressions of Christian Commitment: A Reader in Asian Theology,* ed. T. Dayanandan Francis, 163–72. Madras: Christian Literature Society.

———. 1994. *The Crucified Guru: An Experiment in Cross-Cultural Christology.* Nashville: Abingdon Press.

Thomas, T. K., ed. 1977. *Christianity in Asia: Northeast Asia.* Singapore: Christian Conference of Asia.

Tin, John Jyigiokk. 2002. *Tai-oan Chhui-chhi* ("Christian Commitments and Songs of the Taiwan Democracy Movement"). Ed. Jyin-sek Gwo. Taipei: Bang Chhun-hong Bun-hua.

Tirabassi, Maren C., and Kathy Wonson Eddy. 1995. *Gifts of Many Cultures: Worship Resources for the Global Community.* Cleveland, OH: United Church Press.

Wang, Shenyin. 1993. *Zanmei Shi (xinbian) Shihua* ("Companion to 'Hymns of Praise' [new edition]"). Shanghai: China Christian Council.

Watanabe, Sadao, and Masao Takenaka. 1986. *Biblical Prints by Sadao Watanabe.* Tokyo: Shinkyo Shuppansha.

Williamson, Muriel. 1975a. A Supplement to the Construction and Decoration of One Burmese Harp. *Selected Reports in Ethnomusicology* 2 (2): 111–15.

———. 1975b. Aspects of Traditional Style Maintained in Burma's First 13 Kyo Songs. *Selected Reports in Ethnomusicology* 2 (2): 117–63.

———. 1979. The Correlation Between Speech-tones of Text-syllables and Their Musical Setting in a Burmese Classical Song. *Musica Asiatica* 3: 11–28.

Wren, Brian. 1999. *Praying Twice: The Music and Words of Congregational Song.* Louisville: Westminster John Knox Press.

Young, Carlton, R. 1993. *Companion to The United Methodist Hymnal.* Nashville: Abingdon Press.

Zhao, Qin. 2004. Yu-in liao-liang shang piao kong – Li Bao-zhen zhuan. *Yue-lan* ("Music Browser," Taichung: Guoli Taiwan Jiaoxiangyuetuan) 57 (March 2004): 2–11.

Indexes

Index of Authors, Translators, Paraphrasers, and Sources

The prefix H indicates a number in the hymnal *Sound the Bamboo* (2000). In some instances, the reader may find it helpful to keep in mind the hymnal number rather than the entry term when reading a page.

Index of Composers, Arrangers, and Sources

The prefix H indicates a number in the hymnal *Sound the Bamboo* (2000). In some instances, the reader may find it helpful to keep in mind the hymnal number rather than the entry term when reading a page.

Tune Index

The prefix H indicates a number in the hymnal *Sound the Bamboo* (2000).

Title and First Line Index

Hymn titles are in capitals; first lines are in sentence style. The prefix H indicates a number in the hymnal *Sound the Bamboo* (2000).

Jesus, Jesus, how we adore you, 315, 430, 484, H41

Jesus, lover of my soul!, 513

Jesus, our true Lord of love, 119, 446, 479, H192

Jesus, Savior Lord, lo to you I fly, 316, 338, 472, H59

Jesus, Savior, Spirit, Sun!, 188, 189, 362, 371, H314

Jesus, the Lord stands with the poor, 372, H202

Jesus, your last cry on the cross, 238, 509, H274B

Joy abounds, dear Lord, 316, 466, H309

Joy found in truth surely sets the world free, 120, 437, 438, H66

Joy, O Jesus, crown of all, 283, 390, 466, 487, H28

Juich arde, Juicht alom den Herr, 130

Kyrie eleison, 236, H119

Lamb of God, 142, 517, H129

Let all nations come, praise the LORD, 142, 454, H96

Let all nations praise the LORD, 143, H5

Let us come to worship God, 139, 144, 454, H3

Let us even now go to Bethlehem, 265, 495, H146

Let us now as God's own people, 262, H244

Lift up the Cross, lift up our hearts, 259, 265, H261

"Light and salt" you called your friends, 144, H254

Light of the world, salt of the earth, 144, 486, 506, H254

Light of those whose dreary dwelling, 513

LILIES OF THE FIELD, 236, 237, 454, 463, 507, H201

LIVING IN CHRIST WITH PEOPLE, 145, 372, 473, H202

Lo! He comes with clouds descending, 513

Lo, now ascends the morning sun, 95, 426, H194

Lord Jesus spoke in parables, 236, 237, H201

LORD of life, 359, 434, H267

LORD, as the earth welcomes showers of rain, 120, 507, H90

Lord, before our world was formed, 55

LORD, have mercy, 189, 347, 413, 450, H118, H124, H300

LORD, have mercy on us, 145, 454, H121

Lord, thy word abideth, 9

Lord, we did not live up to your teachings, 27, 284, 493, H43

LORD, we give you heartfelt praise, 146, 502, H112

LORD, we thank you for this food, 146, 171, 454, H163

LORD, your hands have formed this world, 265, 272, H178

Love divine, all loves excelling, 513

Lovely star in the sky, 121, 426, 438, H132

Loving Spirit, 19, 31, 147, 373, 468, H220

Make a joyful noise, all the lands, 67, H93

MARRIAGE SONG, 359, 466, H169

MARY'S SALIDUMMAY, 266, 435, H102

May the grace of Christ, 360, 470, H81

General Index

Page numbers in **bold** are references in commentaries on individual hymns. Part III is not included in this index.